Professional JavaScript® Frameworks

Continued

Professional
JavaScript® Frameworks

Prototype, YUI, Ext JS, Dojo and MooTools

Leslie Michael Orchard

Ara Pehlivanian

Scott Koon

Harley Jones

Wiley Publishing, Inc.

Professional JavaScript® Frameworks: Prototype, YUI, Ext JS, Dojo and MooTools

Published by
Wiley Publishing, Inc.
10475 Crosspoint Boulevard
Indianapolis, IN 46256
www.wiley.com

ISBN: 978-0-470-38459-6

Manufactured in the United States of America

10 9 8 7 6 5 4 3 2 1

For general information on our other products and services please contact our Customer Care Department within the United States at (877) 762-2974, outside the United States at (317) 572-3993 or fax (317) 572-4002.

Wiley also publishes its books in a variety of electronic formats. Some content that appears in print may not be available in electronic books.

Library of Congress Control Number: 2009932978

*Many thanks go to my wife, Alexandra, who somehow put up with
me over the last few years' adventures — of which writing a book was
the least stressful, relatively speaking.*

—Leslie Michael Orchard

*For my wife, Krista, my daughter Emma, and the new one who's on the way!
Thanks for your love and support. I couldn't have done this without you!*

—Ara Pehlivanian

*I want to thank Kim, Amelia, and Naomi for putting up with all the
late nights banging away on the laptop and I dedicate my work on this book to them.*

—Scott Koon

To Marlene, Carolyn, Houston, and my mom.

—Harley Jones

Credits

Acquisitions Editor
Scott Meyers

Development Editor
Kenyon Brown

Technical Editors
Scott Koon
Michael Galloway
Dave Bouwman
Joel Tulloch
Alexei Gorkov

Production Editor
Daniel Scribner

Copy Editor
Mildred Sanchez

Editorial Manager
Mary Beth Wakefield

Production Manager
Tim Tate

Vice President and Executive Group Publisher
Richard Swadley

Vice President and Executive Publisher
Barry Pruett

Associate Publisher
Jim Minatel

Project Coordinator, Cover
Lynsey Stanford

Proofreader
Scott Klemp, Word One
Kyle Schlesinger, Word One

Indexer
Ron Strauss

About the Authors

Leslie Michael Orchard is a tinkerer, writer, and serial enthusiast from the Detroit area. He shares his home with a lovely wife, two spotted Ocicats, and a pair of dwarf bunnies. On rare occasions when spare time is found, he shares and documents odd bits of code and other interests at a web site called 0xDECAFBAD (http://decafbad.com).

Ara Pehlivanian has been working on the Web since 1997. He's been a freelancer, a webmaster, and most recently, a front-end architect and practice lead for Nurun, a global interactive communications agency. Ara's experience comes from having worked on every aspect of web development throughout his career, but he's now following his passion for web standards-based front-end development. When he isn't teaching about best practices or writing code professionally, he's maintaining his personal site at http://arapehlivanian.com/.

Scott Koon has been a professional software developer for over 13 years. He spent the majority of his time in college working with a legacy, undocumented symbolic language (DNA), resulting in a degree in biochemistry. He's been writing JavaScript since it was called LiveScript and remembers when Netscape had a big purple "N" in the upper right-hand corner. He maintains a blog at http://lazycoder.com and has been active in the weblogging community for about 10 years. He is often on Twitter at http://www.twitter.com/lazycoder and has contributed to the development of a WPF .NET Twitter client called Witty. He also cohosts a podcast called Herding Code (http://www.herdingcode.com) that deals with a wide variety of issues in technology. He lives in Seattle, Washington, with his wife and two daughters, adrift in a sea of pink princesses and other girly things.

Harley Jones is currently a lead technical consultant for Perficient, Inc (NASDAQ: PRFT). He graduated from Oglethorpe University in Atlanta, Georgia with an English literature degree but has been programming since he was 10 years old. He has been developing software professionally for more than 10 years and literally consumes programming languages. He actively supports and mentors almost anyone serious in learning modern programming techniques. When not programming, he can be found molding his children into evil scientists. Harley can be reached at harley.333@gmail.com.

Acknowledgments

From Leslie Michael Orchard: This book owes its existence to the Dojo and MooTools communities themselves for the wealth of open source code and resources made available to the Web, as well as answers to random late night questions on IRC.

From Ara Pehlivanian: Thanks to the entire YUI team for writing such a great library. In particular, I want to thank Eric Miraglia, Dav Glass, Nate Koechley, Douglas Crockford, and Todd Kloots for answering my questions and helping me get my brain wrapped around certain issues. I also want to thank the hardworking folks at Wrox for their patience and dedication to putting together a quality product.

From Scott Koon: Thanks to the editors of my chapters for all their help and guidance. Without them, you'd need the Rosetta Stone to read my writing. I also want to thank Brendan Eich for creating this small but powerful language, all of the browser vendors for making JavaScript the most used programming language in the world, and Douglas Crockford for illuminating just how powerful JavaScript is and where there be dragons in JavaScript.

From Harley Jones: Thanks to Ryan Duclos for putting my name in the hat, Jim Minatel for getting the ball rolling, and definitely Kenyon Brown and Scott Meyers for pushing that ball through to the finish. I also want to thank Jack Slocum and Aaron Conran for an awesomely powerful library. And I thank Michael LeComte, Nickolay Platonov, Jozef Sakalos, Nigel White, and the entire Ext community (way too many to list here) for being a sounding board for any and all ideas.

Contents

Contents

Contents

Contents

Contents

Contents

Contents

Contents

Part IV: Dojo

Contents

Contents

Part V: MooTools

Contents

Contents

Introduction

JavaScript is the industry standard client-side scripting language that is used in web applications. *Professional JavaScript Frameworks: Prototype, YUI, Ext JS, Dojo and MooTools* offers an examination of some of the top JavaScript (JS) frameworks that are available, with practical examples and explanations of what each does best.

Over the past few years, there's been a small renaissance in JavaScript as a language. A variety of projects have sprung up to build reusable JS libraries and frameworks — and at this point, a good number of them have matured and shown staying power that they're worth taking a serious look at and relying on in professional projects.

JavaScript has grown in popularity in parallel with the Web and today is supported by all major browsers and new web technologies. JavaScript has been extended over time to deliver high-performing and incredibly impressive Web user experiences, using technologies including Adobe Flash, AJAX, and Microsoft Silverlight.

As JavaScript is used increasingly for "serious" development on the Web, the lessons that have been learned and the tools that have been invented along the way are being consolidated and shared by developers in the form of libraries and frameworks. However, since JavaScript is such a flexible and dynamic language, each framework can present very different approaches to the problems of web development — each with its own pros and cons.

Whom This Book Is For

This book is for web developers who want to get straight into JavaScript and explore the tools and productivity gains offered by the frameworks. A working knowledge of HTML, CSS, and JavaScript are assumed — and also of use will be some experience with object-oriented programming, server-side PHP scripting, and knowledge of web development modern techniques such as AJAX.

What This Book Covers

This book is meant to be a concise and handy companion while you're working, deferring to other sources online and otherwise to fill you in on the more advanced, experimental, and in-progress facets of the JavaScript frameworks.

What You Need to Use This Book

A browser, a text editor, and web hosting are pretty much all you need to make use of the examples in this book. Using Mozilla Firefox as your browser with the Firebug extension installed is highly recommended, since that combination offers a very powerful in-browser development environment with JavaScript logging and DOM exploration tools.

You can download Mozilla Firefox at `http://getfirefox.com/` and Firebug is available at `http://getfirebug.com/` once you've gotten Firefox running.

Additionally, a few examples in this book require a server-side script to fully work, and the example code is in PHP. So, having access to PHP on your web server would help, though the scripts should work on pretty much any version from PHP 4 and up.

Conventions

To help you get the most from the text and keep track of what's happening, the following conventions are used throughout the book:

- ❏ Filenames, URLs, and code within the text are formatted like so: `persistence.properties`.
- ❏ Code is presented in two different ways:

```
In code examples, new and important code is highlighted with a gray background.
```

```
The gray highlighting is not used for code that's less important in the present
context, or has been shown before.
```

Source Code

As you work through the examples in this book, you may choose to either type in all the code manually or use the source code files that accompany the book. All of the source code used in this book is available for download at `http://www.wrox.com`. Once at the site, simply locate the book's title (either by using the Search box or by using one of the title lists) and click the Download Code link on the book's detail page to obtain all the source code for the book.

> *Because many books have similar titles, you may find it easiest to search by ISBN; this book's ISBN is 978-0-470-38459-6.*

Once you download the code, just decompress it with your favorite compression tool. Alternately, you can go to the main Wrox code download page at `http://www.wrox.com/dynamic/books/download.aspx` to see the code available for this book and all other Wrox books.

Errata

We make every effort to ensure that there are no errors in the text or in the code. However, no one is perfect, and mistakes do occur. If you find an error in one of our books, such as a spelling mistake or faulty piece of code, we would be very grateful for your feedback. By sending in errata, you may save other readers hours of frustration and at the same time you will be helping us provide even higher quality information.

To find the errata page for this book, go to `http://www.wrox.com` and locate the title using the Search box or one of the title lists. Then, on the book details page, click the Book Errata link. On this page you can view all errata that has been submitted for this book and posted by Wrox editors. A complete book list including links to each book's errata is also available at `http://www.wrox.com/misc-pages/booklist.shtml`.

If you don't spot "your" error on the Book Errata page, go to `http://www.wrox.com/contact/techsupport.shtml` and complete the form there to send us the error you have found. We'll check the information and, if appropriate, post a message to the book's errata page and fix the problem in subsequent editions of the book.

p2p.wrox.com

For author and peer discussion, join the P2P forums at `http://p2p.wrox.com`. The forums are a Web-based system for you to post messages relating to Wrox books and related technologies and interact with other readers and technology users. The forums offer a subscription feature to e-mail you topics of interest of your choosing when new posts are made to the forums. Wrox authors, editors, other industry experts, and your fellow readers are present on these forums.

At `http://p2p.wrox.com` you will find a number of different forums that will help you not only as you read this book, but also as you develop your own applications. To join the forums, just follow these steps:

1. Go to `http://p2p.wrox.com` and click the Register link.
2. Read the terms of use and click Agree.
3. Complete the required information to join as well as any optional information you wish to provide and click Submit.
4. You will receive an e-mail with information describing how to verify your account and complete the joining process.

You can read messages in the forums without joining P2P but in order to post your own messages, you must join.

Once you join, you can post new messages and respond to messages other users post. You can read messages at any time on the Web. If you would like to have new messages from a particular forum e-mailed to you, click the Subscribe to this Forum icon by the forum name in the forum listing.

For more information about how to use the Wrox P2P, be sure to read the P2P FAQs for answers to questions about how the forum software works as well as many common questions specific to P2P and Wrox books. To read the FAQs, click the FAQ link on any P2P page.

Part I
Prototype

Part I: Prototype

Prototype was one of the first JavaScript libraries to gain prominence during the Web 2.0 resurgence. When the term AJAX was first coined in 2005, making cross-browser XMLHttpRequests was a minefield of browser-specific code. Prototype assists you in your quest for cross-browser compatibility by smoothing out the rough edges of event handling by providing a common method for binding events to their respective handlers and providing a common interface for creating AJAX requests that work in all browsers. It also gives you a cross-browser way to manipulate the DOM, by handling the special cases in all browsers, and allowing you to focus on just writing code without cluttering up your code with browser-specific "if-else" statements.

Prototype extends the JavaScript language as well as the elements. The native JavaScript Object is extended to include methods for determining the type of data the object represents as well as helpful serialization methods. The Enumerable class allows you to easily traverse and manipulate your arrays of both JavaScript objects and DOM elements by providing useful methods such as each() and map() directly on your arrays. The native Function object is also extended with useful methods, such as wrap(), which let you write interceptors for your methods that provide useful features like logging.

Prototype eases inheritance with the Class object. You can easily extend your objects and create hierarchies without the headaches associated with normal inheritance in statically typed languages. All of these features make Prototype the best choice for writing logic in JavaScript, and it provides you with an excellent base for writing your own JavaScript library. Since Prototype does all of the heavy lifting for you, you can focus on the fun parts of library development — creating new widgets and data structures.

Extending and Enhancing DOM Elements

Prototype is an excellent framework to use either as your main JavaScript library or as the foundation of another library. Part of the magic of Prototype is the extension of DOM elements by the framework. By adding new methods to elements, Prototype makes it easier to write cross-browser code in a more eloquent manner. There are also several methods for taking care of the dirty details involved in positioning elements. It is easier to write unobtrusive JavaScript by taking advantage of helper methods such as getElementsByClassName and getElementsBySelectors, making it easy to apply styling or events to groups of elements with something in common.

In this chapter, you'll learn about:

❑ Extending a DOM element with Prototype

❑ Altering and manipulating content and size

❑ Using CSS to style an element

Extending a DOM element

Before Prototype came along, cross-browser code often looked a lot like a road map: a lot of branches and a lot of the same checks over and over again. By extending the elements you are working on, Prototype is able to centralize all of the cross-browser hacks that make JavaScript programming such a chore. Prototype keeps its extension methods for all elements in the Element.Methods and Element.Methods.Simulated object. If the element is an input, select, or textarea tag, the methods in Form.Element.Methods are also included. Form elements themselves are extended with the methods in Form.Methods. Most of these methods return the original element, so you can chain together methods like so: $(myElement).update("updated").show();. It is important to note that not only is the element you choose extended, but all of the child elements of that element are also extended.

In browsers that support modification of the HTMLElement.prototype, Prototype adds the methods to HTMLElement for you. That means you don't have to call Element.extends() on any element you create by hand. You can start using Prototype methods immediately.

```
var newDiv = document.createElement("div");
newDiv.update("Insert some text");
newDiv.addClassName("highlight");
```

Internet Explorer doesn't support modifying HTMLElement, so you have to call Element.extends() or get a reference to the element using the $() or $$() methods.

$() — "The dollar function"

The easiest way to extend a DOM element is to use the $() function to get a reference to the element rather than using document.getElementById or some other method. When you obtain a reference this way, Prototype automatically adds all of the methods in Element.Methods to the element. If you pass a string to the method, it will get a reference to the element with the ID you specify for you. If you pass in a reference to the element, it will return the same reference but with the extension methods. This is the most common way to extend an element.

```
<body>
<div id="myId">Hello Prototype</div>
<script type="text/javascript">
        $("myId").hide();
</script>
</body>
```

$$()

This works in a similar manner to the $() function. It takes a CSS selector as an argument and returns an array of elements that match the selector. CSS selectors are a powerful tool for getting a specific element back from the DOM. The elements in the array will be in the same order as they appear in the DOM and each will be extended by Prototype.

```
$$('input');
// select all of the input elements

$$('#myId');
//select the element with the id "myId"

$$('input.validate');
//select all of the input elements with the class "validate"
```

Prototype does not use the browser's built-in CSS selector parsing, so it is free to implement selectors specified in newer versions of CSS than the browser supports. As a result, version 1.5.1 and higher of Prototype includes support for almost all of CSS3.

```
$$('#myId > input');
//select all of the input elements that are children of the element with the id "myId"

$$('table < tr:nth-child(even)');
//selects all of the even numbered rows of all table elements.
```

Element.extend()

This method accepts an element and extends the element using the methods found in `Element`
`.Methods`. It is very similar to `$()` except it only accepts references to DOM objects and will not fetch
a reference for you if you pass it an id.

Here is a simple example of using `Element.extend()`:

```
Var newDiv = document.createElement("div");
Element.extend(newDiv);
newDiv.hide();
```

Element as a Constructor

You can also use the `Element` object as a way to construct new DOM elements rather than using the
built-in DOM methods. New elements created in this way are automatically extended by Prototype and
can be used immediately.

```
<head>
    <meta http-equiv="Content-Type" content="text/html; charset=utf-8">
    <title>untitled</title>
    <style>
        .redText { color: red;}
    </style>
</head>
<body>
    <div id="myDiv" class="main">Here is my div</div>

    <textarea id="results" cols="50" rows="10"></textarea>
    <script type="text/javascript" src="prototype-1.6.0.2.js"></script>
<script type="text/javascript">
    Event.observe(window,"load", function(e) {
        $("results").value = "";
        $("results").value += $("myDiv").id + "\n";
        $("results").value += $$(".main")[0].id + "\n";
        var newEl = new Element("h1",{"class": "redText"});
        $("myDiv").insert(newEl);
        newEl.update("I'm new here");

        var manuallyCreated = document.createElement("h2");
        $("myDiv").insert(manuallyCreated);
        Element.extend(manuallyCreated);
        manuallyCreated.update("I was extended");
    });
</script></body>
```

5

Since $$() returns a DOM-ordered array of elements, you have to refer to the first element in the array by the ordinal 0.

Here you see some of the ways you can extend an element. First, you use the $() method to grab the element by ID and extend the element. Next, you use the $$() method and pass in a CSS selector to get the element by class name. Now you will use the Element object as a constructor and create a new H1 element with a class of redText, inserting it into the myDiv element and setting the text of the newly created element. Finally, you create an element the old-fashioned way and use Element.extend() to extend the element, as shown in Figure 1-1.

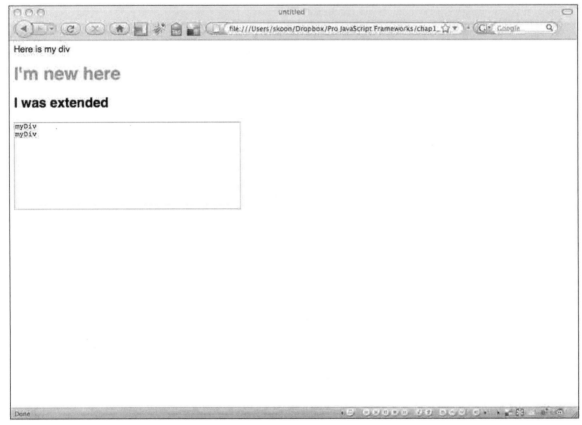

Figure 1-1

Navigating the DOM

Trying to figure out where the element you are interested in is located in the DOM and what elements are surrounding that element is no easy task. Prototype's `Element` object provides a multitude of ways to traverse the DOM. Several methods allow you to specify CSS rules to narrow your search. All of Prototype's DOM navigation methods ignore white space and only return element nodes.

adjacent

This method finds all of an element's siblings that match the selector you specify. This method is useful for dealing with lists or table columns.

```
<body>
    <ul id="PeopleList">
        <li class="female" id="judy">Judy</li>
        <li class="male" id="sam">Sam</li>
        <li class="female" id="amelia">Amelia</li>
        <li class="female" id="kim">Kim</li>
        <li class="male" id="scott">Scott</li>
        <li class="male" id="brian">Brian</li>
        <li class="female" id="ava">Ava</li>
    </ul>
    <textarea id="results" cols="50" rows="10"></textarea>
    <script type="text/javascript" src="prototype-1.6.0.2.js"></script>
    <script type="text/javascript">
        Event.observe(window,"load", function(e) {
            var els =$("kim").adjacent("li.female");
            $("results").value = "";
            for(var i = 0;i < els.length; i++) {
                $("results").value += els[i].id + "\n";
            }
        });
    </script>
</body>
```

Here you start with the list element with the ID "kim" and gather the `li` elements adjacent with the class name `female`, as shown in Figure 1-2.

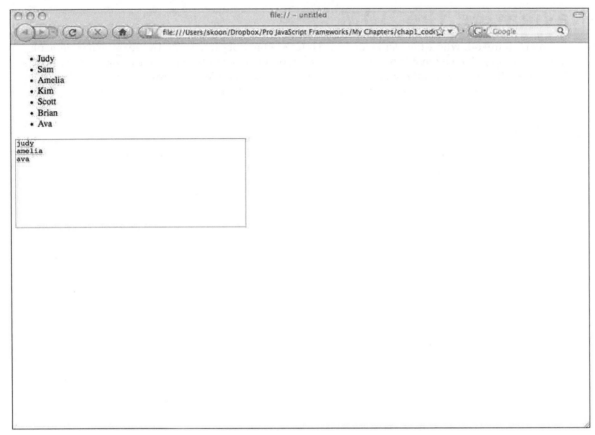

Figure 1-2

ancestors

This collects all of the element's ancestors in the order of their ancestry. The last ancestor of any given element will always be the HTML element. Calling this method on the HTML element will just return an empty array. Given the following HTML snippet:

```
<html>
    <body>
        <div id="myDiv">
            <p id="myParagraph">Hello pops</p>
        </div>
    </body>
</html>
```

The array would be returned with the elements in the following order:

```
DIV @--> BODY @--> HTML
```

You can use the following code to verify this behavior:

```html
<html>
    <body>
        <div id="myDiv">
            <p id="myParagraph">Hello pops</p>
        </div>
        <textarea id="results" cols="50" rows="10"></textarea>
        <script type="text/javascript" src="prototype-1.6.0.2.js"></script>
        <script type="text/javascript">
            Event.observe(window,"load", function(e) {
                var a = $('myParagraph').ancestors();
                $('results').value = "";
                for(var i = 0;i < a.length;i++) {
                    $('results').value += a[i].tagName + "\n";
                }
            });
        </script>

    </body>
</html>
```

up/down/next/previous

These four methods comprise Prototype's core DOM traversal functionality. They allow you to define a starting element, and then walk around the DOM at your leisure. All of the methods are chainable, allowing you to call each in succession on whatever element was returned by the preceding function. If no element can be found that matches the criteria you define, undefined is returned. Each method accepts two arguments: a CSS selector or a numeric index. If no argument is passed, the first element matching the criteria is returned. If an index is passed, the element at that position in the element's corresponding array is returned. For example, the resulting array used for the down() method will match the element's descendants array. If a CSS selector is passed in, the first element that matches that rule is returned. If both an index and a CSS rule are passed in, the CSS rule is processed first and then the index is used to select the element from the array defined by the CSS rule.

up

Returns the first ancestor matching the specified index and/or CSS rule. If no ancestor matches the criteria, undefined is returned. If no argument is specified, the element's first ancestor is returned. This is the same as calling element.parentNode and passing the parent through Element.extend.

down

Returns the first descendant matching the specified index and/or CSS rule. If no descendant matches the criteria, undefined is returned. If no argument is specified, the element's first descendant is returned.

next

Returns the element's siblings that come after the element matching the specified index and/or CSS rule. If no siblings match the CSS rule, all the following siblings are considered. If no siblings are found after the element, undefined is returned.

previous

Returns the element's siblings that come before the element matching the specified index and/or CSS rule. If no siblings match the CSS rule, all the previous siblings are considered. If no siblings are found before the element, undefined is returned.

Take a fragment of HTML that looks like the following example. Here you are defining four elements that relate to each other like this:

```
<div id="up">
        <p id="prevSibling">I'm a sibling</p><div id="start"><p id="down">Start
Here</p></div> <span id="nextSibling">I'm next</span>
    </div>
```

This code starts at the start DIV and looks at the previous, next, up, and down elements. You start at the element with the ID start. The paragraph element containing the text "Start Here" is the first child of the starting element and is returned by calling the down method. The up method returns the topDiv div. The previous method returns the sibling paragraph element and next returns the nextSibling span, as shown in Figure 1-3.

```
<body>
    <div id="up">
        <p id="prevSibling">I'm a sibling</p><div id="start"><p id="down">Start
Here</p></div> <span id="nextSibling">I'm next</span>
    </div>
    <textarea id="results" cols="50" rows="10"></textarea>
    <script type="text/javascript" src="prototype-1.6.0.2.js"></script>
    <script type="text/javascript">
        Event.observe(window,"load", function(e) {
            var startEl = $('start');
            var previousEl = startEl.previous();
            var upEl = startEl.up();
            var downEl = startEl.down();
            var nextEl = startEl.next();

            var resultTextArea = $("results");
            resultTextArea.value = "";
            resultTextArea.value += "start =" + startEl.id + "\n";
            resultTextArea.value += "previous =" + previousEl.id + "\n";
            resultTextArea.value += "next =" + nextEl.id + "\n";
            resultTextArea.value += "down =" + downEl.id + "\n";
            resultTextArea.value += "up =" + upEl.id + "\n";
        });
    </script>
</body>
```

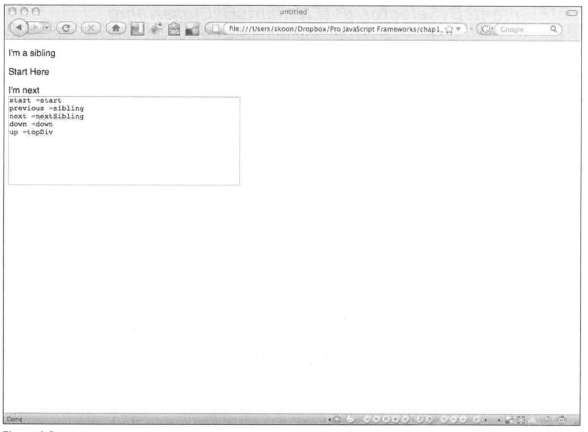

Figure 1-3

descendants/descendantOf/firstDescendant/ immediateDescendants

All of these methods allow you to work with the children of a given element. The methods `descendants` and `immediateDescendants` return arrays of child elements.

❑   **descendants** — This method returns an array containing the children of the element. If the element has no children, an empty array is returned.

❑   **descendantOf** — This method returns a Boolean telling you whether or not the given element is a descendant of the given ancestor.

❑   **firstDescendant** — This method returns the first child of a given element that is itself an element.

❑   **immediateDescendants** — (deprecated) This method returns an array of the elements one level down and no further.

getElementsBySelector/getElementsByClassName

These methods allow you to select groups of elements based on their attributes or position and manipulate the elements however you choose. Both of these methods have been deprecated and you should use the $$() method in place of them.

childElements

This useful function gathers up all the children of an element and returns them as an array of extended elements. The elements are returned in the same order as they are in the DOM. So, the element at index 0 is the closest child to the parent element and so forth.

Altering Page Content

Prototype provides four methods for changing content on a page: insert, remove, replace, and update. These methods can be called using the `Element` object and are added to any element that is extended. They all take an optional argument, which is the element to be altered. The insert and replace methods call `eval()` on any script tags contained in the content passed to them. Any of these methods that take a content argument will accept plain text, an HTML fragment, or a JavaScript object that supports `toString()`.

insert(element, content), insert(element, {position:content)

Insert takes the content you provide and inserts it into an element. If you do not specify a position (such as top, bottom, before, or after), your content will be appended to the element. This method is useful for dynamically inserting content retrieved from a web service or for loading elements into a page one piece at a time for performance reasons.

```
<script type="text/javascript">

    function insertSample() {
        $("MainDiv").insert("New Content added at the end by default");
        $("MainDiv").insert({top:"Added at the top"});
        $("MainDiv").insert({before:"Added before the element"})
        $("MainDiv").insert({after:"Added after the element"});
        $("MainDiv").insert({bottom:"Added at the bottom"});
    };
    insertSample();
</script>
```

remove

Calling remove on an extended element removes it completely from the DOM. The function returns the removed element. This method is most often used to remove an element after a user has chosen to delete whatever item the element represents in the UI.

```
<body>
    <table id="myTable">
        <tr id="firstRow"><td>First Row</td></tr>
        <tr id="secondRow"><td>Second Row</td></tr>
        <tr id="thirdRow"><td>Third Row</td></tr>
    </table>
    <script type="text/javascript" src="prototype-1.6.0.2.js"></script>
    <script type="text/javascript">

        function removeRow() {
            $("secondRow").remove();
        };
        removeRow();
    </script>
</body>
```

replace

Replace takes away the element specified and replaces it with the content provided. This removes the element and its children from the DOM.

```
<body>
    <div id="MainDiv">
        <div id="tempDiv">Place holder</div>
    </div>
    <script type="text/javascript" src="prototype-1.6.0.2.js"></script>
    <script type="text/javascript">
        //simulate loading content from a web service
        setTimeout(function () {
            $("MainDiv").replace("<h1>Replaced Content</h2>");
        }, 1000);
    </script>
</body>
```

update

Update replaces the content of an element with the specified content. It does not remove the element from the DOM, although it does remove any children of the element.

```
<body>
    <div id="MainDiv">Here is some content to be updated</div>
    <script type="text/javascript" src="prototype-1.6.0.2.js"></script>
    <script type="text/javascript">

    //simulate loading content from a web service
    setTimeout(function() {
        $("MainDiv").update("updated the content");
    }, 1000);
    </script>
</body>
```

Manipulating Element Size, Position, and Visibility

One of the hardest things about working with the DOM in different browsers is getting the dimensions of the elements contained in the DOM. Each browser has quirks relating to how it sizes elements in the DOM and how its size affects the flow of the surrounding elements.

Positioning an Element

Setting an element's position is one of the cornerstones of modern web page design. Often when designing dynamic web pages, you need to be able to move elements around and place them on the page exactly where you want them. To place an element precisely on the page, you should first set its position CSS style. Setting the position style rule to absolute means that the element's top and left coordinates are calculated from the top-left corner of the document. Setting the position to relative allows you to position the element using numbers calculated to the containing block's top-left corner. Prototype provides a few methods for easily setting an element's position style.

makePositioned, undoPositioned

These methods allow you to easily make CSS-positioned blocks out of elements in your DOM. Calling `makePositioned` on an element sets its `position` to `relative` if its current position is static or `undefined`. The `undoPositioned` method sets the element's `position` back to what it was before `makePositioned` was called.

```
$("myElement").makePositioned();
$("myElement").undoPositioned();
```

absolutize, relativize

These methods change the positioning setting of the given element by setting the position style to either absolute or relative, respectively.

```
$("myElement").absolutize();
$("myElement").relativize();
```

clonePosition

This method creates a new element with the same position and dimensions as the current element. You specify what settings are applied to the new element by using an optional parameter containing the following options:

Setting	Description
setLeft	Applies the source's CSS left property. Defaults to true.
setTop	Applies the source's CSS top property. Defaults to true.
setWidth	Applies the source's CSS width property. Defaults to true.
setHeight	Applies the source's CSS height property. Defaults to true.
offsetLeft	Lets you offset the clone's left CSS property by n value. Defaults to 0.
offsetTop	Lets you offset the clone's top CSS property by n value. Defaults to 0.

Dealing with Offsets

Prototype has a couple of different methods on its `Element` object that make finding the offset of an element easier.

cumulativeOffset, positionedOffset, viewportOffset

Each of these methods returns two numbers, the top and left values of the given element in the form `{ left: number, top: number}`. The `cumulativeOffset` method returns the total offset of an element from the top left of the document. The positionedOffset method returns the total offset of an element's closest positioned (one whose position is set to `'static'`) ancestor. The viewportOffset method returns the offset of the element relative to the viewport.

getOffsetParent

This method returns the nearest positioned ancestor of the element, and returns the body element if no other ancestor is found.

The following code illustrates how the different offsets are calculated. In it, you have two elements: a parent DIV with one child. The parent has its `position` set to `absolute` and is positioned 240 pixels from the top and 50 pixels from the left side of the document. When you call the `getOffsetParent` method of the element with the ID of `start`, the positioned element `positionedParent` is returned. The `results` textarea has no positioned ancestors. If you call `getOffsetParent` on it, the BODY element is returned. Since the `start` element itself is not positioned, calling `positionedOffset` returns 0,0, as shown in Figure 1-4.

```
<body>
    <div id="positionedParent" style="position:absolute;border:1px solid black;
top:240px;left:50px;">
        <div id="start">Start Here</div>
    </div>

    <textarea id="results" cols="50" rows="10"></textarea>
    <script type="text/javascript" src="prototype-1.6.0.2.js"></script>
    <script type="text/javascript">
        Event.observe(window,"load", function(e) {
            $("results").value = "";
            $("results").value += "offsetParent = " + $("start").getOffsetParent()
.id + "\n";
            $("results").value += "cumulativeOffset = " + $("start")
.cumulativeOffset() + "\n";
            $("results").value += "positionedOffset = " + $("start")
.positionedOffset() + "\n";
            $("results").value += "parent positionedOffset = " + $("start")
.parentNode.positionedOffset() + "\n";
        });
    </script>
</body>
```

15

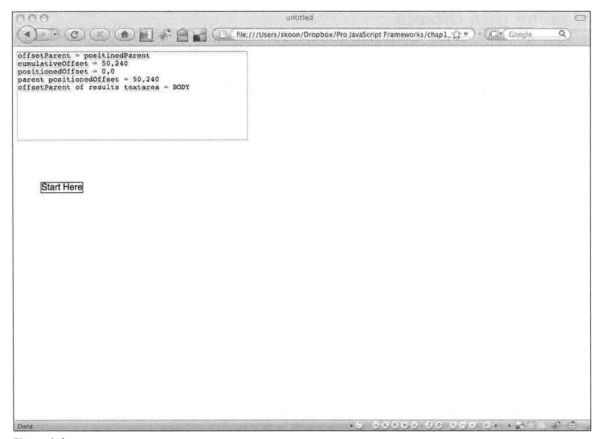

Figure 1-4

Showing/Hiding Elements

Showing and hiding an element has been part of your web developer's toolkit since you typed in your first script tag.

show/hide

These methods allow you to quickly change an element's visibility. They do this by setting the elements `display` CSS style to `none`. Setting the display to none removes the element from the flow of the document and causes the browser to render the other elements in the page as if the element were not present.

```
$("myElement").show();
$("myElement").hide();
```

setOpacity

This method sets the opacity of a given element, while relieving you of the burden of dealing with various browser inconsistencies. It takes a floating-point number, with 0 being totally transparent and 1 being completely opaque. Using this method is the equivalent of setting the opacity via a CSS class or using the `setStyle` method, passing in a value for opacity.

```
$("myElement").setOpacity(0.5);
```

Sizing an Element

Every browser has some kind of quirk associated with the way it represents elements on the screen and how it calculates the element's dimensions. Different browsers calculate an element's computed style differently. Prototype equalizes the differences and returns the correct computed style for the browser.

getDimensions, getHeight, getWidth

Using these methods, you can get the computed dimensions of an element at run time. The `getDimensions` method returns an object containing the computed height and width of the element. When you call `getDimensions`, it's best to save the returned value in a local variable and refer to that rather than making multiple calls. If you just want the width or height, it's best to just call the appropriate method.

```
Var dimensions = $('myDiv').getDimensions();
Var currentWidth = dimensions.width;
Var currentHeight = dimensions.height;
```

makeClipping, undoClipping

The CSS `clip` property allows you to define whether or not the element's content should be shown if the content is wider or taller than the element's width and height will allow. Since the `clip` property is poorly supported amongst the browsers, Prototype provides this method that will set an element's `overflow` property to `hidden` for you. You can use `undoClipping` to allow the element to resize normally.

Working with CSS and Styles

CSS classes are useful for marking elements in response to some event. Say you are creating an online survey form and you want to mark several fields as required, but you don't want to get each element that is required by ID and check them one by one to make sure the user has entered a proper value. You can create a CSS class called "required" and apply it to each of the elements you need the user to enter a value into. Sometimes you need to change an element's style or class at run time in response to a user- or data-driven event, say if you are changing a table row from read-only to editable. Classes are an invaluable tool in any web developer's toolkit. Prototype makes it easier for you to apply and remove CSS classes from elements in your DOM.

addClassName, removeClassName, toggleClassNames

These three methods all alter the className property of a given element. All of them check to make sure the element has the given class name. These methods are useful when you need to set classes on an element or need to turn a CSS style on or off. Their names are self-explanatory.

```
<head>
        <meta http-equiv="Content-Type" content="text/html; charset=utf-8">
        <title>untitled</title>
    <style>
        .invalid { background:red;}
    </style>
</head>
<body>
    <form id="myForm" method="post">
        First Name:<input type="text" id="firstName" class="required"><br/>
        Last Name:<input type="text" id="lastName" class="required"><br/>
        Age:<input type="text" id="age"><br/>
        <input type="button" id="submitButton" value="submit">
    </form>
    <script type="text/javascript" src="prototype-1.6.0.2.js"></script>
    <script type="text/javascript">

        function init() {
            var requiredInputs = $$(".required");
            for(i = 0;i < requiredInputs.length;i++) {
                $(requiredInputs[i]).insert({"after":"*required"});
                Event.observe(requiredInputs[i], "change", function(e) {
                    if(this.hasClassName("invalid")) { this.removeClassName
("invalid")};
                });
            };
            Event.observe("submitButton", "click", validateUserInput);

        };

function validateUserInput() {
            var requiredInputs = $$(".required");
              for(var i = 0; i < requiredInputs.length; i++) {
                if(requiredInputs[i].value == "") {
                    requiredInputs[i].addClassName("invalid");
                } else {
                    if (requiredInputs[i].hasClassName("invalid")) {
                        requiredInputs[i].removeClassName(invalid);
                    };
                };
            };
        };          Event.observe(window, 'load', init);
    </script>
</body>
```

One common task for JavaScript is form validation. Here, you've set up a simple form and defined a simple rule; users have to enter some text into elements that have the "required" class. You can enforce that rule by collecting all of the elements who have the required class using the $$() method and passing in a CSS selector. Once you have an array containing those elements, you iterate over the array and check that the value property of each element does not equal an empty string. If it does, you use the addClass method to add the invalid class to the element. You then also check to see if the class already has the invalid class and the user has entered text. If an element contains text and has the invalid class, you remove the class since it passes the validation rules, as shown in Figure 1-5 and Figure 1-6, respectively.

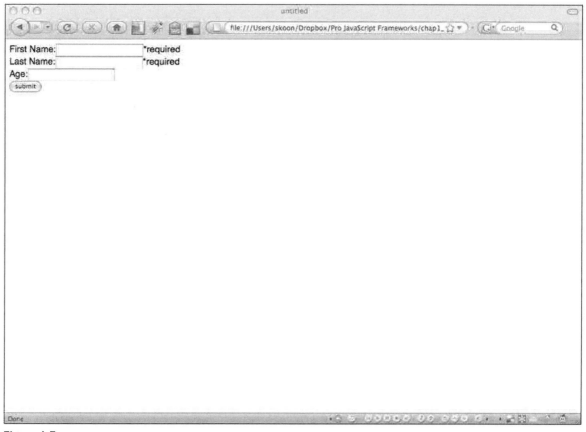

Figure 1-5

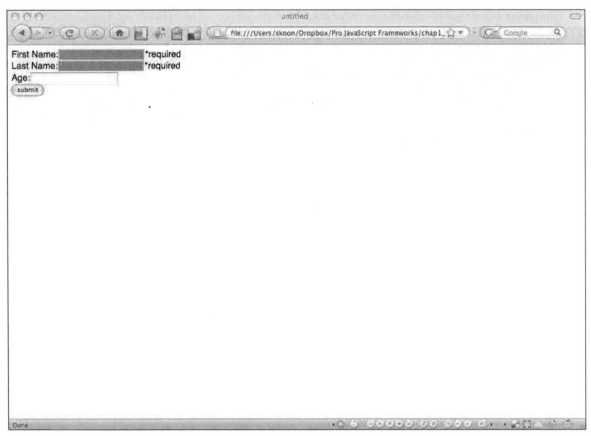

Figure 1-6

hasClassName, classNames

These methods tell you what classes have been applied to the element in question. The hasClassName method allows you to determine if a given element has the class name in its className property. The classNames method has been deprecated; it returns an array containing the classes that have been applied to the element.

setStyle, getStyle

These methods allow you to quickly set styles on your elements and get values for specific styles. You may only query for styles defined by the Document Object Model (DOM) Level 2 Style Specification. To set a style on your element, you pass in an object hash of key-value pairs of the styles you wish to set.

```
El.setStyle( { "font-family": "Arial", "color" : "#F3C" });
```

To get the value for a specific style, pass in the style's name as an argument.

```
El.getStyle("font-size");
```

Internet Explorer returns the literal value while all other browsers return the computed value for styles. For example, if you specify the font-size as 1em, that is what IE will return. Other browsers may return a pixel value for the font-size.

Extending an Element with Your Own Methods

Prototype makes it easy to add your own methods to the `Element` object using the `addMethods` method. The `addMethods` method takes a hash of the methods you want to add. Suppose you want to add a method to any element that will allow you to strip all the whitespace out of the element's text. Here's what that function might look like:

```
function removeWhiteSpace(element) {
    if(element.innerText) {
        return element.innerText.replace(" ", "", "gi");
    } else if(element.textContent){
        return element.textContent.replace(" ", "", "gi");
    }
};
```

First, you need to rewrite the method a little to match what Prototype expects. Then you can call `Element.addMethods`.

```
<body>
    <div id="myDiv">Remove the whitespace</div>
    <script type="text/javascript" src="prototype-1.6.0.2.js"></script>
    <script type="text/javascript">
        var myFunc = {
            removeWhitespace : function (element) {
                if(element.innerText) {
                  return element.innerText.replace(" ", "", "gi");
              } else if(element.textContent){
                  return element.textContent.replace(" ", "", "gi");
              }
            }
        };

    Element.addMethods(myFunc);

    alert($("myDiv").removeWhitespace());
    </script>
</body>
```

What you did here was wrap your function with an intrinsic object so that addMethods can work its magic. You can take this one step further and return the element itself to allow for chaining.

```
var myFunc = {
    removeWhitespace : function (element) {
        if(element.innerText) {
            element.innertText = element.innerText.replace(" ", "", "gi");
        } else if(element.textContent){
            element.textContent = element.textContent.replace(" ", "", "gi");
        }
        return element;
    }
};
```

So now your method is ready to be used by Prototype.

Summary

In this chapter, you looked at how Prototype makes it easy to obtain a reference to DOM elements by ID, CSS class, and their position relative to other elements. Prototype automatically adds helper methods to your elements when possible, and adds the methods when you use the `Element.extends()`, `$()`, or `$$()` methods to get a reference to the element. Prototype also smoothes out some of the bumps associated with positioning elements and finding out the dimensions of a given element.

2

Handling Cross-Browser Events

Event handling is one of the stickier parts of writing modern web applications. Internet Explorer and the W3C have different event handling models. Internet Explorer supports a method called `attachEvent` for adding event handlers to elements. The W3C standard defines a method called `addEventListener` to do the same thing. Prototype provides a cross-browser method for wiring up your event handlers and extends the event object with several useful methods.

In this chapter, you'll learn about:

❑   Using `Event.observe` to wire up your event handlers

❑   Responding to events, including keyboard and mouse events

❑   Periodically firing off events

Registering Event Handlers

Prior to the rise of JavaScript frameworks, most web developers had to wire up event handlers like so:

```
var myInput = document.getElementById("myInput");
    if(myInput.addEventListener ) {
        myInput.addEventListener('keydown',this.keyHandler,false); //W3C
method
    } else if(myInput.attachEvent ) {
        myInput.attachEvent('onkeydown',this.keyHandler); //IE method
    };
```

So why wire up event handlers using either of those methods when all browsers support event attributes like onClick and the DOM level 0 properties like onclick and onload? All of those properties only point to one event handler at a time. If you want to call multiple functions during the window's `onload` event, you have to define one function that calls all of the other functions and assign that to the `window.onload` event. If any other code, say a third-party widget library, assigns an event handler to the `window.onload` event, yours will not be called.

Prototype's Event object provides an easy way to wire up multiple event handlers to an element. It also gives you a cross-browser way to access information about the event, the element that fired the event, the first element with a given tag name near the triggering event, and a way to stop the default action of the event.

Event.observe()

The general form of `Event.observe()` looks like this:

```
Event.observe(element, eventName, handler [,useCapture = false]);
```

The method's arguments are as follows:

❏   `element` — This is the element to bind the event handler to. You can pass in a reference to either the element or just the string ID of the element.

❏   `eventName` — This is the W3C DOM level 2 standard name for the event.

❏   `handler` — This is the function that should handle the event. This can be a pre-declared function or an anonymous function.

❏   `useCapture` — This function determines whether or not to use event capturing or bubbling. Most of the time you won't need to use event capturing and the default of false will work fine.

In order to bind an event handler to an event on an element, the element must exist in the DOM at the time you try to bind it.

```
<body>
    <ul id="PeopleList">
        <li class="female" id="judy">Judy</li>
        <li class="male" id="sam">Sam</li>
        <li class="female" id="amelia">Amelia</li>
        <li class="female" id="kim">Kim</li>
        <li class="male" id="scott">Scott</li>
        <li class="male" id="brian">Brian</li>
        <li class="female" id="ava">Ava</li>

    </ul>

    <textarea id="results" cols="50" rows="10"></textarea>
    <script type="text/javascript" src="prototype-1.6.0.2.js"></script>
<script type="text/javascript">
        $("results").value = "";
        Event.observe("PeopleList", "click", function(e) {
            $("results").value += "clicked on " + e.target.id + "\n";
        });
    </script>
</body>
```

Figure 2-1 shows an unordered list that represents a list of people. You want to know the name of the person, the id of the li element, which the user clicked on.

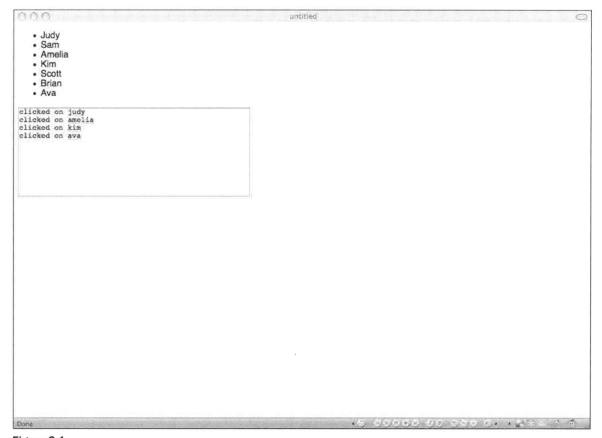

Figure 2-1

Responding to Events

Catching the event when it fires is the first half of the job; now you have to respond to the event. All browsers provide an event object that contains information about the event as well as methods that let you stop the event. Internet Explorer puts the event object in the global window object while the W3C standard says that the event object is passed to the event handler. You end up writing a lot of code that looks like this:

```
function clickHandler(evt) {
      evt = evt || window.event;
target = evt.target || evt.srcElement;
      ///remainder of the event handler goes here
};
```

25

Prototype smoothes out the rough edges of event handling by providing an Event object that gives you access to some common methods and properties. You can access the Event object from within your event handler, pass it the event object for context, and use it instead of writing the branching code shown previously.

Event.target, this, and Event.element

Take a look at the example shown earlier in this chapter, but instead of referring to event.target, change the code to refer to this and the element returned by Event.element(). The result is shown in Figure 2-2.

```
<script type="text/javascript">
        $("results").value = "";
        Event.observe("PeopleList", "click", function(e) {
                e = e || window.event;
                e.target = e.target || e.srcElement;
            $("results").value += "this= " + this.id + "\n";
            $("results").value += "Event.element(event)= " + Event.element(e).id + "\n";
            $("results").value += "event.target= " + e.target.id + "\n";
        });
    </script>
```

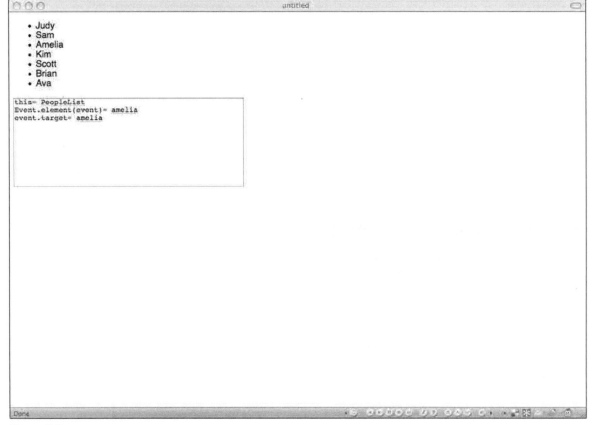

Figure 2-2

You can see that the element returned by the `Event.element()` method is the same element returned by the W3C standard `event.target` property and Internet Explorer's `event.srcElement` property. By using the `Event.element()` method, you can write one line of code to get the element that raised the event instead of having to do object detection on the `event` or `window.event` object.

Event.findElement(element, tagname)

Sometimes you want to find an element near the element that fired an event. The Event.findElement method searches upward from the element that triggered the event and returns the first element that matches the tag name you pass in as a parameter.

Go back to the list example. You can wrap your list in a div tag and obtain a reference to it by calling the `Event.findElement()` method and passing in "div" as your tag name.

```
<body>
    <div id="container">
        <ul id="PeopleList">
            <li class="female" id="judy">Judy</li>
            <li class="male" id="sam">Sam</li>
            <li class="female" id="amelia">Amelia</li>
            <li class="female" id="kim">Kim</li>
            <li class="male" id="scott">Scott</li>
            <li class="male" id="brian">Brian</li>
            <li class="female" id="ava">Ava</li>

        </ul>
    </div>

    <textarea id="results" cols="50" rows="10"></textarea>
    <script type="text/javascript" src="prototype-1.6.0.2.js"></script>
    <script type="text/javascript">
        $("results").value = "";
        Event.observe("PeopleList", "click", function(e) {
                e = e || window.event;
            var container = Event.findElement(e,"div");
            $("results").value = container.id;
        });
    </script>
</body>
```

Event.findElement provides a very simple search functionality. It only searches by tag name. If you need a more complex search, you should get the element the event occurred on by calling the `Event.element()` method and using the `up()` method. You can use CSS selector syntax with the `up()` method.

stopObserving() and unloadCache()

The `stopObserving` method removes the event handler from an element for the event you specify and prevents the event handler from firing in response to that event. You call it with the same arguments as you did when you wired the event up the first time. The `unloadCache()` method unregisters all of the event handlers that were registered using the `Event.observe` method. It will not remove event handlers added any other way; you have to remember to remove those yourself. Internet Explorer has a nasty habit of leaking memory if event handlers are not removed from objects before the objects are removed from the DOM. As of version 1.6, Prototype automatically calls `unloadCache()` for you when the `document` `.unload` event fires, and removes all the event handlers before the DOM objects are cleaned up.

Event.extend(event)

This method extends the event object with the methods in `Event.methods` if it is not already extended. All of the events that are passed to event handlers that were registered using `Event.observe` have already been extended by Prototype. You should only have to call this inside of event handlers that were wired up using the element attributes or by using the native DOM methods `attachEvent` or `addEventListener`.

Event.stop(event)

Suppose you want to prevent the event from bubbling up to an elements parent. Mozilla provides a `stopPropogation` method on the event object and Internet Explorer has a `cancelBubble` method. Stopping the propagation of the event doesn't keep the default action of the event from firing. You have to return false from the event handler to prevent the default action. Prototype serves up a single method that will stop the propagation of the event and prevent the default action of the event from firing.

Here you have a simple input validation script. If the user does not enter the word *pass* in the top input box and tries to tab to the bottom input box, the tab will be blocked and an alert box will pop up instructing the user what to enter.

```html
<body>
    <input type="text" id="input1"><br/>
    <input type="text" id="input2">
    <script type="text/javascript" src="prototype-1.6.0.2.js"></script>
    <script type="text/javascript">
        Event.observe("input1", "keydown", function(e) {
            e = e || window.event;
                if(e.keyCode == 9) {
                    if(Event.element(e).value != "pass") {
                        Event.stop(e);
                        alert("You must enter 'pass!'");
                    }
                }
        });
    </script>
</body>
```

Accepting Keyboard and Mouse Input Across Browsers

Prototype makes it easier to handle keyboard and mouse events by providing a few helper methods on the Event object as well as defining some constants that represent keyboard codes.

isLeftClick

This method tells you if the user has clicked the primary mouse button. This compensates for how the user has configured the system.

pointerX/pointerY

This method returns the absolute horizontal or vertical position of the mouse pointer at the time the event occurred. It is important to note that this is relative to the page and not the viewport. If you scroll down the page some, different coordinates will be returned if the event occurs at the same spot in the viewport.

Keyboard Constants

All of the following constants are defined in the Event namespace.

- ❑   KEY_BACKSPACE

- ❑   KEY_TAB

- ❑   KEY_RETURN

- ❑   KEY_ESC

- ❑   KEY_LEFT

- ❑   KEY_DOWN

- ❑   KEY_RIGHT

- ❑   KEY_UP

- ❑   KEY_DELETE

- ❑   KEY_HOME

- ❑   KEY_PAGEUP

- ❑   KEY_PAGEDOWN

Firing Scheduled Events

Modern browsers provide two methods for executing a function at a timed interval:

- ❑   window.setInterval

- ❑   window.clearInterval

Prototype provides an enhanced version of the setInterval method called PeriodicalExecuter, which ensures that only one callback function is running at a time. The TimedObserver abstract class provides the basis for the `Form.Observer` and `Form.Element.Observer` classes that tell you when elements contained in a form have changed and allow you to react to the changes.

PeriodicalExecuter

This method is very similar to the `window.setInterval` method except that it provides a check to prevent running multiple parallel calls to the callback function. You use the PeriodicalExecuter by creating a new instance of the class and passing in the callback function and the interval in seconds.

```
var pe = new PeriodicalExecuter(callback function, interval);
```

29

The only way to stop a PeriodicalExecuter from running is to reload the page or to call the `stop()` method on the PeriodicalExecuter object.

```
<script type="text/javascript">
        Event.observe(window, "load", function(e) {
            var pe = new PeriodicalExecuter(function(e) {
                if(confirm("Have you filled out your TPS reports?")) {
                    pe.stop();
                }
            }, 5);
        });
</script>
```

TimedObserver

The TimedObserver class is an abstract class that is the basis of two Form helper classes: `Form.Observer` and `Form.Element.Observer`.

Form.Observer

The `Form.Observer` class checks all of the elements on the specified form and calls the function specified by the callback parameter. You can use this class when you want to find out if a group of elements on a form have changed since the last time the callback function was executed. You use it by creating a new instance of the `Form.Observer` class and passing in the form element or ID, the interval in seconds you want the form to be checked, and the callback function.

```
new Form.Observer(element, interval, callback);
```

Here you set up a form containing a single text input in which you want to be notified when the user has typed something different into the text box. The result is shown in Figure 2-3.

```
<body>
    <form id="myForm" action="#">
        <p id="msg" class="message">Current message:</p>
        <div>
          <label for="message">message</label>
          <input id="message" type="text" name="message" value="Hello world!" />
        </div>
    </form>
    <script type="text/javascript">
        new Form.Observer('myForm', 0.3, function(form, value){
          $('msg').update('form changed to ' + value).style.color = 'blue'
          form.down().setStyle({ background:'lime', borderColor:'red' })
        })
    </script>
</body>
```

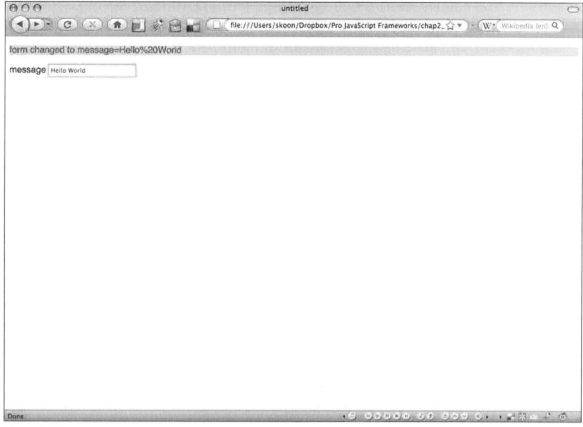

Figure 2-3

Form.Element.Observer

Sometimes you want to be notified when a single element in a form has been changed. The Form.Element.Observer class is an excellent choice. The result is shown in Figure 2-4.

```
<body>
    <form id="myForm" action="#">
        <p id="msg" class="message">Current message:</p>
        <div>
          <label for="message">message</label>
          <input id="message" type="text" name="message" value="Hello world!" />
          <label for="selection">Make a selection</label>
          <select id="selection">
              <option>first</option>
              <option>second</option>
          </select>
        </div>
    </form>
    <script type="text/javascript">
```

```
        new Form.Element.Observer('selection', 0.3, function(form, value){
          $('msg').update('form changed to ' + value).style.color = 'blue'
          form.down().setStyle({ background:'lime', borderColor:'red' })
        })
      </script>
  </body>
```

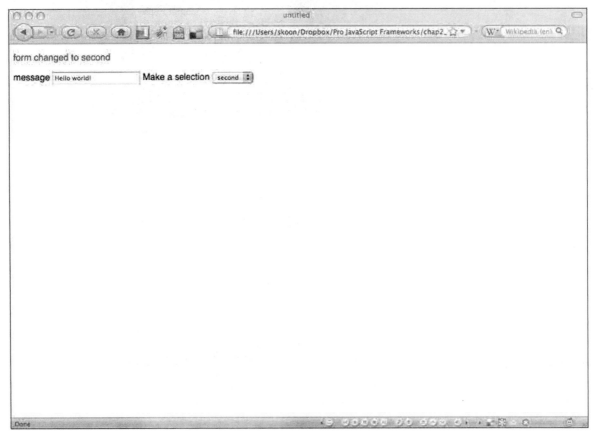

Figure 2-4

Summary

Wiring up and handling events in different browsers is tricky. You have to branch your code to set the event handlers and check different objects with different names for the same properties. Prototype eases that pain by providing a central object that will both wire up events in a cross-browser fashion and give you a central object you can call to get information about the element that triggered the event handler.

3

Simplifying AJAX and Dynamic Data

In 1999, Microsoft released Internet Explorer 5 and included a new type of browser object called XMLHTTP. This new object allowed web developers to request data from the web server without having to reload the entire page. They incorporated the use of XMLHTTP request into their Outlook Web Access product. Three years later, the Mozilla project would release Mozilla 1.0 with support for XMLHttpRequest. Developers started to use the new XMLHttpRequest and the old XMLHTTP objects to make their data more responsive to user interaction. In 2005, Jesse James Garrett coined the term AJAX (Asynchronous JavaScript and XML) to describe the set of technologies and interactions the web developers were using. AJAX tools are powerful tools for building richer, more responsive web applications. In response to the use and popularity of AJAX technologies, more JavaScript libraries and frameworks started to create wrappers around the two different XMLHttpRequest objects to make using them seamless to the developers. Prototype not only makes requesting data from a server with any web browser painless, but it also provides a few different flavors of AJAX requests to meet the needs of current web developers.

In this chapter, you'll learn about:

- ❑ Making requests to a server
- ❑ Setting up responders that will update your web page
- ❑ Setting up periodic updaters to poll your server for new data

Making Requests to a Server

All of the objects that you'll use when you make AJAX calls with Prototype are contained in the Ajax object. The workhorse of Prototype's AJAX is the `Ajax.Request` method. You create a new `Ajax.Request` object and pass in a URL and an options argument. Here is a basic example:

```
//Ajax.Request(url [,options]);

var url = "http://myserver/api/get";

var ajaxCall = new Ajax.Request(url, {
      method: "get",
      onSuccess: function() { alert("success") },
      onFailure: function() { alert("Failed") },
      onComplete: function() { alert("Complete") }
});
```

There are a couple of interesting things going on here. First, you can specify the method of the request using an HTTP verb. HTTP POST and HTTP GET are most commonly used. Second, you are creating new functions to handle the success or failure of the request. Both XMLHttpRequest and XMLHTTP provide a method for setting a callback when a request is completed, but you still have to check the response code manually to see whether or not the request was successful. Prototype looks at the response code and calls the callback specified in `onSuccess` or `onFailure` based on some simple criteria. The `onSuccess` callback is called if the request status is either undefined or in the 200 family; otherwise the `onFailure` callback is called.

In the preceding example, the order of events is as follows:

1. Request is created.
2. Request is initialized.
3. Request is sent.
4. The response is received. This can happen multiple times.
5. If the status code is 2xx, onSuccess is called; otherwise, onFailure is called.
6. Request is completed.

Ajax.Request

Prototype's Ajax object supports a number of options for constructing your requests. These options are passed in when you create a new `Ajax.Request`. Most of the time the default value will be the correct value, but it is good to know what the options are if you need to set them.

Option	Description
asynchronous	Tells Prototype whether or not to make the request asynchronously. Synchronous requests often have unwanted side effects that are generally discouraged. Defaults to "true".
contentType	Specifies the content type of your request. Defaults to "application/x-www-form-urlencoded".
encoding	Specifies the encoding of your request. Defaults to UTF-8.
method	Specifies the HTTP method to be used. Defaults to "post".
parameters	Specifies the parameters to be included along with the request. If the method is set to "get", the parameters will be encoded and appended to the url.
postBody	Specifies the contents of the body if the method of the request is set to "post". If the postBody option is not set, the parameters option will be used instead.
requestHeaders	Either an object, "{header: value}" or an array (even number indexes hold the name of the header and odd indexes hold the value) representing headers to be sent along with the request. Prototype provides 4 default headers that you can override to meet your needs.
	X-Requested-With – Set to "XMLHttpRequest".
	X-Prototype-Version – Set to the version number of the Prototype library you are using.
	Accept – Set to "text/javascript, text/html, application/xml, text/xml, */*"
	Content-type – Set to the current content-type and encoding defined by the request options.
evalJS	If the server response contentType is set to one of the following, the responseText is evaluated:
	* application/ecmascript
	* application/javascript
	* application/x-ecmascript
	* application/x-javascript
	* text/ecmascript
	* text/javascript
	* text/x-ecmascript
	* text/x-javascript
	Defaults to "true". You can force evaluation by passing "force" or cancel it by passing "false".
evalJSON	If the contentType of the response from the server is set to "application/json", the responseText will be evaluated and the responseJSON property of the Ajax.Request will be set to the result. You can force evaluation by passing "force" or cancel it by passing "false".
sanitizeJSON	Sanitizes the responseText before evaluating. Defaults to "false" for local, "true" otherwise.

In order for any JavaScript contained in the responseText to be automatically sent to `eval()`, the AJAX request has to set the content type to one of the JavaScript-related, content-type headers and obey the Same Origin Policy. The Same Origin Policy states that the request must occur from the same domain name, protocol, and port as the server that responds to the request before the data can be used.

Callbacks

Prototype defines a number of callback functions for different stages of the request cycle. All of the callbacks are called with two parameters. The first parameter will be the XMLHttpRequest object that was used for the request. The second parameter will be the result of evaluating the server response if the Content-type is set to a JSON type. You tie into these callbacks by defining or assigning a function in the options that you pass to your request object.

Callback Name	Description
onCreate	Called when the request is initialized but before any of the XHR methods are called.
onComplete	Called when the request is completed.
onException	Called whenever the XHR object throws an exception. Passes the request object as the first argument to the callback and the exception object thrown by the XHR object as the second argument.
onFailure	Called when the status code of the response is not 2xx.
onInteractive	Called when part of the response is received when the response is sent in several parts. Not guaranteed to be called.
onLoaded	Called when the request is set up and the connection is open, but the call has not been made to the server. Not guaranteed to be called.
onLoading	Called when the request is set up and the connection is opened but the request is not ready to be sent. Not guaranteed to be called.
onSucccess	Called when the status code of the response is in the 2xx range.
onUninitialized	Called just after the XHR object is created.
on{status code}	These represent callbacks for specific HTTP status codes, such as on200. If a callback for a status code is specified, onSuccess and onFailure are not called. These callbacks occur before the onComplete callback.

Ajax.Response

`Ajax.Response` is the first parameter passed to all of the `Ajax.Request` callbacks. It is basically a wrapper for the browser-specific XMLHttpRequest object.

Property	Description
status	The HTTP status code from the server.
statusText	The HTTP status text from the server.
readyState	The current state of the request. 0 - "Uninitialized" 1 - "Loading" 2 - "Loaded" 3 - "Interactive" 4 - "Complete"
responseText, responseXML, responseJSON	The body of the HTTP response in the specified format.
headerJSON	The content of the X-JSON header if present.
request	The Ajax.Request or Ajax.Updater used in the request.
transport	The native XMLHttpRequest or XMLHTTP object used in the request.

Methods of Ajax.Response

Prototype provides new implementations of two native XMLHttpRequest methods:
getResponseHeader and getAllResponseHeaders. The main difference being that Prototype's
methods will not throw an error if the header specified is not present, they return null instead. You
should use Prototype's method rather than the wrappers for the native XMLHttpRequest methods:

❏   getHeader(name) — Returns the requested header. If the header specified by "name" is not
present, this method returns null.

❏   getAllHeaders() — Returns a string containing all of the headers separated by line breaks.

❏   getResponseHeader(name) — This is a wrapper around the native
XMLHttp getResponseHeader method and will return the response header specified by
"name" if present.

❏   getAllResponseHeaders() — Returns a string containing all of the headers separated by line
breaks. This is another wrapped method.

Responding Globally to Changing Data

So now you can make an AJAX call using Prototype and respond to the response from the server. There
are some things you want to happen no matter what specific AJAX request you are making, such as
showing a spinning graphic in an overlay to tell the user that something is happening in the background.
Prototype has defined a repository to hold generic responders to Ajax.Request events.

Ajax.Responders

Ajax.Responders is a collection of global callbacks you define. In order to set up a global callback, you define an object and define the function using the same name as the callback you want to register.

```
Ajax.Responders.register({
onCreate: function() {
//do some stuff
        }
});
```

If you define a global callback, it will not be called for AJAX requests that already have that callback defined.

You have to unregister a responder using the exact object you used to register the responder. So if you think you'll want to unregister a responder later, make sure you keep a reference to the responder around to pass to the unregister method.

```
var globalResponders =  {
        onComplete: function() { //hide the "Loading… div },
        onCreate : function() { //show the "Loading …" div. }
};
Ajax.Responders.register(globalResponders);
// code  happens here
Ajax.Responders.unregister(globalResponders);
```

Updating a Page Dynamically

This section describes how to update a page dynamically.

Ajax.Updater

The Ajax.Updater object is a specialized form of the Ajax.Request object. You pass a container element as your first parameter and the Ajax.Updater object will put the contents of the request's responseText in the container you specify. The rest of the arguments are the same as the Ajax.Request object, but also includes two new options to pass to the constructor: evalScripts and insertion.

```
<div id="myDiv">Remove the whitespace</div>
    <script type="text/javascript" src="prototype-1.6.0.2.js"></script>
    <script type="text/javascript">
        var updater = new Ajax.Updater('myDiv', '/getItems'{
            method: "get",
            onSuccess: function() { alert("success") },
            onFailure: function() { alert("Failed") },
            onComplete: function() { alert("Complete") },
            insertion: 'top'
        });
    </script>
```

evalScripts

The `evalScripts` option allows you to specify whether or not `<script>` elements in the `responseText` are passed to the JavaScript `eval()` function. This does not mean that the `<script>` elements are added to the DOM of your page. It means that the JavaScript contained in the `<script>` tag is executed. There are a couple of side effects to this:

❑ The execution scope of the code that is evaluated will be Prototype's internal processing function.

❑ You must use the following syntax to define any functions you want to be accessible to the rest of your page. If you define your functions in the normal fashion, they will be lost once Prototype stops processing your response.

```
Function Myfunction() {}; // This won't work.

Myfunction = function() {};//This will allow other code on your page to call
Myfunction after the response has ended.
```

insertion

Normally, the `Element.update` function is used to put the new content in the container specified in the `Ajax.Updater` initializer. If you pass "insertion" in as an option, you can tell Prototype where to insert the content using the standard strings: `'top'`,`'bottom'`,`'before'`, and `'after'`.

So what happens if your request returns a 404? You don't want the 404 HTML to be inserted into your container. That would look tacky and unprofessional. The `Ajax.Updater` object supports an alternate constructor that takes an object. The object defines the elements to be updated in the case of a successful call or a failed call.

```
<body>
    <div id="myDiv">Remove the whitespace</div>
    <div id="errorDiv"></div>
    <script type="text/javascript" src="prototype-1.6.0.2.js"></script>
    <script type="text/javascript">
        var updater = new Ajax.Updater(
            {
                success: "myDiv",
                failure: "errorDiv"
            }
        , '/getItems'{
                method: "get",
                onSuccess: function() { alert("success") },
                onFailure: function() { alert("Failed") },
                onComplete: function() { alert("Complete") },
                insertion: 'top'
        });
    </script>
</body>
```

Ajax.PeriodicalUpdater

The `Ajax.PeriodicalUpdater` performs a request at an interval that you specify in the request's options. It is not a specialized form of `Ajax.Request` or `Ajax.Updater`:

❏ `frequency` — Defaults to "2". This is the number of seconds between each request.

❏ `decay` — Defaults to "1". Whenever a request's `responseText` is unchanged from the previous request, the current period is multiplied by the decay. This allows you to change the number of requests based on how often you think the data will change. If you think that the data won't change very often, you can set this to a higher number. As soon as the response text changes, the decay is reset to 1.

❏ `Ajax.PeriodicalUpdater` — This is useful when you want to poll the server for new data, but want to throttle down the number of requests your app makes to your server if the data is not changing quickly.

```
<body>
    <div id="myDiv">Remove the whitespace</div>
    <script type="text/javascript" src="prototype-1.6.0.2.js"></script>
    <script type="text/javascript">
        var periodicalUpdater = new Ajax.PeriodicalUpdater('myDiv', '/getItems'
        {
            method: 'get'
            frequency: 3,
            decay: 2
        });
    </script>
</body>
```

In some cases, you may find that you want to stop the requests altogether after a certain frequency has been reached or if the request fails. The `Ajax.PeriodicalUpdater` provides two methods called `start()` and `stop()` for doing just that.

```
<body>
    <div id="myDiv">Remove the whitespace</div>
    <script type="text/javascript" src="prototype-1.6.0.2.js"></script>
    <script type="text/javascript">
        var periodicalUpdater = new Ajax.PeriodicalUpdater('myDiv', '/getItems'
        {
            method: 'get'
            frequency: 3,
            decay: 2,
            onComplete: function() {
                if(periodicalUpdater.frequency > 48) { periodicalUpdater.stop(); }
            },
            onFailure: function() { periodicalUpdater.stop();}
        });
    </script>
</body>
```

Summary

Prototype was one of the first major JavaScript libraries to make cross-browser AJAX calls less painful. It can automatically interpret JavaScript and JSON responses from your server. It makes it easier to update your user interface with data requested from your server at periodic intervals and controls how often requests are made to your server.

Working with Forms

Using forms to gather data from users is part of every web developer's life. Working with forms is a little time consuming and painful. Prototype makes it easier to work with forms and form elements by providing methods for quickly getting their values. You can also check to see if form elements have values and set the focus to any form element you want. Additionally, with Prototype you can easily serialize your form data and submit it to the server using an AJAX call.

In this chapter, you will learn about:

❑ Manipulating form elements and data

❑ Validating form data

❑ Submitting a form using AJAX

Manipulating Form Elements and Data

Before modern JavaScript libraries such as Prototype were widely used, you had to write a lot of time-consuming code that would look at `the document.formName` object and figure out what elements were in the form. Then you could iterate over the form elements and validate them. With Prototype, your form elements are extended the same way your other HTML elements are, but with a few specific methods. Using the `$F()` method, you can quickly get the value of any form element on your page. The `Form.Elements` object contains methods that Prototype uses to extend your form elements. You can easily serialize all of your form elements into an object literal or a string suitable for passing into an AJAX call.

Form

The `Form` object contains all of the methods Prototype provides for dealing with HTML form elements. Much like the `Element.Methods` object, methods in the `Form.Elements` object are used by Prototype to extend the form elements on a page.

disable/enable

These methods iterate over the elements in a form and either enable or disable them. It is important to note that the serialize method will not serialize disabled form elements.

```
$('myForm').enable();
$('myform').disable();
```

findFirstElement

This finds the first non-hidden, non-disabled form element that is an INPUT, SELECT, or TEXTAREA element. It extends the element when it returns the element. The order the element appears in the document, not the tab order, determines whether or not it is considered the first element.

```
var firstElement = $('myForm').findFirstElement();
```

focusFirstElement

This is an aggregate method that gives you a shortcut for putting the focus on the first element in your form. It calls `findFirstElement()` and then calls `activate()` on the returned element. This is a great way to enhance the usability of your web forms by allowing the user to start typing right away instead of having to click on an element.

```
$('myForm').focusFirstElement();
```

reset

This returns all of the elements in a form to their default values.

```
$('myForm').reset();
```

getInputs

This returns an array of all the inputs contained in a form. You can pass in a type and name to restrict the input elements that are returned.

```
var inputs = $('myForm').getInputs('text','firstName');
//returns any text inputs named "firstName"
```

getElements

This returns all of the elements in a form. It will not return OPTION elements, only their parent SELECT elements.

```
var inputsArray = $('myForm').getElements();
```

serialize

The serialize method is the workhorse of the Form object. It gets the values of all of the enabled elements in your form and returns a string of key-value pairs suitable for appending to a URL for a GET or POST request. It accepts an optional getHash Boolean parameter that returns an object representing the form elements and values instead. Take a form like this:

```
<form id="myForm" name="myForm" action="self" method="get">
        <div>Name:<input type="text" id="name" name="name" /></div>
        <div>
            <select id="gender" name="gender">
                <option value="">-=Select a gender</option>
                <option value="M">Male</option>
                <option value="F">Female</option>
            </select><br/>
            <input type="submit" />
    </form>
```

Calling `$('myForm').serialize()` and `$('myForm').serialize(true)` on this form object results in the following values:

```
name=Scott&gender=M //non hashed value
{name:Scott, gender:M} //hash value
```

serializeElements

This method allows you to specify elements by name that you want to include when serializing a form. This is useful if you want to get the values of certain form elements and submit them separately, such as for two SELECT elements where the options in one depend on the selection in another.

```
var formHash = Form.serializeElements([$('name')],true);
```

How It All Works Together

Now you will build a simple form to allow a user to input his or her name and gender. You want to set the focus to the name field when the page loads and serialize the results for submission to your server once the user clicks "Next". Here is how your HTML form looks (see Figure 4-1 and Figure 4-2).

```
<form name="emptyform"><!--this is just a placeholder form so the element will
appear in FF-->
      <div><input type="checkbox" id="chkUseForm" />I want to enter my
      information</div>
</form>
<form id="myForm" name="myForm" action="" method="get">
      <div>Name:<input type="text" id="name" name="name" /></div>
      <div>
          <select id="gender" name="gender">
              <option value="">-=Select a gender</option>
              <option value="M">Male</option>
              <option value="F">Female</option>
          </select><br/>
          <input type="button" id="submitButton" value="submit" />
          <input type="button" id="resetButton" value="reset" />
</form>
```

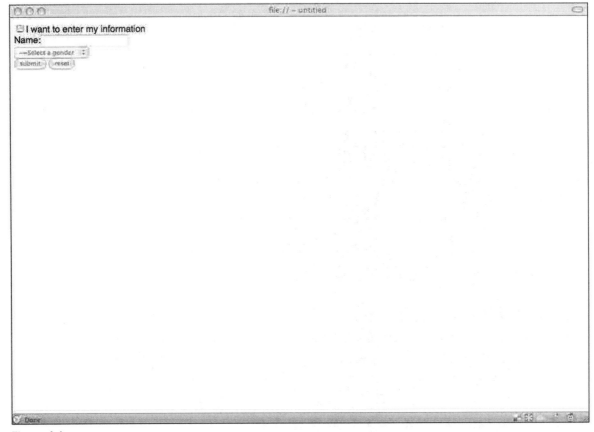

Figure 4-1

Figure 4-2

Since you control how the form is submitted to the server, you use a regular input type="button" rather than a submit button. You provide another button to reset the form elements to their starting values. You also add a checkbox to the page that will enable and disable the form to simulate the form being optional. The form will start off disabled. If the user checks the checkbox, the form should become enabled. When the form is enabled, you will set the focus to the name field. Here is the code to enable this behavior.

```
<script type='text/javascript'>
Event.observe(window, "load", function(e) {
    $('myForm').disable();

});

Event.observe("submitButton", "click", function(e) {
    alert($('myForm').serialize());

});
```

```
Event.observe("chkUseForm", "click", function(e) {
    e.target.checked? function() {$('myForm').enable();$('myForm')
.focusFirstElement();}() :$('myForm').disable();
});

Event.observe("resetButton", "click", function(e) {
    $('myForm').reset();
});
</script>
```

Most of the code is pretty self-explanatory, but you should look at two event handlers that do some interesting things, as shown in the following example:

```
Event.observe("chkUseForm", "click", function(e) {
    e.target.checked? function() {$('myForm').enable();$('myForm')
.focusFirstElement();}() :$('myForm').disable();
});
```

What you are doing here is handling the click event for the checkbox. You have to wrap the checkbox in a FORM tag because some browsers will not recognize form elements, such as inputs and selects, which appear outside of form tags. So you handle the event and you check the checked property of the checkbox. If it is not checked, you disable the form. If it is checked, you want to do two things:

❑   Enable the form.

❑   Set the focus to the first element in the form — in this case, the name field.

Since the ternary operator can only perform one task in each clause, you will wrap the two methods you want to call in an anonymous, self-executing function. You could have rewritten the code to look something like this:

```
Event.observe("chkUseForm", "click", function(e) {
    function enableForm()
    {
        $('myForm').enable();
        $('myForm').focusFirstElement();
    };
    e.target.checked? enableForm() :$('myForm').disable();
});
```

The other function you should look at is the event handler for the "submit" button.

```
Event.observe("submitButton", "click", function(e) {
    alert($('myForm').serialize());

});
```

This method will become the workhorse of your form code. Right now it just serializes the form elements and displays them in a JavaScript alert box so you can view them.

Validating Form Data

So you have your data gathering form. The user can enable and disable the form using the checkbox and when the user clicks the "submit" button, you can serialize the form. Now you want to ensure that the user enters text in the name field, but they do not have to choose a gender. Prototype provides several methods for dealing with individual form elements and will extend a specified form element using either the `$()` or the `$F()` shortcut.

Form.Elements

The `Form.Elements` object contains all of the methods that Prototype uses to extend `input`, `select`, and `textarea` elements. These methods are also aliased to the `Field` object. So anywhere you would use `Form.Elements`, you can use the `Field` shortcut instead.

activate

This sets the focus to the given element and selects the text inside of it if it is a text input.

```
$('name').activate()
```

clear

This clears the contents of the given element.

```
$('name').clear()
```

disable/enable

These two methods work the same as the `Form.disable` and `Form.enable` methods, except they work on individual form elements. Note that calling enable or disable on an element that is already enabled or disabled does not throw an exception.

```
$('name').disable()
$('name').enable()
```

focus

This does exactly what it says — it gives the sets the focus on the given element.

```
$('name').focus()
```

getValue

This returns the value of the given element. It is also aliased by the global shortcut `$F()`. In most cases, this will return a text value. If the element in question is a multiple select box, this method will return an array of values. You can also use the shortcut `$F()` method to quickly get the value of any form element.

```
$('name').getValue()
$F('name');
```

present

This returns true if the given element contains anything and false if it does not.

```
$('name').present()
```

select

This selects the text, if present, in the given element.

```
$('name').select()
```

serialize

This method works the same as the `Form.serialize` method except that it only serializes a single element.

```
$('name').serialize()
```

Validating the Form

Here is your form again.

```
<form name="emptyform"><!--this is just a placeholder form so the element will
appear in FF-->
        <div><input type="checkbox" id="chkUseForm" />I want to enter my
        information</div>
    </form>
    <form id="myForm" name="myForm" action="" method="get">
        <div>Name:<input type="text" id="name" name="name" /></div>
        <div>
            <select id="gender" name="gender">
                <option value="">-=Select a gender</option>
                <option value="M">Male</option>
                <option value="F">Female</option>
            </select><br/>
            <input type="button" id="submitButton" value="submit" />
            <input type="button" id="resetButton" value="reset" />
    </form>
```

If the form is enabled, the user is required to enter his or her name. If the user does not enter his or her name and clicks the "submit" button, you will display a JavaScript alert with a message telling the user to enter his or her name and change the background color of the name field to red.

```
<script type='text/javascript'>
Event.observe(window, "load", function(e) {
    $('myForm').disable();

});

Event.observe("submitButton", "click", function(e) {
    if(!$('name').present()) {
      alert("You must enter  your name");
      $('name').setStyle( {backgroundColor : '#F34851'} );
      return;
    };
    alert($('myForm').serialize());

});
```

```
Event.observe("chkUseForm", "click", function(e) {
    function enableForm()
    {
        $('myForm').enable();
        $('myForm').focusFirstElement();
    };
    e.target.checked? enableForm() :$('myForm').disable();
});

Event.observe("resetButton", "click", function(e) {
    $('myForm').reset();
});
</script>
```

As you can see in Figure 4-3, you have fleshed out the "submit" button click event handler a little bit. You added a call to the `present()` method. This will check the "name" text box and make sure the user has typed some text. If the user has not entered any text, you display a JavaScript alert dialog and then change the background color of the name text box to a light red using the `setStyle` method.

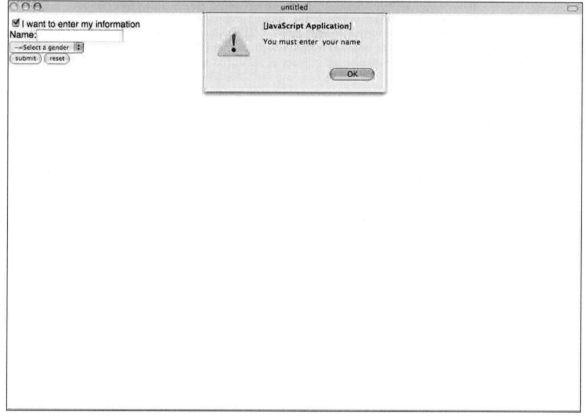

Figure 4-3

Submitting a Form Using AJAX

So now you have validated your user input and you are ready to send the results off to the server. You could use the serialize methods along with Prototype's `Ajax.Request` object, but the Form object provides a method called request, which does all of that for you. You will modify your "submit" button click handler to use the `Form.request` method to send the data back to your server.

```
Event.observe("submitButton", "click", function(e) {
    if(!$('name').present()) {
      alert("You must enter  your name");
      $('name').setStyle( {backgroundColor : '#F34851'} );
      return;
    };
    $('myForm').request(
      {
          onSuccess: function(){alert("form successfully posted")},
          onFailure: function(){alert("form failed to post")}
      });
});
```

The `Form.request` method takes the same options argument as the `Ajax.Request` object. The `Form.request` method infers the method type from the method provided in the form element declaration. If you pass in a method property in the options argument, `Form.request` will use the method you specify instead of the form elements method. The method will default to POST if you do not specify a method and one cannot be inferred from the form element. Parameters that are passed in with the same name as form elements will be used in place of serialized form values.

Summary

You looked at some of the methods Prototype provides for working with forms and form elements. By using the Form object methods, you can decrease the amount of code and the amount of work you have to do to submit your forms to a server using AJAX. You also found ways to validate and manipulate form elements.

Manipulating Common Data Structures and Functions

One of Prototype's greatest strengths is the way it extends native JavaScript objects with methods that make JavaScript easier to use. The native Object, Date, and Array objects are extended with many useful methods. The Function object extensions allow you to perform many advanced tasks such as currying and binding with the functions that you write.

In this chapter, you will learn about:

- ❑ Enhancing a native object and introducing an object hierarchy into code using the Class object
- ❑ Parsing and manipulating strings
- ❑ Using templates to dynamically build the user interface
- ❑ Binding and manipulating functions
- ❑ Introducing the Enumerable class
- ❑ Enhancing JavaScript arrays and introducing the Hash class
- ❑ Dealing with numbers and dates

Enhancing Native Objects and Introducing Classes

One of the strengths of Prototype is that it extends the native JavaScript objects with methods that make it easier to write JavaScript. When you use Prototype, you don't feel like you are using a Framework all the time; you feel like you are just writing JavaScript. The native Object object gains the ability to clone and extend other objects. Several global functions are included that allow you to determine the type of an object. Prototype also includes a Class object that enables you to easily create and maintain an object hierarchy in your JavaScript code.

Extensions to Object

Prototype adds some methods to Object and makes it easier to manipulate or copy objects in your JavaScript code. You can find out what properties an Object has by using the keys collection to convert your Object to any of three formats for transport.

clone

This creates a shallow copy of the object in question.

```
Object.clone(o)
```

extend

This is very similar to the `Element.extend` method. It copies the object's properties to a new object.

```
Object.extend(dest, src)
```

inspect

This looks for an inspect method in the object specified. If one is found, it will be run. Otherwise the `toString` method is called on the object. You can define an inspect method and use it to provide more detailed or better structured information about your object than the `toString` method will give you.

```
Object.inspect(o)
```

isArray, isElement, isFunction, isHash, isNumber, isString, isUndefined

All of these methods determine if the object in question is of the type specified in the method name. If it is, the method will return true. Otherwise it returns false.

```
Object.isArray(o)
Object.isElement(o)
Object.isFunction(o)
Object.isHash(o)
Object.isNumber(o)
Object.isString(o)
Object.isUndefined(o)
```

keys, values

The keys method treats the object like a Prototype Hash object and returns an array of the object's property names. The values method returns the values for each property in the object.

```
Object.keys(o)
Object.values(o)
```

toHTML, toJSON, toQueryString

These three methods convert the specified object into the format specified by the method. These methods come in handy when you need to quickly convert an object with its values into a specific format.

```
var o = {firstName:"Douglas",
lastName:"Crockford",
 toHTML: function(){ return "<p>#{firstName} #{lastName}</p>".interpolate(this);}
};
Object.toHTML(o);
//<p>Douglas Crockford</p>
Object.toJSON(o);
// { "firstName" : "Douglas", "lastName":"Crockford" };
Object.toQueryString(o);
//firstName=Douglas&lastName=Crockford
```

Class

Inheritance in JavaScript usually involves keeping track of your object's prototype chain. You have to remember what objects have inherited from your base object. The Class object in Prototype makes it easier to create and extend objects in your JavaScript code.

create

The `Class.create` method does all of the heavy lifting for you when you want to create a new class. You can pass in an object as a parameter to serve as the superclass of the newly created class. Here is a very simple example that illustrates how to use `Class.create`:

```
var myParentClass = Class.create({ parentFunction: function() { return "parent";}});
        var myClass = Class.create(myParentClass,{ classFunction: function() {return
"class";}});
        var c = new myClass();
        alert(c.classFunction());
        alert(c.parentFunction());
```

Here you create two classes: one called `myParentClass` and one called `myClass`. The `myClass` class inherits the `parentFunction` member from its superclass, `myParentClass`.

Special Properties

Every class object that is created contains two special properties that tell you where the class is in your object hierarchy. The `superclass` property tells you what class your class inherits from, and the `subclasses` array contains all of the objects that inherit from your class.

addMethods

The `addMethods` method is used to mix in new methods to your classes after you create them. It is important to note that you can add the new methods at any time and they will be available to all of the objects you have instantiated using that class. Suppose you add two new methods to the object in the previous example. Add one new method to the parent and one to the class the object is based on after you instantiate the object.

```
var myParentClass = Class.create({ parentFunction: function() { return "parent";}});
var myClass = Class.create(myParentClass,{ classFunction: function() {return "class";}});
var c = new myClass();

myParentClass.addMethods({ newParentMethod: function(){ return "new Method added to
the parent after creating the class";}})
myClass.addMethods({ newMethod: function(){ return "new Method added after creating
the class";}})

alert(c.classFunction());
alert(c.parentFunction());
alert(c.newParentMethod());
alert(c.newMethod());
```

You can see that the methods are available to you even though they were added after you created a new instance of myClass.

Munging and Parsing Strings

As a web developer, you spend a lot of time working with strings. Sometimes you want to sanitize user input to prevent cross-site scripting attacks, and other times you need a better way to match patterns in your strings and return the results. Prototype builds on the String object and provides several useful

methods for munging and parsing your strings.

blank, empty

Both of these methods return a Boolean if the string matches the criteria specified by the method name. It is important to note the difference between the two methods. The blank method returns true when called on an empty string (""). But the empty method does not return true if the string contains one or more spaces, even though the string may look empty.

```
''.blank() // true
' '.blank() //true
' foo'.blank() //false
''.empty() //true
' '.empty() //false
```

camelize, capitalize, dasherize, underscore

All of these methods perform a similar function, although each does something different. All of them take existing strings and modify their format. The following table describes each one:

Method	Description	Code
`camelize`	Takes a string separated by dashes and converts it into its `camelCase` equivalent.	`'first-name'.camelize()` `//firstName`
`capitalize`	Makes sure the first letter of a string is capitalized and makes the remainder of the string lowercase.	`'firstName'.capitalize()` `//Firstname`
`dasherize`	Replaces each underscore character "`_`" with a dash character "`-`"	`'first_name'.dasherize()` `//first-name`
`underscore`	Takes a `camelCased` string and separates each word with an underscore character.	`'firstName'.underscore()` `//first_name`

startsWith, endsWith, include

These methods do what you would expect them to do. They return true or false if the string contains the given substring.

```
'fool'.startsWith('f') // true
'fool'.endsWith('l') //true
'fool'.include('foo') //true
'fool'.include('food') //false
```

evalJSON, toJSON

Prototype provides two methods in the String object for dealing with JSON: `evalJSON` and `toJSON`. The `evalJSON` method attempts to parse the given string and returns a JSON object. If the string is not well-formed JSON data, a syntax error is thrown. It will also take an optional parameter called `sanitize`. If the `sanitize` parameter is passed, `evalJSON` will look for known exploits in the string and will not call `eval()` if any are found. You should always pass the `sanitize` parameter if your string contains data loaded from a remote source. The `toJSON` method will return a JSON encoded string.

```
var person = '{"firstName" : "Douglas", "lastName":"Crockford"}'.evalJSON()
// person .firstName = "Douglas"
var JSONname = 'Johnny "The Killer" Bambam'.toJSON()
//JSONname = 'Johnny \"The Killer\" Bambam'
```

evalScripts, extractScripts, stripScripts

These three methods give you some control over scripts that may be embedded in strings you want to work with. The `stripScripts` method removes any script blocks it finds in your string. You can use this to sanitize user input and prevent cross-site scripting attacks. You can use `extractScripts` to remove scripts embedded in your string and place them in an array for later use. The `evalScripts` method uses the `extractScripts` method to pull the scripts out of the string and then calls `eval` on each script found. The result of calling `eval` on each script is that it returns as an element of an array.

```
"Given this string <script>alert('hiya');</script>".stripScripts()
// will return "Given this string "
"Given this string <script>alert('hiya');</script>".extractScripts()
//retuns ["alert('hiya');"]
"Given this string <script>alert('hiya');</script>".evalScripts()
// will display "hiya" in an alert box.
```

escapeHTML, unescapeHTML

The `escapeHTML` method converts any special characters into their HTML escape sequence. The `unescapeHTML` method strips any HTML tags from the given string and converts escaped HTML characters into their normal form. These two methods can be used to sanitize user input before storing it in a database or an XML file.

```
'1 < 2'.escapeHTML()
//'1 &lt; 2'
'<p> 1 &lt; 2 </p>'.unescapeHTML()
//' 1 < 2 '
```

gsub, sub

Both `sub` and `gsub` look for substrings and replace them with a string you specify in the given string. The `gsub` method looks over the entire string and replaces all of the occurrences of the substring you specify while the `sub` method takes an optional `count` parameter. If you do not pass a `count` parameter, `sub` will only replace the first occurrence of the substring you specify. Otherwise, it will replace the number of occurrences specified in the `count` parameter.

scan

This method allows you to iterate over every match in a string and pass each match to a function. The pattern used to find a match can be either a string or a regular expression.

```
var iCount = 0;
'Mississippi'.scan('i', function(match) { if(match == 'i') { iCount++; }; });
// iCount = 3;
```

Generating Templated Content

Templates are a great way to reuse HTML and separate your data and presentation. Prototype provides an easy-to-use mechanism for creating templates and binding your data. You can define your template using a string. Prototype uses a simple pattern to determine where to insert your data in your template. Just wrap the property name with the text "#{}". For example, if you wanted to insert the firstName property into your template you would put the text "#{firstName}" into your template string.

Here is a simple template that wraps your data with an h1 tag. When you want Prototype to insert your data, call the evaluate method passing in the object you want to bind.

```html
<body>
    <script type="text/javascript">
        var data = {value:'foo'};
        var template = new Template("<h1>#{value}</h1>");
        Event.observe(window, "load", function(e) {
            $("contentHolder").insert(template.evaluate(data));
        });

    </script>
    <div id="contentHolder"/>
</body>
```

Template.evaluate()

The Template.evaluate method binds your objects data to your template and returns a string. Templates are designed to be reused within your code. Let's modify the previous example and bind the template to an array of data objects. You can use the each method on your data array to iterate over your array of data objects and call the evaluate method on your template each time with a new data object. This is a great technique to use if you need to build long lists (see Figure 5-1).

```html
<body
    <script type="text/javascript">
        var data = [{value:'foo'}, {value:'bar'}, {value:'baz'}];
        var template = new Template("<h1>#{value}</h1>");
        Event.observe(window, "load", function(e) {
            data.each(function(value) {
                $("contentHolder").insert(template.evaluate(value));
            });
        });

    </script>
    <div id="contentHolder"/>
</body>
```

Figure 5-1

The `Template.evaluate` method also accepts a second optional parameter that contains a regular expression defining any custom data pattern syntax you want to use.

Binding and Manipulating Functions

In JavaScript, functions are first-class objects. That is, you can manipulate them just as you would any other object. Functions also take a variable number of arguments in JavaScript, meaning you can overload any function at any time. Prototype provides a few methods to extend the native Function object and gives you more flexibility in your JavaScript programming.

Binding Functions

Trying to figure out what the `this` keyword means at any given time can be a little tricky when you are working with JavaScript. Depending on how you have called a function and in what context the function is being called, `this` can refer to the wrapping function, the function itself, or the global `window` object. Prototype gives you a way to bind a function and define what object `this` should refer to.

Take a look at how the element `this` refers to can change depending upon the context a function is called in.

```
window.name = "Global window object";

function showName() {
    return this.name
};

alert(showName()); //shows "Global window object"

var namespace = {
    name : "namespace object",
    showName: function() { return this.name;}
};

alert(namespace.showName());//shows "namespace object"

window.namespaceShowName = namespace.showName;
alert(window.namespaceShowName());//shows "Global window object"
```

Here you declare a function called `showName` that returns the `name` property on whatever object the `this` keyword is referring to at the time it is called. You declare a function contained within the `namespace` object using the same code as the `showName` function. When you call `showName`, it is declared in the global window context and displays the name you assigned to the `window` object in the first line of code. When you call the `namespace.showName` function, it looks at its current execution scope and sees that it is contained within the `namespace` object and returns the name property it finds there. The last few lines are where it gets tricky. You assign the `namespace.showName` function to a new member of the global `window` object and then call the `namespace.showName` function using the new alias. The function looks at its execution scope and sees that it is being called from within the global `window` object and returns the same name as the global `showName` function.

bind

The `bind` method wraps the function specified in another function and locks the scope into whatever you pass in as the second parameter. It returns the `bound` function. It also accepts an optional parameter containing an array of arguments to pass to the `bound` function.

```
function foo(name) {
        this.name = name;
    };

var bar = {
    name : "bar"
};

var fooBound = foo.bind(bar);
alert(bar.name);
fooBound("foo");
alert(bar.name);
```

The `curry` method is very similar to the `bind` method. It works exactly the same except you do not have to pass in the scope parameter.

bindAsEventListener

This is a special case of `bind` that makes sure that the event object is passed to the function being bound.

Function.argumentNames

This returns the function parameters as an array of strings. If the function definition does not specify any parameters, it returns an empty array.

```
function twoParams(foo, bar) {
        //do stuff here
};
var paramNames = twoParams.argumentNames();
//returns ['foo','bar']
```

Other Methods That Manipulate Functions

Sometimes you need to change a function by currying it, scheduling it for later, or by wrapping it with another function. Prototype provides a few handy methods for manipulating your functions.

defer

The `defer` method waits to invoke a function until the interpreter is idle. This can be useful if you want to wait to update a UI element until after unrelated AJAX calls are completed.

wrap

This accepts a function as the parameter and will return a new function wrapped around the first function. This allows you to intercept function calls and perform any action you wish. Here is a simple method that wraps a function and logs some text to the Firebug or Safari console if it exists.

```
var doStuff = function () {
        alert("Do stuff");
    }
doStuff = doStuff.wrap(
        function (func) {
            if(console) { console.log("calling doStuff"); }
            func();
        });

doStuff();
```

delay

This allows you to schedule the invocation of a function until after a set number of seconds. This behaves like the global `setTimeout` method. It even returns an ID that you can pass to the `clearTimeout` method to stop the execution of the function you are delaying. You can also pass an array of arguments to pass to the function when it is called. It is important to note that you specify the delay in seconds rather than milliseconds as when you call the `setTimeout` method.

methodize

The `methodize` function is used when you have a function that accepts an object as a parameter and you want to make the function a member of the object it accepts. This will wrap the function in another function that will pass `this` as the first parameter.

Try.these

This helpful method is not contained in the Function namespace. It accepts *n* number of parameters and will return the result of the first one that does not throw an exception. If none of the functions passed to it execute successfully, this method will return undefined. Sometimes you may want to know if the `Try.these` call was able to execute any of the functions without throwing an exception. In these cases it is useful to use the short-circuit or (||) operator to return false.

```
function tryToExecuteSomeFunctions() {
return Try.these( function() { throw "exception";}, function() { throw "exception";
}) || false;
};
```

Improving Arrays, Hashes, and Iterators

All objects in JavaScript are, at their heart, associative arrays. You can iterate over their properties and methods using a `for` loop. Prototype adds a new Enumerable class and extends the built-in JavaScript Arrays and objects with its methods. Using these new methods, you can easily slice and dice your arrays and collections in any way you see fit. The `each` method provides a reliable means for inspecting the elements in your objects or arrays.

Why Using for-in Can Cause Some Problems

If you have ever tried to use a `for...in` loop to loop over elements in an array, you have noticed that the results are not always what you would expect. The ECMA 262 specification, which is the specification that defines ECMAScript third edition, says that only properties marked as non-enumerable should be ignored by the `for...in` loop. The problem is that Prototype, as well as other JavaScript libraries, does not have any way to mark the methods it adds to Array and Object as non-enumerable. So when you try to use `for...in` to loop over an array extended by Prototype, you also have all of the extension methods returned in addition to your data elements. By using the iterating extension methods that Prototype provides, you avoid this pitfall.

Enumerable

The Enumerable class is a very important class to Prototype and is the basis for all of the collection-based classes or extension to existing objects that act as collections. It provides numerous methods for dealing with the elements in a collection. This class is a module; that is, you do not use it directly. Instead, it is mixed in with other objects using the `Object.extend` method.

Iterators

Iterators are functions that you can pass to certain methods defined in the Enumerable module. These functions can process the data in some way. The following methods in Enumerable support iterators: `all`, `any`, `collect`, `detect`, `each`, `eachSlice`, `find`, `findAll`, `grep`, `inject`, `map`, `max`, `min`, `partition`, `reject`, `select`, `sortBy`, and `zip`.

Setting the Context for the Iterator

All of the Enumerable methods take a second context parameter. The context parameter determines what the `this` keyword refers to inside of the iterator. If no context is specified, the default context of the iterator is used.

all

This method loops through the elements in the Enumerable object and determines if the object is true or false. Once it finds something that evaluates to false, it stops and returns false. Otherwise it returns true. You can provide an iterator to determine whether or not each item should return true or false.

any

The `any` method works in a similar manner to the `all` method except that it stops at the first element that evaluates to true.

collect, map

The `collect` method is a versatile method. It iterates over your Enumerable collection and returns the results, as shown in Figure 5-2. The `map` method is an alias for this method.

```html
<body>
    <script type="text/javascript">
        var data = ['Deoxyribo', 'nucleic', 'acid'];

        function acronymize(dataArray) {
            return dataArray.collect(function(item) {
                return item.charAt(0).toUpperCase();
            }).join('');
        };

        Event.observe(window, "load", function(e) {
            $("contentHolder").insert(acronymize(data));

        });


    </script>
    <div id="contentHolder"/>
</body>
```

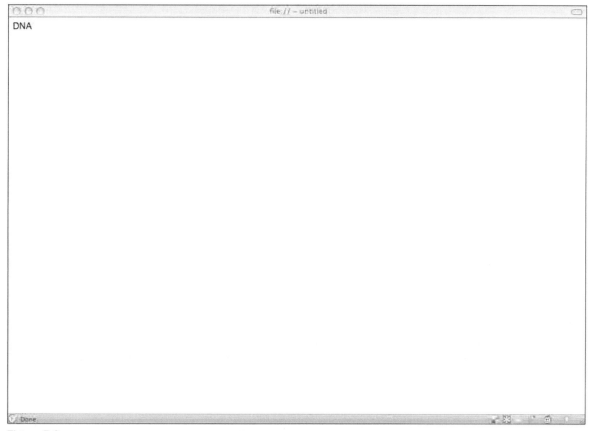

Figure 5-2

detect, reject

The detect method finds the first element of your collection that returns true from your iterator. The reject method is the opposite of the detect method. It returns all of the elements for which the given function returns false.

each

The each method is the backbone of the Enumerable class. This method iterates over your Enumerable class, calling the function you pass to it on each element, and then returns the Enumerable class to allow chaining.

eachSlice

The eachSlice method is useful if you want to break up an Enumerable collection by size. Say you need to call a web method using AJAX, but you are calling a legacy system that has hard coded its parameters to four parameters, such as "name1, name2, name3, name4". You can use eachSlice to iterate over your array and pull out four elements at a time.

entries

This is an alias for the `toArray` method.

find, findAll, select

Both `find` and `findAll` iterate over your Enumerable collection and return elements of your collection that cause your iterator function to return true. The `findAll` method will return each element that returns true from your function while the `find` method, which is an alias for the `detect` method, will only return the first element that meets your criteria. The `select` method is an alias for the `findAll` method.

grep

The `grep` method allows you to search through your collection using a regular expression and returns the results. However, you don't have to use a regular expression; you can use a string pattern or any object that has a `match` method.

inGroupsOf

This is a variant of the `eachSlice` method. It does not take an iterator function. The other main difference is that it fills the final returned array with null values, if need be, to meet the size criteria.

include, member

The `include` method determines if your Enumerable collection contains the value you provide or not. It is important to note that this uses the equality (==) operator and not the identity operator (===), so only the value is checked, not the type and value. The `member` method is an alias for this one.

inject

The `inject` method builds a return value with each iteration over your collection. It is great for building arrays based on Enumerable collections or for performing successive calculations on a range of numbers.

invoke

The `invoke` method executes the given function for each element in the Enumerable collection. Since you do not create a lexical closure over an anonymous function, as you would if you passed in an anonymous function to the `each` method, this performs much better.

max, min

The `max` method returns the maximum element from your collection. The maximum element is determined by either comparing the values directory or by using an iterator. If the Enumerable collection is empty, `undefined` is returned. If equivalent values are present in your collection, the latest one is returned. The `min` method is the opposite of the `max` method and returns the minimum value from your Enumerable collection.

partition

The `partition` method divides your collection into two groups. Group one will be considered true and group two will be considered false. Remember that, in JavaScript, null and `undefined` are considered false. You can provide an iterator function that will determine the trueness or falseness of an element.

pluck

This is an optimized version of the `collect` method. You can use this when you want to select elements from your collection based on a single property for all of the elements.

size

The `size` method returns the number of elements in the Enumerable collection. It is similar to the length property of Arrays.

sortBy

This provides a method for sorting your Enumerable collection. You provide a function that returns the property or calculated value you want to sort by. You should use this only when you cannot use the natural `sort` method.

toArray

This method returns an array representation of the Enumerable collection.

Improvements to Array

In addition to mixing in all of the methods found in the Enumerable module, Prototype enhances the native Array object with some helpful methods, which are shown in the following table:

Method	Description
clear	This removes all of the elements from the array it is called on.
clone	This returns a duplicate of the original array. It leaves the original intact.
compact	This removes any elements that contain a `null` or `undefined` value.
each	This enumerates over the array starting at the lowest index.
first	This returns the first element of the array. It will return `undefined` if the array is empty.
flatten	This returns a one-dimensional array. Any nested arrays will be extracted, and its elements will be inserted at the point the nested array is found.
from	This clones an existing array or creates a new array from an array-like collection. It is also represented by the `$A()` helper method.
indexOf	This works in a similar manner to the `String.indexOf` method. It returns the index of the first occurrence of the value passed to it in the array it is called on. If the value cannot be found in the array, the method will return -1.
inspect	This returns a debug string version of the array.
last	This is the opposite of the `first` method and returns the last element of the array.

(continued)

Method	Description
reduce	This returns the only value of a single element array. Multiple element arrays are left alone.
reverse	This reverses the order of the elements in the array it is called on. By default, it modifies the original array. You can pass in an optional inline method that, if it is set to false, will return a clone of the array reversed.
size	This returns the `Array.length` property.
toArray	This returns an array from any Enumerable object.
toJSON	This converts an array into a JSON string.
uniq	This creates a new array after removing all duplicate elements from the original array. If no duplicates are found, the original array is returned.
without	This creates a new array that does not contain any elements with the specified values.

It is not advisable to use an anonymous function as an iterator when using any of these methods with very large arrays, as the performance suffers. If you have a large array, you are better off writing a regular for loop using a numeric index and performing any operations you need inside of the loop.

Introducing Hash

The Hash class is a helper class introduced by Prototype. A hash can be thought of as an associative array. Since all JavaScript objects are associative arrays, the Hash class defines several extra methods to make working with associative arrays easier. You can create a new instance of a Hash either by using the new keyword or by using the $H() alias and passing in any JavaScript object. If you don't pass in a JavaScript object, a new empty Hash is created for you.

clone

The clone method works the same way as the `Array.clone` method does. It returns an identical copy of the Hash.

each

This method iterates over the Hash and calls the supplied function on each element in the Hash. When the function is called, the key and value are passed as the first two parameters to the function. Unlike using for-in, this method will skip methods found on the object's prototype. There is no guarantee that the elements will be called in any certain order.

get

The get method returns the value found at the element specified by the key passed to this method.

inspect

The inspect method returns a debug-formatted version of the Hash.

keys, values

Both of these methods return arrays containing the specified values. They work the same as the `keys` and `values` methods on the extended Object.

merge

The `merge` method combines the values of an object of Hash with an existing Hash. This is a nondestructive event; the original Hash is cloned before merging. If the destination Hash contains the same key as the source Hash or object, the values will be overwritten.

set

The `set` method assigns the given value to an element with the given `key`.

toJSON, toQueryString

Both of these methods behave in the manner you would expect and work the same as other `toJSON` and `toQueryString` methods.

toObject

This method returns a plain object clone of the Hash.

unset

This method deletes the element with the given `key` and returns its `value` to the caller.

update

The `update` method operates in a similar manner as `merge`; the keys and values of the given object are inserted into the Hash. However, unlike `merge`, this is a destructive operation. The original Hash instance is modified.

Dealing with Numbers and Dates

Because of the dynamic nature of JavaScript, dates and numbers are difficult to deal with. Prototype makes converting numbers and dates to JSON easier, as well as provides several mathematical methods for numbers.

Numbers

By extending numbers in JavaScript, Prototype allows you to use numbers in ranges similar to Ruby and to use numbers to specify how many times a particular action should be executed. Prototype also provides some basic mathematical functions.

abs

This returns the absolute value of the number.

cell

This returns the smallest integer that is greater than or equal to the given number.

floor

The `floor` method is the opposite of the `cell` method. It returns the largest integer that is smaller than or equal to the given number.

round

This rounds the number to the nearest integer. It rounds .5 up.

succ

This returns the successor, the next number on the number line, of the given number.

times

This provides a shortcut method for writing a simple loop. It executes the given function the number of times specified by the number.

```
(3).times(function(n) { alert("hiya " + n)});
```

toColorPart

This method takes a decimal number and returns the hexadecimal representation of the number. This is useful when you need to convert decimal color values to CSS hex values.

toJSON

This method returns a JSON formatted string.

toPaddedString

This returns the number padded with enough zeros to make the entire string of n length.

```
(5).toPaddedString(3) // returns '005'
```

Dates

Prototype provides only one method for working with dates. It extends the Date object with a `toJSON` method that will return the date object as a JSON string. This method is useful for transmitting dates to a server using JSON.

Summary

In this chapter, you looked at how Prototype makes dealing with collections and arrays in JavaScript easier by introducing the Enumerable and Hash classes and extending the native Array object. You also looked at how you can create and maintain object hierarchies using the `Class.create` and `Class.addMethods` methods. Prototype's templating engine can make building your user interface a breeze by allowing you to reuse common HTML markup and bind your data objects.

6

Extending Prototype

Prototype is an excellent base for creating a new JavaScript framework. It takes care of smoothing out the incompatibilities between different DOM implementations and allows you to focus on writing the fun parts of your framework. The lightweight nature of the library means that your users won't have to worry about the download size of their web pages because they have to include Prototype as well as your library.

This chapter looks at three JavaScript frameworks that are based on the Prototype library:

- ❑ Script.aculo.us
- ❑ Moo.fx for Prototype
- ❑ Rico

Script.aculo.us

Script.aculo.us (visit `http://script.aculo.us/`), which is shown in Figure 6-1, is an effects library that's built on top of Prototype. It first rose to fame as the default JavaScript library that's included in Ruby on Rails. It provides excellent visual effects as well as some AJAX controls that build upon the great base that is Prototype's `Ajax.Request` object.

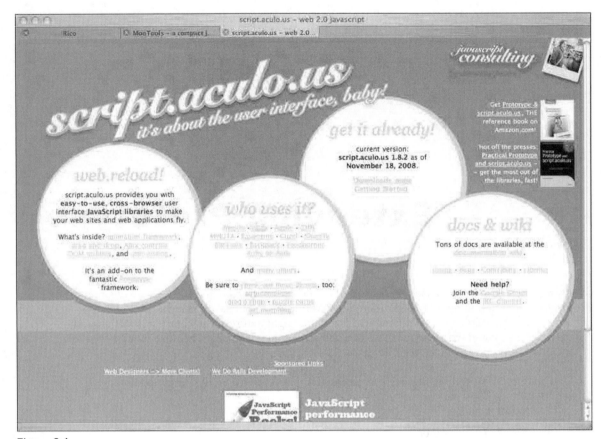

Figure 6-1

Effects

Script.aculo.us provides a library of visual effects that you can either add to your web pages to make them more exciting and usable or to build new visual effects.

The core visual effects are:

- ❑ Effect.Opacity
- ❑ Effect.Scale
- ❑ Effect.Morph
- ❑ Effect.Move
- ❑ Effect.Highlight
- ❑ Effect.Parallel
- ❑ Effect.Tween

There are sixteen other effects that are created by combining two or more of the core effects:

- ❑ Effect.Appear, Effect.Fade
- ❑ Effect.Toggle
- ❑ Effect.Puff
- ❑ Effect.DropOut
- ❑ Effect.Shake
- ❑ Effect.SwitchOff
- ❑ Effect.BlindDown, Effect.BlindUp
- ❑ Effect.SlideDown, Effect.SlideUp
- ❑ Effect.Pulsate
- ❑ Effect.Squish
- ❑ Effect.Fold
- ❑ Effect.Grow
- ❑ Effect.Shrink

The basic way to use any of the effects is to create a new instance of the effect by passing in the element you want to apply the effect to, any required parameters the effect specifies, and any options you want to pass to the effect. There is also an Effect.Toggle that you can use if you want to temporarily apply an effect to an element.

```
new Effect.EffectName(element, required-params, [options]);
```

Say you want to highlight an element when the text inside of it changes. You can use the Effect.Highlight object by passing in the element or the id of the element you want to highlight.

```
<body>
<div id="MainDiv">Change the text</div>
<script type='text/javascript'>
Event.observe(window, "load", function(e) {
    setTimeout(function() { //simulate an AJAX request
        new Effect.Highlight("MainDiv");
        $("MainDiv").update("updated the content");
    }, 1000);
});
</script>
</body>
```

Controls

Script.aculo.us contains a few controls to ease web development. It includes two autocomplete controls, one server based and one local: a slider control, drag-and-drop functionality, and an in-place editing control.

Slider

This is a standard slider control used to select a value from a range of numbers. What's interesting about this slider control is that it allows you to define multiple handlers. You can set its axis to either horizontal or vertical. To use it, create a new instance of the class and pass in a single element, or the id of an element, to use as a handle or an array of elements/ids if you want multiple handles.

```
new Control.Slider('handles','track', [options]);
```

Ajax.InPlaceEditor

The `Ajax.InPlaceEditor` is a great way to enhance your web site by providing single-click editing of data fields on your page. If you have used Flickr, you have seen an in-place editor in use. When you click on text that says, "Click here to add a description", the text changes to an input box and you can enter whatever text you wish. When you hover over the text, the Prototype effects kick in and the background fades in yellow, or whatever color you choose by passing the constructor an options object.

To create a new `Ajax.InPlaceEditor`, just create a new instance of the class and pass in the element/ID that should be editable, pass in a URL for the control to POST the value to, and any options you want to set. The URL you specify should return a value in the response body. This value will replace the default text in the element you specified.

```
<body>
<div id="inPlaceEditorHolder">Click here to edit</div>
<script type='text/javascript'>
Event.observe(window, "load", function(e) {
    var ipe = new Ajax.InPlaceEditor("inPlaceEditorHolder","/");
});
</script>
</body>
```

Here you create a `div` containing the text "Click here to edit" and assign it to a new `Ajax .InPlaceEditor` object (see Figure 6-2). When you click in the text, it is replaced with an input box, an "OK" button, and a "Cancel" link (see Figure 6-3). Entering a value and clicking the "OK" button will POST the value to a URL and replace the text in the div with the value returned in the response body by the server.

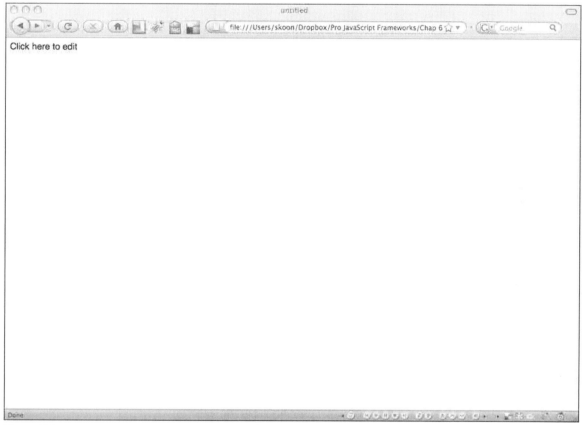

Figure 6-2

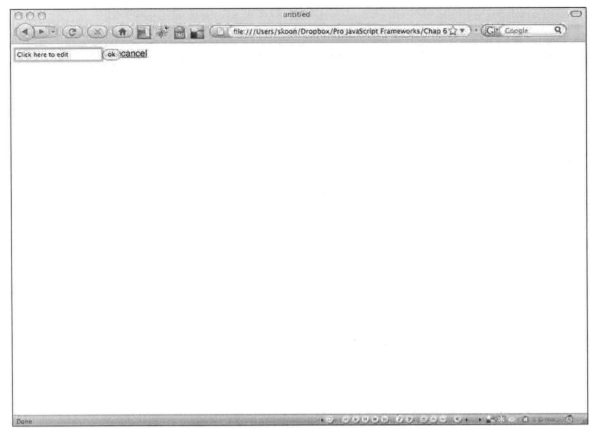

Figure 6-3

Ajax.InPlaceCollectionEditor

This works the same way as the `Ajax.InPlaceEditor`, but replaces the element with a select box instead of a text box. You pass in an array of values to use in the select box.

```
new Ajax.InPlaceCollectionEditor( element, url,
                            { collection: [array], [moreOptions] } );
```

Ajax.Autocompleter, Autocompleter.local

The auto-complete controls in Script.aculo.us are a great addition to forms on your web pages. The `Ajax.Autocompleter` leverages the AJAX objects in Prototype to allow you to easily add auto-complete capabilities to your input elements.

First, you have to style the div that the autocompleter will fill with the results. It's a good idea to initially set the style of the div to `display:none` so that it doesn't show up before it is filled with results and make sure it has the class `autocomplete`. Next, set some kind of indicator for when it is selected.

```
<style>

    div.autocomplete {
      margin:0px;
      padding:0px;
      width:250px;
      background:#fff;
      border:1px solid #888;
      position:absolute;
    }

    div.autocomplete ul {
      margin:0px;
      padding:0px;
      list-style-type:none;
    }

    div.autocomplete ul li.selected {
      background-color:#ffb;
    }

    div.autocomplete ul li {
      margin:0;
      padding:2px;
      height:32px;
      display:block;
      list-style-type:none;
      cursor:pointer;
    }

    </style>
</head>
<body>
<input type="text" id="autocompleteInput">
<div id="autcompleteResults" class="autocomplete" style="display:none;"></div>
<script type='text/javascript'>
Event.observe(window, "load", function(e) {
    var stringArray = ["Alix", "Alice", "Amelia", "Amy"]
   var ac =  new Autocompleter.Local(
      "autocompleteInput",
      "autcompleteResults",
      stringArray);

});
</script>
</body>
```

Finally, set up the `Autocompleter` by creating a new instance of the class. The `Autocompleter` comes in two different flavors. One will query a URL with the values entered in the text box. The second will search a string array that you pass in for the text entered. The preceding example sets up a local `Autocompleter` that will search an array containing female names, as shown in Figure 6-4.

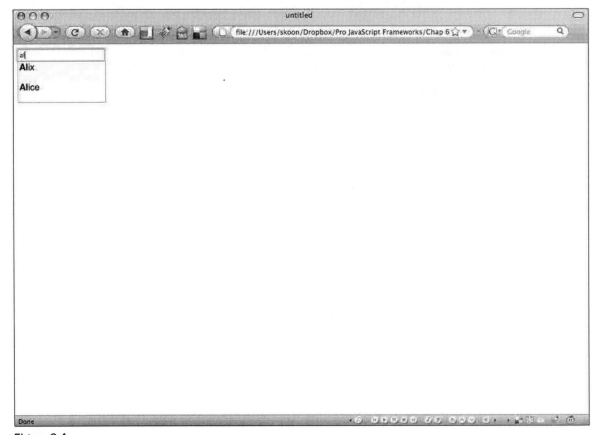

Figure 6-4

Behaviors

Script.aculo.us defines three behaviors that you can apply to elements:

❑ Draggable — Allows the user to drag the element within the page.

❑ Droppable — Defines an area where the user can drop a draggable element and trigger an event.

❑ Sortable — Allows the user to reorder elements inside of a container.

Drag and Drop

Writing drag-and-drop code in JavaScript is a complicated matter and can take a lot of time that could be better spent writing logic code. Script.aculo.us provides two classes that make defining an element as something the user can drag or an area where things can be dropped. To make an element draggable, create a new instance of the Draggable class and pass in the element or id of the element you want to make draggable as well as any options. Script.aculo.us maintains a collection of droppable elements; to create a new droppable element, just add its ID to the current collection.

```
new Draggable('id of element', [options]);
Droppables.add('id_of_element',[options]);
```

Sortable

Making a set of elements sortable is simple. Just call the `Sortable.create` method and pass in the element or ID of the element that contains the elements to be sorted.

You can use almost any container as a container for sortable elements except for a TABLE, THEAD, TBODY *or* TR *element. This is because of a technical restriction in current browsers.*

```
<body>
<div id="MainDiv">
    <ul id="sortableContainer">
        <li>first</li>
        <li>second</li>
        <li>third</li>
    </ul>
</div>
<script type='text/javascript'>
Event.observe(window, "load", function(e) {
    Sortable.create("sortableContainer");
});
</script>
</body>
```

Moo.fx for Prototype

The primary goal of Moo.fx (visit http://moofx.mad4milk.net/), which is shown in Figure 6-5, is to be a small, lightweight effects library. Moo.fx can be used in conjunction with either Prototype or the Mootools JavaScript library. The basic effects in Moo.fx include the following:

❑   Fx.Tween — Allows you to change any CSS properties value to a different value gradually.

❑   Fx.Morph — Allows you to change the values of multiple CSS properties all at once.

❑   Fx.Transitions — Defines a collection of equations that can be used when transitioning an element's property.

❑   Fx.Slide — Allows you to make an element slide in either horizontally or vertically.

Figure 6-5

Fx.Tween

Fx.Tween changes the value of a given CSS property to the ending value you specify. It contains two methods. Set will change the value of the CSS property immediately. Start will gradually change the value of the CSS property to the value you pass. You can optionally provide an ending value when calling the start method and define a range for the value.

```
var myFx = new Fx.Tween(element, [, options]);
myFx.set(property, value);
myFx.start(property, from, [to]);
```

Fx.Morph

Fx.Morph transitions multiple CSS properties all at once. When you call the start method on your Fx.Morph instance, you have to pass it an object containing the CSS properties and the values. You can specify a range to change the property by passing an array with the CSS property.

```
var myFx = new Fx.Morph(element[, options]);
myFx.start({height: [100, 300], width:[100,300]});
```

Fx.Transitions

This is a hash containing a list of equations you can use when transitioning CSS properties of your elements. A partial listing appears in the following table:

Equation	Description
Linear	linear transition
Quad	quadratic transition
Cubic	cubic transition
Quartic	quartic transition
Bounce	bouncy transition
Elastic	elastic curve transition
Circ	circular transition

Fx.Slide

Fx.Slide lets you move an element gradually either horizontally or vertically. You call either the slideIn or slideOut method depending on which you want to do. When you call those methods, you pass in the mode (defaults to "vertical").

```
var myFx = new Fx.Slide(element[, options]);
myFx.slideIn("horizontal");
myFx.slideOut("vertical");
```

Rico

Rico (visit http://openrico.org/), which is shown in Figure 6-6, is a framework that contains some great, pre-built components as well as some style helpers for creating effects such as rounded corners. Development on Rico has been stalled for a while, but they recently released 2.1 on May 3rd, 2009.

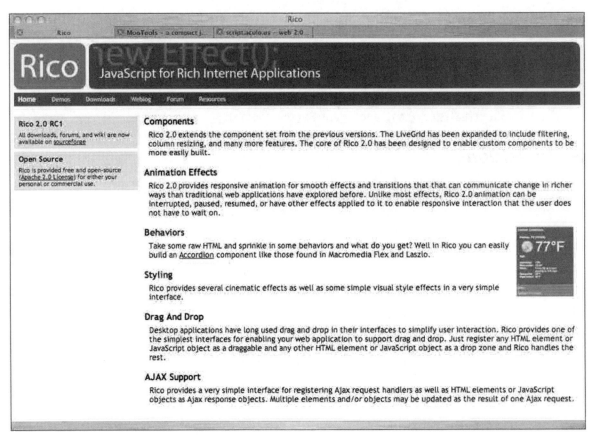

Figure 6-6

Components

Rico components are pre-built widgets you can use to enhance your JavaScript application. Rico contains two types of grid components you can use to display and sort tabular data. An accordion display, calendar, and pop-up window components are also included.

LiveGrid, SimpleGrid

Both of the grid components share some features: column headers that stay fixed at the top of the grid, the first column of the grid that is fixed in place, and resizable columns. They can be loaded with data from a JavaScript array, an XML source, or the result of an AJAX call. Rico provides a number of plug-ins written in various programming languages, including .NET and PHP, which let you load data into your grid from a SQL Query. The simple grid is new in Rico version 2.0 and is a static version of the LiveGrid table that you populate with data either by using one of the plug-ins or by performing an XSLT transformation on a pre-populated HTML table in your web page. You used to be able to perform the XSLT transformation on the client side, but a change in the Prototype library means you have to perform this transformation on the server.

Using a JavaScript array, you can set up a sortable, resizable grid quickly and easily using the LiveGrid component, as shown in Figure 6-7.

Figure 6-7

Accordion component

The accordion component (see Figure 6-8) displays elements stacked on top of each other and allows the users to toggle which one is open.

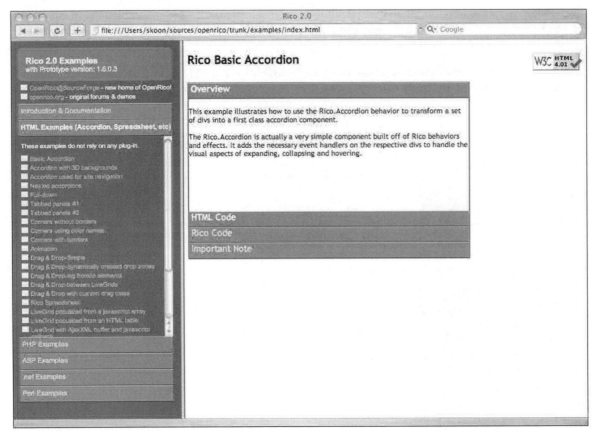

Figure 6-8

Pop-up windows

Rico includes two kinds of pop-up windows, as shown in Figure 6-9. One that can be dismissed with a mouse click and one that cannot.

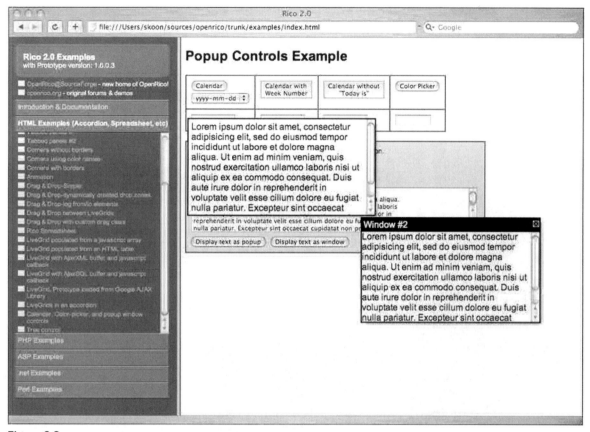

Figure 6-9

Color Picker

You can create a simple color picker (see Figure 6-10), which returns a value that the user selects.

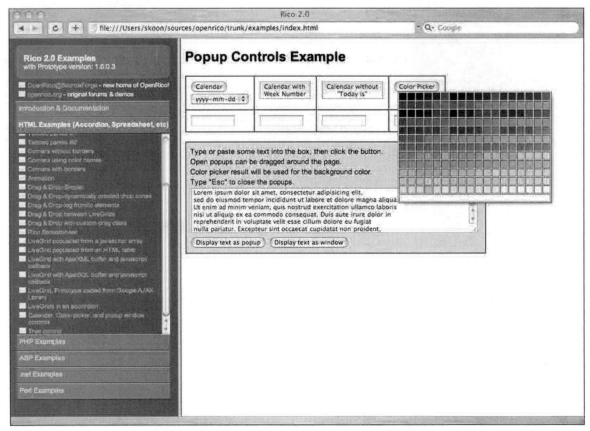

Figure 6-10

Animation Effects

Rico includes three predefined effects: fade in/out, change size, and change position. You can combine these three effects to send your elements zooming around the pages and disappearing when you are finished.

Rounded Corners

One of the more difficult effects to achieve in your web page design is a rounded corner. There are many different ways to achieve this using CSS or sliced-up images. Rico makes it as easy as writing a single line of JavaScript (see Figure 6-11).

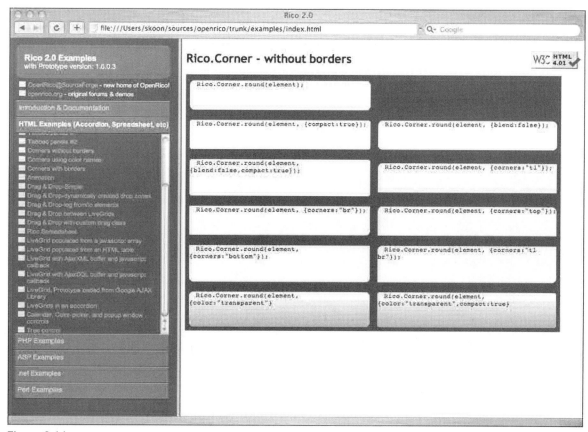

Figure 6-11

Drag and Drop

Rico supports making elements draggable and droppable as well as defining what properties an element should have before it can be dropped in the drop zones.

Summary

You took a brief look at three JavaScript frameworks based on the Prototype library. Script.aculo.us, Moo.fx, and Rico. All three of the frameworks provide excellent visual effects to use in your web pages. Script.aculo.us has a large number of pre-built effects. Moo.fx allows you to easily create new transitions based on equations and create new effects by combining transitions between different CSS properties. Rico provides a number of useful pre-built widgets including static and dynamic grid controls, a tree control, and an accordion control.

Part II

Yahoo! User Interface Library

The entire Yahoo! User Interface Library (YUI), unzipped, is about 50 MB. It includes assets, examples, tests, documentation, and the three flavors of files in which the main library is available. You can find the library at `http://developer.yahoo.com/yui/`.

The library is broken down along four major groups:

❑ YUI Core

❑ Utilities

❑ Controls/Widgets

❑ CSS Tools

Each group in turn is broken down into individual components that can be used as needed without having to include the entire library on a site. All components have a dependency on the YAHOO Global Object which lays out some needed groundwork. After that, most components also need the DOM Collection and the Event Utility. Each component comes in a minified version, a standard version, and a debug version. The latter logs all kinds of information to the logger allowing the inner workings of components to be tracked. The debug version is always the heaviest and should never be used in a production environment. For that matter, neither should the standard version, which is, as its name suggests, a standard JavaScript file filled with whitespace and comments (minus the logging).

Putting either of these versions in a production environment would mean forcing visitors to download at least double the necessary file size required to make the components work. That's because of the minified version. It exists solely for deployment in production environments as it's had all of its whitespace and comments stripped, as well as a few other space-saving operations performed on it. The minified version stops short of obfuscation, a practice the YUI team doesn't believe in because of its propensity to introduce bugs. Nonetheless, the minified versions of YUI components are substantially smaller than their standard and debug counterparts.

If that weren't enough, Yahoo! also offers hosted versions of all of their files through versioned URLs. A comprehensive (and maintained) list of all of the URLs can be found at `http://developer.yahoo .com/yui/articles/hosting/`.

Here is an example of a versioned URL for a hosted YUI file:

```
<script type="text/javascript"
    src="http://yui.yahooapis.com/2.7.0/build/yahoo/yahoo-min.js"></script>
```

The advantage of using the hosted version of the library is performance. These files are served via low latency servers and are cached globally.

Finally, the library offers aggregate versions of their most commonly used files so as to cut down on HTTP requests. There are two of these: `yahoo-dom-event.js` and `utilities.js`. The former obviously contains the YAHOO Global Object, DOM Collection, and Event Utility. The latter contains those as well as the Element Utility, Connection Manager, Drag & Drop Utility, and Animation Utility.

A Note on Namespacing

A basic tenet of the YUI is that global variables are bad, both from a performance standpoint as well as their being prone to colliding with other global variables. That's why the entire YUI Library only uses one global variable, YAHOO, inside which everything else is organized. Components are organized inside nested objects with names that clearly describe their function. Therefore, the DOM collection would be found in YAHOO.util.Dom, and the Event Utility in YAHOO.util.Event. The reason for the YAHOO global variable being in all caps is to further reduce the likelihood of a collision with another global variable with the same name. Since JavaScript variables are case-sensitive, YAHOO can coexist with Yahoo and yahoo without any trouble.

It is an accepted fact that namespacing, although descriptive, can be quite lengthy and cumbersome to type. Therefore, shortcuts can be introduced:

```
var Y = YAHOO.util.Dom;
var foo = Y.get("foo"); // instead of YAHOO.util.Dom.get("foo");
```

To illustrate this technique, some code examples will use shortcuts such as the following:

```
var YD = YAHOO.util.Dom,
    YE = YAHOO.util.Event,
    YEl = YAHOO.util.Element,
    YS = YAHOO.util.Selector;
```

Also, in keeping with the spirit of using as few global variables as possible, the code examples will tend to be wrapped in self-executing anonymous functions. This technique serves the purpose of providing a sort of "sandbox"; the scope of all of the example variables is limited to the anonymous function:

```
(function () {
    var foo = "This variable is not globally available.";
})();
```

Of course, it is also possible to create custom namespaces under the YAHOO Global Object by using the namespace function like this:

```
YAHOO.namespace("foo.bar.baz");
```

This creates the namespace YAHOO.foo.bar.baz. If YAHOO is passed as a part of the namespace string, it will be ignored as it is an implied part of the namespace. Therefore, the following code snippet would also create YAHOO.foo.bar.baz:

```
YAHOO.namespace("YAHOO.foo.bar.baz");
```

7

Traversing and Manipulating the DOM with YUI

Developers have enough to worry about without getting bogged down by the idiosyncrasies of web browsers. Getting blindsided by one can mean time wasted debugging instead of moving ahead with development. It can also mean ugly code forks strewn about throughout a program to get past browser implementation shortfalls. Therefore, the YUI team has put together the DOM collection, a set of "convenience methods for DOM interactions." This of course doesn't do away with code forks, but any forks and shortfall patches are handled in a central library that is easily maintainable. Even better, part of the team's mandate is to test their library against all A-Grade browsers for stability, something the average developer doesn't always have time for. The bottom line is, though you can probably write a lot of the functions found within the YUI DOM collection, these guys have already done it for you, and have made sure it works across all the major browsers.

In this chapter, you'll learn about:

- ❑ Traversing the DOM and finding elements
- ❑ Manipulating content
- ❑ Working with CSS and page styles

Traversing the DOM and Finding Elements

The following elements can be found while traversing the DOM.

get

Consider it `getElementById` but on steroids. The DOM method `getElementById` works great, but it could on occasion benefit from a little flexibility. The self-describing `getElementById` only takes one parameter, a string representing an element's ID. The `get` method, on the other hand, wraps `getElementById` and allows the passing of either a string ID or an `HTMLElement`, or an array containing either of each. If it receives a string ID, it performs a simple `getElementById` and returns the first element it finds. If it receives an array of IDs, it returns an array of `HTMLElements` matching those IDs. If it ever encounters an element as a parameter, it just returns that same element right back.

This last behavior is helpful when the parameter is one that's passed to a constructor, allowing for flexibility in what it can receive from the outside world.

Here's an example:

```
function MyConstructor(id) {
    this.el = YAHOO.util.Dom.get(id);
};

var obj1 = new MyConstructor("foo");

var obj2 = new MyConstructor(document.body);
```

The first instantiation of `MyConstructor` causes it to store an element with the ID "foo". The second passes the body element to the constructor, which passes it to the `get` method. The `get` method recognizes it as an `HTMLElement` and simply returns it right back. The second instantiation of `MyConstructor` therefore stores the body element in its `el` property. This is the sort of flexibility that the `get` method provides.

You can also pass it an array of IDs should you want an array of `HTMLElements` returned. This is helpful in batch operations where you want to be certain that the contents of an array are all elements. Once again, the `get` method will perform `getElementById` on all strings and return an element for each. So the result of the following bit of code will be three elements in an array named `arr`, the first being essentially ignored as it is already an element.

```
var foo = document.getElementById("foo");
var arr = YAHOO.util.Dom.get([foo, "bar", "baz"]);
```

getElementsByClassName

One of the more conspicuous omissions in the W3C DOM spec is a method for getting elements by class name. With `getElementById`, `getElementsByTagName` and even `getElementsByName`, one would think it logical to also include a `getElementsByClassName`, but alas, it isn't there. YUI therefore provides its own `getElementsByClassName` method. It functions like `getElementsByTagName` in that you can call it not only off the `document` element but any other element, making it a starting point for the search. So for example, both of the following are valid:

```
var foo = YAHOO.util.Dom.getElementsByClassName("foo");

var bar = document.getElementById("bar");
var baz = YAHOO.util.Dom.getElementsByClassName("baz", null, bar);
```

Since this is a JavaScript work-around and isn't a method baked into the browser, speed is a consideration. There is a third parameter for this express purpose. Pass the node type that you're searching for like so:

```
var foo = YAHOO.util.Dom.getElementsByClassName("foo", "a");
```

This example gets all anchors within the document with the class name foo. The reason for the optimization has to do with the way getElementsByClassName is constructed. It performs a getElementsByTagName(*) internally, which matches on all elements and then cycles over each looking for the specified class names. If a node name is given, the collection of nodes it needs to cycle over is drastically reduced, making for greater performance.

One final parameter allows for the execution of a function on each of the nodes that are found. Rather than write a second loop to apply a function to the returned collection of elements, it's possible to piggyback onto the loop that's used to find them in the first place. The purpose of this added parameter is once again for the sake of optimization. Using this parameter eliminates the need for a second loop, which, in the case of larger collections of nodes, can result in a noticeable improvement in performance.

Here's an example of how to do it:

```
function addClick(el) {
    el.onclick = function () {
        alert("Click!");
    }
};
var nodes = YAHOO.util.Dom.getElementsByClassName("foo", "a", document, addClick);
```

Internally, the only parameter that gets passed to the addClick function is the current element in the loop (which is trapped with the el variable name).

getFirstChild/getLastChild

A perfect example of cross-browser idiosyncrasies is the firstChild DOM method. In Internet Explorer, it returns the first child node of a given element that is of type HTMLElement. Not so with Firefox, Safari, or Opera. In standards mode, they all follow the W3C spec to the letter and return the first text node inside a given element. That's because, according to the W3C spec, each node in the DOM of type HTMLElement (that is, an HTML tag) has an empty text node for a sibling on either side. This can be a pain because most of the time, when the first child element is needed, it's an HTMLElement and not a text node that's required. getFirstChild normalizes this behavior by ensuring that it always returns a node of type HTMLElement; that is, it skips over the first text node.

Here's an example of its use:

```
<html>
    <head>
        <title>YUI getFirstChild / getLastChild Test</title>
    </head>
    <body>
        <p>Hello World</p>
        <p>This is not the first child.</p>
```

```
        <p>Neither is this.</p>
        <script src="yahoo-dom-event.js"></script>
        <script>
            var helloWorld = YAHOO.util.Dom.getFirstChild(document.body);
            var lastScript = YAHOO.util.Dom.getLastChild(document.body);
        </script>
    </body>
</html>
```

This line of code will return the first HTMLElement that's found inside the document's body. In this case, it's the paragraph that contains the text "Hello World."

Similarly, getLastChild also normalizes the cross-browser text node quirk by making sure that in Firefox, the node before last is returned. In the previous example, the last child happens to be the script tag that contains the example's JavaScript. Hence the variable name lastScript.

getFirstChildBy/getLastChildBy

Sometimes, the node that's needed isn't the first or the last of a set. Rather it's the first or the last of a certain kind in a set. Unfortunately, there aren't any W3C DOM methods available for this sort of node retrieval. Not to worry, the YUI DOM collection has just the thing. And rather than create methods that are specific to a certain criterion, such as getElementById, it leaves the determining of criteria up to the programmer. The two methods that allow this sort of flexibility are getFirstChildBy and getLastChildBy. Both take a start node as their first parameter and a function as their second. The function receives an element and must return either true or false. Here they are in action:

```
<html>
    <head>
        <title>YUI getFirstChildBy / getLastChildBy Test</title>
    </head>
    <body>
        <p>Hello World</p>
        <p class="intro">Hello Planet!</p>
        <p class="intro">This is not the first child.</p>
        <p>Neither is this.</p>
        <p class="outtro">This one is somewhere in the middle.</p>
        <p class="outtro">So is this.</p>
        <script src="yahoo-dom-event.js"></script>
        <script>
            var YD = YAHOO.util.Dom,
                YX = YAHOO.example;
            YX.intro = YD.getFirstChildBy(document.body,
                function (el) {
                    return (el.className === "intro");
                });
            YX.outtro = YD.getLastChildBy(document.body,
                function (el) {
                    return (el.className === "outtro");
                });
        </script>
    </body>
</html>
```

In the previous example, the variable `intro` holds the paragraph containing the text "Hello Planet!" and `outtro` contains the paragraph with the text "So is this." Neither of these paragraphs are the first or the last child of the `body` element. However, they are the first and last of their kinds, respectively.

getChildren/getChildrenBy

More often than not, when dealing with the DOM, the desired type of nodes to be dealing with are element nodes. But `document.body.childNodes` will return text nodes, comment nodes, and every other type of node under the sun. This can be annoying as it requires an extra step to filter out everything but the element nodes when processing the resulting collection. The `getChildren` method however, pre-filters results for element nodes. It also returns an array, which is important because the native DOM method `childNodes` doesn't. It may seem like it does, but in fact it returns a `NodeList`, which looks like an array but lacks several of the array's methods. So for example, though a `NodeList` can be iterated over with a `for` loop, it can't be `sliced`.

Not only does `getChildren` filter for element nodes, but its cousin `getChildrenBy` allows for further filtering through a user-defined Boolean function.

```html
<html>
    <head>
        <title>getChildrenBy</title>
    </head>
    <body>
        <p id="foo">
            Lorem ipsum dolor sit <em>amet</em>, consectetuer adipiscing elit.
            <a href="/vivamus/">Vivamus</a> sed nulla. <em>Donec</em> vitae
            pede. <strong>Nunc</strong> dignissim rutrum nisi.
        </p>
        <script src="yahoo-dom-event.js"></script>
        <script>
            var YD = YAHOO.util.Dom,
                YX = YAHOO.example;
            YX.isEm = function (el) {
                if (el.nodeName.toUpperCase() === "EM") {
                    return true;
                }
                return false;
            };
            YX.init = function () {
                var foo = YD.get("foo");
                var ems = YD.getChildrenBy(foo, YX.isEm);
                var msg = "";
                for (var i = 0; ems[i]; i += 1) {
                    var em = ems[i];
                    msg += "<em>" + (em.innerText || em.textContent) + "</em>, ";
                }
                msg = msg.substring(0, msg.length - 2);
                alert("The following elements are emphasized: " + msg);
            }();
        </script>
    </body>
</html>
```

The previous example gets all em child elements of the paragraph with the ID foo. The isEm function that is used as the Boolean filter receives an element, checks to see if its node name is "EM", and returns either true or false. Once all of the em elements are collected, an alert message is shown, listing the elements that were matched (see Figure 7-1).

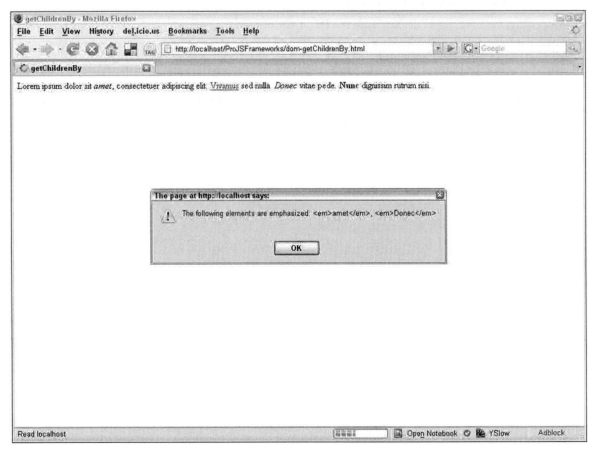

Figure 7-1

getElementsBy

The YUI DOM collection also offers a getElementsBy method, which leaves the door wide open for customization. Rather than be constrained by a particular kind of filtering, that is, "by class name" or "by ID", the getElementsBy leaves the filtering up to the developer. The first parameter it receives is a Boolean function that it passes elements to. If the element passes the test (if the function returns true), then it stores it in the array of elements it eventually returns. If the element fails the test, then it simply moves to the next one. Also, just like with the getElementsByClassName method, a node type can be specified as well as a root node for the starting point. Finally, a function can be passed that will be applied to each node that passes the Boolean function's test.

```
<html>
    <head>
        <title>getElementsBy</title>
    </head>
    <body>
        <ul id="nav">
            <li><a href="/">Home</a></li>
            <li>
                <a href="/products/">Products</a>
                <ul>
                    <li><a href="/products/widget/">Widget</a></li>
                    <li><a href="/products/gadget/">Gadget</a></li>
                    <li><a href="/products/whatzit/">Whatzit</a></li>
                </ul>
            </li>
            <li>
                <a href="/partners/">Partners</a>
                <ul>
                    <li><a href="http://www.widgetsinc.com/">Widgets Inc</a></li>
                    <li><a href="http://www.gadgetsinc.com/">Gadgets Inc</a></li>
                    <li><a href="http://www.whatzitsinc.com/">Whatzits Inc</a></li>
                </ul>
            </li>
            <li><a href="/about/">About Us</a></li>
            <li><a href="/contact/">Contact</a></li>
        </ul>
        <script src="yahoo-dom-event.js"></script>
        <script>
            var YD = YAHOO.util.Dom,
                YX = YAHOO.example;
            YX.isExternal = function (el) {
                if (el.href.substring(0, 4) === "http") {
                    return true;
                }
                return false;
            };
            YX.makePopup = function (el) {
                el.onclick = function () {
                    window.open(el.href);
                    return false;
                };
            };
            YX.externalLinks = YD.getElementsBy(
                YX.isExternal, "a", "nav", YX.makePopup);
        </script>
    </body>
</html>
```

The previous example applies the function isExternal to all anchors within the element with the ID
nav. Each element that passes the test has the function makePopup applied to it. The result of this code is
fairly self-explanatory; any link whose href attribute begins with "http" will open up in a new window.

getAncestorByTagName

Sometimes a parent element acting as a container needs to be affected by an action made on one of its child elements. The trouble is, the child element doesn't know how far up the container is, and therefore can't just point to it by using the parentNode pointer:

```
var parent = this.parentNode;
```

In fact, what it needs to do is loop upward through the DOM until it finds the node it's looking for. That's where the getAncestor family of methods comes in. The getAncestorByTagName does exactly what its name says. It goes up through the DOM starting at a given node and finds a parent node, an ancestor, with a given tag name.

```
<html>
    <head>
        <title>getAncestorByTagName</title>
    </head>
    <body>
        <ul id="nav">
            <li><a href="/" id="home">Home</a></li>
            <li><a href="/contact/" id="contact">Contact</a></li>
            <li><a href="/about/" id="about">About Us</a></li>
        </ul>
        <script src="yahoo-dom-event.js"></script>
        <script>
            var YD = YAHOO.util.Dom,
                YX = YAHOO.example;
            YX.contact = document.getElementById("contact");
            YX.contact.onmouseover = function () {
                var ancestor = YD.getAncestorByTagName(this, "ul");
                if (ancestor) {
                    ancestor.style.border = "solid 1px red";
                }
            };
            YX.contact.onmouseout = function () {
                var ancestor = YD.getAncestorByTagName(this, "ul");
                if (ancestor) {
                    ancestor.style.border = "none";
                }
            };
        </script>
    </body>
</html>
```

In this example, the anchor with the ID contact has two event handlers, onmouseover (see Figure 7-2) and onmouseout (see Figure 7-3), each of which calls getAncestorByTagName and passes the anchor as a starting point. They also state that it should stop at the first UL parent element it encounters. Once the element, or ancestor, is found, its border is manipulated through the style object.

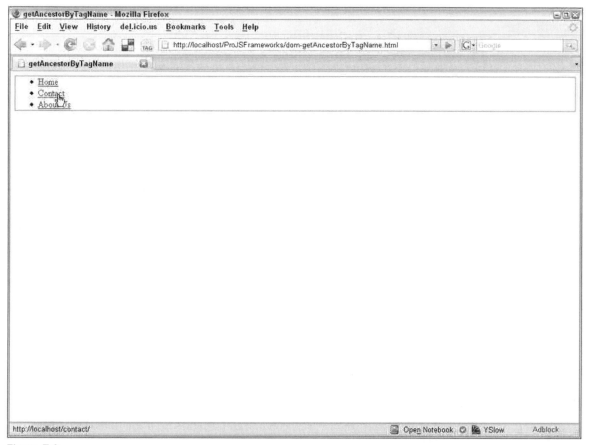

Figure 7-2

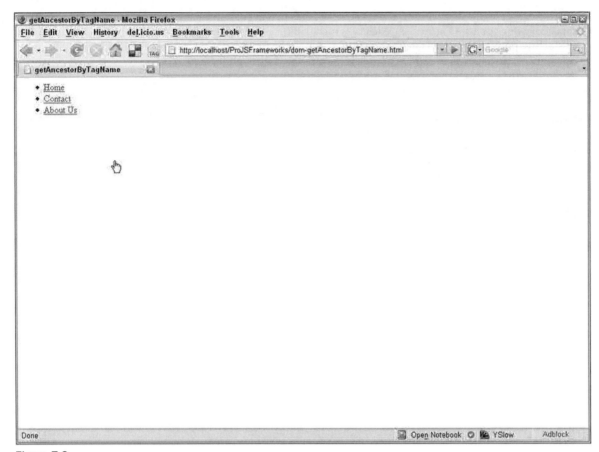

Figure 7-3

getAncestorByClassName

Similarly, getAncestorByClassName starts at a given node and searches up through the DOM for a parent element with a given class name.

```html
<html>
    <head>
        <title>getAncestorByClassName</title>
        <style type="text/css">
            .main {
                border: solid 1px white;
            }
        </style>
    </head>
    <body>
        <div class="main">
            <div class="header">
```

```
            <ul id="nav">
                <li><a href="/" id="home">Home</a></li>
                <li><a href="/contact/" id="contact">Contact</a></li>
                <li><a href="/about/" id="about">About Us</a></li>
            </ul>
        </div>
        <div class="body">
            <p>The page's main content block goes here</p>
        </div>
        <div class="footer">
            <p><small>The page's footer goes here</small></p>
        </div>
    </div>
    <script src="yahoo-dom-event.js"></script>
    <script>
        var YD = YAHOO.util.Dom,
            YX = YAHOO.example;
        YX.contact = document.getElementById("contact");
        YX.contact.onmouseover = function () {
            var ancestor = YD.getAncestorByClassName(this, "main");
            if (ancestor) {
                ancestor.style.border = "solid 1px red";
            }
        };
        YX.contact.onmouseout = function () {
            var ancestor = YD.getAncestorByClassName(this, "main");
            if (ancestor) {
                ancestor.style.border = "solid 1px white";
            }
        };
    </script>
</body>
</html>
```

Here is a similar example as the one for `getAncestorByTagName`. Hovering over the contact link in this case, however, targets the all-encompassing `div` with the ID `main` and manipulates *its* border through the `style` object.

getAncestorBy

Finally, with `getAncestorBy` it's possible to target ancestors by any conceivable criteria just by programming it into a function. The function needs to receive an element, evaluate it, and return either `true` or `false`. So, as `getAncestorBy` cycles up the DOM from its starting point, it passes each parent element it encounters to the Boolean function for evaluation. If the function returns `false`, it moves on to the next element up the chain. If it returns `true`, it stops and returns that element back to its caller.

```
<html>
    <head>
        <title>getAncestorBy</title>
    </head>
    <body>
        <div class="main">
            <div class="header">
```

```
            <ul id="nav">
                <li><a href="/" id="home">Home</a></li>
                <li><a href="/contact/" id="contact">Contact</a></li>
                <li><a href="/about/" id="about">About Us</a></li>
            </ul>
        </div>
        <div class="body">
            <p>The page's main content block goes here</p>
        </div>
        <div class="footer">
            <p><small>The page's footer goes here</small></p>
        </div>
    </div>
    <script src="yahoo-dom-event.js"></script>
    <script>
        var YD = YAHOO.util.Dom,
            YX = YAHOO.example;
        YX.hasBGColor = function (el) {
            if (el.nodeName.toUpperCase() === "DIV" &&
                el.style.backgroundColor) {
                return true;
            }
            return false;
        };
        YX.hasNoBGColor = function (el) {
            if (el.nodeName.toUpperCase() === "DIV" &&
                !el.style.backgroundColor) {
                return true;
            }
            return false;
        };
        YX.contact = document.getElementById("contact");
        YX.contact.onmouseover = function () {
            var ancestor = YD.getAncestorBy(this, YX.hasNoBGColor);
            if (ancestor) {
                ancestor.style.backgroundColor = "red";
            }
        };
        YX.contact.onmouseout = function () {
            var ancestor = YD.getAncestorBy(this, YX.hasBGColor);
            if (ancestor) {
                ancestor.style.backgroundColor = "";
            }
        };
    </script>
    </body>
</html>
```

In this case, hovering over or out of the contact link calls the getAncestorBy method with the Boolean functions hasNoBGColor and hasBGColor, respectively. The hasNoBGColor function finds the first ancestor that is a div and has no background color set. The onmouseover event handler then sets its background color to red. Similarly, hasBGColor finds the first ancestor that is a div and *has* a background color set. The onmouseout event handler then clears its background color.

Element

The YUI Element utility is a wrapper for HTMLElements. One of the more interesting things that it allows for is the deferred assigning of event listeners. It does this by listening for when HTMLElements are added to the DOM and only then attempting to attach events to them. When an HTMLElement becomes available, the contentReady event is fired. And finally, it simplifies the setting and getting of attributes.

In order to use the Element utility, an Element object needs to be instantiated like so:

```
var el = new YAHOO.util.Element("foo");
```

When you use the object instantiated in the previous example, you can add an event handler to el even though the HTMLElement with the ID foo has yet to be added to the DOM. The following example fires an alert when an element with the ID foo is available. It then attaches a mouseover event that changes the element's text to red. Triggering it all is a two-second timer that inserts a div element into the DOM with the ID foo (see Figure 7-4).

```
<html>
    <head>
        <title>YUI Element Utility</title>
    </head>
    <body>
        <script src="yahoo-dom-event.js"></script>
        <script src="element-min.js"></script>
        <script>
            var YE = YAHOO.util.Event,
                YEl = YAHOO.util.Element,
                YX = YAHOO.example;
            YX.el = new YEl("foo");
            YX.el.on("contentReady", function () {
                alert("foo is here!");
            });
            YX.el.on("mouseover", function () {
                this.setStyle("color", "red");
            });
            setTimeout(function () {
                var foo = document.createElement("div");
                foo.id = "foo";
                foo.appendChild(document.createTextNode("foo"));
                document.body.appendChild(foo);
            }, 2000);
        </script>
    </body>
</html>
```

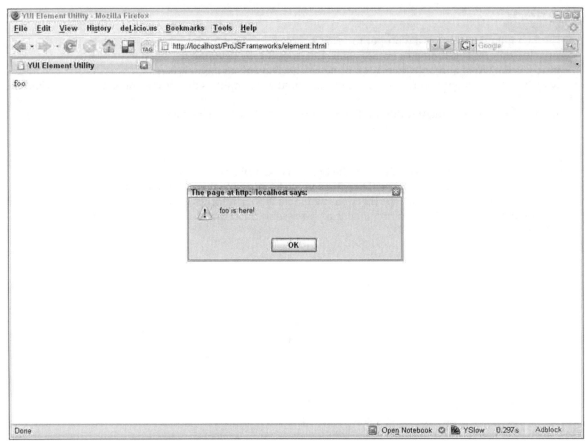

Figure 7-4

Selector

Sometimes, working with DOM methods to get HTMLElements can be a bit cumbersome. Oftentimes, several lines of code are needed to filter for a particular element that is located in a specific hierarchy of nodes or that has a particular attribute. But those familiar with CSS selector syntax know that a simple line of code is all that's needed.

For example, .foo targets all elements with the class name foo, or #foo .bar targets all elements with the class name bar that are a child of an element with the ID foo.

With that in mind, the following block of JavaScript . . .

```
<html>
    <head>
        <title>YUI Selector Utility</title>
    </head>
    <body>
        <h1>YUI Selector Utility</h1>
```

```
<div id="foo">
    <ul>
        <li class="first">This is the first list item</li>
        <li class="second">Here's the second</li>
        <li class="third">And this one's the third</li>
    </ul>
</div>
<script>
    var foo = document.getElementById("foo");
    var listItems = foo.getElementsByTagName("li");
    for (var i = 0; listItems[i]; i += 1) {
        if (listItems[i].className === "second") {
            listItems[i].style.color = "red";
        }
    }
</script>
</body>
</html>
```

. . . can just as easily be written like this, using the Selector utility:

```
<script src="yahoo-dom-event.js"></script>
<script src="selector-min.js"></script>
<script>
    var YS = YAHOO.util.Selector,
        YX = YAHOO.example;
    YX.second = YS.query(".second", null, true);
    YX.second.style.color = "red";
</script>
```

The YUI Selector Utility takes CSS selector syntax and returns an array of elements that match it. In the previous example, an added Boolean parameter is passed telling the engine to return only the first of what it finds. That way, the added step of selecting the first item in an array known to contain only one item is avoided. The second parameter is where a start node ID or reference can be passed. This allows for better performance by narrowing down the number of nodes that need checking. It can be set to null or undefined, and it will default to `Selector.document`. `Selector.document` is actually a reference to the document itself, but it can't be passed as a parameter since the code first checks the value that's passed for a valid tag name (which `document` does not have).

Manipulating Content

Retrieving elements from the DOM is pretty useless unless they're somehow handled. Operations such as moving them around, modifying them, or simply adding new ones can once again be handled through YUI's DOM collection.

insertBefore

Using the `insertBefore` method provided with the DOM not only requires that a new node and a reference node be given, but it also needs to be called from that same reference node's parent.

```
var newNode = refNode.parentNode.insertBefore(newNode, refNode);
```

The YUI `insertBefore` method eliminates the need to mention the reference node twice, and also allows for both the parameters to be either ID strings or actual node references. This can make coding a little easier if ever one is available and not the other. Just like in the case of the native DOM method, YUI's `insertBefore` also returns a reference to the new node.

```
var newNode = YAHOO.util.Dom.insertBefore(newNode, refNode);
```

insertAfter

Although `insertBefore` is offered natively in the DOM, there is no `insertAfter` method. Inserting a new node *after* an existing one requires a bit of extra work.

```
var newNode = refNode.parentNode.insertBefore(newNode, refNode.nextSibling);
```

This works, if the reference node has a `nextSibling`, which isn't always the case. So YUI wraps all of this extra checking and referencing into a neat little method called `insertAfter`.

```
var newNode = YAHOO.util.Dom.insertAfter(newNode, refNode);
```

Working with Class Names

In today's complex web applications, nodes with one class name are a thing of the past. Here's a simple example:

```
<ul id="nav">
    <li class="home selected hover"><a href="/index.html">Home</a></li>
    <!--More list items here -->
</ul>
```

The previous example illustrates how an element can have multiple, equally valid and needed class names. Yet the W3C DOM offers no native methods for adding, replacing, or removing select class names. The only way to work with class names natively is through assignment.

```
el.className = "home";
```

Adding another class name can be done easily enough.

```
el.className += " selected";
```

But there's no way of knowing, for example, if that class name already exists. YUI's DOM collection offers a set of methods for safely working with class names. What's more, these methods accept an element, an element ID, or an array of elements to process. Therefore, if a whole batch of elements need a class name operation performed on them, the entire array can be passed directly as the `el` parameter.

hasClass

Checking to see if an element has a certain class name isn't as simple as it may seem. Elements don't always have just one class name . . .

```
<li class="home selected hover">
```

. . . making checks like this iffy at best:

```
if (el.className === "selected") {  // returns false
```

The element may have `selected` as one of its class names. But in this case it has several, making the `if` statement return `false`. Checking for an `indexOf` can also be iffy:

```
if(el.className.indexOf("select") !== -1) {
```

This can't be a reliable way of checking for the existence of a class name because it will return true on partial matches as well. Even if the element has a class name `selected` or `selection` or `selectable`, checking for `select` will return true. What's needed is an algorithm that breaks the `className` string down into individual class names and checks against each of them. That's what `hasClass` does.

```
if (YAHOO.util.Dom.hasClass(el, "select")) {
```

This line of code returns true only if the full word `select` exists within the element's `className` attribute.

addClass

As mentioned earlier, adding a class name is as simple as this:

```
el.className += " hover";
```

The trouble is, there's no way of knowing if the class name that was just assigned already existed, and since the `className` attribute is a string, it just gets concatenated. So the line in the preceding code may result in something like this:

```
<li class="hover hover">
```

This can result in bugs when trying to remove the `hover` class name because only one of the two will likely be removed, leaving the element with an undesired `hover` class name. YUI's `addClass` method first checks to make sure that the class name that's being added doesn't already exist. If it doesn't, it adds it and returns `true`. If it does exist, it just returns `false` without adding anything.

```
YAHOO.util.Dom.addClass(el, "hover");
```

removeClass

Removing a class name from an element can be one of the more difficult tasks when working with class names. This is where real string processing comes into play. Not only must the whole word representing the class name be found, but the contents of the `className` attribute then needs to be reconstructed minus the class name that is to be removed. Once all that is done, the new string needs to be reassigned to the `className` attribute effectively overwriting the old string with the new one. YUI boils that entire process down to a simple method, `removeClass`.

```
YAHOO.util.Dom.removeClass(el, "hover");
```

replaceClass

Sometimes a class name doesn't need removing so much as replacing. That's where YUI's `replaceClass` comes in. If it doesn't find a class name to replace, it simply adds the new one and returns `true`. If it does find a class name to replace, it replaces it and also returns `true`. If an element happens to have multiple class names that are the same, it replaces them all with the new value.

```
YAHOO.util.Dom.replaceClass(el, "open", "closed");
```

setStyle

Setting style values for a DOM element is relatively straightforward, sort of. For one thing, Internet Explorer 6 manages opacity through a special `filter` rule, whereas Firefox, Opera and Safari don't. Also, using floating elements is a bit touchy since `float` is a reserved word. So Internet Explorer calls it `styleFloat` and the other browsers refer to it as `cssFloat`. These peculiarities can be annoying at best, and can be the source of bugs at worst. Having to remember them and be accommodating can also be a pain. What's more, CSS rule name syntax requires hyphens for the separation of words, but JavaScript, on the other hand, uses camel case.

```
<style type="text/css">
#foo {
    font-size: 2em;
    font-family: arial;
    float: right;
}
</style>

<script>
    foo.style.fontSize = "2em";
    foo.style.fontFamily = "arial";
    foo.style.cssFloat = "right";
</script>
```

Both the `getStyle` and `setStyle` YUI DOM collection methods normalize all of that.

```
<script>
    YAHOO.util.Dom.setStyle(foo, "font-size", "2em");
    YAHOO.util.Dom.setStyle(foo, "font-family", "arial");
    YAHOO.util.Dom.setStyle(foo, "float", "right");
    YAHOO.util.Dom.setStyle(foo, "opacity", "0.5");
</script>
```

Be sure to place this script after the element with the ID foo *in the DOM, preferably right before the closing* </body> *tag. Otherwise, the element won't be found and the code won't work.*

getStyle

Getting an element's style can be problematic since the JavaScript style object only holds values that are set through JavaScript. In other words, style values set through regular CSS won't get picked up by the style object.

```
<script>
    el.style.width = "100px";
    alert(el.style.width); // returns "100px" because it was just set;
    alert(el.style.height); // returns "";
</script>
```

The way to get an element's style value, whether it's been set in the style object or not is to use the getComputedStyle method, unless working with Internet Explorer. In that case, the method to use would be currentStyle, but not before taking care of all of the normalizing that was covered in the setStyle YUI method. Once again, the YUI DOM collection method getStyle provides a cross-browser solution to the insanity.

```
<script>
    YAHOO.util.Dom.getStyle(foo, "font-size");
</script>
```

setXY

Setting an element's x and y position isn't always easy, but setXY takes a good crack at making it just that. It works well, most of the time. Sometimes though, if the element in question is nested deep inside an eccentric layout, setXY doesn't yield the desired result. It does try a second time, however, and allows you to control whether it does or not through a third Boolean parameter. For the most part, however, it's pretty reliable.

```
// set foo's x to 10px and y to 100px and don't retry
YAHOO.util.Dom.setXY(foo, [10, 100], true);
```

Separate setX and setY methods are also available. They follow the same syntax as setXY, except that the x and y value parameters are passed as numbers, not arrays. The previous example can therefore be written as:

```
YAHOO.util.Dom.setX(foo, 10);
YAHOO.util.Dom.setY(foo, 100);
```

New in YUI 3

Apart from a new namespace (it's now YUI, not YAHOO), YUI 3 introduces a whole new approach to DOM traversal and manipulation. It treats DOM nodes as YUI node objects. Node objects have methods and properties that allow for easier access and interaction with the DOM. One major change is its use of the new get method, which is similar to YUI 2.x's selector. Here's an example of it being used (note how it's wrapped in the new script dependency loader called use):

```
YUI().use('node', function(Y) {
    var node1 = Y.get('#main');
    var node2 = Y.get(document.body);
});
```

Source: This code example comes from the YUI 3 Node page.

Summary

As has been made evident throughout this chapter, working with the DOM can be a tenuous undertaking made even more complicated by browser makers' tendency to go off the beaten path to pursue their own interpretations and implementations. YUI goes a long way in bridging the chasm created by these circumstances.

Not only is it a good idea to use YUI for the neutralization of cross-browser issues, but it's advisable to use it for the sake of consistency. Browsers mature and evolve over time. Bugs get fixed, new features are added, and more bugs are introduced. Using a library such as YUI can act as a layer of protection against future issues. For example, if at some point in the future browsers begin to offer native support for the currently nonexistent getElementsByClassName DOM method, the YUI team simply has to replace their code with the DOM method itself, making for a seamless transition for those projects using the library. The alternative would be to hunt down different snippets of code throughout a project in order to make the same change.

Handling Cross-Browser Events

Event handling is a crucial component of modern web development. Unfortunately, modern browsers' implementation of the W3C DOM event model is far from uniform. Internet Explorer in particular handles things quite differently than the other mainstream browsers on the market. What's more, the spec is rather anemic when it comes to certain performance-oriented event handlers that simply don't exist — more on that in a moment. The YUI Event Utility not only does a masterful job of normalizing event handling across browsers, but it also extends the existing model to allow for functionality that would otherwise not exist. Most notable is the Event Utility's tackling of the holy grail of event handling, and that is its ability to add and remove multiple event listeners to an element.

In this chapter you'll learn about:

- ❑ Registering events on page and element readiness
- ❑ Adding event listeners to elements
- ❑ Handling keyboard and mouse input
- ❑ Working with custom events
- ❑ Managing browser history and fixing the back button

Registering Events on Page and Element Readiness

JavaScript functions that get, set, and modify elements in the DOM can't be executed prior to the DOM being ready. If they are, they'll throw an error when they attempt to do something with an element that doesn't exist.

```html
<html>
    <head>
        <title>Hello World - Broken</title>
        <script>
            var hello = document.getElementById("hello");
            var msg = hello.innerText || hello.textContent;
            alert(msg);
        </script>
    </head>
    <body>
        <p id="hello">Hello World</p>
    </body>
</html>
```

This bit of JavaScript will break, because it tries to access a property of the element with the ID `hello` prior to its being created. In this case `getElementById` returns `null`, which obviously has no properties. This happens because JavaScript instructions are executed where they are read. The way around this is to wrap the code in a function and call it later, once that element is ready. Traditionally, this is handled with the `window` object's `onload` event handler.

```html
<html>
    <head>
        <title>Hello World</title>
        <script>
            window.onload = function () {
                var hello = document.getElementById("hello");
                var msg = hello.innerText || hello.textContent;
                alert(msg);
            }
        </script>
    </head>
    <body>
        <p id="hello">Hello World</p>
    </body>
</html>
```

This works just fine, in this example. But on larger pages there will be a noticeable delay before the `onload` event is triggered. That's because a page isn't considered loaded until all of its dependencies are done loading. That includes, among other things, all the images on a page. Most of the time, however, the JavaScript that's to be executed doesn't need the images to be there; all it needs is for the DOM to be ready, that is, for certain elements to be ready. Unfortunately, there is no native W3C DOM method that fires when the DOM is ready.

A Note on Terminology

In this section, when the term *event* is used, it's in reference to a "moment of interest" belonging to a DOM element to which a handler can be attached. An event handler is also known as a listener, or a callback function — these terms are used interchangeably — and is essentially a function that gets executed whenever the event to which it is attached is fired. The terms *attached* and *assigned* are also used interchangeably to describe the association of an event and a handler.

---

onDOMReady

Enter onDOMReady, a YUI Event Utility custom event handler that fires once the DOM is ready. Based on the work of Dean Edwards, John Resig and Matthias Miller, it jumps through a few hoops to check and see if the document is ready, at least for Internet Explorer and early versions of WebKit (Apple's Safari browser). Firefox, Opera, and later versions of WebKit actually have a proprietary event that they fire, which is called DOMContentLoaded which onDOMReady takes advantage of. Unfortunately, there is no such proprietary event that Internet Explorer fires. And of all the browsers, it's the one that could benefit the most from one, since, under certain conditions, modifying the DOM in IE prior to its being ready can cause the page to literally abort with a message from the browser saying as much (see Figure 8-1). It's not pleasant.

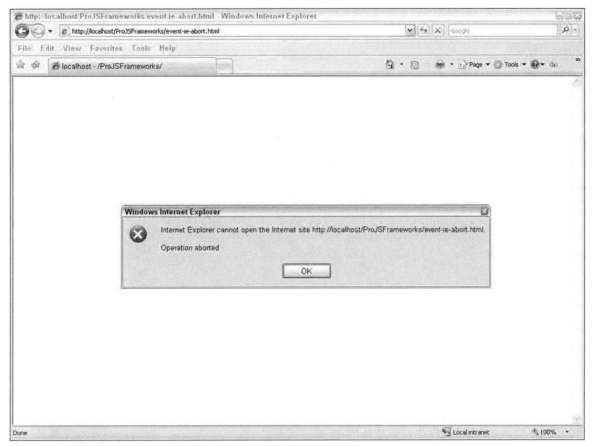

Figure 8-1

Here is an example of some code that causes Internet Explorer to throw its infamous "Operation aborted" message. The reason for this is that IE can't handle an appendChild to the body tag if the script tags aren't direct children of the body tag. Go figure.

115

```html
<html>
    <head>
        <title>Internet Explorer "Operation aborted"</title>
    </head>
    <body>
        <div>
            <script>
                var p = document.createElement("p");
                document.body.appendChild(p);
            </script>
        </div>
    </body>
</html>
```

The problem is easily fixed by wrapping the code with an anonymous function and passing it to YUI's onDOMReady event handler.

```html
<html>
    <head>
        <title>Internet Explorer "Operation aborted" - FIXED!</title>
    </head>
    <body>
        <div>
            <script src="yahoo-dom-event.js"></script>
            <script>
                var YE = YAHOO.util.Event;
                YE.onDOMReady(function () {
                    var p = document.createElement("p");
                    document.body.appendChild(p);
                });
            </script>
        </div>
    </body>
</html>
```

A more common problem however, as mentioned earlier, is having to wait for all of a page's dependencies to finish downloading. This can be a particular problem in the case of image-rich pages. Here is an example where the JavaScript kicks in long before the images are done downloading.

```html
<html>
    <head>
        <title>onDOMReady</title>
        <script src="yahoo-dom-event.js"></script>
        <script>
            var YE = YAHOO.util.Event;
            YE.onDOMReady(function () {
                var images = document.getElementsByTagName("img");
                alert("There will be " + images.length +
                    " images loaded on this page");
            });
        </script>
    </head>
    <body>
```

```
<ol>
    <li><img src="image1.jpg" /></li>
    <li><img src="image2.jpg" /></li>
    <!-- Hundreds of really heavy images go here -->
</ol>
</body>
</html>
```

A Word on Execution Scope and Parameter Passing

Normally, the execution scope of an event handler is the `window` object and the `this` keyword refers to the element whose event triggered the handler. Take for example this code:

```
var el = document.getElementById("foo");
el.onmouseover = function () {
    this.style.color = "red";
};
```

Here, an anonymous function is assigned to an element's `onmouseover` event. When that function is triggered, it accesses the calling element via the `this` keyword. It then modifies its color through the element's `style` object. This is perfectly fine for a simple example such as this. But in more complex constructs, this pattern becomes problematic.

```
<html>
    <head>
        <title>Execution Scope - Broken</title>
    </head>
    <body>
        <a href="/foo/" id="foo">Foo</a>
        <script>
            function DoSomething(id) {
                var foo = document.getElementById(id);
                this.bar = "baz";
                foo.onmouseover = function () {
                    alert(this.bar);
                };
            };
            var doSomething = new DoSomething("foo");
        </script>
    </body>
</html>
```

In this example, an object is instantiated from the function `DoSomething`, which contains a property named `bar` with the value `baz`. There's also an `onmouseover` event handler that is set up on the anchor with the ID `foo`, which alerts the value of the property named `bar`. The trouble is, the event handler's execution scope isn't the `doSomething` object, but the `window` object. Therefore, the `this` keyword refers to the element that called the handler, and not the `doSomething`. As a result, the `alert(this.bar);` returns a value of `undefined` because the anchor in question doesn't have a `bar` attribute from which to return a value. What this event handler needs is a correction of its execution scope. In other words, it needs to be told "run from within `doSomething` and not `window`."

Event Utility Parameter Pattern

All of YUI's Event Utility functions, `addListener`, `onAvailable`, `onContentReady`, and `onDOMReady`, allow for the passing of an optional data object to the callback function. They also all allow for the execution scope of the callback function to be changed. This is done through two parameters called `obj` and `override`. (In the case of `onDOMReady`, the `override` parameter is called `scope`, which is simply a naming inconsistency.)

```
YAHOO.util.Event.onDOMReady(callback, obj, scope/override);
```

These three parameters can be used in different ways to produce different results:

❑   If only the data object is present, then only the data object gets passed to the callback function.

❑   If a data object is present and the override parameter is set to the Boolean value `true`, then the data object becomes the execution scope of the callback function as well as being passed to the callback function.

❑   If a data object is present and the override parameter is also an object, then the data object is passed to the callback function, and the override object becomes the function's execution scope.

Here is an example that corrects the event handler's execution scope.

```
<html>
    <head>
        <title>Execution Scope - Fixed</title>
    </head>
    <body>
        <a href="/foo/" id="foo">Foo</a>
        <script src="yahoo-dom-event.js"></script>
        <script>
            var YE = YAHOO.util.Event,
                YX = YAHOO.example;
            YX.DoSomething = function (id) {
                var foo = document.getElementById(id);
                this.bar = "baz";
                YE.addListener(foo, "mouseover", function () {
                    alert(this.bar);
                }, this, true);
            };
            YX.doSomething = new YX.DoSomething("foo");
        </script>
    </body>
</html>
```

Rather than use a direct assignment technique, this example uses the YUI `addListener` function (more detail on this a little later). The third parameter is the callback function — an anonymous function coded directly inline. The fourth parameter is the data object while the fifth is the Boolean value `true`, which tells `addListener` to make the data object the callback function's execution scope. Since the data object is the `this` keyword, the callback function is being told to execute within the scope of the `doSomething` object. This allows the `mouseover` event handler to access the bar variable's value.

onAvailable

Sometimes pages take a noticeable amount of time to get all of their contents loaded, or their contents aren't all loaded at once. In these cases it becomes very important to be able to detect when a particular piece of expected content becomes available. Having this ability allows a program to begin interacting with an element immediately, without having to wait for either the page to load or even the DOM to be ready. YUI's `onAvailable` function monitors the DOM while it's being built for elements that it's told to keep an eye out for. The moment it finds an element, it executes a callback function. If, however, `onAvailable` is called once page is already done loading, it monitors the DOM for a configurable amount of time (ten seconds by default) before stopping. Here is an example of `onAvailable` catching the insertion of a new node in the DOM after the page has already completed loading.

```
<html>
    <head>
        <title>onAvailable</title>
    </head>
    <body>
        <p id="hello">Hello World!</p>
        <script src="yahoo-dom-event.js"></script>
        <script>
            var YD = YAHOO.util.Dom,
                YE = YAHOO.util.Event,
                YX = YAHOO.example;
            YX.insertNewContent = function () {
                var p = document.createElement("p");
                p.id = "how";
                p.appendChild(document.createTextNode("How's it going?"));
                YD.insertAfter(p, "hello");
            };
            YX.detected = function () {
                alert("New content detected!");
            };
            YE.onAvailable("how", YX.detected);
            setTimeout(YX.insertNewContent, 2000);
        </script>
    </body>
</html>
```

In this example, a new paragraph containing the text "How's it going?" is inserted into the DOM two seconds after the page is done loading (see Figure 8-2). That's what the line with the `setTimeout` does. The new paragraph that gets added to the DOM has the ID how. The `onAvailable` function is set to listen for an element with the ID how and to execute the callback function `detected` once it's found the element. Therefore, it catches the new paragraph the moment it's added to the DOM.

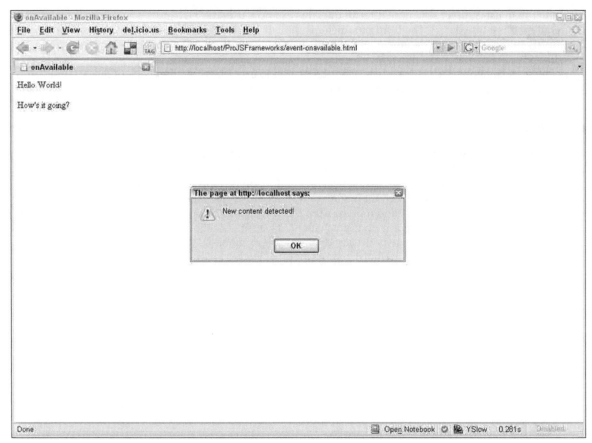

Figure 8-2

onContentReady

Sometimes it isn't enough to know that an element is available. Sometimes the operation that needs to be performed on the element requires its contents to be available as well. The onAvailable function has a fifth Boolean parameter called checkContent. When this parameter is set to true, onAvailable checks the element's child node readiness. It does this by checking the element's siblings, because if the browser has moved on to the next sibling, it stands to reason that it's done with the current one (including all of its children). onContentReady is simply an alias for onAvailable with the checkContent parameter permanently set to true.

Adding Event Listeners to elements can be done easily enough, but adding multiple listeners and then removing them is more difficult, at least consistently across browsers. YUI takes care of this with the functions outlined below.

on/addListener

Adding an event handler to a DOM element can be done very simply by direct assignment. Here is an example of an anonymous function being assigned to an element's `onclick` event.

```
var el = YAHOO.util.Dom.get("foo");
el.onclick = function () {
    // do something
};
```

Similarly, a named function can be assigned like so:

```
function doSomething() {
    // do something
};
var el = YAHOO.util.Dom.get("foo");
el.onclick = doSomething;
```

Both methods of assignment work fine for simple event handling, but can quickly become problematic. For example, an element to which an event needs to be assigned may already have an event assigned to it. The first event may have originated from another programmer and may be completely unknown to the developer who is now about to overwrite it by assigning a new handler to it. This is a problem, because the standard event model allows for only one function to be assigned to one event. Adding multiple event handlers to an event isn't possible.

The YUI `addListener` function allows for exactly what its name suggests: the adding of multiple event handlers to an element.

```
<html>
    <head>
        <title>addListener</title>
    </head>
    <body>
        <p>
            <a href="/dosomething/" id="foo">Do something</a>
        </p>
        <script src="yahoo-dom-event.js"></script>
        <script>
            var YE = YAHOO.util.Event,
                YX = YAHOO.example;
            YX.msg = "Doing something";
            YX.doSomething = function () {
                alert(YX.msg + "!");
            };
            YX.doSomethingElse = function () {
                alert(YX.msg + " else!");
            };
            YE.addListener("foo", "click", YX.doSomething);
            YE.addListener("foo", "click", YX.doSomethingElse);
        </script>
    </body>
</html>
```

In IE7, the `doSomethingElse` *event handler runs before the* `doSomething`. *In Firefox 2 and Safari 3.1, the events fire in the order in which they are added.*

In this example, two event handlers are assigned to the `onclick` event of the element with the ID `foo`. They are executed in the order in which they are assigned. As is the case with most of YUI's functions and constructors, the `addListener` function allows for a string ID, an `HTMLElement`, or an array of either of the two as its first parameter. The second parameter is the event to which the handler (or listener) is to be attached. The function doesn't care whether it's a valid event name or not, it will try and attach the callback function to it nonetheless. It's therefore the programmer's responsibility to make sure that an event with the name provided actually exists. In other words, `addListener` will take, for example, the word "click" and attempt to attach the provided callback function to the `onclick` event. On the other hand, if the word *scream* is passed, then the function will try and attach the callback function to the `onscream` event, which obviously doesn't exist.

Note that in the preceding example, the events will fire in the sequence that they were added except for Internet Explorer. Since YUI maps `addListener` to IE's native `attachEvent`, the events actually fire in the order that IE decides they should. And because of this, they don't fire in a First In First Out order. YUI 3 fixes this issue by wrapping event handlers and treating them as custom events. In other words, YUI 3 handles the triggering itself.

The `addListener` function also allows for the passing of an arbitrary data object:

```
<html>
    <head>
        <title>addListener 2</title>
    </head>
    <body>
        <p>
            <a href="/johndoe/" id="jd">John Doe</a>
        </p>
        <script src="yahoo-dom-event.js"></script>
        <script>
            var YE = YAHOO.util.Event,
                YX = YAHOO.example;
            YX.Person = function (fname, lname) {
                this.fname = fname;
                this.lname = lname;
                this.sayFName = function (e, greeting) {
                    alert(greeting.txt + this.fname);
                };
            };
            YX.johndoe = new YX.Person("John", "Doe");
            YX.init = function () {
                var greeting = {txt: "Hi, my name is "};
                YE.addListener(
                    "jd", "mouseover", YX.johndoe.sayFName, greeting, YX.johndoe);
            }();
        </script>
    </body>
</html>
```

This example illustrates that an object can be passed to an event handler. First, a `Person` object is instantiated into the variable `johndoe`. Then, inside the `init` function an event handler is set up so that whenever the mouse goes over the anchor with the ID `jd`, the `johndoe` object's `sayFName` method is called. That method receives two parameters; the first is the event object, which the browser passes to the callback function (in all browsers except Internet Explorer), and the second is the custom object containing the greeting text.

The `init` function in the previous example is a self-calling function. That is what the brackets at the end of the closing brace brackets do. Once the JavaScript parser finishes parsing the function, it comes across the brackets that tell it to execute the function right away.

Also, YUI provides an alias for `addListener` named `on`. This simply means that this line of code . . .

```
YAHOO.util.Event.addListener("foo", "click", doSomething);
```

. . . can also be written like this:

```
YAHOO.util.Event.on("foo", "click", doSomething);
```

removeListener

Event handlers sometimes need to be removed from the DOM in order to avoid the creation of memory leaks. In Internet Explorer 6 for example, when an event handler is assigned to an element, and then later that element is destroyed, the event handler remains in memory. If this is done several times in the context of a web app, where the user doesn't leave the page but interacts with the app over a long period of time, this can cause a large memory leak. It's therefore advisable to remove event handlers with the `removeListener` YUI function.

```
<html>
    <head>
        <title>removeListener</title>
    </head>
    <body>
        <p>
            <a href="/dosomething/" id="foo">Do something</a>
        </p>
        <script src="yahoo-dom-event.js"></script>
        <script>
            var YE = YAHOO.util.Event,
                YX = YAHOO.example;
            YX.msg = "Doing something";
            YX.doSomething = function () {
                alert(YX.msg + "!");
            };
            YX.doSomethingElse = function () {
                alert(YX.msg + " else!");
            };
            YE.addListener("foo", "click", YX.doSomething);
            YE.addListener("foo", "click", YX.doSomethingElse);
            YE.removeListener("foo", "click", YX.doSomething);
        </script>
    </body>
</html>
```

This is the same `addListener` example with a twist. The first of two handlers is removed, which results in only one being attached to the anchor with the ID `foo`. In the case where multiple event handlers are attached to an element, and no callback function is specified, then `removeListener` removes all handlers from the element that are of the specified type (in this case, "click").

```html
<html>
    <head>
        <title>removeListener 2</title>
    </head>
    <body>
        <p>
            <a href="/dosomething/" id="foo">Do something</a>
        </p>
        <script src="yahoo-dom-event.js"></script>
        <script>
            var YE = YAHOO.util.Event,
                YX = YAHOO.example;
            YX.msg = "Doing something";
            YX.doSomething = function () {
                alert(YX.msg + "!");
            };
            YX.doSomethingElse = function () {
                alert(YX.msg + " else!");
            };
            YE.addListener("foo", "click", YX.doSomething);
            YE.addListener("foo", "click", YX.doSomethingElse);
            YE.removeListener("foo", "click");
        </script>
    </body>
</html>
```

In this example, the anchor with the ID `foo` ends up with no event handlers.

Handling Keyboard and Mouse Input

Sometimes a library doesn't fix a cross-browser problem as much as it just makes life easier. For example, though keyboard handling support is relatively standard across browsers, the code that needs to be written in order to do anything useful with it can get a bit bulky and awkward. Here, YUI simplifies the process by boiling it down into a common pattern found throughout the Event Utility.

KeyListener

The YUI `KeyListener` utility is modeled after `addListener`, in that it allows for an event handler for either a `keyup` or `keydown` event to be attached to a DOM element. The difference is that a new object needs to be instantiated in the case of `KeyListener` whereas with `addListener` it does not. Also, the syntax is slightly but not altogether different. The beauty of `KeyListener`, however, is that the object that's instantiated can be enabled or disabled with methods by the same name. This makes managing key handlers very simple. Also, it simplifies the trapping of modifier keys (Ctrl, Alt, and Shift).

```
<html>
    <head>
        <title>keyListener</title>
    </head>
    <body>
        <script src="yahoo-min.js"></script>
        <script src="event-min.js"></script>
        <script>
            var YX = YAHOO.example;
            YX.cut = function () {
                alert("Cut!");
            };
            YX.copy = function () {
                alert("Copy!");
            };
            YX.paste = function () {
                alert("Paste!");
            };
            YX.cutKey = new YAHOO.util.KeyListener(
                document,
                {ctrl: true, keys: 88},
                YX.cut);
            YX.cutKey.enable();
            YX.copyKey = new YAHOO.util.KeyListener(
                document,
                {ctrl: true, keys: 67},
                YX.copy);
            YX.copyKey.enable();
            YX.pasteKey = new YAHOO.util.KeyListener(
                document,
                {ctrl: true, keys: 86},
                YX.paste);
            YX.pasteKey.enable();
        </script>
    </body>
</html>
```

This example traps the common *Ctrl+X*, *Ctrl+C*, and *Ctrl+V* key combinations and fires different callback functions for each. So for example, a new `KeyListener` object is instantiated into the variable named `cut`. Its first parameter is the `document` object. This means that no matter where the user triggers the event, it will be caught. This parameter, however, can be any DOM element, thus limiting the scope of when the event is caught. As is the pattern in YUI, this parameter can be either a string representing an element's ID or an `HTMLElement` reference. The second parameter is an object referred to as `keyData`. It basically contains the information on what keys and/or key combinations the event handler is to be called. This is where `KeyHandler` differs from `addListener`, since in the case of the latter, an event handler would fire on every triggering of an event (say, for example, on every `onclick` event). `KeyHandler`, on the other hand, traps the `keydown` event by default and only triggers the event handler if the key(s) and/or key combination(s) are the ones specified in the `keyData` object.

The `keyData` object is just a simple object literal. In other words, it isn't an object that needs to be instantiated from an existing class somewhere. It just needs to contain name/value pairs that are recognized by `KeyHandler`. Here are some example forms that the `keyData` object can take.

```
{keys: 88}
```

This traps the X key. 88 is the character code for the X key.

```
{keys: [88, 67, 86]}
```

This traps the X, X, and V keys.

```
{ctrl: true, keys: 88}
```

This traps the X key only when the Ctrl key is also pressed

```
{ctrl: true, alt: true, shift: true, keys: [88, 67, 86]}
```

This traps the X, C, and V keys, but only if Ctrl, Alt, and Shift are also pressed simultaneously.

Since the properties of objects are order independent, the previous example could just as equally be written like this and still be valid:

```
{shift: true, keys: [88, 67, 86], alt: true, ctrl: true}
```

The only difference here is that the properties of the keyData object are in a different order.

Of course, just like the pattern with all of the YUI event handling functions, a data object can be passed to a KeyListener callback function, and its execution scope can also be changed. There is, however, a slight difference in the way it's done with KeyHandler compared with addListener. The pattern is identical in that an object can be passed, and a scope override can be set to set that object as the execution scope, but all of this is done inside one object rather than being separate parameters of the KeyHandler constructor.

Here is a simplified version of the previous KeyHandler code example with a data object being passed to the cut callback function. Note the misleading naming of the object parameter (it's called scope here).

```
<html>
    <head>
        <title>keyListener 2</title>
    </head>
    <body>
        <script src="yahoo-min.js"></script>
        <script src="event-min.js"></script>
        <script>
            var YX = YAHOO.example;
            YX.cut = function (eType, codeAndEv, dataObj) {
                var msg = "The event type responsible for triggering ";
                msg    += "this function is '" + eType + "'.\n";
                msg    += "The key code for the key that was pressed ";
                msg    += "is '" + codeAndEv[0] + "'.\n";
                msg    += "And the message passed through the data object ";
                msg    += "is '" + dataObj + "'.";
                alert(msg);
            };
            YX.cutKey = new YAHOO.util.KeyListener(
                document,
                {ctrl: true, keys: 88},
```

```
                   {fn: YX.cut, scope: "Cutting!"});
          YX.cutKey.enable();
      </script>
   </body>
</html>
```

Since strings are also objects in JavaScript, it's perfectly valid to pass the string `"Cutting!"` as the data object. Also note that the callback function receives three parameters. The first is a string representing the event type. This comes from the YUI Custom Event object, which is covered later in this chapter. In this case, the string value "`keyPressed`" is passed. This can be useful when trying to determine what action was responsible for calling the callback function, when it's assigned to respond to multiple types of events. The second parameter is an array, the first item of which is the key code of the key that was pressed. The second item in the array is the actual event object generated by the browser. Finally, the third parameter is the data object. This can be any object, whether a string or a function. The callback function above yields the following message when the keys Ctrl and X are pressed simultaneously.

```
The event type responsible for triggering this function is 'keyPressed'.
The key code for the key that was pressed is '88'.
And the message passed through the data object is 'Cutting!'.
```

Changing execution scope is just as easily handled with one other parameter.

```
var cut = new YAHOO.util.KeyListener(
    document,
    {ctrl: true, keys: 88},
    {fn: cut, scope: newScope, correctScope: true}
);
```

Likewise, the data object can remain intact and a new scope object can be passed via the `correctScope` parameter.

```
var cut = new YAHOO.util.KeyListener(
    document,
    {ctrl: true, keys: 88},
    {fn: cut, scope: "Cutting!", correctScope: newScope}
);
```

getCharCode

Working with `KeyHandler` to set up event handlers is great, if you know the key (or character) code of the key you want to trap. As always, browser makers seem bent on making life difficult for the developer; thus, doing something as simple as getting the `keyCode` value off of an event object can be tricky. YUI's Event Utility comes with a useful little function called `getCharCode`. It checks the event object for the `keyCode` value, and if it doesn't find what it's looking for there, it looks in `charCode`. It also does a little patch up jog for Safari, since that browser stores the key code in a completely different place. Here's a useful little program that outputs the key code of any key pressed on the keyboard (see Figure 8-3).

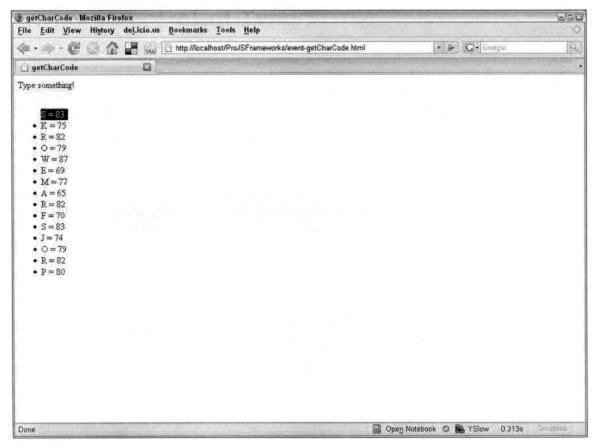

Figure 8-3

Naturally, it uses `getCharCode`.

```html
<html>
    <head>
        <title>getCharCode</title>
        <style type="text/css">
            ul {
                float: left;
            }
            .first {
                color: #fff;
                background: #000;
            }
        </style>
    </head>
    <body>
        <p>Type something!</p>
        <ul id="output">
        </ul>
```

```
<script src="yahoo-dom-event.js"></script>
<script>
    var YD = YAHOO.util.Dom,
        YE = YAHOO.util.Event,
        YX = YAHOO.example;
    YX.output = YD.get("output");
    YE.addListener(document, "keyup", function (e) {
        e = e || event;
        var li = document.createElement("li");
        var cCode = YE.getCharCode(e);
        var txt = document.createTextNode(
            String.fromCharCode(cCode) + " = " + cCode);
        li.appendChild(txt);
        li.className = "first";
        var firstChild = YD.getFirstChild(YX.output);
        if (firstChild) {
            firstChild.className = "";
            YD.insertBefore(li, firstChild);
        } else {
            YX.output.appendChild(li);
        }
    });
</script>
</body>
</html>
```

Note that the same key code value will be returned for both lowercase and uppercase versions of a letter. That's because the key responsible for producing, for example, the letter *a* is the same key whether it's in upper- or lowercase. What makes the difference is the Shift key, which is a modifier. It has its own key code (16), which will come up as a separate line item in the output of the program in the previous example.

Basically, what that program does is set up an event handler on the document element and triggers an anonymous function whenever a keyup event is fired. The anonymous function creates a list item node and populates it with the key code of the key that was just pressed. The code is derived from the event object (e) that's passed to the YUI function getCharCode. It then appends the list item to the unordered list with the ID output that's already in the DOM. The program also converts the character code back into a letter and adds that to the text within the list item. This works fine with alphanumeric keys, but not so well with the others. For example, the left, right, top and down keys produce %, ', &, and (, respectively. Not exactly what's printed on the keyboard.

getXY

The event object contains mouse coordinate data stored in two separate variables. Unfortunately, everyone calls these coordinates pageX and pageY, except for Internet Explorer. It calls them clientX and clientY, to say nothing of the fact that even these numbers aren't accurate in IE as page scroll also needs to be taken into account. getXY does a handy job of neutralizing these issues and making it so the x and y coordinates of the mouse can easily be reported through one function call.

```
<html>
    <head>
        <title>getXY</title>
    </head>
    <body>
        <p id="output"></p>
        <script src="yahoo-dom-event.js"></script>
        <script>
            var YD = YAHOO.util.Dom,
                YE = YAHOO.util.Event,
                YX = YAHOO.example;
            YX.output = YD.get("output");
            YE.addListener(document, "mousemove", function (e) {
                e = e || event;
                YX.output.innerHTML = YE.getXY(e);
            });
        </script>
    </body>
</html>
```

This function sets up a simple event handler that tracks the mouse as it passes over the document element. It reports the mouse's x and y coordinates by outputting the values returned by getXY to a paragraph element with the ID output. The returned value is an array with the x coordinate value being the first item in the array and the y coordinate value being the second.

There are also two functions that report on the x and y values separately. They are called getPageX and getPageY, respectively, in deference to the more popular variable names pageX and pageY. In fact, getXY is simply an alias function that calls getPageX and getPageY, takes their returned values, places them in an array, and returns that array.

getTarget

The event object contains a variable named target, which contains a reference to the element that the mouse clicked. This is useful when performing such things as event delegation, where only one event handler takes care of clicks on multiple objects in the DOM. In keeping with the "we like to be different" theme however, Internet Explorer calls its target variable srcElement. The getTarget function checks for the variable target, and if it doesn't find it, gets the value for srcElement, thus, neutralizing yet another cross-browser issue.

```
<html>
    <head>
        <title>getTarget</title>
    </head>
    <body>
        <p id="output"></p>
        <ul>
            <li>
                <span>Hello World!</span>
            </li>
        </ul>
        <script src="yahoo-dom-event.js"></script>
        <script>
```

```
                      var YD = YAHOO.util.Dom,
                          YE = YAHOO.util.Event,
                          YX = YAHOO.example;
                      YX.output = YD.get("output");
                      YE.addListener(document, "click", function (e) {
                          e = e || event;
                          YX.output.innerHTML = YE.getTarget(e).nodeName;
                      });
                  </script>
              </body>
          </html>
```

This example sets up an `onclick` event handler on the `document` object and reports the node name of any element that was clicked in the document. The `nodeName` value is accessible right off of the `getTarget` function because JavaScript simply substitutes `YAHOO.util.Event.getTarget(e)` with the value it returns and then checks for `nodeName`. This is actually a rather popular pattern in some libraries called chaining.

Note that the previous example will return different values for different browsers when the lower part of the page is clicked. That's because in browsers such as Internet Explorer, the `body` element spans the entire height of the page whereas in browsers such as Firefox, the `body` element only spans the height of the readable content. Clicking the bottom of the page in IE will therefore return `body` whereas in Firefox it will return `html`.

getRelatedTarget

Sometimes, when you track a mouse's movements — especially during a drag-and-drop operation — it's useful to know where the mouse ended up. This isn't as obvious as it may seem. The traditional way of detecting the goings-on of the mouse pointer was to assign `onmouseover` events to all of the elements concerned. This technique, however, becomes very cumbersome because of the complex programming required to juggle the hand-off from element to element. That means the `onmouseout` of one element needs to somehow communicate with the `onmouseover` of another element that it was the one from which the mouse pointer just came. It is possible to detect this type of element-to-element interaction via the `relatedTarget` property of the event object. However, the trouble once again, is that Internet Explorer doesn't call the property the same thing. It also isn't smart enough to know that when the event in question is a `mouseout` it should report the mouse is going *to* and if it's a `mouseover`, it should report where the mouse came *from*. YUI takes care of all of this with one neat function called `getRelatedTarget`. The following program uses `getRelatedTarget` to figure out if the mouse is hovering over the list of items upward or downward. If the mouse is leaving a list item upward, then that item gets an up arrow appended to it, and if it's leaving downward, then the item gets a down arrow.

```
<html>
    <head>
        <title>getRelatedTarget</title>
    </head>
    <body>
        <ul>
            <li id="widget">Widget<span class="dir"></span></li>
            <li id="gadget">Gadget<span class="dir"></span></li>
            <li id="whoozit">Whoozit<span class="dir"></span></li>
```

```
            <li id="foozit">Foozit<span class="dir"></span></li>
            <li id="barzit">Barzit<span class="dir"></span></li>
            <li id="bazzit">Bazzit<span class="dir"></span></li>
        </ul>
        <script src="yahoo-dom-event.js"></script>
        <script>
            var YD = YAHOO.util.Dom,
                YE = YAHOO.util.Event,
                YX = YAHOO.example;
            YX.li = document.getElementsByTagName("li");
            YE.addListener(YX.li, "mouseout", function (e) {
                e = e || event;
                var rTarget = YE.getRelatedTarget(e);
                var dir = YD.getElementsByClassName(
                    "dir", "span", this);
                dir = (dir[0]) ? dir[0] : dir;
                var arrow = "";
                var previous = YD.getPreviousSibling(this);
                var next = YD.getNextSibling(this);
                var first = YD.getFirstChild(this.parentNode);
                var last = YD.getLastChild(this.parentNode);

                if (rTarget === previous) {
                    arrow = "&uarr;";
                } else if (rTarget === next) {
                    arrow = "&darr;";
                } else if (this === first) {
                    arrow = "&uarr;";
                } else if (this === last) {
                    arrow = "&darr;";
                }
                dir.innerHTML = arrow;
            });
        </script>
    </body>
</html>
```

Basically, what this program does is attach an onmouseout event handler to all of the li elements in the page. The handler then determines what the related target is, and based on that assigns each li with either an up or down arrow. The arrows are inserted into a span with the class name dir found in each li. Using a span is simply a matter of convenience, rather than processing the text contents of the li. (The variables within the event handler are simply local vars and don't need to be declared inside the YAHOO.example namespace.) The results are shown in Figure 8-4.

Chapter 8: Handling Cross-Browser Events

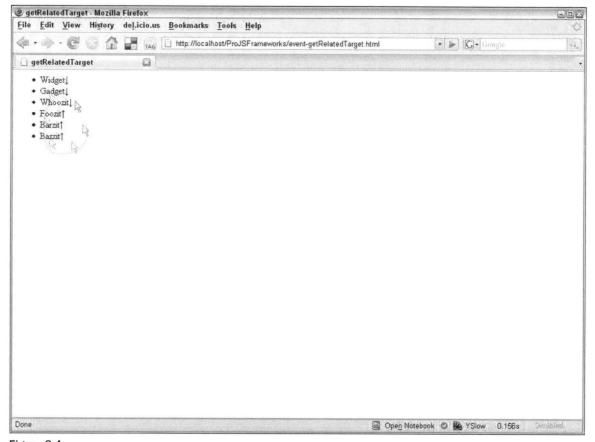

Figure 8-4

Each list item in Figure 8-4 spans the entire width of the browser window. Therefore, they can pick up the mouse pointer's movements even though the visible text content isn't nearly as wide.

preventDefault

Anchors often have `onclick` event handlers assigned to them. Yet anchors pose a bit of a problem in that their default action is to follow the value of their `href` attribute. And therefore, though the anchor's event handler fires, its results never get seen by the user because moments after the click action is completed, a new page begins to load. Now traditionally, returning false to the event stopped the default action.

```
var a = document.getElementById("foo");
a.onclick = function () {
    // do something
    return false;
};
```

There is another way to stop an event's default behavior directly through the event object. In Firefox and other standards-compliant browsers, the event object has a method called `preventDefault`, which when called cancel's the event's default action. Of course, Internet Explorer handles this differently. It requires that a value of `false` be set on `returnValue`, a property of its event object. YUI wraps this difference into a normalized `preventDefault` function.

```
<html>
    <head>
        <title>preventDefault</title>
    </head>
    <body>
        <a href="/about/" id="about">About us</a>
        <script src="yahoo-dom-event.js"></script>
        <script>
            var YD = YAHOO.util.Dom,
                YE = YAHOO.util.Event,
                YX = YAHOO.example;
            YX.doSomething = function (e) {
                e = e || event;
                YE.preventDefault(e);
            };
            var a = YD.get("about");
            YE.addListener(a, "click", YX.doSomething);
        </script>
    </body>
</html>
```

In certain situations it isn't possible to return a `false` value, and in other situations it simply doesn't work, such as in the previous example. Because of the way the YUI `addListener` function attaches the event handler to the element, returning the value `false` doesn't cancel the click action's default action. It's therefore always preferable to cancel the event's default action with `preventDefault`.

stopPropagation

Clicking on an element in the DOM doesn't just trigger its `onclick` event. It triggers the `onclick` events of all the elements under the mouse pointer. So if there's an event handler that fires when the mouse clicks the `document` element, and another on an anchor inside the `document` element, both will fire when the anchor is clicked.

```
<html>
    <head>
        <title>stopPropagation</title>
    </head>
    <body>
        <a href="/about/" id="about">About us</a>
        <script src="yahoo-dom-event.js"></script>
        <script>
            var YD = YAHOO.util.Dom,
```

```
                    YE = YAHOO.util.Event,
                    YX = YAHOO.example;
                YX.msg = function (e, txt) {
                    e = e || event;
                    alert(txt);
                    YE.preventDefault(e);
                };
                YX.about = YD.get("about");
                YE.addListener(YX.about, "click", YX.msg, "About!");
                YE.addListener(document, "click", YX.msg, "Document!");
            </script>
        </body>
    </html>
```

In this example, clicking on the "About us" anchor will trigger the msg function twice, once for the click event of the anchor and once for the click event of the document element. In order to stop this event propagation (as it's called), standards-compliant browsers offer a method off of the event object called stopPropagation. When called, it prevents the action that triggered its event to go any further through the DOM. Internet Explorer's event object doesn't have a stopPropagation method, rather it has a cancelBubble property in which the value false needs to be set in order to stop the event from propagating. Once again, YUI wraps this difference in a convenient stopPropagation function that normalizes the behavior across browsers.

```
    <html>
        <head>
            <title>stopPropagation</title>
        </head>
        <body>
            <a href="/about/" id="about">About us</a>
            <script src="yahoo-dom-event.js"></script>
            <script>
                var YD = YAHOO.util.Dom,
                    YE = YAHOO.util.Event,
                    YX = YAHOO.example;
                YX.msg = function (e, txt) {
                    e = e || event;
                    alert(txt);
                    YE.stopPropagation(e);
                    YE.preventDefault(e);
                };
                YX.about = YD.get("about");
                YE.addListener(YX.about, "click", YX.msg, "About!");
                YE.addListener(document, "click", YX.msg,
                    "Clicking 'About us' won't trigger this");
            </script>
        </body>
    </html>
```

stopEvent

In the previous example, both `stopPropagation` and `preventDefault` were used in order to isolate a click on the anchor and to stop its default behavior of following the URL in the anchor's `href` attribute. YUI offers a convenient method called `stopEvent` that calls both of these in sequence reducing the lines of code needed for this behavior from two to one.

```html
<html>
    <head>
        <title>stopEvent</title>
    </head>
    <body>
        <a href="/about/" id="about">About us</a>
        <script src="yahoo-dom-event.js"></script>
        <script>
            var YD = YAHOO.util.Dom,
                YE = YAHOO.util.Event,
                YX = YAHOO.example;
            YX.msg = function (e, txt) {
                e = e || event;
                alert(txt);
                YE.stopEvent(e);
            };
            YX.about = YD.get("about");
            YE.addListener(YX.about, "click", YX.msg, "About!");
            YE.addListener(document, "click", YX.msg,
                "Clicking 'About us' won't trigger this");
        </script>
    </body>
</html>
```

Working with Custom Events

JavaScript events such as `onclick`, `onmouseover`, and `onload` are very useful. In fact, they're an essential part of modern web development. Event-based programming has become a staple of today's web sites, so much so that JavaScript would benefit from even more events, but which ones to add? Therein lies the problem. There are so many different types of applications being written, and so many different kinds of events that they could conceivably trigger that it wouldn't be feasible to extend the current event model in that way. Enter YUI's custom events. Custom events allow for events to be created and triggered pretty much anywhere in a JavaScript web application. In fact, YUI itself makes heavy use of custom events. For example, the `onDOMReady` function fires a `DOMReady` custom event once it's determined, through its many machinations, that the DOM is in fact ready.

Though JavaScript is an extremely malleable and extensible language, it doesn't allow for the creation of custom events. And so any implementation of the sort has to follow a different syntax. In other words, this wouldn't be possible:

```
el.onmycustomevent = doSomething; // not possible
```

It is, however, possible to put functions into an array and then iterate over that array and fire those events in sequence. And that's essentially what YUI Custom Events are. There's a whole bunch of code that makes sure that custom events can be subscribed and unsubscribed to, that handlers fire with the correct scope, and that errors are caught and managed.

The basic principle behind YUI Custom Events is to allow for functions or objects to expose "interesting moments" to other subscriber functions. In other words, in order to attach an event handler to a custom event, it needs to "subscribe" to that event. This also works like addListener in that multiple event handlers can be attached to (or can subscribe to) a single event.

CustomEvent and subscribe

Creating a custom event is as simple as instantiating an object. This can be done anywhere, though customarily, the object is a member of a function.

```
function Widget(name) {
    this.name = name;
    this.onNameChange = new YAHOO.util.CustomEvent("namechange", this);
};
```

Here, a constructor by the name of Widget contains a custom event named onNameChange. onNameChange is a YUI Custom Event object that has a subscribe method through which functions can subscribe to this event.

```
var gadget = new Widget("foo");
gadget.onNameChange.subscribe(doSomething);
```

When the onNameChange event is fired (through its fire method) all the functions that are subscribers get executed.

```
gadget.onNameChange.fire();
```

The trick is to fire custom events at key moments. As the name of the custom event in the previous example suggests, it should be fired when the Widget object's name gets changed. Otherwise, there isn't much use for an event handler that doesn't fire at the right time and place.

```
<html>
    <head>
        <title>customEvent</title>
    </head>
    <body>
        <a href="/change/" id="change">Change name to "baz"</a>
        <script src="yahoo-dom-event.js"></script>
        <script>
            var YE = YAHOO.util.Event,
```

```
            YX = YAHOO.example;
        YX.Widget = function (name) {
            this.name = name;
            this.onNameChange = new YAHOO.util.CustomEvent("namechange", this);
            this.setName = function (newName) {
                this.name = newName;
                this.onNameChange.fire();
            }
        };
        YX.changeName = function (e, params) {
            params.obj.setName(params.name);
            YE.preventDefault(e);
        };
        YX.announce = function () {
            alert("The object's name is '" + this.name + "'");
        };

        YX.gadget = new YX.Widget("foo");
        YX.gadget.onNameChange.subscribe(YX.announce);
        YX.gadget.setName("bar");

        YE.addListener("change", "click", YX.changeName,
            {obj: YX.gadget, name: "baz"});
    </script>
  </body>
</html>
```

In this example, a class named Widget is instantiated into a variable named gadget. Widget contains a name property, an onNameChanged YUI Custom Event, and a setName method. Though the name property can be set manually by directly accessing it like so: gadget.name = "new name"; there would be no way of triggering the custom event that way. That's why the setName method exists. That way, once it sets the new name value it can go on to trigger the onNameChange custom event.

Though JavaScript isn't an object-oriented language in the classical sense, terms such as constructor, class, *and* method *are used here for the sake of clarity. Essentially, JavaScript behaves enough like a classical object-oriented language for these terms to make relative sense.*

The Widget object is instantiated with the value "foo" in its name property. It is then given the function announce as a subscriber to its onNameChange event. In other words, announce is to be executed when the onNameChange event is fired. Then, its name is changed to "bar" through the setName method. This causes the announce function to execute causing an alert with the message "The object's name is 'bar'" as soon as the page is loaded (see Figure 8-5). After that, an onclick event handler is attached to the anchor with the ID change. The handler is a function called changeName, which receives an object containing a reference to the object whose name it is to change and the text it is to change it to.

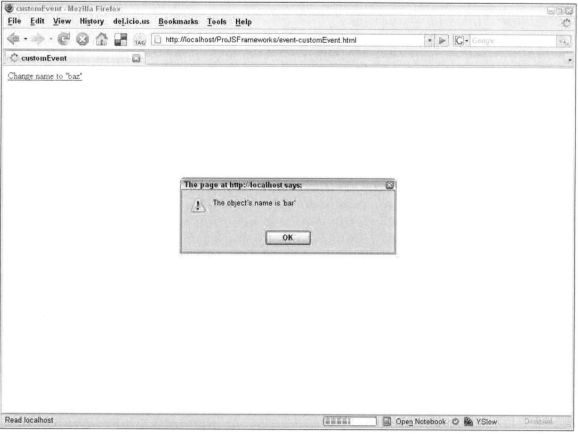

Figure 8-5

So, when the link "Change name to 'baz'" is clicked, it triggers the changeName function, which sets a new name value in the gadget object. This in turn triggers the onNameChanged custom event, which executes its subscribers, of which there is only one, announce. Finally, announce then alerts the user of the change in name (see Figure 8-6).

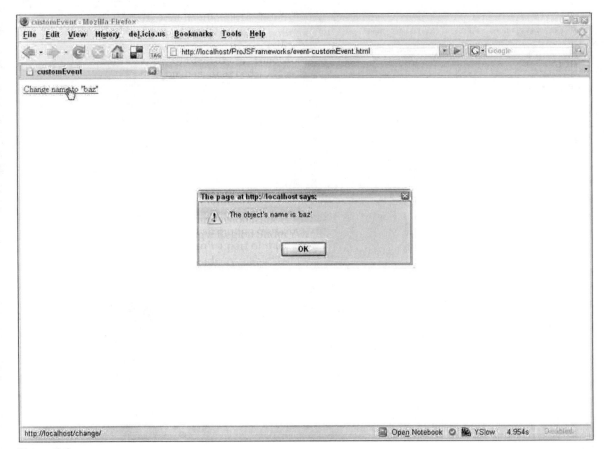

Figure 8-6

unsubscribe

It's only natural that if you can subscribe to a custom event, that you should be able to unsubscribe as well. The unsubscribe method allows for events handlers that have been attached to a custom event to be detached. The syntax is the same as subscribe, except that if the function that is to be detached isn't passed as a parameter, then all subscribers are detached.

```
gadget.onNameChange.unsubscribe(announce);
```

This detaches the function announce from the onNameChange custom event.

```
gadget.onNameChange.unsubscribe();
```

This detaches all functions from the onNameChange custom event.

In fact the latter, on finding that no function was passed, calls unsubscribeAll, which as its name suggests, detaches all functions from the custom event. The unsubscribeAll method can also be called directly.

```
gadget.onNameChange.unsubscribeAll();
```

The difference between `unsubscribe` (without any parameters) and `unsubscribeAll`, and why both options exist to do the same thing, is that if the former is called as a part of an automated process, though a variable may be passed to it, it might not contain anything, which would prompt it to call the latter.

subscribeEvent

YUI Custom Events actually have a custom event of their own. Whenever a new subscriber subscribes to the event, `subscribeEvent` is fired. This allows for scenarios such as the catching of late subscribers to an event that only fires once, and has already fired.

Managing Browser History and Fixing the Back Button

The world has gone Flash and AJAX crazy! Well, not quite, but the prevalence of both has taken a couple of casualties: the back button and bookmarking. Normally, a web site composed entirely inside one Flash object never changes pages. So even though pages inside the Flash object change, the URL of the site remains the same. The same goes with sites that use AJAX heavily. After a user's been on an AJAX-driven site for a while, the page they're on might look nothing like it did when it was first loaded. In both cases, bookmarking the page will bring the user back to a page that starts from scratch, not where they were when they created the bookmark.

The YUI Browser History Manager provides a method by which both of these issues can be fixed. Essentially, the manager tracks key changes to the page in *modules* and stores that information in the URL of the page via its hash property like so:

```
http://localhost/ProJSFrameworks/history.html#step=configure
```

A module is the History Manager's way of segmenting distinct pieces of data that need tracking. Each module is then represented by a key/value pair stored in the URL. Here, the History Manager has saved the state of the module named `step` with the value `configure`.

There is no requirement to save any sort of specific data, just as long as it's a key/value pair. Therefore, the state could represent a step in a process (as in the previous example) whose value can be used as an indicator of what the page should look like on initial load. Since the History Manager supports the storing of multiple modules at a time, they could be used to store the state of multiple components in a page. They could also store multiple pieces of data required by only one component. So for example, if the page was a mapping application, there could be one module for the longitude, a second module for latitude, and a third module for the zoom level.

Now, in the case of an AJAX-driven application, the app would call the manager and save the state at key moments. In the case of a Flash application, the Flash object would have to call JavaScript functions in the page and pass the relevant data to those functions.

Here is an example of a simple AJAX-driven travel booking process (see Figure 8-7). AJAX is in quotes because this code example doesn't contain any AJAX code. Rather, it just outputs some text to the screen where it's supposed to fetch it from the server. This is done to simplify the example.

```html
<html>
    <head>
        <title>History</title>
        <style type="text/css">
            #yui-history-iframe {
                position:absolute;
                top:0; left:0;
                width:1px; height:1px;
                visibility:hidden;
            }
        </style>
    </head>
    <body>
        <iframe id="yui-history-iframe" src="history-iframe.html"></iframe>
        <input id="yui-history-field" type="hidden">
        <h1>Book a vacation</h1>
        <ul id="steps">
            <li id="step1">
                <a href="/choose/">Step 1 - Choose your vacation</a>
            </li>
            <li id="step2">
                <a href="/configure/">Step 2 - Configure it!</a>
            </li>
            <li id="step3">
                <a href="/pay/">Step 3 - Payment</a>
            </li>
            <li id="step4">
                <a href="/confirmation/">Step 4 - Confirmation</a>
            </li>
        </ul>
        <div id="step"></div>
        <script src="yahoo-dom-event.js"></script>
        <script src="history-min.js"></script>
        <script>
            var YD = YAHOO.util.Dom,
                YE = YAHOO.util.Event,
                YH = YAHOO.util.History,
                YX = YAHOO.example;
            YX.initialize = function () {
                YX.loadContents("step", initialState);
            };
            YX.loadContents = function (containerId, state) {
                var step = YD.get(containerId);
                step.innerHTML = "<h2>" + state + "</h2>";
                step.innerHTML += "This is where the AJAX loaded contents of the ";
                step.innerHTML += "step '<strong>" + state + "</strong>' ";
                step.innerHTML += "would be.";
            };
            YX.stateChangeHandler = function (state) {
                YX.loadContents("step", state);
            };
            YX.stepClicked = function (e) {
                var state = this.href.replace(/\/$/, "");
                state = state.substring(state.lastIndexOf("/") + 1);
                try {
```

```
                    YH.navigate("step", state);
                } catch (e) {
                    //History manager not initialized
                }
                YE.preventDefault(e);
            };
            var bookmarkedState = YH.getBookmarkedState("step");
            var initialState = bookmarkedState || "choose";
            YH.register("step", initialState, YX.stateChangeHandler);
            try {
                YH.initialize("yui-history-field", "yui-history-iframe");
            } catch (e) {
                //Browser not supported
            }
            var links = YD.get("steps").getElementsByTagName("a");
            YE.addListener(links, "click", YX.stepClicked);
            YH.onReady(YX.initialize);
        </script>
    </body>
</html>
```

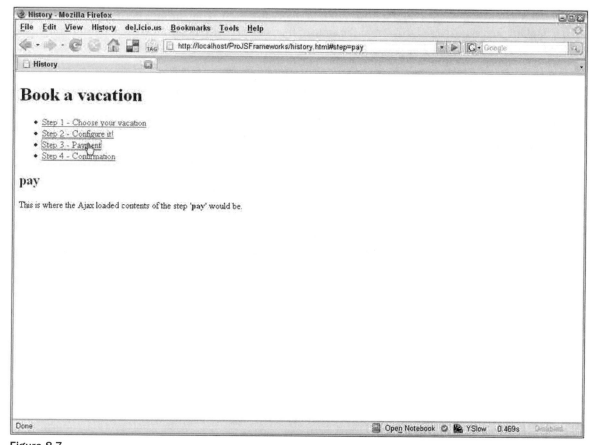

Figure 8-7

The History Manager requires two HTML tags to be put into the markup.

```
<iframe id="yui-history-iframe" src="history-iframe.html"></iframe>
<input id="yui-history-field" type="hidden">
```

These are used to store the current state values. The source of the iframe doesn't have to be anything special, but it does need to be a valid HTML document.

The first thing that needs to be done is to determine what this page's initial state is to be. In order to do that, the first thing to do is to see if the site is being loaded from a bookmark. That can be checked by looking at the URL. If the URL contains a hash with a state name and value, then the visitor is returning from a bookmarked link. The best way to do this is to use the getBookmarkedState method.

```
var bookmarkedState = YH.getBookmarkedState("step");
```

Once getBookmarkedState returns its value, the next thing to do is either accept it or set a default state as a fallback.

```
var initialState = bookmarkedState || "choose";
```

A default value of choose is set if it turns out that the visitor didn't come from a bookmark. Otherwise, the bookmarked state is used. Now that the state of the page has been determined, one or more modules need to be registered with the History Manager. It's important to note that modules can't be registered once the Manager has initialized so now is the time to do it.

```
YH.register("step", initialState, YX.stateChangeHandler);
```

Registering a module with the History Manager is a little bit like adding an event handler using addListener. The first parameter is the name that will identify the module (this ends up as the name of the name/value pair in the URL). The second parameter is the initial state of the module (and consequently the value of the name/value pair in the URL). The third parameter is a callback function that the History Manager will call whenever the state of the module changes. Finally, just like with addListener, it's possible to pass an arbitrary data object as well as set the execution scope of the callback function through a fourth and fifth parameter.

Next, the History Manager needs to be initialized. The trouble here is that it may throw an exception if the browser isn't supported. Therefore, on the recommendation of the YUI team, the initialization is wrapped in a try/catch statement to avoid a possible error message. In fact, an alternative course of action could be programmed into the catch clause if the browser isn't supported. In the case of this example, it just fails silently.

```
try {
    YH.initialize("yui-history-field", "yui-history-iframe");
} catch (e) {
    //Browser not supported
}
```

Now that the History Manager is set up, the actual navigation links in the page need to be wired up to use it. And so, with a simple addListener call, each of the navigation links in the booking process are wired to the stepClicked function. That's the function that comes up with a state for the Manager, and then sets it via its navigate function.

```
YE.addListener(links, "click", YX.stepClicked);
```

In this case, stepClicked reads the href attribute value of the link that was clicked and uses a filtered version of the URL it finds as the state of the step module.

```
YX.stepClicked = function (e) {
    var state = this.href.replace(/\/$/, "");
    state = state.substring(state.lastIndexOf("/") + 1);
    try {
        YH.navigate("step", state);
    } catch (e) {
        //History manager not initialized
    }
    YE.preventDefault(e);
};
```

Again, it's important to note that the navigate function may fail and throw an exception if it wasn't successfully initialized — which is why it's wrapped with a try/catch block.

New in YUI 3

YUI 3 handles events differently than its predecessor. Rather than map to a browser's native event handling scheme, YUI 3 wraps event handlers and triggers them itself. As a pleasant consequence, the First In First Out issue in Internet Explorer mentioned earlier automatically gets fixed. YUI 3 also allows for the simulation of popular events such as click, double-click, mouse over/up/down/out/move. In other words, rather than have the user do it, the code simulates a mouse click on an element.

Summary

Not only does a library like YUI benefit programmers in doing away with the headache of cross-browser issues, but it also extends the sometimes limited functionality of JavaScript when it comes to event-based programming. For one thing, being able to attach multiple event handlers to elements, and detach them at will is lightyears ahead of what JavaScript currently offers. Likewise, being able to create and trigger custom events opens the door wide open to all sorts of previously unconsidered possibilities.

Most importantly, in an age where using JavaScript-based user interfaces that make heavy use of AJAX is the norm, being able to manage the browser history in a reliable way is invaluable. Otherwise, a simple instinctive click of the back button can ruin an otherwise awesome web application.

9

Using Animation and Drag and Drop

The graphical user interfaces of today's operating systems — and consequently desktop applications — have established conventions in regards to what users can expect to see and will be able to do when interacting with applications. For example, people instinctively expect to be able to drag and drop elements on the screen.

Modern web sites are increasingly falling in line with these conventions. Yet up until now, animation has not been a forte of JavaScript. Not because it can't do it, but because it lacks native animation functions. There is no `move`, `fade`, or `bounce` method in the `style` object for example. This made it less likely for programmers, and by extension, designers, to build web apps using these conventions. Yet JavaScript is more than capable of doing the job. What's really needed, however, and what the Yahoo! User Interface Library delivers in spades, is the ability to wrap that raw ability into more programmer-friendly classes and objects.

It's much easier, for example, to declare that an element is to move from one position to another by a certain number of pixels, than to program a custom routine to do so. YUI's Animation component provides a set of generic yet highly customizable classes that make child's play out of animating DOM elements.

In this chapter, you'll learn about:

❑ Composing basic animation sequences

❑ Smoothing animation paths and motion

❑ Interactive animation with drag and drop

Composing Basic Animation Sequences

The YUI Animation component is broken down into four main classes: Anim, Motion, Scroll, and ColorAnim. In fact, Anim is the base animation class, and the other three are subclasses designed to handle different types of animation. The base Anim class handles the heavy lifting, and the subclasses basically leverage that engine by adding new methods to it. So, essentially the animation engine takes care of all the nitty-gritty details such as, among other things, making sure that the animation reports where it is at any given moment; that it exposes key events so that they can be subscribed to by callback functions; that it provides a framework for managing timing and frames; and that the animation is kept in check and on time so that it completes when it's supposed to.

Ultimately, all the base Anim class does is increment or decrement numbers within a certain time frame according to a certain easing formula (See Figure 9-2). So in theory, anything in the browser that relies on numbers for its display properties can be animated. This is why not only the dimensions and position of an element can be animated but also its colors.

Anim

In order to animate a DOM element with YUI, an animation object needs to be instantiated first. This object allows for the animation of dimension-based properties of an element's CSS style (through the style object). Here's a simple example:

```
var anim = new YAHOO.util.Anim("foo");
```

This creates an animation object, but it doesn't do anything else. In order for it to actually animate, the animate method needs to be called.

```
anim.animate();
```

In this case, however, there still won't be any animation because no instructions were given regarding what needs to be animated. Because of the depth and breadth of possible animations, these options are passed through an object literal. That way, one or many different animations can be specified without having to burden the API with an excess of unused parameters. The object literal is two levels deep. The first level defines what aspect of the element is to be animated, height, width, position, and the second level defines the actual units it is to be animated by, or to, or even from.

So for example, animating the width of an element to 100px would look like this:

```
var anim = new YAHOO.util.Anim("foo",
{
    width: {
        to: 100
    }
});
anim.animate();
```

The default animation unit is pixels (px), but it can be overridden like this:

```
var anim = new YAHOO.util.Anim("foo",
{
    width: {
        to: 100,
        unit: "em"
    }
});
anim.animate();
```

Here's an example of a basic height and width animation.

```
<html>
    <head>
        <title>Anim</title>
        <style type="text/css">
            #banner {
                background: #f00;
                border: solid 10px #ff0;
                color: #fff;
                text-align: center;
                width: 350px;
                height: 50px;
                overflow: hidden;
            }
            #banner h1 {
                font-size: 64px;
                margin-top: 42px;
            }
            #banner p {
                font-size: 32px;
            }
        </style>
    </head>
    <body>
        <div id="banner">
            <h1>YUI Wrox!</h1>
            <p>A simple YUI Animation</p>
        </div>
        <script src="yahoo-dom-event.js"></script>
        <script src="animation-min.js"></script>
        <script>
            YAHOO.example.animation = function () {
                var anim = new YAHOO.util.Anim("banner",
                    {
                        width: {to: 976},
                        height: {to: 230}
                    },
                    1.5,
                    YAHOO.util.Easing.easeOutStrong);
                YAHOO.util.Event.addListener(
```

```
                    "banner",
                    "mouseover",
                    anim.animate,
                    anim,
                    true);
          }();
      </script>
    </body>
  </html>
```

This example starts with a `div` element with the ID `doc`. It's set with the height and width values of 50 and 350 pixels, respectively. The animation object is bound to this element and is given the instructions to animate the element's width to 976 pixels and its height to 230 pixels. The animation is triggered with a `mouseover` event (see Figure 9-1).

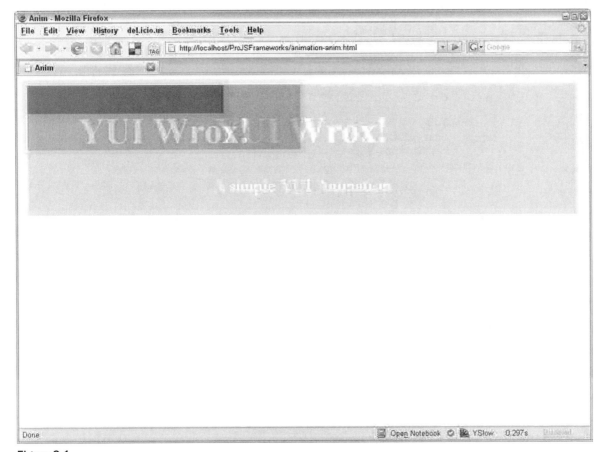

Figure 9-1

The animation object figures out how many frames are needed to get from its initial starting point to its final end point. It then advances both the height and width values accordingly per frame. If it needs to increment the width value a lot more than the height, then each frame will have the width value jump by a larger amount than the height value.

There are two other parameters being passed to the Anim constructor. One is the value 1.5, which is the desired duration in seconds for the animation; the other is the easing effect to be applied to the animation.

Events

The Anim class comes with built-in custom events that can be subscribed to with callback functions. This allows for code to be triggered at key moments in an animation sequence. The three events available are onStart, onTween, and onComplete. Each does as their name suggests so that all callback functions subscribed to onStart are called when the animation begins, those subscribed to onTween are called each time the animation steps forward one frame, and those subscribed to onComplete are called when the animation ends. These custom events are available in all animation subclasses as well as inherited from the Anim base class.

One example for subscribing a callback function to the onTween custom event is to detect element collision. Each time the animation moves the element forward by one frame, the callback function can check its position against all other objects in its vicinity. If a collision is detected, it can further trigger another function in the object it collided with so that it can move out of the way.

Motion

Though the Anim class allows for the moving around of elements by manipulating its top, right, bottom and left values, those dimensions are relative to the elements themselves. Using the Motion subclass allows for the specifying of a point relative to the page where the object is to move to. That way, it doesn't matter where the element is located; it will end up at the specified x and y coordinates on the page. Here's an example:

```
<html>
    <head>
        <title>Motion</title>
        <style type="text/css">
            #doc {
                width: 200px;
                position: absolute;
                top: 0;
                right: 0;
                background: #000;
                padding: 10px;
            }
            #box {
                background: #f00;
```

```
                        border: solid 10px #ff0;
                        color: #fff;
                        width: 100px;
                        text-align: center;
                        font-weight: bold;
                    }
                </style>
            </head>
            <body>
                <div id="doc">
                    <p id="box">YUI Wrox!</p>
                </div>
                <script src="yahoo-dom-event.js"></script>
                <script src="animation-min.js"></script>
                <script>
                    YAHOO.example.motion = function () {
                        var anim = new YAHOO.util.Motion("box",
                            {
                                points: {to: [350, 100]}
                            },
                            1.5,
                            YAHOO.util.Easing.easeOutStrong);
                        YAHOO.util.Event.addListener(
                            "box",
                            "mouseover",
                            anim.animate,
                            anim,
                            true);
                    }();
                </script>
            </body>
        </html>
```

The preceding example sets up a paragraph within a div element. The div is absolutely positioned to the top-right corner of the browser's viewport. It naturally takes along the paragraph (with the ID box) within it. Then, a Motion animation is set up on the paragraph so that when the mouse passes over it, the paragraph moves to 350 pixels by 100 pixels on the page (see Figure 9-2). It will end up there no matter where it starts. So for example, changing the CSS rule from "right: 0;" to "left: 0;" will start the paragraph off on the far left of the screen. Even so, once the mouse passes over it, it will still end up at 350 by 100.

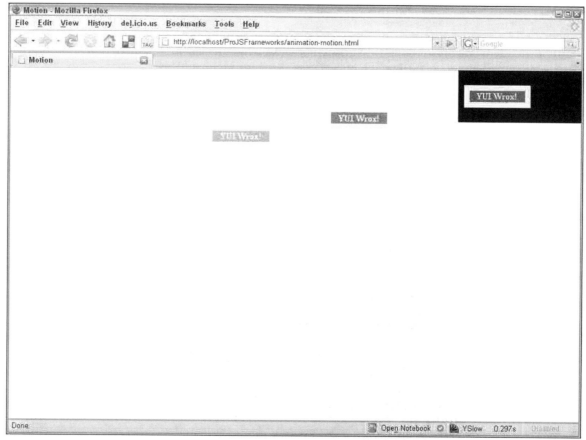

Figure 9-2

The way Motion animation is achieved is through the points parameter. Rather than specifying height, width, top, right, bottom or down, the points parameter is used. And instead of passing a value to be applied to that particular attribute, x/y coordinates are passed through an array.

Although parameters such as this would be used in an Anim object . . .

```
{
    left: {to: 350},
    top: {to: 100}
}
```

. . . this is used in a Motion object:

```
{
    points: {to: [350, 100]}
}
```

Scroll

The `Scroll` animation subclass allows for the animating of overflowed elements, specifically the automated scrolling of overflowed elements. Normally, when an element's `height` value is set in CSS to less than its natural height, and it has a CSS `overflow` rule applied to it, the `Scroll` subclass is able to animate it. The following example illustrates how a paragraph of text can be scrolled inside a `div` element.

```html
<html>
    <head>
        <title>Scroll</title>
        <style type="text/css">
            #box {
                height: 150px;
                width: 200px;
                overflow: auto;
            }
        </style>
    </head>
    <body>
        <div id="box">
            <h1>YUI Wrox!</h1>
            <p>Lorem ipsum dolor sit amet, consectetuer
            adipiscing elit. Donec fermentum, neque et
            ultrices dignissim, est est scelerisque erat,
            sed ornare nisl orci quis tellus. Donec quis
            lacus quis nibh consectetuer dictum. Duis
            fermentum, ligula condimentum congue bibendum,
            dui dolor vehicula lorem, sed congue nisl
            tellus id diam. Sed nulla sem, lacinia vel,
            ullamcorper at, auctor ut, dolor. Praesent
            turpis quam, posuere a, posuere sed, fermentum
            eu, risus. Integer luctus. Maecenas dolor.
            Donec vehicula.<p>
        </div>
        <script src="yahoo-dom-event.js"></script>
        <script src="animation-min.js"></script>
        <script>
            YAHOO.example.scroll = function () {
                var anim = new YAHOO.util.Scroll("box",
                    {
                        scroll: {to: [0, 400]}
                    },
                    1.5,
                    YAHOO.util.Easing.easeOutStrong);
                YAHOO.util.Event.addListener(
                    "box",
                    "mouseover",
                    anim.animate,
                    anim,
                    true);
            }();
        </script>
    </body>
</html>
```

Here a self-executing function called Scroll is set up under the YAHOO.example namespace. Once it executes, a new Scroll animation is created. The animation object is attached to the element with the ID box. The object's attributes parameter is an object containing instructions that the animation is to scroll 0 pixels on its x axis and 400 pixels on its y axis. The animation is also set to run for 1.5 seconds and to be eased using the easeOutStrong easing method. Finally, the object's animate method is attached to the div element as an event handler for the mouseover event. So, the moment the mouse hovers over the div element, it scrolls by 400 pixels (see Figure 9-3).

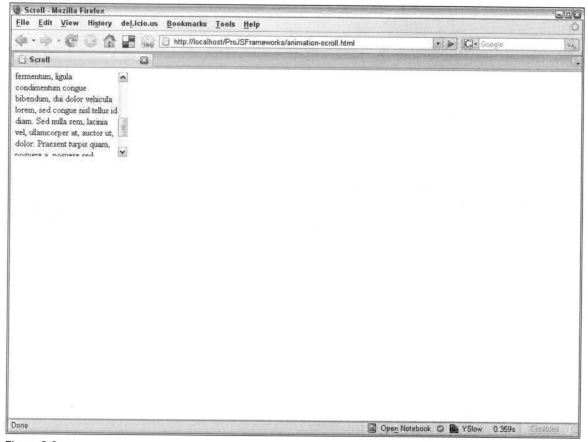

Figure 9-3

ColorAnim

Animating colors may have at one time been a cute addition to a site, though most often overdone and gaudy. Nowadays though, on the "AJAX-driven" web, animating colors is essential to building a usable interface. Specifically, highlighting a change made to a document via AJAX and then fading it out serves as a visual signal to the visitor that something has changed on the page. The most common implementation of this device is highlighting changed content in yellow and then fading it to white (or whatever the page's background color is) after about a second or two. Fading an element's opacity though can be handled through the Anim object directly as it is a property accessible through the style object.

The `ColorAnim` subclass leverages the `Anim` class's main engine and simply passes it a method to execute that increments or decrements from one color value to another. CSS color values come in two different flavors, RGB and Hex. Here is an example of an RGB value in CSS:

```
#foo {
    background-color: rgb(255, 255, 255); /* white */
}
```

Here's the same example but in Hex:

```
#foo {
    background-color: #ffffff; /* white */
}
```

It's possible to feed color values to the `ColorAnim` subclass in four possible patterns: `ffff`, `#ffff`, `[255, 255, 255]`, or `rgb(255, 255, 255)`. These values are taken and passed to a public method called `parseColor` that tries to convert and return them as an rgb 3-tuple, in other words `[255, 255, 255]`. This normalization allows the color values to be processed the same way internally regardless of what form they're passed in.

The following is a real-world use-case where color animation would be used. It's an AJAX-driven comment form (the AJAX part is simulated to save on code). The visitor's comment is dynamically added to the existing list of comments in the page. To indicate that the comment was added, it's given a yellow background color prior to being inserted into the page (See Figure 9-4). A second after it has been inserted, it fades to white, blending into the background.

```
<html>
    <head>
        <title>ColorAnim Comment Demo</title>
        <link rel="stylesheet" type="text/css" href="reset-fonts-grids.css" />
        <link rel="stylesheet" type="text/css" href="base-min.css" />
    </head>
    <body>
        <div id="doc">
            <div id="hd">
                <h1>ColorAnim Comment Demo</h1>
            </div>
            <div id="bd">
                <form id="leave-a-comment" method="post" action="/leaveComment/">
                    <label for="name">Name</label><br />
                    <input type="text" id="name" /><br />
                    <label for="comment">Comment</label><br/>
                    <textarea id="comment"></textarea><br />
                    <input type="submit" value="Submit comment!" />
                </form>
                <h2>Comments</h2>
                <ol id="comments">
                    <li>First!!! -- Anonymous Coward</li>
                    <li>This site is awesome! -- John Doe</li>
                    <li>Yahoo! -- Me</li>
                </ol>
            </div>
        </div>
```

```
<script src="yahoo-dom-event.js"></script>
<script src="animation-min.js"></script>
<script>
    YAHOO.example.colorAnim = function () {
        function addComment(e) {
            var li = document.createElement("li");
            li.appendChild(
                document.createTextNode(
                    comment.value + " -- " + name.value));
            YAHOO.util.Dom.setStyle(li, "background-color", "#ffff00");
            comments.appendChild(li);
            name.value = "";
            comment.value = "";
            var cAnim = new YAHOO.util.ColorAnim(li, {
                    backgroundColor: {
                        to: "#ffffff"
                    }
                }, 1, YAHOO.util.Easing.easeOut);
            setTimeout(function () {
                cAnim.animate();
            }, 1000);
            // AJAX code goes here
            YAHOO.util.Event.preventDefault(e);
        };

        var name = YAHOO.util.Dom.get("name");
        var comment = YAHOO.util.Dom.get("comment");
        var comments = YAHOO.util.Dom.get("comments");
        YAHOO.util.Event.addListener(
            "leave-a-comment", "submit", addComment);
    }();
</script>
</body>
</html>
```

The first thing this code does is set up a self-executing function named `colorAnim` under the YAHOO `.example` namespace. This ensures that all variables that are created are local to the `colorAnim` function and not global. It then sets up an `addComment` function, which is called whenever a new comment is added. The function creates a new list item, sets its background color to yellow, populates it with the visitor's comment and name, and then adds it to the comment list. After it adds the list item to the ordered list, it clears the form fields and sets up a color animation. The animation is set to go from the current background color (since it isn't specified) to white. A `setTimeout` then gets set to trigger the animation object's `animate` method a second later.

A "from" color can also be specified in case the element needs to go from, say, red to white:

```
backgroundColor: {
    from: "#ff0000",
    to: "#ffffff"
}
```

Multiple colors can also be adjusted at the same time. Here's how to set the background color to white and the foreground to red:

```
backgroundColor: {
    to: "#ffffff"
},
color: {
    to: "#ff0000"
}
```

As is obvious, multiple optional attributes can be passed to the animation object. Both `to` and `from` attributes can be set, or just the `to` attribute. Both `color` and `backgroundColor` can be adjusted or just one of them. In fact, even border colors can be set through `borderTopColor`, `borderRightColor`, `borderBottomColor`, and `borderLeftColor`. Each has to be set separately (top, right, bottom and left) since there isn't a simple all-encompassing `borderColor` property. Also, a border color can only be set on an element that has a border style value set (see Figure 9-4).

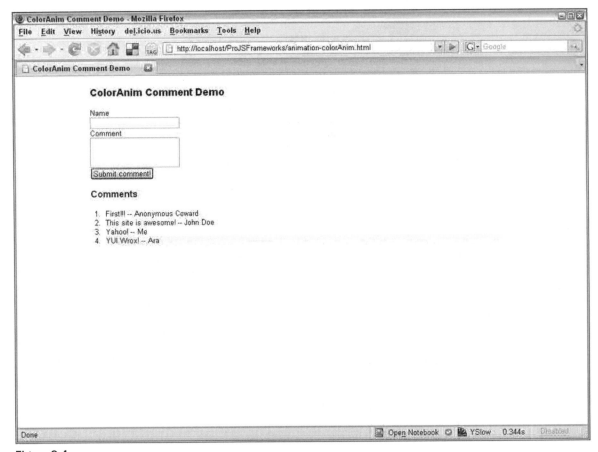

Figure 9-4

Smoothing Animation Paths and Motion

Animations that run at the same speed from beginning to end don't seem natural to the human eye. Human movement for example starts out slow, gets faster, and then slows down before stopping. Of course, there are other types of natural movement as well, such as when objects bounce when they fall, or when they spring back and forth before stopping. The human brain is used to these types of motions as they occur in nature. A computerized, consistent motion from start to finish however seems unnatural and really quite boring.

Easing

Enter easing. Easing is a way for computers to simulate naturally occurring motion by applying mathematical formulae to moving objects. If an easing function is provided to an animation object, then each frame's position calculation gets passed through the easing function, which adjusts its position according to its own formula.

The following table shows all of the available easing effects with short descriptions taken from the API documentation as well as a graphical representation of the formula being applied to the animation:

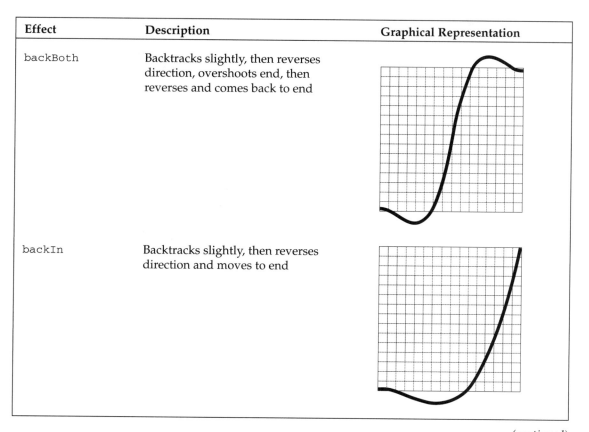

Effect	Description	Graphical Representation
backBoth	Backtracks slightly, then reverses direction, overshoots end, then reverses and comes back to end	
backIn	Backtracks slightly, then reverses direction and moves to end	

(continued)

Effect	Description	Graphical Representation
backOut	Overshoots end, then reverses and comes back to end	
bounceBoth	Bounces off start and end	
bounceIn	Bounces off of start	
bounceOut	Bounces off end	

Effect	Description	Graphical Representation
easeBoth	Begins slowly and decelerates toward end (quadratic)	
easeBothStrong	Begins slowly and decelerates toward end (quartic)	
easeIn	Begins slowly and accelerates toward end (quadratic)	
easeInStrong	Begins slowly and accelerates toward end (quartic)	

(continued)

Effect	Description	Graphical Representation
easeNone	Uniform speed between points	
easeOut	Begins quickly and decelerates toward end (quadratic)	
easeOutStrong	Begins quickly and decelerates toward end (quartic)	
elasticBoth	Snaps both elastic effect	

Effect	Description	Graphical Representation
elasticIn	Snaps in elastic effect	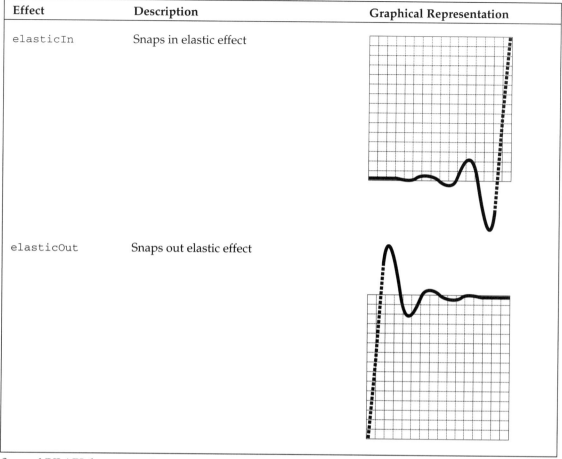
elasticOut	Snaps out elastic effect	

Source: YUI API documentation.

Curved Paths (Bezier)

Sometimes Motion animations need to be animated along more than just a straight line. Bezier curves make that possible. These are most popularly known as *paths* in vector drawing programs such as Adobe's Illustrator. Adding curved paths to YUI Motion animations is as easy as adding an additional attribute to the existing attributes parameter. Just as there are from and to attributes, curved paths are specified through the control parameter.

The following is an example of simple Motion animation:

```
var anim = new YAHOO.util.Motion("obj", {
    points: {
        to: [400, 450]
    }
}, 3);
```

The following is an example of `Motion` animation with curved paths:

```
var anim = new YAHOO.util.Motion("obj", {
    points: {
        to: [400, 450],
        control: [
            [10, 175],
            [650, 30],
            [750, 250],
            [450, 500],
            [125, 350]
        ]
    }
}, 3);
```

In this animation, the element with the ID `obj` will travel from its original position in the document to 400 by 450 on the screen. Along the way it will be "influenced" by the control points specified within the `control` array. The array contains a set of arrays each representing a point with x and y coordinates.

The following is a code example using this animation:

```
<html>
    <head>
        <title>Bezier Demo</title>
        <link rel="stylesheet" type="text/css" href="reset-fonts-grids.css" />
        <link rel="stylesheet" type="text/css" href="base-min.css" />
        <style type="text/css">
            #obj,
            .point,
            .ctrl,
            .end {
                font-size: 77%;
                height: 1.25em;
                width: 1.25em;
                overflow: visible;
                position: absolute;
            }
            #obj {
                z-index: 1;
            }
            #obj,
            .point {
                background: #f00;
            }
            #obj,
            .ctrl,
            .end {
                border: solid 2px #000;
            }
            .end {
                background: #000;
            }
        </style>
    </head>
    <body>
```

```
<div id="doc">
    <div id="hd">
        <h1>Bezier Demo</h1>
    </div>
    <div id="bd">
        <p>Once clicked, the red square at the end of this sentence will
        travel to its end point (black square) while being influenced by
        control points (hollow squares) along the way.
        <span id="obj"></span></p>
    </div>
</div>
<script src="yahoo-dom-event.js"></script>
<script src="animation-min.js"></script>
<script>
    YAHOO.example.bezier = function () {
        function setPoint(xy, cn, txt) {
            var pt = document.createElement("div");
            pt.className = cn || "point";
            if (typeof txt !== "undefined") {
                pt.appendChild(document.createTextNode(txt));
            }
            document.body.appendChild(pt);
            YAHOO.util.Dom.setXY(pt, xy);
            if (pt.className === "point") {
                YAHOO.util.Dom.setStyle(pt, "opacity", "0.25");
            }
        };
        var anim = new YAHOO.util.Motion("obj", {
            points: {
                to: [400, 450],
                control: [
                    [10, 175],
                    [650, 30],
                    [750, 250],
                    [450, 500],
                    [125, 350]
                ]
            }
        }, 3);
        anim.onTween.subscribe(function () {
            setPoint(YAHOO.util.Dom.getXY(this.getEl()));
        });
        for (var i = 0; anim.attributes.points.control[i]; i += 1) {
            setPoint(anim.attributes.points.control[i], "ctrl", i + 1);
        }
        setPoint(anim.attributes.points.to, "end");
        YAHOO.util.Event.addListener(
            "obj",
            "click",
            anim.animate,
            anim,
            true);
    }();
</script>
</body>
</html>
```

This code creates a `Motion` animation and sets its `animate` method as an event handler on the `span` with the ID `obj`. This allows for the element to be animated as soon as it's clicked. Using the animation object's `onTween` event, the code calls the `setPoint` function, which basically leaves a trail behind the animated `span` element. The code also cycles through the control points and sets points representing them as well. This serves to show where those points are in Figure 9-5 and Figure 9-6. Once clicked, the animation will take the `span` element (red square) from its starting point (at the end of the first sentence in the page) to the coordinates 400 by 450 (black square). Along the way, its path will be influenced by the control points (empty squares).

Figure 9-5 shows what the animation looks like.

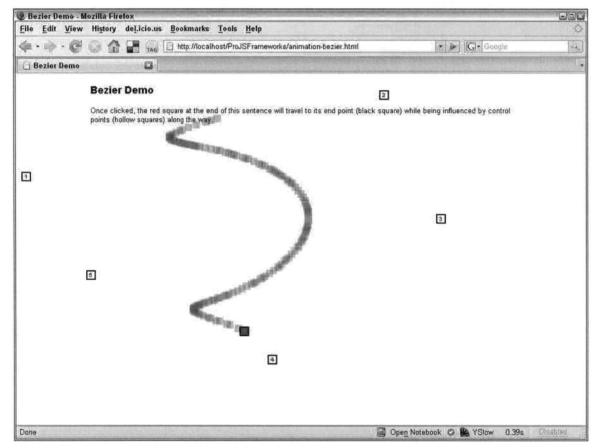

Figure 9-5

The animation can be called again by clicking on the `span` element. This time, however, its starting point is different; therefore, the path it follows will be different (see Figure 9-6). It will start and end at the same point, all the while being influenced by the control points.

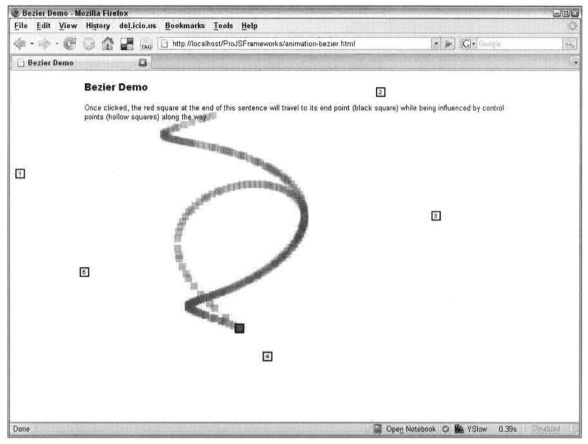

Figure 9-6

Interactive Animation with Drag and Drop

One of the staples of graphical user interfaces is the ability to drag and drop items. All modern operating systems use this convention to allow their users the freedom to move elements around on the screen. Modern web sites are also taking advantage of this convention to allow their visitors the freedom of interaction that they have with their operating systems. The trouble is, JavaScript doesn't have any drag-and-drop functionality built in, and programming it is a complex task. That's where libraries come in to make life easier. YUI has a complete Drag & Drop Utility to help ease the pain of adding drag-and-drop functionality to a web site.

DD

Creating a draggable object is actually quite simple. All that needs to be done is for a DD object to be instantiated with the ID of the element that is to be made draggable. That's it.

```
var el = new YAHOO.util.DD("foo");
```

That one line of code will make the element with the ID `foo` draggable.

The YUI Drag & Drop Utility's base `DragDrop` class is built to be extended. In other words, instantiating directly from `DragDrop` will return a skeleton that doesn't do much. That's why the preceding line of code instantiates from `DD` instead. The `DD` object extends `DragDrop` and provides a much more complete object.

DDProxy

By default, the Drag & Drop Utility makes it so that the element that's being dragged is simply moved across the screen following the mouse wherever it goes. The trouble with this is, if the element is complex in its layout, or just heavy in its contents, the move operation's performance can end up suffering. This is where `DDProxy` comes in. It works just like `DD` except that it creates a separate element that stands in for the draggable element during the `mousemove` operation. This dynamically generated proxy element is a direct child of `document.body` and doesn't contain any content. It's therefore ideal to stand in for elements that would otherwise bog down the user experience were they to be dragged themselves. The proxy element only appears when the element begins to be dragged and is hidden once the operation is complete (see Figure 9-7).

The following code is a simple Drag & Drop demo:

```
<html>
    <head>
        <title>Drag &amp; Drop Demo</title>
        <link rel="stylesheet" type="text/css" href="reset-fonts-grids.css" />
        <link rel="stylesheet" type="text/css" href="base-min.css" />
        <style type="text/css">
            .box {
                border: solid 5px #000;
                height: 5em;
                width: 5em;
                margin: 1em;
                color: #fff;
                font-weight: bold;
                font-size: 123.1%;
                text-transform: uppercase;
                text-align: center;
            }
            .move {
                cursor: move;
            }
            #box1 {
                background: #300;
            }
            #box2 {
                background: #600;
            }
            #box3 {
                background: #900;
            }
            #box4 {
                background: #c00;
            }
```

```
                #box5 {
                    background: #f00;
                }
            </style>
    </head>
    <body>
        <div id="doc">
            <div id="hd">
                <h1>Drag &amp; Drop Demo</h1>
            </div>
            <div id="bd">
                <h2>Boxes</h2>
                <div class="box" id="box1">Box 1</div>
                <div class="box proxy" id="box2">Box 2</div>
                <div class="box" id="box3">Box 3</div>
                <div class="box proxy" id="box4">Box 4</div>
                <div class="box" id="box5">Box 5</div>
            </div>
        </div>
        <script src="yahoo-dom-event.js"></script>
        <script src="dragdrop-min.js"></script>
        <script>
            YAHOO.example.dd = function () {
                var boxes = YAHOO.util.Dom.getElementsByClassName("box");
                for (var i = 0; boxes[i]; i += 1) {
                    var box = boxes[i];
                    if (YAHOO.util.Dom.hasClass(box, "proxy")) {
                        var ddItem = new YAHOO.util.DDProxy(box);
                        box.innerHTML += " (proxy)";
                    } else {
                        var ddItem = new YAHOO.util.DD(box);
                    }
                    ddItem.onMouseDown = function () {
                        var el = this.getEl();
                        if (el) {
                            YAHOO.util.Dom.addClass(el, "move");
                        }
                    };
                    ddItem.onMouseUp = function () {
                        var el = this.getEl();
                        if (el) {
                            YAHOO.util.Dom.removeClass(el, "move");
                        }
                    };
                }
            }();
        </script>
    </body>
</html>
```

This code example grabs all of the elements in the page that have the class name box and iterates over them instantiating an object for each. Before doing so, however, it checks to see whether the element also has the class name proxy assigned to it or not. If so, it instantiates a DDProxy object for it. Otherwise, it goes with DD. Using a class name for a hook makes maintenance and configuration of this sort of program simpler. In the case of an element requiring a `DDProxy` object, the code also adds the words "(proxy)" to the element's contents to denote (for this demo's purposes) which elements will behave differently. As mentioned earlier, DD extends `DragDrop`, which contains a bunch of event handlers that don't do anything by themselves. They're functions that are called at key moments during a drag-and-drop operation. If overridden, they can execute custom code. In the case of the previous example, both the `onMouseDown` and `onMouseUp` event handlers are being overridden to add and remove the `move` class name to the element.

The following table lists all of the available events and their descriptions for `DragDrop`, `DD`, and `DDProxy` according to the API:

Event	Description
b4DragDrop	Fires before the `dragDropEvent`.
b4Drag	Fires before the `dragEvent`.
b4DragOut	Fires before the `dragOutEvent`.
b4DragOver	Fires before the `dragOverEvent`.
b4EndDrag	Fires before the `endDragEvent`. Returning false will cancel.
b4MouseDown	Provides access to the `mousedown` event, before the `mouseDownEvent` gets fired. Returning false will cancel the drag.
b4StartDrag	Fires before the `startDragEvent`. Returning false will cancel the `startDrag` Event.
dragDrop	Fires when the dragged objects are dropped on another.
dragEnter	Occurs when the dragged object first interacts with another targetable drag-and-drop object.
Drag	Occurs on every `mousemove` event while dragging.
dragOut	Fires when a dragged object is no longer over an object that had the `onDragEnter` fire.
dragOver	Fires every `mousemove` event while over a drag-and-drop object.
endDrag	Fires on the `mouseup` event after a drag has been initiated (`startDrag` fired).
invalidDrop	Fires when the dragged object is dropped in a location that contains no drop targets.
mouseDown	Provides access to the `mousedown` event. The `mousedown` does not always result in a drag operation.
mouseUp	Fired from inside `DragDropMgr` when the drag operation is finished.
startDrag	Occurs after a mouse down and the drag threshold has been met. The drag threshold default is either 3 pixels of mouse movement or a full second of holding the mouse down.

Source: YUI API

Figure 9-7 shows what the example looks like in action: The first three boxes have already been moved and the fourth (a box of type DDProxy) is in mid-drag.

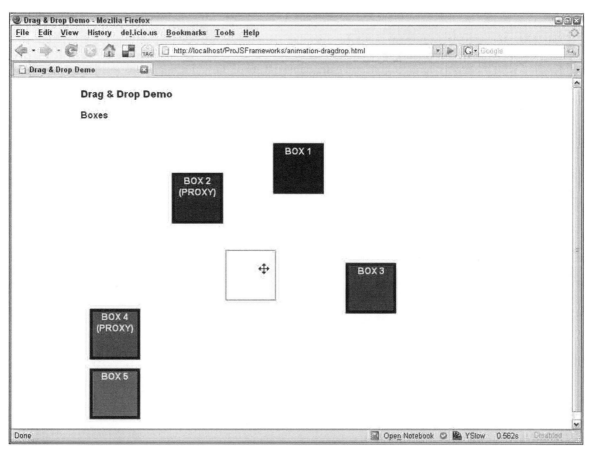

Figure 9-7

New in YUI 3

A new feature in YUI 3's Animation Utility is that the to and from values can actually be functions. The function receives one argument, which is the node object that it's animating, whereupon calculations can be made and a resulting value is returned. This is particularly useful for situations where the node's current width needs to be referred to, for example. Also, the animate method has been renamed to run.

Summary

Even though the norm for desktop applications is to incorporate animation and drag-and-drop ability, web technologies are surprisingly limited in what they can do out of the box. However, libraries such as the YUI provide easy-to-use, powerful, and extendable components that make child's play out of animating the web. An important point to remember with the Animation and Drag & Drop Utilities is their open architecture allowing for custom code to be bound to key events in their execution. This coupled with the highly configurable and extendable nature of these utilities opens the doors wide open to a world of potential.

10

Simplifying AJAX and Dynamic Loading

Traditionally, a browser made an HTTP request to the server, fetched a page, parsed it, and then made some more HTTP requests for resources such as images, JavaScript files, and so forth. This model has been in play since the dawn of the Web. Recently, however, with the emergence of AJAX and new best practices in regards to page optimization, this model is beginning to evolve. No longer are all of the page's contents delivered through the first HTTP request, nor are all of the needed resources downloaded immediately after the page is parsed. Instead, an "on-demand" model of fetching needed data and resources is emerging.

In this chapter, you'll learn about:

- ❑ Requesting and fetching data
- ❑ Loading libraries and components

Making HTTP Requests and Fetching Data

Web 2.0 is all the rage. Asking someone in the industry what "Web 2.0" really means will yield any number of responses, chief among them being AJAX. Although Web 2.0 isn't *all* about AJAX, a lot of the sites being developed today make use of it. So being able to implement AJAX across browsers has become mission critical.

The thing about AJAX is that it isn't actually new. The name is, but the underlying technology is nearly a decade old — older if you include the use of iframes. Microsoft first implemented XMLHTTP in 1999 with the first release of Internet Explorer 5. The Mozilla project then included native support in Mozilla 1.0 and called it XMLHttpRequest (XHR).

In the case where a browser doesn't support XHR natively, such as in Internet Explorer 6, XMLHTTP needs to be invoked through the MSXML ActiveX object. The trouble is, the availability of MSXML varies from machine to machine as does its version. So there's the rub; supporting AJAX across browsers and across operating systems requires a little bit of fancy footwork, a.k.a. code forking.

Once the XHR object has been created, using it can be a bit tricky. One oversight that has yet to be remedied by browser makers is the fact that XHR doesn't have native timeout support. (Internet Explorer 8 has included a timeout property to its native XHR object.) So if a request is made to the server and for whatever reason is never answered, the browser will just sit there waiting for a response and give the user the impression that it has locked up. Of course if the server does respond, it doesn't always mean that the transaction was successful. At this point, what's required is the ability to interpret the server's response to determine if there was a problem or if the transaction was a success. The YUI Connection Manager handles all of this and goes a long way in normalizing and augmenting XHR functionality across browsers.

asyncRequest

All of the heavy lifting done by the YUI Connection Manager is wrapped up into one function called asyncRequest. This function takes four parameters: method, uri, callback, and postData. The method parameter is a string that specifies whether the request is to be of type GET or POST. The uri parameter is a fully qualified path to a resource. This can be anything that produces a response such as a text file, an HTML document, a CGI application, or a server-side script such as a PHP, JSP, ASP, or other similar resource. The callback parameter is a custom object containing callback functions for the possible outcomes of the request that's being made. At the very least it needs to contain a handler for a successful call as well as one for a failed one. Finally, the postData parameter is for requests of type POST. It's used to pass POST data to the server since it can't be tacked onto the path as it can with a GET request. Here's a sample GET call:

```
var callback = {
    success: function (o) {/* do something! */},
    failure: function (o) {/* do something else */}
}
var request = YAHOO.util.Connect.asyncRequest('GET', '/order/', callback);
```

The variable request receives the connection object that is created by asyncRequest. If the transaction with the server is a success, the success event handler is called; otherwise, the failure event handler is called. There are six possible callback events that are available to hook into.

Callback Event	Description
Start	This event fires at the start of a transaction and passes the transaction's ID to its subscribed handler.
Complete	This event fires when a transaction response has completed and passes the transaction's ID to its subscribed handler.
Success	This event fires when a transaction response is complete and determined to be HTTP 2xx. The response object is passed to successEvent's subscribed handler. This event is analogous to the callback success handler. NOTE: This event does not fire for file upload transactions.

Callback Event	Description
Failure	This event fires when a transaction response is complete and determined to be HTTP 4xx/5xx or if an HTTP status is unavailable. The response object is passed to failureEvent's subscribed handler. This event is analogous to the callback failure handler.
Upload	This event fires when a file upload transaction is complete. This event fires only for file upload transaction, in place of successEvent and failureEvent. The response object is passed to the uploadEvent's subscribed handler. This event is analogous to the callback upload handler.
Abort	This event fires when a transaction's callback.timeout triggers an abort. It can also be explicitly fired via YAHOO.util.Connect.abort().

Source: YUI Connection Manager Page.

Here's an example of asyncRequest in action:

```html
<html>
    <head>
        <title>Connection Demo</title>
        <link rel="stylesheet" type="text/css" href="reset-fonts-grids.css" />
        <link rel="stylesheet" type="text/css" href="base-min.css" />
    </head>
    <body>
        <div id="doc">
            <div id="hd">
                <h1>Connection Demo</h1>
            </div>
            <div id="bd">
                <h2>Status</h2>
                <ul id="status">
                </ul>
                <h2>Output</h2>
                <div id="output">
                </div>
            </div>
        </div>
        <script src="yahoo-dom-event.js"></script>
        <script src="connection-min.js"></script>
        <script src="animation-min.js"></script>
        <script>
            YAHOO.namespace("example.proJavaScriptFrameworks");
            YAHOO.example.proJavaScriptFrameworks = function () {
                var status = YAHOO.util.Dom.get("status");
                var output = YAHOO.util.Dom.get("output");

                // Utility functions
                function setStatusMessage(msg) {
                    var li = document.createElement("li");
                    li.appendChild(document.createTextNode(msg));
```

```
                        status.appendChild(li);
                        indicateNewContent(li);
                };
                function indicateNewContent(el) {
                        el = YAHOO.util.Dom.get(el);
                        el.style.backgroundColor = "#ff0";
                        setTimeout(
                                function () {
                                        var anim = new YAHOO.util.ColorAnim(
                                                el, {backgroundColor: {to: "#ffffff"}});
                                        anim.animate();
                                }, 1000);
                };

                // XHR event handlers
                function successHandler(o) {
                        setStatusMessage("Success!");
                        var id = YAHOO.util.Dom.generateId();
                        var content = o.responseText.replace("new-content", id);
                        output.innerHTML += content;
                        indicateNewContent(id);
                };
                function failureHandler(o) {
                        setStatusMessage("Failed");
                };
                var callback = {
                        success: successHandler,
                        failure: failureHandler
                };

                // Timed async requests to the server
                setTimeout(function () {
                        var request1 = YAHOO.util.Connect.asyncRequest(
                                'GET', 'connection-htmlFragment.html', callback);
                }, 1000);
                setTimeout(function () {
                        var request2 = YAHOO.util.Connect.asyncRequest(
                                'GET', 'bogus.html', callback);
                }, 3000);
                setTimeout(function () {
                        var request3 = YAHOO.util.Connect.asyncRequest(
                                'GET', 'connection-htmlFragment.html', callback);
                }, 5500);
        }();
    </script>
  </body>
</html>
```

This example basically makes three different asyncRequests. They're timed in order to simulate user interaction and to make sure that they don't all go through at the same time. Each is a GET request. The second one deliberately fails to show the failure callback function in use. Each block of new content that's added to the DOM also passes through the function indicateNewContent, which causes the content to be briefly highlighted in yellow and then to fade to white. This is the previously mentioned technique that signals to the user that something has changed in the page.

Note how, in the success handler, the ID from the source content is being changed by a generated ID instead. This is because this example uses the same source for its content and, thus, ends up with two elements having the same ID. Replacing the ID with a generated one ensures that the DOM will have only unique IDs and no duplicates.

Figure 10-1 shows an example in action.

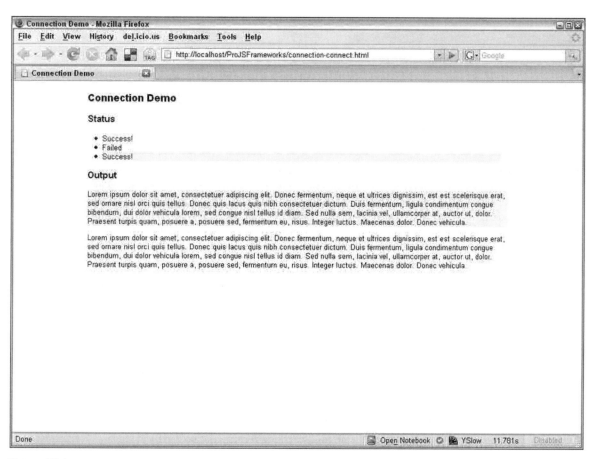

Figure 10-1

Connection Manager examples need to be executed on a web server. Localhost will do, as long as it's a web server because the browser follows a strict "same-origin" policy. Running the example from the file system won't resolve to a domain and the code will fail.

JSON

JavaScript Object Notation, otherwise known as JSON, is a discovery made by Douglas Crockford when he was searching for an ideal data interchange format. JSON simplifies JavaScript's native object literal notation into a form that can easily be produced and consumed by other languages and systems. This lowest common denominator approach is the reason why, for example, JSON requires that the names in its name/value pairs be strings, even though JavaScript allows them not to be.

Here is a bit of simple JSON:

```
{"greeting": "Hello World!"}
```

Once this string is passed through JavaScript's `eval`, it will be transformed into an actual object. So here's a simple example of how that's done:

```
var personString = "{'fname': 'John', 'lname': 'Doe'}";
var person = eval("(" + personString + ")");
alert("Hello, my name is " + person.fname + " " + person.lname);
```

Basically, the string is `eval`ed into an object, and then its contents are accessed via dot notation. It's pretty simple and straight forward except for one thing: `eval`. The `eval` function invokes the JavaScript interpreter and passes it a string. The interpreter then takes that string and parses and executes it, just as if it were code it had read from a trusted HTML or JavaScript file. There is no security model in place whatsoever. So should there be any malicious code serialized in that string, it would get executed as well. This makes for a huge security vulnerability in web sites and is one of the more popular to be exploited in cross-site scripting (XSS) attacks today.

Filtering for malicious code can be difficult and if not properly done, useless. YUI's JSON Utility provides a set of tools to verify the safety of a string of JSON and then to safely proceed in running it through `eval`.

isValid

The `isValid` method is used internally by the JSON Utility as well as exposed for external use. It receives a string as a parameter and runs it through four separate tests:

- ❏ Removes all escape sequences
- ❏ Removes all safe values (true, false, null, carriage return, and so forth)
- ❏ Removes all opening square brackets
- ❏ Verifies if any special characters exist in the remaining string that could cause it to be invalid JSON

Note that step three allows arrays to pass through because they are a valid part of the JSON spec (RFC 4627), even though they are vulnerable to exploits. This is where the responsibility falls on the developer to make sure that the data being passed to the client is secure, and that may require the omission of arrays.

Here is an example of an invalid string of JSON causing isValid to return false:

```
var foo = YAHOO.lang.JSON.isValid("{'foo': 'bar'}");
```

Here's an example a valid string of JSON causing isValid to return true:

```
var foo = YAHOO.lang.JSON.isValid('{"foo": "bar"}');
```

Notice the difference? Even though JavaScript isn't picky about single versus double quote use, JSON is. Even though YUI is parsing the JSON data in JavaScript, JSON isn't limited to JavaScript and so its rules are stricter than those of JavaScript. For example, the name component of the name/value pair needs to be a string in JSON even though object literals don't require them to be in JavaScript. Likewise, strings in JSON are denoted with double quotes.

parse

The traditional way to convert a string of JSON data into a usable JavaScript object is to pass the string through eval. This, as touched on earlier, is highly dangerous as the string could contain malicious code. So the thing to do is to pass it through a validator to make sure that the data is legit. Of course, that extra step is error prone since the developer may forget to validate the data before running it through eval. Enter parse. The parse method first checks to see if the string that it's about to eval is clean by running it through isValid. If it's deemed valid JSON, it then gets run through eval. As an added bonus, the resulting object is passed through a user-defined filter function. This filter is optional and allows for the post-processing of the newly converted JSON data.

So, here's a chunk of JSON data that's ready to be parsed:

```
{
 "author": "Ara Pehlivanian",
 "version": "2.1.3",
 "status": "release",
 "pubDate": "2008-04-07",
 "content": "Lorem ipsum dolor sit amet, consectetuer adipiscing elit. Donec
     fermentum, neque et ultrices dignissim, est est scelerisque erat, sed
     ornare nisl orci quis tellus. Donec quis lacus quis nibh consectetuer dictum.
     Duis fermentum, ligula condimentum congue bibendum, dui dolor vehicula lorem,
     sed congue nisl tellus id diam. Sed nulla sem, lacinia vel, ullamcorper at,
     auctor ut, dolor. Praesent turpis quam, posuere a, posuere sed, fermentum
     eu, risus. Integer luctus. Maecenas dolor. Donec vehicula."
}
```

The following code parses and filters the preceding JSON data:

```html
<html>
    <head>
            <title>JSON parse</title>
    </head>
    <body>
        <h1>JSON parse</h1>
        <ul id="output"></ul>
        <script src="yahoo-dom-event.js"></script>
        <script src="connection-min.js"></script>
        <script src="json-min.js"></script>
        <script>
            YAHOO.namespace("example.ProJSFrameworks.lang.JSON");
            YAHOO.example.ProJSFrameworks.lang.JSON = function () {
                function versionFilter(key, val) {
                    if (key === "version") {
                        return undefined;
                    } else {
                        return val;
                    }
                };
                var callback = {
                    success: function (o) {
                        var parsed = YAHOO.lang.JSON.parse(
                                o.responseText, versionFilter);
                        var output = YAHOO.util.Dom.get("output");
                        for (var key in parsed) {
                            if (parsed.hasOwnProperty(key)) {
                                var li = document.createElement("li");
                                var strong = document.createElement("strong");
                                strong.appendChild(
                                        document.createTextNode(key + ": "));
                                li.appendChild(strong);
                                li.appendChild(
                                        document.createTextNode(parsed[key]));
                                output.appendChild(li);
                            }
                        }
                    }
                };
                var transaction = YAHOO.util.Connect.asyncRequest(
                        'GET', 'lang-json2.json', callback);
            }();
        </script>
    </body>
</html>
```

This code example is very straightforward. It consists of an asynchronous transaction that loads the JSON data from a file named `lang-json2.json`. It then calls the `success` callback function where it parses the returned data found in the `responseText` property of the returned object. Once the JSON data is parsed, it gets run through the `versionFilter` function, which filters out the object's `version` name/value pair.

It's very important to note that the filter function needs to return a value. That's because the `parse` function will remove any node from the original JSON data that receives a value of `undefined` from the `filter` function. So if the node is to be untouched, the `filter` function must return the same value it received.

Once the data has been converted from a string to an object and filtered, it's simply iterated over with a `for in` loop and output to an unordered list in the page.

Dynamically Loading Libraries and Components

Performance is becoming a hot topic in JavaScript circles these days, largely because of the fact that more and more web applications are being written in the language. No longer is JavaScript being used only for simple script tricks on a web page. Nowadays, with desktop applications migrating to the browser, a need for optimally written JavaScript is becoming crucial. One technique to increase performance or the perception of performance is the idea of lazy loading. This is a technique whereby the loading of needed components is deferred to the moment they are actually needed. That way, if a component is never used, the burden of downloading and executing its dependencies is alighted from the page. Another technique for improving performance is to reduce the number of HTTP requests that a page makes. Excluding the actual data transfer, each request still takes a few moments to be made. And, depending on network conditions and server load, those moments can be significant and can add up to a perceivable slowdown. To this end, compressing and combining resources into "aggregate" files allows for the reduction of the number of HTTP requests that a page makes.

Get Utility

YUI offers the Get Utility, which allows for the loading of script and CSS files on the fly. This allows for the ability to load components at the moment that they're needed, instead of on page load in anticipation of their use. It also allows for the loading of cross domain data, which isn't possible through the Connection Utility since `XMLHttpRequest` (XHR) adheres to a strict same-origin policy.

The XHR same-origin policy assumes that only scripts that originate from the same server from which the page was loaded can be trusted. This is both a benefit and a hindrance. The benefit is obviously in the protection that it brings by limiting the possibility of third-party scripts being injected into a site. The hindrance, however, is being felt more and more these days with the advent of third-party APIs and subsequent *mash-ups* of the data that they provide. It isn't possible, for example, to open an XHR connection to a third-party data source. The only way to do so is via a proxy so that the same-origin policy is respected. Setting up proxies isn't always possible. The Get Utility bypasses the same-origin policy altogether by dynamically inserting new script tags into the page that aren't constrained by the same policy. This allows the utility to load scripts from any domain it wants.

> *The Get Utility should* **never** *be used to load JavaScript files from untrusted sources. Any script that's loaded via the Get Utility will execute with* **full** *privileges and cannot be filtered as JSON data can via the Connection Utility.*

The Get Utility goes further than just dumping a `script` or CSS `link` tag into the page. It provides a transaction wrapper that allows for the assigning of callback functions on success and failure, as well as the ability to define the scope in which those functions will execute. It allows for an array of filenames to be passed to it so that one call to Get will load many files. It allows for the targeting of a window into which the `script` or `link` tag is to be loaded. It allows for the specifying of a global variable that it will poll and only advance when it becomes available (this is particularly important in the case of Safari 2.x, which doesn't trigger a loaded event for new script and link tags added to the page). Finally, it allows for the tags to be automatically purged after they're written to the document. This is good for script tags because once they're executed; their code becomes available in memory even after the tag is removed. CSS link tags, however, provide a live link to the style sheet and the moment they're removed, the rules they provided are also removed and the page layout changes accordingly.

The two main methods that Get Utility provides to load dependencies are `script` and `css`:

```
YAHOO.util.Get.script("wrox.js");
YAHOO.util.Get.css("wrox.css");
```

The methods are identical in form and only differ in the tags that they output. Each can receive optional parameters. Here's an example of a fully loaded `script` method:

```
function successHandler(o) {
    // do something
};
function failureHandler(o) {
    // do something
};
var newWin = window.open("/ProJSFrameworks/newPage.html");
YAHOO.util.Get.script("wrox.js", {
    onSuccess: successHandler,
    onFailure: failureHandler,
    win: newWin, // window to insert script into
    scope: newWin, // scope of event handler
    data: "Hello World!", // arbitrary data to pass the event handler
    varName: ["wroxReady"], // var to check in wrox.js to call handler in Safari 2
    autoPurge: true
});
```

This code fragment loads `wrox.js` into the page `newPage.html`, which is opened in a new window. Once that page loads, the Get Utility looks for the availability of the variable named `wroxReady` and then fires its `onSuccess` callback function.

Callback functions can be assigned for two different events, `onSuccess` and `onFailure`. The callback function receives an object containing a unique identifier for the transaction (`tId`), a custom Data object allowing for the passing of arbitrary data to the callback function (`data`), an array of the nodes created by the Get Utility method (`nodes`), a reference to the Window object in which they were created (`win`), and a purge method allowing for the removal of the nodes that were just created (`purge`).

It's important to note that in the case of a loaded script, the tag is purged but the script remains in memory since it's already executed. For CSS however, once the tag is removed, so are the style rules, which will be reflected in the page right away.

The following is a simpler example of Get Utility in action:

```html
<html>
    <head>
        <title>Get Utility</title>
    </head>
    <body>
        <h1>Get Utility</h1>
        <script src="yahoo-min.js"></script>
        <script src="get-min.js"></script>
        <script>
            YAHOO.namespace("example.ProJSFrameworks.get");
            YAHOO.example.ProJSFrameworks.get = function () {
                var successHandler = function (o) {
                    var h1 = YAHOO.util.Selector.query("h1")[0];
                    var txt = document.createTextNode(o.data);
                    h1.insertBefore(txt, h1.firstChild);
                };
                var failureHandler = function (o) {
                    alert("Failed to load Selector Utility");
                };
                var transaction = YAHOO.util.Get.script("selector-min.js", {
                        onSuccess: successHandler,
                        onFailure: failureHandler,
                        data: "The YUI "
                    });
            }();
        </script>
    </body>
</html>
```

The practical purpose that this script serves is to defer the use of the Selector Utility until after it has been dynamically loaded. The Get.script method fetches the selector-min.js file and only after it has loaded does it fire the successHandler function. Inside successHandler it's assumed that the desired JavaScript file has loaded successfully and is therefore safe to execute the Selector.query method. The query gets the page's first h1 tag, creates a text node with text passed through the data property, and prepends it to the h1's existing text. The result is an h1 tag whose contents change from "Get Utility" to "The YUI Get Utility."

YUI Loader Utility

The YUI Get Utility allows for the loading of external script and CSS files on the fly. But in the case of loading YUI files, there is something to take into consideration. Most YUI files have dependencies on other files and need to be loaded in a specific sequence in order to work. With a growing list of components and multiple dependencies per se, it gets to be a challenge remembering each components' individual requirements. This gets even more complicated when there are multiple YUI components in a page, or slider, panel and auto-complete, where each component has its own requirements and shares at least some with another component.

Finally, YUI provides rolled-up, or aggregate files. These are files consisting of the most commonly used set of files all rolled up into one. The reason for this is performance. One of the performance rules put forth by the Yahoo! Exceptional Performance team is to reduce the number of HTTP requests that a page makes. Rolling up the yahoo.js, dom.js, and event.js files into one and minimizing them at the same time (to reduce file size) makes for a more efficient implementation of three of the most commonly required YUI components.

The YUI Loader is a utility that loads YUI components on the fly. It is aware of each of the library's multiple components and their dependencies and is also aware of all of the rolled-up resources so as to be able to choose the optimal combination of files when loading a component. It can detect the parts of YUI that are already loaded so that it doesn't try and wastefully reload existing components.

Using the YUI Loader is very straightforward. A new YUILoader object is instantiated with the parameters telling it what parts of the YUI to load and how to load them. This line, for example, loads container.js as well as its dependencies and optional dependencies.

```
var loader = new YAHOO.util.YUILoader({require: [container], loadOptional: true});
```

Here is a list of all of the YUI components that the YUI Loader is aware of and the names by which they're called. The name value is passed to the require array, which then goes and loads the necessary file as well as its dependencies. If loadOptional is set to true, then the optional dependencies are also loaded. Of course, as mentioned earlier, if a particular dependency happens to already be loaded (such as dom or event), then they aren't loaded again.

Module Name	File	Dependencies	Optional
animation	animation-min.js	dom, event	
autocomplete	autocomplete-min.js	dom, event	connection, animation
base	base-min.css		
button	button-min.js	Element	menu
calendar	calendar-min.js	event, dom	
charts	charts-experimental-min.js	element, json, datasource	
colorpicker	colorpicker-min.js	slider, element	animation
connection	connection-min.js	Event	
container	container-min.js	dom, event	dragdrop, animation, connection
containercore	container_core-min.js	dom, event	
cookie	cookie-beta-min.js	Yahoo	
datasource	datasource-beta-min.js	Event	connection

Module Name	File	Dependencies	Optional
datatable	datatable-beta-min.js	element, datasource	calendar, dragdrop
dom	dom-min.js	Yahoo	
dragdrop	dragdrop-min.js	dom, event	
editor	editor-beta-min.js	menu, element, button	animation, dragdrop
element	element-beta-min.js	dom, event	
event	event-min.js	Yahoo	
fonts	fonts-min.css		
get	get-min.js	Yahoo	
grids	grids-min.css	Fonts	reset
history	history-min.js	Event	
imagecropper	imagecropper-beta-min.js	dom, event, dragdrop, element, resize	
imageloader	imageloader-min.js	event, dom	
json	json-min.js	Yahoo	
layout	layout-beta-min.js	dom, event, element	animation, dragdrop, resize, selector
logger	logger-min.js	event, dom	dragdrop
menu	menu-min.js	containercore	
profiler	profiler-beta-min.js	Yahoo	
profilerviewer	profilerviewer-beta-min.js	yuiloader, element	
reset	reset-min.css		
reset-fonts-grids	reset-fonts-reset-fonts-grids.css		
reset-fonts	reset-reset-fonts.css		
resize	resize-beta-min.js	dom, event, dragdrop, element	animation
selector	selector-beta-min.js	yahoo, dom	

(continued)

Module Name	File	Dependencies	Optional
simpleeditor	simpleeditor-beta-min.js	Element	containercore, menu, button, animation, dragdrop
slider	slider-min.js	Dragdrop	animation
tabview	tabview-min.js	Element	connection
treeview	treeview-min.js	Event	
uploader	uploader-experimental.js	Yahoo	
utilities	utilities.js		
yahoo	yahoo-min.js		
yahoo-dom-event	yahoo-dom-yahoo-dom-event.js		
yuiloader	yuiloader-beta-min.js		
Yuitest	yuitest-min.js	Logger	

Here is an example of YUI Loader fetching style sheets and the container component and then building a panel once all of the necessary components are done loading.

```html
<html>
    <head>
        <title>YUI Loader</title>
    </head>
    <body class="yui-skin-sam">
        <h1>YUI Loader</h1>
        <script src="yuiloader-beta-min.js"></script>
        <script>
            YAHOO.namespace("example.ProJSFrameworks.yuiloader");
            YAHOO.example.ProJSFrameworks.yuiloader = function () {
                var loader = new YAHOO.util.YUILoader({
                    require: ['reset-fonts', 'base', 'container'],
                    loadOptional: true,
                    onSuccess: function () {
                        var pnl = new YAHOO.widget.Panel("hello", {
                            visible: true,
                            modal: true,
                            fixedcenter: true,
                            close: true
                        });
```

```
                                pnl.setHeader("Hello World");
                                pnl.setBody(
                                    "The code for this panel was dynamically loaded");
                                pnl.render(document.body);
                            }
                        });
                        loader.insert();
                    }();
            </script>
        </body>
    </html>
```

The entirety of this program resides in the parameters passed to the YUILoader constructor. Note the onSuccess handler. Of course, this could point to a named function, but in this case an anonymous function is provided inline. Within it, a new panel is created and given some contents. This of course would not have been possible to do prior to YUI Loader's downloading and loading the necessary components.

It's also possible to load non-YUI modules using the YUI Loader via the addModule method.

```
var loader = new YAHOO.util.YUILoader(/* some params here */);
loader.addModule({
    name: "formValidator",
    type: "js",
    fullpath: "http://domain.com/js/form-validator.js",
    varName: "FORMVALIDATOR",
    requires: ['yahoo-dom-event']
});
```

The object literal being passed to addModule is actually the exact same syntax that is used internally by YUI Loader to define its own modules. The name value must be unique and not the same as any of the existing YUI component names. The type tells the Loader what sort of tag to write to the DOM, CSS, or JavaScript. The fullPath value points to the file to be loaded, and varName is a global variable name polled by the Loader in Safari 2.x and older to determine whether or not the module has completed loading.

Also, if the module doesn't belong to a third party, thus being inaccessible, then the YAHOO.register method can be used instead of varName. This is the method by which all YUI components register themselves within the library. Since the register method is called as the last line of code within a module, it does the job of notifying YUI that the module is complete, thus eliminating the need for varName.

Here is an example of YAHOO.register taken directly from the code of connection.js.

```
YAHOO.register("connection",YAHOO.util.Connect, {version: "2.5.0", build: "895"});
```

New in YUI 3

The Connection Manager has been rewritten in YUI 3. It's known as IO and the major difference from its predecessor is that it now supports cross-domain requests or XDR. In order to do this it leverages the ability of Flash to make XDR calls. Also, a cross-domain policy file needs to be deployed to the resource site where the request is being directed. Otherwise the transaction will fail. Finally, YUI 3 splits up IO into smaller chunks so that only what's needed can be loaded rather than the whole utility.

Summary

Gone are the days when JavaScript simply loaded with the main HTTP request and then acted only as the source of a little embellishment on a page. Nowadays, JavaScript is being used to fetch data, dependencies, and even more JavaScript. It's being used to make smaller post-load HTTP requests to the server, and it's being used to dynamically change functionality and contents of a page even after the first HTTP payload has been delivered. YUI's suite of utilities not only normalizes cross-browser issues in this space but goes a long way in extending the baseline functionality provided by the language. It lays a solid foundation for advanced web application development, the likes of which couldn't have even been conceived of just a few years ago.

11

Building User Interfaces with Widgets (Part I)

Since its inception, users of the Web have wanted the same richness they found on the desktop reflected in web sites. The difficulty in delivering such a rich user interface on the Web is that its technologies were never designed with that purpose in mind. The Web's original intention was to deliver linked scientific documents, hence the hyperlink and the name *web*.

It wasn't long after it was created, however, that people were trying to make web pages look prettier. As the web gained in popularity and started hitting more and more desktops, the desire to be able to do more with a web page also grew. It was no longer enough to just have some colored text of varying sizes and a smattering of links. Soon interactivity became a focus, which sparked the creation of Java applets and soon after, the creation of JavaScript (no relation) by Brendan Eich at Netscape. Of course, this was in the time of the so-called browser wars of the mid 1990s, so naturally Microsoft followed suit with JScript, which was essentially a copy of JavaScript, and though it was nearly identical, there were some differences, and the DOM on which both of the browsers acted was also slightly different. To this day, differences exist between browsers, making any serious effort at adding JavaScript to a web page a very circumspect and pragmatic exercise.

Taking into account the hostile environment of the browser, YUI provides several professional-grade, cross-browser components under the `YAHOO.widget` namespace that drag the notion of interactivity in the browser kicking and screaming into the 21st century.

In this chapter, you'll learn about:

- ❑ Using AutoComplete
- ❑ Building containers
- ❑ Using tabs and trees

Using AutoComplete with Form Fields

Forms are a fundamental building block of the Web, second only to hyperlinks. As is well known, forms take the data within their fields and post them to the server. Unfortunately, that's about where the evolution of the form ended — where it started.

The practices of usability and user interaction design, on the other hand, have continued to evolve, and one of the things they've introduced is auto-completion. As great an idea as this may be, it hasn't been formally integrated into the prevailing "specs" that browser makers follow. So it's up to libraries such as YUI to go ahead and fill the gap.

AutoComplete and DataSource

In order for YUI's `AutoComplete` to make any suggestions, it needs to have a data source. That way it can check the value of the input field against a data set and make suggestions accordingly. `AutoComplete` is actually quite versatile allowing for connections to be made to arrays, functions, `XMLHttpRequest`, and `script` nodes.

The four types of data sources are defined as four subclasses that extend the `YAHOO.util.DataSourceBase` class: `LocalDataSource`, `FunctionDataSource`, `ScriptNodeDataSource`, and `XHRDataSource`.

Here's an example of how to set up an array as a data source:

```
var data = [
    "Rock", "Rocket", "Rockets", "Rocket Man", "Rocketeer",
    "Rocketing", "Rocks", "Rocky", "Rocky and Bullwinkle"
];

var dataSource = new YAHOO.util.LocalDataSource(data);
```

Once the data source has been created, it can then be passed to the `AutoComplete` constructor. Here's what that would look like:

```
var autoComplete = new YAHOO.widget.AutoComplete(inputEl, resultsEl, dataSource);
```

The `AutoComplete` constructor requires three parameters: an input field on which to bind itself, a `div` element where results are output, and a data source. Here's a functional example of the preceding code:

```
<html>
    <head>
        <title>AutoComplete</title>
        <link rel="stylesheet" type="text/css" href="reset-fonts-grids.css" />
        <link rel="stylesheet" type="text/css" href="base-min.css" />
        <link rel="stylesheet" type="text/css"
                href="autocomplete/assets/skins/sam/autocomplete.css" />
        <style type="text/css">
            #autocomplete {
                width: 20em;
                height: 1.5em;
```

```
            }
            label,
            #autocomplete,
            #search {
                float: left;
            }
        </style>
    </head>
    <body class="yui-skin-sam">
        <div id="doc">
            <div id="hd">
                <h1>AutoComplete</h1>
            </div>
            <div id="bd">
                <form method="get" action="http://search.yahoo.com/search">
                    <label for="p">Search for:</label>
                    <div id="autocomplete">
                        <input type="text" id="p" />
                        <div id="results"></div>
                    </div>
                    <input type="submit" value="Search!" id="submit" />
                </form>
            </div>
            <div id="ft">
            </div>
        </div>

        <script src="build/yahoo-dom-event/yahoo-dom-event.js"></script>
        <script src="build/datasource/datasource-min.js"></script>
        <script src="build/autocomplete/autocomplete-min.js"></script>
        <script>
        (function () {
            var data = [
                "Rock", "Rocket", "Rockets", "Rocket Man", "Rocketeer",
                "Rocketing", "Rocks", "Rocky", "Rocky and Bullwinkle"
            ];

            var dataSource = new YAHOO.util.LocalDataSource(data);
            var autoComplete = new YAHOO.widget.AutoComplete(
                    "p", "results", dataSource);
        })();
        </script>
    </body>
</html>
```

Note that the AutoComplete utility requires that both the input field and the results div be wrapped by a parent div element. This is done so that the results div is properly placed underneath the input field. Essentially, when the AutoComplete utility binds itself to the input field, it assigns the yui-ac class name to the wrapper div. This causes the wrapper's position to be set to relative in order to contain the results div, which is subsequently set to absolute via the yui-ac-container class name. The rules for these class names are defined in autocomplete.css, which comes with YUI.

The only CSS file required for this example to work is `autocomplete.css`. The others just facilitate the page's layout. Even then, `autocomplete.css` simply dresses up the auto-complete widget as it were. In reality the functionality comes from the code found in `autocomplete-min.js` and `datasource-min.js`. Once these dependencies are in place, instantiating an auto-complete widget is as simple as writing a couple of lines of code.

Figure 11-1 shows what the auto-complete widget looks like in action.

Figure 11-1

Of course, in the case of a search example, it would make more sense to bind the auto-complete widget to a live search engine. As mentioned earlier, `AutoComplete` offers multiple ways to connect to a data source. The seemingly obvious choice in this situation would be to use `XMLHttpRequest` (or `XHR`) except for one major problem: `XHR`'s "same origin" policy. The same origin policy is a security restriction voluntarily put in place by browser vendors in order to protect against cross-site scripting attacks. The idea is that if JavaScript is restricted to only be able to communicate with the server from which its own code originated, the chances of malicious (hijacked) JavaScript sending data to a rogue server can be drastically reduced. But this is a situation where strict security measures actually impede legitimate needs for cross-domain communication. Case in point, only a script originating from the Yahoo! Search domain can access Yahoo! Search via XHR. In order for a third party to access a Yahoo! Search web service, a proxy would need to be put in place. The proxy (a program running on the back-end server) would access the Yahoo! web service, get the response, and then pass it off to the JavaScript. This is cumbersome and a pain. Luckily, both of YUI's DataSource utilities offer an alternative technique to connect to a foreign server via the script tag. Though XHR is restricted, script tags can load JavaScript files from anywhere on the Internet. This sort of freedom comes with the caveat that the data source being accessed needs to be fully trusted. Otherwise, connecting blindly to third-party servers could open a giant security hole in any web application.

YUI uses the Get Utility (described in the previous chapter) under the hood when connecting to scripts via script tags. This ensures uniformity and robust management of dynamically created script tags. Since all of the nitty-gritty is already taken care of, the implementation becomes trivial.

```
<script src="build/yahoo-dom-event/yahoo-dom-event.js"></script>
<script src="build/datasource/datasource-min.js"></script>
<script src="build/autocomplete/autocomplete-min.js"></script>
<script>
    (function () {
        var dataSource = new YAHOO.util.ScriptNodeDataSource(
                "http://search.yahooapis.com/WebSearchService/V1/" +
                "webSearch?appid=YahooDemo&results=10&output=json");
            dataSource.responseSchema = {
                resultsList: "ResultSet.Result",
                fields: ["Title"]
            };
        var autoComplete = new YAHOO.widget.AutoComplete(
                "p", "results", dataSource);
    })();
</script>
```

The two things that change from the prior example are the instantiation of a ScriptNodeDataSource data source as opposed to the prior LocalDataSource as well as the addition of a response schema property. Otherwise, everything else remains the same. Note that the parameter output=json is being passed to the Yahoo! Search API. This specifies that the Yahoo! Search engine is to return results in a JSON string. Of course, DataSource has no way of knowing where to find the results within that object. What it needs is a schema to tell it where to find each result and which property of each result to match its AutoComplete query on.

The parameter that the ScriptNodeDataSource constructor takes is the address of the data source. Next, a schema is assigned to it so that it knows where to find the desired data in the payload it receives:

```
dataSource.responseSchema = {
    resultsList: "ResultSet.Result",
    fields: ["Title"]
};
```

This tells `DataSource` that the root node of the data set is named `ResultSet` and that the results can be found in a node named `Result`. It also tells it to match its queries on a property of each result named `Title`. Here is a sample of the data sent back by the Yahoo! Search API that this schema is defining (data is purposefully truncated with an ellipsis (. . .) for layout reasons):

```
{
  "ResultSet":{
        "type":"web",
        "totalResultsAvailable":26700000,
        "totalResultsReturned":10,
        "firstResultPosition":1,
        "moreSearch":"\/WebSearchService\/V1\/webSearch?query=yui&amp;appid=Ya...",
        "Result":[
            {
                "Title":"The Yahoo! User Interface Library (YUI)",
                "Summary":"The YUI Library also includes several core CSS...",
                "Url":"http:\/\/developer.yahoo.com\/yui\/",
                "ClickUrl":"http:\/\/uk.wrs.yahoo.com\/_ylt=A9iby40zEihIIDEAdS...",
                "DisplayUrl":"developer.yahoo.com\/yui\/",
                "ModificationDate":1209798000,
                "MimeType":"text\/html",
                "Cache":{
                    "Url":"http:\/\/uk.wrs.yahoo.com\/_ylt=A9iby40zEihIIDEAdiz...",
                    "Size":"29225"
                }
            },
            {
                "Title":"Yui - Wikipedia, the free encyclopedia",
                "Summary":"Yui (tribe), a small historical Native American tri...",
```

The data that is displayed within the auto-complete widget's results pane comes from the `Title` property. It could just as easily come from the `DisplayUrl` property were the schema defined like so:

```
dataSource.responseSchema = {
    "ResultSet.Result",
    fields: ["DisplayUrl"]
};
```

Figure 11-2 shows what the auto-complete widget looks like in action when it's plugged into the Yahoo! Search API.

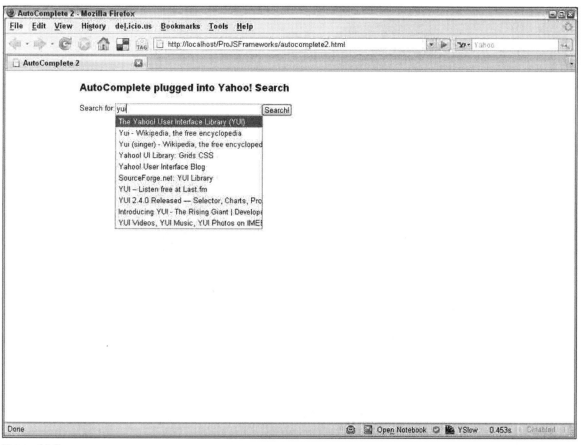

Figure 11-2

Building Containers for Content

A div is a div, is a div, right? Well, if it remains a static div, then yes. However, it is possible for a div to behave more like an interactive module than simply a static DOM element. YUI's Container family of controls provides a set of containers ranging from the complex *SimpleDialog* (A) all the way down to the simplest *Module* (B), both of which are identified in Figure 11-3.

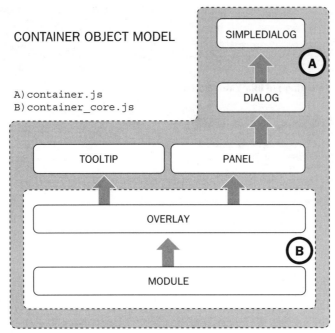

CONTAINER OBJECT MODEL

A) `container.js`
B) `container_core.js`

Figure 11-3

Note how there are two foundation classes, *Module* and *Overlay*, which are available in the lighter `container_core.js` file. Those two, along with the rest of the classes, are also available in the heavier `container.js` file. Note also that if `container.js` is in use, then `container_core.js` is not necessary.

A Container can be built in two possible ways, either from markup or purely from JavaScript. Both have their uses. Sometimes the contents of a Container need to be present in the HTML for search engine indexing or graceful degradation. Other times, the contents of the Container would make no sense without the presence of JavaScript, so generating the Container using nothing but JavaScript makes the most sense.

Module

The `Module` control is a foundational component upon which other controls are built. `Module` is hardly ever used as a standalone control, as its main purpose is to serve as a base on which other controls are built. In its simplest form, the markup for `Module` looks like this:

```
<div id="foo">
    <div class="hd"></div>
    <div class="bd"></div>
    <div class="ft"></div>
</div>
```

Note the class names; this is a recurring nomenclature pattern in YUI where hd represents a header, bd represents a body, and ft represents a footer. Instantiating a Module object based on this markup looks like this:

```
var module = new YAHOO.widget.Module("foo");
```

The markup doesn't need to be present for Module to work. If the ID that is passed to the constructor doesn't point to an element in the DOM, Module will create one and assign *it* the ID that it was passed. However, the new element won't be added to the DOM that requires Module's render method:

```
module.render(document.body);
```

Note the parameter being passed to the render method. This tells Module to render itself as a child of the document's body element. Either a direct reference to (such as in the preceding example) or a string representing an ID of an element can be passed as a parameter. If this parameter is omitted, the render method fails and returns the value false.

To Insert or to Append

As discussed in Chapter 8 (under the "onDOMReady" heading), Internet Explorer suffers from a pretty critical problem when content is added to the DOM prior to it being ready. This happens specifically when the appendChild DOM method is used to append an element to the end of document's body from a script node that is not an immediate child of body. In order to circumvent this issue when Module is built purely via JavaScript, it defaults to adding its contents to the beginning of the body using the YUI insertBefore method.

However, if appendChild is desired because it is determined that it won't cause any problems in IE, then Module's behavior can be changed easily enough through a configuration property passed to the constructor.

```
var module = new YAHOO.widget.Module("foo", {appendtodocumentbody: true});
```

Showing and Hiding

A Module can be set to start out either visible or hidden. That way, if there is content that needs to be hidden from view until a "show" button is clicked, it can be. The default value for the visible parameter is therefore true. In other words, an instance of a Module by default is visible when rendered. It can however be overridden through a parameter passed to the constructor.

```
var module = new YAHOO.widget.Module("foo", {visible: false});
```

Once a Module object is instantiated, showing and hiding it is as simple as calling its show and hide methods.

```
// Instantiate a hidden module
var module = new YAHOO.widget.Module("foo", {visible: false});

// Show the module
module.show();

// Now hide it
module.hide();
```

The Configuration Object — Hidden Gem

Hidden inside the `Module` control, and therefore inherited by all of the other container controls, is the configuration object. The configuration object is a powerful, yet unadvertised component of YUI whose main purpose is to act as overseer of its parent object's properties. It allows for the properties to have default values, to be queued and applied all at once at a given moment, to be reset, and for changes to them to be detected triggering custom events. In `Module`, and therefore all other container controls, the configuration object is named `cfg` and is an immediate child object of the container object.

```
// The configuration object
module.cfg
```

setProperty

So for example, showing or hiding a module is as simple as setting a `true` or `false` value for the `visible` property via the configuration object. This is actually exactly what the `show` and `hide` module methods do.

```
// Instantiate a hidden module
var module = new YAHOO.widget.Module("foo", {visible: false});

// Show the module
module.cfg.setProperty("visible", true);

// Now hide it
module.cfg.setProperty("visible", false);
```

getProperty

Retrieving values is just as straightforward. So the following line of code is used in order to verify whether the module is visible:

```
var isVisible = module.cfg.getProperty("visible");
```

In this case, the `visible` property returns a Boolean value.

Since the amount of configuration that is possible with a Module is limited, more of the configuration object's capabilities are explored in the coming parts on more complex containers.

Overlay

An `Overlay` is an enhanced `Module`. The Overlay control is the first useful container control in that it can be implemented out of the box without the need for any additional programming. Where the `Module` control was quite limited in capability, Overlay offers a bunch of useful properties and methods.

Positioning

For starters, an Overlay control can be positioned via its X, Y, and XY properties (note that positioning values are given in pixels unless specifically noted):

```
// Instantiate an Overlay
var overlay = new YAHOO.widget.Overlay("foo");

// Set the overlay's x position to 250
overlay.cfg.setProperty("x", 250);

// Set the overlay's y position to 100
overlay.cfg.setProperty("y", 100);

// Set both x and y positions at the same time
overlay.cfg.setProperty("xy", [250, 100]);
```

Rather than specifying coordinates, an Overlay can be auto-centered either through the center method or by setting the value of the configuration object's fixedcenter property to true.

Here's how to call the center method:

```
overlay.center();
```

Here's how to set the fixedcenter property:

```
overlay.cfg.setProperty("fixedcenter", true);
```

It's important to note that the center method tells the Overlay to center itself *once*, whereas fixedcenter tells it to maintain its centered position *continually*, even when the browser window size is changed or the page is scrolled.

Another way to position an Overlay without coordinates is by anchoring it to an element in the page via the context property.

```
overlay.cfg.setProperty("context", ["hd", "tl", "br"]);
```

Here, the overlay is being told to anchor its top-left corner (tl) to the bottom-right corner (br) of the element with the ID hd.

Panel

Here is where the Container object really gets interesting. In a time where pop-ups are anathema, being able to rapidly deploy a "faux pop-up" is invaluable. As with the previous two examples, instantiating a new Panel object is as simple as writing the following line of code:

```
var panel = new YAHOO.widget.Panel("foo");
```

Since Panel is simply an extension of Overlay, the same API structure can be expected. In other words, the first parameter is the ID of the element that contains the contents to be displayed in the Panel, or it's the ID to assign to the Panel when it is created dynamically. The second parameter is an object containing user-configurable key value pairs that override the Panel's default configuration values.

```
var config = {
    close: true,
    draggable: true,
    underlay: shadow,
    height: "250px",
    fixedcenter: true,
    modal: true
};
var panel = new YAHOO.widget.Panel("foo", config);
```

Panel also introduces support key listeners to the Container family. With Panel, it's possible to assign keyboard shortcut support that would directly influence the behavior of the Panel. So for example, here's how to assign the Esc key to a Panel so that when it is pressed, the Panel closes.

```
<html>
    <head>
        <title>Container--Panel</title>
        <link rel="stylesheet" type="text/css" href="reset-fonts-grids.css" />
        <link rel="stylesheet" type="text/css" href="base-min.css" />
        <link rel="stylesheet" type="text/css"
            href="container/assets/skins/sam/container.css">
    </head>
    <body class="yui-skin-sam">
        <div id="doc">
            <div id="hd">
                <h1>Container--Panel</h1>
                <p>Hello world, this page contains a modal YUI Panel with a
                close button which also happens to be fixed to the center of
                the viewport.</p>
                <p>Note: Pressing the <kbd>Esc</kbd> key also closes the Panel.</p>
            </div>
            <div id="bd">
                <div id="foo">
                    <div class="hd">Foo Header (from markup)</div>
                    <div class="bd">Foo Body</div>
                    <div class="ft">Foo Footer</div>
                </div>
            </div>
            <div id="ft">
            </div>
        </div>
        <script src="yahoo-dom-event.js"></script>
        <script src="animation-min.js"></script>
        <script src="dragdrop-min.js"></script>
        <script src="container-min.js"></script>
```

```
<script>
    (function () {
        // Instantiate and render a Panel from markup
        //   (panel is deliberately global to break out of sandbox)

        var config = {
            close: true,
            width: "300px",
            fixedcenter: true,
            modal: true
        };
        panel = new YAHOO.widget.Panel("foo", config);

        var keylistener = new YAHOO.util.KeyListener(
                document,
                {keys: 27},
                {fn: panel.hide, scope: panel, correctScope: true});

        panel.cfg.queueProperty("keylisteners", keylistener);

        panel.render();
    })();
</script>
</body>
</html>
```

Here, a Panel is instantiated and passed an object named config containing some custom parameters defining its behavior. After the Panel object is created, a KeyListener is instantiated and told to listen to the Esc key. It's assigned the Panel object's hide method as a callback function. This way, whenever the Esc key is pressed, the Panel gets hidden.

At first it would seem to make sense to simply include the keylistener object to the Panel via the object named config. That isn't possible in this case however, since KeyListener requires a reference to a function to execute and that function wouldn't exist prior to the Panel's instantiation. So what needs to be done is to first instantiate a Panel object, then use it as a reference for the instantiation of the KeyListener object, and then pass it back to the Panel, this time via the queueProperty method.

True to its name, queueProperty queues up properties and fires them at key moments. In this case, when the panel object's render method is called, the keylistener object gets bound to the Panel.

Figure 11-4 shows what the preceding Panel looks like; note that the page behind the Panel isn't white. This is because the Panel was set to be modal, which means everything behind the panel is grayed out while it's active.

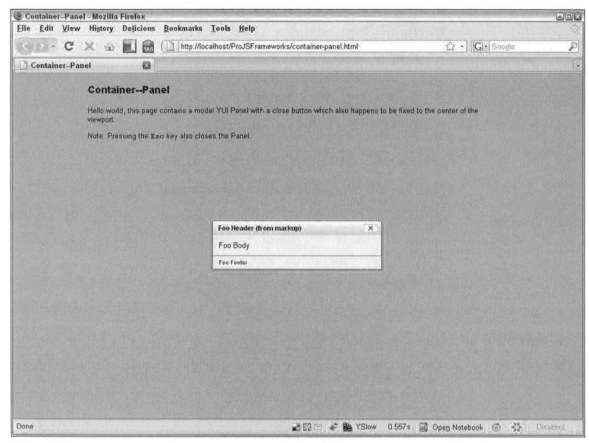

Figure 11-4

Presenting Content in Tabs and Trees

There's only so much real estate available on the screen, and when it's filled, it's filled. So it isn't always possible to display the entirety of the available information in one giant block. One of the most recognized ways of dealing with this shortage of space is to organize the information into smaller chunks and represent them with clickable headings. Clicking a heading reveals the hidden content and most often hides what was previously being viewed. In essence, the information now time-shares the available screen real estate. Two conventions for doing this are the TabView and the TreeView. The former is best suited to organize simple sets of information while the latter is capable of hierarchical organization.

TabView

There are times where the information that needs to be displayed is lengthy and scrolls for several page lengths. The trouble with this is that most people aren't going to read through it all and get overwhelmed at the mass of data being presented to them. To help them in their consumption, the page's contents can be broken up into smaller, more easily digestible chunks. Each chunk can then be represented by a tab, allowing them to cherry-pick what they want to read.

YUI makes both the conversion of existing page data into a TabView, as well as the creation of one purely in JavaScript, a piece of cake. The HTML structure of a TabView is very straightforward. The tabs are organized into an unordered list with each tab being a list item, while the content is separated into divs. Then, both are wrapped by a parent div.

A TabView from Markup

Here's an example of a TabView being created from markup:

```
<html>
    <head>
        <title>Container--Panel</title>
        <link rel="stylesheet" type="text/css" href="reset-fonts-grids.css" />
        <link rel="stylesheet" type="text/css" href="base-min.css" />
        <link rel="stylesheet" type="text/css"
            href="assets/skins/sam/tabview.css"/>
    </head>
    <body class="yui-skin-sam">
        <div id="doc">
            <div id="hd">
                <h1>TabView--Markup</h1>
            </div>
            <div id="bd">

                <!-- START TABVIEW MARKUP -->
                <div id="recipes" class="yui-navset">
                    <ul class="yui-nav">
                        <li>
                            <a href="#seafood">
                                <em>Seafood</em>
                            </a>
                        </li>
                        <li class="selected">
                            <a href="#bbq">
                                <em>BBQ</em>
                            </a>
                        </li>
                        <li>
                            <a href="#pasta">
                                <em>Pasta</em>
                            </a>
```

```
                    </li>
                </ul>
                <div class="yui-content">
                    <div id="seafood">
                        <p>Before you prepare any seafood you
                        need to go fishing!</p>
                    </div>
                    <div id="bbq">
                        <p>Fire up the grill, it's time to BBQ!</p>
                     </div>
                    <div id="pasta">
                        <p>Will it be spaghetti or lasagna?</p>
                    </div>
                </div>
            </div>
            <!-- END TABVIEW MARKUP -->

        </div>
        <div id="ft">
        </div>
    </div>
    <script src="yahoo-dom-event.js"></script>
    <script src="element-min.js"></script>
    <script src="tabview-min.js"></script>
    <script>
        (function () {
            var recipes = new YAHOO.widget.TabView("recipes");
        })();
    </script>
</body>
</html>
```

In fact the only class names that are required are yui-nav on the ul containing the tabs and yui-content on the div containing the content blocks. TabView automatically adds the yui-navset class name to the main div container. It also adds a second class name to the main div container named yui-navset-top.

Tab Orientation

The reason why TabView adds the class name yui-navset-top to the main div container by default is because TabView can be configured to display its tabs on any side of the content block. The class name serves as a hook to style the tabs according to the desired orientation. Here's how to change the TabView's orientation:

```
// tabs on top
var recipes = new YAHOO.widget.TabView("recipes", {orientation: "top"});

// tabs on right
var recipes = new YAHOO.widget.TabView("recipes", {orientation: "right"});

// tabs on bottom
var recipes = new YAHOO.widget.TabView("recipes", {orientation: "bottom"});

// tabs on left
var recipes = new YAHOO.widget.TabView("recipes", {orientation: "left"});
```

YUI comes with a built-in set of CSS rules for positioning and styling TabView for all of these orientations. The rules can be found in the `tabview.css` file found inside the `assets/skins/sam` folder. Figure 11-5, Figure 11-6, Figure 11-7, and Figure 11-8, respectively, show what all four orientations of TabView look like.

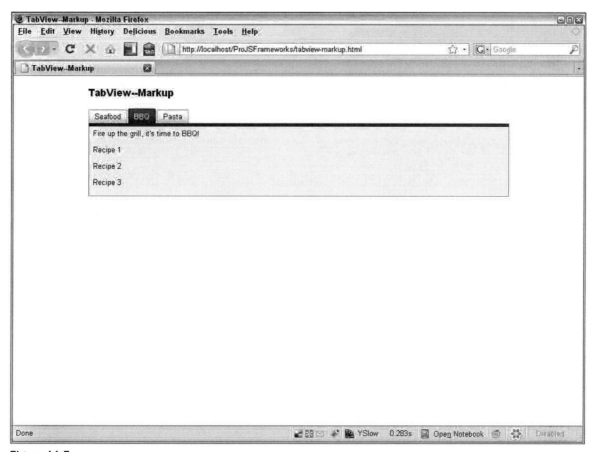

Figure 11-5

Figure 11-6

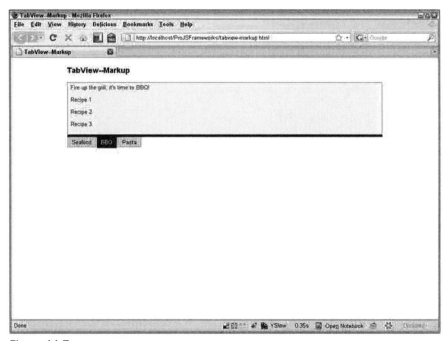

Figure 11-7

Figure 11-8

A TabView Purely from JavaScript

As mentioned earlier, a TabView can also be created entirely from JavaScript. Here's what that would look like:

```html
<html>
    <head>
        <title>TabView--JavaScript</title>
        <link rel="stylesheet" type="text/css" href="reset-fonts-grids.css" />
        <link rel="stylesheet" type="text/css" href="base-min.css" />
        <link rel="stylesheet" type="text/css"
            href="assets/skins/sam/tabview.css"/>
    </head>
    <body class="yui-skin-sam">
        <div id="doc">
            <div id="hd">
                <h1>TabView--JavaScript</h1>
            </div>
            <div id="bd">
                <div id="recipes"></div>
            </div>
            <div id="ft">
            </div>
        </div>
```

```
<script src="yahoo-dom-event.js"></script>
<script src="element-min.js"></script>
<script src="tabview-min.js"></script>
<script>
    (function () {
        var recipes = new YAHOO.widget.TabView("recipes");
        recipes.addTab(new YAHOO.widget.Tab({
            label: "Seafood",
            content: "<p>Before you prepare any seafood you need to " +
                     "go fishing!</p><p>Recipe 1</p><p>Recipe 2</p>" +
                     "<p>Recipe 3</p>"
        }));
        recipes.addTab(new YAHOO.widget.Tab({
            label: "BBQ",
            content: "<p>Fire up the grill, it's time to BBQ!</p>" +
                     "<p>Recipe 1</p><p>Recipe 2</p><p>Recipe 3</p>",
            active: true
        }));
        recipes.addTab(new YAHOO.widget.Tab({
            label: "Pasta",
            content: "<p>Will it be spaghetti or lasagna?</p>" +
                     "<p>Recipe 1</p><p>Recipe 2</p><p>Recipe 3</p>"
        }));
    })();
</script>
</body>
</html>
```

Note how the `recipes div` is now empty since its entire markup is now being generated in JavaScript. Whereas previously the JavaScript for a TabView would end at the instantiation of the TabView object, in this case its `addTab` method is used to add tabs to it. The `addTab` method expects a `YAHOO.widget.Tab` object. A second parameter can be passed indicating the index at which the tab is to be added. If no index is provided, the new tab is simply appended to the existing set.

Creating a new Tab object is pretty straightforward. It can be based on an HTML element (by reference or by ID) or the element can just be created on the fly. Note that if a tab is specified from markup, its HTML needs to follow the same pattern as was specified in the earlier HTML example. In other words, the tab should be a list item containing an anchor and preferably an emphasis (em) tag within that. This is because the TabView to which the tab is being added will append the element to its list of tabs, thereby moving it in the DOM. It will no longer reside in the place where it was originally defined, unless of course it's already in the right place. Also, the reason why it would be preferable to include an emphasis tag within the anchor is because this is what the default YUI CSS rules expect. The emphasis tag isn't needed otherwise. However, the anchor is.

Handling Events

Event handlers can be assigned either to the TabView or Tab objects. In both cases, DOM-based events (such as `onmouseover` and `onclick`) as well as custom events are supported. It is strongly recommended that event handlers not be assigned directly to the HTML element representing the TabView or the Tab. This is to ensure that events on these objects fire in the correct order as well as to maintain the benefits that come from the practice of event delegation. Rather, each object's native `addListener` (or "on" alias) should be used. The following table lists the custom events offered by TabView and Tab:

TabView	Tab
activationEventChange	activeIndexChange
activeChange	activeTabChange
beforeActivationEventChange	beforeActiveIndexChange
beforeActiveChange	beforeActiveTabChange
beforeCacheDataChange	beforeOrientationChange
beforeContentChange	beforeTabsChange
beforeContentElChange	orientationChange
beforeContentVisibleChange	tabsChange
beforeDataLoadedChange	
beforeDataSrcChange	
beforeDataTimeoutChange	
beforeDisabledChange	
beforeHrefChange	
beforeLabelChange	
beforeLabelElChange	
beforeLoadMethodChange	
cacheDataChange	
contentChange	
contentElChange	
contentVisibleChange	
dataLoadedChange	
dataSrcChange	
dataTimeoutChange	
disabledChange	
hrefChange	
labelChange	
labelElChange	
loadMethodChange	

Here's an example of event handlers being added to both Tab and TabView:

```html
<html>
    <head>
        <title>TabView--Events</title>
        <link rel="stylesheet" type="text/css" href="reset-fonts-grids.css" />
        <link rel="stylesheet" type="text/css" href="base-min.css" />
        <link rel="stylesheet" type="text/css"
            href="assets/skins/sam/tabview.css"/>
    </head>
    <body class="yui-skin-sam">
        <div id="doc">
            <div id="hd">
                <h1>TabView--Events</h1>
            </div>
            <div id="bd">

                <!-- START TABVIEW MARKUP -->
                <div id="recipes">
                    <ul class="yui-nav">
                        <li>
                            <a href="#seafood">
                                <em>Seafood</em>
                            </a>
                        </li>
                        <li class="selected">
                            <a href="#bbq">
                                <em>BBQ</em>
                            </a>
                        </li>
                        <li>
                            <a href="#pasta">
                                <em>Pasta</em>
                            </a>
                        </li>
                    </ul>
                    <div class="yui-content">
                        <div id="seafood">
                            <p>Before you prepare any seafood you
                            need to go fishing!</p>
                            <p>Recipe 1</p>
                            <p>Recipe 2</p>
                            <p>Recipe 3</p>
                        </div>
                        <div id="bbq">
                            <p>Fire up the grill, it's time to BBQ!</p>
                            <p>Recipe 1</p>
                            <p>Recipe 2</p>
                            <p>Recipe 3</p>
                         </div>
                        <div id="pasta">
                            <p>Will it be spaghetti or lasagna?</p>
```

```
                                    <p>Recipe 1</p>
                                    <p>Recipe 2</p>
                                    <p>Recipe 3</p>
                                </div>
                            </div>
                        </div>
                        <!-- END TABVIEW MARKUP -->

                    </div>
                    <div id="ft">
                    </div>
                </div>
                <script src="yahoo-dom-event.js"></script>
                <script src="element-min.js"></script>
                <script src="tabview-min.js"></script>
                <script>
                    (function () {
                        function clickHandler() {
                            tab0.set("label", "Seafood: Breaking News!");
                            tab0.set("content", "The ocean is closed. No fishing today.");
                        };
                        function labelChangeHandler(o) {
                            alert("The label changed from '" + o.prevValue +
                                "' to '" + o.newValue + "'");
                        };
                        function overHandler() {
                            // an alert over here would be really annoying
                        };
                        recipes = new YAHOO.widget.TabView("recipies");
                        recipes.on("mouseover", overHandler);
                        var tab0 = recipes.getTab(0);
                        tab0.on("click", clickHandler);
                        tab0.on("labelChange", labelChangeHandler);
                    })();
                </script>
            </body>
        </html>
```

Here, a `mouseover` event handler is added to the `recipes` TabView named `overHandler`. There's also a `click` handler assigned to the first tab in the set named `clickHandler`. Finally, there's a non-DOM event that is specific to the Tab object called `labelChange` to which the `labelChangeHandler` is assigned. Essentially, when the tab is clicked, it calls `clickHandler`, which changes its label and contents. The label change triggers the `labelChange` event, which calls `labelChangeHandler`, which in turn fires an alert with a message stating what the label's old and new values are.

Note that events that are native to the DOM behave as expected when it comes to the way the event object is passed to their handlers. Conversely, non-DOM events that are unique to Tab and TabView (as listed the previous table) will pass a custom object as its first parameter consisting of the properties `newValue`, `prevValue` and `type`, which allow for the detection of value changes.

Figure 11-9 displays what things look like once the first tab in the set is clicked.

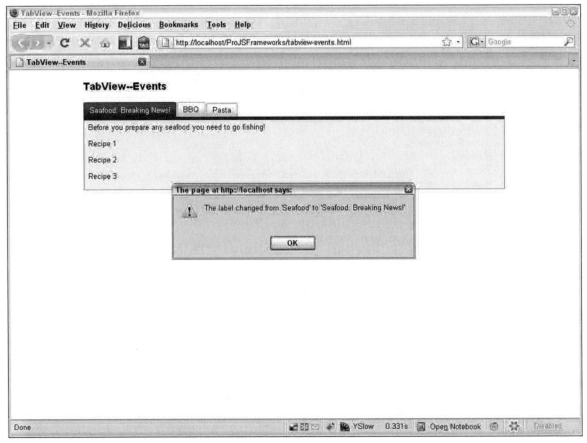

Figure 11-9

Note how the first tab's label has already changed but the contents below it have not. This is because the label change is called first within `clickHandler` and the `alert`, which halts all JavaScript operations, keeps the content change from executing until the OK button is clicked.

TreeView

TreeViews are generated entirely through JavaScript; there is no "from markup" option. That being said, the task of creating a TreeView is really quite simple. First, a TreeView object needs to be instantiated:

```
var tree = new YAHOO.widget.TreeView("tree");
```

Then, the TreeView object's root node needs to be put into a variable so as to attach branch and leaf nodes to it.

```
var root = tree.getRoot();
var chocolate = new YAHOO.widget.TextNode("Chocolate", root, true);
```

Here, a new `TextNode` is created with the label "Chocolate" and added to the tree's `root` node. The third parameter tells the node whether or not to remain open when child nodes are added to it. In other words, should it render in an expanded or retracted state? In this case, the node will remain open when child nodes are added to it. Here's an example of a child node being added to the "Chocolate" node.

```
var sugarless = new YAHOO.widget.TextNode("Sugarless", chocolate, true);
```

Note how this new node is added to the TreeView. Its second parameter is the variable name of the node to which it should be added, in this case `chocolate`.

Though the first parameter in these examples is a string, it can also be an object containing much more information about the node. So for example, in order to create a node that is clickable and has an ID, the following can be done:

```
var dark = new YAHOO.widget.TextNode(
                {
                    label: "Dark",
                    href: "http://search.yahoo.com/search?p=Dark+Chocolate"
                }, chocolate, false);
```

Here, a `TextNode` object is being created with a `label` of "Dark" and an `href` that opens up a Yahoo! Search for the term "Dark Chocolate."

The `TextNode` object stores this information in a property called `data`. However, it's important to note that `data` can be either a string or an object depending on the information contained within it. If the label has anything more than a label, `data` will be an object. Otherwise, `data` will be a string. So, for example:

```
sugarless.data // returns "Sugarless"

dark.data // returns an object
dark.data.label // returns "Dark"
```

It's also possible to pass along arbitrary values to the data object like so:

```
var dark = new YAHOO.widget.TextNode(
                {
                    label: "Dark",
                    href: "http://search.yahoo.com/search?p=Dark+Chocolate",
                    oldmacdonald: "had a farm"
                }, chocolate, false);
```

Arbitrary values can be accessed the same way the standard `label` and `href` values can.

```
dark.data.oldmacdonald // returns "had a farm"
```

Here's a full TreeView example and how it would render (see Figure 11-10).

```
<html>
    <head>
        <title>TreeView</title>
        <link rel="stylesheet" type="text/css" href="reset-fonts-grids.css" />
        <link rel="stylesheet" type="text/css" href="base-min.css" />
        <link rel="stylesheet" type="text/css"
            href="assets/skins/sam/treeview.css"/>
    </head>
    <body class="yui-skin-sam">
        <div id="doc">
            <div id="hd">
                <h1>TreeView</h1>
            </div>
            <div id="bd">
                <div id="tree"></div>
            </div>
            <div id="ft">
            </div>
        </div>
        <script src="yahoo-dom-event.js"></script>
        <script src="element-min.js"></script>
        <script src="treeview-min.js"></script>
        <script>
            (function () {
                var tree = new YAHOO.widget.TreeView("tree");
                var root = tree.getRoot();

                var trees = new YAHOO.widget.TextNode("Trees", root, true);
                var oak = new YAHOO.widget.TextNode(
                    {
                        id: "oaktree",
                        label: "Oak",
                        href: "http://search.yahoo.com/search?p=Oak+Trees",
                        oldmacdonald: "had a farm"
                    }, trees, false);
                var birch = new YAHOO.widget.TextNode("Birch", trees, false);
                var pine = new YAHOO.widget.TextNode("Pine", trees, false);
                var spruce = new YAHOO.widget.TextNode("Spruce", trees, false);
                var cedar = new YAHOO.widget.TextNode("Cedar", trees, false);

                var flowers = new YAHOO.widget.TextNode("Flowers", root, true);
                var rose = new YAHOO.widget.TextNode("Rose", flowers, true);
                var carnation = new YAHOO.widget.TextNode("Carnation",
                        flowers, false);
                var tulip = new YAHOO.widget.TextNode("Tulip", flowers, false);

                tree.subscribe("labelClick", function (node) {
                    console.log("label clicked", node, node.data, node.data.id);
                });

                tree.draw();
            })();
        </script>
    </body>
</html>
```

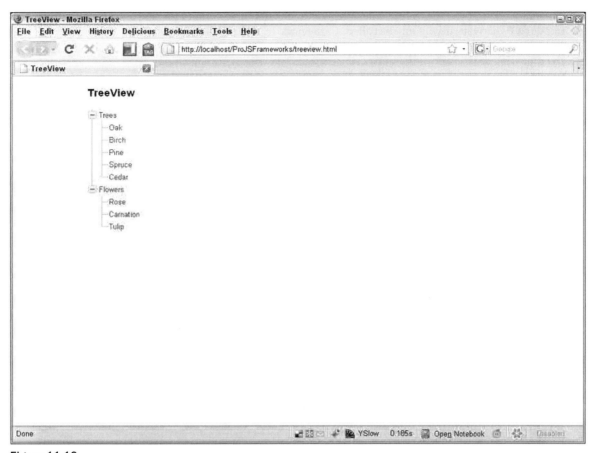

Figure 11-10

Dynamic Loading

A really useful feature of the TreeView object is that it allows for the dynamic loading of its node data both at the tree level as well as the node level.

The way this is achieved is by assigning a callback function to the setDynamicLoad method either directly to the TreeView object or any of its nodes.

```
tree.setDynamicLoad(loadDataForNode); // assigned to the treeview

textNode.setDynamicLoad(loadDataForNode); // assigned to a text node
```

The callback function receives two parameters, a reference to the current node as well a function to execute once all processing is complete. The latter tells the TreeView that the callback's work is done.

```
function loadDataForNode(node, nodesAreReady) {
    var newNode = new YAHOO.widget.TextNode("New Node", node, false)
    nodesAreReady();
}
```

In the case where `loadDataForNode` is assigned to the TreeView, it will be called for each node in that TreeView. Otherwise, it will only be called for the node to which it is assigned.

The following is an example of nodes being loaded dynamically for an entire tree and how it renders (see Figure 11-11).

```html
<html>
    <head>
        <title>TreeView--Dynamic (Tree)</title>
        <link rel="stylesheet" type="text/css" href="reset-fonts-grids.css" />
        <link rel="stylesheet" type="text/css" href="base-min.css" />
        <link rel="stylesheet" type="text/css"
            href="assets/skins/sam/treeview.css"/>
    </head>
    <body class="yui-skin-sam">
        <div id="doc">
            <div id="hd">
                <h1>TreeView--Dynamic (Tree)</h1>
            </div>
            <div id="bd">
                <div id="tree"></div>
            </div>
            <div id="ft">
            </div>
        </div>
        <script src="yahoo-dom-event.js"></script>
        <script src="element-min.js"></script>
        <script src="treeview-min.js"></script>
        <script src="json-min.js"></script>
        <script src="connection-min.js"></script>
        <script>
            (function () {
                function loadDataForNode(node, nodesAreReady) {
                    var callback = {
                        success: function (o) {
                            var data = YAHOO.lang.JSON.parse(o.responseText);
                            for (var key in data) {
                                if (data.hasOwnProperty(key)) {
                                    var newNode = new YAHOO.widget.TextNode(
                                            {
                                                label: data[key].label,
                                                id: key
                                            }, node, false)
                                }
                            }
                            nodesAreReady();
                        }
                    };
                    var transaction = YAHOO.util.Connect.asyncRequest(
                            "GET",
                            "treeview-dynamic-" + node.data.id + ".json",
                            callback);
                }
                var tree = new YAHOO.widget.TreeView("tree");
```

```
                    tree.setDynamicLoad(loadDataForNode);
                    var root = tree.getRoot();
                    var links = new YAHOO.widget.TextNode({
                        label: "Links",
                        id: "links"}, root, false);
                    var morelinks = new YAHOO.widget.TextNode({
                        label: "More Links",
                        id: "morelinks"}, root, false);
                    var evenmorelinks = new YAHOO.widget.TextNode({
                        label: "Even More Links",
                        id: "evenmorelinks"}, root, false);
                    var silly = new YAHOO.widget.TextNode({
                        label: "OK, this is getting silly",
                        id: "silly"}, root, false);
                    tree.draw();
                })();
            </script>
        </body>
    </html>
```

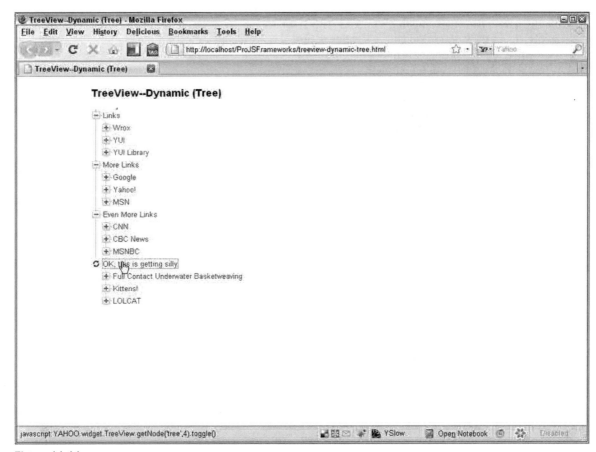

Figure 11-11

The first thing that this example does, after defining the `loadDataForNode` callback function, is to create a TreeView object named `tree`. After that, it is assigned the `loadDataForNode` function using its `setDynamicLoad` method. Next, a few root-level nodes are created to which the dynamic nodes will be appended.

The `loadDataForNode` function in this example is slightly complex in that it makes an XHR call for its data via the YUI Connection Utility. This is to demonstrate the extent of how data can be fetched. First, the Connection Utility's own `callback` object is defined. For the sake of simplicity, it only contains a function to treat successes (in other words, there is no error handling). Since each node that is processed gets passed to `loadDataForNode`, and each node is created with an `id` parameter, the value of the node's `id` is used in calling up the right data. (This is done in lieu of passing parameters to a real back end so as to allow this code to function on its own.) This example uses four text files as data sources:

❑   treeview-dynamic-**links**.json

❑   treeview-dynamic-**morelinks**.json

❑   treeview-dynamic-**evenmorelinks**.json

❑   treeview-dynamic-**silly**.json

Note the part of each filename that's in bold. This is where the node's `id` value is inserted. Once the data is received and the Connection Utility's callback function is executed, it's a simple matter of iterating over the new data, creating new nodes and finally, executing the `nodesAreReady` function to signal to the TreeView that the work is complete.

Here is the data that's used by the previous example:

treeview-dynamic-links.json

```
{
    "wrox": {
        "label": "Wrox",
        "href": "http://www.wrox.com"
    },
    "yui": {
        "label": "YUI",
        "href": "http://developer.yahoo.com/yui"
    },
    "yuilibrary": {
        "label": "YUI Library",
        "href": "http://yuilibrary.com"
    }
}
```

treeview-dynamic-morelinks.json

```
{
    "google": {
        "label": "Google",
        "href": "http://www.google.com"
    },
    "yahoo": {
```

```
            "label": "Yahoo!",
            "href": "http://www.yahoo.com"
        },
        "msn": {
            "label": "MSN",
            "href": "http://www.msn.com"
        }
    }
```

treeview-dynamic-evenmorelinks.json

```
    {
        "cnn": {
            "label": "CNN",
            "href": "http://www.cnn.com"
        },
        "cbcnews": {
            "label": "CBC News",
            "href": "http://www.cbcnews.ca"
        },
        "msnbc": {
            "label": "MSNBC",
            "href": "http://www.msnbc.com"
        }
    }
```

treeview-dynamic-silly.json

```
    {
        "basketweaving": {
            "label": "Full Contact Underwater Basketweaving",
            "href": "http://search.yahoo.com/search?p=full+contact+underwater+basket"
        },
        "kittens": {
            "label": "Kittens!",
            "href": "http://search.yahoo.com/search?p=kittens"
        },
        "lolcat": {
            "label": "LOLCAT",
            "href": "http://search.yahoo.com/search?p=lolcat"
        }
    }
```

Note that the scope of this example is limited by the fact that it calls flat files for its data. Therefore, once "Links" is clicked and its child nodes are loaded, there is no more data to display.

As mentioned earlier, there's a more precise approach to dynamic loading rather than the "carpet bombing" example that was just given. A loader can be assigned to each node that is created rather than a catch-all assigned to the whole tree. Here's an example of node-level dynamic loading:

```html
<html>
    <head>
        <title>TreeView--Dynamic (Node)</title>
        <link rel="stylesheet" type="text/css" href="reset-fonts-grids.css" />
        <link rel="stylesheet" type="text/css" href="base-min.css" />
        <link rel="stylesheet" type="text/css"
            href="assets/skins/sam/treeview.css"/>
    </head>
    <body class="yui-skin-sam">
        <div id="doc">
            <div id="hd">
                <h1>TreeView--Dynamic (Node)</h1>
            </div>
            <div id="bd">
                <div id="tree"></div>
            </div>
            <div id="ft">
            </div>
        </div>
        <script src="yahoo-dom-event.js"></script>
        <script src="element-min.js"></script>
        <script src="treeview-min.js"></script>
        <script src="json-min.js"></script>
        <script src="connection-min.js"></script>
        <script>
            (function () {
                function loadDataForNode(node, nodesAreReady) {
                    var callback = {
                        success: function (o) {
                            var data = YAHOO.lang.JSON.parse(o.responseText);
                            for (var key in data) {
                                if (data.hasOwnProperty(key)) {
                                    var newNode = new YAHOO.widget.TextNode(
                                            {
                                                label: data[key].label,
                                                id: key
                                            }, node, false);
                                }
                            }
                            nodesAreReady();
                        }
                    };
                    var transaction = YAHOO.util.Connect.asyncRequest(
                            "GET", "treeview-dynamic-flowers.json", callback);
                }

                var tree = new YAHOO.widget.TreeView("tree")
                var root = tree.getRoot();
                var oak = new YAHOO.widget.TextNode("Oak", root, false);
                var pine = new YAHOO.widget.TextNode("Pine", root, false);
```

```
                    var ash = new YAHOO.widget.TextNode("Ash", root, false);
                    var flowers = new YAHOO.widget.TextNode("Flowers", root, false);
                    flowers.setDynamicLoad(loadDataForNode);
                    tree.draw();
                })();
            </script>
        </body>
    </html>
```

There isn't too much difference in this example from the previous one. As before, it sets up a callback function named `loadDataForNode`, except in this case, it is only assigned to the text node named `flowers`. The resulting behavior is that only the node with the label "Flowers" loads child nodes dynamically, as shown in Figure 11-12.

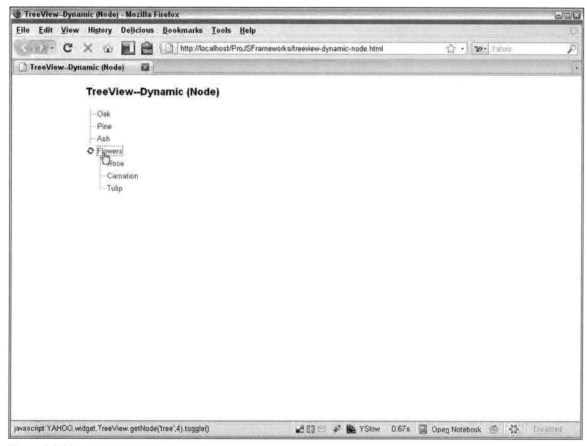

Figure 11-12

Finally, it's possible to move and remove nodes from a tree. The following example shuffles a few nodes around and removes one completely (see Figure 11-13). It does this by using the `appendTo`, `insertBefore`, and `removeNode` methods. Note that none of the changes are reflected on the screen until the tree's `draw` method is called. Similarly, it's possible to refresh only one node (as in the case of appending `pine` to `oak`) by calling that node's `refresh` method.

```
<html>
    <head>
        <title>TreeView--Move/Remove</title>
        <link rel="stylesheet" type="text/css" href="reset-fonts-grids.css" />
        <link rel="stylesheet" type="text/css" href="base-min.css" />
        <link rel="stylesheet" type="text/css"
            href="assets/skins/sam/treeview.css"/>
    </head>
    <body class="yui-skin-sam">
        <div id="doc">
            <div id="hd">
                <h1>TreeView--Move/Remove</h1>
            </div>
            <div id="bd">
                <div id="tree"></div>
            </div>
            <div id="ft">
            </div>
        </div>
        <script src="yahoo-dom-event.js"></script>
        <script src="element-min.js"></script>
        <script src="treeview-min.js"></script>
        <script src="json-min.js"></script>
        <script src="connection-min.js"></script>
        <script>
            (function () {
                var tree = new YAHOO.widget.TreeView("tree")
                var root = tree.getRoot();
                var oak = new YAHOO.widget.TextNode("Oak", root, false);
                var pine = new YAHOO.widget.TextNode("Pine", root, false);
                var ash = new YAHOO.widget.TextNode("Ash", root, false);
                var spruce = new YAHOO.widget.TextNode("Spruce", root, false);
                var birch = new YAHOO.widget.TextNode("Birch", root, false);
                var willow = new YAHOO.widget.TextNode("Willow", root, false);
                // Draw the tree with its original nodes
                tree.draw();

                // Remove Oak and append it to Pine as a child
                tree.removeNode(oak);
                oak.appendTo(pine);

                // Remove Birch and insert it before Spruce
                tree.removeNode(birch);
                birch.insertBefore(spruce);

                // Remove Willow altogether
```

```
                    tree.removeNode(willow);

                    // Re-render the tree
                    tree.draw();
                })();
        </script>
    </body>
</html>
```

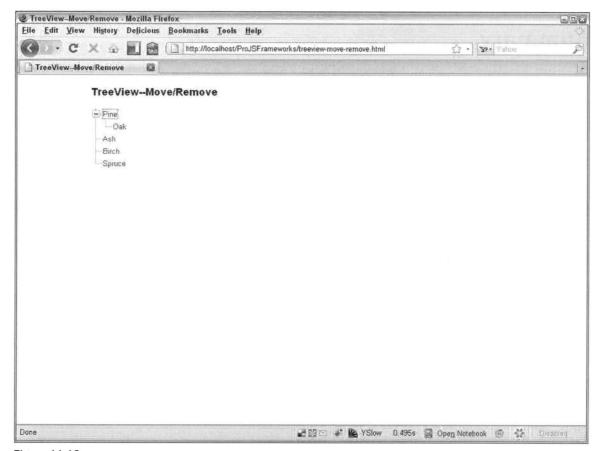

Figure 11-13

> ### New in YUI 3
>
> Widgets in YUI 3 inherit from a base Widget class that standardizes all widgets with `render`, `init`, and `destroy` methods. The Widget class uses "abstract rendering methods to support a consistent MVC structure across widgets, a common set of base widget attributes, consistent class-name generation support, and plugin support."

Source: YUI 3 Widget Page.

Summary

Browsers don't natively support auto-completion, panels and overlays, tab views or tree views, yet all of these are needed components of modern web design. YUI bridges the gap with a cross-browser and extensible set of widgets that do the job quite nicely.

12

Building User Interfaces with Widgets (Part II)

Sometimes the controls that come with the browser don't fully meet the needs of a particular project, and a little extra is required. In this chapter, you'll learn about:

❑   Using controls

❑   Coding menus

❑   Adding dates to forms

❑   Editing rich content

Wiring up Buttons, Sliders, and Menus

The YUI Library offers several controls to bridge the gap between what's currently available and what modern projects need.

Buttons

Buttons, radio buttons, and checkboxes are relatively limited in their presentational and behavioral abilities. For example, regular buttons can't behave like radio buttons or checkboxes. Nor can they behave like split or menu buttons (see Figure 12-7 and Figure 12-8, respectively). None of that is possible with regular HTML buttons. The YUI Button Control, however, makes all of that possible. Not only can YUI Buttons *do* more than regular buttons, but they can even be dressed up to *look* different. As far as their behavior goes, they act just like their browser default counterparts. In other words, a YUI submit button will submit its parent form, and a YUI reset button will reset its parent form.

Styling

The root element of every YUI Button has two classes, the generic .yui-button and the specific .yui-[type]-button where [type] is the type of the button. (For a complete list of types, see the table in the "Event Handling" section later in this chapter.) Button root elements will also receive two class names for state management, once again the generic .yui-button-[state] and the specific .yui-[type]-button-[state]. Valid states are focus, hover, active, and disabled. Note that it's possible for multiple state classes to be assigned to an element at once, for example focus and hover.

Types of Buttons

The following types of buttons can be created with the YUI Button Control. Figures 12-1 to 12-8 illustrate the default styles. However, it is possible to change the look of any of these buttons with CSS.

Name: Push Button

Type: Push

Figure 12-1

Name: Link Button

Type: Link

Figure 12-2

Name: Checkbox

Type: Checkbox

Figure 12-3

Name: Radio Button

Type: Radio

Figure 12-4

Name: Reset Button

Type: Reset

Reset Form

Figure 12-5

Name: Submit Button

Type: Submit

Submit Form

Figure 12-6

Name: Split Button

Type: Split

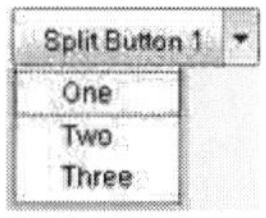

Split Button 1 ▼
One
Two
Three

Figure 12-7

Name: Menu Button

Type: Menu

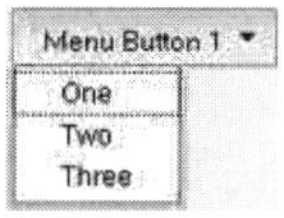

Menu Button 1 ▼
One
Two
Three

Figure 12-8

Buttons from HTML

The `<input>`, `<button>`, or `<a>` tags are valid as well as predefined YUI Button HTML when creating buttons based on markup. Here's an example of what the predefined markup looks like:

```
<span id="yuilinkbutton" class="yui-button">
    <span class="first-child">
        <a href="http://developer.yahoo.com/yui">YUI</a>
    </span>
</span>
```

Once the markup is ready and available in the DOM, it's a simple case of instantiating a Button object and pointing it to an element via its ID, which in this case is yuilinkbutton:

```
var linkbutton1 = new YAHOO.widget.Button("yuilinkbutton");
```

Rather than nesting the anchor above in two span tags, the anchor itself could have just as easily been the reference:

```
<a href="http://developer.yahoo.com/yui" id="yuilinkbutton">YUI</a>
```

This is the reason why the first example of markup (the predefined YUI Button HTML) isn't really recommended since pointing to a simple anchor will suffice. The YUI Button's constructor creates the necessary markup when instantiated.

Buttons from JavaScript

The only markup requirement, when you're creating YUI Buttons via JavaScript, is to provide a reference to an element within which the button will be rendered.

```
var linkbutton2 = new YAHOO.widget.Button({
    id: "yuilinkbutton2",
    type: "link",
    label: "YUI",
    container: "foo"
});
```

In this case, the Button constructor takes only one parameter: an object literal containing information used in the creation of the button. The first value is the ID, which will be assigned to the button upon its creation. The second is the type (see the table in the "Event Handling" section later in this chapter for a complete list of available types). The third is the text to be displayed inside the button, and the fourth is the ID of the element within which the button is going to be rendered. Note that when creating a Button based on existing markup, the constructor takes pains to figure out what kind of button needs to be created (based on the element it's being pointed to). In this case, however, it's necessary to specify a type.

Button Groups

The YUI Button Control equivalent of the radio button is the Button Group. Once more, it's possible to point to a set of radio buttons via the ID of its containing element, or to simply generate them from scratch in JavaScript.

```
<div id="radiogroup1">
    <input type="radio" id="radio1" name="radio" value="one" checked="checked" />
    <input type="radio" id="radio2" name="radio" value="two" />
    <input type="radio" id="radio3" name="radio" value="three" />
    <input type="radio" id="radio4" name="radio" value="four" />
</div>
```

This set of radio buttons can be converted into a Button Group with the following line of code:

```
var radio1 = new YAHOO.widget.ButtonGroup("radiogroup1");
```

Here's how to generate a set of four radio buttons using only JavaScript:

```
var radio1 = new YAHOO.widget.ButtonGroup({
    id: "radiogroup1",
    name: "somechoice",
    container: "radiogroup1"
});

radio1.addButtons([
    {label: "One", value: "1"},
    {label: "Two", value: "2"},
    {label: "Three", value: "3"},
    {label: "Four", value: "4"}
]);
```

Menu and Split Buttons

Finally, a common desktop application convention is the split button, which is a button that behaves normally when clicked but also presents multiple alternative options when its down-arrow icon is clicked (see Figure 12-7). The main difference between a menu button (Figure 12-8) and a split button is that the former doesn't have a default click value, whereas the latter does.

The base markup for both types of button is identical, consisting of a button and select element. The Menu Button and Split Button controls collapse the input and select elements into one button. Here is what the markup of a split (or menu) button looks like:

```
<input type="submit" id="menubutton1" name="menubutton1" value="Menu" />
<select id="menubutton1select" name="menubutton1select" multiple="multiple">
    <option value="1">One</option>
    <option value="2">Two</option>
    <option value="3">Three</option>
</select>
```

Instantiating an object is as simple as pointing to the elements and specifying the type of button to build:

```
var menubutton1 = new YAHOO.widget.Button(
    "menubutton1",
    {
        type: "menu",
        menu: "menubutton1select"
    });
```

Event Handling

Just like regular form elements, it's also possible to bind event handlers to YUI Buttons. It's actually quite simple to do. In addition to standard DOM events such as onclick, there are other YUI Button-specific events that are available.

Here's an example of an event handler being assigned to a YUI Button's standard DOM:

```
function clickHandler () {
    alert("click");
};
var pushbutton1 = new YAHOO.widget.Button("pushbutton1");
pushbutton1.on("click", clickHandler);
```

The following table lists all of the YUI Button-specific events that are available:

Event	Description
beforeCheckedChange	Fires before the value for the configuration attribute 'checked' changes. Return false to cancel the attribute change.
beforeContainerChange	Fires before the value for the configuration attribute 'container' changes. Return false to cancel the attribute change.
beforeDisabledChange	Fires before the value for the configuration attribute 'disabled' changes. Return false to cancel the attribute change.
beforeFocusmenuChange	Fires before the value for the configuration attribute 'focusmenu' changes. Return false to cancel the attribute change.
beforeHrefChange	Fires before the value for the configuration attribute 'href' changes. Return false to cancel the attribute change.
beforeLabelChange	Fires before the value for the configuration attribute 'label' changes. Return false to cancel the attribute change.
beforeLazyloadmenuChange	Fires before the value for the configuration attribute 'lazyloadmenu' changes. Return false to cancel the attribute change.
beforeMenuChange	Fires before the value for the configuration attribute 'menu' changes. Return false to cancel the attribute change.
beforeMenuclassnameChange	Fires before the value for the configuration attribute 'menuclassname' changes. Return false to cancel the attribute change.
beforeNameChange	Fires before the value for the configuration attribute 'name' changes. Return false to cancel the attribute change.
beforeOnclickChange	Fires before the value for the configuration attribute 'onclick' changes. Return false to cancel the attribute change.
beforeSelectedMenuItemChange	Fires before the value for the configuration attribute 'selectedMenuItem' changes. Return false to cancel the attribute change.

Event	Description
beforeSrcelementChange	Fires before the value for the configuration attribute 'srcelement' changes. Return false to cancel the attribute change.
beforeTabindexChange	Fires before the value for the configuration attribute 'tabindex' changes. Return false to cancel the attribute change.
beforeTargetChange	Fires before the value for the configuration attribute 'target' changes. Return false to cancel the attribute change.
beforeTitleChange	Fires before the value for the configuration attribute 'title' changes. Return false to cancel the attribute change.
beforeTypeChange	Fires before the value for the configuration attribute 'type' changes. Return false to cancel the attribute change.
beforeValueChange	Fires before the value for the configuration attribute 'value' changes. Return false to cancel the attribute change.
Blur	Fires when the menu item loses the input focus. Passes back a single object representing the original DOM event object passed back by the event utility (YAHOO.util.Event) when the event was fired.
checkedChange	Fires when the value for the configuration attribute 'checked' changes.
containerChange	Fires when the value for the configuration attribute 'container' changes.
disabledChange	Fires when the value for the configuration attribute 'disabled' changes.
Focus	Fires when the menu item receives focus. Passes back a single object representing the original DOM event object passed back by the event utility (YAHOO.util.Event) when the event was fired.
focusmenuChange	Fires when the value for the configuration attribute 'focusmenu' changes.
hrefChange	Fires when the value for the configuration attribute 'href' changes.
labelChange	Fires when the value for the configuration attribute 'label' changes.
lazyloadmenuChange	Fires when the value for the configuration attribute 'lazyloadmenu' changes.

(continued)

Event	Description
menuChange	Fires when the value for the configuration attribute 'menu' changes.
menuclassnameChange	Fires when the value for the configuration attribute 'menuclassname' changes.
nameChange	Fires when the value for the configuration attribute 'name' changes.
onclickChange	Fires when the value for the configuration attribute 'onclick' changes.
Option	Fires when the user invokes the button's option. Passes back a single object representing the original DOM event (either "mousedown" or "keydown") that caused the "option" event to fire.
selectedMenuItemChange	Fires when the value for the configuration attribute 'selectedMenuItem' changes.
srcelementChange	Fires when the value for the configuration attribute 'srcelement' changes.
tabindexChange	Fires when the value for the configuration attribute 'tabindex' changes.
targetChange	Fires when the value for the configuration attribute 'target' changes.
titleChange	Fires when the value for the configuration attribute 'title' changes.
typeChange	Fires when the value for the configuration attribute 'type' changes.
valueChange	Fires when the value for the configuration attribute 'value' changes.

Source: YUI Button API documentation.

With the exception of blur, focus, and option, all other events receive an event object containing two properties: prevValue and newValue. Since all of these events are triggered when an attribute is changed, the old and new value properties can be useful when tracking changes to a button.

Here's an example of how to set and then trigger a non-DOM event:

```
function changeHandler (e) {
    alert("Changing from " + e.prevValue + " to " + e.newValue);
};
var pushbutton1 = new YAHOO.widget.Button("pushbutton1");
pushbutton1.on("labelChange", changeHandler);
pushbutton1.set("label", "Something new");
```

Sliders

One feature that definitely does not come standard on any browser is a slider control, like a volume control or a color slider. To date, the only way to have a draggable control that returns a value is to do it with some fancy mouse-tracking JavaScript. But dragging and mouse tracking are notoriously difficult to code. That being said, the YUI Slider component provides vertical, horizontal, and region sliding controls that just work.

Horizontal and Vertical Sliders

Setting up a YUI Slider is simple. The first thing that's needed is some basic HTML consisting of two nested containers and an image. The first container serves as the area within which the second will slide, and the image serves as the actual "thumb" element that's to be dragged. Here is what that HTML looks like:

```
<div id="sliderbg">
    <div id="sliderthumb"><img src="sliderthumb.gif" /></div>
</div>
```

Once the HTML is in place, instantiating a slider requires no more than one line of JavaScript:

```
var slider = YAHOO.widget.Slider.getHorizSlider("sliderbg", "sliderthumb", 0, 275);
```

Here, rather than using the new keyword for object instantiation, the getHorizSlider function returns a new slider object. The first two parameters tell it where to find the two slider container elements, and the next two tell it how far it can slide. In this example the slider can't slide left at all (the 0 value), and it can slide 275 pixels to the right. In the complete example that follows, the sliderthumb.gif image is 75 pixels wide, while the sliderbg element is 350 pixels wide. Therefore, limiting the thumb's horizontal sliding distance to 275 pixels means that the thumb image will remain within the sliderbg element at all times.

Once a slider is instantiated, it's possible to give it an initial value by simply setting it like so (Figure 12-9 has an initial value of 0):

```
slider.setValue(50);
```

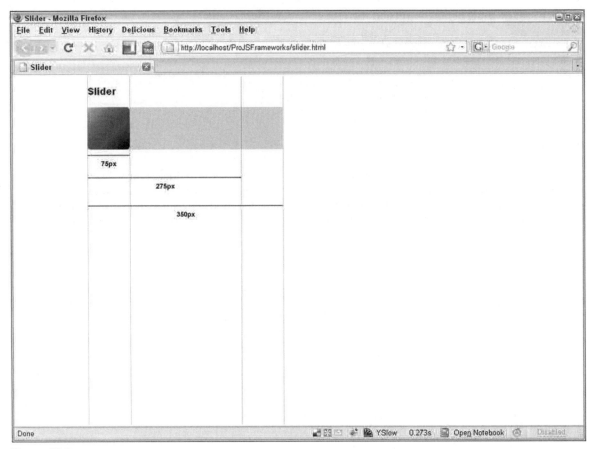

Figure 12-9

The following is the code listing for Figure 12-9:

```
<html>
    <head>
        <title>Slider</title>
        <link rel="stylesheet" type="text/css" href="reset-fonts-grids.css" />
        <link rel="stylesheet" type="text/css" href="base-min.css" />
        <style type="text/css">
            #sliderbg {
                background: #ccc;
                width: 350px;
            }
            #sliderthumb {
                width: 75px;
            }
        </style>
    </head>
    <body class="yui-skin-sam">
```

```
<div id="doc">
    <div id="hd">
        <h1>Slider</h1>
    </div>
    <div id="bd">
        <div id="sliderbg">
            <div id="sliderthumb"><img src="sliderthumb.gif" /></div>
        </div>
    </div>
    <div id="ft">
    </div>
</div>
<script src="yahoo-dom-event.js"></script>
<script src="dragdrop-min.js"></script>
<script src="slider-min.js"></script>
<script>
    (function () {
        var slider = YAHOO.widget.Slider.getHorizSlider("sliderbg",
                "sliderthumb", 0, 275);
    })();
</script>
</body>
</html>
```

A vertical slider can just as easily be created by using the `getVertSlider` function. The constructor takes the same parameters producing the same results, just up and down instead of left and right.

In fact, the `getHorizSlider` and `getVertSlider` constructors both take a fifth parameter and that is in order to apply ticks to the slider. In other words, if a value of 25 were to be passed as the fifth parameter, then the slider's thumb would jump 25 pixels every time it was dragged horizontally or vertically. This can be useful for situations where the value a user selects needs to be in increments of x rather than any value between a and b.

One of the features of the YUI Slider is that clicking on either side of `sliderthumb` within `sliderbg` will cause the thumb to move in that direction. This is, in fact, a normal and expected behavior of sliders (such as a browser's scroll bar). If the YUI Animation Utility is present, then the thumb will animate by easing to the position where the click was made rather than simply snapping there. If this behavior isn't desired, it can be disabled like so:

```
var slider = YAHOO.widget.Slider.getHorizSlider("sliderbg", "sliderthumb", 0, 275);
slider.animate = false;
```

Of course, a slider is of no use if the information it generates can't be accessed. The YUI Slider exposes three events, `slideStart`, `slideEnd`, and `change`, to which handlers can be attached. Neither `slideStart` nor `slideEnd` pass any arguments to the callback function. However, `change` does pass one argument, the current pixel position of the slider. So in the case of the previous example, 100 percent would be 275.

Here is how to attach event handlers to a slider:

```
var slider = YAHOO.widget.Slider.getHorizSlider("sliderbg", "sliderthumb", 0, 275);
slider.subscribe("slideStart", function () {
    // slide action has started
});
slider.subscribe("slideEnd", function () {
    // slide action has ended
});
slider.subscribe("change", function (val) {
    // val contains the current slider value
});
```

Region Sliders

It's also possible to have two-dimensional sliders with a thumb element that can move both vertically and horizontally. Implementing a Region Slider is as easy as using a different constructor and adding a couple of more parameters.

```
var slider = YAHOO.widget.Slider.getSliderRegion("sliderbg", "sliderthumb",
        0, 275, 0, 275);
```

The first two parameters are once more the IDs to the slider elements in the DOM. The third and fourth parameters are for the left and right limits, and the fifth and sixth parameters are for the top and bottom limits (see Figure 12-10). As in its one-dimensional counterparts, this slider uses the same dimensions, a thumb that measures 75 pixels square, and a slider that's 350 pixels wide (and tall).

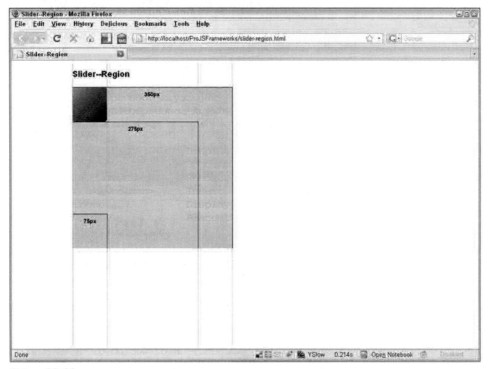

Figure 12-10

The initial value of a Region Slider can be set like so:

```
slider.setRegionValue(50, 100);
```

where the first value is the x offset and the second is the y offset.

In addition to receiving coordinate value(s), both setValue (for one-dimensional sliders) and setRegionValue can take three optional Boolean parameters. The first one determines whether or not this action will be animated (assuming animation-min.js is present); the second whether to force the value on the slider even if it's locked; and the third whether it should set the values silently. If the last parameter is set to true, then none of the slider's events will fire as a result of this action.

Since a Region Slider's thumb moves along the x- *and* y-axes, the change event handler receives two values in the form of an object. So rather than receiving a value like this:

```
function changeHandler(val) {
    // handler code here
}
```

a Region Slider's change handler would receive both x and y values like this:

```
function regionChangeHandler(vals) {
    var x = vals.x;
    var y = vals.y;
}
```

Dual Sliders

Finally, there's the Dual Slider, which is essentially two horizontal or vertical sliders sharing the same background container. Rather than manipulating just one value, Dual Sliders allow for the manipulation of a min and a max value.

Figure 12-11 demonstrates a Dual Slider in action with the value of each thumb being updated below the slider.

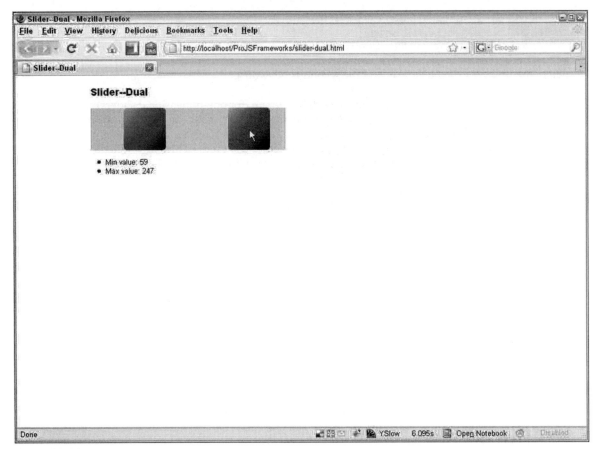

Figure 12-11

A Word About Positioning

In previous examples, it wasn't necessary to explicitly position the slider background or its thumb element. In other words, the slider background could remain static (the CSS default for all nonpositioned elements) while the thumb gets automatically set to relative by the Slider code. The trouble with this when it comes to the Dual Slider is that two thumbs can't be on the same line when positioned relatively (see Figure 12-12). It is therefore necessary to explicitly position the thumbs as absolute. Doing this, however, requires that the slider background be set to relative in order to properly contain the absolutely set thumbs.

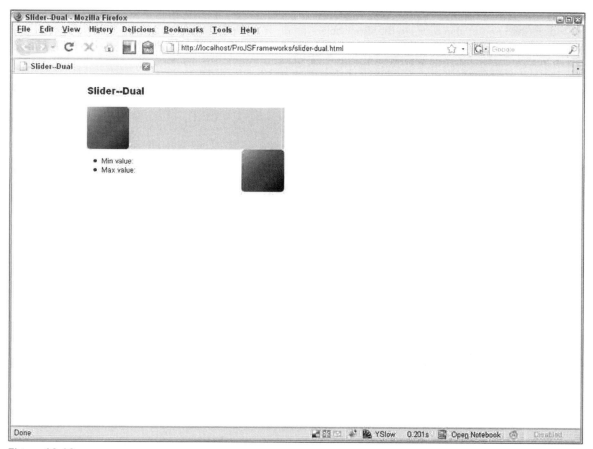

Figure 12-12

Instantiating a Dual Slider takes four required parameters and two optional ones. The first three are IDs: the slider background element's ID, the min thumb's ID, and the max thumb's ID, respectively. The fourth required parameter is the range value, which tells the slider how high the values can go. The first optional parameter is the tick size. If set to zero, then sliding is smooth; otherwise, the thumbs snap to points along the way that are multiples of the specified tick size. So if the value of the tick size is 50, then the thumbs will snap to 50, 100, 150, and so on. Finally, the second optional parameter is an array of two values, which are the initial values for the min and max thumbs.

As with the other sliders, it's possible to manually set both thumbs' values. However, the method names are slightly different to accommodate the presence of two thumbs:

```
slider.setMinVal(50); // sets the min thumb's value to 50
slider.setMaxVal(125); // sets the max thumb's value to 125
slider.setValues(50, 125); // does the same thing as the first to lines of code
```

Accessing thumb values from a Dual Slider isn't much harder than accessing them from regular sliders. The same events are fired and, as with the others, the work of accessing thumb values is done in the change event handler. The main difference is that instead of being passed a thumb's value(s), a Dual

Slider's `change` handler gets passed a reference to the slider object itself. In fact, the `this` keyword within the handler also refers to the slider object, so it isn't even necessary to refer to the reference being passed as a parameter. The slider object contains two properties of interest, minVal and maxVal, which obviously contain the min thumb's value and the max thumb's value, respectively. The following code listing is an example of this in action. It is also illustrated in Figure 12-11.

```html
<html>
    <head>
        <title>Slider--Dual</title>
        <link rel="stylesheet" type="text/css" href="reset-fonts-grids.css" />
        <link rel="stylesheet" type="text/css" href="base-min.css" />
        <style type="text/css">
            #sliderbg {
                position: relative;
                background: #ccc;
                width: 350px;
                height: 75px;
            }
            #minthumb,
            #maxthumb {
                position: absolute;
                width: 75px;
            }
        </style>
    </head>
    <body class="yui-skin-sam">
        <div id="doc">
            <div id="hd">
                <h1>Slider--Dual</h1>
            </div>
            <div id="bd">
                <div id="sliderbg">
                    <div id="minthumb"><img src="sliderthumb.gif" /></div>
                    <div id="maxthumb"><img src="sliderthumb.gif" /></div>
                </div>
                <ul>
                    <li>Min value: <span id="minVal" /></li>
                    <li>Max value: <span id="maxVal" /></li>
                </ul>
            </div>
            <div id="ft">
            </div>
        </div>
        <script src="yahoo-dom-event.js"></script>
        <script src="dragdrop-min.js"></script>
        <script src="slider-min.js"></script>
        <script>
            (function () {
                var slider = YAHOO.widget.Slider.getHorizDualSlider("sliderbg",
                        "minthumb", "maxthumb", 275);

                var minVal = YAHOO.util.Dom.get("minVal");
                var maxVal = YAHOO.util.Dom.get("maxVal");

                slider.subscribe("change", function () {
```

```
                minVal.innerHTML = this.minVal;
                maxVal.innerHTML = this.maxVal;
            });
        })();
    </script>
  </body>
</html>
```

Menus

Menus, particularly flyout menus, are a staple of user interface design and they can be found everywhere, whether it's desktop applications, operating systems, or web sites. They're popular because they clean up UIs by hiding away subnavigation items and commands until they're needed by the user.

Yet, as useful and in demand as flyout menus are, they're notoriously difficult to code in web browsers. The main problem is event handling, in particular the `mouseover` and `mouseout` events. Different browsers fire them at different moments and in different situations and not always when they're wanted. Take the following snippet of HTML, for example (see Figure 12-13):

```
<ul>
    <li><a href="/home/">Home</a></li>
    <li>
        <a href="/products/">Products</a>
        <ul>
            <li><a href="/products/widget/">Widget</a></li>
            <li><a href="/products/gadget/">Gadget</a></li>
            <li><a href="/products/gizmo/">Gizmo</a></li>
        </ul>
    </li>
</ul>
```

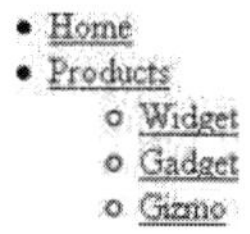

Figure 12-13

Converting this markup into a flyout menu so that the list of products appears when the "Products" item is hovered over is relatively easy. Detecting when to close that flyout, however, is where things get tricky. Common sense dictates that the appropriate moment to close the flyout is when the mouse leaves the submenu area that it occupies — in other words, "on mouseout, close." This is great except for one problem: When the mouse hovers over child items of that submenu, it also triggers a mouseout event. So the simple act of hovering over a submenu's links will cause it to close. Oops. To work around this, different checks need to be made to ensure that the submenu only closes at the appropriate time.

On the flip side, there are some simpler solutions made purely in CSS, but these fall short in the area of configurability. Once these solutions are implemented, it usually doesn't take long for the client to request a delay in the showing or hiding of menu and submenu items. This need is fairly self-evident; humans aren't as precise as computers and will accidentally leave the menu for a second or two as they navigate to a submenu item. Without a delay, the submenu will close when the mouse momentarily leaves the menu, causing the user unneeded frustration. So CSS solutions are out.

YUI's Menu family of components takes all of these issues into account and provides a relatively simple implementation with a wide range of possible configurations. There are three flavors of menus available: Menu, ContextMenu, and MenuBar.

Menu

The Menu component is essentially a fly-out menu. The main difference between it and the MenuBar component is that Menu renders vertically (Figure 12-14), whereas MenuBar renders horizontally (Figure 12-15).

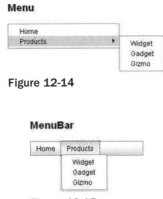

Figure 12-14

Figure 12-15

The basic structure from which a menu is derived is a nested unordered list:

```
<ul>
    <li><a href="/home/">Home</a></li>
    <li>
        <a href="/products/">Products</a>
        <ul>
            <li><a href="/products/widget/">Widget</a></li>
            <li><a href="/products/gadget/">Gadget</a></li>
            <li><a href="/products/gizmo/">Gizmo</a></li>
        </ul>
    </li>
</ul>
```

The YUI Menu family of controls extends YUI Overlay. This way, each flyout inherits all of the goodness built into the YUI Overlay, such as positioning, iframe protection for IE6, and alignment. In order to accommodate Menu's use of Overlay, the markup listed in the previous example needs to be modified slightly:

```
<div id="nav">
    <div class="bd">
        <ul>
            <li><a href="/home/">Home</a></li>
            <li>
                <a href="/products/">Products</a>
```

```
<div id="products">
    <div class="bd">
        <ul>
            <li><a href="/products/widget/">Widget</a></li>
            <li><a href="/products/gadget/">Gadget</a></li>
            <li><a href="/products/gizmo/">Gizmo</a></li>
        </ul>
    </div>
</div>
        </li>
    </ul>
</div>
</div>
```

Essentially, each unordered list (ul) gets wrapped with two div elements and becomes a Menu object (see Figure 12-16). This is the structure of a basic YUI Overlay. The first div serves to define the Overlay container and the second its body (as is evident by its class name bd). Both also have IDs. The first is needed as it is passed the Menu constructor on instantiation; the others are there for convenience (so that programmers can access menus directly rather than traversing a menu's hierarchy). If no IDs are found in the nested Overlay divs, then YUI will generate and assign IDs to them.

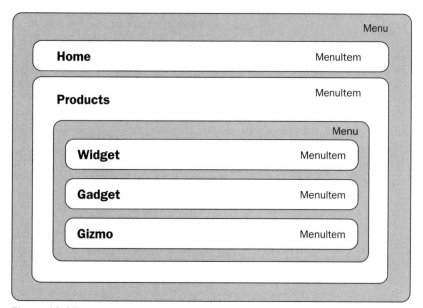

Figure 12-16

Once the basic markup is defined, creating a menu is a simple matter of instantiating a Menu object:

```
var menu = new YAHOO.widget.Menu("nav");
```

One final piece is needed to tie everything together: CSS. The YUI Menu family comes with a basic CSS skin file (the results of which are seen in Figures 12-14 and 12-15). But even more than just making the menus pretty, the menu.css file serves to set up a lot of important positioning rules. Finally, a width value on the container `div` (nav) tames its width and voila! Here's what the complete code listing for Figure 12-14 looks like:

```html
<html>
    <head>
        <title>Menu</title>
        <link rel="stylesheet" type="text/css" href="reset-fonts-grids.css" />
        <link rel="stylesheet" type="text/css" href="base-min.css" />
        <link rel="stylesheet" type="text/css"
                href="menu/assets/skins/sam/menu.css" />
        <style type="text/css">
            #nav {
                width: 200px;
            }
        </style>
    </head>
    <body class="yui-skin-sam">
        <div id="doc">
            <div id="hd">
                <h1>Menu</h1>
            </div>
            <div id="bd">
                <div id="nav">
                    <div class="bd">
                        <ul>
                            <li><a href="/home/">Home</a></li>
                            <li>
                                <a href="/products/">Products</a>
                                <div>
                                    <div class="bd">
                                        <ul>
                                            <li>
                                                <a href="/products/widget/">
                                                    Widget
                                                </a>
                                            </li>
                                            <li>
                                                <a href="/products/gadget/">
                                                    Gadget
                                                </a>
                                            </li>
                                            <li>
                                                <a href="/products/gizmo/">
                                                    Gizmo
                                                </a>
                                            </li>
                                        </ul>
                                    </div>
                                </div>
                            </li>
                        </ul>
                    </div>
                </div>
            </div>
            <div id="ft">
```

```
            </div>
        </div>
        <script src="yahoo-dom-event.js"></script>
        <script src="container_core-min.js"></script>
        <script src="menu/menu-min.js"></script>
        <script>
            (function () {
                var menu = new YAHOO.widget.Menu("nav");
            })();
        </script>
    </body>
</html>
```

Rendering a MenuBar using the same markup and basic CSS is as simple as changing constructors:

```
var menu = new YAHOO.widget.MenuBar("nav", {
    autosubmenudisplay: true
});
```

Note the added `autosubmenudisplay` property. This is so that the submenu flys out when the mouse hovers over "Products" rather than waiting for a click since "Products" has a link toward "/products/" and clicking on it would load that page. So setting `autosubmenudisplay` to `true` makes sure the submenu is accessible. In the case where a top-level MenuBar item doesn't have a link, a # would suffice. YUI Menu detects the # and makes sure the link doesn't try and load it when clicked since it's obviously a placeholder.

The reason why menu items are links and in fact need to be links is for accessibility's sake. Anchors can be tabbed too, thus allowing a whole menu to be navigable via the keyboard.

Without Markup

It's also possible to render a Menu identical to the one in Figure 12-14 without any markup, only JavaScript. Assuming that the page's body (the `div` with the ID `bd`) is empty, the following JavaScript would render the same Menu as in the first example.

```
// Instantiate a Menu to hold the product links
var productsMenu = new YAHOO.widget.Menu("products");

// Populate the products Menu with items
productsMenu.addItems([
    {
        "text": "Widget",
        "url": "/products/widget/"
    },
    {
        "text": "Gadget",
        "url": "/products/gadget/"
    },
    {
        "text": "Gizmo",
        "url": "/products/gizmo/"
    }
]);
```

```
// Instantiate the main Menu and set its position to "static"
var menu = new YAHOO.widget.Menu("nav", {
    position: "static"
});

// Populate the main Menu with links and the submenu
menu.addItems([
    {
        "text": "Home",
        "url": "/home/"
    },
    {
        "text": "Products",
        "url": "/products/",
        "submenu": productsMenu
    }
]);

// Render the menu in the main body div
menu.render("bd");

// Show the menu
menu.show();
```

Once again, changing from Menu to MenuBar is as easy as changing constructors.

```
var menu = new YAHOO.widget.MenuBar("nav", {
    position: "static",
    autosubmenudisplay: true
});
```

Note that, as before, `autosubmenudisplay` is added to the configuration object.

Events

The following table lists both Menu and MenuBar inherit events, which come from YUI Module and YUI Overlay. (Actually, Menu is a subclass of Overlay, which is itself a subclass of Module, and MenuBar is a subclass of Menu.) Menu has a set of unique events that MenuBar inherits:

Event	Description
Click	Fires when the user clicks the menu. Passes back the DOM Event object as an argument.
itemAdded	Fires when an item is added to the menu.
itemRemoved	Fires when an item is removed from the menu.
Keydown	Fires when the user presses a key when one of the menu's items has focus. Passes back the DOM Event object as an argument.
Keypress	Fires when the user presses an alphanumeric key when one of the menu's items has focus. Passes back the DOM Event object as an argument.

Event	Description
Keyup	Fires when the user releases a key when one of the menu's items has focus. Passes back the DOM Event object as an argument.
Mousedown	Fires when the user mouses down on the menu. Passes back the DOM Event object as an argument.
Mouseout	Fires when the mouse has left the menu. Passes back the DOM Event object as an argument.
Mouseover	Fires when the mouse has entered the menu. Passes back the DOM Event object as an argument.
Mouseup	Fires when the user releases a mouse button while the mouse is over the menu. Passes back the DOM Event object as an argument.

Source: API documentation.

Likewise, the following table describes how MenuItem and MenuBarItem share custom events:

Event	Description
Blur	Fires when the menu item loses the input focus.
Click	Fires when the user clicks the menu item. Passes back the DOM Event object as an argument.
Destroy	Fires when the menu item's <li> element is removed from its parent <ul> element.
Focus	Fires when the menu item receives focus.
Keydown	Fires when the user presses a key when the menu item has focus. Passes back the DOM Event object as an argument.
Keypress	Fires when the user presses an alphanumeric key when the menu item has focus. Passes back the DOM Event object as an argument.
Keyup	Fires when the user releases a key when the menu item has focus. Passes back the DOM Event object as an argument.
Mousedown	Fires when the user mouses down on the menu item. Passes back the DOM Event object as an argument.
Mouseout	Fires when the mouse has left the menu item. Passes back the DOM Event object as an argument.
Mouseover	Fires when the mouse has entered the menu item. Passes back the DOM Event object as an argument.
Mouseup	Fires when the user releases a mouse button while the mouse is over the menu item. Passes back the DOM Event object as an argument.

Source: API documentation.

Here are a few examples of how to wire up events to Menus and their items.

```
menu.subscribe("beforeShow", function () {
    alert("beforeShow"); // beforeShow is inherited from YAHOO.widget.Module
});
menu.subscribe("mouseover", function () {
    alert("This will get annoying really fast.");
});
```

Here, two event handlers are being attached, one to beforeShow and the other to mouseover. It's important to note that event handlers that are assigned to a menu will also be assigned to all of its submenus.

Traversing a Menu's Hierarchy

The family of Menu and MenuItem objects offers methods and properties for the traversal of a menu's hierarchy. As mentioned before, the Menu constructor also assigns IDs to Menu and MenuItem elements as a convenience in order to bypass the need for manual traversal of a hierarchy. IDs make it easier to target elements directly.

Retrieving a Menu object's items can be done by using either the getItem or getItems methods as well as the getProperty config method. Once a desired object is retrieved, accessing its element in the DOM is as simple as referencing its element property. It's also possible to traverse a Menu in the opposite direction using the parent property and getRoot method. The following code listing demonstrates, somewhat verbosely, the traversal of the nav menu built earlier.

```
// Instantiate a Menu object (based on the root HTML element with the ID "nav")
var menu = new YAHOO.widget.Menu("nav");

// Retrieve the Menu object's element
var menuElement = menu.element;

// Retrieve the Menu object's first item, "Products"
var productsItem = menu.getItem(1);

// Retrieve the Products item's element
var productsItemElement = productsItem.element;

// Retrieve the Products item's label text
var productsItemText = menu.getItem(1).cfg.getProperty("text");

// Retrieve the Products item's submenu object
var productsSubMenu = menu.getItem(1).cfg.getProperty("submenu");

// Retrieve the Products item's submenu object's element
var productsSubMenuElement = menu.getItem(1).cfg.getProperty("submenu").element;
```

```
// Retrieve the menu items belonging to the Products submenu (returns an array)
var productsSubMenuItems = menu.getItem(1).cfg.getProperty("submenu").getItems();

// Retrieve the first Products submenu item (widget)
var widget = menu.getItem(1).cfg.getProperty("submenu").getItem(0);

// Retrieve the widget menu item's label text ("Widget")
var widgetElement = widget.element;

// Retrieve the parent menu object of the widget element
var parent = widget.parent;

// Retrieve the main menu object
var root = productsSubMenu.getRoot();
```

As mentioned earlier, key elements in a menu are automatically assigned IDs (if they didn't already have them) so that accessing the Products submenu element, for example, would be as simple as:

```
var productsSubMenuElement = document.getElementById("products");
```

Or, it would be as simple as using the YUI DOM Collection:

```
var productsSubMenuElement = YAHOO.util.Dom.get("products");
```

Context Menus

Creating a context menu (Figure 12-17) is as easy as creating a Menu or a MenuBar. The main difference is that in the ContextMenu constructor, a target needs to be specified. The value passed as the target parameter can be a reference to an element in the DOM, an ID, or an array of either.

```
var contextMenu = new YAHOO.widget.ContextMenu("cmenu", {trigger: document});
```

In this case, the trigger is set to be the document. Therefore, right-clicking anywhere on the document will cause the context menu to appear. Once the context menu object is instantiated, adding menu items and submenu items is the same as before. Here is a complete ContextMenu example:

```
<html>
    <head>
        <title>Context Menu</title>
        <link rel="stylesheet" type="text/css" href="reset-fonts-grids.css" />
        <link rel="stylesheet" type="text/css" href="base-min.css" />
        <link rel="stylesheet" type="text/css"
                href="menu/assets/skins/sam/menu.css" />
    </head>
    <body class="yui-skin-sam">
        <div id="doc">
            <div id="hd">
                <h1>Context Menu</h1>
            </div>
            <div id="bd">
```

```
            </div>
            <div id="ft">
            </div>
        </div>
    <script src="yahoo-dom-event.js"></script>
    <script src="container_core-min.js"></script>
    <script src="menu/menu-min.js"></script>
    <script>
        (function () {
            var contextMenu = new YAHOO.widget.ContextMenu("cmenu",
                {trigger: document});

            var sub = new YAHOO.widget.Menu("sub");
            sub.addItems(["Un", "Deux", "Trois", "Quatre"]);

            contextMenu.addItems(
                [
                    "One",
                    {
                        text: "Two",
                        url: "http://www.wrox.com"
                    },
                    {
                        text: "Three",
                        onclick: {
                            fn:function () {
                                alert("Three!")
                            }
                        }
                    },
                    {
                        text: "Four",
                        submenu: sub
                    }
                ]
            );
            contextMenu.render(document.body);
        })();
    </script>
    </body>
</html>
```

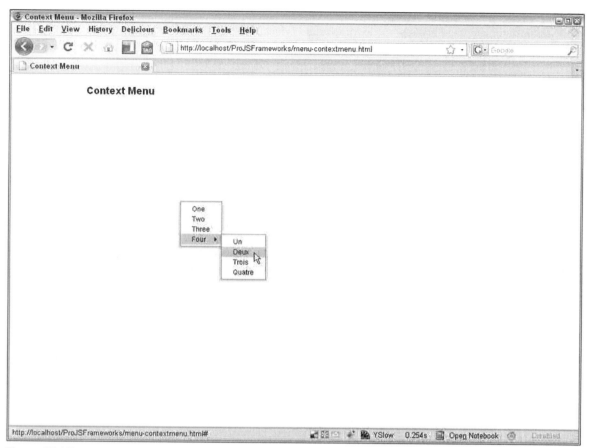

Figure 12-17

Note that Opera does not currently support the right-click event that triggers the Context Menu. To call up a context menu, Opera users on Windows need to hold down *Ctrl* and then click the left mouse button. Users of Opera on OSX need to hold down the Command key and click the left mouse button.

Offering Date Selection

Filling in forms can best be described as a chore. Having to enter information according to a certain pattern just makes the experience more annoying. For example, when you enter a departure date on a travel site, does the date need to be formatted as YYYY-MM-DD or DD-MM-YY or MM-DD-YYYY? Should the values be separated by hyphens, spaces, or slashes? Most sites specify the required format next to the field, and some don't. Either way, people aren't used to thinking of dates in formats like that. Rather, they think of 2008-07-01 as being "July first, two thousand and eight." Asking people to convert that into numbers just adds to the frustration of filling out the form.

Enter date selection. Providing a calendar icon next to a date field whereby a user can select a date from a small pop-up calendar makes the whole experience of filling in a date in a form that much more pleasant.

But programming calendars can be tricky, especially when it comes to doing date math in a client-side programming language that's prone to localization issues. The YUI Calendar component takes all of that pain away. It's a fully customizable solution that provides simple-to-implement, simple-to-use calendars that can also act as foundations for much more complex applications built off of them.

A Simple Calendar

Setting up a simple calendar is pretty straightforward. First some dependencies need to be loaded. These consist of the `calendar.css` sample skin file as well as the `yahoo-dom-event.js` and `calendar-min.js` JavaScript files. With these loaded, the creation of a calendar boils down to two lines of code:

```
var cal = new YAHOO.widget.Calendar("calendar");
cal.render();
```

Here, a new Calendar object is being instantiated. Its constructor is being passed ID "calendar," which is the ID of the element into which the calendar is to render. However, instantiating a Calendar object doesn't automatically cause it to be rendered. This is so that the object can be configured between its instantiation and its rendering. Another reason for the render method is to make it possible to adjust the calendar's look-and-feel at a later time via its configuration object and calling its render method again.

In the previous code, the calendar is being rendered with its default configuration. Figure 12-18 shows a default rendering of a Calendar object. Today's date is highlighted with a black border, the selected date has a light blue background and the hover state has a dark blue background. In order to apply the sample skin provided by YUI, the class name `yui-skin-sam` needs to be assigned to an element somewhere higher up in the DOM on an ancestor element to the one in which the calendar is going to be rendered. It's commonly recommended by the YUI team to place this class name on the `body` tag.

There are three ways to set a Calendar object's configuration properties: through its constructor, the `queueProperty` method, or the `setProperty` method. Here are examples of all three techniques:

```
// Constructor
var cal = new YAHOO.widget.Calendar("calendar", {title: "Pick a date"});
cal.render();

// Using queueProperty
var cal = new YAHOO.widget.Calendar("calendar");
cal.cfg.queueProperty("title", "Pick a date");
cal.cfg.fireQueue();
cal.render();

// Using setProperty
var cal = new YAHOO.widget.Calendar("calendar");
cal.cfg.setProperty("title", "Pick a date");
cal.render();
```

Each technique has a reason for why it exists. The first is a simple, no-hassle way of doing everything on instantiation. The `queueProperty` method makes it possible to assign multiple values and set them all at once (for example, from inside a loop). Finally, `setProperty` just allows for a value to be set immediately. Note that in the second example, calling `fireQueue` is not needed since render automatically applies all queued properties, but it's in the example for the sake of clarity. Also note that most configuration properties that set or modify a visual aspect of the calendar will require a call of the `render` method in order to make the change visible on the screen (see Figure 12-18).

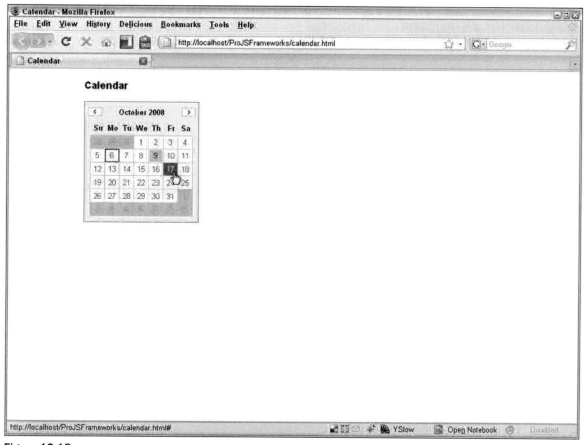

Figure 12-18

The following table lists all of the possible configuration properties including a column that specifies whether the `render` method needs to be called when the property is adjusted.

Name	Type	Default	Description	Render Required
pagedate	String/Date	Current month	Sets the calendar's visible month and year. If set using a string, the default string format is "mm/yyyy".	Yes
selected	String	null	Sets the calendar's selected dates. The built-in default date format is MM/DD/YYYY. Ranges are defined using MM/DD/YYYY-MM/DD/YYYY. Month/day combinations are defined using MM/DD. Any combination of these can be combined by delimiting the string with commas. (e.g., "12/24/2 005,12/25/2005,1/18/2006-1/21/2006").	Yes
mindate	String/Date	null	Sets the calendar's minimum selectable date, either in the form of a JavaScript Date object or a string date (e.g., "4/12/2007").	Yes
maxdate	String/Date	null	Sets the calendar's maximum selectable date, either in the form of a JavaScript Date object or a string date (e.g., "4/12/2007").	Yes
Title	String	null	Sets the calendar's title, displayed at the top of the container.	No
Close	Boolean	false	When set to true, displays a close icon that can be used to dismiss the calendar.	No
iframe	Boolean	true	Places an iframe shim underneath the calendar to prevent select elements from bleeding through.	No
multi_select	Boolean	false	Determines whether the calendar should allow for the selection of multiple dates.	No
navigator	Boolean/Object	null	Configures the CalendarNavigator (Year Selector) feature for the calendar. If set to true, the calendar's Year Selector functionality is enabled. The CalendarNavigator's configuration can be customized (strings, month, format, and so on) by setting this property to an object literal as defined in the Navigator Configuration Object documentation.	Yes

Name	Type	Default	Description	Render Required
show_weekdays	Boolean	true	Determines whether to display the weekday headers.	Yes
locale_months	Array	"long"	The format of the month title to be displayed. Possible values are "short", "medium", and "long".	Yes
locale_weekdays	Array	"short"	The format of the weekday title to be displayed. Possible values are "1char", "short", "medium", and "long".	Yes
start_weekday	Integer	0	0-6, representing the day on which a week begins.	Yes
show_week_header	Boolean	false	Determines whether to display row headers.	Yes
show_week_footer	Boolean	false	Determines whether to display row footers.	Yes
hide_blank_weeks	Boolean	false	Determines whether to hide extra weeks that are completely outside the current month.	Yes

Source: YUI Calendar page.

Events

Interacting with a Calendar object at key moments is possible by hooking into its events. This is done via the custom event object's subscribe method like so:

```
cal.selectEvent.subscribe(function (eventType, args) {
});
```

The arguments returned by the custom event follow the YUI Custom Event pattern where the first property is a string denoting the type of event that just occurred, and the second is a collection of arguments being passed to the handler.

In the case of the select event, which gets fired when a date is selected, the second argument contains an array of dates (since Calendar also supports multiple date selection). An example (see Figure 12-19) of accessing the day, month, and year values of the first date passed to the handler would be done like so:

```
cal.selectEvent.subscribe(function (eventType, args) {
    var datesArray = args[0],
        firstDate = datesArray[0],
        year = firstDate[0],
        month = firstDate[1],
        day = firstDate[2];
    alert(
        "Event Type: " + eventType + "\n" +
        "Year: " + year + "\n" +
        "Month: " + month + "\n" +
        "Day: " + day);
});
```

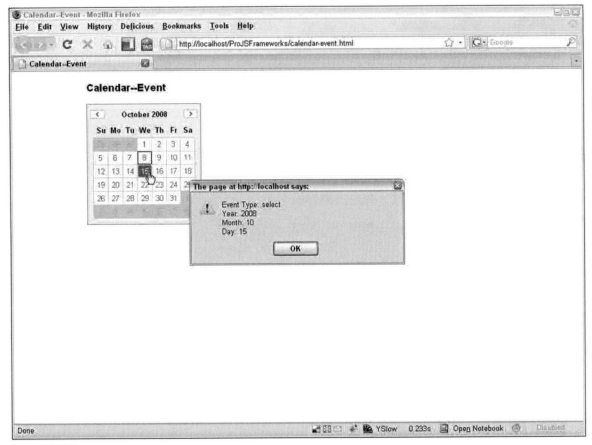

Figure 12-19

The only other custom event that passes arguments to the handler is `deselectEvent` which, as its name suggests, is fired when a date is deselected. A complete list of the Calendar's custom events is as follows:

❑ `selectEvent`

❑ `beforeSelectEvent`

❑ `deselectEvent`

❑ `beforeDeselectEvent`

❑ `renderEvent`

❑ `beforeRenderEvent`

❑ `changePageEvent`

❑ `clearEvent`

❑ `resetEvent`

❑ `beforeHideEvent`

❑ `hideEvent`

❑ `beforeShowEvent`

❑ `showEvent`

❑ `beforeShowNavEvent`

❑ `showNavEvent`

❑ `beforeHideNavEvent`

❑ `hideNavEvent`

As mentioned before, the names of these events are self-explanatory.

Multiple Pages

Sometimes it's necessary to present the user with a calendar containing multiple months, or pages. This is done very easily by simply calling the CalendarGroup constructor instead of the Calendar constructor.

```
var cal = new YAHOO.widget.CalendarGroup("calendar");
cal.render();
```

By default, CalendarGroup renders a two-page calendar. It is possible, however, to specify any number of pages by simply passing the value via the constructor's config object.

```
var cal1 = new YAHOO.widget.CalendarGroup("calendar1");
cal1.render();
var cal2 = new YAHOO.widget.CalendarGroup("calendar2", {pages: 3});
cal2.render();
```

Here, two calendar groups are being rendered in the same page. The first is a standard two-page calendar while the second is a three-pager (see Figure 12-20).

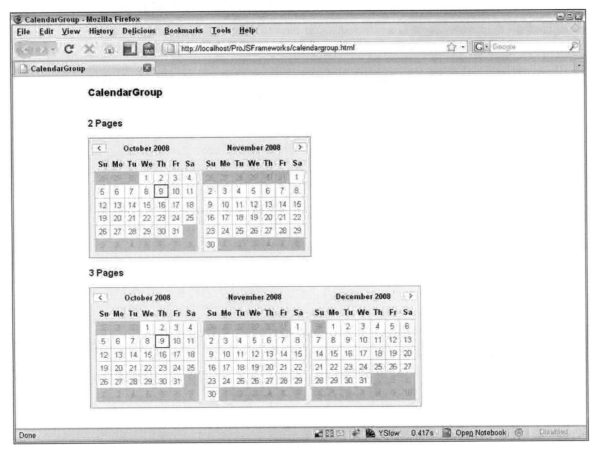

Figure 12-20

Enabling Rich Content Editing

The textarea form field only allows for basic text to be entered within it. It doesn't have the ability to format in any way. Yet some applications may require more than a simple textarea; some applications may require a rich text editor. Unfortunately, a rich text editor isn't provided in modern browsers. However, there is a way to make a document act like it's an editor, and that's by setting the document's designMode property to on. So the trick is to set the designMode property of a document loaded in an iframe to on; that way, only it is editable instead of the whole host page.

Of course, even a simple thing as setting the value of a property is troublesome here. Internet Explorer has a known bug where the value has to be set to true rather than on. And it doesn't get any prettier going forward. Every modern browser, from Firefox to Opera to Adobe AIR, has some oddity or quirk that prevents this trick from being used as a straightforward, cross-browser solution. Yet the YUI Rich

Text Editor does just that. Braving the myriad browser issues, it patches, bypasses, and normalizes its way to providing a simple, easy-to-use API for a Rich Text Editor. The end result is a stable widget that's straightforward to implement, with all of the fun and none of the headache.

To begin with, the YUI Editor comes in two flavors: SimpleEditor and Editor. The latter extends the former and offers more features at the cost of having to load more dependencies.

SimpleEditor's dependencies are: YAHOO, DOM, Event, Element, as well as the optional Container_Core, Animation, DragDrop, and Resize.

Editor's dependencies are: YAHOO, DOM, Event, Element, Container_Core, Menu, Button, as well as the optional Animation, DragDrop, and Resize.

Though it is possible to skin the Editor, the examples in this chapter use the default YUI sample skin. The default CSS that is used here is both functional as well as visual.

Once the CSS and JavaScript files are loaded, setting up an Editor is pretty straightforward. First, a `textarea` element is needed as a base, to provide both a position to render the Editor as well as a source of rich content to preload into the Editor.

```
<textarea name="message" id="message" cols="60" rows="20">
    <strong>Testing</strong>, <em>testing</em>, 1, 2, 3.
</textarea>
```

Note that the `textarea` in the preceding example contains HTML content even though the `textarea` can't natively render it. Using a `textarea` for its base element, the YUI Rich Text Editor becomes a *progressive enhancement* in that it enhances a standard, accessible HTML element via JavaScript. The contents of the `textarea` are therefore still available to the user who doesn't have JavaScript enabled or available.

Once the markup is ready, an Editor object can be instantiated by simply passing the Editor or SimpleEditor's constructor the `textarea`'s ID.

```
// Render a SimpleEditor
var simpleEditor = new YAHOO.widget.SimpleEditor("message");
simpleEditor.render();

// Or render a full Editor
var editor = new YAHOO.widget.Editor("message");
editor.render();
```

Though these examples both render fully functional editors, their appearance will be somewhat limited. For starters, their height and width values will be determined by what the `textarea`'s dimensions are. Setting height and width values, as well as other settings, can be achieved through a config object passed as a second parameter to the constructor.

```
var editor = new YAHOO.widget.SimpleEditor("message", {
    height: "250px",
    width: "650px",
    dompath: true,
    autoHeight: true
});
editor.render();
```

Here, the editor is being given a height of 250 pixels and a width of 650 pixels (see Figure 12-21 and Figure 12-22). It's also being told to display a dompath bar at the bottom of the editor. A dompath bar serves to show the cursor's current position in the DOM. So for example, if it's over the word "Testing", which is in a `strong` tag, the dompath bar will display `body < strong`. Finally, the Editor is being told to adjust its height as the height of the contents within it increases, as opposed to just displaying a scroll bar.

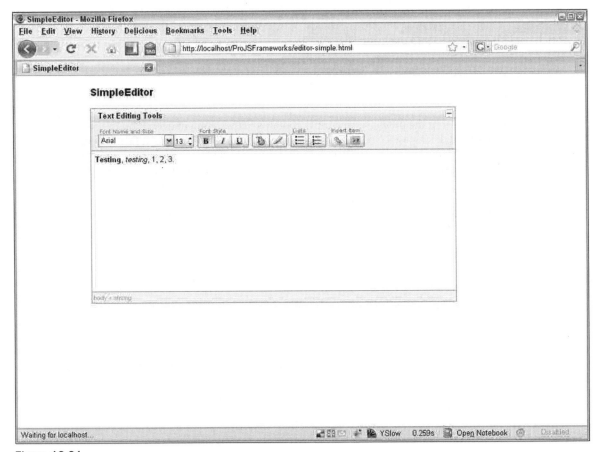

Figure 12-21

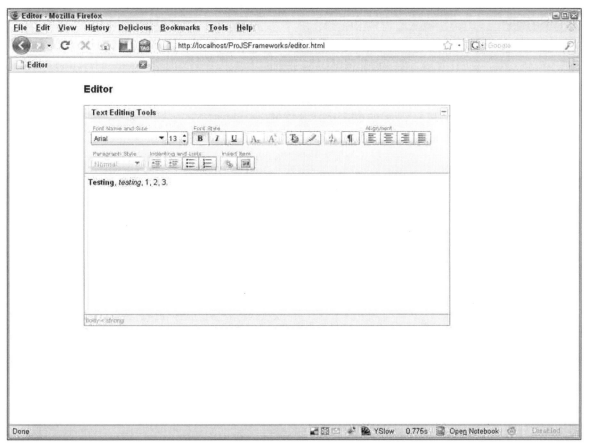

Figure 12-22

The following table lists all of the different possible configuration attributes that can be set for an Editor or SimpleEditor object.

Attribute	Description	Default Value
allowNoEdit - Boolean	Should the editor check for non-edit fields. It should be noted that this technique is not perfect. If the user does the right things, he or she will still be able to make changes, such as highlighting an element below and above the content and hitting a toolbar button or a shortcut key.	Default Value: false

(continued)

Attribute	Description	Default Value
animate - Boolean	Should the Editor animate window movements.	Default Value: false unless Animation is found, then true
autoHeight - Boolean || Number	Remove the scroll bars from the edit area and resize it to fit the content.	Default Value: false
blankimage - String	The URL for the image placeholder to put in when inserting an image.	Default Value: The yahooapis.com address for the current release + 'assets/blankimage.png'
css - String	The Base CSS used to format the content of the Editor. Default Value:	

```
html {
    height: 95%;
}
body {
    height: 100%;
    padding: 7px;
    background-color: #fff;
    font:13px/1.22 arial,helvetica,clean,sans-serif;
    *font-size:small;
    *font:x-small;
}
a {
    color: blue;
    text-decoration: underline;
    cursor: pointer;
}
.warning-localfile {
    border-bottom: 1px dashed red !important;
}
.yui-busy {
    cursor: wait !important;
}
img.selected { //Safari image selection
    border: 2px dotted #808080;
}
img {
    cursor: pointer !important;
    border: none;
}
```

Attribute	Description	Default Value
disabled - Boolean	Toggle the Editor's disabled state. When the Editor is disabled, designMode is turned off and a mask is placed over the iframe so no interaction can take place. All Toolbar buttons are also disabled so they cannot be used.	Default Value: false
dompath - Boolean	Toggle the display of the current DOM path below the editor.	Default Value: false
element_cont - HTMLElement	Internal config for the Editor's container.	Default Value: false
extracss - String	Extra user-defined CSS to load after the default SimpleEditor CSS.	Default Value: ''
focusAtStart - Boolean	Should the Editor focus the window when the content is ready?	Default Value: false
handleSubmit - Boolean	Config handles if the Editor will attach itself to the textareas parent form's submit handler. If it is set to true, the Editor will attempt to attach a submit listener to the textareas parent form. Then it will trigger the Editor's save handler and place the new content back into the text area before the form is submitted.	Default Value: false
height - String	The height of the Editor iframe container, not including the toolbar.	Default Value: Best-guessed size of the textarea; for best results use CSS to style the height of the textarea or pass it in as an argument.

(continued)

Attribute	Description	Default Value

html - String	The default HTML to be written to the iframe document before the contents are loaded (Note that the DOCTYPE attr will be added at render item).
	
	Default Value: This HTML requires a few things if you are to override:
	
	`{TITLE}`, `{CSS}`, `{HIDDEN_CSS}`, `{EXTRA_CSS}` and `{CONTENT}` need to be there; they are passed to YAHOO.lang.substitute to be replace with other strings.
	`onload="document.body._rteLoaded = true;"`: the onload statement must be there or the Editor will not finish loading.
	
	<pre><html>
	<head>
	<title>{TITLE}</title>
	<meta http-equiv="Content-Type" content="text/html;
	charset=UTF-8" />
	<style>
	{CSS}
	</style>
	<style>
	{HIDDEN_CSS}
	</style>
	<style>
	{EXTRA_CSS}
	</style>
	</head>
	<body onload="document.body._rteLoaded = true;">
	{CONTENT}
	</body>
	</html></pre>	

limitCommands - Boolean	Should the Editor limit the allowed execCommands to the ones available in the toolbar: If true, then execCommand and keyboard shortcuts will fail if they are not defined in the toolbar.	Default Value: false
markup - String	Should the Editor try to adjust the markup for the following types: semantic, CSS, default, or xhtml.	Default Value: "semantic"
nodeChangeThreshold - Number	The number of seconds that need to be in between nodeChange processing.	Default Value: 3
panel - Boolean	A reference to the panel you are using for windows.	Default Value: false

Attribute	Description	Default Value
plainText - Boolean	Process the initial textarea data as if it was plain text. Accounting for spaces, tabs and line feeds.	Default Value: false
removeLineBreaks - Boolean	Should the editor remove linebreaks and extra spaces on cleanup.	Default Value: false
toolbar - Object	The default toolbar config.	
toolbar_cont - Boolean	Internal config for the toolbars container.	Default Value: false
width - String	The width of the Editor container.	Default Value: Best-guessed size of the textarea; for best results use CSS to style the width of the textarea or pass it in as an argument.

Source: API documentation.

Events

It's possible to interact with the Editor via events that are triggered at key moments. The Rich Text Editor uses the more recent Event Provider model of custom event handling. This simplifies the syntax by turning something like this: `obj.customEventName.subscribe(callback)` into something like this: `obj.on("customEventName", callback)`. Therefore, in order to detect if the Editor's toolbar is loaded, the following code would be used:

```
editor.on("toolbarLoaded", function () {
    alert("Toolbar is loaded!");
});
```

Likewise, accessing toolbar events can be done through the toolbar object like so:

```
editor.on("toolbarLoaded", function () {
    this.toolbar.on("buttonClick", function () {
        alert("Click!");
    });
});
```

Note how the `toolbar` event assignment is being done inside the `toolbarLoaded` callback. This is because it takes time for the `toolbar` to be initialized, and trying to assign an event handler to it before it is ready will cause an error to be thrown. Also note that the toolbar object is being accessed via the `this` keyword. In this case, the `this` keyword refers to the Editor object itself.

Some of the more common Editor events are listed in the following table; a full list, including the arguments passed to each event, can be found in the API documentation that's included in the YUI zip file.

SimpleEditor Events	Editor Events
Editor Render Events: ❑ toolbarLoaded ❑ afterRender ❑ editorContentLoaded Editor HTML Event Mapping: ❑ editorMouseUp ❑ editorMouseDown ❑ editorDoubleClick ❑ editorKeyUp ❑ editorKeyPress ❑ editorKeyDown ❑ Editor Command Execution Events: ❑ beforeNodeChange ❑ afterNodeChange ❑ beforeExecCommand ❑ afterExecCommand Toolbar Events (accessed via Editor Obj.toolbar.on()): ❑ toolbarExpanded ❑ toolbarCollapsed ❑ colorPickerClicked ❑ cmdClick (dynamic event) ❑ menucmdClick (dynamic event) ❑ buttonClick	Editor Render Events: ❑ toolbarLoaded ❑ afterRender ❑ editorContentLoaded Editor HTML Event Mapping: ❑ beforeEditorMouseUp ❑ editorMouseUp ❑ beforeEditorMouseDown ❑ editorMouseDown ❑ beforeEditorClick ❑ editorClick ❑ beforeEditorDoubleClick ❑ editorDoubleClick ❑ beforeEditorKeyUp ❑ editorKeyUp ❑ beforeEditorKeyPress ❑ editorKeyPress ❑ beforeEditorKeyDown ❑ editorKeyDown Editor Command Execution Events: ❑ beforeNodeChange ❑ afterNodeChange ❑ beforeExecCommand ❑ afterExecCommand ❑ Editor Window Events: ❑ beforeOpenWindow ❑ afterOpenWindow ❑ closeWindow ❑ windowCMDOpen (dynamic event) ❑ windowCMDClose (dynamic event) ❑ windowRender ❑ windowInsertImageRender ❑ windowCreateLinkRender Toolbar Events (accessed via EditorObj. ❑ toolbar.on()): ❑ toolbarExpanded ❑ toolbarCollapsed ❑ colorPickerClicked ❑ cmdClick (dynamic event) ❑ menucmdClick (dynamic event) ❑ buttonClick

Source: API documentation.

Putting It to Use

Once an Editor or SimpleEditor is set up, it's of no use unless the text entered into it can be accessed. Getting the data from the Editor can be done in a couple of different ways. One way to do it is to simply set the configuration property handleSubmit to true. This causes the Editor to try and bind itself to its parent form and transfer its contents to the textarea when the submit button is clicked. It's also possible to access the Editor's contents manually by first calling its saveHTML method, which transfers its contents to the textarea, and then simply references the textarea's value property.

New in YUI 3

As mentioned in the previous chapter, widgets in YUI 3 inherit from a base Widget class, which standardizes all widgets with render, init, and destroy methods. The Widget class uses "abstract rendering methods to support a consistent MVC structure across widgets, a common set of base widget attributes, consistent class-name generation support, and plug-in support."

Source: YUI 3 Widget Page.

At the time this book went to print, the only widget that was fully rewritten for YUI 3 was Slider. The following example taken from the YUI 3 web site illustrates the new slider in action by rendering two sliders (one horizontal and one vertical).

```
// Create a YUI instance and request the slider module and
// its dependencies
YUI({base:"../../build/", timeout: 10000}).use("slider",
        function (Y) {

// store the node to display the vertical Slider's current
// value
var v_report = Y.get('#vert_value'),
    vert_slider;

// instantiate the vertical Slider.  Use the classic thumb
// provided with the Sam skin
vert_slider = new Y.Slider({
    axis: 'y', // vertical Slider
    value: 30, // initial value
    railSize: '10em', // range the thumb can move through
    thumbImage: Y.config.base+
            '/slider/assets/skins/sam/thumb-classic-y.png'
});

// callback function to display Slider's current value
function reportValue(e) {
    v_report.set('innerHTML', 'Value: ' + e.newVal);
}

vert_slider.after('valueChange', reportValue);
```

(continued)

```
// render the slider into the first element with
// class vert_slider
vert_slider.render('.vert_slider');



// instantiate the horizontal Slider, render it, and
// subscribe to its valueChange event via method chaining.
// No need to store the created Slider in this case.
new Y.Slider({
        railSize: '200px',
        thumbImage: Y.config.base+
                    '/slider/assets/skins/sam/thumb-classic-x.png'
    }).
    render('.horiz_slider').
    after('valueChange',function (e) {
        Y.get('#horiz_value').set('innerHTML', 'Value: ' +
                e.newVal);
    });

});
```

Some points to note are YUI 3's use of a loader for its dependencies via the use method, its heavy use of method chaining (i.e., Object.method1().method2(). method3()), and its heavy use of the get and set node wrapper methods. In the case of the get method, it acts basically like YUI 2.x's selector, which fetches DOM elements based on CSS selector values.

Summary

Though web browser controls haven't evolved much since the early days, JavaScript libraries such as YUI have stepped in and filled the gap quite nicely, as the previous two chapters attest. There are many different configurations and combinations that are possible with these controls. With the configurability, extendability, and modularity YUI offers, the sky really is the limit.

13

Enhancing Development with the YUI Core

In this chapter, you'll learn about:

- ❑   Applying namespaces and modularity
- ❑   Detecting browser environment and available modules
- ❑   Logging and debugging

Applying Namespaces and Modularity

A big strength of the YUI Library is how it's organized. Each component, be it a utility or a widget, is shipped as a standalone package within the YUI archive. That way, if a project requires only a couple of components, the user isn't forced to download them all. What's more, in order to avoid complicated naming conventions or potential conflicts in function names, the entire YUI library is namespaced. The YUI core, which is loaded in the yahoo.js file, consists of several key functionalities including the namespace function and extensions to the JavaScript language itself.

Namespacing

JavaScript doesn't support native namespacing as such, but it does support nested object literals that can be accessed via dot notation. This makes creating namespaces fairly simple. For example, creating the namespace TEST.testing.tester is as easy as writing the following:

```
var TEST = {
    testing: {
        tester: {
        }
    }
};
```

Note the uppercase root variable name, TEST, just like the root YUI variable name is YAHOO. This is done to lessen the probability of colliding with an existing variable name in the global variable space. Variables don't tend to be fully uppercase, so the odds that there will already be one named YAHOO are pretty low compared to one named yahoo.

YUI has a core function called namespace, which allows for the creation of namespaces on the fly. The one thing about it, however, is that it's biased toward the YUI Library, so whatever namespace it produces is always off of the root YAHOO variable.

```
YAHOO.namespace("YAHOO.test");    // Creates the namespace YAHOO.test
YAHOO.namespace("test");          // Creates the namespace YAHOO.test
```

Note how both uses of the namespace function produce the same thing.

The namespace function will skip over existing objects and only create the ones that don't exist.

```
YAHOO.namespace("YAHOO.wrox");
YAHOO.wrox.important = "Don't delete me!";
YAHOO.namespace("YAHOO.wrox.books.ProJSFrameworks");
```

This code creates the wrox object off of the YAHOO variable. It then creates a variable off of wrox, which contains the string "Don't delete me!" and then continues to create the books.ProJSFrameworks objects off of the existing wrox object. In other words, calling the namespace function the second time does not recreate the entire chain of objects, and therefore does not destroy the variable named important.

Language Extensions

JavaScript is not a perfect language; at the very least it's missing some nice-to-haves, which the YUI team has gone ahead and included under the YAHOO.lang namespace. For example, there's a whole set of type verification functions that either fix or wrap buggy native JavaScript code or fill in the gap where a similar function doesn't already exist but is needed (see the following table). Some of these are there for convenience's sake while others fill a real need. For example, the YAHOO.lang.isFunction function corrects Internet Explorer's sometimes false assertion that some functions are objects.

Function	Description
hasOwnProperty	Wraps the existing hasOwnProperty function by adding support for Safari 1.3.
isArray	Tests whether the provided object is an Array. This isn't natively possible in JavaScript, so YUI tests for known Array properties instead.
isBoolean	Tests whether the provided object is a Boolean.
isFunction	Tests whether the provided object is a function.
isNull	Tests whether the provided object is null.
isNumber	Test whether the provided object is a number.

Function	Description
isObject	Tests whether the provided object is of type Object or Function.
isString	Tests whether the provided object is of type String.
isUndefined	Tests whether the provided object is undefined.
isValue	Tests whether the provided object contains a non-null value.

Simulating Classical Inheritance

Unlike conventional object-oriented programming languages such as C++, JavaScript uses prototypical inheritance rather than classical inheritance. Though that subject is beyond the scope of this book, achieving a semblance of classical inheritance in JavaScript requires a bit of fancy code. YUI has a few functions that allow for the imitation of classical inheritance such as extend and augment — which JavaScript's native prototypical inheritance doesn't support.

The extend Function

The YUI extend function allows for the chaining of constructors and methods. Note that static members aren't inherited. The following code listing illustrates a use of the extend function to extend an Employee class by inheriting from a Person class.

```
// Define a Person "class"
var Person = function (config) {
    this.name = config.name;
    this.gender = config.gender;
    this.height = config.height;
    this.weight = config.weight;
    alert(
        "Person: " + this.name + ", " + this.height + ", " + this.weight);
};

// Define a method for Person called init
Person.prototype.init = function () {
    alert("Person Initialized!");
};

// Define an Employee "class"
var Employee = function (config) {
    Employee.superclass.constructor.call(this, config);
    this.employeeId = config.employeeId;
    this.position = config.position;
    this.seniority = config.seniority;
    alert(
        "Employee: " + this.employeeId + ", " + this.position + ", " +
        this.seniority + "\n" +
        "Person: " + this.name + ", " + this.gender + ", " +
```

```
                this.height + ", " + this.weight);
    };

    // Employee inherits from Person
    YAHOO.lang.extend(Employee, Person);

    // Define a method for Employee called init
    Employee.prototype.init = function () {
        // Call Person's init function
        Employee.superclass.init.call(this);
        alert("Employee Initialized");
    };

    // Instantiate an Employee object
    var john = new Employee({
        name: "John",
        gender: "Male",
        height: "5'11\"",
        weight: "190lbs",
        employeeId: "424242",
        position: "Senior Basket Weaver",
        seniority: "17 years"
    });

    // Initialize the Employee object
    john.init();
```

Essentially, what extend does is it copies a base class's members to another class and creates a reference to the base class via the superclass keyword. This way, the base class's constructor and methods can be called from the class that inherited from it. This is illustrated in both the Employee constructor as well as its init method.

The previous code example creates a base classed named Person. The Person base class receives an argument called config, which is an object containing values for name, gender, height, and weight. These can be considered attributes that are generic enough so as to belong to any person. Finally, the constructor triggers an alert to notify the user of the values it received. Its init method is defined immediately after the constructor. This simple method just triggers an alert stating that it was executed.

Next, the Employee class is created. The Employee class is meant to inherit from the Person class. In order to do this, the YAHOO.lang.extend function is called immediately after the Employee class definition. This ensures that the reference to superclass within Employee (which is the Person class) will exist when the Employee constructor is executed.

Once extend has been run, the Employee class will have a reference to Person via the superclass keyword and can therefore call the Person constructor, which it does as soon as it is executed. Likewise, methods belonging to Employee can access Person methods via the superclass keyword. This way, when the Employee class's init method is called, the first thing it does is trigger the Person's init method. In effect, this chains the methods (just like in the case of the constructors being chained via the same principle).

In the case of this code example, creating the `Employee` object named `john` triggers the `Employee` constructor, which in turn calls the `Person` constructor. This throws the `Person` class's alert to the screen after which the `Employe` class's alert will pop up. Once the constructors are done executing, `john`'s init method is called, which will again, call the `Person` class's init method and then the `Employee init` method. These calls once more throw an alert message from the `Person` class first, and then from the `Employee` class.

The augmentObject and augmentProto Functions

Sometimes all that's needed is to augment an existing object with the members of another object. This is where the `augment` and `augmentObject` functions come in.

augmentObject

The following code listing demonstrates `augmentObject` in action (see Figure 13-1).

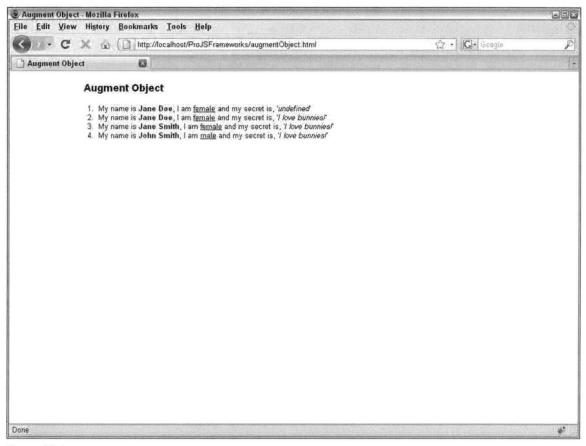

Figure 13-1

Here two objects of type `Person` are instantiated: one named `john` and the other, `jane`. The `augmentObject` function is used to progressively give more and more of john's properties to `jane`.

```
(function () {
    var Person = function (fname, lname, gender) {
        this.fname = fname;
        this.lname = lname;
        this.gender = gender;
    };

    Person.prototype.speak = function (elId, nodeName) {
        var el = document.getElementById(elId);
        el = el || document.body;
        nodeName = nodeName || "p";
        el.innerHTML += "<" + nodeName + ">" +
                        "My name is " +
                        "<strong>" +
                            this.fname + " " + this.lname +
                        "</strong>" +
                        ", I am " +
                        "<u>" +
                            this.gender +
                        "</u> " +
                        "and my secret is, " +
                        "'<em>" +
                            this.secret +
                        "</em>'" +
                        "</" + nodeName + ">";
    };

    // Instantiate a Person object named John Smith
    var john = new Person("John", "Smith", "male");

    // Give John a secret
    john.secret = "I love bunnies!";

    // Instantiate a Person object named Jane Doe
    var jane = new Person("Jane", "Doe", "female");

    /*
     * Output jane's properties to the screen.
     * Yields: "My name is Jane Doe, I am female and my secret is, 'undefined'"
     */
    jane.speak("output", "li");

    /* Copy properties from john that jane doesn't already have
     *    and output jane's properties to the screen.
     * Yields: "My name is Jane Doe, I am female and my secret is,
     * 'I love bunnies!'"
     */
    YAHOO.lang.augmentObject(jane, john);
    jane.speak("output", "li");

    /*
```

```
 * Copy the value of john's "lname" property to jane
 *    whether she has a value in her "lname" porperty or not.
 *    Output jane's properties to the screen.
 * Yields: "My name is Jane Smith, I am female and my secret is,
 * 'I love bunnies!'"
 */
YAHOO.lang.augmentObject(jane, john, "lname");
jane.speak("output", "li");

/*
 * Overwrite all of jane's properties with john's and
 *    output jane's properties to the screen.
 * Yields: "My name is John Smith, I am male and my secret is,
 * 'I love bunnies!'"
 */
YAHOO.lang.augmentObject(jane, john, true);
jane.speak("output", "li");
})();
```

First, the `Person` class is created and given a `speak` method. The `speak` method takes two optional parameters: a target output element ID and a node name to wrap its output in. If neither is provided, it will render paragraph tags directly in the document body.

Next, a `Person` object is instantiated with the first name "John", the last name "Smith" and the gender "male", which are stored in the `fname`, `lname` and `gender` properties, respectively. Finally, John is given a secret. The `secret` property is not native to the `Person` class. It's being added dynamically to demonstrate the default behavior of `augmentObject`. The following object to be created is `jane`. It is also instantiated from the `Person` class and given the first name "Jane", last name "Doe", and gender "female." Jane however isn't given a secret.

When Jane's `speak` method is called, she outputs the following text to the screen:

My name is **Jane Doe**, I am <u>female</u> and my secret is, '*undefined*'

Note how Jane's secret is "undefined." This is naturally because of the fact that the `jane` object doesn't contain a property named `secret`. Once `augmentObject` is run, however, `jane` receives `john`'s secret. This is because `augmentObject`'s default behavior is to augment an object with only the members of another object that its target is missing. That way it doesn't accidentally overwrite members in the target object without explicitly being told to do so.

The next time Jane speaks, she yields the following text to the screen:

My name is **Jane Doe**, I am <u>female</u> and my secret is, '*I love bunnies!*'

Jane has now demonstrated that she's received John's secret. Next, `augmentObject` is run once more but this time with a third parameter, "lname." This tells `augmentObject` to overwrite the value of the `lname` member in the target object regardless of whether it already contains a value or not.

This time Jane reveals that her last name has changed to "Smith":

```
My name is Jane Smith, I am female and my secret is, 'I love bunnies!'
```

Finally, `augmentObject` is run one last time, this time with the third property set to `true`. This tells `augmentObject` to overwrite everything in the target object.

Telling Jane to speak now reveals that she is in fact "John Smith", "male", and loves bunnies:

```
My name is John Smith, I am male and my secret is, 'I love bunnies!'
```

augmentProto (a.k.a. augment)

Sometimes what's needed is to inherit members of another class's prototype but nothing else. The following example illustrates this by allowing an `Animal` class to inherit the `speak` method from the `Person` class. It doesn't however inherit the `fname`, `lname`, and `gender` properties from `Person` since they aren't assigned to its prototype. The following example uses `augment` (an alias for `augmentProto`) to accomplish this.

```
(function () {
    var Person = function (fname, lname, gender) {
        this.fname = fname;
        this.lname = lname;
        this.gender = gender;
    };

    Person.prototype.speak = function (msg) {
        var n = (this.fname) ? this.fname + " " + this.lname : this.name;
        alert(n + " says '" + msg + "'");
    };

    var Animal = function (name, species) {
        this.name = name;
        this.species = species;
    };

    YAHOO.lang.augment(Animal, Person);

    var john = new Person("John", "Smith", "male");
    john.speak("Hello world!");

    var spot = new Animal("Spot", "dog");
    spot.speak("Woof!");
})();
```

The first thing this example does is to create a `Person` class with the properties `fname`, `lname`, and `gender`. Then, a method called `speak` is created and added to `Person`'s prototype. Finally, an `Animal` class is created with `name` and `species` properties. Note how `Animal` doesn't have a `speak` method. The YUI `augment` function is used in order to give `Animal` a `speak` method. Once the inheritance operation is complete, both `john` and `spot` objects are able to speak.

More Language Extensions: merge, dump, and substitute

Three more useful language extensions, `merge`, `dump` and `substitute`, are illustrated in the following code example. The first two help work with objects while the latter is a tool for reusing strings of text.

```
(function () {
    function out(tag, msg) {
        var html = "<" + tag + ">" + msg + "</" + tag + ">";
        document.getElementById("bd").innerHTML += html;
    };

    var heading = "The following is a dump of the <em>{objName}</em> data object:";

    var addressData = {
        streetNumber: "711",
        streetName: "de la Commune W.",
        city: "Montreal",
        province: "Quebec",
        country: "Canada",
        postalCode: "H3C 1X6"
    };

    var personData = {
        firstName: "John",
        middleName: "Connor",
        lastName: "Doe",
        age: 32
    };

    var combined = YAHOO.lang.merge(addressData, personData);

    out("h2", YAHOO.lang.substitute(heading, {"objName": "address"}));
    out("p", YAHOO.lang.dump(addressData));

    out("h2", YAHOO.lang.substitute(heading, {"objName": "person"}));
    out("p", YAHOO.lang.dump(personData));

    out("h2", YAHOO.lang.substitute(heading, {"objName": "combined"}));
    out("p", YAHOO.lang.dump(combined));
})();
```

The primary purpose of this code example is to merge two objects, addressData and personData, together (see Figure 13-2). The dump function is used to serialize object data for output to the screen, while the substitute function is used to update some heading text with the appropriate object name in order to reuse it. A utility function called out is created to simplify the task of outputting content to the screen while ensuring legible code.

Figure 13-2

Trim

A staple of most modern programming languages, the `trim` function, is oddly missing from JavaScript. YUI fills the gap with its own `trim` function. It receives a string and removes any leading or trailing whitespace that it finds. If what it receives is not a string, it simply returns it untouched.

The following example illustrates `trim` in action by parsing an array of words, each with leading and trailing whitespace. The first time it is output to the screen (once again using the `out` utility function introduced in the previous example), all of the whitespace is conserved. The second time, however, all of the whitespace is eliminated (see Figure 13-3).

```
(function () {
    function out(tag, msg) {
        var html = "<" + tag + ">" + msg + "</" + tag + ">";
        document.getElementById("bd").innerHTML += html;
    };

    function makeMsg(arr, trim) {
        var msg = "", word;
        for (var i = 0; arr[i]; i += 1) {
            if (trim) {
                word = YAHOO.lang.trim(arr[i]);
            } else {
                word = arr[i];
            }
            msg += word + " ";
        }
        return msg;
    };

    var words = [
        "    These    ",
        " words          ",
        "    are         ",
        "  really     ",
        "        spaced    ",
        "               apart!    "
    ];

    out("h2", "Untrimmed");
    out("pre", makeMsg(words));
    out("h2", "Trimmed");
    out("pre", makeMsg(words, true));
})();
```

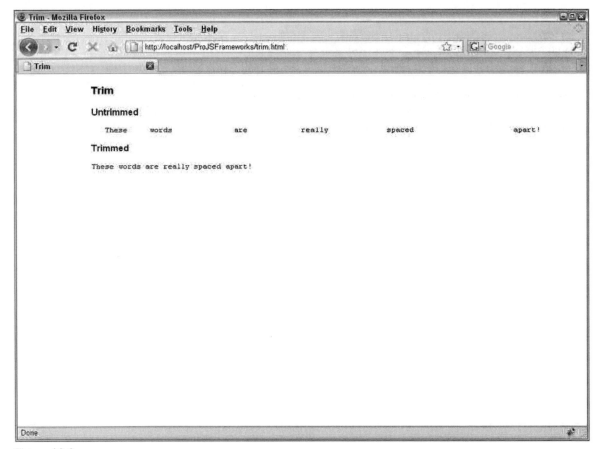

Figure 13-3

Later

Finally, the YUI team has put together a wrapper for the native JavaScript `setTimeout` and `setInterval` functions called `later`. The main purpose for this function is to provide the ability to define what the keyword `this` refers to within the functions called by either `setTimeout` or `setInterval`.

The following example illustrates both the delayed and repeated execution of functions using YUI's `later`. In both instances the syntax is the same except for an additional Boolean value of true in the latter, signaling that the call must be repeated. Also note that the first use of `later` is assigned to a variable named `repeat`. This is done so that it can later be canceled (within the second use of `later`).

```
(function () {
    // Set scoped vars with initial values
    var message = "Warning, this message will self-destruct in {sec} seconds!";
    var counter = 5;

    // Message class constructor
    function Message(targetEl, msg) {
        this.target = YAHOO.util.Dom.get(targetEl);
        this.msg = msg;
    };

    // Method to output message to screen
    Message.prototype.say = function () {
        this.target.innerHTML = this.msg;
    };

    // Message to clear output
    Message.prototype.clear = function () {
        this.target.innerHTML = "";
    };

    // Instantiate a Message object, set initial message and output it
    var destruct = new Message("output");
    destruct.msg = YAHOO.lang.substitute(message, {sec: counter});
    destruct.say();

    // Set up a repeater that decrements counter and updates message every second
    var repeat = YAHOO.lang.later(1000, destruct, function () {
        counter -= 1;
        this.msg = YAHOO.lang.substitute(message, {sec: counter});
        this.say();
    }, null, true);

    // Clear the output and cancel the repeater after 5 seconds
    YAHOO.lang.later(counter * 1000, destruct, function () {
        this.clear();
        repeat.cancel();
    });
})();
```

This example displays the message "This message will self-destruct in 5 seconds!" and then proceeds to count the seconds down, replacing 5 with 4, then 3, and so on (see Figure 13-4), until it reaches 0 at which point the message is erased from the screen.

In order to accomplish this, two implementations of later are used. The first updates the message on the screen once per second while the second clears the message and cancels the repeating later function.

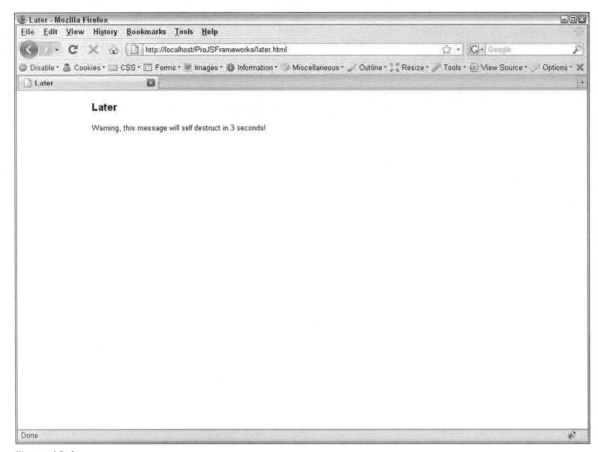

Figure 13-4

Detecting Browser Environment and Available Modules

Effective DOM programming relies on JavaScript code being aware of the environment in which it's running. This not only includes its ability to determine the availability of needed DOM members but what browser (a.k.a. user agent) that it's running in. It also should be able to determine what library components are currently loaded and available.

YAHOO.env.ua

The best practice regarding environment awareness is called *feature detection*, where a feature (or DOM member) is tested prior to being used. This is preferred to browser detection since determining which browser is running the script doesn't guarantee the existence of needed DOM members. However, even though browser (or user agent) detection isn't a recommended practice, it is sometimes a necessary evil. Sometimes differences in browser behavior simply can't be tested for, such as the select box issue in IE 6 where no HTML content except for an `iframe` can be positioned over a select box element. In cases like these, knowing which browser is running the code allows for specialized routines to be run in order to compensate for known issues.

Normally, detecting the browser means parsing the `userAgent` string, which can be daunting, if not tricky. YUI simplifies this by parsing the `userAgent` string and populating the `YAHOO.env.ua` object with the results. The object contains the following properties: `air`, `gecko`, `ie`, `mobile`, `opera`, and `webkit`. Each property, except `mobile`, will contain either a float value representing the detected version or `0`, the latter in the case that the given browser wasn't detected at all. Since the mobile market is so diverse, the `mobile` property contains a string with relevant user agent information. Currently, the only mobile user agents that are detected are Safari, iPhone/iPod Touch, Nokia N-series devices with the WebKit-based browser, and Opera Mini.

Here's an example of how to use YUI's user agent detection:

```
if (YAHOO.env.ua.ie > 5 && YAHOO.env.ua.ie < 7) {
    // iframe code for IE6
}
```

YAHOO.env.getVersion

In keeping with the theme of environment awareness, YUI also offers the ability to detect the version and build number of all loaded YUI modules. The `getVersion` method verifies if a given YUI module is loaded and, upon finding it, returns an object containing version information for that module. Here's an example of `getVersion` in action:

```
<html>
    <head>
        <title>YAHOO.env.getVersion</title>
        <link rel="stylesheet" type="text/css" href="reset-fonts-grids.css" />
        <link rel="stylesheet" type="text/css" href="base-min.css" />
    </head>
    <body class="yui-skin-sam">
        <div id="doc">
            <div id="hd">
                <h1>YAHOO.env.getVersion</h1>
            </div>
            <div id="bd">
            </div>
            <div id="ft">
            </div>
        </div>
        <script src="build/yahoo-dom-event/yahoo-dom-event.js"></script>
```

```
<script src="build/json/json-min.js"></script>
<script>
    (function () {
        function verify(moduleName) {
            var module = YAHOO.env.getVersion(moduleName);
            var msg = "";
            if (module) {
                msg += "Module Name: " + module.name + " [LOADED]\n";
                msg += "Version: " + module.version + "\n";
                msg += "Build: " + module.build + "\n";
                msg += "--\n";
            } else {
                msg += "Module Name: " + moduleName + " [NOT LOADED]\n";
                msg += "--\n";
            }
            return msg;
        };

        var status = "";
        status = verify("json");
        status += verify("yahoo");
        status += verify("container");
        status += verify("event");
        status += verify("dom");
        status += verify("history");

        alert(status);
    })();
</script>
</body>
</html>
```

This code example basically calls the `getVersion` function six times via a wrapper function called `verify`. Each time `verify` is called, it evaluates the module name that it's passed using `getVersion` and depending on whether the given module is loaded or not, it returns an appropriate message. Once all of the messages returned by the multiple `verify` calls are accumulated in a variable named `status`, they're output to the screen via an `alert` (see Figure 13-5).

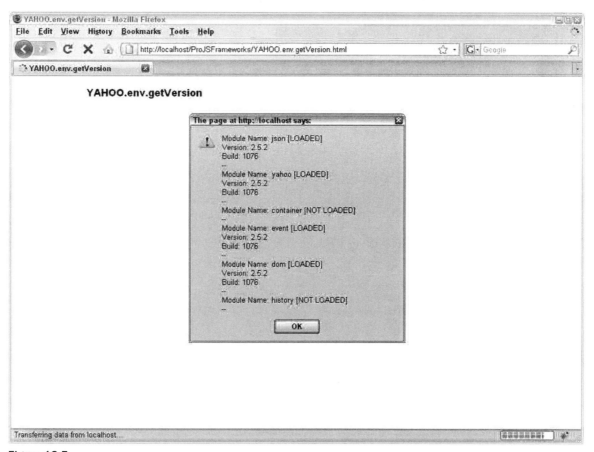

Figure 13-5

YAHOO_config

Finally, there are situations where YUI modules may be loaded at unknown points in time. The global object YAHOO_config allows for the detection of modules the moment they're loaded.

```html
<html>
    <head>
        <title>YAHOO_config</title>
        <link rel="stylesheet" type="text/css" href="reset-fonts-grids.css" />
        <link rel="stylesheet" type="text/css"
            href="container/assets/container.css" />
        <link rel="stylesheet" type="text/css" href="base-min.css" />
        <script>
            YAHOO_config = {
                listener: function (module) {
```

```
                    if (module.name === "container") {
                        YAHOO.util.Dom.addClass("yui-skin-sam", document.body);
                        var panel = new YAHOO.widget.Panel("hello", {
                            width: "350px",
                            fixedcenter: true,
                            modal: true
                        });

                        var msg = "The code for this panel was defined " +
                                  "at the top of this page but it was only " +
                                  "called once the container module was loaded, " +
                                  "at the end of this page.";
                        panel.setHeader("YAHOO_config");
                        panel.setBody(msg);
                        panel.render("bd");
                    };
                }
            };
        </script>
    </head>
    <body class="yui-skin-sam">
        <div id="doc">
            <div id="hd">
                <h1>YAHOO_config</h1>
            </div>
            <div id="bd">
            </div>
            <div id="ft">
            </div>
        </div>
        <script src="build/yahoo-dom-event/yahoo-dom-event.js"></script>
        <script src="build/container/container-min.js"></script>
    </body>
</html>
```

This example assigns a callback function YAHOO_config.listener, which gets called each time a module gets loaded. Here the code only checks for the existence of the container module where in fact it gets called a total of five times, once each for yahoo, dom and event; and then for yahoo-dom-event; and finally for container. Upon detecting the existence of the container module, a new panel is created and rendered on screen (see Figure 13-6).

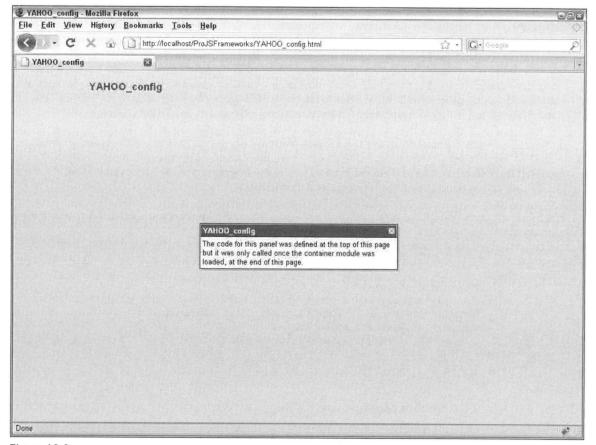

Figure 13-6

Logging and Debugging

A long-standing debugging technique of JavaScript programmers is to output debug data via the alert function.

```
var apples = 100;
var oranges = 200;
alert(apples + oranges); // outputs 300
```

This works fine for small, isolated instances like the previous example. But using alert quickly becomes impractical when, for example, a loop is introduced.

```
var fruit = 300;
for (var i = 1; i <= fruit; i += 1) {
    alert(i);
}
```

This example would cause 300 alerts to appear in succession, making any attempt to work with this code highly annoying. What's needed is a way to output the value of i somewhere that doesn't interrupt the program's flow. In past examples in this section, custom functions (such as out) were written to output messages to the page. Although this works fine, it isn't really practical in a debugging situation. Rather, what's needed is a console that can easily be turned on or off and doesn't interfere with the page that's being debugged. The trouble is that although most browsers have a built-in JavaScript console (such as Firefox and Safari), others don't. What's more, the supported syntax for each console isn't always the same. This can result in JavaScript errors from code trying to access an inexistent console.

Enter YUI's Logger Control. With the YUI Library loaded, calls to YAHOO.log won't cause any errors, even if a Logger object doesn't exist. YUI is smart enough to quietly suppress calls it can't output — though it does keep a record of them. So in cases where the Logger script file isn't even loaded, YAHOO.log calls won't throw "log is not defined" errors.

The following is an example of how to implement LogReader, the object responsible for displaying log messages.

```html
<html>
    <head>
        <title>Logger</title>
        <link rel="stylesheet" type="text/css" href="reset-fonts-grids.css" />
        <link rel="stylesheet" type="text/css" href="base-min.css" />
        <link rel="stylesheet" type="text/css"
            href="build/logger/assets/skins/sam/logger.css" />
    </head>
    <body class="yui-skin-sam">
        <div id="doc">
            <div id="hd">
                <h1>Logger</h1>
            </div>
            <div id="bd">
            </div>
            <div id="ft">
            </div>
        </div>
        <script src="build/yahoo-dom-event/yahoo-dom-event.js"></script>
        <script src="build/logger/logger-min.js"></script>
        <script>
            (function () {
                var logger = new YAHOO.widget.LogReader("bd");
                YAHOO.log("Hello World!");
            })();
        </script>
    </body>
</html>
```

Note that `log` method isn't associated with the `logger` object. This allows for the decoupling of debug messages from the logger, meaning they can be safely left in production code without the worry of debug messages appearing on the site. The only real impact is that YUI is still logging messages, so this could impact performance — more on that in Chapter 16.

In the previous code listing, the first thing that is done is the inclusion of the `logger.css` file, which contains basic CSS for the LogReader. It won't work, however, unless it has the `yui-skin-sam` class name to hook on to. This is added to the body tag. Finally, a LogReader object is instantiated and given the ID for where to render itself as its sole parameter. Note how the "Hello World!" log comes after the LogReader instantiation. This isn't necessary. In fact, if the two lines were reversed, the logger would just output the stored log message once it was done rendering itself, as shown in Figure 13-7.

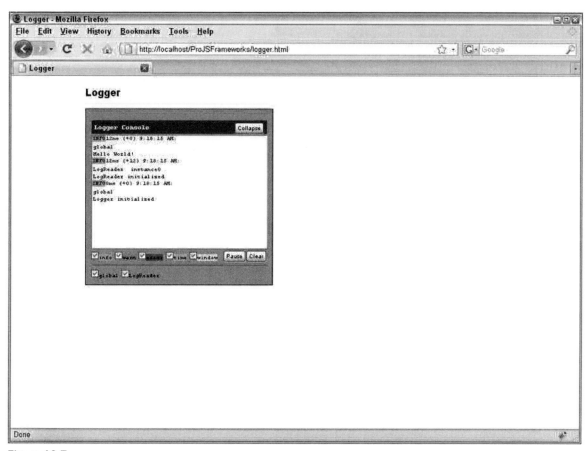

Figure 13-7

LogReader can output five different types of messages: info, warn, error, time, and window (see Figure 13-7). They allow for the customization of different types of messages displayed under different circumstances. So for example, if a `try` fails and the code falls into a `catch`, it might be a good idea to output a message of type "warn", which is easily recognizable by its unique color. The syntax for defining a type of log message is as follows:

```
YAHOO.log("Oops, something went wrong!", "warn");
```

Summary

JavaScript and the DOM's native functionality may be limited, but libraries such as YUI have stepped up and filled the gap between what's natively possible and what's needed. These advances make building and debugging modern web sites a lot easier.

14

Dealing with Data, Tables, and Charts

In this chapter, you'll learn about:

❑ Formatting dates and numbers

❑ Acquiring sources of data

❑ Presenting tabular data

❑ Drawing charts and graphs

Formatting Dates and Numbers

Formatting dates and numbers is essential when displaying content. Unfortunately, JavaScript doesn't support date or number formatting natively. YUI has a couple of hidden gems within the DataSource Utility as formatting helpers for the DataTable control. The first is the equivalent to `strftime` while the second provides a flexible way to format numbers. They can be found under `YAHOO.util.Date` and `YAHOO.util.Number`, respectively. Granted, loading up all 30KB of `datasource-min.js` simply for the formatting isn't a sensible option, but if it's already loaded, then using it certainly makes sense!

Dates

The following table lists the formatting options that `YAHOO.util.Date.format` supports:

Format	Description
%a	Abbreviated weekday name according to the current locale.
%A	Full weekday name according to the current locale.
%b	Abbreviated month name according to the current locale.

(continued)

Format	Description
%B	Full month name according to the current locale.
%c	Preferred date and time representation for the current locale.
%C	Century number (the year divided by 100 and truncated to an integer, range 00 to 99).
%d	Day of the month as a decimal number (range 01 to 31).
%D	Same as %m/%d/%y.
%e	Day of the month as a decimal number, a single digit is preceded by a space (range ' 1' to '31').
%F	Same as %Y-%m-%d (ISO 8601 date format).
%g	Like %G, but without the century.
%G	The 4-digit year corresponding to the ISO week number.
%h	Same as %b.
%H	Hour as a decimal number using a 24-hour clock (range 00 to 23).
%I	Hour as a decimal number using a 12-hour clock (range 01 to 12).
%j	Day of the year as a decimal number (range 001 to 366).
%k	Hour as a decimal number using a 24-hour clock (range 0 to 23); single digits are preceded by a blank. (See also %H.)
%l	Hour as a decimal number using a 12-hour clock (range 1 to 12); single digits are preceded by a blank. (See also %I.)
%m	Month as a decimal number (range 01 to 12).
%M	Minute as a decimal number.
%n	Newline character.
%p	Either 'AM' or 'PM' according to the given time value, or the corresponding strings for the current locale.
%P	Like %p, but lowercase.
%r	Time in a.m. and p.m. notation equal to %I:%M:%S %p.
%R	Time in 24-hour notation equal to %H:%M.
%s	Number of seconds since the Epoch, i.e., since 1970-01-01 00:00:00 UTC.
%S	Second as a decimal number.
%t	Tab character.
%T	Current time, equal to %H:%M:%S.
%u	Weekday as a decimal number [1,7], with 1 representing Monday.
%U	Week number of the current year as a decimal number, starting with the first Sunday as the first day of the first week.

Format	Description
%V	The ISO 8601:1988 week number of the current year as a decimal number, range 01 to 53, where week 1 is the first week that has at least 4 days in the current year, and with Monday as the first day of the week.
%w	Day of the week as a decimal, Sunday being 0.
%W	Week number of the current year as a decimal number, starting with the first Monday as the first day of the first week.
%x	Preferred date representation for the current locale without the time.
%X	Preferred time representation for the current locale without the date.
%y	Year as a decimal number without a century (range 00 to 99).
%Y	Year as a decimal number including the century.
%z	Numerical time zone representation.
%Z	Time zone name or abbreviation.
%%	A literal '%' character.

Text in the table is from datasource-debug.js.

Here is a simple example of how to use the `format` method:

```
YAHOO.util.Date.format(
    new Date()
    {
        format: "Today's date is %A, %B %C, %G. The time is currently %l:%m%p."
    });
/*
 * Returns:
 *    Today's date is Tuesday, February 20, 2009. The time is currently 9:02PM.
 */
```

Essentially, a date object is passed to the formatter along with formatting instructions via a config object. The config object contains one parameter, "format", and a string containing the formatting codes that will be replaced with the correct data. So for example, in the previous code listing, %A gets replaced with Tuesday, %B with February, and so on. The complete list of supported formatting options is listed in the previous table.

Numbers

YUI's number formatter provides the expected flexibility when trying to format numbers. For example, it allows for the appending of a prefix (such as $ when formatting currency), the number of decimal places to round the number to, the decimal separator, the thousands separator, and a suffix.

The following code listing outputs the U.S. national debt formatted for both English and French readers (see Figure 14-1). It takes the number 10773608518631.0509482739 and outputs the following:

```
The U.S. national debt at the time of this book's writing was
approximately $10,773,608,518,631.05 USD
La dette nationale des États-Unis au moment d'écriture de ce livre été
environs 10 773 608 518 631,05$ USD
```

```html
<html>
    <head>
        <title>Number Formatting</title>
        <link rel="stylesheet" type="text/css" href="reset-fonts-grids.css" />
        <link rel="stylesheet" type="text/css" href="base-min.css" />
        <style type="text/css">
        </style>
    </head>
    <body>
        <div id="doc">
            <div id="hd">
                <h1>Number Formatting</h1>
            </div>
            <div id="bd">
            </div>
            <div id="ft">
            </div>
        </div>
        <script src="build/yahoo-dom-event/yahoo-dom-event.js"></script>
        <script src="build/datasource/datasource-min.js"></script>
        <script>
            (function () {
                var num = 10773608518631.0509482739;
                var bd = document.getElementById("bd");

                // In English

                var msg = "The U.S. national debt at the time of this book's " +
                        "writing was approximately ";
                msg += YAHOO.util.Number.format(num, {
                    prefix: "$",
                    decimalPlaces: 2,
                    decimalSeparator: ".",
                    thousandsSeparator: ",",
                    suffix: " USD"
                });
                bd.innerHTML = "<p>" + msg + "</p>";

                // In French

                msg = "La dette nationale des États-Unis au moment d'écriture " +
                    "de ce livre été environs "
                msg += YAHOO.util.Number.format(num, {
                    prefix: "",
                    decimalPlaces: 2,
                    decimalSeparator: ",",
                    thousandsSeparator: " ",
```

```
                        suffix: "$ USD"
              });
              bd.innerHTML += "<p>" + msg + "</p>";
         })();
       </script>
     </body>
   </html>
```

Figure 14-1

Acquiring Sources of Data

In today's world of web applications, dealing with data sources is becoming an unavoidable reality. Building reusable components that rely on external data can become an issue when the type of data and its format aren't known in advance, or may change over time. Being able to abstract the connection is an essential way to deal with this issue. YUI's DataSource Utility makes the abstraction process possible with very little effort (see Figure 14-2).

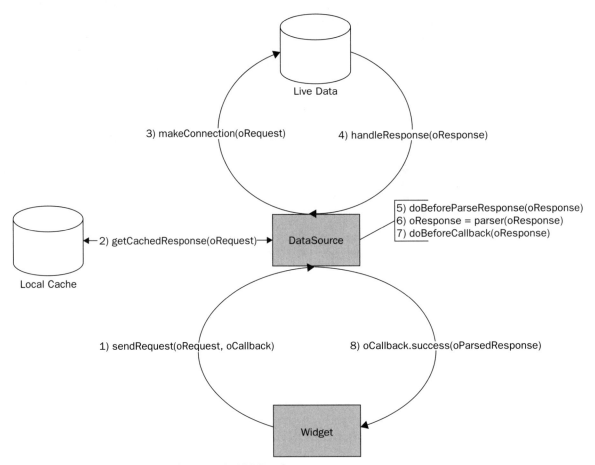

Figure 14-2 is based on the figure found on the YUI DataSource page.

Figure 14-2

1. First, a request is made to the `DataSource` object via its `sendRequest` method.

The `sendRequest` method takes two parameters. The first is a string that's pertinent to the request. So in the case of remote data, it would be something like `"id=abc&show=all"` while for local data, it could be something simpler like `"xyz."` This parameter may actually be irrelevant to the call, so it can be left as `null`.

The second parameter for `sendRequest` is an object literal specifying callback information for a `success` function, a `failure` function, the callback execution `scope`, and an arbitrary `argument` object. The callback object's parameters are named `success`, `failure`, `scope`, and `argument`.

2. The `DataSource` object verifies if it has the requested data already stored in its cache.

3. If the requested data isn't in cache, the `DataSource` object makes a call to the live data source.

4. The requested data is returned in raw form.

5. At this point, it is possible to access and modify the returned data via `doBeforeParseResponse`.

6. This is where `DataSource` does all of its heavy lifting and parses the raw data according to the specified `dataType` and schema.

7. `doBeforeCallback` allows access to modify the parsed data before it gets cached.

8. The parsed data is returned to the requesting widget with the following arguments: `oRequest`, `oParsedResponse`, and `oPayload`.

The first argument mirrors the first value that was sent to the `sendRequest` method while the last mirrors the `oCallback` object. The `oParsedResponse` argument, however, is new and is an object containing the following properties: `tId`, `results`, `error`, `cached`, `meta`.

The following is an example of `DataSource` hooking into a simple array:

```html
<html>
    <head>
        <title>DataSource--Simple Array</title>
        <link rel="stylesheet" type="text/css" href="reset-fonts-grids.css" />
        <link rel="stylesheet" type="text/css" href="base-min.css" />
    </head>
    <body>
        <div id="doc">
            <div id="hd">
                <h1>DataSource--Simple Array</h1>
            </div>
            <div id="bd">
            </div>
            <div id="ft">
            </div>
        </div>
        <script src="build/yahoo-dom-event/yahoo-dom-event.js"></script>
        <script src="build/datasource/datasource-min.js"></script>
        <script>
            (function () {
                var simple = ["red", "orange", "yellow", "green", "blue"];
                var ds = new YAHOO.util.LocalDataSource(simple);
                ds.responseType = YAHOO.util.LocalDataSource.TYPE_JSARRAY;
                ds.responseSchema = {fields: ["color"]};

                function out(target, msg) {
                    target = YAHOO.util.Dom.get(target);
                    if (target) {
                        target.innerHTML += "<p>" + msg + "</p>";
                    }
                };

                function dataLoadedCallback(request, payload) {
                    var tId = payload.tId;
                    var results = payload.results;
                    var meta = payload.meta;

                    var msg = "request: " + request;
```

```
                    msg += "<br \/>tId: " + tId;
                    msg += "<br \/>results: " + YAHOO.lang.dump(results);
                    msg += "<br \/>meta: " + YAHOO.lang.dump(meta);
                    out("bd", msg);
                };

                // Get simple array
                ds.sendRequest(null, dataLoadedCallback);

                // Add a new color and get array again
                out("bd", "Adding indigo");
                simple.push("indigo");
                ds.sendRequest(null, dataLoadedCallback);

                // Add a new color and get array again
                out("bd", "Adding violet");
                simple.push("violet");
                ds.sendRequest(null, dataLoadedCallback);
            })();
        </script>
    </body>
</html>
```

The core functionality of this code listing is actually isolated to a couple of lines. First, a simple array is created containing the names of five different colors. The array is aptly named *simple*. Next, a `LocalDataSource` object is instantiated using the array as its sole parameter. This causes the object to bind to the array. Finally, a response schema is defined in order to tell the `DataSource` object where to find the desired data within the payload it receives. Response schemas are what make the YUI DataSource so versatile in that it allows for the data that's received to be structured independently of what the ultimate consumer requires. The response schema tells `DataSource` where to find the desired data within the payload. It then maps identifying names to the desired data in order to make it readily accessible to the receiving widget. In this case, the data is stored in a simple array and so the mapping is equally simple. The name "color" is assigned to the values found within the array. In other words, the data that is retrieved from the array is returned like so:

```
[
    {
        color: "red"
    },
    {
        color: "orange"
    },
    {
        color: "yellow"
    },
    {
        color: "green"
    },
    {
        color: "blue"
    }
]
```

Each entry in the array is converted to an object, within which is a name/value pair. The value is that which is found in the array and the name is the one specified in the response schema.

In the case of a slightly more complex data set, (this time a bilingual set of colors), the response schema gets a little more complex too, but not that much. Take the following data set:

```
var simple = [
    "red", "rouge",
    "orange", "orange",
    "yellow", "jaune",
    "green", "vert",
    "blue", "bleue"
];
```

Here, the colors are alternately in English and in French. Their position denotes their language, so in this case, position is very important. The schema's name positions must match the positions of the values found in the array:

```
ds.responseSchema = {fields: ["color", "couleur"]};
```

This way the `DataSource` knows to assign "color" to the even values, then "couleur" to the odd ones, yielding the following data set:

```
[
    {
        couleur => red,
        color => red
    },
    {
        couleur => rouge,
        color => rouge
    },
    {
        couleur => orange,
        color => orange
    },
    {
        couleur => orange,
        color => orange
    },
    {
        couleur => yellow,
        color => yellow
    },
    {
        couleur => jaune,
        color => jaune
    },
    {
        couleur => green,
        color => green
    },
```

```
    {
        couleur => vert,
        color => vert
    },
    {
        couleur => blue,
        color => blue
    },
    {
        couleur => bleue,
        color => bleue
    }
]
```

Accessing the data is fairly straightforward. For one thing, a DataSource can be simply instantiated and passed along to another YUI widget, letting it take care of accessing the data by itself:

```
// Set up a DataSource
var ds = new YAHOO.util.LocalDataSource(simple);
ds.responseSchema = {fields : ["color"]};

// Set up an AutoComplete
var ac = new YAHOO.widget.AutoComplete("myInput", "myContainer", ds);
...
```

However, if the data isn't destined for a YUI widget, interacting with the DataSource is fairly straightforward. Interaction with the DataSource object is done asynchronously, so a callback function is always needed, as illustrated in the previous code listing. Here's a clipping of that same code:

```
(function () {
    var simple = ["red", "orange", "yellow", "green", "blue"];
    var ds = new YAHOO.util.LocalDataSource(simple);
    ds.responseType = YAHOO.util.LocalDataSource.TYPE_JSARRAY;
    ds.responseSchema = {fields: ["color"]};

    ...

    function dataLoadedCallback(request, payload) {
        ...
    };

    // Get simple array
    ds.sendRequest(null, dataLoadedCallback);

    ...
})();
```

This way, regardless of the data source's type, the live data source is queried and the callback function is executed once the data is ready.

Here's an example of some JSON data being retrieved with `DataSource`. Note how both `connection-min.js` and `json-min.js` are now required in order to enable the `DataSource` object to make the remote calls to the data.

```html
<html>
    <head>
        <title>DataSource--XHR</title>
        <link rel="stylesheet" type="text/css" href="reset-fonts-grids.css" />
        <link rel="stylesheet" type="text/css" href="base-min.css" />
    </head>
    <body>
        <div id="doc">
            <div id="hd">
                <h1>DataSource--XHR</h1>
            </div>
            <div id="bd">
                <h2>Employees</h2>
                <ul id="employees"></ul>
            </div>
            <div id="ft">
            </div>
        </div>
        <script src="build/yahoo-dom-event/yahoo-dom-event.js"></script>
        <script src="build/datasource/datasource-min.js"></script>
        <script src="build/connection/connection-min.js"></script>
        <script src="build/json/json-min.js"></script>
        <script>
            (function () {
                var ds = new YAHOO.util.XHRDataSource("employees.json?");
                ds.responseType = YAHOO.util.DataSource.TYPE_JSON;
                ds.connXhrMode = "queueRequests";
                ds.responseSchema = {
                    resultsList: "resultset.results",
                    fields: ["fname", "lname", "title"]
                };

                function out(target, msg) {
                    target = YAHOO.util.Dom.get(target);
                    if (target) {
                        target.innerHTML += "<li>" + msg + "</li>";
                    }
                };

                function callback(request, response) {
                    for (var i = 0; response.results[i]; i += 1) {
                        var employee = response.results[i];
                        out("employees", employee.fname + " " + employee.lname +
                            " (" + employee.title + ")");
                    }
                };
```

```
                    var callbackObj = {
                        failure: callback,
                        success: callback
                    };

                    ds.sendRequest("count=all", callbackObj);
                })();
            </script>
        </body>
    </html>
```

Here is the data found in the `employees.json` file:

```
{"resultset":{
    "results":[
        {
            "fname": "John",
            "lname": "Doe",
            "title": "CEO"
        },
        {
            "fname": "Jane",
            "lname": "Doe",
            "title": "CFO"
        },
        {
            "fname": "Jack",
            "lname": "Smith",
            "title": "CIO"
        },
        {
            "fname": "Jen",
            "lname": "Smith",
            "title": "CTO"
        }
    ]}
}
```

This example is largely the same as the prior one except here, a `resultsList` is defined in order to tell the `DataSource` object where to find the results within the JSON data it receives. Also, since the data is within a JSON object and not an array, the order of the values found in the response schema doesn't need to match the order of the data. In other words, rather than being defined as `"fname"`, `"lname"`, `"title"`, they could have just as easily been defined as `"lname"`, `"title"`, `"fname"` and everything would still work. Once the data is retrieved, the callback function gets called, which in this case follows the YUI Connection object's pattern with functions for when either a `failure` or `success` occur. For the sake of simplicity, they both point to the same callback function in this example. Once the data is received, it's a simple matter of looping over it and outputting it to the screen (see Figure 14-3).

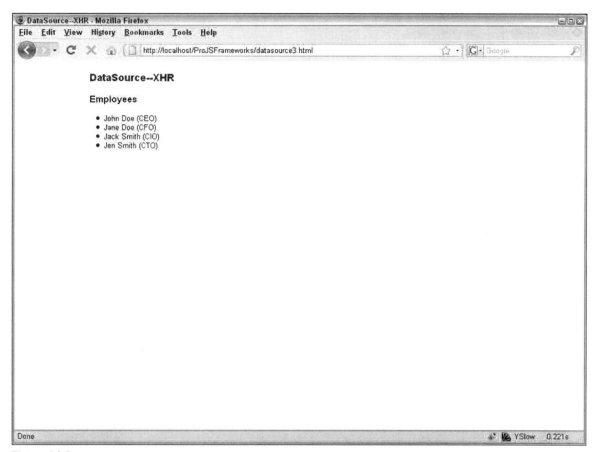

Figure 14-3

Presenting Tabular Data

Everyone knows how to build a table in HTML. If anything, for too long all people did on the Web was build tables — even when it wasn't to display tabular data. But a simple HTML table doesn't cut it in today's Web. Site visitors have come to expect a certain level of richness and interactivity whenever presented with data sets. Sometimes data visualization is employed (more on that in the section on charts) and sometimes the raw data is presented. In the case of the latter, it's good to enable the visitor the ability to interact with the data in front of them — whether this means sorting or filtering the data or even updating it in real time. YUI's DataTable allows for all that and more.

One of the great features of DataTable is that it can be plugged into a source of data via the `DataSource` object, turning raw data into a rich, interactive data table (see Figure 14-4).

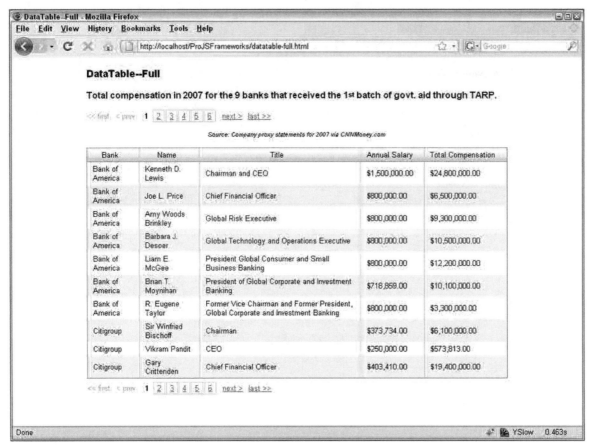

Figure 14-4

Here's how it's done:

```html
<html>
    <head>
        <title>DataTable--Full</title>
        <link rel="stylesheet" type="text/css"
            href="reset-fonts-grids.css" />
        <link rel="stylesheet" type="text/css"
            href="base-min.css" />
        <link rel="stylesheet" type="text/css"
            href="build/paginator/assets/skins/sam/paginator.css" />
        <link rel="stylesheet" type="text/css"
            href="build/datatable/assets/skins/sam/datatable.css" />
    </head>
    <body class="yui-skin-sam">
        <div id="doc">
            <div id="hd">
            </div>
            <div id="bd">
                <h1>DataTable--Full</h1>
```

```html
            <h2>
                Total compensation in 2007 for the 9 banks
                that received the 1<sup>st</sup> batch of govt.
                aid through TARP.
            </h2>
            <div id="data">
            </div>
        </div>
        <div id="ft">
        </div>
    </div>
    <!-- Required -->
    <script type="text/javascript"
        src="build/yahoo-dom-event/yahoo-dom-event.js"></script>
    <script type="text/javascript"
        src="build/element/element-min.js"></script>
    <script type="text/javascript"
        src="build/datasource/datasource-min.js"></script>

    <!-- Optional -->
    <script type="text/javascript"
        src="build/paginator/paginator-min.js"></script>
    <script type="text/javascript"
        src="build/json/json-min.js"></script>
    <script type="text/javascript"
        src="build/connection/connection-min.js"></script>
    <script type="text/javascript"
        src="build/get/get-min.js"></script>
    <script type="text/javascript"
        src="build/dragdrop/dragdrop-min.js"></script>

    <!-- Required -->
    <script type="text/javascript"
        src="build/datatable/datatable-min.js"></script>

    <script>
        (function () {
            /*
             * Sort function for currency values
             */
            function totalSort(a, b, desc) {
                return moneySort("total", a, b, desc);
            };

            function salarySort(a, b, desc) {
                return moneySort("salary", a, b, desc);
            };

            function moneySort(val, a, b, desc) {
                a = a.getData()[val];
                b = b.getData()[val];

                if (desc) {
                    return b - a;
```

```
                } else {
                    return a - b;
                }
            };

            /*
             * Instantiate data source
             */
            var dataSource = new YAHOO.util.XHRDataSource("bonuses.json?");
            dataSource.responseType = YAHOO.util.DataSource.TYPE_JSON;

            dataSource.connXhrMode = "queueRequests"; /* handles requests
                                                         synchronously */
            dataSource.responseSchema = {
                resultsList: "resultset.results",
                fields: ["bank", "name", "title", "salary", "total"]
            };

            /*
             * Define columns
             */
            var columnDefs = [
                {key: "bank", label: "Bank", sortable:true, resizeable:true},
                {key: "name", label: "Name", sortable:true, resizeable:true},
                {key: "title", label: "Title", sortable:true, resizeable:true},
                {key: "salary", label: "Annual Salary", sortable:true,
                    resizeable:true,
                    formatter:YAHOO.widget.DataTable.formatCurrency,
                    sortOptions:{sortFunction:salarySort}},
                {key: "total", label: "Total Compensation", sortable:true,
                    resizeable:true,
                    formatter:YAHOO.widget.DataTable.formatCurrency,
                    sortOptions:{sortFunction:totalSort}}
            ];

            /*
             * Instantiate data table
             */
            var config = {

                    caption: "Source: Company proxy statements for 2007 via " +
                        "CNNMoney.com",
                    paginator: new YAHOO.widget.Paginator({
                        rowsPerPage: 10
                    }),
                    draggableColumns:true
            };

            var dtable = new YAHOO.widget.DataTable("data", columnDefs,
                    dataSource, config);
        })();
    </script>
    </body>
</html>
```

After including all of the necessary CSS and script files, the process of tying a data source to a data table is fairly straightforward. In this case, for the sake of illustrating the widget's abilities, the `DataTable` in question is doing a lot of different things.

The first thing that's done is the creation of a custom sort function. This is done in order to make sure that the columns with currency information are sorted as numbers and not as strings. In other words, it's to make sure a set of values such as 15, 4, 1, 7 don't end up getting sorted as 1, 15, 4, 7 but rather as 1, 4, 7, 15. Since there's no way of knowing which column called the sort algorithm, a unique function must be created for each in order for the algorithm to know which values to sort. The unique functions in turn call the main sort function adding the name of the column on which the sort is being applied.

Next, a `DataSource` object is instantiated pointing it to a file named `bonuses.json`. This file contains data that looks like this:

```
{"resultset":{
    "results":[
        {
            "bank": "Bank of America",
            "name": "Kenneth D. Lewis",
            "title": "Chairman and CEO",
            "salary": 1500000,
            "total": 24800000
        },
        {
            "bank": "Bank of America",
            "name": "Joe L. Price",
            "title": "Chief Financial Officer",
            "salary": 800000,
            "total": 6500000
        },
        ...
    ]}
}
```

Now that the data source is created, all that's left to do is to instantiate a `DataTable` object and connect the two. Rather than doing all of the configuration for the `DataTable` object inline, it's done in a couple of variables, `columnDefs` and `config`. The final product of this exercise is a data table that is sortable, has pagination, and has columns that can be resized and dragged.

Drawing Charts and Graphs

Rendering data in tables is nice, but nothing gets an immediate reaction like a visual. Turning data into a chart used to be the realm of spreadsheet software. Not anymore. YUI's Charts control plugs into a `DataSource`, turning its data into visually appealing charts and graphs. The Charts control is capable of displaying line charts, bar charts, column charts, pie charts, stacked bar charts, and stacked column charts. Choosing between them is as simple as choosing between the following constructors:

❑   `YAHOO.widget.LineChart`

❑   `YAHOO.widget.BarChart`

❑   `YAHOO.widget.ColumnChart`

❑   `YAHOO.widget.PieChart`

❑   `YAHOO.widget.StackedBarChart`

❑   `YAHOO.widget.StackedColumnChart`

For example, take the following partial data set:

```
{"resultset":{
    "results":[
        {
            "bank": "Merrill Lynch",
            "name": "E. Stanley O'Neal",
            "title": "Former Chief Executive Officer",
            "salary": 584231,
            "total": 24300000
        },
        {
            "bank": "Merrill Lynch",
            "name": "Ahmass L. Fakahany",
            "title": "Former Co-President and Co-Chief Operating Officer",
            "salary": 350000,
            "total": 4600000
        },
        {
            "bank": "Merrill Lynch",
            "name": "Dow Kim",
            "title": "Former Executive Vice President",
            "salary": 309615,
            "total": 14500000
        },
        ...
    ]}
}
```

This data set can be turned into a chart (see Figure 14-5) with the following code:

```
<html>
    <head>
        <title>Charts</title>
        <link rel="stylesheet" type="text/css" href="reset-fonts-grids.css" />
        <link rel="stylesheet" type="text/css" href="base-min.css" />
        <style type="text/css">
            #chart {
                height: 450px;
                width: 750px;
            }
        </style>
    </head>
```

```html
<body class="yui-skin-sam">
    <div id="doc">
        <div id="hd">
        </div>
        <div id="bd">
            <h1>Charts</h1>
            <h2>
                Total compensation in 2007 for the 9 banks
                that received the 1<sup>st</sup> batch of govt.
                aid through TARP. (partial list)
            </h2>
            <div id="chart">
            </div>
        </div>
        <div id="ft">
        </div>
    </div>
    <!-- Required -->

    <script type="text/javascript"
            src="build/yahoo-dom-event/yahoo-dom-event.js"></script>
    <script type="text/javascript"
            src="build/element/element-min.js"></script>
    <script type="text/javascript"
            src="build/datasource/datasource-min.js"></script>
    <script type="text/javascript"
            src="build/json/json-min.js"></script>

    <!-- Optional -->

    <script type="text/javascript"
            src="build/connection/connection-min.js"></script>

    <!-- Required -->
    <script type="text/javascript" src="build/charts/charts-min.js"></script>

    <script>
        (function () {
            /*
             * Instantiate data source
             */

            var dataSource = new YAHOO.util.XHRDataSource(
                    "bonuses-short.json?");
            dataSource.responseType = YAHOO.util.DataSource.TYPE_JSON;

            dataSource.connXhrMode = "queueRequests"; /* handles requests
                                                        synchronously */
```

```
                        dataSource.responseSchema = {
                            resultsList: "resultset.results",
                            fields: ["bank", "name", "title", "salary", "total"]
                        };

                        /*
                         * Instantiage chart
                         */
                        function formatCurrencyAxisLabel( value )
                        {
                            return YAHOO.util.Number.format( value,
                            {
                                prefix: "$",
                                thousandsSeparator: ",",
                                decimalPlaces: 2
                            });
                        }
                        var currencyAxis = new YAHOO.widget.NumericAxis();
                        currencyAxis.labelFunction = formatCurrencyAxisLabel;

                        var seriesDef =
                        [
                            { displayName: "Salary", yField: "salary" },
                            { displayName: "Total Compensation", yField: "total" }
                        ];


                        var chart = new YAHOO.widget.StackedColumnChart( "chart",
                        dataSource,
                        {
                            xField: "name",
                            yField: "total",
                            yAxis: currencyAxis,
                            series: seriesDef
                        });
                    })();
            </script>
        </body>
    </html>
```

Once the required files are in place, it's a simple case of instantiating a data source and tying it to a chart object. There is some customization that's being done here in that the y-axis labels are being touched up so as to apply currency formatting to them via the NumericAxis object's labelFunction property. It's also possible to create a TimeAxis object in order to display time-based values along an axis.

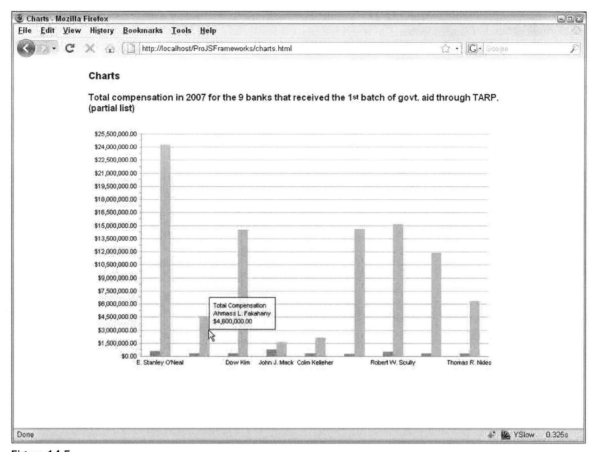

Figure 14-5

Chart customization is done through a style object passed to the constructor via the config parameter taking the following form:

```
var seriesDef =
[
    {
        displayName: "Salary",
        yField: "salary",
        style: {
            color: 0xff0000
        }
    },
    {
        displayName: "Total Compensation",
        yField: "total",
        style: {
            color: 0x00ff00
        }
    }
];
```

These new values found within the `style` object will turn the Salary bars red and the Total Compensation bars green (since 0xff0000 is the hex value for red and 0x00ff00 is the hex value for green).

Here's a table of all of the available styling attributes:

Style	Substyle	Description
padding		A numeric value that specifies the spacing around the edge of the chart's contents. Unlike CSS padding in HTML, the chart's padding does not increase the dimensions of the chart.
animationEnabled		A Boolean value that specifies whether marker animations are enabled or not. The default value is true, meaning that markers will animate when data changes.
font		One may declare a font style to customize the default axis text, including the font name, size, color, and more. It is represented as an Object value that contains several substyles.
	Name	Accepts a String that is either the name of the font or a list of comma-delimited font names, similar to the way `font-family` works in CSS.
	Color	A hex number value like 0xff0000.
	Size	Accepts a numeric value for the point size. No other font size units are available.
	Bold	Boolean value to set if the font is displayed in bold.
	Italic	Boolean value to set if the font is displayed in italics.
	Underline	Boolean value to set if the font is displayed with an underline.
border		The border style allows a developer to add a colored border around the chart. The chart itself decreases in dimensions to accommodate the border. It is represented as an Object value that contains several substyles.
	Color	A hex-formatted string or number value like "ff0000" or 0xff0000.

Style	Substyle	Description
	Size	The border thickness in pixels.
background		The background style allows one to customize the background color or image. It is represented as an Object value that contains several substyles.
	Color	Specifies the background fill color. If an image is present, this fill color will appear behind the image. Accepts a hex-formatted string or number value like "ff0000" or 0xff0000.
	Alpha	A value from 0.0 to 1.0 that refers to the transparency of the background color. This is most useful when used on the data tip background.
	Image	The URL of a JPG, PNG, GIF, or SWF image. May be relative or absolute. Relative URLs are relative to the HTML document in which the chart is embedded.
	Mode	The method used to display the background image. May be "repeat" (default), "repeat-x", "repeat-y", "no-repeat", or "stretch".
legend		The legend style lets a developer customize the appearance of the legend. It is represented as an Object value that contains several substyles.
	Display	Specifies the location where the legend will be drawn. Accepted values include "none", "left", "right", "top", and "bottom". The default value is "none".
	Spacing	A value that specifies the number of pixels between each of the items displayed in the legend.
	Padding	Same as the padding style described above.
	Border	Same as the border style described above.
	Background	Same as the background style described above.
	Font	Same as the font style described above.

(continued)

Style	Substyle	Description
dataTip		The dataTip style lets a developer customize the appearance of the data tip. It is represented as an Object value that contains several substyles.
	Padding	Same as the padding style described above.
	Border background	Same as the border style described above. Same as the background style described above.
	Font	Same as the font style described above.
xAxis and yAxis		The xAxis and yAxis styles allow one to customize the appearance of either axis. They are represented as Object values that contain several substyles.
	Color	The color of the axis itself. Accepts a hex-formatted string or number value like "ff0000" or 0xff0000.
	Size	A numeric value that represents the thickness of the axis itself. A value of 0 hides the axis (but not the labels).
	showLabels	If true, the labels are displayed. If false, they are hidden.
	hideOverlappingLabels	Indicates whether or not to hide overlapping labels. This style is used on the Category Axis when calculateCategoryCount is false. The style is used on the TimeAxis and NumericAxis when the user specifies the majorUnit. Otherwise, the axes place the labels so that they do not overlap.
	labelSpacing	The distance, in pixels, between labels on an axis. The default value is 2.
	labelDistance	The distance, in pixels, between a label and the axis. The default value is 2.
	titleRotation	Indicates the rotation of the title on the axis.
	titleDistance	The distance, in pixels, between a title and the axis labels. The default value is 2.

Style	Substyle	Description
	`majorGridLines`	Described below.
	`minorGridLines`	Described below.
	`zeroGridLine`	Described below.
	`majorTicks`	Described below.
	`minorTicks`	Described below.
`majorGridLines` and `minorGridLines`		The majorGridLines and minorGridLines styles have a couple of substyles that need extra explanation. As shown above, majorGridLines and minorGridLines are substyles of the xAxis and yAxis styles.
	`Color`	The color of the grid lines. Accepts a hex-formatted string or number value like "ff0000" or 0xff0000.
	`Size`	A numeric value that represents the thickness of the grid lines. To hide the grid lines, set the size substyle to 0 (zero). If the grid lines are hidden by default, a thickness greater than zero must be specified to show them.
`zeroGridLine`		The zeroGridLine style allows for emphasis on the zero grid line when it falls beyond the origin of the axis. The zeroGridLine style has the following substyles:
	`Color`	The color of the zero grid line. Accepts a hex-formatted string or number value like "ff0000" or 0xff0000.
	`Size`	A numeric value that represents the thickness of the zero grid line. To hide the grid line, set the size substyle to 0.
`majorTicks` and `minorTicks`		The majorTicks and minorTicks styles have a couple of substyles that need extra explanation. As shown above, majorTicks and minorTicks are substyles of the xAxis and yAxis styles.
	`Color`	The color of the ticks. Accepts a hex-formatted string or number value like "ff0000" or 0xff0000.

(continued)

Style	Substyle	Description
	Size	A numeric value that represents the thickness of the ticks. This style may need to be set to a valid numeric value greater than zero if the ticks are not shown by default.
	Length	The number of pixels the ticks extend from the axis. This style may need to be set to a valid numeric value greater than zero if the ticks are not shown by default.
	Display	Specifies how the ticks are drawn. Accepted values include "none", "inside", "outside", and "cross". In many cases, "none" is the default.

Table comes from the Charts page on the YUI web site.

Summary

Dealing with data is practically a breeze with YUI's DataSource component, which easily plugs into other YUI widgets. It also makes developing custom data-driven widgets very simple since it abstracts data to an easily manageable object. What's more, visualizing data acquired with DataSource is so easy with DataTable and Charts. It's a wonder how this sort of thing was done before the advent of these components.Figure 14-2 is based on the figure found on the YUI DataSource page.

15

Working with YUI CSS Tools

In this chapter, you'll learn about:

❑   Establishing cross-browser consistency

❑   Getting control of typography

❑   Building layouts from grids

Establishing Cross-Browser Consistency

Every browser maker builds their own layout algorithm, which is surprisingly close to, but not exactly the same as that of its competitors. So it's no surprise that distances between objects on the page and even font kerning can be slightly different form browser to browser. In fact, with the current state of browsers, it's impossible to have exactly identical renderings from one browser to the next.

Take the following markup for example:

```
<h1>Base Render</h1>
<p>
    Lorem ipsum dolor sit amet, consectetur adipiscing elit. Donec lectus.
    Curabitur malesuada purus vitae tellus. Quisque feugiat volutpat enim.
    Donec tempor mauris et nunc.
</p>
<ul>
    <li>
        Etiam nunc turpis, placerat a, aliquam non, vestibulum in, odio.
    </li>
    <li>
        Nulla scelerisque, nisl in tincidunt iaculis, quam ante malesuada
        purus, ac interdum tortor elit sed sapien.
    </li>
</ul>
```

```
        <li>
            Ut auctor, diam at bibendum accumsan, felis nisi porttitor enim,
            sed feugiat nibh mi sagittis dolor.
        </li>
    </ul>
    <h2>Nulla fringilla turpis ac nibh.</h2>
    <blockquote>
        <p>
            Vivamus tempus turpis adipiscing nibh. Ut nec orci. Etiam vitae
            ante nec nunc ornare tincidunt. Ut tortor nunc, adipiscing vel,
            semper at, tincidunt et, lectus.
        </p>
    </blockquote>
    <table>
        <thead>
            <tr>
                <th>Donec</th>
                <th>non orci</th>
            </tr>
        </thead>
        <tbody>
            <tr>
                <td>
                    ut sem dapibus mollis. Donec nunc ipsum, pellentesque
                    consectetur, congue non, faucibus bibendum, lectus.
                </td>
                <td>
                    In hac habitasse platea dictumst. Sed fringilla.
                    Quisque tristique leo eu risus.
                </td>
            </tr>
        </tbody>
    </table>
```

Here is what this markup looks like in IE7, Firefox 3, and Chrome side by side (and overlapped to show the differences), as shown in Figure 15-1.

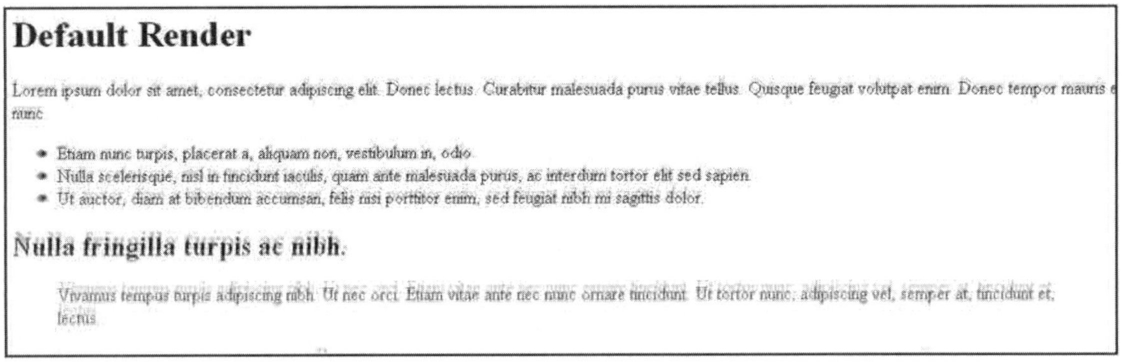

Figure 15-1

YUI's CSS files try to reign in rendering engines as much as possible, the first of which is `reset.css`. This file strips the browser's default rendering values so that all font sizes for all elements are the same, all margins and padding values are set to zero, and so on. Though the outcome isn't perfect (see Figure 15-2), it does establish a clean slate upon which some default values can be set. If nothing more, it ensures that developers don't take default values for granted. In other words, if a list item needs a bullet and a left padding of `1em`, then it's up to the developer to specify that value, instead of assuming that it's the same across all browsers.

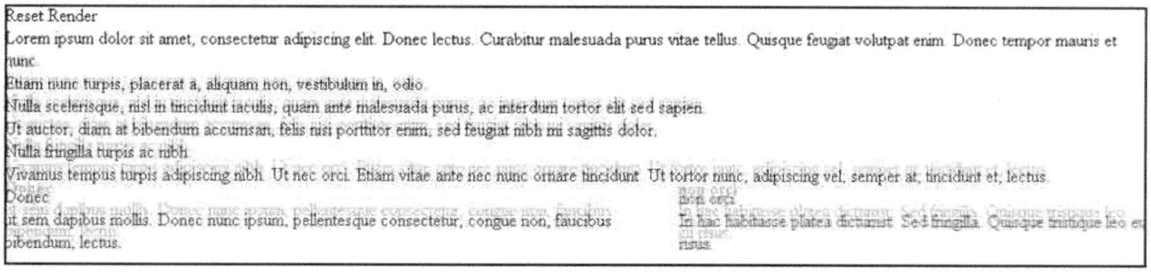

Figure 15-2

As is fairly obvious in Figure 15-2, however, even stripping the default rendering of its size and positioning values doesn't quite line up the different browsers' outputs. But assigning new and consistent margin, padding, and font size values to the reset rendering does actually go a long way to bringing all browsers to a much more similar rendering (see Figure 15-3). Note that the font values being assigned to Figure 15-3 actually come from `fonts.css` (discussed later).

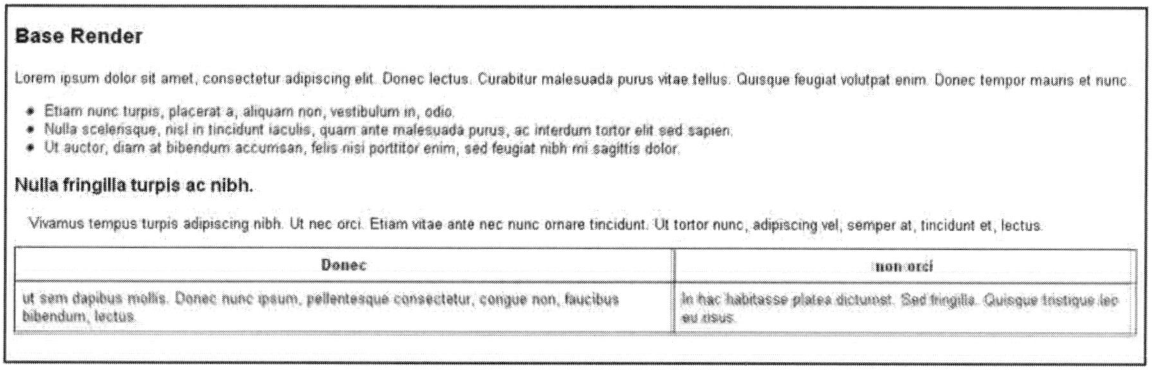

Figure 15-3

Though `base.css` does a good job of straightening everything out, it isn't really recommended for production use, the reason being that most production sites will have specific layout needs, which will require specific CSS rules. As it is, using `reset.css` and `fonts.css` (to be covered next) to bring everything to a baseline adds a bunch of rules to a page just to get it to a usable state. Weighing it down further with `base.css` only to later override *it* with a site's specific CSS doesn't make much sense.

Getting Control of Typography

Typography has always been a weakness of web publishing. Browsers rely on the local presence of fonts for their rendering needs. In other words, a font file can't be sent to the browser along with the HTML, CSS, and JavaScript files. This puts the page at the mercy of the platform on which it's being rendered. To make things worse, different browsers treat the *same* font differently when it comes to kerning and other calculations.

In order to bring a little sanity to the game, YUI has a `fonts.css` file which normalizes — as much as possible — the typographical discrepancies between browsers. It sets the default font family to Arial and sets up a degradation path for commonly available font families (if one isn't available, its known equivalent is requested instead). It also sets the baseline font size to 13 pixels with a line height of 16 pixels.

Here are the font families that are set to degrade well across multiple operating systems:

```
#demo1 {}
#demo2 {font-family:monospace;}
#demo3 {font-family:georgia;}
#demo4 {font-family:verdana;}
#demo5 {font-family:times;}
```

This example comes from the YUI fonts page.

With that done, font sizes can now be set reliably enough across browsers using the following lookup table:

Pixels	Percent
10	77
11	85
12	93
13	100
14	108
15	116
16	123.1
17	131
18	138.5
19	146.5
20	153.9
21	161.6
22	167

Pixels	Percent
23	174
24	182
25	189
26	197

So, in order to achieve a 12-pixel font size, the value to set in CSS is 93 percent. However, be advised that font values are inherited in CSS, so setting nested percentages will yield unexpected results. So for example, setting a container element's font size to 93 percent, and then a child element's to 93 percent as well will actually be setting the child to 93 percent *of* 93 percent, or 11.2 pixels. It's therefore very important to set font sizes wisely, making sure to never nest them unless expressly intended. Figure 15-4 and Figure 15-5 show how `fonts.css` brings the three aforementioned browsers in line.

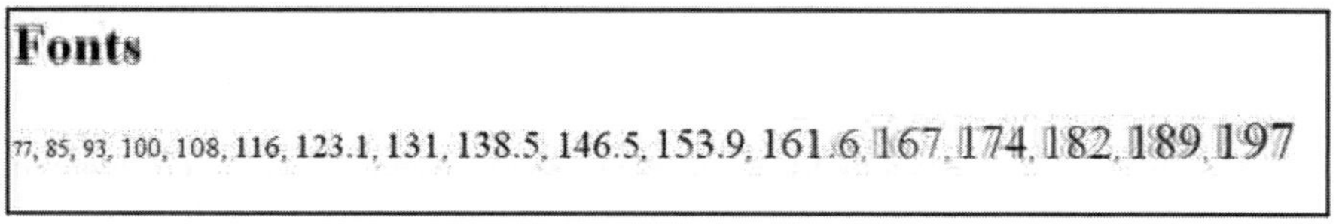

Fonts

77, 85, 93, 100, 108, 116, 123.1, 131, 138.5, 146.5, 153.9, 161.6, 167, 174, 182, 189, 197

Figure 15-4

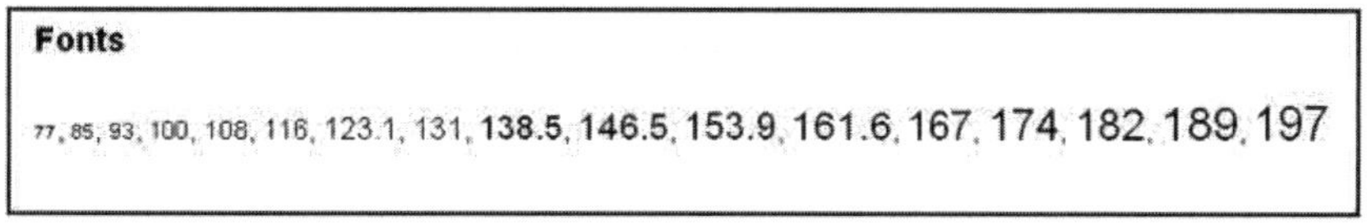

Fonts

77, 85, 93, 100, 108, 116, 123.1, 131, 138.5, 146.5, 153.9, 161.6, 167, 174, 182, 189, 197

Figure 15-5

Building Layouts from Grids

Layout has long been the source of friction in the web development world. Stemming largely from the now settled debate of whether to use tables for layout or not, it's now left purely to CSS to properly place content on the page. This should be good news, except that browsers have traditionally been notorious for going out of their way to be different from each other. This translates into a huge headache for web developers who just want one layout to bind them.

YUI's `grids.css` provides the ability to lay out pages in a cross-browser, robust, and flexible manner. The base dimensions offered by the *grids* system accommodate the Interactive Advertising Bureau's (IAB) *Ad Unit Guidelines* for common ad dimensions. In other words, it's possible to choose a "column" or "cell" width (to use `table` parlance) that coincides with IAB standard ad sizes. The YUI team even provides a "Grid Builder" tool available at `http://developer.yahoo.com/yui/grids/builder/` that puts together all of the markup, described next, with only a few clicks of the widget (see Figure 15-6).

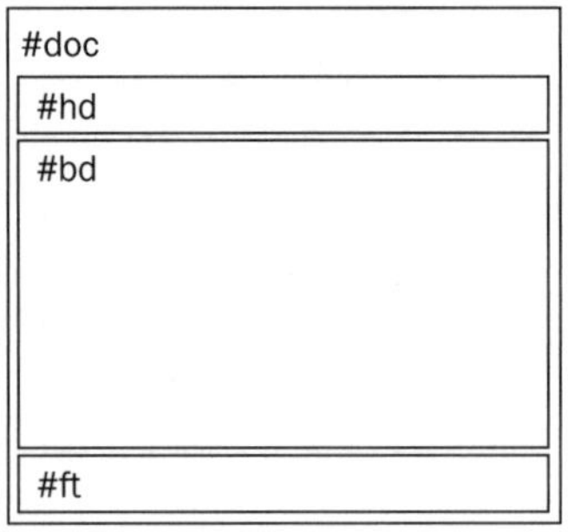

Figure 15-6

YUI grids come in four main flavors that are represented by four root IDs:

❏   **div#doc** creates a 750px page width.

❏   **div#doc2** creates a 950px page width.

❏   **div#doc3** creates a 100 percent page width. (Note that the 100 percent page width also sets 10px of left and right margins so that content had a bit of breathing room between it and the browser chrome.)

❏   **div#doc4** creates a 974px page width, and is a new addition to Grids in YUI version 2.3.0.

The contents of this bullet list come directly from the YUI (750px page width) example page.

The 10px margin on either side of the 100 percent width layout keeps the content from bleeding into the browser's chrome. It can however be reset with the following CSS:

```
#doc3 {margin: auto}
```

Customizing the width of a grid layout is simple. Since YUI's grid layouts are based on em values, which are in turn tied into the baseline font size, a simple bit of arithmetic is all it takes to convert the desired width into an em value. Widths are set in ems because ems scale with the baseline font size — in other words, when the user adjusts their font size, the entire grid will respond accordingly. Since the baseline font size is set to 13 pixels, converting a pixel width to em values is as simple as dividing the width by 13. At least it's that simple for all non-IE browsers. For IE, the division must be made by 13.3333. Here's an example of how to go about implementing an override value:

```
<style>
#custom-doc {
      margin:auto;text-align:left; /* leave unchanged */
      width:46.15em;/* non-IE */
      *width:45.00em;/* IE */
      min-width:600px;/* optional but recommended */
}
</style>
```

This example comes directly from the YUI Grids page.

The basic structure of a grids-based document has been present throughout the examples in this section, and is as follows:

```
<html>
    <head>
        <title></title>
        <link rel="stylesheet" type="text/css" href="reset-fonts-grids.css" />
    </head>
    <body>
        <div id="doc">
            <div id="hd">
                <!-- Header content goes here -->
            </div>
            <div id="bd">
                <!-- Body content goes here -->
            </div>
            <div id="ft">
                <!-- Footer content goes here -->
            </div>
        </div>
    </body>
</html>
```

First, the `grids.css` file is included in the document head. Then a `div` with the desired doc ID is created; in this case it's simply "doc", which yields a 750-pixel width layout. Within it are included three `div`s with the IDs `hd`, `bd`, and `ft` for head, body and foot, respectively (see Figure 15-6).

Templates

Most sites have a columnar layout with one column representing the main content and another representing the secondary content. YUI Grids has a set of prebuilt templates built around this concept (the dimensions are based on the IAB guidelines). The two initial columns are created with two `div`s given the `yui-b` class name, the "b" standing for "block." In order to achieve source-order independence (in other words, letting either primary or secondary content be first in the source but not first in the layout), the main content block is surrounded by a `div` with the ID `yui-main`. Finally, in order to trigger one of the six preset templates, one of the following class names is given to the root `div`.

Template Class	Preset Description
`yui-t1`	160 on left
`yui-t2`	180 on left
`yui-t3`	300 on left
`yui-t4`	180 on right
`yui-t5`	240 on right
`yui-t6`	300 on right

Here is a code listing for a basic template layout using preset yui-t4 (see Figure 15-7):

```
<div id="doc" class="yui-t4">
    <div id="hd">
        <! - Header content goes here -->
    </div>
    <div id="bd">
        <div id="yui-main">
            <div class="yui-b">
                <!-- Primary content goes here -->
            </div>
        </div>
        <div class="yui-b">
            <!-- Secondary content goes here -->
        </div>
    </div>
    <div id="ft">
        <! - Footer content goes here -->
    </div>
</div>
```

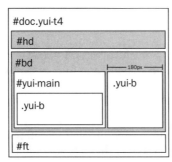

Figure 15-7

Nesting Grids

Content blocks can further be divided in half by using what YUI calls grids. A grid can, in a limited way, be equated to an HTML table's row element. Within a grid are placed two unit elements, which can be equated to a table's cells. Grids are identified by the yui-g class name and units are identified by the yui-u class name (see Figure 15-8). The code for two units in a grid looks like this:

```
...
<div class="yui-g">
    <div class="yui-u first">
        <!-- Unit content here -->
    </div>
    <div class="yui-u">
        <!-- Unit content here -->
    </div>
</div>
...
```

The code for four units looks like this:

```
<div class="yui-g">
    <div class="yui-g first">
        <div class="yui-u first">
            <!-- Unit content here -->
        </div>
        <div class="yui-u">
            <!-- Unit content here -->
        </div>
    </div>
    <div class="yui-g">
        <div class="yui-u first">
            <!-- Unit content here -->
        </div>
        <div class="yui-u">
            <!-- Unit content here -->
        </div>
    </div>
</div>
```

Note how the outer grid (yui-g) contains another two grids. Since each grid only holds two units, this is the way to put four of them together. Note also the presence of the first class name. Whenever there's a series of items such as two or more yui-u or yui-g elements, the first class name tells YUI to treat the first in the series slightly different when it comes to its margins, and so on. In short, the first class name makes sure things get laid out properly.

Grid units (yui-u) split the available space fifty-fifty. But there are cases where one unit needs to be bigger, or you need to have three units. This is where special grids come in.

Special Grid Class	Description
yui-gb	1/3 - 1/3 - 1/3
yui-gc	2/3 - 1/3
yui-gd	1/3 - 2/3
yui-ge	3/4 - 1/4
yui-gf	1/4 - 3/4

With grids and special grids used in combination, it's possible to build very complex layouts. The following is a code listing for just such a complex layout (see Figure 15-8).

```
<html>
    <head>
        <title></title>
        <link rel="stylesheet" type="text/css" href="reset-fonts-grids.css" />
        <link rel="stylesheet" type="text/css" href="base-min.css" />
    </head>
```

```
<body>
    <div id="doc" class="yui-t4">
        <div id="hd">
            <h1>Header</h1>
        </div>
        <div id="bd">
            <div id="yui-main">
                <h2>Primary Col</h2>
                <div class="yui-b">
                    <div class="yui-g">
                        <div class="yui-g first">
                            <div class="yui-u first">
                                <h3>Row 1, Col 1</h3>
                                <p>Lorem ipsum dolor sit amet, consectet...</p>
                            </div>
                            <div class="yui-u">
                                <h3>Row 1, Col 2</h3>
                                <p>Lorem ipsum dolor sit amet, consectet...</p>
                            </div>
                        </div>
                        <div class="yui-g">
                            <div class="yui-u first">
                                <h3>Row 1, Col 3</h3>
                                <p>Lorem ipsum dolor sit amet, consectet...</p>
                            </div>
                            <div class="yui-u">
                                <h3>Row 1, Col 4</h3>
                                <p>Lorem ipsum dolor sit amet, consectet...</p>
                            </div>
                        </div>
                    </div>
                    <div class="yui-gc">
                        <div class="yui-u first">
                            <h3>Row 2, Col 1</h3>
                             <p>Lorem ipsum dolor sit amet, consectet...</p>
                        </div>
                        <div class="yui-u">
                            <h3>Row 2, Col 2</h3>
                            <p>Lorem ipsum dolor sit amet, consectet...</p>
                        </div>
                    </div>
                </div>
            </div>
            <div class="yui-b">
                <h2>Secondary Col</h2>
                <p>Lorem ipsum dolor sit amet, consectetur adipiscing... </p>
            </div>
        </div>
        <div id="ft">
            <p>Footer</p>
        </div>
    </div>
</body>
</html>
```

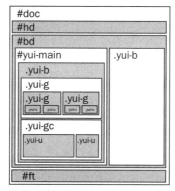

Figure 15-8

New in YUI 3

Apart from renaming the CSS folders and files with the prefix "css" for clarity's sake (now they're called cssreset, cssfonts, and cssgrids), YUI 3 CSS files now also include context. This means that rather than being forced to apply the CSS files to the whole page, it's now possible, through -context.css versions of the library files to apply them to only a part of the page. This makes retrofitting existing pages that don't use YUI a whole lot easier. Also, rather than having one grids document defined by an ID, it's possible to have multiple layouts per page that coexist now that all ID-based CSS selectors have been replaced with class names.

Summary

CSS implementations across browsers tend to be more of an art than a science. The result of this is that rendering engines don't always spit out the exact same layout from one browser to another. The YUI Library's set of CSS files goes a long way in reigning browsers' rendering engines in and normalizing their output to something a little more predictable. The basic ground that these files cover help developers and designers hit the ground running and enable them to focus on their site designs rather than rendering engine differences.

16

Building and Deploying

JavaScript is an uncompiled language that gets sent over the wire in clear text to be interpreted and executed by the browser on the receiving end. Code that exists in its written form, with all of its whitespace, comments, and indentation, is great for developers who need to read it. But all it does for computers is slow them down. Whitespace and comments are completely useless to browsers and can account for up to 60 percent of a JavaScript file's weight. This sort of thing can be responsible for crippling performance issues when dealing with potentially large library files.

YUI offers a couple of solutions in order to combat the weight and delivery issues of JavaScript.

In this chapter, you'll learn about:

❑   Using shared YUI files from Yahoo!

❑   Shrinking and optimizing loading times

Shared YUI Files from Yahoo!

Caching files has long been a technique used by browsers for improving page load times. Though caching a file doesn't help the speed with which it's loaded the first time around, once it's in the browser's cache, the speed with which it's accessed is dramatically improved. It's basically a proximity game; bringing the resources closer to the browser reduces the time needed to load them. Obviously, the hard drive is the closest a file can get to the browser, but there are other levels of closeness that can be achieved. Rather than delivering the files from the hosting server, they can be moved geographically to a server closer to the visitor. A network of such servers is called a Content Delivery Network, or CDN. Yahoo!, being the large company that it is, has its own CDN and in February, 2007, with the release of YUI 2.2.0, opted to host YUI files on it. Incidentally, Google also hosts YUI files on their servers along with various other libraries (more information here: http://code.google.com/apis/ajaxlibs/documentation/#AjaxLibraries). The main difference between Yahoo!'s CDN and Google's CDN is that Yahoo! supports combo-handling and Google supports SSL.

Not only are files hosted on the Yahoo! CDN closer to visitors, but they're also served up much faster than if they were served by normal servers. This is because CDN servers are configured to do nothing but spit out static, cached files. They're optimized for it. A site that's processing a bunch of server-side scripts and maybe accessing a database can't hope to keep up with a streamlined CDN server.

Another performance bonus that is gained through the use of hosted YUI files is that if a visitor has already been on a site using a hosted YUI file, then it will already be on his or her computer (since its signature will be determined by the URL of the file, which comes from the same source). In other words, they've already got the file on their computer so they don't need to download it again.

The easiest way to use the YUI hosted files is to visit the YUI Dependency Configurator at `http://developer.yahoo.com/yui/articles/hosting/`. The tool on that page allows for the selection of all the needed dependencies via an easy-to-use set of buttons, and spits out the necessary code ready to be copied and pasted into a page. The good thing about using the configurator is that it's aware of the needed dependencies of certain library components. For example, clicking the "AutoComplete Control" button will generate code to load `autocomplete.css`, `yahoo-dom-event.js`, `datasource-min.js`, and `autocomplete-min.js` (see Figure 16.1). The fact that minimized files are being output by the configurator can also be adjusted. The option to output minimized, raw, or debug versions of the files is available via another click of a button.

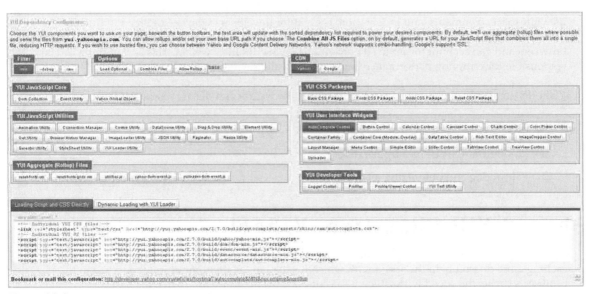

Figure 16-1

Here's a quick example of how to load the core Yahoo, DOM, and event files. Make sure that all your `src=` expressions are declared on a single line.

```
<script type="text/javascript" src=
"http://yui.yahooapis.com/2.7.0/build/yahoo/yahoo-min.js"></script>
<script type="text/javascript" src="
http://yui.yahooapis.com/2.7.0/build/dom/dom-min.js"></script>
<script type="text/javascript" src=
"http://yui.yahooapis.com/2.7.0/build/event/event-min.js"></script>
```

It's also possible to load all three in the rolled up `yahoo-dom-event.js` file like so:

```
<script type="text/javascript" src=
"http://yui.yahooapis.com/2.7.0/build/yahoo-dom-event/yahoo-dom-event.js"></script>
```

The hosted files are versioned (in this case they belong to version 2.7.0), so there's no chance of them being changed without notice. New versions of the library will simply be hosted under new version number folders. As with the downloadable library, the hosted files come in three flavors: minimized, debug, and raw. These can be accessed by simply changing the filenames in the request URL and adding -min or -debug or nothing at all to the base filenames. Here is an example of the `yahoo.js` file being loaded in the three different ways:

Minimized

```
<script type="text/javascript" src=
"http://yui.yahooapis.com/2.7.0/build/yahoo/yahoo-min.js"></script>
```
Debug

```
<script type="text/javascript" src=
"http://yui.yahooapis.com/2.7.0/build/yahoo/yahoo-debug.js"></script>
```
Raw

```
<script type="text/javascript" src=
"http://yui.yahooapis.com/2.7.0/build/yahoo/yahoo.js"></script>
```

Combining Files

Though serving files from a CDN increases the speed with which they make it to the browser, making multiple requests for files can become another performance bottleneck. Each HTTP request represents time lost in making a request to the server and waiting for a response. Worse still, only two HTTP connections can be made from a browser to a server at any given time, so multiple calls will have to wait for those connections to free up. Also, the additional HTTP header data as well as file header data (in the case of images for example) just adds to the payload that needs to be transferred back and forth.

The solution is to combine the needed files into aggregate files so that the number of HTTP requests get reduced to as few as possible. In the case of images, this means creating sprites (which falls out of the scope of this book). In the case of JavaScript and CSS files, what's needed is to concatenate the files into one big JavaScript or CSS file. YUI already does this with its `yahoo-dom-event.js` file, which is an aggregate of the `yahoo.js`, `dom.js`, and `event.js` files. But what about other dependencies? Well, YUI has introduced a combo handler that allows for the on-the-fly concatenation of YUI files. Here's what the `AutoComplete` scripts look like when loaded with the combo handler:

```
<script type="text/javascript" src=
"http://yui.yahooapis.com/combo?2.7.0/build/yahoo-dom-event/yahoo-dom-event
.js&2.7.0/build/datasource/datasource-min.js&2.7.0/build/autocomplete/
autocomplete-min.js"></script>
```

Granted, it makes for a long URL, but the end result is only one HTTP request. The same can be done with CSS files as well. Here's an example of both the `AutoComplete` control and the Button control CSS files being loaded via the combo handler:

```
<link rel="stylesheet" type="text/css" href=
"http://yui.yahooapis.com/combo?2.7.0/build/autocomplete/assets/
skins/sam/autocomplete.css&2.7.0/build/button/assets/skins/sam/button.css">
```

Shrink and Optimize Loading Times

Along with CDNs and file concatenation, the actual weight of the files being transferred can also be reduced as a performance-optimization measure. Anywhere from 40 percent to 60 percent of a JavaScript or CSS file's weight comes from whitespace, comments, and verbose variable names.

Though not a part of the YUI distribution files, the YUI Compressor is YUI's answer to needless weight in JavaScript and CSS files. It isn't a part of the distributable because the distribution itself already comes with minimized files, but it's made available to anyone wanting to optimize his or her own code alongside YUI. A link to the compressor can be found on the YUI Library homepage.

The YUI Compressor strips JavaScript and CSS files of all comments and unnecessary whitespace. In the case of JavaScript, it can even rename local variables to one-letter names, further reducing the file's weight. (The reason it only renames local variables is so that it doesn't get into obfuscating the actual API of the code and by extension inadvertently introduce bugs.)

The YUI Compressor requires Java to run. It uses the latter to parse the JavaScript file. Here's an example of how to run it (x.y.z represents the Compressor's version number):

```
java -jar yuicompressor-x.y.z.jar myfile.js -o myfile-min.js
```

Here is a listing of all of the available options that the Compressor offers:

```
$ java -jar yuicompressor-x.y.z.jar
Usage: java -jar yuicompressor-x.y.z.jar [options] [input file]

    Global Options
      -h, --help                Displays this information
      --type <js|css>           Specifies the type of the input file
      --charset <charset>       Read the input file using <charset>
      --line-break <column>     Insert a line break after the specified column number
      -v, --verbose             Display informational messages and warnings
      -o <file>                 Place the output into <file>. Defaults to stdout.

    JavaScript Options
      --nomunge                 Minify only, do not obfuscate
      --preserve-semi           Preserve all semicolons
      --disable-optimizations   Disable all micro optimizations

GLOBAL OPTIONS

  -h, --help
      Prints help on how to use the YUI Compressor
```

--line-break

    Some source control tools don't like files containing lines longer than, say 8000 characters. The linebreak option is used in that case to split long lines after a specific column. It can also be used to make the code more readable, easier to debug (especially with the MS Script Debugger) Specify 0 to get a line break after each semi-colon in JavaScript, and after each rule in CSS.

--type js|css

    The type of compressor (JavaScript or CSS) is chosen based on the extension of the input file name (.js or .css) This option is required if no input file has been specified. Otherwise, this option is only required if the input file extension is neither 'js' nor 'css'.

--charset character-set

    If a supported character set is specified, the YUI Compressor will use it to read the input file. Otherwise, it will assume that the platform's default character set is being used. The output file is encoded using the same character set.

-o outfile

    Place output in file outfile. If not specified, the YUI Compressor will default to the standard output, which you can redirect to a file.

-v, --verbose

    Display informational messages and warnings.

JAVASCRIPT ONLY OPTIONS

--nomunge

    Minify only. Do not obfuscate local symbols.

--preserve-semi

    Preserve unnecessary semicolons (such as right before a '}') This option is useful when compressed code has to be run through JSLint (which is the case of YUI for example)

--disable-optimizations

    Disable all the built-in micro optimizations.

This text comes from the YUI Compressor page and is an output of the actual YUI Compressor application.

When and Where to Run It

YUI Compressor is best used in a build process. In other words, JavaScript and CSS files should remain in their full forms in the development environment where they were written. But when the time comes to move them to a staging or QA environment, that's when the Compressor should be run on them. This way, the source files remain untouched, but the delivered versions get optimized. Ideally, they shouldn't be compressed and pushed directly into production (a live site) since there's always the possibility that something might go wrong with the compression. Instead, the files should be compressed and pushed to an environment where they can be tested and verified. Once it's confirmed that all is well with the files, then they can be safely pushed to the live site.

Summary

The natural growth in size of JavaScript libraries that occurs over time creates weight and performance problems that the YUI team has dealt with handily. Not only do they provide lightweight versions of their library's files, but they offer a free CDN service to host them as well as tools to optimize code that isn't even a part of their library.

Part III
Ext JS

Near the beginning of 2006, the Yahoo! User Interface (YUI) Library was released with an emphasis on a strong, stable, and well-documented library of general JavaScript functionality. The YUI team succeeded in each of its original goals. However, the library was offering little in the way of a control library. Browsers were now capable of rendering rich and attractive interfaces to rival the traditional desktop. And Internet clients and users alike were clamoring for a rich and high-performing experience on the Web.

A Little History...

In mid-2006, an individual named Jack Slocum appeared on the YUI scene sporting an attractive data grid based on the YUI foundation. The grid was responsive to users, offered several advanced features that desktop users had come to expect, and was visually appealing. Based on the object-oriented design of the YUI foundation, developers found Slocum's code easy to learn and customize.

About a year later, Slocum officially branched off of the YUI Library and was offering a control library known as Ext JS 1.0. Rather than anchor his library to the YUI foundation, Slocum decided to create an "adapter" abstraction layer, offering developers a choice between several modern and mature JavaScript libraries. Ext JS now had a large control library available to developers using jQuery, Prototype, and of course YUI. Using the simple technique of namespacing, developers could rest assured the Ext JS control library would not conflict with their core JavaScript library of choice. A few months after the release of Ext JS 1.0, a version 1.1 was released offering a new "adapter" based solely on Ext JS code (free of external dependencies). Since then, the Ext JS team has maintained the "adapter" abstraction layer while continuing to add to its rich control library.

Even with its humble beginnings of a single data grid, the Ext JS library is not your typical JavaScript library of functions. Of course, Ext JS has all the general functionality that developers have come to expect from JavaScript libraries (high-performing traversal of the DOM, manipulating CSS and HTML, simplified AJAX execution, handling of XML and JSON data, and so on). But Ext JS has aimed at providing developers with a complete, themed control library, which is easy to extend, easy to use á la carte, and is so visually attractive that it virtually sets the standard. To date, Ext JS has surpassed each of these goals.

Before You Begin...

First, you must realize that JavaScript is an object-oriented language. Most JavaScript code existing on the Internet today ignores the full potential and flexibility of object-oriented design. And while even beginning developers can easily understand concepts such as inheritance and modularity, the concepts of polymorphism (scope) and encapsulation (private members) can be particularly difficult. The Ext JS library uses all of these object-oriented concepts extensively and benefits from each.

It is also important to note that the Ext JS library is guilty of a sharp learning curve. More often than not, however, this learning curve is caused by developers jumping head first into the "coolest" parts of the Ext JS widget library. Certainly, the Ext Grid is awesome in power. But jumping from a simple HTML table to such a complex beast is obviously foolish. In this section, you will spend quite a bit of time understanding the building blocks of the library before you dive into the "coolest" parts.

17

Architecture and Library Conventions

In this chapter, you'll dip into the core of Ext JS and discover:

- ❑ When to use Ext JS
- ❑ How to use Ext JS
- ❑ Ext JS's object-oriented design
- ❑ Utility functions to take over the world
- ❑ Ext JS's event-based design

When to Use Ext JS

Ext JS is squarely aimed at the next generation of enterprise-level web applications. As such, Ext JS is a large and comprehensive library. It can seem quite daunting to new developers. But rest assured that the library is well thought out and modular. Whether you're creating a simple content site (blog, CRM, document repository) or a fully interactive database application, it's easy to cut Ext JS down to your size.

As you'll see in this chapter, Ext JS is extensible. If you don't like the way that Ext JS performs a particular task, override it, augment it, or just flat out replace it.

Ext JS plays well with others. If you're already using another framework, Ext JS is designed to work alongside other well-playing frameworks. In fact, Ext JS's core libraries can be swapped out with other popular frameworks (this can save time with developer training, preexisting code maintenance, and end-user bandwidth).

Ext JS doesn't have any monolithic classes solving dozens of problems. Each class in Ext JS is designed to solve a small handful of problems. Isolating the pieces you want is easy, and excluding the pieces you don't need is equally easy. And the classes build upon each other; there is very little code duplication.

All of this comes together as a well-maintained and cohesive body of code that is suitable for almost every HTML-based project on the Web today.

How to Use Ext JS

To use Ext JS, you need to download the Ext JS library. For this section, you will use the full Ext JS 2.2 SDK, which can be found on the Ext web site (http://extjs.com/). The Ext JS web site also offers a "Build-Your-Own" feature where you can pick and choose which features you need. The complete feature list is too lengthy to list here, but it's important to note that the "Ext Core" feature is the only required portion of the library. You will not use a customized version of the library for this book. However, if you choose to use the "Build-Your-Own" feature, you will have a single, specialized script file that results in a very small footprint.

The full Ext JS SDK comes with documentation, a library of working examples, all of the Ext JS resources (images, CSS files, themes), the third-party adapters (jQuery, Prototype, and YUI), each original source file (complete with comments), a minimized version of each source file, and a few compilation files. The compilation files are as follows:

- ❏ ext-all.css – all CSS files in minimized form
- ❏ ext-all.js – the complete library in minimized form
- ❏ ext-all-debug.js – the complete library without comments (but not minimized)
- ❏ ext-core.js – the "core" group of files in minimized form
- ❏ ext-core-debug.js – the "core" group of files without comments (but not minimized)

The CSS files used by the Ext JS library expect a typical web site folder hierarchy as shown in Figure 17-1.

Figure 17-1

The images folder contains a folder for each Ext JS theme. Creating new themes is a simple matter creating a new CSS file (in the CSS folder). If images need to be overridden, create a new folder in the images folder containing the replacement images. Unfortunately, creating new themes is outside the scope of this book, but the Ext JS SDK contains the "default" and "gray" themes. Both are completely full featured, and can be used as a learning tool for creating new themes.

The SDK also comes with an INCLUDE_ORDER.txt file describing which files to include, depending on your choice of adapter. For this section, you will use the Ext JS core adapter. As such, you need to include three files:

```
<link type="text/css" rel="stylesheet" href="css/ext-all.css" />
<!-- the Ext adapter (as opposed to a 3rd Party adapter) -->
<script type="text/javascript" src="scripts/ext-base.js"></script>
<script type="text/javascript" src="scripts/ext-all.js"></script>
<script type="text/javascript">
    Ext.onReady(function() { // the web-page is now loaded
        alert("Hello, World!");
    });
</script>
```

With these lines you have included the *entire* Ext JS library, and have used the global Ext.onReady event handler to start an application safely. Before you dive into the deep end, the next section covers some of the library's more foundational aspects.

Stylistic Conventions

The Ext JS library has adopted a fairly run-of-the-mill coding style convention. This consistency helps with the developer learning curve. While each developer certainly has his or her own habits and conventions, it's extremely helpful when a library is consistent with itself:

❑   Class names are capitalized (GridPanel, Observable, and so on).

❑   Event names are lowercase (click, dblclick, and so on).

❑   Constants are uppercase (DAY, HOUR, and so on).

❑   All other identifiers are camel case (ext, doSomething, myValue, and so on).

If you venture into the Ext JS source code, you will see the following code conventions:

❑   Opening braces appear on the end of the preceding line.

❑   All control blocks are explicit.

```
if (condition) code(); // this will not be seen

if (condition) { // this is preferable
    code();
}
```

The Ext JS library is event based. Any events that are "cancelable" will be named **"before*Event*."** When handling these events, the developer can simply return false from the event handler to prevent the rest of the event's processing from occurring.

There are quite a few "singleton" classes within the Ext JS library. Singleton classes do not need to be instantiated by the developer, and usually consist of an organizational library of methods. As such, singleton classes are usually utility classes (Ext.DomHelper) or managers of a collection of similar classes (Ext.WindowMgr).

Here's a typical technique for creating a singleton class that can be found in the Ext JS library:

```
MyClass = function() {
    var arg = 5; // a private variable
    return {
        myMethod: function() { // a public method
            return arg;
        }
    }
}();
// no need to instantiate
var myValue = MyClass.myMethod();
```

Ext JS's Object-Oriented Design

One of the original goals of Ext JS has always been to maintain the ability to coexist with any other responsible JavaScript library and still remain extensible. To this end, the Ext JS class offers a handful of simple methods to assist developers in organizing, creating, and extending classes. Although these methods were written for the Ext JS library, they will work on all JavaScript objects.

Ext.namespace

```
namespace( String namespace1, String namespace2, String etc ) : void
```

In JavaScript, a namespace is simply an object, which only contains properties that are object definitions. Using proper namespaces ensures that your code is encapsulated from other libraries. Of course, proper namespaces become very deep, very fast. It's not unusual to see a well-named class like Ext.ux.graphing.GraphPanel. The Ext.namespace convenience method can define all your namespaces in a single call. Not only does this help your code to play with others, but it shaves precious bytes off the size of your script.

Here is some traditional JavaScript code creating a namespace hierarchy:

```
var Ext = Ext || {};
Ext.ux = Ext.ux || {};
Ext.ux.graphing = Ext.ux.graphing || {};
Ext.ux.soundFx = Ext.ux.soundFx || {};
Ext.ux.maps = Ext.ux.maps || {};
```

This single call to the Ext.namespace method achieves the same result:

```
Ext.namespace("Ext.ux.graphing", "Ext.ux.soundFx", "Ext.ux.maps");
```

Ext.override

```
override( Object origclass, Object overrides ) : void
```

JavaScript is a very flexible language and overriding a method is as simple as reassigning the method's name:

```
// let's create a function
function doesStuff() {
    alert("I do it!");
}
// now, let's override that function
doesStuff = function() {
    alert("I did it!");
};
```

Reassigning the method of a class definition is just as simple by using the class's prototype:

```
function MyClass() {
    // class constructor
}
MyClass.prototype.myMethod = function() {
    alert("hey");
};
var x = new MyClass();
x.myMethod(); // displays "hey"
MyClass.prototype.myMethod = function() {  // replace the method
    alert("hello");
};
x.myMethod(); // displays "hello"
```

Using this same method, a developer can also add his or her own custom functions to a preexisting class.

The Ext.override method is a convenience method intended to help developers redefine entire classes in one fell swoop. The following example replaces two methods of a class definition. Following traditional JavaScript convention, if the methods are not in the class's original definition, the methods are added. The first parameter is the class being modified, and the second parameter is a JavaScript object containing the members being overridden:

```
Ext.override(MyClass, {
    myMethod: function() {
        // do something different
    }
});
```

This simple method certainly has great value in keeping code maintenance concerns to a minimum. For example, experienced JavaScript developers are familiar with using and customizing third-party libraries. But each new release of those third-party libraries ensures a fresh round of customization. Using the Ext.override method, developers can keep the original third-party files intact. Their customizations can easily be placed in a separate and self-contained file.

Ext.extend and Constructor Conventions

```
extend( Function superclass, Object overrides ) : Function
extend( Function subclass, Function superclass, [Object overrides] ) : Function
```

While the Ext.override method *replaces* functionality, the Ext.extend method is Ext JS's solution to object-oriented inheritance. There are two ways to call the method, and each results in a new class definition that is inherited from the class defined by the superclass parameter and overrides any methods defined by the overrides parameter. The Ext.extend method has three side effects, which apply to the new class definition. First, an override method is added to the new class, which simply calls Ext.override. Second, an override method is added to each instance of the new class. This method takes a single parameter and copies all members from this object to the current instance (overriding any preexisting members of the same name). Third, a property called superclass is added to each instance of the new class, which allows access to the parent object's definition.

As noted before, Ext JS has several coding conventions that improve the library's consistency and ease of adoption. One of these conventions is the library's constructor interface. Nearly all of Ext JS's constructors have a single parameter and this parameter is an object containing configuration options appropriate for the class being instantiated. This code convention flies in the face of traditional OOP languages. Traditionally, all method signatures (including constructors) have explicit parameter names with explicit parameter types. The traditional convention leverages the power and safety of the compiler. However, JavaScript parameters do not have data types and there is no compiler. The benefits of the traditional convention are nonexistent for JavaScript in modern browsers.

In fact, the traditional convention actually hinders JavaScript code maintenance. For example, version 1 of methodA is expecting the first parameter to be a String. Three months later, version 2 of methodA is released, and the first parameter is now a Date. Without a compiler, developers are forced to sift through all of their code, trying to find and correct something that simply shouldn't be a problem. And while we all know that the author of classA has caused all this unnecessary pain, there's simply nothing we can do about it now.

This is a very common, real-world JavaScript development problem. So, Ext JS has chosen a simple, one-parameter signature convention, which leverages the innate power of JavaScript and eases code maintenance. In addition, developers can easily derive Ext JS objects without fear that the constructor of the base class is going to change and break their inherited object.

With all that said, there is a fourth possible side effect of Ext.extend: the creation of a constructor method. The first method of calling Ext.extend only accepts two parameters. The first parameter is the superclass, and the second parameter (overrides) is an object containing the methods to add to or override the superclass. If the overrides parameter contains a definition for the constructor, this will be used for the new class definition's constructor. If a constructor property is not defined, Ext.extend will create a constructor following the convention already described. This automatic constructor will also call the superclass's constructor, passing any parameters. This practice of executing the superclass's constructor is very consistent with traditional OOP conventions, and is future-compatible when using Ext JS's convention of a single configuration object.

Here is an example of each use of Ext.extend; each accomplishes the same goal. Note the use of the superclass and the different methods of defining the constructor:

```
var NewClass = Ext.extend(MyClass, {
    constructor: function(config) { // explicit constructor
        config.name = config.name || "Bob";
        NewClass.superclass.constructor.call(this);
        this.name = config.name;
    },
    myMethod: function() {
        NewClass.superclass.myMethod.call(this);
        alert(this.name);
    }
});
function NewClass(config) { // constructor
    config.name = config.name || "Bob";
    NewClass.superclass.constructor.call(this);
    this.name = config.name;
}
Ext.extend(NewClass, MyClass, {
    myMethod: function() {
        NewClass.superclass.myMethod.call(this);
        alert(this.name);
    }
});
```

Since nearly all Ext JS objects have the same constructor signature, it makes sense that each constructor is going to perform a very similar operation. In fact, the majority of all constructors copy each member of the config parameter to the new object being constructed. Ext JS provides two convenience methods that can accomplish this task.

Ext.apply

```
apply( Object obj, Object config, [Object defaults] ) : Object
```

Ext.apply copies each member of the config parameter to the obj parameter. Optionally, defaults can be specified, which are copied to obj before the config values.

Ext.applyIf

```
applyIf( Object obj, Object config ) : Object
```

Ext.applyIf copies each member of the config parameter to the obj parameter, but only if that member does not already exist within obj.

When developers inherit an object, the purpose is usually to add functionality. That added functionality may require more configuration. The developer can leverage Ext JS's constructor convention, and calling the superclass's constructor (while retaining the necessary config information) becomes a simple task:

```
MyClass = Ext.extend(MyBase, {
    constructor: function(config) {
        // provide some default values, but only if they do not exist in 'config'
        config = Ext.applyIf(config, {
            someValue: 5
        });
        // provide some default values, overriding any that are already in 'config'
        config = Ext.apply(config, {
            someOtherValue: 10
        });
        // call the superclass's constructor, passing our modified configuration
        MyClass.superclass.constructor.call(this, config);
    }
});
```

The power of the apply methods is often overlooked. While these methods are helpful for object constructors, they have uses in several places throughout the library.

Utility Functions to Take Over the World

Each of the following methods has been added to the Function object's prototype. This means that the developer can use these methods on any JavaScript function to alter its original behavior.

Function.createCallback

```
createCallback() : Function
```

As you will see, events and event handlers are a major part of Ext JS. The Function.createCallback function is primarily used when assigning event handlers. For example, here is a simple sayHi function with one parameter:

```
function sayHi(name) {
    alert("Hi " + name);
}
```

This function is used in several places throughout the application. One such place is on the click of a Button. When the Button is clicked, you want "Fred" passed to the sayHi function. However, the event handler config option is expecting a function pointer. The following code *won't* work:

```
new Ext.Button({
    text: "Say Hi",
    renderTo: Ext.getBody(),
    handler: sayHi("Fred") // this won't work!
});
```

This code uses the `Function.createCallback` function to achieve the desired result:

```
new Ext.Button({
    text: "Say Hi",
    renderTo: Ext.getBody(),
    handler: sayHi.createCallback("Fred") // much better
});
```

The function returned by `Function.createCallback` can handle any number of parameters and always executes in the scope of the browser's `window` object.

"Setting scope" is the ability to control what the `this` keyword is referencing. As already stated, `Function.createCallback` does not set scope; it uses the global scope of the browser's `window` object.

Function.createDelegate

```
createDelegate( Object obj, [Array args], [Boolean/Number appendArgs] ) : Function
```

The `Function.createCallback` function is useful, but there are often occasions when the affected function needs to have a scope other than `window`. That's where `Function.createDelegate` comes into play. The `Function.createDelegate` method creates a new function that, when executed, sets the `this` keyword to the value of the `obj` parameter. In the following examples, notice how the reference for `this` changes:

```
function MyClass(color) {
    this.color = color;
};
MyClass.prototype.myMethod = function(name) {
    alert("My name is " + name + ", and I like the color " + this.color);
};

// here, we instantiate a new object, which has its own scope
var x = new MyClass("red");
x.myMethod("Fred"); // displays "My name is Fred, and I like the color red"

// here, we create an object that is NOT derived from MyClass
//   but it has a 'color' property
var inlineObject = {color: "green"};
var func = MyClass.prototype.myMethod.createDelegate(inlineObject);
func("Sally"); // displays "My name is Sally, and I like the color green"

// this version of createDelegate uses an array of pre-defined parameters
var func2 = MyClass.prototype.myMethod.createDelegate(inlineObject, ["Sam"]);
func2(); // displays "My name is Sam, and I like the color green"
```

As you can see, `Function.createDelegate` gives developers an easy method for code reuse without modifying class definitions or jumping through hoops.

Function.createInterceptor

```
createInterceptor( Function fcn, [Object scope] ) : Function
```

Using `Function.createInterceptor`, a developer can intercept a method call and conditionally continue execution. Intercepting a method without deriving a class can be quite useful. Code auditing, for example, can be quite difficult in any language. But using the `Function.createInterceptor` method is a quick and easy way to audit specific methods.

```
// a VERY simple Logger class
function Logger() {
    this.messages = [];
}

// here's the method we want to audit
function myMethod(color) {
    alert(color);
}

// create an instance of the logger
var myLogger = new Logger();

// create an interceptor to be used in place of the original method
myMethod = myMethod.createInterceptor(function(color) {
    this.messages[this.messages.length] = color;  // write value to log
    return color != "yellow"; // if the color is yellow, we don't want to continue
}, myLogger);

myMethod("red"); // alert is displayed
myMethod("yellow"); // alert is NOT displayed
```

Function.createSequence

```
createSequence( Function fcn, [Object scope] ) : Function
```

Another method for simple code auditing is the `Function.createSequence` method. Here, the developer creates a new function, which executes the original function and then the function passed by the `fcn` parameter. For example:

```
function repeat() {
    var s = "";
    for (var x = 0; x < arguments.length; x++) {
        s += arguments[x] + ",";
    }
    alert("The arguments: " + s);
}
repeat(1, 2, 3); // displays "The arguments: 1,2,3,"
repeat = repeat.createSequence(function() {
    alert("There were " + arguments.length + " arguments.");
});
repeat(1, 2, 3); // displays "The arguments: 1,2,3,", and then
                 // displays "There were 3 arguments."
```

The optional scope parameter can also be used (like in the Function.createInterceptor example). While Function.createInterceptor could be used to log each method call, Function.createSequence could be used to log each method call, which completes without throwing an unhandled exception. With these two methods and very little effort, you could have a pretty useful code auditor.

Function.defer

```
defer( Number millis, [Object obj], [Array args], [Boolean/Number appendArgs] ) :
    Number
```

Function.defer schedules the original function to execute after the specified number of milliseconds. You can optionally set the scope of the function and pass an array of arguments. This method returns a Number, which is compatible with the browser's clearTimeout function. A sample use might be for an auto-completion text box. As the user types, you'd want to check the data-store for any string that might complete what the user is typing in. But if the user is a fast typist, you'd be checking for strings that the user has already finished typing. Instead, you could call getPossibleStrings a second after the text box's keyup event. If the user presses another key before getPossibleStrings executes, you would cancel the first call by calling clearTimeout:

```
function getPossibleStrings(value) {
    alert("checking for " + value);
}
var x = null;
var txt = Ext.get("textbox");
txt.on("keyup", function() {
    if (x) {
        clearTimeout(x); // abort the previously deferred call
    }
    x = getPossibleStrings.defer(1000, window, [this.getValue()]);
}, txt);
```

Ext JS's Event-Based Design

In addition to providing a consistent object-oriented design, Ext JS provides a simple and well thought out event-based design. The heart of Ext JS's event-based design is the Ext.util.Observable class, which forms an abstract base class for anything that needs to fire events.

Ext.util.Observable.addEvents

```
addEvents( Object object ) : void
```

Usually called within the constructor of a class derived from Observable, the addEvents method defines a collection of all the events that the class might fire. However, if a developer attempts to call addListener or fireEvent on an undefined event, the event will automatically get added to the collection. Because of this, this method is now primarily used to self-document code.

```
MyClass = Ext.extend(Ext.util.Observable, {
    constructor: function() {
        this.addEvents({
            click: true,
            keyUp: true,
            keyDown: true
        });
    }
});
```

Ext.util.Observable.addListener / .on

```
addListener( String eventName, Function handler, [Object scope], [Object options] )
    : void
on( String eventName, Function handler, [Object scope], [Object options] ) : void
```

Here's your typical addListener method which takes an eventName and a handler. For lazy programmers, like me, you can cut down on typing by using the on method. You can optionally specify a scope object. There are also a few options for the fourth parameter:

❑   delay — Number — The number of milliseconds to delay the invocation of the handler after the event fires (see Function.defer).

❑   single — Boolean — true to handle the next firing of the event, and then automatically remove the handler.

❑   buffer — Number — Behaves like the delay option. However, if the event fires more than once within the specified number of milliseconds, the handler is only executed once.

Here's the simplest form of the method:

```
var instance = new MyClass();
instance.on("click", onClick);
```

It's also possible to add several handlers at one time:

```
instance.on({
    click: onClick,
    keyUp: onKeyUp
});
```

If you're fancy, add multiple handlers with options:

```
instance.on({
    click: {fn: onClick, single: true}, // handle the click event once
    keyUp: {fn: onKeyUp, buffer: 1000} // handle the keyUp event after a second of
                                       // no other keyUp events
});
```

Ext.util.Observable.removeListener / .un

```
removeListener( String eventName, Function handler, [Object scope] ) : void
un( String eventName, Function handler, [Object scope] ) : void
```

This method stops the specified `handler` from executing for the specified `eventName`. Internally, the `Observable` class maintains a collection of handlers keyed on `eventName`, `handler`, and `scope`. So, if a handler was added for a particular `scope`, you must specify the `scope` when removing it.

Ext.util.Observable.fireEvent

```
fireEvent( String eventName, Object... args ) : Boolean
```

This method fires the specified `eventName` and passes the specified parameters to each handler. Each handler is executed in the order that they were added. If a handler returns `false`, the remaining handlers are not executed and `fireEvent` returns `false`. The following example code executes the `click` event with two parameters:

```
if (!instance.fireEvent("click", 1, 2)) {
    alert("a handler returned false");
}
```

Ext.util.Observable.hasListener

```
hasListener( String eventName ) : Boolean
```

This method checks to see if the object has any handlers for the specified `eventName`.

Ext.util.Observable.purgeListeners

```
purgeListeners() : void
```

This method removes all handlers from the object.

Ext.util.Observable.relayEvents

```
relayEvents( Observable o, Array events ) : void
```

This method relays the specified events from the object to the specified `Observable`.

In the following example, each time `anotherInstance` fires the `click` or `keyUp` events, `instance` also fires the same event:

```
instance.relayEvents(anotherInstance, ["click", "keyUp"]);
```

The two instance objects used in `relayEvents` *do NOT have to be of the same type.*

Ext.util.Observable.suspendEvents / .resumeEvents

```
suspendEvents() : void
resumeEvents() : void
```

The suspendEvents method prevents events from firing, and resumeEvents restores normal execution. Once suspendEvents has been called, calls to fireEvent do nothing.

Ext.util.Observable.capture / .releaseCapture

```
capture( Observable o, Function fn, [Object scope] ) : void
releaseCapture( Observable o ) : void
```

These two methods are static utility methods which are contained in the Ext.util.Observable namespace, but are not part of an instance of Observable. The capture method is used to add a single handler for all events on the specified Observable object. This handler is executed before any of the normal handlers. An optional scope object may be used. In effect, the capture method creates an interceptor function on the fireEvent method of the specified object (see Function.createInterceptor).

Summary

This chapter has been a quick introduction into some of the core concepts behind Ext JS. In the next chapter, you continue to look at the building blocks of the Ext JS library. The browser platform and the HTML DOM do not always behave as one would like, and Ext JS has a strong foundation for making developers lives easier.

18

Elements, DomHelper, and Templates

Assuming that the reader is an experienced web developer, no time is wasted on covering the myriad of problems that exist in the world of HTML today. With ever-changing CSS and HTML specifications as well as new browser versions being released every quarter, each web developer is inevitably asked to solve the same problem a half dozen different ways.

Whether it's traversing the DOM to find one piece of text, or simply figuring out which mouse button the user has clicked, everything is a headache for the web developer. Fortunately, the Ext JS library solves these cross-browser/cross-version issues.

Furthermore, Ext JS gives the developer a solid foundation with which to build a rich UI. This chapter briefly demonstrates how Ext JS solves the cross-browser issues and lays a solid foundation for the Ext JS Component System.

In this chapter, you'll learn about:

❑ Element manipulation

❑ DOM traversal

❑ DOM manipulation

❑ CSS manipulation

Element Manipulation

HTML documents are composed of HTML elements. Traditionally, the web server creates an entire HTML document and the browser downloads it. The HTML document contains everything it needs. And if the screen needs to change, the browser asks the server for a new HTML document. However, when the change is small (enabling a button, for example), the cost of talking to the server is expensive. The obvious and inexpensive solution is changing the HTML document from within the browser. To this end, the Ext JS library offers a class, which can represent each HTML element.

Ext.Element

Because HTML elements are the heart of the HTML document, every browser vendor has done its best to create a DOM API centered around those elements. Each browser offers the HTMLElement class for this purpose. Unfortunately, great minds do not think alike, and we end up with a myriad of browsers all offering different techniques to solve the same problem. At this point, most authors of JavaScript libraries begin augmenting the HTMLElement class. The Ext JS library, however, does not change the built-in HTMLElement class. Instead, the Ext JS library has built the Ext.Element class to re-centralize and simplify the functionality needed to modify elements. One reason for keeping the HTMLElement class "pure" is so other libraries, which have no knowledge of Ext JS, can continue functioning as if Ext JS were never there. By being unobtrusive in this manner, the Ext JS library can be added to an existing project without major impact to the existing codebase.

The Ext.Element is a cross-browser abstraction class offering all the common functionality that is offered by the native HTMLElement class. Experienced JavaScript developers will immediately understand the methods supplied by the Ext.Element class. If necessary, the unchanged HTMLElement is also accessible from the Ext.Element's dom property. The following code example constructs an instance of Ext.Element:

```
// here's the old-fashioned way to get an HTMLElement
var domElement = document.getElementById("someId");

var el;
// here, we're constructing an Ext.Element by ID
el = new Ext.Element("someId");
// here, we're constructing an Ext.Element by dom node
el = new Ext.Element(domElement);

// let's prove we got the right HTMLElement
if (domElement == el.dom) {
    alert("We got it!");
} else {
    alert("We don't got it.");
}
```

There is also a helper function (get) for constructing/retrieving an Element. The get method works like the constructor except that it keeps a cache of all Elements that have been "got." This simple cache ensures that the developer receives the same Element object each time (instead of constructing new instances and consuming memory). This cache is routinely garbage-collected (along with any events handlers on the Elements) so browser memory leaks are avoided.

```
// the helper function works with IDs and dom nodes too
el = Ext.get("someId");
el = Ext.get(domElement);
```

In reality, the Ext.Element object has virtually no properties of its own (it is merely a cross-browser wrapper for the native HTMLElement). Even so, when operating on a large number of HTMLElements (every cell in a table, for example), constructing an instance of Element for each HTMLElement can be expensive. To alleviate this, there is another helper function (`Ext.fly`), which maintains a "flyweight" instance of `Ext.Element`.

```
// the 'fly' method works just like 'get'
el = Ext.fly("someId");
el = Ext.fly(domElement);
```

The "flyweight" instance of `Ext.Element` takes advantage its "wrapper" architecture and merely swaps the value of its `dom` property. All the `Element` methods continue to function as expected without the overhead of hundreds of instantiated objects. However, developers must be aware that the flyweight object is used throughout the application. This means, the `dom` property *will* get swapped out. In other words, use the `fly` method in cases such as a tight loop where performance is vital.

```
// make all the inputs transparent without constructing
//   unnecessary Element instances
var col = document.getElementsByTagName("input");
for (var i = 0, el; el = Ext.fly(col[i++]);) {
    el.setOpacity(0);
}
```

The "flyweight" object is actually an instance of `Ext.Flyweight`, and the developer can actually create multiple flyweight objects. This could be useful for separating your own code from Ext JS's (and improve the predictability of your own flyweight element). To create and access your own instance of `Ext.Flyweight`, simply specify a name:

```
var el = Ext.fly("someId", "myFlyweight");
```

The `Ext.Element` class exposes several DOM manipulation methods (`createChild`, `replace`, `replaceWith`, `insertHtml`, `insertFirst`, and so on). And each of these methods uses the `Ext.DomHelper` class, which is discussed later in this chapter.

DOM Event Handling

The `Element` class does *not* inherit from `Ext.util.Observable`. But `Element` uses the `Ext.EventManager` class internally, and has the familiar methods of `addListener`/`on` and `removeListener`/`un`. The `Ext.EventManager` class is another cross-browser class intended to eliminate developer woes. All browsers share a single interface to the DOM, and all fired events result in a common, cross-browser object (`Ext.EventObject`). The parameters to `Ext.Element.addListener` are the same as `Ext.util.Observable`. The `options` parameter still allows `scope`, `delay`, `single`, and `buffer`; but the following are also offered:

❑   `delegate` — a simple selector, which finds an ancestor of the target (if a matching ancestor is not found, the original target is used).

❑   `normalized` — `false` to pass a browser event to the handler function instead of an `Ext.EventObject`.

❑   `preventDefault` — `true` to prevent the browser's default action.

❑   `stopEvent` — `true` to stop the event. Same as `preventDefault: true` and `stopPropagation: true`.

❑   `stopPropagation` — `true` to prevent event propagation (event bubbling).

These extra options are specific to DOM events and therefore unnecessary for Ext.util.Observable. If you use preventDefault, stopEvent, or stopPropagation, your handler is still invoked.

And while normal Ext JS event handlers have function signatures specific to their purpose, the DOM event handlers all have the same signature (an Ext.EventObject or the browser's event object, an Ext.Element, and the options object).

The Ext.EventObject class contains several helper methods for obtaining cross-browser information about the event (getKey, getWheelDelta, getPageX, getPageY, and so on). But more importantly, the browserEvent property exposes the original, raw browser event object.

Element Animations

Many methods of the Ext.Element class accept an optional animate parameter. Setting this parameter performs a visible animation while the method executes. The animate parameter can be set to true for a default behavior, or an object can be passed with options for fine control. The options object has the following properties:

❑ duration — Determines how long the animation lasts (in seconds) (default is .35)

❑ easing — Determines how the animation should behave (valid values are: easeNone, easeIn, easeOut, easeBoth, easeInStrong, easeOutStrong, easeBothStrong, elasticIn, elasticOut, elasticBoth, backIn, backOut, backBoth, bounceIn, bounceOut, bounceBoth)

❑ callback — This is a function to execute when the animation is done

❑ scope — Determines the scope of the callback

Here's an example of operating on an Element with animation:

```
// by default, no animation
el.moveTo(50, 50);
// here, we use the default animation settings
el.moveTo(100, 100, true);
// here, we slow down the animation (default duration is .35)
el.moveTo(150, 150, {
    duration: .5
});
```

Since you're assuming the entire Ext JS library, the Ext.Element class comes with a whole library of animation effects. This library of functions is maintained in the Ext.Fx class and includes effects such as fadeIn, fadeOut, highlight, scale, and so on. As with other Ext.Element methods, the effects methods can also be chained together:

```
el.hide(); // hide the element
el.slideIn().puff(); // the element drops into view from the top and then
                     // slowly fades while growing larger (like smoke)
```

Chaining visual effect methods with nonvisual effect methods must be used with caution, however. The Ext.Fx methods return immediately (even if the effect has not completed). Internally, each effect is added to a sequencer (so effects do not trample each other). Nonvisual methods are not added to this sequence.

```
el.fadeIn().setVisible(false); // the element is hidden before
                               // the fadeIn method can complete

el.fadeIn({
    callback: function() { // callbacks are called when the animation is complete
        el.setVisible(false);
    }
}); // the user now gets the intended effect
```

Manipulating Collections of Elements

The `Ext.Element` class allows you to manipulate single `HTMLElement` objects and the `Ext.FlyWeight` class enables you to save precious browser resources by using fewer objects. However, maintaining a collection of elements is a common requirement. `Ext.Flyweight` is intended to hold only one element, and `Ext.Element` can become too costly. Here is where the `Ext.select` method comes into play:

```
var col = Ext.select("div"); // grab ALL div tags on the page
```

The `Ext.select` method returns an instance of the `Ext.CompositeElementLite` class. This class keeps its own internal instance of `Ext.Flyweight` and an array of DOM nodes. The class exposes all the methods of the `Ext.Element` class and executes all method calls on each DOM node in the array:

```
var col = Ext.select("div"); // grab ALL div tags on the page
col.setStyle({border: "solid 1px green"}); // give them all a border
```

The `Ext.CompositeElementLite` class inherits from the lesser used `Ext.CompositeElement` class. `CompositeElement` stores an array of `Ext.Elements` and does not take advantage of the flyweight technique. To create a `CompositeElement`, use `Ext.select` with its second parameter:

```
var col = Ext.select("div", true); // true for unique elements (non-flyweight)
```

Both `CompositeElement` and its descendant, `CompositeElementLite`, have several utility methods for manipulating the collection of elements. These are standard collection-style methods, such as `add`, `contains`, `clear`, `each`, `item`, and so on.

Ext.Element Methods

Almost all methods of the `Element` class have a return value of the `Element` itself. This enables the technique of method chaining:

```
// set height, then set color
el.setHeight(50).setStyle({color: "red"});
```

The following is a categorized listing of all the methods on the `Ext.Element` class (without the extraneous parameter descriptions).

General Purpose Utilities

These methods allow low-level access to any attribute of the HTMLElement.

```
getAttributeNS( String namespace, String name ) : String
getValue( Boolean asNumber ) : String/Number
set( Object o, [Boolean useSet] ) : Ext.Element
```

DOM Structuring

As already discussed, the DOM structure is the backbone of the HTML document. These methods assist the developer in moving, adding, removing, and replacing elements within the structure of the HTML document. Internally, these methods are using the Ext.DomHelper and Ext.DomQuery classes (which are also discussed in this chapter).

```
appendChild( String/HTMLElement/Array/Element/CompositeElement el ) : Ext.Element
appendTo( Mixed el ) : Ext.Element
child( String selector, [Boolean returnDom] ) : HTMLElement/Ext.Element
clean( [Boolean forceReclean] ) : void
contains( HTMLElement/String el ) : Boolean
createChild( Object config, [HTMLElement insertBefore], [Boolean returnDom] )
    : Ext.Element
createProxy( String/Object config, [String/HTMLElement renderTo],
    [Boolean matchBox] ) : Ext.Element
createShim() : Ext.Element
down( String selector, [Boolean returnDom] ) : HTMLElement/Ext.Element
findParent( String selector, [Number/Mixed maxDepth], [Boolean returnEl] )
    : HTMLElement
findParentNode( String selector, [Number/Mixed maxDepth], [Boolean returnEl] )
    : HTMLElement
first( [String selector], [Boolean returnDom] ) : Ext.Element/HTMLElement
insertAfter( Mixed el ) : Ext.Element
insertBefore( Mixed el ) : Ext.Element
insertFirst( Mixed/Object el ) : Ext.Element
insertHtml( String where, String html, [Boolean returnEl] )
    : HTMLElement/Ext.Element
insertSibling( Mixed/Object/Array el, [String where], [Boolean returnDom] )
    : Ext.Element
is( String selector ) : Boolean
last( [String selector], [Boolean returnDom] ) : Ext.Element/HTMLElement
next( [String selector], [Boolean returnDom] ) : Ext.Element/HTMLElement
parent( [String selector], [Boolean returnDom] ) : Ext.Element/HTMLElement
prev( [String selector], [Boolean returnDom] ) : Ext.Element/HTMLElement
query( String selector ) : Array
remove() : void
replace( Mixed el ) : Ext.Element
replaceWith( Mixed/Object el ) : Ext.Element
select( String selector, [Boolean unique] ) : CompositeElement/CompositeElementLite
up( String selector, [Number/Mixed maxDepth] ) : Ext.Element
update( String html, [Boolean loadScripts], [Function callback] ) : Ext.Element
wrap( [Object config], [Boolean returnDom] ) : HTMLElement/Element
```

Positioning

These methods assist the developer in changing the visible position of the Element.

```
alignTo( Mixed element, String position, [Array offsets],
    [Boolean/Object animate] ) : Ext.Element
anchorTo( Mixed element, String position, [Array offsets],
    [Boolean/Object animate], [Boolean/Number monitorScroll], Function callback )
    : Ext.Element
autoHeight( [Boolean animate], [Float duration], [Function onComplete],
    [String easing] ) : Ext.Element
center( [Mixed centerIn] ) : void
clearPositioning( [String value] ) : Ext.Element
getAlignToXY( Mixed element, String position, [Array offsets] ) : Array
getAnchorXY( [String anchor], [Boolean local], [Object size] ) : Array
getBox( [Boolean contentBox], [Boolean local] ) : Object
getCenterXY() : Array
getComputedHeight() : Number
getComputedWidth() : Number
getHeight( [Boolean contentHeight] ) : Number
getLeft( Boolean local ) : Number
getOffsetsTo( Mixed element ) : Array
getPositioning() : Object
getRegion() : Region
getRight( Boolean local ) : Number
getScroll() : Object
getSize( [Boolean contentSize] ) : Object
getTextWidth( String text, [Number min], [Number max] ) : Number
getTop( Boolean local ) : Number
getViewSize() : Object
getWidth( [Boolean contentWidth] ) : Number
getX() : Number
getXY() : Array
getY() : Number
move( String direction, Number distance, [Boolean/Object animate] ) : Ext.Element
moveTo( Number x, Number y, [Boolean/Object animate] ) : Ext.Element
position( [String pos], [Number zIndex], [Number x], [Number y] ) : void
scroll( String direction, Number distance, [Boolean/Object animate] ) : Boolean
scrollIntoView( [Mixed container], [Boolean hscroll] ) : Ext.Element
scrollTo( String side, Number value, [Boolean/Object animate] ) : Element
setBottom( String bottom ) : Ext.Element
setBounds( Number x, Number y, Number width, Number height,
    [Boolean/Object animate] ) : Ext.Element
setBox( Object box, [Boolean adjust], [Boolean/Object animate] ) : Ext.Element
setHeight( Number height, [Boolean/Object animate] ) : Ext.Element
setLeft( String left ) : Ext.Element
setLeftTop( String left, String top ) : Ext.Element
setLocation( Number x, Number y, [Boolean/Object animate] ) : Ext.Element
setPositioning( Object posCfg ) : Ext.Element
setRegion( Ext.lib.Region region, [Boolean/Object animate] ) : Ext.Element
setRight( String right ) : Ext.Element
setSize( Number width, Number height, [Boolean/Object animate] ) : Ext.Element
setTop( String top ) : Ext.Element
setWidth( Number width, [Boolean/Object animate] ) : Ext.Element
setX( Number The, [Boolean/Object animate] ) : Ext.Element
```

```
setXY( Array pos, [Boolean/Object animate] ) : Ext.Element
setY( Number The, [Boolean/Object animate] ) : Ext.Element
translatePoints( Number/Array x, [Number y] ) : Object
```

Appearance

These methods assist the developer in changing the appearance of the `Element`.

```
addClass( String/Array className ) : Ext.Element
addClassOnClick( String className ) : Ext.Element
addClassOnFocus( String className ) : Ext.Element
addClassOnOver( String className ) : Ext.Element
applyStyles( String/Object/Function styles ) : Ext.Element
boxWrap( [String class] ) : Ext.Element
clearOpacity() : Ext.Element
clip() : Ext.Element
enableDisplayMode( [String display] ) : Ext.Element
getBorderWidth( String side ) : Number
getBottom( Boolean local ) : Number
getColor( String attr, String defaultValue, [String prefix] ) : void
getFrameWidth( String sides ) : Number
getMargins( [String sides] ) : Object/Number
getPadding( String side ) : Number
getStyle( String property ) : String
getStyles( String style1, String style2, String etc. ) : Object
hasClass( String className ) : Boolean
hide( [Boolean/Object animate] ) : Ext.Element
isBorderBox() : Boolean
isDisplayed() : Boolean
isMasked() : Boolean
isScrollable() : Boolean
isVisible( [Boolean deep] ) : Boolean
radioClass( String/Array className ) : Ext.Element
removeClass( String/Array className ) : Ext.Element
repaint() : Ext.Element
replaceClass( String oldClassName, String newClassName ) : Ext.Element
setDisplayed( Mixed value ) : Ext.Element
setOpacity( Float opacity, [Boolean/Object animate] ) : Ext.Element
setStyle( String/Object property, [String value] ) : Ext.Element
setVisibilityMode( visMode Element.VISIBILITY ) : Ext.Element
setVisible( Boolean visible, [Boolean/Object animate] ) : Ext.Element
show( [Boolean/Object animate] ) : Ext.Element
toggle( [Boolean/Object animate] ) : Ext.Element
toggleClass( String className ) : Ext.Element
unclip() : Ext.Element
```

Events and Behaviors

These methods assist the developer with event handling and how the `Element` behaves. Internally, each DOM event that is subscribed to is handled by the `Ext.EventManager` class. Each time the browser fires a DOM event, it passes an object filled with properties indicating the current state of the browser. Ext JS has wrapped this object in a cross-browser class called `Ext.EventObject`. These two classes create a predictable, reusable, and extensible cross-browser, event-based platform. These classes are discussed in more depth later in this chapter.

```
addKeyListener( Number/Array/Object/String key, Function fn, [Object scope] )
    : Ext.KeyMap
addKeyMap( Object config ) : Ext.KeyMap
addListener( String eventName, Function fn, [Object scope], [Object options] )
    : void
blur() : Ext.Element
focus() : Ext.Element
hover( Function overFn, Function outFn, [Object scope] ) : Ext.Element
mask( [String msg], [String msgCls] ) : Element
on( String eventName, Function fn, [Object scope], [Object options] ) : void
relayEvent( String eventName, Object object ) : void
removeAllListeners() : Ext.Element
removeListener( String eventName, Function fn, [Object scope] ) : Ext.Element
swallowEvent( String eventName, [Boolean preventDefault] ) : Ext.Element
un( String eventName, Function fn ) : Ext.Element
unmask() : void
unselectable() : Ext.Element
```

Animations

These helper methods were covered in the previous section. They simply wrap the functionality of the Ext.Fx class.

```
animate( Object args, [Float duration], [Function onComplete], [String easing],
    [String animType] ) : Ext.Element
// the following methods are added from the Ext.Fx class
fadeIn( [Object options] ) : Ext.Element
fadeOut( [Object options] ) : Ext.Element
frame( [String color], [Number count], [Object options] ) : Ext.Element
ghost( [String anchor], [Object options] ) : Ext.Element
hasActiveFx() : Boolean
hasFxBlock() : Boolean
highlight( [String color], [Object options] ) : Ext.Element
pause( Number seconds ) : Ext.Element
puff( [Object options] ) : Ext.Element
scale( Number width, Number height, [Object options] ) : Ext.Element
sequenceFx() : Ext.Element
shift( Object options ) : Ext.Element
slideIn( [String anchor], [Object options] ) : Ext.Element
slideOut( [String anchor], [Object options] ) : Ext.Element
stopFx() : Ext.Element
switchOff( [Object options] ) : Ext.Element
syncFx() : Ext.Element
```

Server Communication

These methods assist the developer with AJAX-style communication with the server.

```
getUpdater() : Ext.Updater
load() : Ext.Element
```

Drag and Drop

Drag-and-drop functionality can be a major headache to the web developer. These three convenience methods are provided for added simplicity.

```
initDD( String group, Object config, Object overrides ) : Ext.dd.DD
initDDProxy( String group, Object config, Object overrides ) : Ext.dd.DDProxy
initDDTarget( String group, Object config, Object overrides ) : Ext.dd.DDTarget
```

DOM Traversal

When it comes to using JavaScript within a web application, even the most complicated tasks can be boiled down to dynamically modifying the structure HTML document. And this means manipulating the document object model. Modifying the HTML document involves three steps:

1. Locate the position for the new content.

2. Build the new content.

3. Insert the new content.

Traditionally, DOM modification from the browser is a complicated process of determining which browser is being used, which version of that browser, and then executing the proper method on the browser's document object. You already know how to locate a single element (using Ext.get or Ext.fly), and you've also had a brief look at locating a collection of elements (using Ext.select). When you use the Ext.select method to create a collection of elements, an array of DOM nodes, Ext.Elements, or DOM node ids can be used. However, if a string is used, the Ext.select method uses the Ext.DomQuery class.

Ext.DomQuery

The Ext.DomQuery class is a singleton class, which contains utility methods for creating and executing high-performance selector functions. The DomQuery class is used throughout the Ext JS library and accepts several forms of selectors including XPath and CSS (many of which are not yet supported by contemporary browsers). Here's a quick rundown of each selector.

Element Selectors

```
*  -- any element
E  -- an element with the tag E
E F -- all descendant elements of E that have the tag F

    These four are considered "non-simple"
E > F or E/F -- all direct children elements of E that have the tag F
E + F -- all elements with the tag F that are immediately preceded by an
    element with the tag E
E ~ F -- all elements with the tag F that are preceded by a sibling element
    with the tag E
```

Attribute Selectors

The use of @ and quotes is optional. For example, div[@foo='bar'] is also a valid attribute selector.

```
E[foo] -- has an attribute "foo"
E[foo=bar] -- has an attribute "foo" that equals "bar"
E[foo^=bar] -- has an attribute "foo" that starts with "bar"
E[foo$=bar] -- has an attribute "foo" that ends with "bar"
E[foo*=bar] -- has an attribute "foo" that contains the substring "bar"
E[foo%=2] -- has an attribute "foo" that is evenly divisible by 2
E[foo!=bar] -- has an attribute "foo" that does not equal "bar"
```

Pseudo Classes

```
E:first-child -- E is the first child of its parent
E:last-child -- E is the last child of its parent
E:nth-child(n) -- E is the nth child of its parent (1 based)
E:nth-child(odd) -- E is an odd child of its parent
E:nth-child(even) -- E is an even child of its parent
E:only-child -- E is the only child of its parent
E:checked -- E is an element that is has a checked attribute that is true
     (e.g. a radio or checkbox)
E:first -- the first E in the resultset
E:last -- the last E in the resultset
E:nth(n) -- the nth E in the resultset (1 based)
E:odd -- shortcut for :nth-child(odd)
E:even -- shortcut for :nth-child(even)
E:contains(foo) -- E's innerHTML contains the substring "foo"
E:nodeValue(foo) -- E contains a textNode with a nodeValue that equals "foo"
E:not(S) -- an E element that does not match simple selector S
E:has(S) -- an E element that has a descendant that matches simple selector S
E:next(S) -- an E element whose next sibling matches simple selector S
E:prev(S) -- an E element whose previous sibling matches simple selector S
```

CSS Value Selectors

```
E{display=none} -- css value "display" that equals "none"
E{display^=none} -- css value "display" that starts with "none"
E{display$=none} -- css value "display" that ends with "none"
E{display*=none} -- css value "display" that contains the substring "none"
E{display%=2} -- css value "display" that is evenly divisible by 2
E{display!=none} -- css value "display" that does not equal "none"
```

Each selector is available to the developer and can be combined with other selectors in any way imaginable. Each selector is evaluated in the order in which the developer specifies. These features give the developer complete control to optimize the selector definition for his or her specific DOM structure requirements. Internally, a large amount of regular expression evaluations are being processed. By using the compile method, the developer can improve the query's performance (which is quite useful for often-used queries).

Ext.DomQuery methods

In this section, several methods are described.

compile

```
compile( String selector, [String type] ) : Function
```

This method compiles a selector/xpath query into a reusable function. This method returns a function, which takes one parameter (root) and returns an array of DOM nodes. The root parameter (which defaults to document) is the context node where the query should start.

```
var fn = Ext.DomQuery.compile("input:checked");
var a = fn(); // check the entire document
alert("I found " + a.length + " elements!");
```

The type parameter accepts "select" or "simple", and defaults to "select". This parameter indicates *how* ID and tagName attributes are searched for. "simple" is slightly faster, but it does *not* support the following element selectors:

```
E > F or E/F
E + F
E ~ F
```

filter

```
filter( Array el, String selector, [Boolean nonMatches] ) : Array
```

This method accepts an array of elements and returns the elements from that array, which matches the specified *simple* selector. Optionally, you can pass the value of true to the nonMatches (default to false) parameter to get the elements that do *not* match the specified selector.

is

```
is( String/HTMLElement/Array el, String selector ) : Boolean
```

This method returns true if the passed element(s) matches the specified *simple* selector.

select

```
select( String selector, [Node root] ) : Array
```

This method returns an array of DOM nodes, which match the specified selector. The selector parameter in this method can contain multiple selector definitions (delimited by commas). An optional parameter allows the searching to start at a specified DOM node (defaults to document).

```
// grabs all the text boxes on the document
var col = Ext.DomQuery.select("input[type=text],input:not([type]),textarea");
```

selectNode

```
selectNode( String selector, [Node root] ) : Element
```

This method returns the first element from Ext.DomQuery.select and accepts the same parameters.

selectNumber

```
selectNumber( String selector, [Node root], [Number defaultValue] ) : Number
```

This method executes selectValue and attempts to parse its return value into a Number. If no value is found, a defaultValue can be specified (defaults to 0). An optional parameter allows the searching to start at a specified DOM node (defaults to document).

selectValue

```
selectValue( String selector, [Node root], [String defaultValue] ) : String
```

This method selects the value of the first node found by the selector definition. If there is no value, the optional defaultValue (defaults to null) can provide one. An optional parameter allows the searching to start at a specified DOM node (defaults to document).

DOM Manipulation

Now you know how to find elements and manipulate them. The next step for total DOM domination is creating and inserting new DOM nodes. The Ext.DomHelper, Ext.Template, and Ext.XTemplate classes all help the developer to achieve this step.

Ext.DomHelper

The Ext.DomHelper singleton class accomplishes the task of creating new elements and placing them into the HTML document. Each of the methods in DomHelper accepts a parameter containing an HTML fragment, or an object containing the definition of the new element(s). This object would look something like this:

```
var html = {
    tag: "div",
    children: [
        {
            tag: "input",
            type: "submit",
            value: "Click Me!"
        },
        {
            html: "some <i>inner</i> HTML"
        }
    ],
    cls: "someCssClass"
};
```

There are a few special properties that you need to be aware of in the definition object:

❑   tag — This is the element type to be created (defaults to "div").

❑   children — This is an array of definitions that will be placed within the new element.

❑   cls — This is a CSS class name. (This special name avoids conflicts with "class," which is a reserved word.)

❑   html — This is an HTML fragment, which is assigned to the new element's innerHTML value.

❑   style — See Ext.DomHelper.applyStyles on the next page.

If `children` and `html` are both used, `children` are created and `html` is discarded.

The `DomHelper` class also has a `useDom` property (defaults to `false`). By default, `DomHelper` uses string concatenation to build an HTML fragment and inserts the one string (this usually results in the best performance). However, if the `useDom` property is set to `true`, `DomHelper` builds HTML DOM nodes and uses the browser's DOM methods to insert each node.

Ext.DomHelper.append

```
append ( Mixed el, Object/String o, [Boolean returnElement] )
    : HTMLElement/Ext.Element
```

This method appends the new element(s) (defined by `o`) before the closing tag of the specified element (defined by `el`). `el` can be the `id` of a DOM node, a DOM node, or an `Ext.Element`. It returns a DOM node (by default) or an `Ext.Element` (if `returnElement` is `true`).

Ext.DomHelper.applyStyles

```
applyStyles ( String/HTMLElement el, String/Object/Function styles ) : void
```

This method accepts the `id` of a DOM node or a DOM node (`el`) and applies the specified CSS styles (`styles`) to it. Styles can be specified by a string, an object, or a function which returns a string or an object. For example:

```
function getStyles(useObj) {
    if (useObj) {
        return {width: "100px", color: "#000000"};
    } else {
        return "width:100px;color:#000000;";
    }
}

var style = getStyles(false);
Ext.DomHelper.applyStyles(myEl, style); // set styles using a string

var styleObj = getStyles(true);
Ext.DomHelper.applyStyles(myEl, styleObj); // set styles using an object

Ext.DomHelper.applyStyles(myEl, getStyles); // set styles using a function
```

Ext.DomHelper.createTemplate

```
createTemplate ( Object o ) : Ext.Template
```

This method calls `Ext.DomHelper.markup` and then returns a new `Ext.Template`. See later in this chapter for more information on `Ext.Template`.

Ext.DomHelper.insertAfter

```
insertAfter ( Mixed el, Object o, [Boolean returnElement] )
    : HTMLElement/Ext.Element
```

This method appends the new element(s) (defined by o) after the closing tag of the specified element (defined by el). el can be the id of a DOM node, a DOM node, or an Ext.Element. It returns a DOM node (by default) or an Ext.Element (if returnElement is true).

Ext.DomHelper.insertBefore

```
insertBefore ( Mixed el, Object/String o, [Boolean returnElement] )
    : HTMLElement/Ext.Element
```

This method appends the new element(s) (defined by o) before the opening tag of the specified element (defined by el). el can be the id of a DOM node, a DOM node, or an Ext.Element. It returns a DOM node (by default) or an Ext.Element (if returnElement is true).

Ext.DomHelper.insertFirst

```
insertFirst ( Mixed el, Object/String o, [Boolean returnElement] )
    : HTMLElement/Ext.Element
```

This method appends the new element(s) (defined by o) after the opening tag of the specified element (defined by el). el can be the id of a DOM node, a DOM node, or an Ext.Element. It returns a DOM node (by default) or an Ext.Element (if returnElement is true).

Ext.DomHelper.insertHtml

```
insertHtml ( String where, HTMLElement el, String html ) : HTMLElement
```

This method inserts an HTML fragment into the document where specified in relation to the specified DOM node (el). The where parameter can have the following values: "beforeBegin", "afterBegin", "beforeEnd", or "afterEnd". A new DOM node is returned. When useDom is false, this method is used internally by append, insertAfter, insertBefore, and insertFirst.

Ext.DomHelper.markup

```
markup ( Object o ) : String
```

This method takes an element definition object and returns an HTML fragment.

Ext.DomHelper.overwrite

```
overwrite ( Mixed el, Object/String o, [Boolean returnElement] )
    : HTMLElement/Ext.Element
```

This method overwrites the contents of the specified element (defined by el) with the new element(s) (defined by o). el can be the id of a DOM node, a DOM node, or an Ext.Element. It returns a DOM node (by default) or an Ext.Element (if returnElement is true). (This method ignores the useDom property.)

Ext.Template

The cross-browser methods in DomHelper are definitely better than dealing with all the browser-specific issues. And the simple method of defining HTML as a definition object increases productivity and performance. But the Ext JS library goes a few steps further. The Ext.Template class was introduced to enable developers to create reusable HTML templates where different values can be plugged into the template each time it executes (for example, table rows have different values and attributes, but the HTML structure is identical).

However, the Ext.Template class is simply a string generator. While its intended goal was building HTML fragments, its usage can be much broader (for example, generating paragraphs of text).

Moreover, the Ext.Template class is aware of the Ext.util.Format class. Ext.util.Format is a singleton class containing utility functions for string formatting. For example, to format a date string, you would use:

```
var d = new Date(); // current date/time
var s = Ext.util.Format.date(d, "m/d/Y");
alert(s); // you'll see a user-friendly date string
```

Now, here's an example of using Ext.Template:

```
var t = new Ext.Template("{myDate:date('m/d/Y')}");
var s = t.apply({myDate: new Date()});
alert(s); // you'll see the same user-friendly date string
```

Obviously, this simple example would be a waste of processing power. Ext.Template's real strength lies in generating large HTML fragments and binding those fragments to complex data.

Template.from

```
Template.from ( String/HTMLElement el, [Object config] ) : Ext.Template
```

This static method takes the textual value of the specified element (either the value attribute or the innerHTML value) and calls the Ext.Template constructor.

constructor

```
Template ( String/Array html, [Object config] )
```

The constructor creates an instance of the Ext.Template class based on the html parameter. Each property of the config parameter will be copied to the new instance (see Ext.apply). There is only one configuration option, compiled. The compiled configuration option forces the compile method to be called during construction. Any other configuration options get copied to the class instance.

The constructor also allows an infinite number of string parameters (used for increased readability). Internally, these strings get joined together.

```
var t;
// each of the following constructor calls gets identical results
t = new Ext.Template("<div>{text}</div>");
t = new Ext.Template(
    "<div>",
        "{text}",
    "</div>"
);
// this line compiles the template
t = new Ext.Template("<div>{text}</div>", {compiled: true});
```

append

```
append( Mixed el, Object/Array values, [Boolean returnElement] )
    : HTMLElement/Ext.Element
```

Applies the values to the template (see `Ext.Template.applyTemplate`) and invokes `Ext.DomHelper` to insert the new HTML before the closing tag of the specified element. `el` can be the `id` of a DOM node, a DOM node, or an `Ext.Element`. It returns a DOM node (by default) or an `Ext.Element` (if `returnElement` is `true`).

applyTemplate/apply

```
applyTemplate( Object/Array values ) : String
```

This method returns an HTML fragment containing the template with the specified values. The values can be specified as a definition object or as an array.

compile

```
compile() : Ext.Template
```

Like the `Ext.DomQuery` class, `Ext.Template` uses a large amount of regular expression evaluations internally. And like `Ext.DomQuery`, this class offers a `compile` method for better performance. This method merely returns the current instance of the class (not a new instance of `Ext.Template`).

insertAfter

```
insertAfter( Mixed el, Object/Array values, [Boolean returnElement] )
    : HTMLElement/Ext.Element
```

Applies the values to the template (see `applyTemplate/apply`) and invokes `Ext.DomHelper` to insert the new HTML after the closing tag of the specified element. `el` can be the `id` of a DOM node, a DOM node, or an `Ext.Element`. It returns a DOM node (by default) or an `Ext.Element` (if `returnElement` is `true`).

insertBefore

```
insertBefore( Mixed el, Object/Array values, [Boolean returnElement] )
    : HTMLElement/Ext.Element
```

Applies the values to the template (see `applyTemplate/apply`) and invokes `Ext.DomHelper` to insert the new HTML before the opening tag of the specified element. `el` can be the `id` of a DOM node, a DOM node, or an `Ext.Element`. It returns a DOM node (by default) or an `Ext.Element` (if `returnElement` is `true`).

insertFirst

```
insertFirst( Mixed el, Object/Array values, [Boolean returnElement] )
    : HTMLElement/Ext.Element
```

Applies the values to the template (see `applyTemplate/apply`) and invokes `Ext.DomHelper` to insert the new HTML after the opening tag of the specified element. `el` can be the `id` of a DOM node, a DOM node, or an `Ext.Element`. It returns a DOM node (by default) or an `Ext.Element` (if `returnElement` is `true`).

overwrite

```
overwrite( Mixed el, Object/Array values, [Boolean returnElement] )
    : HTMLElement/Ext.Element
```

Applies the values to the template (see `applyTemplate/apply`) and completely replaces the innerHTML value of the specified element with the new HTML. `el` can be the `id` of a DOM node, a DOM node, or an `Ext.Element`. It returns a DOM node (by default) or an `Ext.Element` (if `returnElement` is true).

set

```
set( String html, [Boolean compile] ) : Ext.Template
```

This method allows the developer to reset the template by supplying new HTML and optionally compiling the template. Unlike the constructor, the `html` parameter must be a single string.

Ext.XTemplate

The powerful `Ext.Template` class is capable of binding complex data to HTML fragments in very few lines of code. This saves the developer time, eases maintenance, and increases readability. However, the Ext JS library takes you one more step with the `Ext.XTemplate` class. Deriving from the `Ext.Template` class, `XTemplate` has all the power and ease of use, but can handle hierarchical data.

The set method should not be used on an instance of `Ext.XTemplate`. Doing so will effectively break the template.

All of the `XTemplate` methods are derived from `Template`, so there is no need to repeat them here. However, the template syntax now supports a new tag: `tpl`. The `tpl` tag allows the developer to perform looping, conditionals, and execution of code. For example:

```
var t;
t = new Ext.XTemplate(
    "<div>",
        "<span>{name:capitalize}</span>", // use method from Ext.util.Format
        "<tpl for='scores'>", // looping
            "<p>",
                "{#}: {[this.round(score)]}", // execute code in square brackets
                "<tpl if='score &lt; 60'>", // conditional
                    " AWFUL!",
                "</tpl>",
            "</p>",
        "</tpl>",
    "</div>"
, {
    round: function(value) {
        return Math.round(value);
    }
});
```

The `tpl` tag has three attributes, which *cannot* be used together:

```
<tpl for="string"> - The contents of the tpl tag execute for each member of the
    named child array.
<tpl if="condition"> - If the condition returns true, the contents of the tpl tag
    execute.  The basic math operators (+, -, /, and *) can also be used here.
<tpl exec="executable code"> - Executes the specified code (ignores the contents
    of the tpl tag).
```

Within a `tpl` tag, there are several keywords that can also be used:

```
{string} - Binds the named value of the current object.
{parent.string} - When looping, binds the named value of the parent object.
{#} - When looping, binds the index of the current object (1 based).
{.} - When looping through an array of values (not objects), binds the current
    value.
{[executable code]} - Executes the specified code in the scope of the current
    XTemplate instance.  The following variables are available for use (these
    are also available to <tpl if> and <tpl exec>):
    this - the current XTemplate instance
    values - the current object - ex: values.score
    parent - the current object's parent object - ex: parent.name
    xindex - when looping, the current object's index
    xcount - when looping, the total number of items
    fm - shortcut to Ext.util.Format - ex: fm.trim(values.name)
```

Because the `{[...]}` block executes in the scope of the current XTemplate instance, all of the instance's methods and properties are available. This can be quite useful, as seen in the previous code example where the `round` method is being used for custom formatting.

These features make `Ext.XTemplate` one of the most powerful classes in the Ext JS library.

CSS Manipulation

True DOM-manipulation domination isn't complete without controlling the cascading style sheets, and Ext JS has a solution for that as well.

Ext.util.CSS

This simple singleton class gives the developer cross-browser control over the CSS attached to the HTML document. Accessing the CSS information can be expensive on some browsers, so Ext JS caches the information for better performance. This cache is only used for this class (it doesn't affect `Ext.DomQuery` or any other part of the Ext JS library). If you are dynamically removing CSS information, make sure you call `refreshCache`, if necessary.

Ext.util.CSS.createStyleSheet

```
createStyleSheet( String cssText, String id ) : StyleSheet
```

This method creates a style sheet from a text blob of rules (`cssText`). These rules will be wrapped in a style tag and appended to the head of the document with the supplied `id`.

Ext.util.CSS.getRule

```
getRule( String/Array selector, [Boolean refreshCache] ) : CSSRule
```

This method returns the first CSSRule that matches one of the specified selectors. The developer can optionally rebuild the internal CSSRule cache. This method returns null if the specified selector cannot be found.

Ext.util.CSS.getRules

```
getRules( [Boolean refreshCache] ) : Object
```

This method returns an object containing all CSSRules for the document. The object has the following structure:

```
{
    selector1: definition1,
    selector2: definition2
}
```

The developer can optionally rebuild the internal CSSRule cache.

Ext.util.CSS.refreshCache

```
refreshCache() : Object
```

This method refreshes the rule cache if you have dynamically added style sheets. It is equivalent to getRules(true).

Ext.util.CSS.removeStyleSheet

```
removeStyleSheet( String id ) : void
```

This method removes a style or link tag using the specified id. If the specified id cannot be found, nothing happens.

Ext.util.CSS.swapStyleSheet

```
swapStyleSheet( String id, String url ) : void
```

This method executes removeStyleSheet (using the specified id), and then creates a link tag with the specified id and url.

Ext.util.CSS.updateRule

```
updateRule( String/Array selector, String property, String value ) : Boolean
```

This method updates the property of the CSSRule(s), which match the supplied selector(s) with the supplied value.

```
Ext.util.CSS.updateRule([".invalid", ".error"], "color", "red");
```

Summary

This chapter has briefly covered Ext JS's technique for DOM traversal and DOM manipulation. With a solid object model in place, a well thought out event system, and a normalized interface to the browser, you are now prepared to tackle the real business of building Internet applications. It's important to note that most JavaScript libraries stop here in terms of HTML generation. In fact, you now have all the building blocks in place to generate large, valid HTML fragments and place them accurately into the DOM. In the next chapter, you dive into the Ext Component system, which is the backbone of all UI widgets in the Ext JS library and builds directly on the foundation outlined here.

19

Components, Layouts, and Windows

This chapter covers the real meat of the Ext JS library. Everything up to this point has been mere building blocks for the Ext JS Component system. HTML elements are nice and all, but for even the most basic "widget," the DOM is simply too bulky and time consuming to deal with. For example, creating an Auto-Complete ComboBox (which is often viewed as a *basic* control by customers) requires several accurately placed HTML elements, which must all coordinate both visually and behaviorally. Of course, that ComboBox needs to be placed on a form and in the context of several other data entry controls. And all the controls must flow together with labels and validation markup. To a customer, this is all basic; but to a web developer, this can quickly turn into a rather large headache. The Component system provides a very elegant solution to this overwhelming problem.

In this chapter, you'll learn about:

❑   The Ext JS Component system

❑   The Ext JS Component life cycle

❑   Ext.Viewport

❑   Ext.Container layouts

❑   Panels and windows

The Ext JS Component System

The Ext JS Component system is described here.

Ext.Component

The Ext JS Component starts with the `Ext.Component` class. It is the mother of all widgets and the base class for all "widgets" of the Ext JS toolkit. Whether a developer needs a simple checkbox or a complex three-column layout with nested grids, the `Ext.Component` class is at the heart of it all. Internally, each `Component` has an instance of `Ext.Element` (which, in turn, contains a reference to an old-fashioned DOM `HTMLElement`).

The `Ext.Component` class provides a very nice foundation for developers to build off of. For nested components, the `Component` class has several methods for traversing up the component hierarchy. (For traversing down the component hierarchy, see the "Ext.Container" class section.) `Component` also enforces a simple life cycle, which assists in event listener cleanup and reduces browser memory leaks. Common tasks such as show/hide, enable/disable, and saving/restoring state are all supported by simple methods.

For further extensibility, a powerful plug-in [ ] t system. Each `Component` accepts a collection of plug[ ] is simply a class that has an `init` method. The plug-in[ ] e `Component`. And from there, the plug-in can [ ] job done. This is an extremely simple method of augm[ ] erive.

In addition to all of this, `Ext.Component` de[ ] s all `Components` to fire their own custom events[ ] d to HTML elements. Several events come in pai[ ] restate). In these cases, the first event fires before the[ ] rom an event handler, the developer can cancel t[ ] rs, the second event is fired.

Some developers may question the value of [ ] tive HTML. But consider a simple ComboBox "widget."[ ] an input tag (to display the selected text), a hidden i[ ] div tag to display all the options, a `div` and hidden `input` tag for each option, a `button` tag (to display the scrolling div), and a wrapping `div` tag to put it all in. This is a typical solution; there are probably better ones. But the point is, this one "widget" can easily balloon to hundreds of `HTMLElements`. Add to this browser incompatibilities and traversing, manipulating, and interacting with all of these `HTMLElements` can quickly become a major headache.

It is clear that authoring raw, native HTML has become a hurdle to rapid development. Developing with a "widget" interface can significantly improve your productivity, and the `Ext.Component` class provides a simple and extensible foundation.

Ext.ComponentMgr

As each `Component` is created, it is registered with the `Ext.ComponentMgr` singleton class (`Ext.ComponentMgr.register`). Likewise, as each `Component` is destroyed, it is removed from the `ComponentMgr` collection (`Ext.ComponentMgr.unregister`). The `Component` constructor ensures that each `Component` has a unique ID (this is not a DOM node ID). By using this ID, `Ext.ComponentMgr` provides simple access to every `Component`:

```
var cmp = Ext.ComponentMgr.get("myComponent");
cmp = Ext.getCmp("myComponent"); // short-hand
```

The `ComponentMgr` class also provides a read-only property (`Ext.ComponentMgr.all`), which is the collection of all instantiated `Components`. `all` is an instance of the `Ext.util.MixedCollection` class. `MixedCollection` (derived from `Observable`) is a name/value style collection. And events are fired whenever the collection is modified. This allows developers to have full knowledge of all instantiated `Components` in the application.

To be clear, the Ext Component system is best used by single-page applications. Forcing the end user to waste time waiting for the web server to produce screen layouts for a dozen different screens is a waste of bandwidth. Instead of needless post-backs, Ext developers can create `Components` on demand and redraw selected portions of the screen when necessary. This is not to say that Ext `Components` cannot be used on a traditional web page. The `Tree` and `Grid` classes are fantastic components that behave well wherever they are used. However, to take full advantage of all widgets and to have them cooperate in the best fashion, a single-page application is preferred.

With that in mind, each class derived from `Component` has an `xtype` configuration option. The `xtype` can be used for lazy instantiation and lazy rendering of nested components. This can be extremely useful for added performance on large applications. For example, a user of a large single-page application (containing dozens of screens) might only need to open one screen. With lazy instantiation, only the `Components` necessary are created, and lazy rendering prevents the browser from wasting processing power on DOM nodes that are never seen. This technique allows your Ext application to scale properly. Your single-page application doesn't become a memory hog and slow your user's system to a crawl.

To further illustrate the `xtype` concept, here is an example of a `Window` with a form `Panel` and three `TextFields`:

```
var window = new Ext.Window({
    items: [
        new Ext.Panel({
            layout: "form",
            items: [
                new Ext.form.TextField({
                    fieldLabel: "First Name"
                }),
                new Ext.form.TextField({
                    fieldLabel: "Middle Name"
                }),
                new Ext.form.TextField({
                    fieldLabel: "Last Name"
                })
            ]
        })
    ],
    title: "Sample Window"
});
window.show(); // display the window
```

Here is the same example using xtypes:

```
var window = new Ext.Window({
    items: [
        {xtype: "panel",
            layout: "form",
            items: [
                {xtype: "textfield",
                    fieldLabel: "First Name"
                },
                {xtype: "textfield",
                    fieldLabel: "Middle Name"
                },
                {xtype: "textfield",
                    fieldLabel: "Last Name"
                }
            ]
        }
    ],
    title: "Sample Window"
});
window.show(); // display the window
```

If the window is displayed, each of these samples will produce identical results to the user. However, if the window is *not* displayed, the xtype sample will have a smaller memory footprint. In addition, the xtype sample wastes no time in instantiating objects that are never used. This memory and performance savings can be added up for larger applications.

> *In the preceding code example, the* "window" *xtype is not being used. xtype instantiation occurs from the container. Normally, windows are intended to float above all other content and would not necessarily have a container.*

xtypes are also registered with the ComponentMgr class (Ext.ComponentMgr.registerType). If a Component class's xtype is not registered with the ComponentMgr, it will not be able to take advantage of lazy instantiation and lazy rendering.

```
Ext.ComponentMgr.registerType("textfield", Ext.form.TextField);
// now, the "textfield" xtype will be recognized
```

All built-in Components register their own xtypes. However, if you develop your own Components and want them to take advantage of lazy instantiation and lazy rendering, you must register them.

Ext.BoxComponent

There are several classes that inherit directly from Component (Ext.Button, Ext.ColorPalette, Ext.DatePicker, and so on), but the Ext.BoxComponent, also derived from Component, is another foundational base class that adds functionality. Basically, the BoxComponent adds simple functionality for positioning, moving, and resizing a Component. Methods such as getSize, setPosition, setHeight, are available to any classes deriving from BoxComponent. The BoxComponent class ensures accurate and consistent positioning of all Components.

Ext.Container

Deriving from BoxComponent, the Ext.Container class adds functionality for nested Components. Creating entire Component hierarchies in one call is a simple matter of specifying an array of Components for the items configuration option. Once created, nested Components can be accessed through the read-only items property (an instance of Ext.util.MixedCollection). But there are several methods added to the Container class that make finding nested Components easier. Here's a quick summary of these methods.

getComponent

```
getComponent(String/Ext.Component id) : Ext.Component
```

This method searches the items property for the specified id or Component. This method does not search recursively.

findBy

```
findBy(Function func, [Object scope]) : Ext.Component[]
```

This method uses the supplied function recursively to determine which nested Components should be returned:

```
// find all the hidden components
var hiddenComponents = comp.findBy(function(innerComp) {
    return innerComp.hidden;
});
```

find

```
find(String name, Object value) : Ext.Component[]
```

This method uses the supplied property name and value recursively to determine which nested Components should be returned:

```
// find all the hidden components
var hiddenComponents = comp.find("hidden", true);
```

findById

```
findById(String id) : Ext.Component
```

This method uses the supplied id recursively to determine which nested Component should be returned.

findByType

```
findByType(String/Class xtype, []) : Ext.Component[]
```

This method uses findBy (which is recursive) to find all nested Components that have the specified xtype (or Component class type):

```
// find all TextFields
var texts = comp.findByType("textfield");
// or
texts = comp.findByType(Ext.form.TextField);
```

Creating Nested Components

Items can be added to the Container (or one of its derivatives) using the add or insert methods, but it is easiest to use the items configuration option during construction. The defaults configuration option can also be used to specify common, overrideable configuration options on one items at once:

```
var window = new Ext.Window({
    defaults: {
        allowBlank: false, // all fields are required
        xtype: "textfield" // all nested items are text boxes by default
    },
    items: [
        {fieldLabel: "First Name"},
        {fieldLabel: "Last Name", allowBlank: true}, // not a required field
        {fieldLabel: "Has Hair", xtype: "checkbox"} // not a textfield
    ],
    layout: "form"
});
window.show();
```

By using the items configuration option and taking advantage of each item's xtype configuration option, the developer has saved valuable browser memory and increased performance.

The Ext JS Component Life Cycle

The Component Life Cycle controls the initialization, rendering, and destruction of each Component. As designed, the end developer doesn't need to worry about the inner workings on the Component Life Cycle. By default, Ext.Container (and its subclasses) automatically destroys any nested Components, and each Component is responsible for any Elements that it creates. Although the life cycle works as designed for typical usage, it is useful to have a deeper understanding.

Initialization

As soon as a Component has been instantiated, the Initialization phase of its life cycle begins.

First, a Component ID is generated if one was not specified in the configuration options. The Component is then registered with the ComponentMgr, and the base class (Ext.util.Observable) constructor is called (which creates any event listeners specified in the configuration options).

The initComponent method is called next and is the heart of the Initialization phase. By default, initComponent does nothing and is intended to be overwritten by Component subclasses. However, when deriving, be sure to call the base class's initComponent method. This method should perform the actions typical of a constructor (allocate collection classes, attach default event listeners, and so on). By performing these actions here (instead of the constructor), your Component will enforce a predictable architecture, which allows subsequent subclasses a chance to override (and this is a good thing).

The plug-in architecture is now initialized. Each plug-in in the plugins configuration option has its init method called, with the Component as the only argument.

If the `Component` is participating in state management, its state is now restored. The `beforestaterestore` event is fired (allowing the entire state restoration process to be canceled), state is restored, and then the `staterestore` event is fired. State management is turned on by setting the `Component`'s `stateful` configuration option to `true`. All state is accessed through the singleton class, `Ext.state.Manager` (which is covered later in this section).

If the `renderTo` or `applyTo` configuration options have been set, the Rendering phase begins immediately. Otherwise, rendering occurs on demand. `renderTo` is used to render the `Component` *into* a DOM node where it is added after any existing content. `applyTo` is used to specify a DOM node, which already contains valid markup. `applyTo` takes precedence over `renderTo`, and `renderTo` will be ignored if both of these configuration options are used.

Rendering

The Rendering phase begins when the `render` method is called. The `render` method takes two optional parameters: `container` (an `Ext.Element`, a DOM node, or a DOM node id specifying a containing DOM node for the `Component`) and `position` (specifying where in the container to add the `Component`). Once a `Component` has been rendered, the `Component`'s `rendered` property will return `true`. If you find you need to re-render a `Component`, you will need to set this property to `false`.

For example:

1. The `render` method first calls the `beforerender` event. The developer can cancel the entire phase by handling this event and returning `false`.

2. Usually, the `render` method is called with a `container` argument (the `Component` that will contain the newly render `Component`). However, if the `container` argument is not set, the `Component` is required to have an `Element` reference (in its `el` property). If there is no `container` argument, the `Element`'s `parentNode` is used as the container. (Usually, the `el` property has been set within the `initComponent` method.) In either case, the `container` property of the `Component` is now set.

3. Even though DOM manipulation has not yet occurred, the `rendered` property is now set to `true`.

4. The `onRender` method is now executed. Like the `initComponent` method, this method is intended to be overwritten (be sure to call the base class's `onRender` method) and does most of the heavy lifting. The `onRender` method should place the `Component` officially into the DOM.

5. Depending on the Boolean `autoShow` configuration option, the `Component` is now unhidden (which merely removes the `x-hidden` CSS class from the underlying element). The `cls` configuration option is added and the `style` configuration option is applied.

6. Rendering is now considered complete, and the `render` event is fired. After this, the `afterRender` method is called. `afterRender` does nothing by default and is intended to be overwritten by subclasses.

7. The `hidden` and `disabled` configuration options are applied. These options are used to set the initial state of the `Component`. Obviously, setting `hidden` and `autoShow` would needlessly tax your system and end up with a hidden `Component`.

8. Finally, `stateEvents` are created. The `stateEvents` configuration option is used to specify an array of `Component` events that should invoke the `Component`'s `saveState` method. For example, the `GridPanel` class will store the width of each column (along with other information). If you wanted to store this information each time a column is resized, you would specify the following:

```
stateEvents: ["columnresize"]
```

Destruction

The Destruction phase begins when the `destroy` method is executed. Generally, the `destroy` method is called from within the framework and doesn't need to be executed directly. For example:

1. The `beforedestroy` event is fired, allowing the developer to cancel the entire phase.

2. The `beforeDestory` method is called. By default, this method does nothing, and it is intended to be overridden by subclasses.

3. All event listeners are removed from the `Component`'s underlying `Element` and the `Element` is removed from the DOM.

4. Now that the underlying `Element` is truly destroyed, the `onDestroy` method is called. Again, this method does nothing by default and it is intended to be overwritten by a subclass.

5. The `Component` is unregistered from the `ComponentMgr` and the `destroy` event is fired.

6. Finally, all event listeners are removed from the `Component`.

Please note, a `Component` can only have one primary `Element`. If you author your own `Component` subclass, and it has multiple `Elements`, you will need to properly destroy those `Elements` as well. This can be done using the `beforeDestroy` or `onDestroy` method.

Ext.Viewport

To facilitate the next few examples, this section jumps ahead and discusses the `Ext.Viewport` class. The `Viewport` class is a specialized `Ext.Panel` (which is discussed later in the chapter) that is intended to render itself in the entire browser's viewport. The `Viewport` renders itself directly in the document's `body` and automatically resizes itself when the browser resizes.

A complete example would look something like this:

```
<!DOCTYPE html PUBLIC "-//W3C//DTD XHTML 1.0 Strict//EN"
 "http://www.w3.org/TR/xhtml1/DTD/xhtml1-strict.dtd">
<html xmlns="http://www.w3.org/1999/xhtml">
    <head>
        <title>Viewport Sample</title>
        <meta content="text/html; charset=UTF-8" http-equiv="Content-Type" />
        <link type="text/css" rel="stylesheet" href="css/ext-all.css" />
```

```
        </head>
        <body>
            <form>
                <script type="text/javascript" src="js/ext-base.js"></script>
                <script type="text/javascript" src="js/ext-all.js"></script>
                <script type="text/javascript">
TheApp = {
    init: function() {
        Ext.BLANK_IMAGE_URL = "images/default/s.gif";

        new Ext.Viewport({
            items:[
                {
                    xtype: "panel",
                    border: false,
                    html: "Hello World!"
                }
            ]
        });
    }
};
Ext.onReady(TheApp.init, TheApp, true);
                </script>
            </form>
        </body>
</html>
```

Ext.Container Layouts

Not only does the Ext.Container class allow nested items, it also handles the tricky concept of *layout*. The full power of Ext's Component System really begins to shine with the Container's handling of different layouts.

The Ext.Container's layout configuration option supports several values, which specify how the items are to be laid out within the Container. Each possible layout value represents a different class, which is instantiated when the Container is rendered. (These classes do not need to be instantiated by the developer.) Depending on the type of layout, each of the Container's items may support additional configuration options. In addition, developers can create their own layout classes to provide custom and complex multi-Component layout.

Figure 19-1 displays a list of the built-in layout types.

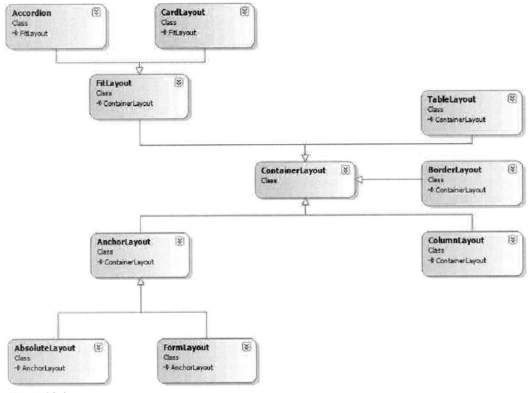

Figure 19-1

Ext.layout.ContainerLayout

If no `layout` value is specified, an `Ext.layout.ContainerLayout` is instantiated. The
`ContainerLayout` simply displays all of its items as is. No attempt is made to reformat
the `items`. The `Container` class also supports the `layoutConfig` configuration option. Because a
`ContainerLayout` is not instantiated by the developer, the `layoutConfig` configuration option is
used to pass configuration options to the layout. The `ContainerLayout` supports the `extraCls` (a CSS
class that is added to each item in the layout) and the `renderHidden` (a Boolean that determines if the
`items` of the layout should be hidden when first rendered) configuration options. This class also has a
read-only `activeItem` property, but it is only used by the `Accordion` and `CardLayout` classes.

```
// the default layout
new Ext.Viewport({
    layout: "auto",
    layoutConfig: {
        renderHidden: true    // each nested item is hidden when rendered
    },
    items:[{  // three nested panels
        title: "Test 1",
```

```
                xtype: "panel"
        }, {
            title: "Test 2",
            xtype: "panel"
        }, {
            title: "Test 3",
            xtype: "panel"
        }]
    });
```

Ext.layout.BorderLayout

The Ext.layout.BorderLayout (that is derived from Ext.layout.ContainerLayout) uses five regions (north, south, east, west, and center) to render its Container's items. Each item can specify its region configuration option (defaults to center). Internally, the BorderLayout class creates an Ext.layout.BorderLayout.Region for each of its items. Adding more than one item that specifies the same region is not supported and unknown behavior will result. In other words, a BorderLayout should only have up to five items (one for each Region). Of course, each Region can have as many items (and nested items) as necessary.

```
new Ext.Viewport({
    layout: "border",
    items:[{  // three nested panels
        title: "Center Region",
        xtype: "panel",
        region: "center"
    }, {
        title: "North Region",
        xtype: "panel",
        region: "north",
        height: 150,
        minHeight: 100,
        split: true  // this region is resizable
    }, {
        title: "East Region",
        xtype: "panel",
        collapsible: true,
        region: "east",
        width: 200
    }]
});
```

Ext.layout.ColumnLayout

The Ext.layout.ColumnLayout (that is derived from Ext.layout.ContainerLayout) allows the developer to create column layouts. Each item in the items configuration option represents a column. Each item can specify its width in pixels (using the width configuration option) or as a percentage (using the columnWidth configuration option). Percentage widths are specified using a value between zero and one. While rendering, absolute widths are first taken into account with percentage widths taking up the rest of the available space. To get predictable results, all percentage-width-based columns must add up to one. An item that does not specify a width or a columnWidth value will use its underlying Element's getWidth method (which returns a number of pixels). This item will then be treated as if it had a width value.

```
new Ext.Viewport({
    layout: "column",
    items:[{  // three columns
        title: "Test 1",
        xtype: "panel",
        width: 250  // this column is exactly 250 pixels
    }, {
        title: "Test 2",
        xtype: "panel",
        columnWidth: .2  // this column is 20% of the remaining total width
    }, {
        title: "Test 3",
        xtype: "panel",
        columnWidth: .8  // this column is 80% of the remaining total width
    }]
});
```

Ext.layout.TableLayout

The Ext.layout.TableLayout (that is derived from Ext.layout.ContainerLayout) uses a standard HTML table to provide traditional rowspan and colspan functionality. The TableLayout class requires a columns configuration option. This option specifies the total number of columns that the table is to have and is passed to the TableLayout constructor through the Container's layoutConfig configuration option. The developer specifies rowspan and colspan values on each item, if desired. As each item is rendered, an HTML td element is rendered to contain each item. The developer can use the cellCls configuration option (which should contain a CSS class name) to adjust the appearance of the table cell (as opposed to the item itself). For programmatic control of the table cell, the developer can use the cellId configuration option.

```
new Ext.Viewport({
    layout: "table",
    layoutConfig: {
        columns: 3  // this option is passed to the TableLayout class
    },
    items:[{ // three columns, two rows
        title: "Test 1",
        xtype: "panel",
        cellId: "theFirstCell",  // for easy recall
        rowspan: 2,  // this item takes up column 1 of rows 1 and 2
        html: "rowspan = 2"
    }, {
        title: "Test 2",
        xtype: "panel",
        colspan: 2,  // this item takes up columns 2 and 3 of row 1
        html: "colspan = 2"
    }, {
        title: "Test 3",  // this item takes up column 2 of row 2
        xtype: "panel"
    }, {
        title: "Test 4",  // this item takes up column 3 of row 2
        xtype: "panel"
    }]
});
var myCell = Ext.get("theFirstCell");
```

Ext.layout.AnchorLayout

The Ext.layout.AnchorLayout (that is derived from Ext.layout.ContainerLayout) allows the developer to create very fluid designs. Each item is anchored to the left side of the container and stacked vertically. The width and height of each item can be specified using the anchor configuration option (a string with two values separated by a space). The values in the anchor configuration option can be an offset from the right-bottom side of the container (specified in a number of pixels), or a percentage of the total width of the container. To create a "virtual" space within the container, the developer can use the anchorSize configuration option. anchor values are now computed based on the anchorSize (rather than the actual size of the container).

```
new Ext.Viewport({
    layout: "anchor",
    anchorSize: {  // a virtual "box"
        width: 800,
        height: 800
    },
    items:[{  // three nested panels
        title: "Test 2",
        xtype: "panel",
        anchor: "-200 -600" // 200 pixels from the right, 600 from the bottom
    }, {
        title: "Test 1",
        xtype: "panel",
        anchor: "50% 25%" // 50% of the width, 25% of the height
    }, {
        title: "Test 3",
        xtype: "panel",
        anchor: "-10 5%" // 10 pixels from the right, 5% of the height
    }]
});
```

Ext.layout.AbsoluteLayout

The Ext.layout.AbsoluteLayout (that is derived from Ext.layout.AnchorLayout) uses each items' x and y configuration options in conjunction with the anchor configuration option.

```
new Ext.Viewport({
    layout: "absolute",
    anchorSize: {  // a virtual "box"
        width: 800,
        height: 800
    },
    items:[{  // two nested panels
        title: "Test 1",
        xtype: "panel",
        anchor: "-200 50%",
        x: 50,
        y: 50
    }, {
```

```
            title: "Test 2",  // height and width are based on the panel's contents
            xtype: "panel",
            x: 100,
            y: 100
        }]
    });
```

Ext.layout.FormLayout

The Ext.layout.FormLayout (that is derived from Ext.layout.AnchorLayout) gives the developer fine control over the appearance of traditional form data entry screens (label and value pairs). To achieve this control, configuration options have been added to the layout, the Container, and each item.

Here are the configuration options for the layout:

❑ elementStyle — Allows the developer to specify a string of CSS style specification, which is applied to all field values

❑ labelSeparator — Allows the developer to specify text (defaults to a colon) to appear between the label and the value

❑ labelStyle — Allows the developer to specify a string of CSS style specification, which is applied to all field labels

Here are the configuration options that are added to the container:

❑ hideLabels — This is a Boolean to hide all labels and label separators.

❑ itemCls — This allows the developer to specify a CSS class, which is applied to the special div that is wrapped around each label and value.

❑ labelAlign — By default, labels are rendered to the left of the values. This option accepts "top" in order to render labels above their values.

❑ labelPad — Used with labelWidth, this option specifies the pixel distance between the labels and their values (defaults to 5). (This option has no effect if labelAlign is set to "top".)

❑ labelWidth — This is the total pixel width of labels (defaults to 100). (This option has no effect if labelAlign is set to "top".)

Here are the configuration options that are added to each item:

❑ clearCls — Allows the developer to specify a CSS class, which is applied to the special clearing div to the left of the field

❑ fieldLabel — Contains the text for the item's label

❑ hideLabel — A Boolean value that hides an item's label and label separator

❑ itemCls — Allows the developer to specify a CSS class, which is applied to the special div that is wrapped around both the label and the value (If specified, this will override the container's itemCls configuration option.)

❑ labelSeparator — Allows the developer to specify text to appear between the label and the value (If specified, this will override the layout's labelSeparator configuration option.)

❑ labelStyle — Allows the developer to specify a string of CSS style specification, which is applied to the label (If specified, this will override the layout's labelStyle configuration option.)

```
new Ext.Viewport({
    layout: "form",
    layoutConfig: {
        labelSeparator: ","
    },
    labelAlign: "top",
    items:[{  // three nested text boxes
        fieldLabel: "Test 1",
        xtype: "textfield"
    }, {
        fieldLabel: "Test 2",
        xtype: "textfield"
    }, {
        fieldLabel: "Test 3",
        xtype: "textfield",
        labelSeparator: ":" // overrides layoutConfig
    }]
});
```

Even with all this fine control, the FormLayout class simply stacks each item vertically. If the developer needs a more complex layout, it is a simple matter of combining layouts.

```
new Ext.Viewport({
    layout: "column",
    items: [{  // two columns of text boxes with labels
        xtype: "panel",
        title: "Column 1",
        columnWidth: .5,
        layout: "form",  // this column has a form layout
        items: [{
            xtype: "textfield",
            fieldLabel: "Textbox 1"
        }, {
            xtype: "textfield",
            fieldLabel: "Textbox 2"
        }]
    }, {
        xtype: "panel",
        title: "Column 2",
        columnWidth: .5,
        layout: "form",  // this column has a form layout
        items: [{
            xtype: "textfield",
            fieldLabel: "Textbox 3"
        }, {
```

```
            xtype: "textfield",
            fieldLabel: "Textbox 4"
        }]
    }]
});
```

It should also be noted that the `Ext.layout.FormLayout` class does not accomplish the behavior of a form (data binding, input validation, and so on). Those tasks are separated out to their logical places, and are covered in later chapters.

Ext.layout.FitLayout

The `Ext.layout.FitLayout` (that is derived from `Ext.layout.ContainerLayout`) forces the container to display one item and for that item to expand to fill the entire width and height of the container. If more than one item is added, the extra items will be rendered, but never displayed:

```
new Ext.Viewport({
    layout: "fit",
    items:[{
        title: "Test 1",
        xtype: "panel"
    }]
});
```

Ext.layout.Accordion

The `Ext.layout.Accordion` (that is derived from `Ext.layout.FitLayout`) allows more than one item to be added to the `Container`, but only one is displayed at a time. Other items' `title` can be seen stacked vertically. A collapse toolbar button is added to the title bar of each item (this button is located on the right of other buttons). The `ContainerLayout`'s `activeItem` property is set with the selection of a new item.

The following configuration options are supported by the layout to customize appearance and behavior:

❑   `activeOnTop` — A Boolean value that indicates whether the newly selected item should move to the top of the accordion (defaults to `false`).

❑   `animate` — A Boolean value that indicates whether to show animation when a new item is selected (defaults to `false`).

❑   `autoWidth` — A Boolean value, which forces all items to be the width of the container (defaults to `true`).

❑   `collapseFirst` — A Boolean value that indicates whether to render the collapse toolbar button to the left of other buttons (defaults to `false`).

❑   `fill` — A Boolean value, which forces all items to be the height of the container (defaults to `true`).

❑ `hideCollapseTool` — A Boolean value, which hides the collapse toolbar button (defaults to `false`).

❑ `titleCollapse` — A Boolean value, which allows users to click anywhere on the title bar of each item (defaults to `true`). If both `hideCollapseTool` and `titleCollapse` are `false`, the user will not be able to swap items.

```
new Ext.Viewport({
    layout: "accordion",
    layoutConfig: {
        animate: true
    },
    items:[{  // three nested panels
        title: "Test 1",
        xtype: "panel"
    }, {
        title: "Test 2",
        xtype: "panel"
    }, {
        title: "Test 3",
        xtype: "panel"
    }]
});
```

Ext.layout.CardLayout

The `Ext.layout.CardLayout` (that is derived from `Ext.layout.FitLayout`) allows more than one item, but displays only one at a time. However, to swap between the items, the developer must execute the `setActiveItem` method. This class presents an excellent base for a wizard-style interface or perhaps a timed presentation of slides. The developer must make sure the `Container`'s `activeItem` configuration option is set. Otherwise, nothing will display by default.

```
var viewport = new Ext.Viewport({
    layout: "card",
    layoutConfig: {
        deferredRender: true  // render each card as it is selected
    },
    activeItem: 0, // make sure there is default active item
    items:[{  // three nested panels
        title: "Test 1",
        xtype: "panel",
        html: "Content Page 1"
    }, {
        title: "Test 2",
        xtype: "panel",
        html: "Content Page 2"
    }, {
        title: "Test 3",
        xtype: "panel",
        html: "Content Page 3"
    }]
});
viewport.layout.setActiveItem(1);  // display the second card
```

Creating Your Own Custom Layouts

In addition to these built-in layout classes, it is simple to create your own. To achieve such a streamlined and extensible rendering mechanism, the `Ext.Container` and `Ext.ContainerLayout` classes are tightly coupled. Container layouts are instantiated and executed by the `Ext.Container`'s render method. Much like the Component life cycle, there is a predictable pattern to how layout classes work. But to roll your own, you need to know some of the inner workings:

❑ `constructor(layoutConfig)` — The `Container`'s `layoutConfig` configuration option is passed to the Layout's constructor.

❑ `setContainer(container)` — This method initializes the Layout. Usually, this is used by the Layout to attach event listeners to the `Container`.

❑ `setActiveItem(item)` — The `Container` will call this method if the `Container` has the `activeItem` configuration option set. However, only the `CardLayout` currently supports this method.

At this point, the `Container`'s render method calls the `doLayout` method. `doLayout` recalculates the `Container`'s layout, as well as any nested `Containers`, until all `Containers` have been recalculated. This method is useful for refreshing selected portions of the screen. The `doLayout` method calls the following methods of the Layout:

❑ `layout()` — This method calls the `Container`'s `getLayoutTarget()` method, and then calls the Layout's `onLayout` method. When the process is complete, the `afterlayout` event is fired.

❑ `onLayout(container, target)` — This method simply calls the `renderAll(container, target)` method, which calls the `renderItem(container, position, target)` method. These render methods are responsible for executing the `render` method on each item (`Ext.Components`), which actually places them into the DOM. By wrapping your own HTML fragments around items, you can easily customize the resulting layout.

Finally, the `Container`'s destruction phase will execute the Layout's `destroy()` method (for any necessary cleanup).

As you can see, creating your own custom layouts is a simple matter of deriving `Ext.layout.ContainerLayout` (or any other built-in layout type) and overriding the methods necessary. To have your custom layout recognized by the `Container`'s `layout` configuration option, you also need to create a name and add it to the `Ext.Container.LAYOUTS` collection:

```
// this makes "mine" a valid layout value
Ext.Container.LAYOUTS['mine'] = Ext.ux.layout.MyLayout;
```

Panels and Windows

Panels and windows are described here.

Ext.Panel

The `Ext.Panel` class derives from `Ext.Container` and adds several useful features that users have come to expect from rich GUI applications. Panels can be dragged, resized, have toolbars, rounded corners, and a header, footer, and body. Plus, being `Containers`, they are capable of all the Layouts previously discussed with nested `Components` and all of their functionalities.

The `Panel` class also comes with several built-in "tool" buttons. These tool buttons do nothing by default, and the developer must provide a handler containing functionality. But the buttons are provided so developers have an easy repository that seamlessly fits the rest of the selected UI theme.

In addition, `Panels` are capable of being updated. Updating is covered in the Chapter 20. For now, take a look at how simple a complex `Panel` can be. The following example is a panel that can be dragged, collapsed, and has a header (with a title and all the tools), a toolbar above the body, a body, a toolbar below the body, and a footer (with an `Ext.Button`):

```
var toolClick = function(event, toolEl, panel) {
    // do something here
};

var layout = new Ext.Viewport({
    layout: "absolute",
    items:[{
        bbar: ["Bottom Toolbar"],
        buttons: [ // this creates the footer automatically
            {text: "Footer"}
        ],
        collapsible: true,
        draggable: true,
        frame: true, // adds a frame around the entire panel
        height: 300,
        html: "Here's the body",
        tbar: ["Top Toolbar"],
        title: "Header", // this creates the header automatically
        tools: [
            // the "toggle" tool is created automatically when collapsible=true
            // {id: "toggle", qtip: "toggle", handler: toolClick},
            {id: "close", qtip: "close", handler: toolClick},
            {id: "minimize", qtip: "minimize", handler: toolClick},
            {id: "maximize", qtip: "maximize", handler: toolClick},
            {id: "restore", qtip: "restore", handler: toolClick},
            {id: "gear", qtip: "gear", handler: toolClick},
            {id: "pin", qtip: "pin", handler: toolClick},
            {id: "unpin", qtip: "unpin", handler: toolClick},
            {id: "right", qtip: "right", handler: toolClick},
            {id: "left", qtip: "left", handler: toolClick},
            {id: "up", qtip: "up", handler: toolClick},
```

```
                    {id: "down", qtip: "down", handler: toolClick},
                    {id: "refresh", qtip: "refresh", handler: toolClick},
                    {id: "minus", qtip: "minus", handler: toolClick},
                    {id: "plus", qtip: "plus", handler: toolClick},
                    {id: "help", qtip: "help", handler: toolClick},
                    {id: "search", qtip: "search", handler: toolClick},
                    {id: "save", qtip: "save", handler: toolClick},
                    {id: "print", qtip: "print", handler: toolClick}
                ],
                width: 500,
                x: 100,
                xtype: "panel",
                y: 100
            }]
        });
```

Besides inheriting all of the properties, methods, and events from `Container`, `BoxComponent`, and `Component`, the `Ext.Panel` class also adds several events and methods that the developer would expect. Methods such as `collapse`, `expand`, `addButton`, and `setTitle` help with everyday tasks. But there's also `getTopToolbar`, `getInnerHeight`, `getFrameWidth`, and so on, which offer the developer a natural object model to the most immediate needs. Much of the `Panel`'s functionality has been covered in this chapter.

Ext.Window

Directly on top of `Ext.Panel` is the `Ext.Window` class. Being more specialized, `Windows` have quite a bit more functionality built into them. `Windows` can be modal, resizable, and constrained to the browser's viewport. Several of the built-in tools now have default functionality (minimize, maximize, close, and so on).

When `Windows` are closed, the default action is to destroy the `Window` and remove it from the DOM. However, many applications have `Windows` that are used over and over again. In this case, the developer can simply set the `Window`'s `closeAction` configuration option to "hide." This option does not destroy the `Window`, but merely hides it. The `show` method will restore the `Window`. This can drastically reduce the overhead associated with recreating large groups of controls.

Because `Windows` traditionally float, the `Ext.Window` class has several methods that are involved with positioning. `alignTo`, `anchorTo`, `center`, `toBack`, and `toFront` are helper functions that are more suitable for a traditional `Window`.

Perhaps most exciting of all (for end users, anyway), the `Ext.Window` class has a `manager` configuration option. The manager configuration option accepts an instance of `Ext.WindowGroup` (by default, this is set to `Ext.WindowMgr`).

Ext.WindowGroup

A `WindowGroup` is simply a collection class of `Window` instances. When a `Window` is created it is automatically added to a `WindowGroup`. When the `Window` is destroyed, it is removed from the group. The `WindowGroup` class manages the "active" `Window` of the group, and a z-order of all `Windows` in the group. There are also a few helper functions for iterating through the group (`each`), dealing with z-order (`sendToBack` and `bringToFront`), and retrieving a specific Window (`get` and `getBy`). All of these methods are similar to previously discussed methods.

Ext.WindowMgr

The `Ext.WindowMgr` class is the global singleton instance of `Ext.WindowGroup`. If the developer chooses not to create his own `WindowGroup`, this group will be used as the default manager for all Windows. By creating your own `WindowGroups`, you could easily create several "desktops" within a single browser page.

Summary

In the previous chapters, you learned about the building blocks that have laid the foundation for the Ext JS widget library. This chapter is an introduction to that library. While most JavaScript libraries restrict themselves to a well thought out foundation, Ext has actually done something with it. Using classes such as `Ext.DomQuery`, `Ext.DomHelper`, and `Ext.Template`, the Ext Component system has created a robust and yet simple basis for the entire widget library. The full benefits of a concise and organized Object hierarchy can already be seen in classes such as `Ext.Panel` and `Ext.Window`.

In the next chapter, you begin digging into the classes that help developers send and retrieve data from the server and model data within the browser.

20

Handling Data and Talking with the Server

The main purpose of HTML and the Internet in general has always been about distributing data. Whether it's scientific documents, a family photo album, or video news clips, almost all forms of data have found their place on the Web. As data has grown, the performance of the Web has suffered. Waiting five seconds for page two of the family photo album is simply too long. While the techniques of loading data without reloading the entire page has been around for about a dozen years, it has only been in the past couple of years that these techniques have really been used to the fullest extent possible.

Now, every JavaScript framework on the planet has added some helper functions for performing these fancy AJAX jobs, and Ext JS is no exception. However, the Ext JS authors realize that AJAX techniques do not solve all the data access problems. Getting the data is only part of the problem. Issues such as data format, data schema, and data deserialization have all been addressed by Ext. In this chapter, you'll learn about:

- ❑ Getting data
- ❑ Remodeling data
- ❑ Storing data locally
- ❑ Putting it all together

You'll also see how Ext JS has simplified the entire data-access issue. There are three categories of classes that accomplish the majority of the data-access issues. You'll examine the classes that retrieve data (proxies); the classes that deserialize and model data (readers); and the classes that cache the remodeled data (stores). All of these classes have tight dependencies on the others and work in conjunction to form a high-performing and flexible data engine.

Getting the Data

As mentioned earlier, AJAX techniques do not solve every data-access problem. To be precise, AJAX relies on the browser's XMLHttpRequest object. AJAX techniques do not retrieve data on servers other than the current page's server. However, developers expect a consistent interface for all types of data-access techniques. In order to create this consistency, the Ext authors have created the `Ext.data.DataProxy` abstract base class.

Ext.data.DataProxy

By itself, the `DataProxy` class does nothing (see Figure 20-1). It merely exposes two events (`beforeload` and `load`) that subclasses can fire. And each of the `DataProxy` subclasses has been written to address a specific data-access technique. When a `DataProxy` subclass fires each of the events, it is expected to conform to the following signatures:

❑ `beforeload(this,params)` — `this` is the current instance of `Ext.data.DataProxy`, and `params` are usually the parameters sent to the server. This event can be canceled by returning `false` from an event listener.

❑ `load(this,o,arg)` — `this` is the current instance of `Ext.data.DataProxy`, `o` is the data loaded from the server, and `arg` is a developer supplied object.

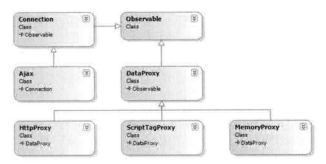

Figure 20-1

Ext.data.HttpProxy

Since AJAX is the technique used by most developers, take look at the `Ext.data.HttpProxy` class first.

The `HttpProxy` class exposes one method:

> `load : function(params, reader, callback, scope, arg)` — `params` are parameters sent to the server; `reader` is an instance of the `Ext.data.DataReader` class; `callback` is a method that is called when communication with the server has ended; `scope` determines the scope of the callback; and `arg` is a developer-defined object that is passed to the callback. The callback method has the following three parameters: `result` (the object resulting from successful deserialization); `arg` (the optional `arg` parameter from the `load` method); and `success` (a Boolean value indicating if the entire load process completed successfully).

The `HttpProxy` class exposes one new event:

> `loadexception : function(this, options, response, e)` — `this` is the current instance of `Ext.data.HttpProxy`; `options` is an object containing all values sent to the `HttpProxy`'s `load` method; `response` is the browser's XMLHttpRequest object that performed the actual communication with the server; and `e` is either `null` or an `Error` encountered during the deserialization process.

When the `load` method is called, the `HttpProxy` does all of its server communication through an instance of the `Ext.data.Connection` class. The `HttpProxy` constructor optionally accepts an instance of the `Connection` class or an object, which is passed to the `Ext.Ajax.request` method. `Ext.Ajax` is a global instance of `Ext.data.Connection`, which is used in the absence of an explicit `Connection` object.

As soon as the `HttpProxy`'s `load` method is called, its `beforeload` event is fired, allowing developers a chance to cancel the load process. If not canceled, the load process continues by executing the `request` method of the `Connection` object. The `request` method is an asynchronous call to the server, and is covered in more detail in the "Ext.data.Connection and Ext.Ajax" section. If the `request` is successful, the `HttpProxy` continues by invoking the supplied `reader` (an instance of `Ext.data.DataReader`) to deserialize the data. If the `DataReader` succeeds, the `HttpProxy`'s `load` event is fired. Otherwise, the `HttpProxy`'s `loadexception` event is fired. Finally, the supplied `callback` method is executed.

```
var proxy = new Ext.data.HttpProxy({  // we're not using an explicit Connection
    url: "getData.html"
});
proxy.on({
    beforeload: {
        fn: function(proxy, params) {
            // here's a chance to cancel the load process
        }
    },
    load: {
        fn: function(proxy, data, arg) {
            // loading has completed successfully
        }
    },
    loadexception: {
        fn: function(proxy, options, response, e) {
            if (e) {
                // there has been a deserialization error (examine the e argument)
            } else {
                // there has been a server error (examine the response argument)
            }
        }
    }
});
proxy.load(params, reader, callback, scope, arg);
```

Ext.data.Connection and Ext.Ajax

The `Ext.data.Connection` class is your typical AJAX class and the foundation of Ext's server connectivity. The class is used internally by the `Ext.data.HttpProxy` class for access to the server. But the `Connection` class can also be used alone for more controlled data access. All requests to the server are done asynchronously with a simple and flexible method for attaching callbacks. The Ext.Ajax class is a global instance of Connection, which is provided for convenience. Here's a simple one-line call to the server:

```
Ext.Ajax.request({
    url: "getData.html",
    callback: function(options, success, response) {
        if (success) {
            alert("Yea!");
        } else {
            alert("Boo!");
        }
    }
});
```

As you can see, a response parameter will always be passed to the callback method. In the previous example, the developer examines the success flag. In addition to the all-purpose callback method, there are also success and failure methods where the success flag is unnecessary.

The Connection class can be used and reused for multiple requests. The constructor accepts configuration options that can be reused for all calls to the request method. Here's a listing of all the constructor's configuration options:

❑ autoAbort — A Boolean that indicates whether to abort any pending requests (defaults to false).

❑ defaultHeaders — An object that contains headers to add to each request (defaults to undefined).

❑ disableCaching — A Boolean that indicates whether or not to add a time stamp to the QueryString when making a request (this will defeat browser caching). This is only used when the method option is set to "GET" (defaults to true).

❑ disableCachingParam — A string value for the name of the QueryString time stamp, which disables caching (defaults to "_dc").

❑ extraParams — An object that contains values that will be added to each request (defaults to undefined).

❑ method — The HTTP method used for each request (defaults to "GET", but if params are present, defaults to "POST").

❑ timeout — The number of milliseconds to allow before aborting a request (defaults to 30000–30 seconds).

❑ url — The location of server resource. The resource must be within the current page's originating domain.

The request method also accepts a configuration option object. The request method overrides any conflicting configuration options from the constructor. Here are the options for the request method:

❑ `headers` — An object that contains HTTP header values (defaults to `undefined`).

❑ `disableCaching` — Used to override the `disableCaching` option from the constructor.

❑ `params` — An object that contains values that will be added to the request (defaults to `undefined`).

❑ `method` — Used to override the `method` option from the constructor.

❑ `timeout` — Used to override the `timeout` option from the constructor.

❑ `url` — Used to override the `url` option from the constructor.

❑ `callback` — A method that is called on completion or failure of the request.

❑ `success` — A method that is called on completion of the request.

❑ `failure` — A method that is called on failure of the request.

❑ `scope` — An object that is the scope of the `callback`, `success`, and `failure` methods.

❑ `form` — `Ext.Element`, `HTMLElement`, or DOM node ID of the HTML Form tag that needs to be serialized.

❑ `isUpload` — Set to `true` to allow file uploads. See the "File Uploads" section below for more information.

❑ `xmlData` — An XML document that is sent in the body of the request (if `params` are being used, they are appended to the QueryString). This cannot be used with `jsonData`.

❑ `jsonData` — A JavaScript string or object that is sent in the body of the request (if `params` are being used, they are appended to the QueryString). This cannot be used with `xmlData`.

This configuration object is always merged with the constructor's configuration object and passed to the callback methods (`callback`, `success`, and `failure`). This can come in handy when the callback method needs information that doesn't need to be sent to the server:

```
var conn = new Ext.data.Connection();
conn.request({
    myValues: { // these values are NOT sent to the server
        value1: "test"
    },
    url: "getData.html",
    params: { // these values ARE sent to the server
        dataType: "user"
    },
    callback: function(options, success, response) {
        if (success) {
            // all the options are still here
            alert(options.myValues.value1);
        }
    }
});
```

The `Connection` class is also derived from `Ext.util.Observable` and offers three events. These events are fired for all requests executed from the current instance of `Connection`:

❏ `beforerequest(Connection conn, Object options)` — This is fired right before the request is sent to the server. Returning false from an event listener will result in the event being canceled (and no request being sent to the server).

❏ `requestcompleted(Connection conn, Object response, Object options)` — This is fired as soon as a successful response is received from the server.

❏ `requestexception(Connection conn, Object response, Object options)` — This is fired as soon as a failure response is received from the server.

In all three of the events (as well as the three callback methods), the `response` parameter is the browser's native XMLHttpRequest object. This contains all of the raw information that the developer could ever have access to. The `request` method also returns a transaction ID, which can be passed back to the `Connection`'s `isLoading` or `abort` methods. As always, the developer is in full control.

File Uploads

Performing file uploads is the Achilles' heel of AJAX. The XMLHttpRequest object does not support file attachments for a variety of reasons. To work around this issue, Ext creates a hidden IFRAME, posts the data (along with any file attachments) through the IFRAME, and destroys the IFRAME once the request is completed. Ext also creates a fake XMLHttpRequest object, which is populated with the data returned from the server. This gives the developer a consistent object model for all requests (whether they are done through AJAX or IFRAME).

However, this work-around may require special attention from the developer as well. When returning JSON data from an IFRAME request, it is necessary to send that data with a MIME type of "`text/html`." This tells the browser to leave the data alone and allows Ext to parse it as necessary. Also, uploading files requires that the browser use the "`multipart/form`" content type, which can cause grief for some web servers. Both of these issues are necessary evils of the browser HTTP platform and can be easily solved on the web server.

Ext.data.MemoryProxy

The `MemoryProxy` class is by far the simplest proxy class. Its sole purpose is to uphold the consistent interface of data access. The `MemoryProxy` accesses data, which is held in local JavaScript objects. As simple as this is, the `MemoryProxy` can be extremely useful when loading data from third-party JavaScript or Flash libraries.

The `MemoryProxy`'s constructor accepts the JavaScript object, which needs loading. The class also exposes a `load` method and a `loadexception` event with the same signatures as found in the `HttpProxy`. The `MemoryProxy` class has no need for either the `params` argument on the `load` method or the `response` argument of the `loadexception` event, but they are still available for consistency and extensibility purposes. The `beforeload` and `load` events are completely absent, however.

```
var data = [
    {
        FirstName: "Bob",
        LastName: "Smith"
    }, {
        FirstName: "Gary",
        LastName: "Robertson"
    }
];
var proxy = new Ext.data.MemoryProxy(data);
proxy.on({
    loadexception: {
        fn: function(proxy, options, response, e) {
            // response will always be null
            if (e) {
                // there has been a deserialization error
            }

        }
    }
});
proxy.load(null, reader, callback, scope, arg);
```

Ext.data.ScriptTagProxy

The Ext.data.ScriptTagProxy addresses a third data-access problem: retrieving data from a remote server. Behind the scenes, the ScriptTagProxy class creates a hidden callback method and passes the name of the callback method to the remote server on the QueryString. The remote server then generates valid JavaScript to execute this callback method and passes it the JSON formatted data. Here is some sample server-side pseudo-code:

```
Response.ContentType = "text/javascript";
String theData = getData().toJson();
String callbackName = Request.QueryString["callback"];
Response.Write(callbackName + "(" + theData + ");");
```

Of course, using the ScriptTagProxy from the browser side is very similar to the other proxies. There is a load method (same as HttpProxy), and a loadexception event. The beforeload and load events also behave as expected. The only oddity here is that the loadexception event has replaced the response parameter with the arg parameter (which was passed to the load method). Once the data has been retrieved (or the timeout has been reached), the hidden callback method is destroyed.

The ScriptTagProxy constructor accepts a configuration object with the following options:

- ❏ url — The location of the remote server resource
- ❏ timeout — The number of milliseconds allowed before the proxy gives up (defaults to 30000)
- ❏ callbackParam — The name of the QueryString parameter, which will contain the name of the hidden JavaScript callback method (defaults to "callback")
- ❏ nocache — A Boolean that determines whether a time stamp is added to the QueryString to make this request unique (which defeats browser caches) (defaults to true)

The `load` method accepts the same parameters as the `HttpProxy` `load` method and behaves in the same fashion. The only difference here is that the `params` argument is serialized as JSON and placed on the QueryString when sent to the remote server (in essence, this data request is required to be an HTTP GET).

```
var proxy = new Ext.data.ScriptTagProxy({
    url: "www.remoteServer.com"
});
proxy.on({
    beforeload: {
        fn: function(proxy, params) {
            // here's a chance to cancel the load process
        }
    },
    load: {
        fn: function(proxy, data, arg) {
            // loading has completed successfully
        }
    },
    loadexception: {
        fn: function(proxy, options, arg, e) {
            if (e) {
                // there has been a deserialization error (examine the e argument)
            } else {
                // there has been a server error
            }
        }
    }
});
proxy.load(params, reader, callback, scope, arg);
```

Remodeling the Data

As discussed previously, each `DataProxy` subclass has a `load` method, which accepts a `reader` argument. The `reader` is the object that deserializes the data. And to do the deserialization, the reader needs to know the data model that it's dealing with. That's where the `Ext.data.Record` class comes into play.

Ext.data.Record

The `Ext.data.Record` class is another abstract base class, but it uses a factory pattern for creating new `Record` types. The `Record` class also has a dual purpose. It is used to define a data row (modeling), and it is also used to store the original and modified values of a single data row (deserialization). For the moment, modeling is discussed. The deserialization mechanics of the `Record` class is discussed later in the chapter.

It is important to understand that there is no such thing as a generic `Record` definition. All definitions are custom made, but they must behave in a similar fashion. Because of this, it makes sense to have a factory pattern for creating `Record` types. To create a new custom `Record`, you should execute the `Ext.data.Record.create` method. This method accepts an array of field definitions.

Ext.data.Field

Internally, the field definitions are used to create an array of `Ext.data.Field` instances. The `Field` class isn't used anywhere in the Ext library except from within `Ext.data.Record`, but each `Field` will contain a custom `convert` method for transforming the original data value into something more appropriate. This `convert` method is usually constructed based on the `type` of data, but it can be easily overwritten from the field definition:

```
var userRecordDefinition = Ext.data.Record.create([
    {name: "FirstName", mapping: "FName", type: "string"},
    {name: "LastName", mapping: "LName", type: "string"},
    {name: "DateOfBirth", mapping: "DOB", type: "date", dateFormat: "m/d/Y"},
    {name: "FavoriteColor", defaultValue: "Green"},
    {name: "ShirtSize", mapping: "size", convert: function(value, row) {
        switch (value) {
            case 1:
                return "X-Large";
            break;
            case 2:
                return "Large";
            break;
            case 3:
                return "Medium";
            break;
            default:
                // we have access to the original data row
                if (!row["DOB"]) {
                    return "Small";
                }
            break;
        }
    }}
]);
```

As seen in the previous example, each `Field` definition has the following properties (`name` is the only required value):

❑   `name` — This is the name that is used within your code to access the field's value.

❑   `mapping` — This method obtains the value relative to its record's root. This value is specific to the type of data being read. For example, the `XmlReader` class expects a path expression understood by the `Ext.DomQuery` object, such as "firstName" or "name/first" (note that hierarchical data is supported). If the `mapping` value is the same as the `name` value, `mapping` may be excluded.

❑   `type` — This is the data type that is used for default conversions. The available options are `auto` (no conversion), `string`, `int`, `float`, `boolean`, and `date`.

❑   `sortType` — This defines how records should be sorted when sorted by the current `Field`. Valid values are contained in the `Ext.data.SortTypes` class (see the "Ext.data.SortTypes" section for more details). Default values are based on the `type` value.

❑   `sortDir` — ASC (ascending) or DESC (descending) (defaults to ASC).

❑   `convert` — This is a custom conversion function that obtains the displayable value.

Ext.data.SortTypes

The `Ext.data.SortTypes` class is a simple helper class. It contains functions that are used to convert raw data values before comparing them for sorting purposes. It is important to realize that converting data so it can be sorted is different than converting data to be viewed. For example, dates must be formatted in very special ways for end users, but that same formatting will not sort as logic dictates. The built-in sorting conversion functions are as follows:

❏   `none` — Does nothing to the value

❏   `asText` — Strips any HTML tags from the value

❏   `asUCText` — Strips any HTML tags and uppercases (for case-insensitive sorts)

❏   `asUCString` — Uppercases (for case-insensitive sorts)

❏   `asDate` — Returns a date (or zero)

❏   `asFloat` — Returns a float (or zero)

❏   `asInt` — Returns an integer (or zero)

Ext.data.DataReader

The `Ext.data.DataReader` is yet another abstract base class that provides more code consistency. The JSON objects resulting from `DataReaders` are highly customizable (using `Ext.data.Record`) and perform extremely well, even with large amounts of data. The Ext library offers several data caching classes (discussed later in the chapter), which use the formatted JSON objects to populate virtually every UI component in the Ext widget library.

There are three built-in subclasses: `Ext.data.XmlReader`, `Ext.data.JsonReader`, and `Ext.data.ArrayReader`. Each subclass has a constructor that accepts two arguments:

❏   `meta` — Information specific to the subclass

❏   `recordType` — A custom `Ext.data.Record` definition that is sent to the `Ext.data.Record` `.create` method

Each subclass also has a `readRecords` method, which only has one argument, the data. This method deserializes the data and creates a `Record` instance for each row. The return value is an object with the following structure:

❏   `records` — An array of `Record` instances (which are typed using the `recordType` configuration option)

❏   `totalRecords` — Either the total number of rows in the `records` array or the total number of rows on the server (used when paging data)

❏   `success` — A Boolean value that indicates whether a form submission was successful (which is discussed in more detail in Chapter 33)

For the three built-in `DataReader` subclasses, similarly structured data are used in the examples in this chapter (see Figure 20-2). Notice how little the Ext code needs to change given a selected `DataReader`.

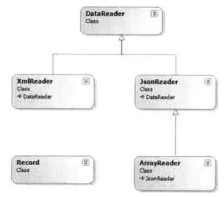

Figure 20-2

Ext.data.XmlReader

The Ext.data.XmlReader is used to read XML documents. Use the following XML document for the code example:

```xml
<?xml version="1.0" encoding="UTF-8"?>
<table>
    <count>4</count>
    <person>
        <firstName>Bob</firstName>
        <lastName>Smith</lastName>
        <age>16</age>
        <userId>bsmith</userId>
    </person>
    <person>
        <firstName>Gary</firstName>
        <lastName>Johnson</lastName>
        <age>22</age>
        <userId>gjohnson</userId>
    </person>
    <person>
        <firstName>Susan</firstName>
        <lastName>Brown</lastName>
        <age>32</age>
        <userId>sbrown</userId>
    </person>
    <person>
        <firstName>Leslie</firstName>
        <lastName>Harris</lastName>
        <age>18</age>
        <userId>lharris</userId>
    </person>
</table>
```

The meta configuration object has five properties (all are optional):

❑ totalRecords — An Ext.DomQuery path expression pointing to the value containing the total number of rows. This value is useful when paging.

❑ record — An Ext.DomQuery path expression pointing to the repeating element, which represents a row.

❑ id — An Ext.DomQuery path expression pointing to the field containing each row's unique identifier (this is relative to the record expression).

❑ fields — The Record definition sent to the Ext.data.Record.create method (by using this, you can exclude the DataReader constructor's recordType argument).

❑ success — An Ext.DomQuery path expression pointing to the value representing a successful form submission (see Chapter 33 for more details).

```
var reader = new Ext.data.XmlReader({
    totalRecords: "count",
    record: "person",
    id: "userId",
    fields: [
        {name: "firstName"},
        {name: "lastName"},
        {name: "age", type: "int"}
    ]
});
```

Ext.data.JsonReader

The Ext.data.JsonReader is used to read JSON objects. Use the following JSON object for the code example:

```
var data = {
    count: 4,
    person: [
        {firstName: "Bob", lastName: "Smith", age: 16, userId: "bsmith"},
        {firstName: "Gary", lastName: "Johnson", age: 22, userId: "gjohnson"},
        {firstName: "Susan", lastName: "Brown", age: 32, userId: "sbrown"},
        {firstName: "Leslie", lastName: "Harris", age: 18, userId: "lharris"}
    ]
};
```

The meta configuration object has five properties (all are optional):

❑ totalProperty — A JavaScript expression pointing to the value containing the total number of rows. This value is useful when paging.

❑ root — A JavaScript expression pointing to the array containing all rows.

❑ id — A JavaScript expression pointing to the field containing each row's unique identifier (this is relative to the root expression).

❑ fields — The Record definition sent to the Ext.data.Record.create method (by using this, you can exclude the DataReader constructor's recordType argument).

❏   successProperty — JavaScript expression pointing to the value representing a successful form submission (see Chapter 33 for more details).

```
var reader = new Ext.data.JsonReader({
    totalProperty: "count",
    root: "person",
    id: "userId",
    fields: [
        {name: "firstName"},
        {name: "lastName"},
        {name: "age", type: "int"}
    ]
});
```

The JsonReader also exposes an onMetaChange method (which is executed internally). When the data has been received from the DataProxy, the data object may include a metaData property, which can redefine the underlying Record structure as well as any of the configuration options for the current JsonReader. When the metaData property is received, the onMetaChange method is executed.

Here is an example of such an object (as returned from the DataProxy):

```
{
    metaData: {
        totalProperty: "length", // changes the totalProperty value
        root: "person",
        id: "userId",
        fields: [ // redefines the Record structure
            // reverses the mapping of the name fields
            {name: "firstName", mapping: "lastName"},
            {name: "lastName", mapping: "firstName"},
            {name: "age", type: "int"}
        ]
    }
}
```

This can be an incredibly powerful feature when used properly. For example, if a user hides a column from a grid, the server can save valuable bandwidth by not sending those values. And with the Record structure redefined, the browser won't waste processing power on values that are no longer there.

Ext.data.ArrayReader

The Ext.data.ArrayReader is a specialized JsonReader and is used to read complex JavaScript arrays. The following code example shows a JavaScript array:

```
var data = [
    ["Bob", "Smith", 16, "bsmith"],
    ["Gary", "Johnson", 22, "gjohnson"],
    ["Susan", "Brown", 32, "sbrown"],
    ["Leslie", "Harris", 18, "lharris"]
];
```

The meta configuration object has one property (which is optional): id, which is the ordinal position of the row's unique identifier

```
var reader = new Ext.data.ArrayReader({id: 3}, [
    {name: "firstName", mapping: 0},
    {name: "lastName", mapping: 1},
    {name: "age", mapping: 2, type: "int"}
]);
```

Storing the Data Locally

Up to this point, this chapter has covered the various methods for retrieving data. You've also seen how to remodel and deserialize that data. Now, you need to store that data locally so it can be used in grids, trees, forms, and so on. The Ext.data.Store class uses all of the classes and technologies discussed so far in this chapter (see Figure 20-3).

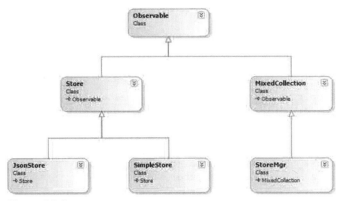

Figure 20-3

Ext.data.Store

The Store class is a one-stop shop for almost all data-access concerns. It has no knowledge of the underlying structure (Ext.data.Record), what it originally looked like (Ext.data.DataReader), or where it came from (Ext.data.DataProxy). But using these classes internally, the Store is capable of serving up indiscriminate data in a very consistent fashion.

Ext.data.JsonStore

Derived from Ext.data.Store, the Ext.data.JsonStore class is simply a helper class with a built-in Ext.data.JsonReader. To properly construct the JsonReader, the JsonStore constructor accepts all the Ext.data.Store options as well as a fields option (which is passed to the JsonReader constructor).

Ext.data.SimpleStore

Derived from `Ext.data.Store`, the `Ext.data.SimpleStore` class is simply a helper class with a built-in `Ext.data.ArrayReader`. To properly construct the `ArrayReader`, the `SimpleStore` constructor accepts all the `Ext.data.Store` options as well as `fields` and `id` options (which are passed to the `ArrayReader` constructor).

The following is a thorough rundown of the `Store` class (and its subclasses).

Ext.data.Store Options

The `Store` constructor has the following configuration options:

❑ `storeId` — A unique value that is used with the `Ext.StoreMgr` (a collection of cached data; see the "Ext.StoreMgr" section for more details).

❑ `url` — A URL that is used to construct an internal instance of `Ext.data.HttpProxy` (ignored if the `proxy` configuration option is also supplied).

❑ `autoLoad` — Either a Boolean value that determines if the `Store`'s `load` method should be executed immediately after construction, or an object that is passed to the `Store`'s `load` method (which will be executed immediately after construction). This value is ignored if the `data` configuration option is also supplied (defaults to `false`).

❑ `proxy` — An instance of `Ext.data.DataProxy` that is used for data access.

❑ `data` — Inline data that is loaded immediately after construction. An instance of `Ext.data.DataProxy` is completely unnecessary, because the data is already here.

❑ `reader` — An instance of `Ext.data.DataReader`, which will deserialize the data.

❑ `baseParams` — An object that contains values to be sent to the `DataProxy`'s `load` method (merged with the `DataProxy` `load` method's `params` argument).

❑ `sortInfo` — An option that determines the default sort for the data (example: `{field: "fieldName", direction: "DESC"}`). If `remoteSort` is set to true, this information is sent to the `DataProxy`.

❑ `remoteSort` — A Boolean value that determines whether or not sorting is to be handled by the `DataProxy`. If `remoteSort` is `true`, a `sort` value and a `dir` value are both sent to the `DataProxy`'s `load` method (merged with the `load` method's `params` argument).

❑ `pruneModifiedRecords` — The `Store` class has the ability to track changes made to the underlying `Records`. If this value is set to true, modified `Records` will be destroyed as soon as possible (by deleting the original `Record` or by reloading the `DataProxy`).

Ext.data.Store Events

The `Store`, derived from `Ext.util.Observable`, also has several events:

❑ `datachanged(store)` — Fires when the underlying `Records` have changed because of reloading, filtering, or sorting.

❑ `metachange (store, metadata)` — Fires when the `store`'s `DataReader` executes its `onMetaChange` method.

❑ add(store, records) — Fires when a Record(s) has been added to the Store. records is an array of Ext.data.Record.

❑ remove(store, record, index) — Fires when a Record has been removed from the Store.

❑ update(store, record, operation) — Fires when a Record's value(s) has been updated. The operation argument may be one of the following: "edit" (Ext.data.Record.EDIT), "reject" (Ext.data.Record.REJECT), or "commit" (Ext.data.Record.COMMIT).

❑ clear(store) — Fires when the Store's RemoveAll method is executed.

❑ beforeload(store, options) — Fires before the DataProxy's load method is executed. The developer can return false from any event listener to bypass the load process. The options argument contains the options object that was sent to the Store's load method.

❑ load(store, records, options) — Fires after successfully executing the DataProxy's load method. The records argument contains an array of Ext.data.Record, which will be added to the Store. The options argument contains the options object that was sent to the Store's load method.

❑ loadexception — Relays the DataProxy's loadexception event.

Ext.data.Store Methods

The Store has several useful methods as well, which are discussed next.

Adding and Removing Records Manually

❑ add(Records[]) — The array of Ext.data.Record is added to the Store. The add event is fired.

❑ addSorted(Record) — The instance of Ext.data.Record is added to the Store using the current sort information. The insert method is called to add the record at the proper position.

❑ insert(index, Record[]) — Inserts the array of Record at the specified index. The add event is fired.

❑ remove(Record) — Removes the specified Record. The remove event is fired.

❑ removeAll() — Removes all Records from the Store. The clear event is fired.

Filtering and Locating Records

❑ filter(field, value, anyMatch, caseSensitive) — Filters the Records based on the specified Field (field) and compared against the value (which can be a string or RegEx). anyMatch is a Boolean determining if the comparison can match anywhere within the Field's value or just at the beginning. caseSensitive is a Boolean determining if the comparison is case-sensitive.

❑ filterBy(func, scope) — Each Record in the Store is passed to the specified function (func), using the optional scope. The function must return true for the Record to be included in the filter.

❑ clearFilter(suppressEvent) — All filtered data is restored. The suppressEvent argument is a Boolean determining whether or not to fire the datachanged event.

❏ `isFiltered()`, `Boolean` — Returns a Boolean value indicating if a filter is currently in effect.

❏ `find(field, value, startIndex, anyMatch, caseSensitive)`, `Number` — Works like `filter`, but returns the first matching index.

❏ `findBy(func, scope, startIndex)`, `Number` — Works like `filterBy`, but returns the first matching index.

❏ `query(field, value, anyMatch, caseSensitive)`, `Record[]` — Works like `filter`, but returns an array of matching `Records`.

❏ `queryBy(func, scope)`, `Record[]` — Works like `filterBy`, but returns an array of matching `Records`.

❏ `getAt(index)`, `Record` — Returns the `Record` at the specified `index`.

❏ `getById(id)`, `Record` — Returns the `Record` with the specified unique identifier.

❏ `getRange(startIndex, endIndex)`, `Record[]` — returns an array of `Records`.

❏ `indexOf(Record)`, `Number` — Returns the index of the specified `Record`.

❏ `indexOfId(id)`, `Number` — Returns the index of the `Record` with the specified unique identifier.

Sorting Records

❏ `getSortState()`, `Object` — Returns an object containing the current sort field and the direction on which to sort (`ASC` or `DESC`). For example, `{field: "name", dir: "ASC"}`.

❏ `setDefaultSort(field, direction)` — Sets up sort information for the next load process.

❏ `sort(field, direction)` — Sorts the data.

Loading Records

❏ `load(options)`, `Boolean` — The `options` argument is passed to the `DataProxy`'s `load` method (that method is detailed earlier in the chapter). These `options` are stored for later use with the `reload` method. The `beforeload` event is fired, giving developers a chance to cancel the entire load process. This method returns `false` if the load process is canceled.

❏ `loadData(data, append)` — This uses the `Store`'s `Ext.data.DataReader` to model the data and then populates the `Store`. The append Boolean value indicates whether or not to clear the current data before populating. The `load` event is fired, and the `datachanged` event is fired if appending.

❏ `reload(options)` — This works identically to the `load` method, but reuses the `options` from the previous call to `load`. The developer can override `options`, if necessary.

Miscellaneous

❏ `collect(dataIndex, allowNull, bypassFilter)` — Returns an array of all unique values found in the `Records`' specified column. `dataIndex` is a string specifying the name of the `Ext.data.Field` to be searched. `allowNull` is a Boolean determining if null values should be included. `bypassFilter` is a Boolean determining if filtered records should be included.

❑ each(func, scope) — Each Record in the Store is passed to the specified function (func), using the optional scope. Returning false from the function will stop the iteration.

❑ getCount(), Number — Returns the number of Records in the Store.

❑ getTotalCount(), Number — Returns the total value (which is returned by the DataReader).

❑ sum(field, startIndex, endIndex), Number — Returns the sum value of all Records within the specified range of indexes (the range is optional).

Ext.data.Record (Revisited)

Earlier, the Ext.data.Record class was discussed in terms of data modeling and deserialization. When coupled with the Ext.data.Store class, however, the Record class becomes more than a simple definition.

Each row that is deserialized by the Ext.data.DataReader is stored in a custom-typed instance of Record. The Record not only stores the data; it also tracks which values are being changed. When coupled with a Store, Record methods can fire events from the Store, and vice versa. Each Record exposes a set of methods to assist in this change-management.

❑ get(name), Object — Returns the value of the named field.

❑ isModified(name), Boolean — Returns a true if the named field has been modified.

❑ getChanges(), Object — Returns a hash Object of only modified Fields.

❑ set(name, value) — Applies the value to the named field. If the Record is not in 'edit' mode, this method fires the Store's update event with an operation of 'edit.'

❑ beginEdit() — Puts the Record into 'edit' mode.

❑ endEdit() — Removes the Record from 'edit' mode. If any Field value has been modified, the Store's update event is fired immediately with an operation of 'edit.'

❑ cancelEdit() — Removes the Record from 'edit' mode and prevents the reject method from restoring original values.

❑ commit(silent) — Removes the Record from 'edit' mode and accepts all modified values. Depending on the Boolean silent value, the Store's update event is fired with an operation of 'commit.'

❑ reject(silent) — Removes the Record from 'edit' mode and restores original values. Depending on the Boolean silent value, the Store's update event is fired with an operation of 'reject.'

The Store class has a few helper methods for dealing with all Records at once:

❑ commitChanges() — Executes the commit method on each Record

❑ rejectChanges() — Executes the reject method on each Record

❑ getModifiedRecords(), Record[] — Returns the Array of a modified Record

When you use this handful of methods, determining which `Records` have changed (and even which `Fields`) can be a simple task.

```
var records = store.getModifiedRecords();
var line = [];
line[line.length] = "The following Records have been modified...";
for (var i = 0, rec; rec = records[i++];) {
    line[line.length] = "Record " + rec.id + ": ";
    var fields = rec.getChanges();
    for (var name in fields) {
        line[line.length] = "  Field: " + name + " Value: " + fields[name];
    }
}
alert(line.join("\n"));
```

Ext.StoreMgr

The singleton `Ext.StoreMgr` class is intended to be a repository of cached data. If the `Ext.data.Store`'s configuration option `storeId` is set, the `Store` is automatically registered with the `StoreMgr`. Once registered, the `Store` can be accessed at anytime using the `storeId`.

The `Ext.StoreMgr` class offers the `register` method, which accepts an instance of `Ext.data.Store`, and the `unregister` method, which accepts an instance of `Ext.data.Store` or a `storeId`. There is also a `lookup` method, which accepts a `storeId` and returns an instance of `Ext.data.Store`.

This simple class eases the job of creating a local data cache in a straightforward and no-nonsense manner.

Putting It All Together

Here is a fairly typical example to demonstrate how all these classes fit together.

```
var storeId = "adminUsers";
var store = new Ext.data.Store({
    storeId: storeId, // we'll cache this store instance for later
    baseParams: {
        userType: "admin" // we only want Admin users
    },
    sortInfo: {field: "lastName"}, // default sort by lastName
    // here's the DataProxy!
    proxy: new Ext.data.HttpProxy({url: "getUsers.html"}),
    // here's the DataReader!
    reader: new Ext.data.JsonReader({
        root: "person",
        id: "userId",
        // here's the Ext.data.Record structure!
        fields: [
            {name: "firstName", type: "string"},
            {name: "lastName", type: "string"},
            {name: "age", type: "int"}
```

```
                ]
        })
    });

    // let's use some events of the Store
    store.on({
        load: {
            fn: function(store, records, options) {
                // when loading is done, get some Records
                var family = store.queryBy(function(record, id) {
                    if (record.get("lastName") == "Jones") {
                        return true;
                    }
                    return false;
                });
                // then, filter the grid
                store.filter("firstName", "Bob");
                // and re-sort on age
                store.sort("age");
            }
        },
        loadexception: {
            fn: function(proxy, options, response, error) {
                alert("Something bad happened while loading");
            }
        }
    });

    // let's load this sucker up!
    store.load();

    // even if we delete the store variable, it's still available in the Ext.StoreMgr
    //  this happens because we created a store with a storeId config option
    delete store;
    var store2 = Ext.StoreMgr.lookup(storeId);
```

Summary

This chapter briefly discussed several of the data-centric Ext classes. Advanced topics such as a common data-access interface and data deserialization were covered. You also looked at custom data-modeling and simple data-caching.

In the next chapter, you'll see how all these classes simplify common (yet complicated) tasks such as rendering Grids and Trees.

21

DataViews and Grids

This chapter covers the Ext JS components used for displaying large amounts of data. DataViews and GridPanels both take advantage of the classes covered in previous chapters.

These classes rely on the data classes discussed in the Chapter 20 to gather and model the data, and they continue the object and event-based architecture found throughout the Ext JS library.

In this chapter, you'll learn about:

- ❑ Ext.DataView
- ❑ Ext.grid.GridPanel

Ext.DataView

Chapter 18 covers the `Ext.XTemplate` class and its ability to render arbitrary HTML based on hierarchical data. Chapter 19 covers the Ext Component system, and its flexibility and ease of use. In Chapter 20, the data-handling power of the `Ext.data.Store` class is discussed. When you use these three techniques, the Ext JS library is already offering more than the average JavaScript library. With all of the foundation in place, Ext JS's methodology of incremental improvements really begins to shine.

The Ext.DataView class derives from the Ext.BoxComponent class and uses an Ext.XTemplate to render the data from an Ext.data.Store. The following code renders a list of users:

```
var theData, theStore, theTemplate, theView;

theData = [
    ["Bob", "Smith", 16, "bsmith"],
    ["Gary", "Johnson", 22, "gjohnson"],
    ["Susan", "Brown", 32, "sbrown"],
    ["Leslie", "Harris", 18, "lharris"]
];

theStore = new Ext.data.Store({
    proxy: new Ext.data.MemoryProxy(theData),
    reader: new Ext.data.ArrayReader(
        {id: 3},
        [
            {name: "id", mapping: 3, type: "string"},
            {name: "firstName", mapping: 0, type: "string"},
            {name: "lastName", mapping: 1, type: "string"},
            {name: "age", mapping: 2, type: "int"}
        ]
    ),
    sortInfo: {field: "lastName"}
});

theTemplate = new Ext.XTemplate(
    "<tpl for=\".\">",
        "<div id=\"{id}\">Name: {lastName}, {firstName}",
            // do not show age for anyone over 21
            "<tpl if=\"age &lt; 21\"> - Age: {age}</tpl>",
        "</div>",
    "</tpl>"
);

theView = new Ext.DataView({
    itemSelector: "div", // every DIV is a unique and selectable item
    singleSelect: true,
    store: theStore,
    tpl: theTemplate
});
theStore.load();

new Ext.Viewport({items: [theView]});
```

Because the Store class is derived from Ext.util.Observable, the DataView class is able to listen for events and redraw itself when necessary. As seen in the previous example, the DataView class also supports item selection. By default, a selected item is assigned a CSS class of `x-view-selected`, but this class is purposefully omitted by the Ext JS designers. Add the following to the code example:

```
<style type="text/css">
    .x-view-selected {
        color: blue;
    }
</style>
```

Now, you can click an item and see its appearance change.

The `DataView` is a simple, and yet incredibly powerful method of rendering and providing user interaction with arbitrary data. As discussed in Chapter 19, the `Ext.BoxComponent` base class provides a mechanism for state persistence (using the `stateEvents` configuration option) and custom extensibility (using the `plugins` configuration option) while still providing access to the underlying `HTMLElement` (using the `getEl` method).

In addition to the functionality inherited from the `BoxComponent` class, the following configuration options can be used to customize the `DataView`'s behavior:

❏ `autoAbort` — A Boolean that indicates whether to abort any pending requests (defaults to `false`).

❏ `deferEmptyText` — A Boolean that indicates whether to defer showing the `emptyText` until the `Store`'s first load operation (defaults to `true`).

❏ `emptyText` — A string that contains text to be shown when the `Store` is empty (defaults to "").

❏ `itemSelector` — (required) A simple CSS selector that indicates which Template nodes represent a selectable item (defaults to `undefined`).

❏ `loadingText` — A string that contains text to be shown while the `Store` is loading (defaults to `undefined`).

❏ `multiSelect` — A Boolean that indicates whether to allow multiple selections (defaults to `false`).

❏ `overClass` — A CSS class that is applied as the mouse hovers over each item (defaults to `undefined`).

❏ `selectedClass` — A CSS class that is applied as each item is selected (defaults to `x-view-selected`).

❏ `simpleSelect` — A Boolean that indicates whether the user is required to hold down Shift or Ctrl to perform multiselection (defaults to `false`).

❏ `singleSelect` — A Boolean that indicates whether to restrict users to one selection at a time (defaults to `false`). This option will be overridden by `multiSelect` if both are set to `true`.

❏ `store` — (required) The `Ext.data.Store` used for binding (defaults to `undefined`).

❏ `tpl` — (required) The `Ext.XTemplate` used for rendering (defaults to `undefined`).

❏ `trackOver` — A Boolean that indicates whether to fire the `mouseenter` and `mouseleave` events for each item (defaults to `false`).

The itemSelector *configuration option is required. The Ext JS designers always intended for end developers to use the DataView for item manipulation and end-user interaction. The* itemSelector *determines what an item is exactly. If no manipulation or interaction is required, the* Ext.XTemplate *class is probably a better fit.*

Manipulating the DataView

Once rendered, each node in the DataView is a simple HTMLElement. And each node is rendered with the attributes defined within the template. In the example template shown earlier, each node is a DIV tag, and each DIV tag has a defined ID attribute. Manipulating a DataView after being rendered is a simple matter of selecting the nodes and changing them however desired. Because the developer has full control over the rendered content, he can use a selection method that best suits his purpose. This is all covered in Chapter 18 (Ext.DomQuery, Ext.DomHelper, and Ext.Element).

Finding Nodes of the DataView

In addition to using Ext.DomQuery directly, there are several methods to assist the developer in locating DataView nodes. These methods have been optimized for use with the DataView.

findItemFromChild

```
findItemFromChild( HTMLElement node ) : HTMLElement
```

For a complicated rendering template, this method locates the DataView node containing the specified HTMLElement.

getNode

```
getNode( HTMLElement/String/Number nodeInfo ) : HTMLElement
```

This method locates the DataView node (using the HTMLElement of the node, its ID, or its node index).

getNodes

```
getNodes( [Number start], [Number end] ) : Array
```

This method returns an array of DataView nodes based on a range of node indices.

indexOf

```
indexOf( HTMLElement/String/Number nodeInfo ) : Number
```

This method returns the index of the specified node (using the HTMLElement of the node, its ID, or its node index).

Selecting Nodes of the DataView

The `DataView` class also offers several methods to support programmatic selection of nodes.

clearSelections

```
clearSelections( [Boolean suppressEvent] ) : void
```

This method clears all selections (which removed the `selectionClass` from each node). The optional `suppressEvent` argument is used to prevent the `selectionchange` event from firing.

deselect

```
deselect( HTMLElement/Number node ) : void
```

This method deselects the specified node (by `HTMLElement` or node index). The `selectionchange` event is fired.

getSelectedIndexes

```
getSelectedIndexes() : Array
```

This method returns an array of all selected node indices.

getSelectedNodes

```
getSelectedNodes() : Array
```

This method returns an array of all selected nodes.

getSelectedRecords

```
getSelectedRecords() : Array
```

This method returns an array of all selected `Ext.data.Records` (as defined by the `Ext.data.Store` from the `DataView`'s configuration options).

getSelectionCount

```
getSelectionCount() : Number
```

This method returns a count of the selected nodes.

isSelected

```
isSelected( HTMLElement/Number node ) : Boolean
```

This method returns a Boolean indicating if the specified node (by `HTMLElement` or node index) is currently selected.

select

```
select( Array/HTMLElement/String/Number nodeInfo, [Boolean keepExisting],
    [Boolean suppressEvent] ) : void
```

This method selects a node (using its HTMLElement or its node index). Optionally, an array of nodes can be selected. Use the keepExisting argument to prevent currently selected nodes from being deselected. Use the suppressEvent argument to prevent the selectionchange event from firing.

selectRange

```
selectRange( Number start, Number end, [Boolean keepExisting] ) : void
```

This method selects all nodes within the node index range of start to end, inclusively. The selectionchange event is fired.

Manipulating the DataView's Underlying Data

Of course, playing with HTMLElements is only part of a true data-bound Component. When an Ext.data.Store is attached to a DataView, the DataView listens for several events from the Store (beforeload, datachanged, add, remove, update, and clear).

These event handlers ensure that the DataView is current with all data changes. However, occasions may arise where the developer needs full control. The following methods can be helpful to access the underlying Ext.data.Records.

getRecord

```
getRecord( HTMLElement node ) : Record
```

This method returns the Ext.data.Record for the specified DataView node (using the node's HTMLElement).

getRecords

```
getRecords( Array nodes ) : Array
```

This method returns an array of Ext.data.Records for the specified array of DataView nodes (using each node's HTMLElement).

refresh

```
refresh() : void
```

This method reloads all Ext.data.Records and completely re-renders the DataView using the template. Executing the reload method of the DataView's store will also result in a DataView refresh.

refreshNode

```
refreshNode( Number index ) : void
```

This method re-renders a single node (specified using a node index). This can be quite useful when modifying a single Record's data. For example:

```
// 'dv' is an instance of Ext.DataView
var index = dv.indexOf("someElementId");
var node = dv.getNode(index);
var rec = dv.getRecord(node);
rec.set("someField", "newValue");
dv.refreshNode(index);
```

However, this is usually unnecessary because the DataView listens for the Ext.data.Store's update event and automatically re-renders nodes as their Records are modified.

setStore

```
setStore( Store store ) : void
```

This method attaches the DataView to a new Ext.data.Store. The refresh method is called automatically.

DataView Events

In addition to manipulating the nodes of the DataView, several events are supplied so developers can have their system react to item selection and typical mouse events (click, mouseenter, mouseleave, selectionchange, and so on). Here is the previous example with a click event listener:

```
var theData, theStore, theTemplate, theView;

theData = [
    ["Bob", "Smith", 16, "bsmith"],
    ["Gary", "Johnson", 22, "gjohnson"],
    ["Susan", "Brown", 32, "sbrown"],
    ["Leslie", "Harris", 18, "lharris"]
];

theStore = new Ext.data.Store({
    proxy: new Ext.data.MemoryProxy(theData),
    reader: new Ext.data.ArrayReader(
        {id: 3},
        [
            {name: "id", mapping: 3, type: "string"},
            {name: "firstName", mapping: 0, type: "string"},
            {name: "lastName", mapping: 1, type: "string"},
            {name: "age", mapping: 2, type: "int"}
        ]
    ),
    sortInfo: {field: "lastName"}
});
```

```
theTemplate = new Ext.XTemplate(
    "<tpl for=\".\">",
        "<div id=\"{id}\">Name: {lastName}, {firstName}",
            // do not show age for anyone over 21
            "<tpl if=\"age &lt; 21\"> - Age: {age}</tpl>",
        "</div>",
    "</tpl>"
);

theView = new Ext.DataView({
    itemSelector: "div", // every DIV is a unique and selectable item
    singleSelect: true,
    store: theStore,
    tpl: theTemplate,
    listeners: {
        click: function(view, index, node, e) {
            alert(theView.getRecord(node).data.lastName);
        }
    }
});
theStore.load();

new Ext.Viewport({items: [theView]});
```

Ext.grid.GridPanel

While the DataView offers total flexibility for displaying data in any layout, the Ext.grid.GridPanel class solves the common problem of displaying tabular data. The GridPanel derives from Ext.Panel but does not require a layout configuration setting. Instead, the GridPanel displays data in the traditional grid fashion (see Figure 21-1).

Figure 21-1

The `GridPanel` offers dozens of configuration options. Most of them are self-explanatory flags, which determine the various behaviors of the grid (`disableSelection`, `enableColumnHide`, `enableColumnResize`, and so on). However, there are a few configuration options that require some attention. Obviously, the `store` option is important since it points to an `Ext.data.Store` and provides data to the grid (the `Store` class is covered in Chapter 20). Other configuration options to note are the `colModel`, `selModel`, and `view`.

Ext.grid.ColumnModel

Here is the definition for the grid shown in Figure 21-1 (the `store` object has been omitted for brevity):

```
var store = new Ext.data.Store(...);

// a function to help render the pctChange column
function pctChange(val, metadata, record, rowIndex, colIndex, store) {
    var color;
    if (val >= 0) {
        color = "green";
    } else {
        color = "red";
    }
    return "<span style=\"color:" + color + ";\">" + val + "%</span>";
}
// a function to help render the change column
function change(val, metadata, record, rowIndex, colIndex, store) {
    if(val >= 0){
        return "<span style=\"color:green;\">" + val + "</span>";
    } else {
        return "<span style=\"color:red;\">" + val + "</span>";
    }
    return val;
}
var grid = new Ext.grid.GridPanel({
    autoExpandColumn: "company",
    columns: [
        {
            header: "Company",
            width: 160,
            sortable: true,
            dataIndex: "company",
            id: "company"
        }, {
            header: "Price",
            width: 75,
            sortable: true,
            renderer: "usMoney",
            dataIndex: "price"
        }, {
            header: "Change",
            width: 75,
            sortable: true,
            renderer: change,
            dataIndex: "change"
```

```
        }, {
            header: "% Change",
            width: 75,
            sortable: true,
            renderer: pctChange,
            dataIndex: "pctChange"
        }, {
            header: "Last Updated",
            width: 85,
            sortable: true,
            renderer: Ext.util.Format.dateRenderer("m/d/Y"),
            dataIndex: "lastChange"
        }
    ],
    height: 350,
    store: store,
    stripeRows: true,
    title: "Array Grid",
    width: 600
});
new Ext.Viewport({items: [grid]});
```

The `columns` configuration option contains an array of column definitions. Internally, this array is passed to the constructor of the `Ext.grid.ColumnModel` class. The `ColumnModel` class tells the grid how each column should look and behave.

A column definition is a simple object supporting the following options:

❑ `align` — A string that sets the CSS text-align property of the column (defaults to `undefined`).

❑ `css` — A string that sets CSS for all table cells in the column (but not the header cell) (defaults to `undefined`).

❑ `dataIndex` — A string that indicates which `Ext.data.Field` the column binds to. By default, the column will bind to the `Field` with the same ordinal position (for example, Column 1 binds to Field 1).

❑ `editor` — An `Ext.form.Field` that is used when editing values within the column (defaults to `undefined`). (Form controls are discussed in Chapter 22.)

❑ `header` — A string that contains the text to display in the column's header cell (defaults to `undefined`).

❑ `hidden` — A Boolean that indicates if the column should be hidden when first rendered (defaults to `false`).

❑ `hideable` — A Boolean that indicates if the column is capable of being hidden (defaults to `true`).

❑ `id` — A string that is used in the construction of a CSS class name, which is applied to each cell in the column. The resulting CSS class name will look like "x-grid3-td-{id}". By default, the column's ordinal position is used (for example, "x-grid3-td-1").

❑ `menuDisabled` — A Boolean that indicates if the column's menu should be disabled (defaults to `false`).

❑ renderer — A custom function that is used to generate the HTML markup within each cell of the column. By default, the raw data value is displayed. See "Rendering Data with Custom Functions" for a full discussion of custom rendering functions.

❑ resizable — A Boolean that indicates if the column is resizable (defaults to true).

❑ sortable — A Boolean that indicates if the column is sortable (defaults to the GridPanel's defaultSortable property). The Ext.data.Store determines if local or remote sorting is used.

❑ tooltip — A string that contains the text to be the column header's tooltip (defaults to undefined).

❑ width — A number that contains the column's width (in pixels) when first rendered (defaults to undefined).

Notice, there are no required properties for a column. If you have a DataReader with three defined fields, and you simply want to display the three fields in order (with no header), your ColumnModel definition could look like this:

```
columns: [{}, {}, {}]
```

Rendering Data with Custom Functions

Ext JS gives the developer complete control while rendering each cell of a grid. This is done through custom renderer functions. Each renderer function is passed the following arguments:

❑ value — The raw data value

❑ metadata — An object that contains two properties

❑ css — A string that contains a CSS class name to add to the TD tag of the current cell

❑ attr — A string that contains HTML attribute markup to add to the TD tag of the current cell (for example, 'id="cell1" style="color: red;"')

❑ record — The Ext.data.Record that contains all Ext.data.Fields for the current row

❑ rowIndex — Index of the Ext.data.Record within the Ext.data.Store

❑ colIndex — Index of the grid column (not the index of the Ext.data.Field)

❑ store — The Ext.data.Store that is used to bind the entire GridPanel

In the previous code example, you may have noticed that the values in the "Change" column are either red or green. Looking at the column's definition, you can see that a custom renderer is being used. Here it is:

```
function change(val, metadata, record, rowIndex, colIndex, store) {
    if(val >= 0){
        return "<span style=\"color:green;\">" + val + "</span>";
    } else {
        return "<span style=\"color:red;\">" + val + "</span>";
    }
    return val;
}
```

In addition to custom-rendered functions, there are several built-in rendering functions. In the code example shown earlier, the "Price" column uses the rendering function known as "usMoney". The Ext.util.Format class houses these pre-built rendering functions. When the grid data is rendered and a string value has been specified as a renderer (such as "usMoney"), the grid looks in the Format class for a function by that name. This means, adding your own custom renderers to be used throughout your application is as simple as the following:

```
Ext.util.Format.change = function(val) {
    if(val >= 0){
        return "<span style=\"color:green;\">" + val + "</span>";
    } else {
        return "<span style=\"color:red;\">" + val + "</span>";
    }
    return val;
};
```

Now, to use your new custom renderer, you simply need to specify the function's name on the column's definition:

```
renderer: "change"
```

The Ext.util.Form.dateRenderer function (as seen on the "Last Updated" column) is a factory function, which creates a customized renderer function using the date format specified.

When you use these simple techniques, creating a truly customized and attractive grid is no longer a large undertaking.

Ext.grid.AbstractSelectionModel

Most likely, selections need to be made within the grid. The GridPanel's SelectionModel configuration option solves this requirement. Ext JS provides three different pre-built selection models (cell, row, and row-based checkboxes). Each selection model is derived from the simple Ext.grid.AbstractSelectionModel. In addition to the inherited members (from Ext.util.Observable), the AbstractSelectionModel class provides three methods: isLocked, lock, and unlock.

isLocked

```
isLocked() : Boolean
```

This method returns a Boolean indicating if the current user selections are locked.

lock

```
lock() : void
```

This method prevents any further user selections to be made.

unlock

```
unlock() : void
```

This method allows further user selections to be made.

Ext.grid.CellSelectionModel

The `CellSelectionModel` class enables users to select a single individual cell (typical of traditional spreadsheet applications). This class does exactly what the developer would expect and supplies simple methods for manipulating selections (`clearSelections`, `getSelectedCell`, `hasSelection`, and `select`).

Ext.grid.RowSelectionModel

The `RowSelectionModel` class enables users to select rows within the `GridPanel`. Like the `CellSelectionModel` class, this class does exactly what the developer would expect and supplies several familiar methods for manipulating selections (`clearSelections`, `deselectRow`, `each`, `getCount`, `getSelections`, `selectRows`, and so on).

Ext.grid.CheckboxSelectionModel

The `CheckboxSelectionModel` class derives from `Ext.grid.RowSelectionModel` and works the same. However, the `CheckboxSelectionModel` can also be used as a column definition, which results in a column of checkboxes (providing users with a familiar and useful UI convention):

```
// create the selection model
var sm = new Ext.grid.CheckboxSelectionModel();

var grid = new Ext.grid.GridPanel({
    selModel: sm, // apply the selection model
    columns: [
        sm, // add the selection model as a column definition
        {
            header: "Last Name",
            dataIndex: "lastName"
        }, {
            header: "First Name",
            dataIndex: "firstName"
        }, {
            header: "Age",
            dataIndex: "age"
        }
    ]
    ... more config settings
});
```

The results are shown in Figure 21-2.

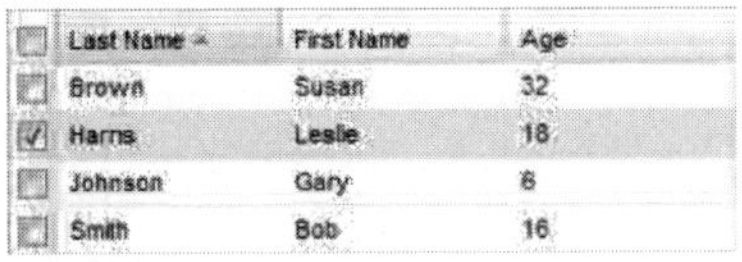

Figure 21-2

Ext.grid.GridView

While the `ColumnModel` handles the rendering of the contents of each individual cell, the `Ext.grid.GridView` class handles the rendering of the entire grid. The appearance of the table, headers, each row, and each cell are controlled by the `GridView`. The `GridView` derives from `Ext.util.Observable` and fires several events during the rendering of a `GridPanel` (such as, `refresh`, `rowremoved`, and so on).

The built-in `GridView` does a fantastic job at presenting the grid in a very attractive fashion. However, requirements often arise that ask you to present data in a tabular, yet nontraditional way. The `templates` property of a `GridView` contains all the various templates (see Chapter 18 for a discussion of the `Ext.XTemplate` class) used to render the `GridPanel`.

Ext.grid.GroupingView

The `Ext.grid.GroupingView` class extends the default `GridView` class by adding a hierarchical level of data grouping, as shown in Figure 21-3. Each group within the grid is expandable and allows for simple summaries to be displayed for large amounts of data.

Figure 21-3

Other Avenues for Customization

The ColumnModel and SelectionModel architectures already give the developer quite a bit of control. However, there's always a requirement that seems just out of reach. Fortunately, there are still a couple techniques for customizing a GridPanel.

The most obvious technique for modifying the GridPanel is to simply derive from it and add your custom functionality. The Ext.grid.EditorGridPanel class does just that by adding a simple editing API. The Ext.grid.PropertyGrid extends it further by offering a solution to the typical property grid requirement (an editable grid of name/value pairs).

You can also use the plug-in architecture, as mentioned in Chapter 19. The plug-in architecture belongs to anything deriving from the Ext.Component class. For the GridPanel, this is an excellent way to encapsulate custom, reusable logic. Once the grid is constructed, the init method of each plug-in will be executed and passed a reference to the grid. Each plug-in can now listen to any grid event and basically alter the grid's behavior in any way imaginable.

The beauty of the Ext JS library is that everything has a logical place. For example, the EditorGridPanel class knows very little about input controls. In Ext JS, there is an entire namespace devoted to input controls (as discussed in Chapter 22). So, there is no need to bloat the Ext.grid namespace with a bunch of logic that is defined elsewhere and can be reused. The same is also true for the context menu found on the grid's header row. The Ext.menu namespace is completely separate and reusable.

Extending each piece of the grid is a simple matter of identifying your requirements and targeting the classes that need extending. Although this may seem like common sense, it is painful to extend most JavaScript libraries. And most JavaScript widgets simply fall apart when used outside their originally intended purpose.

Summary

This chapter provided a brief overview of the DataView and GridPanel classes. Both of these classes offer solutions for presenting large amounts of data. The DataView class gives developers complete control over the rendering of that data, and the GridPanel class gives developers a wealth of commonly requested tools. Both solutions are extensible and perform very well with even the largest sets of data.

22

Form Controls, Validation, and a Whole Lot More

You've entered the home stretch of this section of the book, and you've arrived at some of the most interesting and visually attractive pieces of the Ext JS library. Indeed, when it comes to an application's success, much depends on the little things. Users expect immediate feedback on field validation, auto-complete textboxes, and so on. And developers have finally started to demand well thought out frameworks, instead of a bunch of disconnected function libraries. This chapter will blitz through the entire collection of form widgets and how they validate, and will conclude with a sampling of some of the more interesting pieces that this book simply doesn't have space to delve into.

In this chapter, you'll learn about:

❑ Form controls
❑ Field and Form validation

and a whole lot more!

Introduction to the Form Controls

The Ext JS library is intended to be used as a front end for enterprise-level applications. As such, all of the typical primitive controls need to be accounted for. Form controls are a necessity to any enterprise-level application. Unfortunately, most JavaScript libraries lean on the basic HTML controls and almost ignore this vital piece of the puzzle. And although some JavaScript libraries provide a validation API, most libraries leave the complex job of correct, cross-browser rendering up to the developer.

For those libraries that attempt to tackle the problem of consistent rendering, a memory and processor-intensive API is usually the solution. Developers find the API straightforward, but as the application scales to larger and more complex designs, the user experience suffers. Fortunately, the authors of Ext JS have taken this difficult job seriously, and have provided a rather satisfactory API.

The following sample is a full-functioning example of an `Ext.form.FormPanel` with three fields, a Save button, and validation baked in. You'll dive into the details next, but it's impressive to see how much can be accomplished without compromising the user experience. In fact, this sample is only a simple object. Until this object is passed to the `Ext.form.FormPanel` constructor and rendered, the browser merely stores it; and it has no references to DOM elements or other heavy objects, so memory consumption is not a problem.

```
{
    xtype: "form",
    defaults: {
        msgTarget: "side"
    },
    monitorValid: true,
    buttons: [
        {
            formBind: true,
            text: "Save",
            handler: function() {
                alert("Saved!");
            }
        }
    ],
    items:[
        {
            fieldLabel: "Checkbox",
            xtype: "checkbox"
        }, {
            fieldLabel: "TextField",
            xtype: "textfield",
            allowBlank: false
        }, {
            fieldLabel: "DateField",
            xtype: "datefield"
        }
    ]
}
```

Now, take a quick look at each of the form controls.

Ext.form.Label

Usually, you will not create a `Label` manually. However, if you run into such an occasion, the `Label` class has only a few configuration options. (`Ext.form.Label` inherits from `Ext.BoxComponent` and derives all the properties and functionality of that class.)

❑   `text` — A simple string to be rendered

❑   `forId` — The `ID` attribute of an HTML element to be used for the `htmlFor` attribute

❑   `html` — An HTML fragment to be rendered (This is ignored if the `text` configuration option is also set.)

```
var myLabel = new Ext.form.Label({text: "First Name", forId: "fname"});
```

Ext.form.Field

As with the `Label` class, you will not usually create a `Field` manually. All other form controls inherit from the `Field` class, and it is normally best to use those classes directly. By default, the `Field` class renders as a regular HTML text box. However, the `Field` class offers the `autoCreate` configuration option (a `DomHelper` element specification; see Chapter 18) for those rare occasions where you want the benefits of the class, but need complete control over the HTML. The `Field` class handles focusing and blurring events, as well as delivering a very nice validation API.

The following example is an entire Ext JS application using JavaScript best practices. While simple, this example demonstrates just how lightweight Ext JS can truly be.

```
// We create a single object to contain our entire application.
//   (No need to clutter the global namespace.)
TheApp = (function() {
    // Private variables can go here and be used throughout our application.
    //   These variables are global to our application, but hidden from the outside.
    var myLabelText = "Field Label";
    return {
        // The init method initiates our application.
        init: function() {
            // Remember, always set this value.
            Ext.BLANK_IMAGE_URL = "images/default/s.gif";

            var theForm = new Ext.form.FormPanel({
                renderTo: Ext.getBody(),
                // By using xtypes, we avoid creating heavy objects.
                //   The objects are created when they are actually needed.
                xtype: "form",
                buttons: [
                    // Our FormPanel has one button.
                    {
                        text: "Save",
                        handler: function() {
                            alert("Saved!");
                        }
                    }
                ],
                items:[
                    // Our FormPanel has only one element - a Field.
                    {
                        // No need to create a Label manually, the Field
                        //   class does it for us.
                        fieldLabel: myLabelText, // our private variable!
```

```
                    xtype: "field"
                }
            ]
        });
    }
};
})();
// The onReady method will fire our app's init method when the HTML document is
//  ready.
Ext.onReady(TheApp.init, TheApp);
```

The field and label are shown in Figure 22-1

Figure 22-1

The preceding example simply shows the Field; it doesn't show any of the Field's abilities. To see the Field class's validation API in action, you'd have to write some code. But why do that, when Ext JS already provides such a rich library?

Ext.form.TextField

The TextField class derives from the Field class and adds some really great functionality, such as automatically growing to match the user's input; requiring a minimum length, as well as enforcing a maximum length; and using a regular expression to limit the valid characters.

Next, you add a TextField to the preceding example (the comments are removed here):

```
TheApp = (function() {
    return {
        init: function() {
            Ext.BLANK_IMAGE_URL = "images/default/s.gif";

            var theForm = new Ext.form.FormPanel({
                renderTo: Ext.getBody(),
                xtype: "form",
                buttons: [
                    {
                        text: "Save",
                        handler: function() {
                            alert("Saved!");
                        }
                    }
                ],
                items:[
                    {
```

```
                                fieldLabel: "Field Label",
                                xtype: "field"
                    }, {
                                // Here's our TextField!
                                fieldLabel: "Text Field",
                                xtype: "textfield",
                                // This TextField cannot be blank.
                                allowBlank: false
                    }
                ]
            });
        }
    };
})();
Ext.onReady(TheApp.init, TheApp);
```

The text boxes are shown in Figure 22-2

Figure 22-2

When executing this example, you now see two text boxes. As you tab through the text boxes (leave them empty), the second one (the `TextField`) turns red and gets underlined. Place a value in the text box, press Tab, and voila! The `TextField` is now valid.

Ext.form.FormPanel & Ext.form.BasicForm

Before you go too far into the different `Field` classes, take a look at the `FormPanel` class. The `FormPanel` derives from the `Ext.Panel` class and uses an `Ext.layout.FormLayout` to render its components (see Chapter 19 for a discussion of containers and their layouts). In addition to drawing a pretty picture, the `FormPanel` adds a collection of `Ext.Buttons` (seen in the previous example), some basic form validation monitoring, and encapsulates the `Ext.form.BasicForm` class.

The `BasicForm` (derived from `Ext.util.Observable`) contains all the mechanisms for loading and submitting typical form data. In a nutshell, the `FormPanel` creates a `BasicForm` internally and adds all Fields to the `BasicForm`. When the `BasicForm` submits data, it serializes the `Fields` and uses an AJAX request to submit to the server. (If necessary, there is a configuration option to submit data using an old-fashioned FORM submission.) To simplify matters, the `FormPanel` accepts all the configuration options of the `BasicForm` and passes them along when creating the `BasicForm`.

The AJAX data loading and data submission are done using the `Ext.form.Action` classes. Directly out of the box, there is an `Ext.form.Action.Load` class and an `Ext.form.Action.Submit` class. These classes behave very much like the `HttpProxy` class (see Chapter 20), but add several configuration options for finer control. Each `Action` has a `run` method, which performs the AJAX request. However, both of these classes are fully encapsulated by the `BasicForm` class, and usually you will not need to be bothered by them.

So, even though there's a lot going on under the hood of the `FormPanel` (the `BasicForm` and its `Actions`), you probably don't need to get your hands too dirty.

Now, go back to the example. Your new requirements are:

❑ Display a validation icon with an error message next to each invalid Field.

❑ Disable the Save button whenever the form is invalid.

❑ Have the Save button actually submit your data.

```
TheApp = (function() {
    return {
        init: function() {
            Ext.BLANK_IMAGE_URL = "images/default/s.gif";
            // a utility class for displaying fancy tooltips
            Ext.QuickTips.init();

            var theForm = new Ext.form.FormPanel({
                renderTo: Ext.getBody(),
                // see Chapter 19 about the defaults option
                defaults: {
                    // Validation messages are now on the left.
                    msgTarget: "side"
                },
                // This makes the FormPanel monitor all Field's validity.
                monitorValid: true,
                // This tells the FormPanel where to submit to
                url: "http://ourserver/ourpage",
                buttons: [
                    {
                        // This makes this button aware of the Form's
                        // validity.
                        formBind: true,
                        text: "Save",
                        handler: function() {
                            // Get the BasicForm and submit!
                            var formPanel = this.findParentByType("form");
                            if (formPanel) {
                                formPanel.getForm().submit();
                            }
                        }
                    }
                ],
                items:[
                    {
                        fieldLabel: "Field Label",
                        xtype: "field",
                        name: "Field1"
                    }, {
                        fieldLabel: "Text Field",
                        xtype: "textfield",
                        name: "Field2",
```

```
                        allowBlank: false
                    }
                ]
            });
        }
    };
})();
Ext.onReady(TheApp.init, TheApp);
```

The result is shown in Figure 22-3.

Figure 22-3

That's it! Add a few configuration options and the rest is handled for you. Please note, HTTP requires that each `Field` have a `name`. (Unfortunately, the server-side code to handle a submission is outside the scope of this book.)

Other Form Controls

The rest of the form controls are simply more of the same.

Ext.form.NumberField

The `NumberField` class is a specialized `TextField`, allowing only digits to be entered (a decimal point and a negative sign are optional), as shown in Figure 22-4.

```
new Ext.form.NumberField();
```

or

```
{xtype: "numberfield"}
```

NumberField:

Figure 22-4

Ext.form.TextArea

The `TextArea` class is another specialized `TextField`, rendering as a multiline text box and allowing carriage returns, as shown in Figure 22-5.

```
new Ext.form.TextArea();
```

or

```
{xtype: "textarea"}
```

Figure 22-5

Ext.form.TriggerField

The `TriggerField` class derives from `TextField` but is a base class for text boxes, which have an accompanying "trigger" button, as shown in Figure 22-6. Creating a `TriggerField` directly will render as a `ComboBox`, but you must provide the functionality yourself.

```
new Ext.form.TriggerField();
```

or

```
{xtype: "trigger"}
```

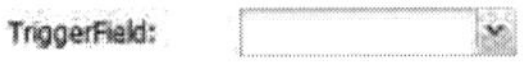

TriggerField:

Figure 22-6

Ext.form.DateField

The `DateField` class is a specialized `TriggerField`, providing a fully featured date-lookup control. The "trigger" button displays a calendar for user-friendly date selection, as shown in Figure 22-7. The calendar can also be easily customized to prevent users from selecting dates outside a certain range; to prevent users from selecting certain days; or even to prevent the selection of an array of specific dates, as shown in Figure 22-8.

```
new Ext.form.DateField();
```

or

```
{xtype: "datefield"}
```

Figure 22-7

Figure 22-8

Ext.form.ComboBox

The ComboBox class is another specialized TriggerField, providing full functionality to bind to an Ext.data.Store (just like an Ext.grid.GridPanel). The ComboBox provides optional auto-complete functionality and optional ad hoc text entry, as shown in Figure 22-9.

```
new Ext.form.ComboBox();
```

or

```
{xtype: "combo"}
```

Figure 22-9

Ext.form.TimeField

The TimeField class is a specialized ComboBox, which does not bind to an Ext.data.Store. All aspects of time-formatting are easily customizable, as shown in Figure 22-10.

```
new Ext.form.TimeField();
```

or

```
{xtype: "timefield"}
```

Figure 22-10

Ext.form.Checkbox

The Checkbox class is exactly what you would expect (see Figure 22-11).

```
new Ext.form.Checkbox();
```

or

```
{xtype: "checkbox"}
```

Checkbox:

Figure 22-11

Ext.form.Radio

The Radio class, derived from the Checkbox class, represents a single radio button (see Figure 22-12). By specifying the same name for multiple radio buttons, they become mutually exclusive.

```
new Ext.form.Radio();
```

or

```
{xtype: "radio"}
```

Radio:

Figure 22-12

Ext.form.CheckboxGroup

The CheckboxGroup class is a convenience class for grouping Checkboxes together. They are rendered within a table in either horizontal or vertical fashion. The following examples create a 3x3 table of checkboxes, as shown in Figure 22-13.

```
new Ext.form.CheckboxGroup({
    fieldLabel: "CheckboxGroup",
    columns: 3,
    defaults: {
        labelStyle: "{width: 5px}"
    },
    items: [
        {fieldLabel: "one"},
        {fieldLabel: "two"},
        {fieldLabel: "three"},
        {fieldLabel: "four"},
        {fieldLabel: "five"},
        {fieldLabel: "six"},
        {fieldLabel: "seven"},
        {fieldLabel: "eight"},
```

```
                {fieldLabel: "nine"}
            ]
        });

    or

        {
            xtype: "checkboxgroup",
            fieldLabel: "CheckboxGroup",
            columns: 3,
            defaults: {
                labelStyle: "{width: 5px}"
            },
            items: [
                {fieldLabel: "one"},
                {fieldLabel: "two"},
                {fieldLabel: "three"},
                {fieldLabel: "four"},
                {fieldLabel: "five"},
                {fieldLabel: "six"},
                {fieldLabel: "seven"},
                {fieldLabel: "eight"},
                {fieldLabel: "nine"}
            ]
        }
```

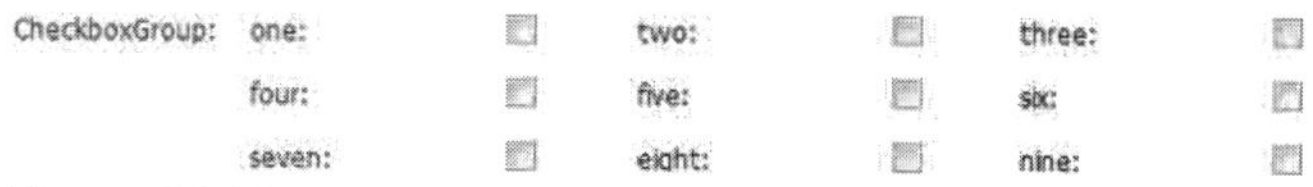

CheckboxGroup:	one:	☐	two:	☐	three:	☐
	four:	☐	five:	☐	six:	☐
	seven:	☐	eight:	☐	nine:	☐

Figure 22-13

Ext.form.RadioGroup

The RadioGroup class, derived from the CheckboxGroup class, is a convenience class for grouping Radios together. They are rendered within a table in either horizontal or vertical fashion. The following examples create a 3x3 table of radio buttons, as shown in Figure 22-14. (This layout is vertical.)

```
    new Ext.form.RadioGroup({
        fieldLabel: "RadioGroup",
        columns: 3,
        vertical: true,
        defaults: {
            labelStyle: "{width: 5px}"
        },
        items: [
            {fieldLabel: "one"},
            {fieldLabel: "two"},
            {fieldLabel: "three"},
            {fieldLabel: "four"},
```

```
                    {fieldLabel: "five"},
                    {fieldLabel: "six"},
                    {fieldLabel: "seven"},
                    {fieldLabel: "eight"},
                    {fieldLabel: "nine"}
                ]
        });
```

or

```
        {
            xtype: "radiogroup",
            fieldLabel: "RadioGroup",
            columns: 3,
            vertical: true,
            defaults: {
                labelStyle: "{width: 5px}"
            },
            items: [
                {fieldLabel: "one"},
                {fieldLabel: "two"},
                {fieldLabel: "three"},
                {fieldLabel: "four"},
                {fieldLabel: "five"},
                {fieldLabel: "six"},
                {fieldLabel: "seven"},
                {fieldLabel: "eight"},
                {fieldLabel: "nine"}
            ]
        }
```

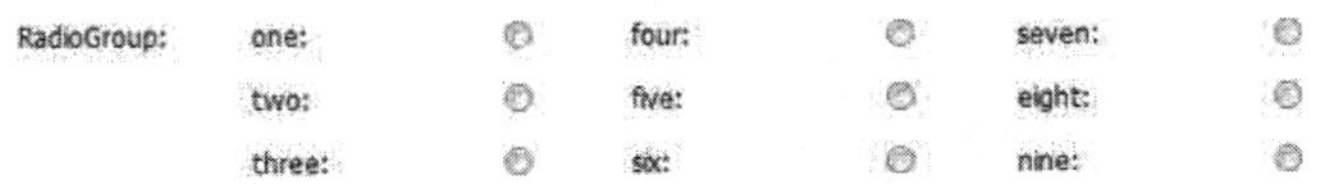

Figure 22-14

Ext.form.HtmlEditor

The HtmlEditor class is a lightweight and customizable rich-text editor. Its value will be returned as formatted HTML, as shown in Figure 22-15.

```
        new Ext.form.HtmlEditor();
```

or

```
        {xtype: "htmleditor"}
```

HtmlEditor:

Figure 22-15

Ext.form.Hidden

The `Hidden` class is a typical hidden field. It does not render, but its value will be submitted with the rest of the form element (as long as it has a `name` property setting).

```
new Ext.form.Hidden();
```

or

```
{xtype: "hidden"}
```

Field and Form Validation

Most of the form controls have typical validation techniques built in. For example, the `NumberField` allows the developer to specify a `minValue` and a `maxValue` as well as whether decimals and negatives should be allowed. The `DateField` allows fine control over the selectable dates and days. The `TextField` offers the `allowBlank`, `minLength`, and `maxLength` options. All of these techniques are simple and self-explanatory.

Validation Messages

Usually, each of the validation techniques will display the text of the `invalidText` option (by default, "This value in this field is invalid."). However, each validation technique also has an option for a more specific message. For example, the `NumberField`'s `minValue` validation option has a matching `minText` option. If the `minValue` validation fails, the `minText` will be displayed.

All of these messages are customizable and completely optional. Plus, how these messages are reported to the user is customizable. The `Ext.ux.Field` class exposes a `msgTarget` option, which determines the location of the `Field`'s validation errors. There are five built-in values for the `msgTarget` option:

```
{xtype: "textfield", allowBlank: false, msgTarget: "qtip"}
```

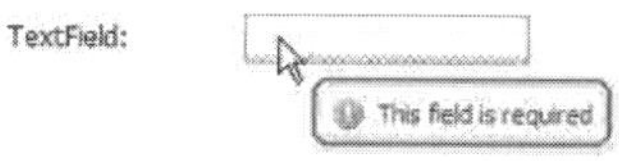

TextField: 🛈 This field is required

Figure 22-16

Please note, the `qtip` value requires that you call the `Ext.QuickTips.init` method.

```
{xtype: "textfield", allowBlank: false, msgTarget: "title"}
```

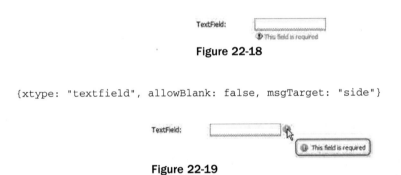

Figure 22-17

```
{xtype: "textfield", allowBlank: false, msgTarget: "under"}
```

Please note, the `under` value will render the error message directly under the field and push other content down.

Figure 22-18

```
{xtype: "textfield", allowBlank: false, msgTarget: "side"}
```

Figure 22-19

Please note, the `side` value requires that you call the `Ext.QuickTips.init` method.

The fifth option is the `ID` of any HTML element. The error text will simply replace the `innerHTML` of this element; it is a complete replacement. In other words, do not use this method if you want a single element to contain all error messages of all fields.

Of course, the unsupported sixth option is to take complete control. The easiest method to do this is to use the `title` value and to listen for the `valid` and `invalid` events:

```
{xtype: "textfield", allowBlank: false, msgTarget: "title",
    listeners: {
        invalid: function(field, msg) {
            field.el.dom.title = ""; // undo the built-in mechanism
            // this field is now invalid
            //   do whatever you want
        },
        valid: function(field) {
            // this field is now valid
            //   do whatever you want
        }
    }
}
```

Advanced Validation Techniques

In addition to the various built-in validation techniques, the `TextField` (and all controls that derive from it) also offers three extensible options: `regex`, `validator`, and `vtype`.

First off, the `regex` option is fairly typical of a modern `TextField` control. When the `TextField`'s value is tested for validity, the value is tested against the `regex` expression.

```
{xtype: "textfield", regex: /^[0-9a-zA-Z]*$/ // alphanumerics ONLY
```

Second, the `validator` option is simply a developer-supplied function. The function accepts a single parameter (the value of the `TextField`), and returns a Boolean indicating validity.

```
// the value must be "red" or "green"
{xtype: "textfield", validator: function(value) {
    return (value == "red" || value == "green";
}}
```

Finally, the `vtype` is used as a shortcut to common validation function. A few basic `vtype` functions are already built-in, but you can easily create your own. For example, the following `TextField` is required to be a valid URL:

```
{xtype: "textfield", vtype: "url"}
```

That's pretty simple and can save a lot of typing.

Creating a new `vtype` function to be used throughout your application is a simple matter. For example, to create a simple `vtype` function for U.S. Social Security Numbers, use the following code:

```
Ext.apply(Ext.form.VTypes, {
    ssn:  function(v) {
        return /^\d{3}\-\d{2}\-\d{4}$/.test(v);
    },
    ssnText: "Must be a valid SSN."
});
```

Now, use the new `vtype`:

```
{xtype: "textfield", vtype: "ssn"}
```

That's it! Now, you have a custom validation function with a custom error message that is available application-wide.

Form-Level Validation

Everything you've seen so far is considered "field-level" validation (validation performed on a single field). Unfortunately, the Ext JS library doesn't provide any out-of-box "form-level" validation (validation performed on an entire form). However, it can be achieved without too much hassle.

The easiest method to achieve "form-level" validation is to simply override the `BasicForm`'s `isValid` method:

```
isValid: function() {
    var isValid = Ext.form.BasicForm.prototype.isValid.call(this);
    if (isValid) {
        // perform your custom "form-level" validation here
        // you'll also have to report any errors
    }
    return isValid;
}
```

Of course, reporting form-level validation errors to the user is your responsibility. Do you insert text at the top of the form? Do you display a modal dialog? The best course of action all depends on your specific needs.

The Other Stuff

There are literally dozens of little tools and techniques to be found within the Ext JS library. A book dedicated to Ext JS would have a difficult job of covering them all. This last section quickly presents a few of the precious gems that may entice you.

State Management

Once enterprise-level applications reach a certain level of maturity, users begin to expect the application to remember certain things (sort orders on grids, where movable columns were placed, and so on). Unfortunately, the Ext JS designers have no idea what is important to you or your users, so they have only added state management to the `GridPanel`.

However, as with the rest of the library, there is a simple and robust technique for expanding the base library's abilities. In fact, every widget derived from the `Ext.Component` class (and that's all of them) has the following configuration options, methods, and events.

Configuration Options

The configuration options are:

❑   `stateEvents` — An array of event names that trigger the `saveState` method.

❑   `stateId` — A unique name used with saving and restoring state for the current component; if you have already specified a unique `id` for the component, this is unnecessary.

❑   `stateful` — A flag, which determines whether the component should restore its state when the component is constructed. Construction is the only moment when state is restored.

Methods

❑   `applyState(state)` — When state is being restored, this method is called in order to perform the actual state restoration. For example, when restoring which columns were hidden on a grid, this method examines the state object and hides the appropriate columns.

❑ `getState()`, `state` — When state is being saved, this method is called in order to gather the state information, which needs to be saved. The structure of the state object is determined by the component author. This structure can be any valid object.

Events

❑ `beforestaterestore(component, state)` — Fires before the component's state is restored. Returning false prevents the state from being restored (the `applyState` method will not be called).

❑ `beforestatesave(component, state)` — Fires before the component's state is saved. Returning false prevents the state from being saved (the `getState` method will not be called).

❑ `staterestore(component, state)` — Fires after the component's state is restored.

❑ `statesave(component, state)` — Fires after the component's state is saved.

Now you know how state is saved and restored, but *where* is it saved? Ext JS has only one state provider implementation built into the library. The `Ext.state.CookieProvider` saves state to browser cookies. The `CookieProvider` is derived from `Ext.state.Provider`, which provides all the mechanisms needed for encoding and decoding. Obviously, the `CookieProvider` is not sufficient for all applications, but it demonstrates how easy it is to create a more robust state provider.

Browser History

In addition to Component State Management, Ext JS offers a simple mechanism for handling browser state management (in other words, the Browser's history). The `Ext.History` class allows you to perform whatever tasks necessary to take your user into the past/future. In other words, Ext JS doesn't make a full record of your application's current state. Ext JS merely provides you with a mechanism for recording a simple token, which represents your application's current state.

Methods

❑ `add(token, preventDuplicates)` — The token is a string representing the current state of the browser. This value can be whatever is meaningful to your application. The `preventDuplicates` parameters (defaulting to true) does exactly what you expect.

❑ `back()` — Takes one step back in the history.

❑ `forward()` — Takes one step forward in the history.

❑ `getToken()`, `token` — Returns the token representing the current state of the browser.

Events

❑ `change(token)` — Fires whenever the history token changes. It's important to point out that the `change` event fires every time the token changes, even on `add`s.

Visual Effects

The `Ext.Fx` namespace contains several built-in visual effects. As with most of the Ext JS library, this namespace is optional. If you do not have a need for visual effects, by all means, exclude the `Ext.Fx` namespace from your application. However, the visual effects found here are very simple to execute and have a low performance overhead.

When included, the methods found in this namespace are automatically added to the `Ext.Element` class. The `Ext.Fx` methods may be chained together, which is a very simple way to create some impressive presentations.

```
myElement.highlight(); // a simple highlight animation
```

Please take note, `Ext.Fx` methods may be chained together, and `Ext.Element` methods may be chained together. But you must take care when chaining `Ext.Fx` and `Ext.Element` methods together. All `Ext.Fx` methods are asynchronous in nature and must therefore be queued (so they execute in the correct order, and not on top of each other). However, `Ext.Element` methods are synchronous and have no need for such a queue.

For example, the focus method is from the `Ext.Element` class and places input focus into the element (presumably, a `TextField`). The highlight method is from the `Ext.Fx` class.

```
// I want to highlight the field and then set focus to it

myTextField.highlight("00FF00").focus(); // this won't work

myTextField.highlight("00FF00", { // this WILL work
    callback: function(el) {
        el.focus();
    }
});
```

The first example won't work because focus is set before the highlight animation has finished. The second example uses a simple callback function, which is executed when the animation is complete.

Drag and Drop

While drag and drop sounds simple enough to users (I want to grab this and drag it over there), it is usually a headache for developers. Fortunately, Ext JS has supplied a very thorough foundation for identifying drag zones and drop zones. Helper classes for simple drag-and-drop operations are included, as well as helper classes for rendering a proxy element that follows the mouse cursor during the drag operation.

There are also several classes to simplify some of the more commonly requested features: dragging to/from grids, forms, panels, and so on.

Toolbars and Menus

Toolbars are already baked into every Panel in the Ext JS library (that includes grids, tabs, forms, and so on). However, the `Ext.Toolbar` class derives from `Ext.BoxComponent`, which means it can be rendered virtually anywhere. There are a few `Toolbar`-specific controls (specialized buttons and the like) that make common jobs easy. In addition, there are a couple specialized `Toolbars`: `Ext.StatusBar` and `Ext.PagingToolbar`.

Of course, every mature JavaScript widget library offers a menu control. The `Ext.menu.Menu` class is fully featured and quite robust, offering icons, infinitely nested submenus, radio items, checkboxes, and so on. It's all supported and simple to implement. Of course, Menus can be added to Toolbars to create a complete menu system.

However, the `Ext.menu.Menu` class does not derive from the `Ext.Component` class. This is a good thing because it avoids needless code bloat, and shouldn't be a problem.

Themes

The entire look of Ext JS is done using CSS and image sprites. All the widget classes allow the developer to specify CSS class names for almost every conceivable situation (`selectedClass`, `invalidClass`, `hoverClass`, and so on). And the Ext JS designers have obviously done a lot of work to take advantage of the cascading nature of CSS. However, creating your own theme is no small undertaking.

Fortunately, by targeting one widget at a time (concentrating on the base widgets first), it can be done. And the Ext JS community offers dozens of pre-made themes.

Trees

Other commonly requested controls are trees (navigation trees, data trees). Ext JS offers a simple and extensible mechanism for presenting trees, and there are several examples that demonstrate different techniques for loading and rendering trees. Obviously, the `Ext.tree.TreePanel` uses the `Store` class for gathering and modeling data. And the tree's selection model is very similar to the grid's selection model.

Keyboard Navigation

The `Ext.KeyMap` and `Ext.KeyNav` classes both offer simple solutions to the problem of keyboard navigation. The `KeyNav` class is a targeted solution, which allows the developer to handle typical keyboard navigation requirements (left, right, up, down, Page Up, Page Down, Enter, Esc, and so on). However, the `KeyMap` class offers a simple mechanism with a more general solution.

For example, whereas the `KeyNav` class is suitable for handling the navigation within a component (tabstrip, grid, and so on), the `KeyMap` class is suitable for a more general component (menu, editor, and so on). Being so general, there are helper methods on the `Ext.Element` class for creating `KeyMaps` (`addKeyListener` and `addKeyMap`).

Too Much to List

Of course, the list goes on and on. There are common things such as the `Ext.MessageBox` class and the `Ext.Slider` control, and then there are cutting-edge things such as the `Ext.air` namespace (which adds support for Adobe AIR) and the `Ext.sql` namespace (which adds support for SQLite). And there are still dozens of helper classes, which assist in everyday tasks: `Ext.Layer`, `Ext.Shadow`, `Ext.Resizable`, `Ext.ColorPalette`, `Ext.util.ClickRepeater`, `Ext.util.DelayedTask`, `Ext.util.TaskRunner`, and many more.

Summary

This chapter covered the entire Ext JS form widget library. You also looked at how those form controls are validated. Of course validation is more than a simple Boolean value; users need to know which fields are invalid and why. You also looked at the built-in mechanisms for displaying that information to users.

You took a brief glimpse at some of the lesser known classes within the Ext JS library. With a library as large in breadth as Ext JS, it seems amazing that the library isn't larger in size. However, a proper object-oriented code base makes reusing code a snap. With JavaScript best practices and techniques, the entire library performs well on all browsers.

It's no wonder that the Ext JS library works well on small projects, but has excellent scalability for even the largest projects.

Part IV
Dojo

Dojo is an open-source framework that began life as an effort to unify a handful of separate DHTML toolkits and JavaScript utility libraries. As such, the Dojo toolkit offers all the amenities expected from modern JavaScript frameworks. You'll find basic language enhancements, as well as the usual tools for dealing with DOM manipulation and AJAX requests.

Where Dojo really shines, though, is with its facilities for building user interfaces and whole applications using declarative HTML markup. Rather than piecing together applications with long stretches of object initialization code and wiring up DOM elements, Dojo offers the ability to scan the page itself for setup cues in Dojo-specific attributes and conventions. Though you still can choose to build things without this declarative style, it can help speed development.

Another major pillar of the toolkit is its packaging system, organizing a rich set of libraries, components, widgets, and extensions. All modules are laid out in a clear namespaces not unlike the standard library you'd find in languages like Java or Python.

And having a clear structure is good, because Dojo offers a lot. Fortunately, you don't have to use it all at once: In conjunction with the organizational facets of the packaging system, Dojo offers facilities for dynamically loading modules and any declared dependencies — all of which can be later optimized away through custom builds that bundle required code together into a single compact JS include. Additionally, Dojo's packaging system can be used to organize and locate CSS, images, and other assets associated with widgets and code in your projects.

And finally, no introduction to Dojo would be complete without mentioning the nonprofit Dojo Foundation, which was established to sponsor the project as well as to bring clarity and consistency to the licensing under which each contribution is covered. Each contributor to the project is required to sign what's called, appropriately enough, a Contributor License Agreement. This agreement makes explicit the desire to allow work to be offered as part of the Dojo framework.

Subsequently, the Dojo framework can be licensed under either the terms of the BSD license or the Academic Free License — both of which, among other things, allow the clear use of Dojo in commercial projects without separate licensing or fees and helps promote liability-free contributions from the community.

23

Enhancing Development with Dojo Core

In this chapter, you'll be shown the Dojo core of basic JavaScript language enhancements that provides the foundation for all of the other tools and systems offered by the toolkit. But first, you'll be shown how to get a copy of Dojo, either from current releases or leading-edge development versions. Then, you'll be taken on a tour through the basic packaging, markup declaration, and object-oriented programming features.

You'll learn about:

❑   Declaring, loading, and providing dependencies

❑   Defining classes and using inheritance

❑   Declaring objects in markup

Getting Dojo

It's time to dig in and start playing with it for yourself. There are several ways to do this, and each way offers its own advantages.

Using Dojo via the AOL CDN

The easiest way to start using Dojo is by way of the AOL Content Delivery Network.

In short, the AOL CDN is a widely distributed and highly available network of web servers hosting static assets — and among these assets are the code and collateral for the Dojo toolkit. What this means is that you can get started using Dojo with an include like the following:

```
<script type="text/javascript" src="http://o.aolcdn.com/dojo/1.1.1/dojo/dojo.xd.js">
</script>
```

This single JavaScript include pulls in an optimized build of the Dojo core, which is enough to get you rolling thanks to the Dojo packaging system and dynamic module loading.

Downloading the Latest Dojo Release

If relying on someone else's servers for a JS framework isn't quite your style — even if (or because) they are as big as AOL — you can download the complete Dojo framework to host your own way.

You can find the latest Dojo release here:

```
http://dojotoolkit.org/downloads
```

From that page, you can find a distribution package of everything Dojo — as well as a few other support tools such as Dojo ShrinkSafe, handy for use later in building your own compressed version of the bits of Dojo you end up using.

Once you've downloaded the distribution archive, you'll need to unpack it somewhere convenient on your web server. Make a note of the URL at which you've made it available, for use throughout the rest of this part of the book.

Trying Dojo Under Development

If you're really feeling adventurous, you can skip the release version and head straight for a cut of the current code under development. The easiest way to do this is to check out a nightly build, available here:

```
http://archive.dojotoolkit.org/nightly/
```

But, if you'd like to track Dojo development even more closely, you can check out code directly from the project's Subversion repository. As of this writing, you can find details on this repository here:

```
http://dojotoolkit.org/book/dojo-book-0-9/part-4-meta-dojo/get-code-subversion
```

If you have a command-line Subversion client, the following as of this writing will assemble and check everything out for you from all the subprojects:

```
svn co http://svn.dojotoolkit.org/src/view/anon/all/trunk dojodev
```

After this command, you should have a `dojodev/` directory organized in the same way as a release package. The rest of the examples here refer to this `dojodev/` directory in using Dojo locally, but keep the following in mind: Grabbing a copy of Dojo this close to the bleeding-edge might not quite be what you want to deal with on a regular basis.

Sampling Dojo

If you grabbed a local copy of Dojo, whether from a release download or checked out from the development repository, you should notice that there are several directories in the root of the package directory, including the following:

- ❏ `dojo/` — Here lives the core of Dojo, including basic JS extensions, dynamic module loading, DOM and AJAX utilities, and a host of other useful bits.

- ❏ `dijit/` — Residing in this directory is Dijit, the Dojo widget system.

- ❏ `dojox/` — Under this path, you'll find optional yet powerful extensions to Dojo that provide charting facilities, cryptographic routines, offline application support, and more.

Getting to Hello World

Possibly the best way to get a flavor for the Dojo way is to jump right into a quick example page that loads up the toolkit and tries a few things out:

```html
<html>
    <head>
        <title>Hello Dojo</title>

        <style type="text/css">
            @import "../dojodev/dojo/resources/dojo.css";
            @import "../dojodev/dijit/themes/tundra/tundra.css";
        </style>

        <style type="text/css">
            .accord { margin: 1em; height: 300px; }
        </style>

        <script type="text/javascript" src="../dojodev/dojo/dojo.js"
            djConfig="isDebug: true, parseOnLoad: true"></script>
```

Note that the CSS and JavaScript paths in the previous code assume that this page resides in a folder devoted to this chapter — `ex-dojo-core/` for example — in the same directory as the `dojodev/` folder.

The code itself is fairly mundane stuff so far — the page opens with a title and the inclusion of a couple of Dojo style sheets. What's worth noting, though, is that Dojo does include a baseline "reset" CSS like the one offered by YUI and others, though not nearly as ambitious.

The second CSS import is somewhat more interesting: `tundra.css` defines a complete theme for Dijit widgets, and can be swapped out for another. For example, `soria/soria.css` is one you might try. For more details about this feature, see Chapter 28.

The final bit of CSS is just a little tweak to an element that will appear further along in the page.

After the CSS, take a look at the first JavaScript import of the page. This loads up the core of Dojo. Notice that there's a custom `djConfig` attribute on the `<script>` tag — this is your first hint that there's something different going on here. The `djConfig` attribute may contain flags and settings used globally to configure the Dojo toolkit. In this case, the `isDebug` flag enables debug logging and messages, and the `parseOnLoad` flag tells Dojo to scan the DOM for setup cues once the page has finished loading.

Continuing on, here's markup to finish off the `<head>` element:

```
<script type="text/javascript">
    dojo.require("dojo.parser");
    dojo.require("dijit.form.TextBox");
    dojo.require("dijit.form.CheckBox");
    dojo.require("dijit.form.DateTextBox");
    dojo.require("dijit.form.NumberSpinner");
    dojo.require("dijit.form.Slider");
    dojo.require("dijit.layout.AccordionContainer");
</script>
</head>
```

The `dojo.require()` calls you see in this `<script>` block use the Dojo module system. For each of these, if the named module has not already been loaded, the Dojo core attempts to locate and load it dynamically to satisfy each dependency. If any of these modules declares further requirements — and these, in particular, do — Dojo will scoop them up as well.

In fact, if you happen to use Firefox as your browser, and have the Firebug extension installed, you can take a look at the network activity tab and monitor all the requests generated by the requirements specified. Figure 23-1 shows an example of what you might see. There's quite a lot going on here, but keep in mind that there are tools for optimizing this later on.

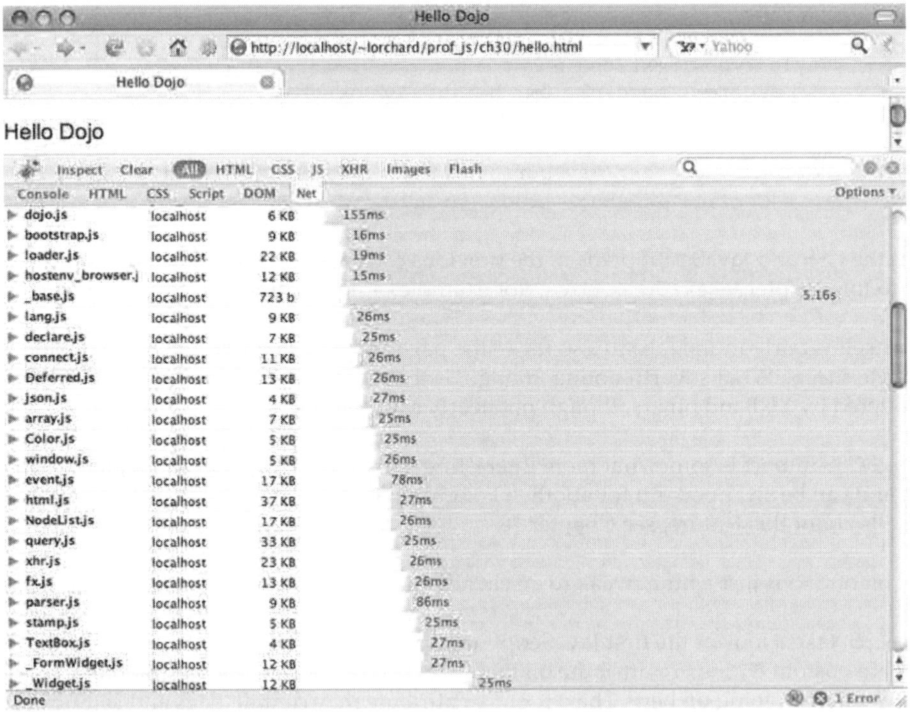

Figure 23-1

Using Firebug

In case you've never been introduced to it, Firebug is an invaluable Firefox extension for web developers.

Firebug is useful in every aspect of the job — you can inspect elements in the page, view and manipulate live CSS, access a JavaScript shell for trying out small snippets, as well as view a log of debugging messages from your code. Firebug can be found at `http://getfirebug.com`.

It's also worth noting that Dojo, at least in development, comes with a copy of Firebug Lite for non-Firefox browsers. It can be activated by the Dojo config setting isDebug. Read more about Firebug Lite at `http://getfirebug.com/lite.html`.

Next begins the `<body>` of the page:

```
<body class="tundra">


    <h1>Hello Dojo</h1>
```

Note that the `<body>` tag has a `class="tundra"` attribute. This corresponds to the theme loaded in CSS earlier. Now you're starting to get into some meaty bits:

```
<div class="accord"
    dojoType="dijit.layout.AccordionContainer"
    duration="200">

    <div dojoType="dijit.layout.AccordionPane" selected="true"
        title="Intro" class="apane">
        <p>Hello world - welcome to Dojo!</p>
    </div>
```

There hasn't been much JavaScript in this page yet, but the HTML in the previous example will cause quite a bit to happen. Thanks to the requirements loaded in the `<head>` — as well as `djConfig="parseOnLoad: true"` appearing on the `<script>` tag loading Dojo — the markup here is interpreted on page load as declarative cues for object initialization.

In particular, this markup declares that an accordion-style layout widget be constructed. Although there are some caveats, this widget can be styled like any bit of HTML on the page, as seen with the `.accord` selector appearing in CSS earlier, back in the `<head>` element.

Notice that each of the `<div>` elements comes with a custom `dojoType` attribute that defines what Dijit class should be instantiated and wrapped around each. The parent `<div>` becomes an `AccordionContainer`, and the first child `<div>` becomes an `AccordionPane`. Additionally, each of these comes with configuration for the widgets in the form of custom attributes. For instance, the animation speed with which the accordion panes open and close is specified by `duration="200"`, and the title of a pane is specified with `title="Intro"`.

Figure 23-2 shows an example of what all the previous code produces.

Figure 23-2

To reinforce the ideas, take a look at a few more widgets declared in markup:

```
<div dojoType="dijit.layout.AccordionPane"
    title="Form #1" class="apane">
  <form>

      <label for="fname">First Name</label><br />
      <input name="fname" type="text" length="10"
          trim="true" propercase="true"
          dojoType="dijit.form.TextBox" /><br />

      <label for="lname">Last Name</label><br />
      <input name="lname" type="text" length="10"
          trim="true" propercase="true"
          dojoType="dijit.form.TextBox" /><br />
```

Here's another AccordionPane, this time containing a `<form>`. The form starts off with two input fields, which are also declared to be TextBox widgets. These both include parameters in the form of trim="true" and propercase="true" attributes — which cause whitespace to be trimmed and the first letter to be capitalized, respectively.

Next, it's time to try a slightly more interesting widget:

```
<label for="bday">Birthday</label><br />
<input name="bday" type="text" length="10"
    dojoType="dijit.form.DateTextBox" /><br />
```

Although the markup for this DateTextBox is simpler than the previous two, it does dramatically more. Figure 23-3 shows what happens when a user clicks on this new input field. Without much fuss at all, a full-featured calendar date selection widget can be integrated into a simple HTML form.

Figure 23-3

Finally, it's time to see a little bit of scripting make an appearance in the page:

```
<label for="fnum">Favorite Number</label><br />
<input name="fnum" id="fnum" type="text" length="15"
    dojoType="dijit.form.TextBox" /><br />

<div dojoType="dijit.form.HorizontalSlider"
    id="horiz1" name="horiz1" value="10"
    maximum="100" minimum="0"
    intermediateChanges="true" showButtons="false"
    onChange="dojo.byId('fnum').value=arguments[0]"
    style="width:10em; height: 20px;">
</div>

    </form>

</div>
</div>
</body>
</html>
```

If you missed the scripting, look for the onChange attribute of the HorizontalSlider widget. That small bit of glue code copies updates of the widget as a number to the TextBox before it. Otherwise, the two widgets used here aren't much more complex than those found in the rest of the sample page. Figure 23-4 shows the end result.

Figure 23-4

While it might seem strange to introduce a JavaScript framework mostly through HTML, this is a major part of the Dojo magic. In the coming chapters, you'll see that many aspects of Dojo can be used through both declarative and programmatic means. You can do it all strictly through JavaScript, but you may eventually find it useful to tie into this system and build your own widgets and declaratively driven modules.

Examining Dojo Core

Now that you've gotten a foot in the Dojo, it's time to back up a little and take a closer look at what Dojo core offers to a JavaScript developer. The other aspects touched upon in the initial sample will return throughout the rest of this part of the book.

Declaring, Loading, and Providing Dependencies

Defining modules, declaring dependencies, and dynamically loading code is a key facet of Dojo. What's especially nice, though, is that you can use these facilities in your own projects.

Using dojo.require() to Declare and Load Dependencies

You've already seen part of this system in action with dojo.require(), used like so:

```
dojo.require("dojo.parser");
dojo.require("dijit.form.TextBox");
dojo.require("dijit.form.CheckBox");
dojo.require("dijit.form.DateTextBox");
dojo.require("dijit.form.NumberSpinner");
dojo.require("dijit.form.Slider");
dojo.require("dijit.layout.AccordionContainer");
```

These statements resulted in dynamically constructed `<script>` inserted into the `<head>` of the page. There's a bit more to it than that, but this is the basic idea. To derive URL for include, the following was done: Dots in the module names were replaced with slashes, a `.js` was added, and a base URL prefix was constructed from the location of `dojo.js`.

Most of these modules themselves include further `dojo.require()` statements, which in turn result in more includes. The thing is, though, many of these `dojo.require()` statements end up asking for the same things. Luckily, `dojo.require()` has enough smarts to know when something has already been loaded and won't try loading it again.

Providing Dependencies with dojo.provide()

Actually, the smarts don't lie completely within `dojo.require()`. Rather, they depend upon convention in the use of `dojo.provide()`. Each module in Dojo starts with a call to `dojo.provide()`, which registers that module as having been loaded. For example, `dijit/form/TextBox.js` begins with the following:

```
dojo.provide("dijit.form.TextBox");
```

There's another benefit to using `dojo.provide()` in your own code, though. Consider whether you've ever seen or written something like the following:

```
if (typeof window.decafbad == 'undefined')
    window.decafbad = {};
if (typeof decafbad.util == 'undefined')
    decafbad.util = {};
if (typeof decafbad.util.foo == 'undefined')
    decafbad.util.foo = {};

decafbad.util.foo.aMethod = function() {
    // method body
}
```

This is the convention by which namespaces are established in many modern JavaScript applications, ensuring the existence of each part of the namespace before trying to use it. Sometimes only the last part of the namespace is created because all the parent namespaces have been created in other dependencies loaded earlier, but this is the general form of the dance.

This can be replaced with a more concise and descriptive call to `dojo.provide()`, like so:

```
dojo.provide("decafbad.util.foo")

decafbad.util.foo.aMethod = function() {
    // method body
}
```

Not only does this call register the namespace as loaded with respect to `dojo.require()`, it also ensures that the full namespace itself is created as necessary. This provides both an implementation and a readability benefit for your code.

Telling Dojo Where to Find Your Modules

There's one more piece to the dependencies story: How does Dojo find your code? By default, `dojo.require()` attempts to load all modules from the parent URL where `dojo.js` was found. This means that Dojo will orient itself with respect to relative paths from wherever you've installed Dojo and its subprojects — which could mean the AOL CDN, if you chose to go that route.

Thus, consider that a `dojo.require("decafbad.util.foo")` might resolve to the following:

```
http://o.aolcdn.com/dojo/1.1.1/decafbad/foo/bar.xd.js
```

It's highly unlikely that you can host your project on the AOL CDN, so you'll want Dojo to look for your code elsewhere. And, even if you're using a locally downloaded installation of Dojo, it's cleaner to keep your code out of that directory in case you plan on ever upgrading Dojo in the future. So, here's where `dojo.registerModulePath()` comes in:

```
dojo.registerModulePath('decafbad', '../../ex-dojo-core/decafbad');
```

If you're using a local installation of Dojo, this statement will cause any `dojo.require()` call for `decafbad` or any of its child modules to be loaded from the given path relative to the `dojo` module directory. For example, consider this as a directory structure for your project:

- ❑ `dojodev/`
    - ❑ `dojo/dojo.js`
- ❑ `ex-dojo-core/`
    - ❑ `hello.html`
    - ❑ `decafbad/foo/bar.js`

Since `dojo.js` resides under the `dojodev/dojo/` directory, the registered relative module path `../../ex-dojo-core/decafbad` would be found outside the Dojo installation itself.

Where things get a little trickier is if you're using the AOL CDN version of Dojo, which is an *XDomain build*. That means this particular build of Dojo is geared toward loading its resources from a different domain (that is, `o.aolcdn.com`) versus where it's been included (that is, yours). Because of the particulars of implementation of cross-domain module loading, the situation is slightly different than what a local Dojo install allows.

For the most part, you don't need to worry too much about what this implies — but in this case, it means you need to include a base URL for your modules, relative to the *current page* instead of a local Dojo installation, in `djConfig`:

```
<script type="text/javascript"
    src="http://o.aolcdn.com/dojo/1.1.1/dojo/dojo.xd.js"
    djConfig="isDebug: true, parseOnLoad: true, baseUrl: './'"></script>

<script type="text/javascript">
    dojo.registerModulePath('decafbad', './decafbad');
    dojo.require("dojo.parser");
```

```
        dojo.require("dijit.layout.AccordionContainer");
        dojo.require("decafbad.foo.bar");
    </script>
```

This sets the base URL for all modules loaded with relative paths, which exclude those that are part of the Dojo XDomain build — because those modules in the XDomain build all have absolute paths to the AOL CDN "burned in" as part of the build process for that version of Dojo.

And, since you're now up to two settings in djConfig, it's worth noting that you can also define djConfig more fully in a JavaScript block rather than an attribute:

```
    <script type="text/javascript">
        djConfig = {
            isDebug: true,
            parseOnLoad: true,
            baseUrl: './',
            modulePaths: {
                "decafbad": "./decafbad",
            },
        };
    </script>
    <script type="text/javascript"
        src="http://o.aolcdn.com/dojo/1.1.1/dojo/dojo.xd.js"></script>
```

Notice that the dojo.registerModulePath() call can be replaced by defining modulePaths in djConfig. This offers a bit more clarity and efficiency up front if you know you're going to define a series of paths or do a bit of advanced Dojo configuration anyway.

More About Dojo XDomain Builds

In order to avoid a lengthy digression, this chapter glosses over the Dojo build system. The build system is covered in a later chapter — but if you'd like to know about XDomain builds in particular, read more at the following web site:

```
http://dojotoolkit.org/book/dojo-book-0-9/part-4-meta-dojo/
package-system-and-custom-builds
```

Defining Classes and Using Inheritance

Something that's important to understand about JavaScript is that while it does deal with objects, it's a prototype-based language. It doesn't natively offer classes and inheritance like other languages focused on object-oriented programming. In many ways, a prototype-based language can be more expressive because multiple forms of code reuse can be employed — including classes and inheritance — but with the caveat that you need to implement those facilities yourself.

Defining Classes with dojo.declare()

With that in mind, take a look at the following code, which defines a JavaScript class the usual way:

```
decafbad.school.PersonClassic = function(name) {
    this.name = name;
};
decafbad.school.PersonClassic.prototype = {
    getName: function() {
        return this.name;
    }
};
```

Now, consider this functionally similar code from a module defined in decafbad/school.js:

```
dojo.provide("decafbad.school")

dojo.declare("decafbad.school.Person", null, {
    constructor: function(name) {
        this.name = name;
    },
    getName: function() {
        return this.name;
    }
});
```

The dojo.declare() method does all the behind-the-scenes work necessary to create a JavaScript class with inheritable constructors and methods. The arguments to the method are the following:

❑   Name of the class, complete with namespace.

❑   Parent class from which to inherit, if any. In this case, it's null, which indicates there are no parent classes for this class.

❑   Object literal defining the class, including all of its data members and methods.

Among the methods defined in a Dojo class, constructor is called whenever a new instance of the class is created. This plays the same roll as the initial function definition in native JS prototype-based classes.

Declaring Subclasses and Overriding Methods

Considering further what Dojo does beyond standard JavaScript prototypes, take a look at this declaration of a Person subclass:

```
dojo.declare("decafbad.school.Student", decafbad.school.Person, {
    constructor: function(name, grade) {
        // Note that the inherited constructor is automatically called.
        this.grade = grade;
    },
    getGrade: function() {
        return this.grade;
    }
});
```

The new `Student` class is a subclass of `Person` — thanks to Dojo, `Student` inherits all the methods of `Person`, including the constructor. When a new instance of `Student` is created, the `Person` class `constructor` method is automatically called before `constructor` is called for `Student`.

This is sort of class-based programming supported by other languages — though it requires a little extra work within JavaScript's prototype-based environment to support inheritance and other typical OOP facilities. This is what `dojo.declare()` provides.

Now, consider the following code to see how you can override methods inherited from parent classes:

```
dojo.declare("decafbad.school.MaleStudent", decafbad.school.Student, {
    getName: function() {
        var name = this.inherited(arguments);
        return "Mr. " + name;
    }
});
```

This `MaleStudent` class inherits the `getName()` method from `Student`, but overrides it. The new implementation uses `this.inherited(arguments)` provided by Dojo to call the parent class method and put its own spin on the return value. Other than the special case of `constructor`, no overridden parent methods are automatically called in subclasses.

Note that the `arguments` parameter to `this.inherited()` is a built-in JavaScript feature. This call convention allows you to easily pass along all of the arguments originally given to the current method.

Using Multiple Inheritance Through Mixins

Dojo also supports multiple-inheritance in the form of *mixins*. Take a look at this new example:

```
dojo.declare("decafbad.school.DoorUnlocker", null, {
    canUnlockDoors: true,
    constructor: function() {
        this.doorsUnlocked = [];
    },
    unlockDoor: function(door) {
        this.doorsUnlocked.push(door);
        return door + " now unlocked";
    }
});

dojo.declare("decafbad.school.DormAssistant",
    [ decafbad.school.Student, decafbad.school.DoorUnlocker ], { });
```

Two classes are defined here: `DoorUnlocker` and `DormAssistant`.

The first class, `DoorUnlocker`, does not inherit from any parent classes but defines a property `canUnlockDoors`, a constructor, and a method `unlockDoor`.

The second class, `DormAssistant`, uses an array literal to declare inheritance from both `Student` and `DoorUnlocker`. These are called *mixin* classes. This means that Dojo mixes them in — it adds all of the properties and methods from each mixin into the `DormAssistant` class, in the order that they appear in the inheritance list. The exception to this is constructors: They're accumulated in an internal list for the new class and each is called in order whenever a new instance is created.

Thus, in this example, DormAssistant is a Student given the additional add-on capability to perform unlockDoor(). The Student class, first in the inheritance list, is the official parent class of DormAssistant. The DoorUnlocker class is treated as extra capabilities sprinkled in.

Extending Existing Classes with dojo.extend()

Using multiple inheritance in declaring new classes with mix-and-match functionality is handy, but what can be even handier is the ability to augment existing classes. This is where dojo.extend() comes in:

```
dojo.extend(decafbad.school.Person, {
    _studying: null,
    study: function(subject) {
        this._studying = subject;
        return "Now studying "+subject;
    }
});
```

The previous code augments the Person base class with a new study() method and a new data member to keep track of what's being studied. What's particularly nice is that additions to the base class carry down to subclasses. Take this creation of a DormAssistant object, for example:

```
var bar = new decafbad.school.DormAssistant('kim', 'senior');
bar.study('physics');
```

Using dojo.extend() allows you to layer in custom functionality in a powerful way atop existing widgets and classes. This post-declaration augmentation of existing classes offers a way to package up alterations and tweaks to your own classes — as well as those belonging to Dojo itself.

The dojo.extend() call in the example shown earlier doesn't even need to be in the same module as the original Person class. You can include dojo.extend() statements as part of an external package for use with dojo.require(), with no preplanned coordination with other existing packages and classes.

Declaring Objects in Markup

As you've already seen in the first part of this chapter, part of the mojo of Dojo is the declaration of objects in HTML markup. This is most immediately useful in the context of widgets that wrap DOM elements with additional functionality. However, this feature is not limited to widgets: Using the Dojo parser, you can declare the instantiation of *any* Dojo class through HTML markup.

The dojo.parser module provides the Dojo parser. You can enable it by ensuring that parseOnLoad is true in djConfig, and that dojo.require("dojo.parser") appears in your page scripts. This is all true for the sample offered at the start of the chapter.

On page load, the parser scans through the DOM looking for elements bearing a dojoType attribute — the existence of the attribute signifies that the element is an object declaration, and the value of the attribute specifies the class of the object to instantiate.

Declaring an Object

Diving right into object declaration, take a look at the following HTML code:

```html
<html>
    <head>
        <title>Hello Dojo Parser</title>

        <script type="text/javascript">
            djConfig = {
                isDebug: true,
                parseOnLoad: true,
                modulePaths: {
                    "decafbad": "../../ex-dojo-core/decafbad",
                },
            };
        </script>

        <script type="text/javascript"
            src="../dojodev/dojo/dojo.js"></script>

        <script type="text/javascript">
            dojo.require("dojo.parser");
            dojo.require("decafbad.things");
        </script>

    </head>
    <body>

        <h1>Hello Dojo Parser</h1>

        <div dojoType="decafbad.things.thingA" jsId="decafbad.stuff.someThingA"
            class="someThingA" alpha="true" beta="three, four"
            foo="bar" baz="123" xyzzy="hello">

            <p>Alpha: <span class="alpha">default</span></p>
            <p>Beta:  <span class="beta">default</span></p>
            <p>Foo:   <span class="foo">default</span></p>
            <p>Baz:   <span class="baz">default</span></p>
            <p>Xyzzy: <span class="xyzzy">default</span></p>

        </div>

    </body>
</html>
```

Most of this should look familiar with respect to what you've seen so far in this chapter: The first `<script>` block sets up `djConfig` before loading up the Dojo core in the next `<script>` element. After that comes a pair of `dojo.require()` calls to load in the Dojo parser and a new module named `decafbad.thingA`.

In the page `<body>`, you can see an object instance declared with `dojoType="decafbad.thingA"`, bearing a number of custom attributes and some paragraphs contained within.

As one of those attributes, `jsId` makes its first appearance: The value of this attribute identifies a variable in the global namespace where the parser should store the newly instantiated object. In this case, `decafbad.stuff.someThingA` is where the new object will be found. This feature is very useful for referring to and connecting multiple objects declared in markup — more of this is covered in later chapters when working with Dijit widgets.

Defining a Class to Support Declaration in Markup

Now, take a look at this implementation for the `decafbad/thingA.js` module:

```
dojo.provide("decafbad.things");

dojo.declare("decafbad.things.thingA", null, {

    alpha: false,
    beta:  [ 'one', 'two' ],
    foo:   'default',
    baz:   456,

    constructor: function(args, node) {

        dojo.mixin(this, args);

        dojo.query('span', node).forEach(function(ele) {

            var name = ele.className;
            var val  = this[name];

            ele.innerHTML = val ?
                '[' + (typeof val) + "] " + val :
                'undefined';

        }, this);

    }

});
```

This isn't much code, but there's a lot going on here — this is a theme throughout Dojo.

First, the module itself is established with a call to `dojo.provide()`, then the declaration of the class `decafbad.things.thingA` is begun.

The class starts off with several properties, each a different JavaScript type. This is important to note, because the parser peeks into the class and performs type conversions from attribute character data as appropriate based on the original types of the default values. Hopefully, this feature will make more sense once you've seen it in action.

After the property definitions comes the constructor, whose parameters are supplied by the parser:

❑   `args` — An object collecting the attributes from markup

❑   `node` — A reference to the DOM element declaring the object instance.

In the constructor implementation, the first thing is a call to `dojo.mixin(this, args)`. This is a quick way to take all of the incoming converted attributes from `args` and assign them to object properties — like mixin classes, `dojo.mixin()` mixes the given properties into the given object.

The next part is a `dojo.query()` chained with a `forEach()` call. This sort of construct is explored in more detail in the Chapter 24. In short, it searches the contents of `node` for `<span>` elements and applies an anonymous function to each of them. The final parameter, `this`, causes the anonymous function to execute in the context of the object being constructed.

With each `<span>`, the anonymous function examines the class name and attempts to update its `innerHTML` property with a representation of the object property bearing the same name. So, if there's a `<span class="alpha">`, it should be changed to represent the type and contents of `this.alpha` if such a property has a value in the object. Otherwise, the `<span>` should read "undefined".

Seeing Markup Object Declaration in Action

Figure 23-5 shows what this code should end up doing when you put it all together.

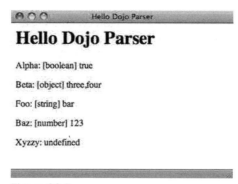

Figure 23-5

Here are some things to notice about the output and what happened:

❑   Thanks to the `dojoType="decafbad.things.thingA"` attribute in the markup, an instance of `decafbad.things.thingA` was created by the Dojo parser on page load.

❑   Because of `jsId="decafbad.stuff.someThingA"`, other code can refer to this newly instantiated object as `decafbad.stuff.someThingA`.

❑   Each attribute on the `<div>` was handed to the constructor for `decafbad.things.thingA` in a single JavaScript object, with type conversions to match the default values of properties existing in the class declaration.

❑   As part of constructing the `decafbad.things.thingA` instance, the contents of the `<div>` declaring the object were modified to reflect the properties of the new instance.

❑   Oh, and there's one more thing: The property `xyzzy` appears to be undefined.

That last item is true because not *all* of the attributes from the markup were converted and passed to the constructor. Take a look at the implementation for decafbad.things.thingA again, and you may notice that xyzzy is missing from the list of properties in the class declaration.

Since the parser does introspection into the properties and their types defined by the class declaration, it only converts and provides data for those attributes named in the declaration. So, although xyxxy — and even class — appear as attributes on the object declaration <div>, they're not given to the constructor because they're not part of the class declaration. In other words, if the class didn't ask for it, the parser won't provide it.

Designing Classes for Both Declarative and Programmatic Use

It's perfectly fine to bypass the parser and programmatically create a new instance of a class designed for declaration in markup. For example, you could write something like this:

```
var new_thing = new decafbad.things.thingA(
    { alpha: true },
    dojo.byId('someDiv')
);
```

This is basically what dojo.parser does, after all. However, there are cases where it would be nice to have a simpler constructor for use in code and still support declaration in markup. This is where a special "static" class method named markupFactory comes in:

```
dojo.declare("decafbad.things.thingB", null, {

    alpha: false,
    beta:  [ 'one', 'two' ],
    foo:   'default',
    baz:   456,

    constructor: function(alpha, beta, foo, baz) {
        this.alpha = alpha;
        this.beta  = beta;
        this.foo   = foo;
        this.baz   = baz;
    },

    markupFactory: function(args, node, thisClass) {
        var instance = new thisClass(
            args.alpha, args.beta, args.foo, args.baz
        );
        return instance;
    }

});
```

In this new decafbad.things.thingB class, you can see that there's both a constructor and a markupFactory method. The Dojo parser instantiates objects using the constructor, *unless* it finds a markupFactory method to use instead.

The `markupFactory` method works like a "static" class method in other languages in that it is not called on individual object instances of a class, but is instead called on the class prototype itself. The parameters for this method, which are similar to the signature for `constructor` seen earlier, include:

- ❑ `args` — The set of parameters collected from markup attributes
- ❑ `node` — A reference to the DOM node declaring the object instance
- ❑ `thisClass` — A reference to the class for which an instance should be created

When called, this method is responsible for creating and returning a new instance of `thisClass`, and is free to do whatever it needs to do in between. This lets you maintain two separate means for creating an instance of a class based on whether the context is programmatic or whether it's declared in markup.

Considering mixin classes and `dojo.mixin()`, the availability of `markupFactory` also affords the possibility to augment existing classes that were not previously designed for use in markup by way of a newly mixed-in implementation for `markupFactory`.

Declaring Objects in Markup Versus Validating HTML

There's an elephant in the room with regards to this whole section explaining Dojo's parser and declaring objects in markup: If you're using all these custom attributes, how will your pages ever pass the test of HTML validation?

The short answer is that your pages won't validate, but it might be okay.

The longer answer is that you need to choose between the convenience of the Dojo parser and non-validating custom attributes versus programmatic creation of objects and validating markup.

Custom attributes work in browsers, practically speaking, and the current implementation of the Dojo parser is considered a trade-off between convenience and performance. Introducing XML namespaces or using some CSS class naming convention — both of which seem to be common suggestions — fall on the nonperforming side of the equation, and so the Dojo team has drawn this pragmatic line in the sand and punted on satisfying everyone in what's a very noisy religious debate.

So, if you're willing to give up strict HTML validity, you may find the benefits of declaring networks of objects and widgets in markup worth your while.

On the other hand, if you really do adhere to the discipline of validating all of your markup, then `dojo.parser` is not for you. This is one more reason why the `constructor` / `markupFactory` arrangement is useful, because any object that can be declared in markup can also be instantiated in plain old JS code. Alternatively, you can look into the option of extending or replacing the `dojo.parser` module to work within your own acceptable constraints.

If you're interested, you can read some of the background surrounding this issue here:

```
www.dojotoolkit.org/book/dojo-porting-guide-0-4-x-0-9/widgets/general
```

Summary

In this chapter, you were given a quick tour of core Dojo — including how to get Dojo working in your own pages, how to manage modules and dependencies, and how Dojo's class system and page parser build on top of JavaScript's prototype-based system. This is the foundation upon which just about everything else in the Dojo framework builds — but this foundation is available for you to do the same with your own code.

Coming up in the next chapter, you'll be able to get down to business with Dojo's DOM manipulation facilities.

24

Manipulating the DOM

It wasn't until browsers began introducing Dynamic HTML that JavaScript really became useful in building web applications. Sure, in earlier days, you could use it to do some primitive form validation, spawn dubious pop-up windows, and enable scrolling text in the status bar — but it wasn't until JavaScript developers could really treat the browser window as a canvas (albeit still primitive) and develop client-side user interfaces that the language started to come into its own.

You'd be hard pressed to find a developing or mature framework today that doesn't have at its core an effort to bring cross-browser consistency and work-saving abstraction to the job of navigating and manipulating the browser document object model and handling the events generated by user actions on a page. Dojo is, of course, no exception. In fact, despite the breadth of capabilities you'll find in the Dojo toolkit which themselves have no direct relation to Dynamic HTML, you'll find Dojo called a DHTML toolkit throughout its documentation.

And in Dojo, you'll find means for finding, altering, and creating elements in the DOM. Beyond basics, though, you'll find a host of convenient methods and conventions both original and inspired by other JS libraries that allow you to apply sweeping changes with concise and clear code. Dojo also offers a very flexible set of event handling abstractions to do everything from handling simple button clicks to orchestrating whole applications driven by custom events.

In this chapter, you'll learn about:

- ❑ Finding DOM elements
- ❑ Handling lists
- ❑ Processing lists

Finding DOM Elements

Most Dynamic HTML and DOM scripting starts from a complete web page, working from there to alter and augment the page. So, one of the fundamental building blocks of DOM scripting is the ability to find elements within the page upon which to perform desired operations.

Finding Elements with dojo.byId

The first and simplest way to find something in the DOM is to give it a literal ID in markup and use `document.getElementById()` in JavaScript to fetch it.

In Dojo, the method `dojo.byId()` is a shortcut built atop this basic DOM feature. Take a look at the following HTML:

```
<div id="sect1">
    <h2>Section 1</h2>
    <p id="para1">
        Lorem ipsum dolor sit amet, consectetuer adipiscing elit.
    </p>
</div>
```

In order to get a handle on the <div> and <p> elements in the preceding example, you'd write the following:

```
var sect1 = dojo.byId('sect1');
var para1 = dojo.byId('para1');
```

Beyond brevity, the main difference between `dojo.byId()` and `document.getElementById()` is that if you pass a non-string into it as a parameter — say, an element that's already been fetched — `dojo.byId()` simply returns the parameter. For example:

```
var sect1_dup = dojo.byId(sect1); // sect1_dup == sect1
```

Sometimes it's easy to come up with a known ID or derive one by some naming convention. At other times you've already got a reference to an element during the course of navigating the DOM. To build flexible functions that can accommodate both scenarios, element handling code can just wrap the incoming parameter in a call to `dojo.byId()` and carry on from there like so:

```
function getTagName(id_or_ele) {
    var ele = dojo.byId(id_or_ele);
    return ele.tagName;
}
```

Finding Elements with dojo.query

Locating a single element by ID is great, but rarely do things stop there. Most often, it's useful to operate on large groups and ranges of elements. But, it takes a lot of coordination and cluttered markup to ensure that every relevant element on the page has been given an ID.

To this end, the DOM offers methods such as document.getElementsByTagName() and document.getElementsByName() in order to get sets of elements. Additionally, individual elements offer properties such as childNodes and parentNode to navigate through the page hierarchy. Using these in well-constructed loops, looking for semantic hooks in markup like tag names and CSS class names, you can pretty much locate and manipulate any arrangement of elements you like.

The problem, however, is that code written to deal DOM navigation can quickly grow in size and complexity — and that's before you even get down to doing what you wanted to do with the elements in the first place.

But, wait a minute: Isn't identifying groups of elements on a page a problem already solved by another part of the web development suite — namely, with CSS selectors? You use CSS selectors to declare the patterns by which elements should be found and on which CSS styles should be applied. What if you could do the same thing for finding and processing DOM nodes in JavaScript?

As it turns out, this is just what dojo.query() offers. Consider the following HTML fragment:

```
<div id="ex1">
    <ul>
        <li><a href="http://decafbad.com">Item #1</a></li>
        <li class="seconditem dojolink">
            <a href="http://dojoproject.org">Item
                <span class="num">#2</span></a>
        </li>
        <li>
            <span>Sub-list</span>
            <ul>
                <li><a href="http://delicious.com">Item
                    <span class="num letter">B</span></a></li>
                <li><a href="http://mozilla.org">Item C</a></li>
            </ul>
        </li>
        <li><a href="http://wrox.com">Item
            <span class="num">#5</span></a></li>
    </ul>
</div>
```

Now, take a look at this attempt to scoop up some elements the hard way:

```
var num_spans = [];
var root_ele = document.getElementById('ex2');
var spans = root_ele.getElementsByTagName('span');
for (var i=0,span; span=spans[i]; i++) {
    if (/\s?num\s?/.test(span.className)) {
        num_spans.push(span);
    }
}
```

First of all, it might take you a minute or two to even decipher what this code is meant to do, and it's not even written in an intentionally obfuscated way.

The previous code finds the `<div id="ex2">` element by ID, then searches inside it for `<span>` elements. Next, the collection of `<span>` elements are processed, searching for those with CSS class names of 'num'. Note that a regular expression is used here because class names can be space-separated lists — and one of the `<span>` elements in the sample HTML bears just such an attribute with multiple classes.

Once found, the matching `<span>` elements are collected into an array. The highlighted lines show where the items will be found:

```
<div id="ex1">
    <ul>
        <li><a href="http://decafbad.com">Item #1</a></li>
        <li class="seconditem dojolink">
            <a href="http://dojoproject.org">Item
                <span class="num">#2</span></a>
        </li>
        <li>
            <span>Sub-list</span>
            <ul>
                <li><a href="http://delicious.com">Item
                    <span class="num letter">B</span></a></li>
                <li><a href="http://mozilla.org">Item C</a></li>
            </ul>
        </li>
        <li><a href="http://wrox.com">Item
            <span class="num">#5</span></a></li>
    </ul>
</div>
```

Now, take a look at code using `dojo.query()` to accomplish the same thing:

```
var num_spans = dojo.query('span.num', 'ex2');
```

This is quite a reduction in code and offers a much greater degree of clarity. The first parameter to `dojo.query()` is a CSS3 selector describing what to look for, and the optional second parameter can be an element or an ID which has child elements that the search will be constrained to.

There are more advanced selectors supported by `dojo.query()`, as well. For example:

```
var dot_org_links = dojo.query('a[href$=".org"]', 'ex2');
var li_the_first  = dojo.query('li:first-child', 'ex2');
var li_the_third  = dojo.query('li:nth-child(3)', 'ex2');
```

The first of these finds all links with URLs that end in `.org`.

The second finds each `<li>` element appearing first in its parent list.

The last statement finds all `<li>` elements that appear third in their respective lists.

The implementation of `dojo.query()` does not support the full CSS3 specification, but it does support a useful subset. For reference, the following table lists the selectors that are known to work at the time of this writing:

Selector	Purpose
*	Matches all elements
.class	Matches elements whose CSS classes contain 'class'
#foo	Matches elements with id="foo"
E	Matches <E> elements
E F	Matches elements <F> that are descendants of elements <E>
E>F	Matches elements <F> that are direct descendants of elements <E>
E[foo]	Matches elements <E> bearing attribute foo
E[foo="bar"]	Matches elements <E foo="bar">
E[foo~="bar"]	Matches elements <E> whose attribute foo is a space-separated list containing the value bar — useful for attributes constructed like CSS class names.
E[foo^="bar"]	Matches elements <E> whose attribute foo begins with bar
E[foo$="bar"]	Matches elements <E> whose attribute foo ends with bar
E[foo*="bar"]	Matches elements <E> whose attribute foo contains bar
E:nth-child(n)	Matches elements <E> that are the nth child of the parent element
E:nth-child(odd)	Matches elements <E> that are the odd-numbered children of the parent element
E:nth-child(even)	Matches elements <E> that are the even-numbered children of the parent element
E:nth-child(3n+1)	Matches every third element <E>, starting with the first child.
E:first-child	Matches elements <E> that are their parent element's first child
E:last-child	Matches elements <E> that are their parent element's last child
E:not(. . .)	Negates any of the above selectors

Handling Lists of DOM Elements

Working with `dojo.query()` is somewhat similar to expressing database queries in SQL — rather than programmatically stepping through collections and searching for things, you can declare what you need and want to do. To this point, you've seen how to declare what you need — now it's time to see how Dojo lets you refine the results and declare what you want to do with them.

At the core of this is the `dojo.NodeList` class, an instance of which is returned by a call to `dojo.query()`. The `dojo.NodeList` class offers a set of methods useful for filtering, refining, and processing the results contained within. What's more is that most of these methods themselves each return a `dojo.NodeList` reference, so that you can chain method calls together in a way that can read like a declarative query language.

Filtering and Refining Lists of Nodes

Once you've got the basics down in finding elements with CSS selectors and `dojo.query()`, you can further refine and filter the results from a simple call with `NodeList` methods.

Filtering NodeList Results with .filter()

The first and simplest of the `NodeList` methods is `.filter()`. It gives you a way to exclude nodes from the list, either by using a CSS selector or by applying a callback function where the return value is a yes or no decision on whether to include that node in the output list.

Take a look at the following markup:

```
<ul id="ex1">
    <li><a href="http://decafbad.com">Item #1</a></li>
    <li class="seconditem dojolink">
        <a href="http://dojoproject.org">Item
            <span class="num">#2</span></a>
    </li>
    <li class="thirditem">
        <a href="http://w3.org">Item #3</a>
    </li>
    <li>
        <span>Sub-list</span>
        <ul>
            <li><a href="http://yahoo.com">Item A</a></li>
            <li><a href="http://delicious.com">Item
                <span class="num letter">B</span></a></li>
            <li><a href="http://mozilla.org">Item C</a></li>
        </ul>
    </li>
    <li id="item4"><a href="http://getfirebug.com">Item #4</a></li>
    <li><a href="http://wrox.com">Item
        <span class="num">#5</span></a></li>
</ul>
```

With that in mind, consider what the following code will do:

```
var items = dojo
    .query('a')
    .filter('a[href$=".org"]');
```

Since JavaScript doesn't mind whitespace in the midst of its dot-notation in chained function calls, you can introduce a bit more formatting clarity to your code to make it easier to tell what should be going on and give the appearance of a declarative query language within JavaScript.

The first `.query()` finds all links in the page, and then the `.filter()` narrows those results to just those links with URLs that end in `.org`:

```
<ul>
    <li><a href="http://decafbad.com">Item #1</a></li>
    <li class="seconditem dojolink">
        <a href="http://dojoproject.org">Item
            <span class="num">#2</span></a>
    </li>
<li class="thirditem">
    <a href="http://w3.org">Item #3</a>
</li>
<li>
    <span>Sub-list</span>
    <ul>
        <li><a href="http://yahoo.com">Item A</a></li>
        <li><a href="http://delicious.com">Item
            <span class="num letter">B</span></a></li>
        <li><a href="http://mozilla.org">Item C</a></li>
    </ul>
</li>
<li id="item4"><a href="http://getfirebug.com">Item #4</a></li>
<li><a href="http://wrox.com">Item
        <span class="num">#5</span></a></li>
</ul>
```

Admittedly, this isn't a very practical example. You could have just lead off with the filter selector as the query itself. The utility of `.filter()` becomes more apparent when you can chain it with other calls that modify results beyond what the initial `.query()` could have found, as you'll see with the `.map()` call in a little bit.

Next, take a look at what the following `.filter()` call will do with the markup in the previous example:

```
var items = dojo
    .query('a[href$=".org"]')
    .filter(function(el) {
        return dojo.hasClass(el.parentNode, 'dojolink');
    }, this);
```

Same as before, the results of the `.query()` come up with all the links on the page. The `.filter()` call in the chain then narrows the results to only those links whose parent list items' CSS classes include `'dojolink'`. Which, in the above HTML, is the following single result:

```
<ul id="ex1">
    <li><a href="http://decafbad.com">Item #1</a></li>
    <li class="seconditem dojolink">
        <a href="http://dojoproject.org">Item
```

```
                <span class="num">#2</span></a>
    </li>
    <li class="thirditem">
        <a href="http://w3.org">Item #3</a>
</li>
  <li>
    <span>Sub-list</span>
  <ul>
        <li><a href="http://yahoo.com">Item A</a></li>
        <li><a href="http://delicious.com">Item
            <span class="num letter">B</span></a></li>
     <li><a href="http://mozilla.org">Item C</a></li>
  </ul>
  </li>
  <li id="item4"><a href="http://getfirebug.com">Item #4</a></li>
  <li><a href="http://wrox.com">Item
      <span class="num">#5</span></a></li>
</ul>
```

Going further, here's something else that a .query() call can't do:

```
var items2 = dojo
    .query('a')
    .filter(function(el) {
        return (Math.random() > 0.5);
    }, this);
```

This code returns a random sample of all the links on the page, with a 50 percent chance of any particular item appearing in the list. Although this one is pretty silly, you can use practically any selection criteria you like in a .filter() call, adding just a little more complexity to your code.

But, speaking of complexity — if you find your situation requires a bit more, the .filter() method actually supplies two more parameters to your callback function:

```
var items3 = dojo
    .query('a[href$=".com"]')
    .filter(function(item, index, arr) {
        return index % 2;
    }, this);
```

This code returns every other link on the page with a URL that ends in .com, which demonstrates the full parameter set passed to the callback:

❑   item — the current DOM node being processed.

❑   index — the zero-based index of the current node in the list.

❑   arr — an array of all nodes considered by the .filter() call, such that the following is always true: arr[index] === item

Among other things, you can use the index and the full array provided to do things such as look ahead or behind the current position to make decisions on whether or not to include the current item.

Performing Subqueries with .query()

Another way to either narrow or expand `NodeList` results is with the `.query()` method, which performs a `dojo.query()` with each element in the `NodeList` as root and collects the results. Take a look at the following markup:

```
<div>
    <h2>Example HTML Code</h2>
    <ul id="ex2">
        <li class="foo bar baz"><strong>One</strong></li>
        <li>2
            <span>Sublist</span>
            <ul>
                <li>Alpha</li>
                <li>Beta</li>
            </ul>
        </li>
        <li>
            <span>Yet another sublist</span>
            <ul>
                <li>Foo</li>
                <li>Bar</li>
            </ul>
        </li>
        <li>
            <span>An ordered sublist</span>
            <ol>
                <li>One</li>
                <li>Two</li>
            </ol>
        </li>
    </ul>
</div>
```

Given the preceding HTML, consider this code:

```
var items = dojo.query('div > ul').query('ul > li');
```

This query returns all the `<li>` elements found in `<ul>` lists that are themselves members of lists.

The first `.query()` call finds `<ul>` elements that are direct children of `<div>` elements, of which there is one in this HTML.

Note that the second chained `.query()` operates upon each result found by the first, searching for `<li>` elements as children of `<ul>` elements. This second `.query()` does not include the results of the first, because each element of the original results was used as a base for a subquery and was not itself a part of that subquery's results.

The items in the NodeList at the end of the chain include the following highlighted items:

```
<div>
    <h2>Example HTML Code</h2>
    <ul id="ex2">
        <li class="foo bar baz"><strong>One</strong></li>
        <li>
            <span>Sublist</span>
            <ul>
                <li>Alpha</li>
                <li>Beta</li>
            </ul>
</li>
<li>
    <span>Yet another sublist</span>
    <ul>
        <li>Foo</li>
        <li>Bar</li>
    </ul>
</li>
<li>
    <span>An ordered sublist</span>
    <ol>
        <li>One</li>
        <li>Two</li>
    </ol>
  </li>
 </ul>
</div>
```

The items <li>One</li> and <li>Two</li> will not be returned, because they are in an <ol> ordered list, and the others were all in the required <ul> lists.

This is a very contrived example, but it's not one that a simple CSS selector might have gotten you. Also, keep in mind that .query() is just a method of NodeList — and that most methods of NodeList return further NodeLists. Thus, subqueries can appear just about anywhere in a NodeList call chain, and not just immediately after another .query().

This means that you can not only perform subqueries on the results of queries, but also on the results of lists produced by other list modifications in the rest of this chapter.

Transforming NodeLists with .map()

The .map() method offered by NodeList allows you to apply a callback function to each node in the list, the return value of which will replace that node in the NodeList returned after the .map() call. This allows you to perform a node-by-node transformation to the entire list.

Take a look again at the markup used to illustrate the `.filter()` method. Given that markup, consider what this will do:

```
var items = dojo
    .query('a[href$=".org"]')
    .map(function(el) {
        return el.parentNode;
    }, this);
```

The selector in the `dojo.query()` call was used earlier in the chapter — it finds all the links on the page with URLs that end in `.org`. What the chained `.map()` call does is replace each of those links with a reference to their respective `<li>` parent nodes.

With the example HTML, these are the items the code will find:

```
<ul id="ex1">
    <li><a href="http://decafbad.com">Item #1</a></li>
    <li class="seconditem dojolink">
        <a href="http://dojoproject.org">Item
            <span class="num">#2</span></a>
    </li>
    <li class="thirditem">
        <a href="http://w3.org">Item #3</a>
    </li>
    <li>
        <span>Sub-list</span>
        <ul>
            <li><a href="http://yahoo.com">Item A</a></li>
            <li><a href="http://delicious.com">Item
                <span class="num letter">B</span></a></li>
            <li><a href="http://mozilla.org">Item C</a></li>
        </ul>
    </li>
    <li id="item4"><a href="http://getfirebug.com">Item #4</a></li>
    <li><a href="http://wrox.com">Item
        <span class="num">#5</span></a></li>
</ul>
```

This transformation by callback function allows you to perform refinement on a selection of nodes from the document. You can examine any property of a node, perform complex lookups and comparisons for each, and do any number of other things not easily expressed in CSS.

Note that the `.map()` method also passes an index and the full array as parameters to your callback, just like `.filter()` does:

```
var items2 = dojo
    .query('a[href$=".org"]')
    .map(function(el, index, arr) {
        return (index % 2) ? el : el.parentNode;
    }, this);
```

This code maps a list of links into an alternating set of links and parent list items.

Combining NodeLists with .concat()

Whereas a `.filter()` call reduces the nodes in a list, the `.concat()` method allows you to add to it. Take a look at this HTML:

```
<ul id="ex3">
    <li class="foo bar baz"><strong>One</strong></li>
    <li class="bar baz"><em>Two</em></li>
    <li class="foo baz"><u>Three</u></li>
    <li class="baz"><small>Four</small></li>
    <li class="foo">Five</li>
</ul>
```

Think about the results of the following query chain, including a series of `.concat()` calls:

```
var items = dojo
    .query("strong")
    .concat(dojo.query("em"))
    .concat(dojo.query("u"))
    .concat(dojo.query("small"))
    .map(function (el) {
        return el.parentNode;
    });
```

Each `.concat()` call concatenates the results of the nested `dojo.query()` call onto the `NodeList`. The result, after the `.map()` transformation at the end, includes these highlighted nodes:

```
<ul id="ex3">
    <li class="foo bar baz"><strong>One</strong></li>
    <li class="bar baz"><em>Two</em></li>
    <li class="foo baz"><u>Three</u></li>
    <li class="baz"><small>Four</small></li>
    <li class="foo">Five</li>
</ul>
```

Using dojo.extend() to Enhance NodeLists

If you often find yourself combining NodeLists with .concat() or anything similar in your code, you may want to customize your Dojo environment to make things more elegant.

Rather than using .concat(dojo.query()) calls, the following code could serve you better:

```
dojo.extend(dojo.NodeList, {
    also: function(queryStr) {
        return this.concat(dojo.query(queryStr))
    }
});

var items2 = dojo
    .query("strong")
    .also("em")
    .also("u")
    .also("small")
    .map(function (el) {
        return el.parentNode;
    });
```

The call to dojo.extend() installs into dojo.NodeList a new method named .also (), which shortens the .concat(dojo.query()) call seen earlier.

Consider this as an extension point for the dojo.query() and NodeList system. It's a reminder of the language enhancements introduced in the previous chapter, and that those enhancements can themselves be turned back upon the Dojo toolkit to make your own improvements and customizations as needed.

Extracting Subsets of NodeLists with slice()

The .slice() method offered by NodeList allows you to specify exact start and end positions in the list to extract a subset. This can be useful in situations such as building a paginated window on a larger set of nodes. Returning to the HTML list presented in the discussion on .map(), consider what this code will do:

```
var items = dojo
    .query('a')
    .map(function(el) {
        return el.parentNode;
    }, this)
    .slice(1,4);
```

The parameters to `.slice()` are zero-based array indexes. The first indicates where to start including nodes and the second optional parameter specifies where to stop. The node at the index of the first parameter will be included, whereas the final index will not.

The previous example includes list items with the second through the fourth links found on the page, highlighted in the following example:

```html
<ul id="ex1">
    <li><a href="http://decafbad.com">Item #1</a></li>
    <li class="seconditem dojolink">
        <a href="http://dojoproject.org">Item
            <span class="num">#2</span></a>
    </li>
    <li class="thirditem">
        <a href="http://w3.org">Item #3</a>
    </li>
    <li>
        <span>Sub-list</span>
        <ul>
            <li><a href="http://yahoo.com">Item A</a></li>
            <li><a href="http://delicious.com">Item
                <span class="num letter">B</span></a></li>
            <li><a href="http://mozilla.org">Item C</a></li>
        </ul>
    </li>
    <li id="item4"><a href="http://getfirebug.com">Item #4</a></li>
    <li><a href="http://wrox.com">Item
        <span class="num">#5</span></a></li>
</ul>
```

Editing NodeLists in Place with splice()

The `.splice()` method available with `NodeList` can be used to edit a list in place and cut subsets of items out of lists entirely.

This method is a little different than the others. Although, `.splice()` returns a `NodeList` like other methods, it has side effects that leave the incoming `NodeList` modified as well. For example, consider this variation on the previous example with `.slice()`:

```javascript
var orig_items = dojo
    .query('a')
    .map(function(el) {
        return el.parentNode;
    }, this);

var sub_items = orig_items
    .splice(1,4);
```

The resulting list in sub_items at the end of this code looks just like the results of .slice(). However, whereas before the .splice() the list orig_items contained all list items with links, the contents of the list was altered by .splice() like so:

```
<ul id="ex1">
    <li><a href="http://decafbad.com">Item #1</a></li>
    <li class="seconditem dojolink">
        <a href="http://dojoproject.org">Item
            <span class="num">#2</span></a>
    </li>
    <li class="thirditem">
        <a href="http://w3.org">Item #3</a>
    <li>
        <span>Sub-list</span>
        <ul>
            <li><a href="http://yahoo.com">Item A</a></li>
            <li><a href="http://delicious.com">Item
                <span class="num letter">B</span></a></li>
            <li><a href="http://mozilla.org">Item C</a></li>
        </ul>
    </li>
    <li id="item4"><a href="http://getfirebug.com">Item #4</a></li>
    <li><a href="http://wrox.com">Item
        <span class="num">#5</span></a></li>
</ul>
```

In other words, whereas .slice() just extracts a copied subset of items, .splice() removes the subset of items from the original list entirely.

A call to .splice() also accepts a variable number of optional parameters after the start and end index parameters, the values of which will be inserted as replacements for the removed items. Check out this modified version of the earlier code:

```
var orig_items = dojo
    .query('a')
    .map(function(el) {
        return el.parentNode;
    }, this);

var replacements = dojo.query('span');

var sub_items = orig_items
    .splice(1, 4, replacements[0], replacements[1]);
```

This code will result in link items removed from the list, replaced by a pair of <span> elements:

```html
<ul id="ex3">
    <li><a href="http://decafbad.com">Item #1</a></li>
    <li class="seconditem dojolink">
        <a href="http://dojoproject.org">Item
            <span class="num">#2</span></a>
    </li>
    <li class="thirditem">
        <a href="http://w3.org">Item #3</a>
    <li>
        <span>Sub-list</span>
        <ul>
            <li><a href="http://yahoo.com">Item A</a></li>
            <li><a href="http://delicious.com">Item
                <span class="num letter">B</span></a></li>
            <li><a href="http://mozilla.org">Item C</a></li>
        </ul>
    </li>
    <li id="item4"><a href="http://getfirebug.com">Item #4</a></li>
    <li><a href="http://wrox.com">Item
        <span class="num">#5</span></a></li>
</ul>
```

Processing Lists of Nodes

Now that you've seen how to find, filter, refine, and transform lists of DOM nodes using the quasi-declarative syntax offered by dojo.query() and NodeList — it's time to explore what you can *do* with the nodes in these lists.

Applying Functions to Nodes with forEach

The most basic of methods made available for operating on NodeList contents is the .forEach() method. This method accepts a callback function and applies it to each of the nodes in the list. Take this code for example:

```javascript
dojo.query("a[href$='.org']")
    .forEach(function(el) {
        el.style.backgroundColor = "#8f8";
    });
```

The previous code finds every link with a URL that ends in .org and gives each a light green background color.

A second parameter is accepted by .forEach() — this defines the context in which the anonymous function will be called. Consider the following:

```javascript
dojo.declare("decafbad.exForEach", null, {

    the_color: "#f88",

    doTheThing: function() {
```

```
dojo.query('a')
    .map(function(el) {
        return el.parentNode;
    })
    .forEach(function(el) {
        el.style.backgroundColor = this.the_color;
    }, this);

}

});
var obj = new decafbad.exForEach();
obj.doTheThing();
```

In this code, a new class `decafbad.exForEach` is defined, which contains a data member named `the_color` and a method named `doTheThing()`.

In the implementation for `doTheThing()`, there's a `.forEach()` call with a callback function that needs to use the value of `the_color`. That's where the second parameter to `.forEach()` comes in — by passing the method's value for `this`, the anonymous function in `.forEach()` is called with the same scope context for `this`. If that parameter to `.forEach()` had been omitted, the anonymous function's value for `this` would have pointed at the browser's `window` object rather than the `exForEach` instance.

Note that this is also useful for passing a reference to an object method instead of an anonymous function like so:

```
dojo.declare("decafbad.exForEach2", null, {

    the_colors: [ "#f88", "#8f8" ],

    mapNode: function(el, index, arr) {
        return el.parentNode;
    },

    processNode: function(el, index, arr) {
        el.style.backgroundColor =
            this.the_colors[ (index % 2) ? 0 : 1 ];
    },

    doTheThing: function() {
        dojo.query('a', 'ex1')
            .map(this.mapNode, this)
            .forEach(this.processNode, this)
    }

});
var obj2 = new decafbad.exForEach2();
obj2.doTheThing();
```

In this example, the `processNode()` method does the work of processing nodes in the `.forEach()` call as a separate object method from `doTheThing()`. This is useful when you find yourself composing very similar callbacks as inline anonymous functions and see an opportunity to create a new shared method to handle all of those cases. You can see that the same thing is supported by the `.map()` method, as well.

Also notice that, thrown in as a bonus in this example, the `.forEach()` method passes the index and array parameters to your callback functions, just as `.filter()` and `.map()` do. The `processNode()` method of the class defined in the previous example refers to an array of colors, which it applies in an alternating fashion to the nodes.

One last interesting feature of `.forEach()` is that it also accepts a more concise snippet of code as a string rather than a function reference:

```
dojo.query("a:not([href$='.org'])")
    .forEach('item.style.backgroundColor="#ff8"');
```

This code finds all links with URLs that do *not* end in `.org`, and gives each a light yellow background color.

Since the desired action to perform was a simple one-liner, it's easy to pass code as a string to `.forEach()`. The `.forEach()` method then evaluates the code in a context offering the following pre-defined variables:

❑   `item`— The current DOM node being processed.

❑   `index`— The zero-based index of the current node in the list.

❑   `arr`— An array of all nodes considered by the `.forEach()` call, such that the following is always true: `arr[index] === item`

These pre-defined variables are essentially the same thing as the parameters passed to callback functions, but made available in a way that the code snippet can use.

Manipulating Node Styles with .style()

The `.forEach()` method allows you to do anything with a DOM node, though there are some specific tasks more commonly needed than others. For these, the `NodeList` class offers a few more shortcuts in the `.style()`, `.attr()`, and `.addContent()` methods.

Getting straight to a demonstration, consider this markup:

```
<ul id="ex4">
    <li><a href="http://decafbad.com">Link #1</a></li>
    <li><a href="http://dojoproject.org">Link #2</a></li>
    <li><a href="http://getfirebug.com">Link #3</a></li>
    <li><a href="http://delicious.com">Link #4</a></li>
    <li><a href="http://mozilla.org">Link #5</a></li>
    <li><a href="http://wrox.com">Link #6</a></li>
    <li><a href="http://w3.org">Link #7</a></li>
    <li id="mary">
        <span>Mary</span>
        <span>had</span>
```

```
        <span>a</span>
        <span>lamb</span>
    </li>
</ul>
```

The `.style()` method can be used to tweak CSS style properties:

```
dojo.query('a[href$=".org"]', 'ex4')
    .map(function(el) { return el.parentNode })
    .style('border', '2px solid #000');
```

This code finds all the links with URLs that end in .org and applies a border to their list item parents. As seen in the previous example, the `.style()` method takes two parameters:

❑   A CSS style property's name

❑   The value to set for the style

Manipulating Node Attributes with .attr()

The `.attr()` method can be used to change node attributes:

```
dojo.query('a[href$=".com"]', 'ex4')
    .attr('target', '_new');
```

In the previous code, all links with URLs that end in `.com` are set to open in a new window. Just like the `.style()` method, `.attr()` accepts two parameters:

❑   An attribute name

❑   The attribute value

Adding Node Content with .addContent()

A little more complex and interesting is the `.addContent()` method. You can use this method to inject new content into the DOM:

```
dojo.query('a[href^="http://de"]', 'ex4')
    .addContent(' [New!] ', 'after');
```

This code finds all links with URLs that start with "`http://de`" and inserts [New!] after each, as a child of the parent list item. The `.addContent()` method accepts two parameters:

The content to insert

The position at which to insert the content

Both of these parameters have some interesting features to them:

```
var img = document.createElement('img');
```

```
img.src = 'http://decafbad.com/images/globe.jpg';

dojo.query('a[href^="http://de"]', 'ex4')
    .addContent(img, 'first');
```

The `.addContent()` method accepts either raw HTML content in a string or preconstructed DOM nodes as content for insertion. Demonstrating this, the previous code creates a new image element and supplies that as the content for the `.addContent()` call.

As for the second parameter, the value "`first`" causes the content to be inserted as first child of the selected element. Several named values are supported for this parameter:

❑   `before`— Inserts before the selected node, as a child of the parent node

❑   `after`— Inserts after the selected node, as a child of the parent node

❑   `last` or `end`— Inserts as the last child of the selected node

❑   `first` or `start`— Inserts as the first child of the selected node

This parameter can also be a numeric index, counting through the child nodes in the selected node:

```
dojo.query('li#mary', 'ex4')
    .addContent('<span>little</span> ', 6);
```

Note that though there were only four `<span>` elements making up "Mary had a lamb" in the markup, the list of child nodes for an element includes text nodes and, thus, the index counts those as well.

Figure 24-1 shows the results of the code samples exercising the `.style()`, `.attr()`, and `.addContent()` methods.

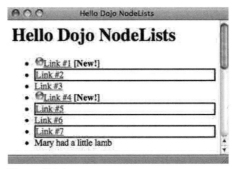

Figure 24-1

Manipulating CSS Classes with .addClass() and .removeClass()

Some of the examples shown earlier manipulated style properties on elements directly, which is really something you should do sparingly (if at all) in a non-trivial web application. Instead, such styles should be declared separately in CSS with class-based selectors. Then, class names on elements can be manipulated to choose which pre-defined styles are applied. This offers more of a loose coupling between markup, style, and behavior.

The .addClass() and .removeClass() methods get specific in facilitating the arrangement outlined earlier. To demonstrate, check out this markup:

```
<style type="text/css">
    .foo       { list-style-type: none }
    .baz       { font-family: monospace; font-weight: bold; font-size: 200% }
    .warning   { background-color: #ffc; border: 3px solid #000;  }
    .selected  { background-color: #cfc; border: 3px dotted #000; }
</style>

<ul id="ex3">
    <li class="foo bar baz"><strong>One</strong></li>
    <li class="bar baz"><em>Two</em></li>
    <li class="foo baz"><u>Three</u></li>
    <li class="baz"><small>Four</small></li>
    <li class="foo">Five</li>
</ul>
```

And now, consider this code as applied to the previous code:

```
var list_kids = dojo.query('li > *', 'ex3');

list_kids
    .filter(function(el) { return /^T/.test(el.innerHTML); })
    .map(function(el) { return el.parentNode; })
    .addClass('warning');

list_kids
    .filter(function(el) { return /^F/.test(el.innerHTML); })
    .map (function(el) { return el.parentNode; })
    .addClass('selected');
```

First, a dojo.query() call scoops up all the first child nodes of list items under <ul id="ex3"> and stashes the results in an intermediate variable list_kids. Next, all the list items whose first child's contents begins with the letter "T" are given the CSS class "warning". Then, the CSS class "selected" is added to those whose contents start with the letter "F".

Figure 24-2 shows what this looks like in a browser. Notice that, perhaps surprisingly, the list item reading "Five" did not get the 'selected' class added — thus the lack of a dotted border or any background color. This is because the selector 'li > *' matches child element nodes, and not text nodes. This is just a small "gotcha" to stay aware of.

Also notice that .addClass() properly *added* the class without disturbing the others — this is apparent in the trio of list items with class "foo", which have hidden list bullets thanks to the style property declaration "list-style-type: none" under the ".foo" selector.

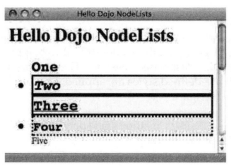

Figure 24-2

Finally, consider that all the above applies to .removeClass(), which is simply the inverse of .addClass(). For example, here's code that removes the class "baz" on every list item of class "bar":

```
dojo.query('li.bar', 'ex3').removeClass('baz');
```

Look at Figure 24-3 and note that the first two items, which were marked up with both classes "bar" and "baz", are no longer covered by "baz" — their respective contents are no longer monospaced or large.

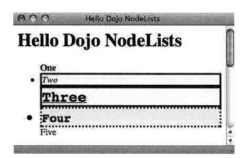

Figure 24-3

Repositioning Nodes in the DOM

So far, all of these methods for processing nodes have focused on attribute and styling changes, largely leaving the DOM structure unmodified. But beyond those simple in-place tweaks, the NodeList methods .orphan(), .adopt(), and .place() provide the means to remove, move, and insert nodes in the DOM structure, respectively. Combined with all the means for working with lists presented so far, these can offer some very powerful sweeping changes to a document in a minimum of code.

Take a look at this markup sample:

```
<ul id="ex5">
    <li>
        <h2>.com links</h2>
        <ul id="dotcom"></ul>
    </li>
    <li>
        <h2>.org links</h2>
        <ul id="dotorg"></ul>
    </li>
    <li><a href="http://decafbad.com"><span>Link #1</span></a></li>
    <li><a href="http://dojoproject.org"><span>Link #2</span></a></li>
    <li><a href="http://getfirebug.com"><span>Link #3</span></a></li>
    <li><a href="http://delicious.com"><span>Link #4</span></a></li>
    <li><a href="http://mozilla.org"><span>Link #5</span></a></li>
    <li><a href="http://wrox.com"><span>Link #6</span></a></li>
    <li><a href="http://w3.org"><span>Link #7</span></a></li>
</ul>
```

Now, consider this demonstration of the `.orphan()` method:

```
var dot_orgs = dojo.query('a[href$=".org"]', 'ex5')
    .map(function(el) { return el.parentNode; })
    .orphan();
```

The `.orphan()` method used in the previous example "plucks out" all list items containing links ending in `.org` from the document, but leaves the now-orphaned nodes in a list in the `dot_orgs` variable:

```
<ul id="ex5">
    <li>
        <h2>.com links</h2>
        <ul id="dotcom"></ul>
    </li>
    <li>
        <h2>.org links</h2>
        <ul id="dotorg"></ul>
    </li>
    <li><a href="http://decafbad.com"><span>Link #1</span></a></li>
    <li><a href="http://dojoproject.org"><span>Link #2</span></a></li>
    <li><a href="http://getfirebug.com"><span>Link #3</span></a></li>
    <li><a href="http://delicious.com"><span>Link #4</span></a></li>
    <li><a href="http://mozilla.org"><span>Link #5</span></a></li>
    <li><a href="http://wrox.com"><span>Link #6</span></a></li>
    <li><a href="http://w3.org"><span>Link #7</span></a></li>
</ul>
```

With the orphaned nodes in `dot_orgs`, you can find them a home with the `.adopt()` method like so:

```
dojo.query('#dotorg').adopt(dot_orgs);
```

This code inserts all the orphaned nodes into the list with an ID of "dotorg", resulting in a document structure like the following:

```
<ul id="ex5">
    <li>
        <h2>.com links</h2>
        <ul id="dotcom"></ul>
    </li>
    <li>
        <h2>.org links</h2>
        <ul id="dotorg">
            <li><a href="http://dojoproject.org"><span>Link #2</span></a></li>
            <li><a href="http://mozilla.org"><span>Link #5</span></a></li>
            <li><a href="http://w3.org"><span>Link #7</span></a></li>
        </ul>
    </li>
<li><a href="http://decafbad.com"><span>Link #1</span></a></li>
<li><a href="http://getfirebug.com"><span>Link #3</span></a></li>
<li><a href="http://delicious.com"><span>Link #4</span></a></li>
<li><a href="http://wrox.com"><span>Link #6</span></a></li>
</ul>
```

Finally, consider this call to .place(), which is basically the inverse of the .adopt() method in the previous example:

```
dojo.query('a[href$=".com"]', 'ex5')
    .map(function(el) { return el.parentNode; })
    .place('#dotcom');
```

This call moves all list items containing .com links into the list with the ID 'dotcom', leaving the following document structure as an end result:

```
<ul id="ex5">
    <li>
        <h2>.com links</h2>
        <ul id="dotcom">
            <li><a href="http://decafbad.com"><span>Link #1</span></a></li>
            <li><a href="http://getfirebug.com"><span>Link #3</span></a></li>
            <li><a href="http://delicious.com"><span>Link #4</span></a></li>
            <li><a href="http://wrox.com"><span>Link #6</span></a></li>
        </ul>
    </li>
    <li>
        <h2>.org links</h2>
        <ul id="dotorg">
            <li><a href="http://dojoproject.org"><span>Link #2</span></a></li>
            <li><a href="http://mozilla.org"><span>Link #5</span></a></li>
            <li><a href="http://w3.org"><span>Link #7</span></a></li>
        </ul>
    </li>
</ul>
```

It's also worth noting that both `.place()` and `.adopt()` accept as an optional second parameter the same positional argument as the `.addContent()` method. This includes the named values `after`, `before`, `first`, and `last` as well as numeric index positions. For example:

```
dojo.query('ul#ex5 > li:first-child')
    .place('ul#ex5 > li:last-child', 'after');
```

This code will swap the lists of .com and .org links in the markup above. And, as for the `.adopt()` method, try this example:

```
var node = dojo.query('ul#ex5 > li:last-child').orphan();
dojo.query('ul#ex5').adopt(node, 'first');
```

The code above will reverse the previous example, moving the last of the two lists into the position of first child.

Using Other Array Methods with NodeLists

There is a handful of other array methods supported by `NodeList` that this chapter will not give an in-depth treatment. These include things like the following:

❑   `.indexOf()` — Finds the first numeric index of a given node

❑   `.lastIndexOf()` — Finds the last numeric index of a given node

❑   `.every()` — Applies a callback function to each node in the list and return whether that function returned true for every node

❑   `.some()` — Applies a callback function to each node in the list and return whether that function returned true for some nodes

❑   `.coords()` — Returns the on-page coordinates for each node

As always, your best bet for finding documentation on these and potentially more methods not covered here is in the official Dojo API documentation:

```
http://dojotoolkit.org/docs/api
```

Summary

This chapter gave you a working tour of the DOM manipulation methods offered by Dojo, including the ability to easily find elements with `dojo.query()` and then refine lists and act upon them with the chainable methods offered by `dojo.NodeList` to alter and restructure the contents of a page.

In the next chapter, you'll see the variety of tools Dojo gives you to wire up a page with handlers to react to user interaction.

25

Handling Events

Up to this point, you've seen how to find elements in the document object model with `dojo.query()`, refine and filter lists of nodes with the methods of `NodeList`, as well as make batch changes to the content and structure of the DOM. However, these things have all been largely autonomous and instantaneous with no input from a user.

While useful, these things don't make up the whole picture in building a responsive user interface. At its base, the Dojo event system provides flexible and cross-browser means to connect to user input and actions that trigger DOM events from button and link clicks, other mouse gestures, and keyboard activity.

However, Dojo builds upon this native foundation and offers further abstraction and flexibility by allowing you to connect handlers not only to DOM events, but also to other handlers and object methods. This allows you to build complex yet loosely coupled reactions to input and happenings in your application. Dojo also provides a broadcast messaging system involving publishers and subscribers to loosen coupling even further.

And, to assist in constructing the patterns of handlers needed in a user interface, Dojo offers additional `NodeList` methods to bring handler connections into the realm of chained `dojo.query()` calls discussed in the previous chapter. Alongside these, Dojo also offers a "behavior" facility that allows you to map out events and handlers in a declarative fashion akin to CSS style sheets.

In this chapter, you'll learn about:

- ❑ Reacting to page load and unload
- ❑ Connecting to DOM events
- ❑ Connecting to methods
- ❑ Publishing and subscribing

Reacting to Page Load and Unload

Reacting to the successful load and unload of a page are two basic event hooks that are the most convenient in setting up and tearing down a user interface. Dojo offers two methods to allow registration of handlers on these events, named `dojo.addOnLoad()` and `dojo.addOnUnload()`, used like so:

```
dojo.addOnLoad(function() {
    console.log("** Inline onload handler fired!");
});

dojo.addOnUnload(function() {
    alert("** Inline onunload handler fired!");
});
```

If you haven't already done so, now would be a good time to install Firebug (`http://getfirebug .com`) — or for all other browsers, ensure that `isDebug` is set to true in your `djConfig`. This will ensure that you see the output of these `console.log()` statements, which will be used throughout this chapter to illustrate some of the less visible aspects of Dojo's event handling.

Each of the inline anonymous functions in the code above will be called when the page loads up and is navigated away from, respectively. Using `console.log()` in the page load handler will cause a message to appear either in your Firebug log, or in the on-page debug log supplied by the version of Firebug Lite that comes with Dojo.

The page unload handler opts for an `alert()`, because it temporarily interrupts the transition to the next page — a `console.log()` statement's output would be lost before you could see it as the browser loads the next page. Once you understand how this works, you may want to comment out this `alert()`, mainly because it makes each page reload a bit tedious as you play with the code.

Another way to register handlers for page load and unload is to use object methods like this:

```
dojo.declare('decafbad.eventsanim.events.pageHandlers', null, {
    handleOnLoad: function() {
        // this == handlers
        console.log("** Object onload handler fired!");
    },
    handleOnUnload: function() {
        // this == handlers
        //alert("** Object onunload handler fired!");
        console.log("** Object onunload handler fired!");
    }
});
var handlers = new decafbad.eventsanim.events.pageHandlers();

dojo.addOnLoad(handlers, 'handleOnLoad');
dojo.addOnUnload(handlers, 'handleOnUnload');
```

Note that in this case, the context for `this` within these functions is automatically set to a reference to `handlers`, thus keeping them in their original object context.

> ### The window.onload Problem
>
> Something very interesting about `dojo.addOnLoad()` is that it fires registered handlers after the successful load of the DOM, Dojo, and its initial batch of `dojo.require()` statements — but before all the CSS and images included on the page have loaded in.
>
> This is important, because a simple `window.onload` handler fires after every referenced asset on the page has arrived.
>
> The distinction is useful, because it allows you to get page initialization done earlier. Widgets can be constructed, events wired up, and page changes applied before more visual styling takes effect — thus hopefully preempting any confusing flashes of content or other ugly intermediate setup artifacts that appear while long-loading images roll in.
>
> The other thing worth reinforcing is that `dojo.addOnLoad()` fires after Dojo has loaded.
>
> This is important because Dojo may still be finishing up some loading tasks even after the native window.onload event has fired. Dojo may still be working on resolving a few last remaining `dojo.require()` statements, or any number of other things. For this reason `dojo.addOnLoad()` is really a replacement for `window.onload` in the Dojo context.

Connecting to DOM Events

Conceptually, Dojo solves the problem of responding to user interface events with connections and subscriptions. This distinction is important because, as you'll soon see, both connections and subscriptions can apply to happenings outside the realm of just DOM events.

To prepare for some demonstrations, take a look at the following markup, which offers some CSS and HTML for use by the event handlers coming up:

```css
<style type="text/css">
    #ex1 .clickme {
        padding: 0.5em; margin: 0.5em;
        display: block; background-color: #ddf;
        border: 2px dashed #fff;
        color: #000;
    }
    #ex1 .clickcolor {
        background-color: #dfd;
        border: 2px dashed #000;
    }
</style>

<div id="ex1">
    <a id="link1" class="clickme color0" href="#">Click me!</a>
    <a id="link2" class="clickme color0" href="#">Click me!</a>
    <a id="link3" class="clickme color0" href="#">Click me!</a>
    <a id="link4" class="clickme color0" href="#">Click me!</a>
    <a id="link5" class="clickme color0" href="#">Click me!</a>
</div>
```

Figure 25-1 shows what this will look like in a browser before any event handlers are introduced.

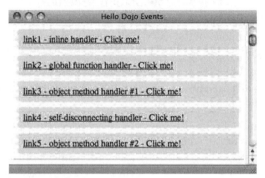

Figure 25-1

Connecting Inline Handlers to Events

To connect some code up to the first link, consider this code example:

```
dojo.connect(dojo.byId('link1'), 'click', function(ev) {
    dojo.stopEvent(ev);
    dojo.toggleClass(ev.target, 'clickcolor');
    // this == ev.target
    console.log(this);
    console.log('Clicked link #1');
});
```

In the preceding example, you see a call to `dojo.connect()`, which is at the heart of Dojo DOM event handling. Its first parameter is a reference to a DOM node, acquired here by way of an inline call to `dojo.byId('link1')`. Next there's the name of a DOM event, "`click`," which captures any clicks on the link.

Finally, there's an inline anonymous callback function that handles any clicks on the link. In this function, there's a call to `dojo.stopEvent(ev)` — this is a shortcut that calls both `ev.preventDefault()` and `ev.stopPropagation()`, which in turn will respectively stop the default action of the DOM event (that is, navigate away from the page) and stop event propagation to any other DOM nodes with handlers listening for this event.

The rest of handler is simple: A call to `dojo.toggleClass()` causes the "`clickcolor`" CSS class to be alternately added and removed with each click, and a couple of messages are sent to the log. One of these will report the current context of the variable `this` for the function, which in this case is equal to the element target of the event. Figure 25-2 shows what things should look like after the handler is connected and the first link is clicked.

Figure 25-2

Connecting Global Functions to Events

Next, here's a slight tweak in evolution to the previous code:

```
function clickFunc(ev) {
    dojo.stopEvent(ev);
    dojo.toggleClass(ev.target, 'clickcolor');
    // this == ev.target
    console.log(this);
    console.log(ev);
}

var link2 = dojo.byId('link2');
dojo.connect(link2, 'click', clickFunc);
```

This event handler setup is identical to the previous one. The only difference is that the handler function connected to the event is a globally declared function rather than one defined inline. The functionality and the context for this are the same.

The advantage of this form of dojo.connect() over the previous one is that it allows you to define a handler that's reusable for connection to many nodes' events. Figure 25-3 shows the effect of this second handler connected to its respective link.

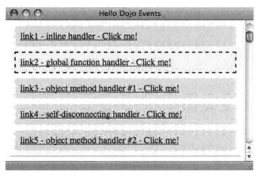

Figure 25-3

Connecting Object Methods to Events

Moving further down the road to reusability, take a look at this code:

```
dojo.declare('decafbad.eventsanim.events.connectHandlers', null, {
    color_toggle: 'clickcolor',

    clickMethod: function(ev) {
        dojo.stopEvent(ev);
        // this == handlers
        dojo.toggleClass(ev.target, this.color_toggle);
        console.log(this);
        console.log(ev);
    }
});
var handlers = new decafbad.eventsanim.events.connectHandlers();

var link3 = dojo.byId('link3');
dojo.connect(link3, 'click', handlers, 'clickMethod');
```

Here, an object containing handlers is created, which has a single property `color_toggle` and a single method `clickMethod`. And, in the `dojo.connect()` statement, the third parameter changes into two: a reference to the object, and the name of the handler method to which the event should be connected.

The big difference here is that, within the `clickMethod` handler, the context of this has changed to point to `handlers`, the object to which the handler method belongs. Therefore, it is able to access the object's `color_toggle` property. This third handler appears to accomplish the same as the previous two, as shown in Figure 25-4.

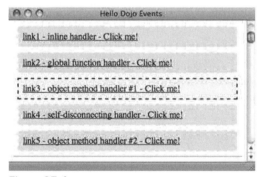

Figure 25-4

Disconnecting from Events

Finally, note that `dojo.connect()` is paired with a method named `dojo.disconnect()` — the return value from a `dojo.connect()` method returns a handle you can use with `dojo.disconnect()` to cancel the event connection like so:

```
var conn1 = dojo.connect(dojo.byId('link4'), 'click',
    function(ev) {
        dojo.stopEvent(ev);
        dojo.toggleClass(ev.target, 'clickcolor');
        console.log("This connection will now self-destruct");
        dojo.disconnect(conn1);
    });
```

This code offers a bit of self-reference, in that the function declared inline as the handler to the `click` event is a closure that has access to the `conn1` variable. The value of the `conn1` variable is defined at the time of event connection. Thus, from within the handler, it can disconnect itself from the DOM event that triggered it.

Figure 25-5 shows that this latest handler does the same as the last three. The thing you can't see in the Figure, however, is that once you've clicked this link, the handler disconnects — and, thus, subsequent clicks will not further toggle the styling.

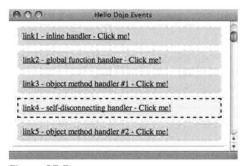

Figure 25-5

Special Event Handling and Event Objects

Dojo supports all the DOM events offered by the browser for use with `dojo.connect()`, which vary a bit between browsers — but there is a common normalized set that's included in the following table:

Event	Purpose
click	Generates when the user clicks the mouse button
keydown	Generates when the user starts holding down a key
keypress	Generates when the user presses a key, down and up
keyup	Generates when the user releases a key that was held
mousedown	Generates when the user starts holding the mouse button
mouseenter	Generates when the user moves the mouse into the bounds of an element on the page
mouseleave	Generates when the user moves the mouse out of the bounds of an element on the page
mousemove	Generates when the user moves the mouse inside an element on the page
mouseup	Generates when the user releases the mouse button

Certainly, there are more DOM events available. However, the preceding table is a useful list and is used throughout the rest of the chapter. You can find more details on events available in various browsers at these pages:

❑   http://en.wikipedia.org/wiki/DOM_Events

❑   http://developer.mozilla.org/en/docs/DOM:event

❑   http://msdn2.microsoft.com/en-us/library/ms533022.aspx

❑   www.w3.org/TR/DOM-Level-2-Events/

There are several notable things about Dojo's handling of these events and their names:

❑   The prefix 'on' in event names is optional, and will be added or removed by Dojo as needed.

❑   Some events, notably 'keypress', get special cross-browser treatment to normalize behavior.

❑   Efforts are made to account for and clean up notable memory leaks in browsers such as Internet Explorer.

The other important thing is that event handlers are given a cross-browser event object bearing the normalized properties and methods in the following table:

Normalized Property / Method	Purpose
target	Element that generated the event
currentTarget	Element with handler that is responding to the event
layerX	The mouse x coordinate, relative to currentTarget
layerY	The mouse y coordinate, relative to currentTarget
pageX	The mouse x coordinate, relative to the viewport
pageY	The mouse y coordinate, relative to the viewport
relatedTarget	The object the mouse has just moved in or out of for mouseout and mouseover, respectively
charCode	The character code of the keypress detected
preventDefault()	Method that stops the element's default handling of the event
stopPropagation()	Method that stops the propagation of the event to parent node

There are other properties available that the Dojo event object passed to handlers. They're composed of the unmodified properties from the browser's native DOM Event object. The following table includes a small subset of additional properties that are somewhat reliable across browsers:

Non-Normalized Property	Purpose
type	Indicates the type of event fired (such as "click")
ctrlKey	Indicates whether the control modifier key was pressed
shiftKey	Indicates whether the shift modifier key was pressed
altKey	Indicates whether the alt modifier key was pressed
metaKey	Indicates whether the meta modifier key was pressed (i.e. command key on Mac OS X machines)
button	Indicates which mouse button was detected
keyCode	Indicates the unicode value of a noncharacter key in a keyboard event

Connecting to Methods

Now that you've seen how Dojo supports simple connections between DOM events and handler callbacks, it's time to introduce another form of `dojo.connect()` — connecting callback handlers to generic object methods. Take a look at the following code example:

```
dojo.connect(handlers, 'clickMethod', function(ev) {
    // this == handlers
    console.log(this);
    console.log("Hey, me too!  I'm anonymous!");
});
```

Remember the handlers object defined earlier, bearing a method named `clickMethod()`? Well, this code attaches another handler onto *that* handler. Thus, whenever `handlers.clickMethod()` is called, the function in the preceding example gets called right after it.

This useful because `clickMethod` can be connected to multiple DOM methods like so:

```
dojo.connect(dojo.byId('link3'), 'click', handlers, 'clickMethod');
dojo.connect(dojo.byId('link5'), 'click', handlers, 'clickMethod');
```

In this case, when either `link3` or `link5` is clicked, both `clickMethod` *and* the inline callback defined in the preceding code will fire. Since the connection is made to the method rather than to a DOM event, all DOM event connections — or even direct method calls — that fire the method will also fire the additional attached handler.

Following the form for connecting to DOM events, `dojo.connect()` can be used with both global functions and further object methods like so:

```
function clickMeTooFunc(ev) {
    // this == handlers
    console.log(this);
    console.log("Hey, me too!  I'm a function!");
}
dojo.connect(handlers, 'clickMethod', clickMeTooFunc);

dojo.extend(decafbad.eventsanim.events.connectHandlers, {
    clickMeTooMethod: function(ev) {
        // this == handlers
        console.log(this);
        console.log("Hey, me too!  I'm a method!");
    }
});
dojo.connect(handlers, 'clickMethod', handlers, 'clickMeTooMethod');
```

In the preceding code, both a global function and a newly defined object method are connected to an existing handler method. Just as more than one handler can be connected to the same element's DOM event, more than one handler can be connected to the same method, all firing in the order of connection.

In fact, if you have Firebug installed or `djConfig.isDebug` enabled — and you really should have one or the other or both — trying the code in the previous example will produce a series of log messages like the following if you click either `link3` or `link5`:

```
Object color_toggle=clickcolor
click clientX=170, clientY=254
Object color_toggle=clickcolor
Hey, me too! I'm anonymous!
Object color_toggle=clickcolor
Hey, me too! I'm a function!
Object color_toggle=clickcolor
Hey, me too! I'm a method!
```

Notice that the `handlers` object was the context for `this` in all of the connections to the `handlers.clickMethod()` method.

This ability to connect to handlers, as well as DOM events, offers a lot of flexibility in post hoc extension and augmentation with a minimum of pre-planned coordination. You can find widgets and handlers already registered in multiple places across the page and simply hook onto them, minimizing the number of connections needed and without needing the pre-approval of the code to which you're connecting. Figure 25-6 shows this final link as wired up for a second application of the object method handlers.

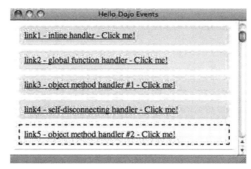

Figure 25-6

Making Connections with NodeLists

Once you start making a lot of `dojo.connect()` calls with `dojo.byId()` calls, things start to look less and less elegant as they did back when you were locating DOM nodes with native navigation methods. Using `dojo.query()` and `NodeList` methods helped clean things up there — and as it turns out, they can help clean things up for event connections as well.

To set the stage for the coming demonstration, consider this HTML:

```
<style type="text/css">
    .canvas {
        padding: 1em; margin: 1em;
        width: 100px; height: 100px;
        background-color: #ddf;
        border: 2px dashed #fff;
        float: left;
    }
    .entered, .selected {
        background-color: #dfd;
        border: 2px dashed #000;
    }
</style>

<form id="coord_canvas">

    <label for="coord_x">x:</label>
    <input name="coord_x" id="coord_x" type="text" size="5" />
    <label for="coord_y">y:</label>
    <input name="coord_y" id="coord_y" type="text" size="5" />
    <label for="status">status:</label>
    <input name="status" id="status" type="text" size="35" />

    <br />

    <div id="c1" class="canvas"> </div>
    <div id="c2" class="canvas"> </div>
```

```
          <div id="c3" class="canvas"> </div>
          <div id="c4" class="canvas"> </div>

          <br style="clear: both" />

    </form>
```

The markup in the preceding code is shown in Figure 25-7. It's a simple layout consisting of a few form fields and a set of small squares. This demonstration wires up the squares with a set of mouse event handlers and updates the form fields with properties of the events handled.

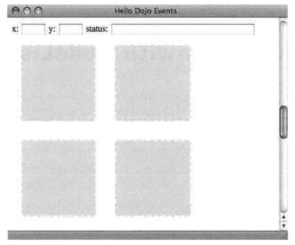

Figure 25-7

Now, take a look at the following code:

```
var canvases = dojo.query('#coord_canvas .canvas');

canvases
    .onmousemove(function(ev) {
        dojo.byId('coord_x').value = ev.pageX;
        dojo.byId('coord_y').value = ev.pageY;
    })
    .onclick(function(ev) {
        var el = ev.target;
        // this == el
        dojo.byId('status').value =
            'Mouse clicked '+el.id+' at '+ev.pageX+' x '+ev.pageY;
    });
```

Using dojo.query(), the code finds all the elements with a class of "canvas", which encompass the squares to which event handlers need to be connected.

The NodeList class offers a number of helpers that employ partially applied dojo.connect() calls to each element in the list. In particular, two used here are .onmousemove() and .onclick(). The first handles the mouse moving across one of the squares by updating the coord_x and coord_y text fields with the event's reported coordinates. The second handles clicks in the squares with a message update in the status field.

This short bit of code replaces a series of dojo.byId() and dojo.connect() pairs. Using the NodeList helpers, you can cleanly declare the connection of event handlers to dojo.query() results and keep things short and sweet.

Event connection helper methods offered by NodeList include the following:

- ❏   connect(event, func or object[, method name])
- ❏   onclick(func or object[, method name])
- ❏   onmousedown(func or object[, method name])
- ❏   onmouseenter(func or object[, method name])
- ❏   onmouseleave(func or object[, method name])
- ❏   onmousemove(func or object[, method name])
- ❏   onmouseup(func or object[, method name])
- ❏   onkeydown(func or object[, method name])
- ❏   onkeypress(func or object[, method name])
- ❏   onkeyup(func or object[, method name])

As you can see, the pattern for these helper methods is fairly predictable.

The first one, .connect(), works like dojo.connect() except the first parameter is shifted off to be filled in with each node in the list by Dojo.

The rest of the methods shift off the second parameter as well, since the event name is derived from the name of the helper method itself.

The final two parameters to each of these can be either a handler callback function or an object and the name of a method to use as the callback.

This last bit of code demonstrates the use of .onmouseenter() and .onmouseleave() with handlers belonging to an object:

```
dojo.declare('decafbad.eventsanim.events.nodelistHandlers', null, {

    highlight_class: 'entered',

    handleOnMouseEnter: function(ev) {
        var el = ev.target;
        // this == handlers
```

```
        dojo.addClass(el, this.highlight_class);
        dojo.byId('status').value = 'Mouse entered '+el.id;
    },

    handleOnMouseLeave: function(ev) {
        var el = ev.target;
        // this == handlers
        dojo.removeClass(el, this.highlight_class);
        dojo.byId('status').value = 'Mouse left '+el.id;
    }

});
var handlers = new decafbad.eventsanim.events.nodelistHandlers();

canvases
    .onmouseenter(handlers, 'handleOnMouseEnter')
    .onmouseleave(handlers, 'handleOnMouseLeave');
```

This code wires up every square in the markup with events that track when the mouse enters and leaves the element, adding or removing a highlight class as appropriate and updating the status text field. You can see a snapshot of this all in action in Figure 25-8.

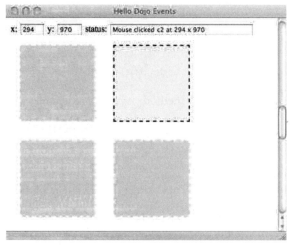

Figure 25-8

Publishing and Subscribing to Event Topics

As shown earlier in the chapter, connecting methods to methods offers a degree of post hoc extension and loose coordination. Additionally, Dojo provides a generic event publish/subscribe facility that offers an even more powerful mechanism in the form of the dojo.publish(), dojo.subscribe(), and dojo.unsubscribe() methods.

Using Event Topics with DOM Event Handlers

Getting right into a demonstration, consider the following markup:

```
<style type="text/css">
    .canvas {
        padding: 1em; margin: 1em;
        width: 100px; height: 100px;
        background-color: #bbf;
        float: left;
    }
    .entered, .selected {
        background-color: #bfb;
    }
</style>

<form id="broadcaster">

    <label for="source">select:</label>
    <select name="source" id="source">
        <option value="none">None</option>
        <option value="sel1">Square 1</option>
        <option value="sel2">Square 2</option>
        <option value="sel3">Square 3</option>
        <option value="sel4">Square 4</option>
    </select>

    <label for="source_status">status:</label>
    <input name="source_status" id="source_status" type="text" size="35" />


    <br />

    <div id="sel1" class="canvas"> </div>
    <div id="sel2" class="canvas"> </div>
    <div id="sel3" class="canvas"> </div>
    <div id="sel4" class="canvas"> </div>

    <br style="clear: both" />

</form>
```

As shown in Figure 25-9, this HTML consists of a drop-down selection box with options corresponding to the IDs belonging to a set of boxes on the page.

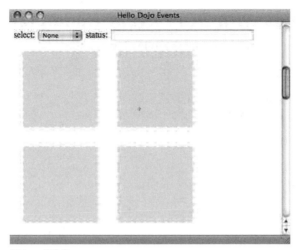

Figure 25-9

The following code connects a handler to the selection box change event that will broadcast a message about any selection value changes:

```
var select_topic = '/decafbad/eventsanim/squareselected';

dojo.connect(dojo.byId('source'), 'change', function(ev) {
    var el  = ev.target;
    var idx = el.selectedIndex;
    var val = el.options[idx].value;
    console.log("Announcing selection of " + val);
    dojo.publish(select_topic, [ val ]);
});
```

The first thing to do is to establish a shared *event topic* — an arbitrary string identifying a custom event that can fire on the page. All event publishers and subscribers pivot on this shared string constant: Publishers send messages using it, and subscribers register interest using it.

Next, a dojo.connect() connects a handler to the change event for the drop-down selection box. This handler figures out what option was selected and then uses dojo.publish() and the established event topic to broadcast a message indicating the value selected. Note that the contents of the message, as second parameter to dojo.publish(), is an array.

Now, to respond to messages published by the aforementioned, take a look at this:

```
dojo.subscribe(select_topic, function(sel_id) {
    console.log("Selection changed to " + sel_id);
    dojo.byId('source_status').value =
        "Selected changed to " + sel_id;
});
```

This code subscribes an inline function callback to the event topic published whenever the drop-down selection is changed. Notice that the array sent out with `dojo.publish()` is converted into parameters to the subscribing function — if the array had been two or more elements, the subscribing callback could have expected two or more parameters.

Inside this callback, the received selection is sent to the log, and the value of the text field `source_status` is updated with a message reporting the current selection.

That was easy — now it's time for a bit more complexity:

```
function respondToSelection(el_id, sel_id) {
    var el = dojo.byId(el_id);
    if (el_id == sel_id) {
        console.log("Selecting " + el_id);
        dojo.addClass(el, 'selected');
    } else {
        console.log("Deselecting " + el_id);
        dojo.removeClass(el, 'selected');
    }
}

dojo.forEach([ 'sel1', 'sel2', 'sel3', 'sel4' ], function(el_id) {
    dojo.subscribe(select_topic, function(sel_id) {
        respondToSelection(el_id, sel_id);
    });
});
```

The function `respondToSelection()` is defined in the preceding code. It expects an element ID and a selection ID as parameters. The function grabs the identified element, compares its ID with the selection ID, and then adjusts the 'selected' class on the element as appropriate.

After this, there's a `dojo.forEach()` call iterating over the known IDs for selectable squares. For each square, it creates a new subscribed handler that responds to the selection box event topic. Since the inline function here is a closure, it has access to the `el_id` parameter from `dojo.forEach()`. And, since the first parameter of the callback handler expects the selection ID, these are all the parameters needed for the `respondToSelection()` call fired off in the handler.

Putting it all together, a number of things happen when the selection is changed and the resulting message is published. Figure 25-10 shows the effect of selecting a box.

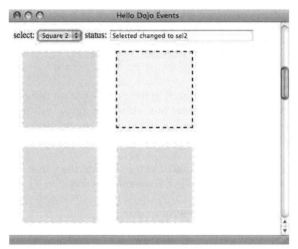

Figure 25-10

Along with the visible user interface changes, you should see a transcript like the following in the Firebug log:

```
Announcing selection of sel2
Selection changed to sel2
Deselecting sel1
Selecting sel2
Deselecting sel3
Deselecting sel4
```

All the above serves to create a loosely coupled system where selection changes result in broadcast messages on a shared topic. There's a status field that responds to the messages, and each selectable square is subscribed to the shared topic and individually decides whether to become highlighted or drop its highlight.

None of this needed to be decided up front: You can add as many subscribers responding to selection box changes as you need — the selection box itself requires no modifications to see that other parts of the system are updated. Furthermore, you can plan out any number of event topics as necessary for important happenings in the workings of your user interface.

Using Object Methods as Subscribers

The previous demonstration shows how to build a loosely coupled system with broadcast events using inline function handlers. For the sake of completeness, it's worth noting that object methods work just as well, promoting reuse:

```
console.log("*** Adding subscribers from object...");

var the_topic = '/decafbad/eventsanim/sample';
var subs = [];

dojo.declare('decafbad.eventsanim.events.pubsubHandlers', null, {
    foo: function(a, b) {
        console.log("foo: received event with args "+a+" and "+b);
    },
    bar: function(a, b) {
        console.log("bar: received event with args "+a+" and "+b);
    },
    baz: function(a, b) {
        console.log("baz: received event with args "+a+" and "+b);
    }
});
var handlers = new decafbad.eventsanim.events.pubsubHandlers();

dojo.forEach(['foo', 'bar', 'baz'], function(name) {
    var sub = dojo.subscribe(the_topic, handlers, name);
    subs.push(sub);
});

dojo.publish(the_topic, ['hello again', 'pubsub']);
```

This code declares a new class with the methods `foo()`, `bar()`, and `baz()`. Each of these methods is then subscribed via `dojo.forEach()` to respond to the event topic "/decafbad/eventsanim/ sample". Immediately after that, a broadcast is made on that event topic. The resulting Firebug log transcript should look something like this:

```
*** Adding subscribers from object...
foo: received event with args hello again and pubsub
bar: received event with args hello again and pubsub
baz: received event with args hello again and pubsub
```

Unsubscribing from Published Messages

Also, note that there's a `dojo.unsubscribe()` call, which accepts the return value of `dojo.subscribe()` as a handle and destroys that subscription like so:

```
console.log("*** Unsubscribing every other subscriber...");

for (var i=0; i<subs.length; i++) {
    if (i % 2) dojo.unsubscribe(subs[i]);
}

dojo.publish(the_topic, ['private', 'pubsub']);
```

After running this code, the Firebug transcript will change to reflect the missing second subscriber:

```
*** Adding subscribers from object...
foo: received event with args hello again and pubsub
baz: received event with args hello again and pubsub
```

Turning Object Methods into Publishers

Another useful trick is to listen in on preexisting object method calls with published events. Dojo offers an easy way to do this with the dojo.connectPublisher() utility. Take a look at this code that offers a demonstration:

```
console.log("*** Connecting publishers to object methods...");

dojo.declare('decafbad.eventsanim.events.methodPub', null, {
    quux: function(a, b) {
        console.log("quux says "+a+" and "+b);
    },
    xyzzy: function(a, b) {
        console.log("xyzzy mentions "+a+" and "+b);
    },
    foobar: function(a, b) {
        console.log("foobar announces "+a+" and "+b);
    }
});
var some_obj = new decafbad.eventsanim.events.methodPub();

var method_topic = '/decafbad/eventsanim/methodCalled';

dojo.forEach(['quux', 'xyzzy', 'foobar'], function(name) {
    var conn = dojo.connectPublisher(method_topic, some_obj, name);
});

var sub = dojo.subscribe(method_topic, function(a, b) {
    console.log("subscriber overheard "+a+" and "+b);
});

some_obj.quux('hello', 'world');
some_obj.xyzzy('again', 'hello');
some_obj.foobar('what', 'where');
```

The preceding example creates a new class with a set of simple methods and creates an instance of this new methodPub class. Each method just emits a log message summarizing the method name and its two parameters.

Next, the event topic /decafbad/eventsanim/methodCalled is established. This event topic is used by dojo.connectPublisher() calls in a dojo.forEach() loop to convert each object method into a publisher. The method signature of dojo.connectPublisher() is the following:

```
dojo.connectPublisher(event topic, object, method name)
```

Note that this utility returns a handler usable with dojo.disconnect() to unhook the publisher.

After enabling the publishers, a `dojo.subscribe()` call sets up a listener for the event topic. This handler will just report its success at eavesdropping on method calls.

Finally, calls to the object methods are made. When you put it all together, you'll see log messages like these appear in your transcript:

```
*** Connecting publishers to object methods...
quux says hello and world
subscriber overheard hello and world
xyzzy mentions again and hello
subscriber overheard again and hello
foobar announces what and where
subscriber overheard what and where
```

Using Dojo Behaviors

If using CSS selectors in `dojo.query()` and `NodeList` methods to wire up event handlers seems like a declarative style of coding, Dojo behaviors go further by offering an approach that makes attaching code to elements feel just like declaring styles with style sheets.

Consider this slight variant to the HTML presented earlier:

```html
<form id="coord_canvas_2">

    <label for="coord_x_2">x:</label>
    <input name="coord_x_2" id="coord_x_2" type="text" size="5" />
    <label for="coord_y_2">y:</label>
    <input name="coord_y_2" id="coord_y_2" type="text" size="5" />
    <label for="status_2">status:</label>
    <input name="status_2" id="status_2" type="text" size="35" />

    <br />

    <div id="c1_2" class="canvas"> </div>
    <div id="c2_2" class="canvas"> </div>
    <div id="c3_2" class="canvas"> </div>
    <div id="c4_2" class="canvas"> </div>

    <br style="clear: both" />

</form>
```

In the preceding markup, the IDs were changed from the earlier example so that they can coexist on the same page for side-by-side comparison. Accordingly, there are a number of form text fields available for reporting on events as they happen, as well as a number of `<div>`s that will be styled as colored squares and onto which event handlers will be connected.

Using Behaviors to Find Nodes and Make Connections

Even more elegant than using chained `NodeList` methods, the `dojo.behavior` module offers a way to cleanly declare and map out all the event handlers and event topics needed by your web application. Take a look at this code, which demonstrates some of the things the module affords:

```
dojo.require('dojo.behavior');

dojo.behavior.add({

    '#coord_canvas_2 label': function(el) {
        console.log("Found label "+el.getAttribute('for'));
    },

    '#coord_canvas_2 .canvas': {

        found: function(el) {
            console.log("Found canvas "+el.id);
        },

        onmousemove: function(ev) {
            dojo.byId('coord_x_2').value = ev.pageX;
            dojo.byId('coord_y_2').value = ev.pageY;
        },

        onclick: function(ev) {
            var el = ev.target;
            // this == el
            dojo.byId('status_2').value =
                'Mouse clicked '+el.id+' at '+ev.pageX+' x '+ev.pageY;
        }

    }

});

dojo.behavior.apply();
```

First, since `dojo.behavior` is not a part of the base `dojo` module, it needs to be loaded with a `dojo.require()` call. Then, a call to `dojo.behavior.add()` is made with an object literal as its only parameter. This object literal lays out a set of CSS selectors and rules to be applied to elements matching the selector. The final call, `dojo.behavior.apply()`, fires up the Dojo behavior engine. which applies all the rules defined in the `add()` call.

The data structure passed to `dojo.behavior.add()` is a set of rules, akin to a CSS style sheet. The top-level properties are named with CSS selectors, and the value of each can be either a function or a further nested data structure.

If the value is a function, either defined inline or from a variable, the Dojo behavior engine will call that function once for each element found matching the CSS selector. Thus, when the `apply()` method is called in the previous example, you'll see messages like the following in your Firebug log transcript:

```
Found label coord_x_2
Found label coord_y_2
Found label status_2
```

The second rule in the preceding code constructs a nested data structure as the value for the CSS selector rule. The names of each property in this structure reflect DOM events, with `onmousemove` and `onclick` used in the example shown earlier. Each of these results in a `dojo.connect()` call connecting the supplied function as handler for the named event on each element found by the CSS selector. Note that in defining behaviors, the prefix "on" is not optional as it is in `dojo.connect()` calls.

The exception to this is the property named "`found`" — this one works just like the previous rule, in that the supplied function will be called for each element found. This code produces log messages like the following in Firebug:

```
Found canvas c1_2
Found canvas c2_2
Found canvas c3_2
Found canvas c4_2
```

The end results of this behavior set being applied are the aforementioned log messages, and event handlers connected to the `click` and `mousemove` events of the `<div>` squares on the page.

Using Behaviors to Connect Object Methods

A little more complex, but even more useful is the ability to connect handlers from an object to DOM events like so:

```
dojo.declare('decafbad.eventsanim.events.behaviorHandlers', null, {

    highlight_class: 'entered',

    handleOnMouseEnter: function(ev) {
        var el = ev.target;
        // this == handlers
        dojo.addClass(el, this.highlight_class);
        dojo.byId('status_2').value =
            'Mouse entered '+el.id;
    },

    handleOnMouseLeave: function(ev) {
        var el = ev.target;
        // this == handlers
        dojo.removeClass(el, this.highlight_class);
        dojo.byId('status_2').value =
            'Mouse left '+el.id;
    }

});
var handlers = new decafbad.eventsanim.events.behaviorHandlers();
```

```
dojo.behavior.add({
    '#coord_canvas_2 .canvas': {
        onmouseenter:
            dojo.hitch(handlers, 'handleOnMouseEnter'),
        onmouseleave:
            dojo.hitch(handlers, 'handleOnMouseLeave')
    }
});

dojo.behavior.apply();
```

This code example declares a new class, `behaviorHandlers`. The instances of this class provide two handler methods for `mouseenter` and `mouseleave` events. The `dojo.behavior.add()` call connects these two handlers to their respective events on the square canvas `<div>`'s as appropriate.

The Dojo documentation mentions that the following construct should do the trick for declaring behavior rules to connect objects as handlers:

```
onmouseenter: { targetObj: handlers, targetFunc: 'handleOnMouseEnter' }
```

However, that doesn't seem to work at the time of this writing. Thus, the code uses a call to `dojo.hitch()` — this Dojo utility returns a wrapper function that calls the appropriate method on the given object. It's an extra step, but works basically the same way. Still, by the time you read this, you may want to try the more declarative approach instead of the `dojo.hitch()` call and see if it works.

Using Behaviors to Publish Event Topics

For the last `dojo.behavior` trick, take a look at this code:

```
dojo.behavior.add({
  '#coord_canvas_2 div': '/decafbad/eventsanim/div',
  '#coord_canvas_2 input': {
      'found': '/decafbad/eventsanim/foundInput',
      'onchange': '/decafbad/eventsanim/inputChanged',
      'onkeypress': '/decafbad/eventsanim/inputKeypress'
    }
});

dojo.subscribe('/decafbad/eventsanim/div', function(el) {
    console.log("Found a div "+el.id);
});

dojo.subscribe('/decafbad/eventsanim/div', function(el) {
    console.log("Found a div (again) "+el.id);
});
```

```
dojo.behavior.apply();

dojo.subscribe('/decafbad/eventsanim/foundInput', function(el) {
    console.log("Found an input "+el.id);
});

dojo.subscribe('/decafbad/eventsanim/inputChanged', function(ev) {
    console.log("Detected change on "+ev.target.id);
});

dojo.subscribe('/decafbad/eventsanim/inputKeypress', function(ev) {
    console.log("Detected keypress on "+ev.target.id);
});
```

As this code illustrates, you can use event topic strings instead of functions in behavior rules. Some of these rules result in events published upon elements being found, and others will automatically connect handlers to DOM events that publish events to the given topics.

However, notice that the subscription for the "/decafbad/eventsanim/foundInput" topic appears after the dojo.behavior.apply() call. As such, it will never receive any messages published on that topic by the behavior rules. You can, of course, establish subscriptions to the topics at any point — even after calling apply() — but any events related to elements found for selectors will have already been published past that point.

Upon application, these rules and the subsequent events published will result in a Firebug log transcript like the following:

```
Found a div c1_2
Found a div (again) c1_2
Found a div c2_2
Found a div (again) c2_2
Found a div c3_2
Found a div (again) c3_2
Found a div c4_2
Found a div (again) c4_2
```

Given the last couple of subscriptions, playing around with the input fields on the page will trigger log messages like these:

```
Detected keypress on coord_x_2
Detected keypress on coord_x_2
Detected change on coord_x_2
Detected keypress on coord_y_2
Detected keypress on coord_y_2
Detected keypress on coord_y_2
Detected change on coord_y_2
Detected keypress on status_2
Detected change on status_2
```

Summary

In this chapter, you were introduced to the tools Dojo offers for connecting handlers to DOM events — including simple `dojo.connect()` calls, batch event connections using `dojo.NodeList` methods, as well as the use of `dojo.behavior` to declare maps of events and handlers in a way similar to CSS style sheets. The system of publishing and subscribing to abstract event topics was also explored, offering another way to flexibly decouple handlers from DOM events.

The next chapter introduces the animation system provided by Dojo. You'll see demonstrations of the various animation primitives in Dojo, paired with ways to chain and combine animations and apply easings to the flow of animations. Extended `NodeList` methods will be introduced, showing how `dojo.query()` can be used to construct animations with specific sets of nodes.

26

Composing Animations

Receiving and operating upon user input is a vital part of a responsive user interface, but there's more to the story. The ability to provide feedback and grab attention to highlight results and new information is just as important. Following the maxim of "Show, don't tell," animation is one of the easiest and most effective ways to do this: You can fade or wipe in status messages, depict the results of an operation by sliding elements into new positions, or even compose a whole chain of motions and transitions to tell a story.

The Dojo toolkit offers an animation system that provides a mix of simplicity in use and flexibility in tweaking. The overall system and a few animation primitives are available in the Dojo core, with additional capabilities available on demand from loadable modules.

The animation engine itself is tuned for performance, managing multiple simultaneous animations with a single JavaScript timer and working to keep transitions and motions smooth. Animation primitives managed by the engine are all based on a common class whose instances describe transitions between CSS style properties — which includes positions, colors, and sizes.

These animation objects also offer a set of methods and synthetic events for altering animations in-flight and reacting to various points in their lifecycles. And finally, Dojo provides the means for chaining animations together end-to-end and combining them in parallel.

In this chapter, you'll learn about:

- ❑ Animating CSS style properties
- ❑ Using fade and wipe transitions
- ❑ Using slide animations

Animating CSS Style Properties

The foundation of all Dojo animation is based on transitions between CSS style properties. Since these include position, opacity, color, size, and a number of other rendering aspects, this is a very powerful way to express motion and transitions.

Setting the stage for the first demonstration, consider the following HTML:

```
<style type="text/css">
    #toAnim, .toAnim {
        position: relative;
        width: 100px;
        text-align: center;
        padding: 1em;
        border: 2px dotted #000;
        background-color: #ddf;
    }
</style>

<div id="anim_property">

    <form>
        <button id="doAnim1">Anim Out</button>
        <button id="doAnim2">Anim Back</button>
    </form>

    <div id="toAnim">Watch me!</div>

    <br style="clear: both" />

</div>
```

In this example, a simple bit of CSS is included to style the `<div>` that's about to get animated. The rest of the markup introduces two buttons as a user interface: the lucky `<div>` itself, and a line break to round out the small layout. See Figure 26-1 for an example of what this markup looks like.

Figure 26-1

Now, take a look at this first bit of animation code:

```
dojo.connect(dojo.byId('doAnim1'), 'click', function(ev) {
    dojo.stopEvent(ev);
    var anim = dojo.animateProperty({
        node: dojo.byId('toAnim'),
```

```
              duration: 1000,
              properties: {
                  left: { start: '0', end: '300', unit: 'px' },
                  width: { start: '100', end: '300', unit: 'px' },
                  backgroundColor: { start: '#dfd', end: '#ddf' }
              }
          });
          anim.play();
      });

      dojo.connect(dojo.byId('doAnim2'), 'click', function(ev) {
          dojo.stopEvent(ev);
          var anim = dojo.animateProperty({
              node: dojo.byId('toAnim'),
              duration: 1000,
              properties: {
                  left:  { start: '300', end: '0', unit: 'px' },
                  width: { start: '300', end: '100', unit: 'px' },
                  backgroundColor: { start: '#ddf', end: '#dfd' }
              }
          }).play(500); // delay 500ms before starting animation
      });
```

Using what you've just read about handling events, these two dojo.connect() calls wire up the buttons on the page so that, when clicked, each fires off an animation involving the <div> in the layout.

In each case, dojo.animateProperty() is used to create an animation object, assigned to the variable anim. The specific methods and properties of these objects will be explored in depth later in the chapter, but note for now that these animations do not start upon creation and require a call to the .play() method to begin the process.

Also note that the .play() method returns the animation object itself, allowing for some call chaining. Additionally, the method accepts a parameter defining in milliseconds how long it should wait before beginning the actual animation.

Looking deeper into the code, notice that each dojo.animateProperty() call accepts an object literal as its parameter. This is treated as a set of properties used to instantiate the new animation object, which are included in the following table:

Animation Property	Purpose
node	DOM node to be animated
duration	Time in which animation should be completed, in milliseconds
delay	Time to wait before which animation starts, in milliseconds
repeat	How many times to repeat the animation
easing	Function used to translate linear progress into dynamic motion
properties	Declaration of CSS properties and their transitions

In each of the animations in the previous code, `dojo.byId('toAnim')` provides the node, while the `duration` is set to one second. No `delay` or `repeat` is defined, and so defaults of zero are used for each.

Also, no `easing` is defined, so the default one will be used — easings in particular will be covered a little later in this chapter, so don't worry too much about that for now. Some additional properties are not mentioned here — some of these include the assignment of event handlers and will be covered toward the end of the chapter, while others can be found in the Dojo API documentation.

Finally, there's the nested data structure defining `properties`. This is a list of CSS property names associated with `start`, `end`, and `unit` properties.

Note that expressing CSS property names in JavaScript follows a general production rule of converting from hyphen separation to CamelCase, so that the property "`background-color`" converts to the JS name "`backgroundColor`".

So, over the course of the time specified in `duration`, Dojo will figure out how to get each CSS property transitioned from the `start` value to the `end` value in the given `unit` type. Thus, in the previous code, each animation will move the node horizontally, change its width, and blend its background color all at once. Dojo has code internally to work out the transitions between just about any pair of values for any kind of CSS property, so feel free to try various combinations to get a feel for what it can do.

Using Fade Transitions

While you can set up just about any transition you like using `dojo.animateProperty()`, there are a few that are particularly useful or common. So, Dojo has a few helpers that simplify the process of using them. Offered in the Dojo core is the first pair of these helpers: `dojo.fadeOut()` and `dojo.fadeIn()` — each of these animates the opacity of an element to provide a fade effect.

Like the markup in the previous example, here's some HTML to provide a basic interface:

```
<style type="text/css">
    #toFade {
        border: 2px dotted #000;
        background-color: #ddf;
    }
</style>

<div id="anim_fade">
    <form>
        <button id="fadeItOut">Fade Out</button>
        <button id="fadeItIn">Fade In</button>
    </form>
    <div id="toFade">
        <h3>Watch me fade in and out!</h3>
    </div>
</div>
```

In this example, there are two buttons to fire off animations, accompanied by a `<div>` to be subject to the animations. Figure 26-2 shows how this is rendered in a browser.

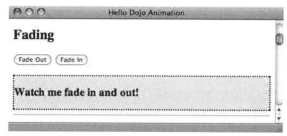

Figure 26-2

The following code wires up the buttons with the simplified animation helpers for fading:

```
dojo.connect(dojo.byId('fadeItOut'), 'click', function(ev) {
    dojo.stopEvent(ev);
    var anim = dojo.fadeOut({
        node: dojo.byId('toFade'), duration: 1000
    }).play();
});

dojo.connect(dojo.byId('fadeItIn'), 'click', function(ev) {
    dojo.stopEvent(ev);
    var anim = dojo.fadeIn({
        node: dojo.byId('toFade'), duration: 1000
    }).play();
});
```

The effect here is that pressing the first button will cause the element to fade into the background, yet still occupy space. The second button will bring the element back to full opacity.

Notice that the code is much simpler than using `dojo.animateProperty()`, though it actually does more: As part of preparing for manipulating opacity, these helpers tweak a few other styles to ensure that the effect works across browsers.

With the exception of the `properties` value, which the helpers manage themselves, the parameters to these helpers are identical to those used with the `dojo.animateProperty()` utility. This includes `node`, `duration`, `delay`, `repeat`, `easing`, and the rest.

Using Wipe Transitions

Having mentioned that the faded element still occupies space is significant with respect to the next pair of animation helpers, named `dojo.fx.wipeOut()` and `dojo.fx.wipeIn()` from the `dojo.fx` module.

These two shrink and grow the height of an element, respectively, making it either appear to insert itself into the page or to roll up and vanish. As opposed to fading, this effect removes the element from view and the flow of layout altogether. This can come in handy for transient alert panes or other momentary messages dismissed shortly after appearing. Note that this transition does not actually remove the element from the DOM — whether or not you want that to happen, you need to do that separately.

The following markup should look familiar with respect to the other animation demonstrations so far:

```html
<style type="text/css">
    #anim_fx_wipe .toAnim div {
        padding: 1em;
        border: 2px dashed #000;
        background-color: #dfd;
    }
</style>

<div id="anim_fx_wipe">

    <form>
        <button id="doWipeOut">Wipe Out</button>
        <button id="doWipeIn">Wipe In</button>
    </form>

    <div class="toAnim">
        <div>Watch me!</div>
    </div>

</div>
```

The HTML in this example includes two buttons to drive animations, as well as an element to be the subject of those animations. You can see the rendering of this markup in Figure 26-3.

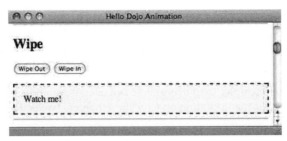

Figure 26-3

Consider this code that exercises the `dojo.fx.wipeOut()` and `dojo.fx.wipeIn()` helpers:

```javascript
dojo.require('dojo.fx');

dojo.connect(dojo.byId('doWipeOut'), 'click', function(ev) {
    dojo.stopEvent(ev);
    var anim = dojo.fx.wipeOut({
        node: dojo.query('.toAnim', 'anim_fx_wipe')[0], duration: 250
    }).play();
});

dojo.connect(dojo.byId('doWipeIn'), 'click', function(ev) {
    dojo.stopEvent(ev);
    var anim = dojo.fx.wipeIn({
        node: dojo.query('.toAnim', 'anim_fx_wipe')[0], duration: 250
    }).play();
});
```

Following the pattern established so far, this code connects the click event of the two buttons in the interface each to a handler that will instantiate a wipe-in and a wipe-out animation, respectively. The effect will be that the element subject to animation will either shrink vertically until it is removed from visibility on the page, or grow vertically to insert itself into the layout.

Although very similar in use to `dojo.fadeOut()` and `dojo.fadeIn()`, the major difference is that these come from a module separate from the Dojo code — namely `dojo.fx`. This module is loaded in with the `dojo.require()` statement. The `dojo.fx` module offers a few more enhancements including these helpers, as you'll soon see.

Using Slide Animations to Move Elements

Fades and wipes are animation of a kind, but they don't impart any motion to an element. This is where the `dojo.fx.slideTo()` helper comes in.

Consider this markup, and also note the `position: relative` in the styles:

```
<style type="text/css">
    .toAnim {
        position: relative;
        width: 100px;
        text-align: center;
        padding: 1em;
        border: 2px dotted #000;
        background-color: #ddf;
    }
</style>

<div id="anim_fx_slide">

    <form>
        <button id="doSlideOut">Slide Out</button>
        <button id="doSlideBack">Slide Back</button>
    </form>

    <div class="toAnim">
        <div>Watch me!</div>
    </div>

    <br style="clear: both" />

</div>
```

As before, this markup provides two buttons to exercise two animations. The `<div>` with a CSS class of "toAnim" awaits the application of motion. Figure 26-4 presents a rendering of this markup.

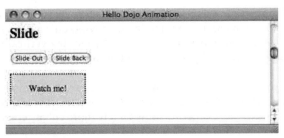

Figure 26-4

The motion is supplied by the following code:

```
dojo.require('dojo.fx');

dojo.connect(dojo.byId('doSlideOut'), 'click', function(ev) {
    dojo.stopEvent(ev);
    var anim = dojo.fx.slideTo({
        node: dojo.query('.toAnim', 'anim_fx_slide')[0],
        duration: 1000,
        left: '200', top: '100', unit: 'px'
    }).play();
});

dojo.connect(dojo.byId('doSlideBack'), 'click', function(ev) {
    dojo.stopEvent(ev);
    var anim = dojo.fx.slideTo({
        node: dojo.query('.toAnim', 'anim_fx_slide')[0],
        duration: 1000,
        left: '0', top: '0', unit: 'px'
    }).play();
});
```

The first of these animations using `dojo.fx.slideTo()` moves the element 200 pixels to the left, and 100 pixels down. The second moves the element back to its origin.

Something important to notice, if you recall the `position: relative` shown earlier, is that while `dojo.fx.slideTo()` can move an element with absolute positioning on the page, it can also deal with relative positioning. If the element has neither positioning type applied, Dojo will calculate the location of the element, set its `position` property to `absolute`, and work from there.

Following in the footsteps of the wipe animation helpers, `dojo.fx.slideTo()` lives in the `dojo.fx` module and as such, it also requires loading.

Well, actually, it doesn't need to be loaded twice if you have caught it with a `dojo.require()` statement previously. However, since the combination of `dojo.require()` and `dojo.provide()` are smart enough to keep track of what's been loaded, duplicate declarations of dependencies won't hurt anything — and in fact are necessary at times, especially in different modules that aren't dependencies of each other.

Controlling Motion with Easings

Linear motion and transitions are boring. They don't catch the eye very well and aren't fun to watch. Instead, it's nice to be able to vary things while an animation is in flight. For example, instead of just sliding evenly from point A to point B, imagine an element that shoots out dramatically and then slows down to coast in for a landing. Or, picture an element snapping back to a position elastically with a little bounce to its path. Without overdoing it, a little seasoning can do a lot to make a user interface a pleasure to use.

The simplest, most boring easing formula just produces a linear, unchanging march toward completion:

```
var linear_easing = function(n) { return n; }
```

As mentioned earlier, all animations accept a property named easing, with a default used if none is supplied. As it turns out, this is what the default formula looks like:

```
dojo._defaultEasing = function(/*Decimal?*/ n){
    // summary: The default easing function for dojo._Animation(s)
    return 0.5 + ((Math.sin((n + 1.5) * Math.PI))/2);
}
```

This default easing produces motion that looks a bit more natural with inertia and momentum: Motion is slow to start, picks up speed, and then gradually brakes to a halt at the end.

To help let that sink in, consider that Dojo synchronizes everything in a single animation by tracking the overall percentage of completion. A decimal number evenly incremented from 0.0 to 1.0 measures this percentage over the amount of time specified by the value of duration. Dojo works out the details on how to perform the transition between one or more CSS properties specified for animation. The progress of each individual transition at any given point is calculated as a multiple of the overall percentage.

Actually, that's not quite the whole picture: An *easing* represents a transformation on the overall percentage of completion before it's handed to the individual transitions. So, while the percentage of completion tracked by Dojo marches smoothly from 0.0 to 1.0, an easing function gets to have some fun with the value along the way — and thus with the apparent effects in motion and transition during the in-flight course of the animation.

Probably the easiest way to understand how easings work is to build a laboratory in which to play with them. Start by considering this markup as a user-interface framework:

```
<div id="anim_easing">

    <form>
        <select class="slideEase"></select>
        <button class="doSlideOut">Ease Out</button>
        <button class="doSlideBack">Ease Back</button>
    </form>

    <div class="toAnim">
        <div>Watch me!</div>
    </div>

    <br style="clear: both" />

</div>
```

The first thing in the form defined in this markup is an empty `<select>` element. In the code coming up, this will be dynamically populated with available easings. The selected easing will be used with the two animations that will be connected to the buttons in the interface. In case you're interested, this markup looks something like Figure 26-5.

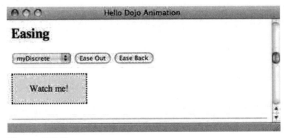

Figure 26-5

Speaking of available easings, the following code defines a few:

```
// Build a set of simple easings.
var my_easings = {
    myPlainLinear: function(n) {
        return n;
    },
    myDiscrete: function(n) {
        return Math.floor( n * 10 ) / 10;
    },
    myPower: function(n) {
        return (n==0) ? 0 : Math.pow(2, 10 * (n - 1));
    }
};
```

There are three easings defined in `my_easings`:

❑ `myPlainLinear` — Simple and boring choice

❑ `myDiscrete` — An easing that locks the animation down to discrete marching steps

❑ `myPower` — An easing that fires the animation off with increasing speed until stopping abruptly

To explore more choices, you can turn to a DojoX module:

```
// Sprinkle in some more experimental easings from dojox.
dojo.require('dojox.fx.easing');
dojo.mixin(my_easings, dojox.fx.easing);
```

This code pulls in the `dojox.fx.easing` module and merges its contents into `my_easings`, which provides about 30 more easings for you to play with. A few particularly dramatic choices include `elasticOut`, `bounceOut`, and `backOut` — keep an eye out for them when this lab is ready to use.

The following code makes these choices available in the user interface:

```
// Populate the selection box with available easings.
dojo.query('.slideEase', 'anim_easing')
    .forEach(function(el) {
        for (var name in my_easings) {
            if (dojo.isFunction(my_easings[name])) {
                el.options[el.options.length] =
                    new Option(name, name);
            }
        }
    }, this);
```

This locates the empty selection box and iterates through available easings, adding each as a new choice option in the menu. Next up, it's time to implement an animation that uses the selected easing:

```
dojo.require('dojo.fx');

// Simple helper to perform a slide to some horizontal coord
function performSlideTo(left_coord) {
    var sel  = dojo.query('.slideEase', 'anim_easing')[0];
    var name = sel.options[sel.selectedIndex].value;
    console.log("Using selected easing " + name);

    var anim = dojo.fx.slideTo({
        node:     dojo.query('.toAnim', 'anim_easing')[0],
        duration: 1000,
        easing:   my_easings[name],
        left:     left_coord
    }).play();
}
```

In this- code, the first thing is a `dojo.require()` to pull in `dojo.fx`, just in case you haven't done so before. Then, the function `performSlideTo()` is defined.

The first half of `performSlideTo()` finds the easing selection box and digs out the currently selected value, sending a message to the log reporting the choice. Then, a `dojo.fx.slideTo()` animation is created, this time with the easing property supplied by looking up the function in `my_easings` named by the selection box choice.

Finally, this code wires everything up to the two buttons for launch:

```
// Wire up the buttons to each perform a slide.
dojo.query('.doSlideOut', 'anim_easing')
    .onclick(function(ev) {
        dojo.stopEvent(ev);
        performSlideTo(300);
    });
dojo.query('.doSlideBack', 'anim_easing')
    .onclick(function(ev) {
        dojo.stopEvent(ev);
        performSlideTo(0);
    });
```

The first button sends the element out 300 pixels to the right, while the second brings it back to origin. Both use the `performSlideTo()` function to honor the selected easing in a common spot.

This lab framework lets you try out easings in a way that can't easily be described here in text; put it together and try selecting each of the available easings and see if you can't find a use for one or more of them to replace the default.

Chaining Animations in Serial

So far, you've seen how to fire off various kinds of single animations. However, Dojo also offers a facility in the `dojo.fx` module to build chains of animations that fire off in serial order.

Getting right into it, consider this HTML as a test bed for this feature:

```
<style type="text/css">
    #anim_chain .fader {
        margin: 0.25em;
        width: 100px;
        float: left;
        border: 2px dotted #000;
        background-color: #ddf;
    }
    #anim_chain span {
        display: block;
        padding: 1em;
    }
</style>


<div id="anim_chain">

    <div class="fader" id="play1"><span>Click me to fade</span></div>
    <div class="fader" id="play2"><span>Click me to fade</span></div>
    <div class="fader" id="play3"><span>Click me to fade</span></div>
    <div class="fader" id="play4"><span>Click me to fade</span></div>

    <br style="clear: both" />

</div>
```

This user interface consists of four squares, each of which when clicked will fade in and out thanks to the next bit of code coming. Figure 26-6 shows what this looks like.

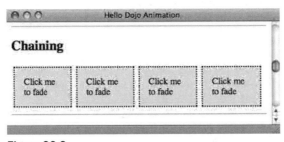

Figure 26-6

Putting the plan into action is fairly simple, with the following code:

```
dojo.require('dojo.fx');

dojo.query('.fader', 'anim_chain')
    .onclick(function(ev) {
        dojo.fx.chain([
            dojo.fadeOut({ node: ev.currentTarget, duration: 1000 }),
            dojo.fadeIn({ node: ev.currentTarget, duration: 1000 })
        ]).play();
    });
```

The preceding code uses dojo.query() to find all the fader squares, chained with a .onclick() call to connect the given handler to each. This inline handler makes a call to dojo.fx.chain(), which accepts as its only parameter an array of animations. The call to dojo.fx.chain() itself returns an animation, which is fired up with a call to .play().

You can use dojo.fx.chain() to build strings of animations of any size you like. Each animation fires in sequence, each starting after the end of the one before it. With this tool, you can build up paths and loops for elements to move through, as well compositions like the fade-out/fade-in effect demonstrated earlier.

Combining Animations in Parallel

Along with firing animations in series, dojo.fx also offers a way to play animations in parallel together with dojo.fx.combine().

To prepare for a quick demonstration, take a look at the following markup:

```
<div id="anim_combine">
    <div class="toAnim" id="toAnim1"><span>Click me</span></div>
    <br style="clear: both" />
    <div class="toAnim" id="toAnim2"><span>Watch me</span></div>
    <br style="clear: both" />
</div>
```

This HTML presents two squares, one of which will be made clickable and both of which will animate. Figure 26-7 shows a rendering of this markup.

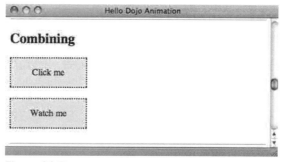

Figure 26-7

Consider the following code, building on both chaining and combining animations:

```
dojo.require('dojo.fx');

dojo.connect(dojo.byId('toAnim1'), 'click', function(ev) {
    dojo.fx.chain([
        dojo.fx.combine([
            dojo.fadeOut({
                node: dojo.byId('toAnim1'), duration: 1000
            }),
            dojo.fx.slideTo({
                node: dojo.byId('toAnim2'), duration: 1000, left: 300
            })
        ]),
        dojo.fx.combine([
            dojo.fadeIn({
                node: dojo.byId('toAnim1'), duration: 1000
            }),
            dojo.fx.slideTo({
                node: dojo.byId('toAnim2'), duration: 1000, left: 0
            })
        ])
    ]).play();
});
```

There's a lot going on in the preceding code, but in short this is what to expect: When the first element is clicked, it fades out and back in while the element below it slides to the right and back.

Dissecting the code itself, the initial `dojo.connect()` call wires up the inline handler to the first of the two elements. Inside this handler, a call to `dojo.fx.chain()` sets up a series of animations to play.

Each of these chained animations is returned by a call to `dojo.fx.combine()`, the star of this particular show. This method accepts a list of other animations, provided here by other animation helpers you've seen so far in this chapter. Each of these animations is applied to a different element, but thanks to `dojo.fx.combine()` they will both fire in synch.

With `dojo.fx.combine()`, you can mash together any number of animations working on separate elements — or even the same elements. Wipe out a message while fading in a new data item, or even just build up intricate simultaneous movement paths. This gives you one more tool for composing complex animations from the available primitives and helpers.

Using NodeList Animation Methods

Having gone through much of what the Dojo animation facilities have to offer in composing single animations, it's time to introduce what's available in `dojo.NodeList` extensions to apply animations to sets of nodes located by `dojo.query()`.

Take a look at this markup, based on what was used in the previous chapter to put `dojo.query()` through its paces:

```
<div id="anim_nodelist">

    <form>
        <button class="doAnim">Animate!</button>
    </form>

    <ul>
        <li><a href="http://decafbad.com">Item #1</a></li>
        <li class="seconditem dojolink">
            <a href="http://dojoproject.org">Item
                <span class="num">#2</span></a>
        </li>
        <li class="thirditem">
            <a href="http://w3.org">Item #3</a>
        <li>
            <span>Sub-list</span>
            <ul>
                <li><a href="http://yahoo.com">Item A</a></li>
                <li><a href="http://delicious.com">Item
                    <span class="num letter">B</span></a></li>
                <li><a href="http://mozilla.org">Item C</a></li>
            </ul>
        </li>
        <li id="item4"><a href="http://getfirebug.com">Item #4</a></li>
        <li><a href="http://wrox.com">Item
            <span class="num">#5</span></a></li>
    </ul>

</div>
```

Though you've seen it before, Figure 26-8 provides a refresher peek at what this looks like in a browser.

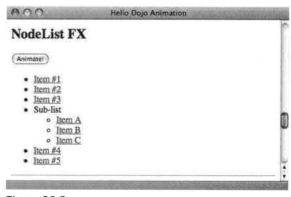

Figure 26-8

Diving in headfirst, consider the following code as applied to the HTML in the preceding example:

```
dojo.require('dojo.NodeList-fx');

dojo.query('.doAnim', 'anim_nodelist').onclick(function(ev) {
    dojo.stopEvent(ev);

    dojo.fx.chain([

        dojo.query('a[href^="http://d"]')
            .fadeOut({ duration: 500 }),

        dojo.query('a[href^="http://d"]')
            .fadeIn({ duration: 500 }),

        dojo.fx.combine([

            dojo.query('a[href$=".com"]')
                .map(function (el) { return el.parentNode })
                .animateProperty({
                    duration: 500,
                    properties: {
                        backgroundColor: { start: '#fff', end: '#ff8' }
                    }
                }),

            dojo.query('a[href$=".org"]')
                .map(function (el) { return el.parentNode })
                .animateProperty({
                    duration: 500,
                    properties: {
                        backgroundColor: { start: '#fff', end: '#8f8' }
                    }
                })

        ])
    ]).play();
});
```

First things first, the `dojo.NodeList-fx` module is required. When loaded, this module extends the `dojo.NodeList` class with a load of new methods, including the following familiar favorites:

- ❑ `.animateProperty()`
- ❑ `.wipeIn()`
- ❑ `.wipeOut()`
- ❑ `.slideTo()`
- ❑ `.fadeIn()`
- ❑ `.fadeOut()`

Each of these methods operates just like their non-`NodeList` equivalents presented so far in the chapter. The difference is that each of these methods iterates through the `NodeList` and is applied to each of the list's nodes in turn.

Rather than a `NodeList` like the other chainable methods, the return value from these methods is an animation object. This object is built using `dojo.fx.combine()`, composing a set of parallel animations applied to each node in the set. This caps off method chaining in the `NodeList` context, but allows you to use the results of `NodeList`-built animations in other combined and chained animations.

The code in the previous example puts everything together. The handler connected to the animate button composes an animation chain of several steps. First in the chain is to cause all links whose URLs start with "`http://d`" to fade out, followed by the inverse animation causing the same links to fade back in.

Then, a parallel set of animations is composed: All of the list items containing links with URLs that end with ".`com`" have their background colors cycled from white through to a light yellow color. Meanwhile, all the list items with ".`org`" links cycle from white to light green backgrounds.

This all aims to demonstrate how you can combine the power of declarative `dojo.query()` lookups with creating, chaining, and combining any number and arrangements of animations with just a few twists and turns of code.

Examining Animation Objects

Each animation example in this chapter has so far treated the object returned by the various animation helpers and builders as a black box with a `.play()` method. As it turns out, each animation object exposes a number of methods for manipulating its progress in flight, including the following:

- ❏ `.play(delay, gotoStart)`— Starts the animation with an optional delay. Animation will start from the beginning if `gotoStart` is `true`, or from wherever it last left off or was paused (the default).

- ❏ `.pause()`— Pauses the animation.

- ❏ `.gotoPercent(percent, andPlay)`— Jumps the animation to the given `percent` of completion, a decimal number between 0.0 and 1.0. If `andPlay` is `true`, the animation will also start playing from there.

- ❏ `.stop(gotoEnd)`— Stops the animation. If `gotoEnd` is `true`, the animation will jump to the end while stopping.

- ❏ `.status()`— Returns the current status of the animation, with one of the following strings: `paused`, `playing`, or `stopped`.

Additionally, there are a half-dozen or so synthetic events available for connection, which report on various points throughout the animation's lifecycle. Among these are:

- ❏ `beforeBegin`— Fired before the animation begins playing.

- ❏ `onBegin`— The animation has begun playing.

- ❏ onAnimate— Fired for each tick of the clock during the course of an animation.
- ❏ onPause— Fired when the .pause() method has been called.
- ❏ onStop— Fired when the .stop() method has been called.
- ❏ onEnd— Fired when the animation has completed its course.

Between these methods and events, you can build progress bars tracking actual completion of a process, string together complex animations with interrelated cues, or build animated timers — just to field a few ideas.

As mentioned earlier with easings, building a small laboratory is probably the easiest way to get a feel for how these methods and events work. Consider the following markup to kick off the project:

```
<div id="anim_events">

    <form>

        <button class="reset">Reset</button>
        <button class="play">Play</button>
        <button class="pause">Pause</button>
        <button class="stop">Stop</button>
        --
        Jump to:
        <button class="go0">0%</button>
        <button class="go25">25%</button>
        <button class="go50">50%</button>
        <button class="go75">75%</button>

        <br style="clear: both" />

        <label for="status">Status:</label>
        <input class="status" type="text" size="40" />

        <br style="clear: both" />

        <div class="toAnim">Watch me!</div>

    </form>

</div>
```

To exercise the methods exposed by an animation, this interface offers a set of buttons that will be wired up to trigger them. There's also a text field that will be used to report on events as they fire. The Firebug log will come in handy for this as well. Finally, there's a lone <div> at the end — this will be the subject of the experiment. You can see a rendering of this HTML in Figure 26-9.

Figure 26-9

Getting down to code, the following begins the definition of a new class to drive the interface:

```
dojo.declare('decafbad.ch4.animation.withEvents', null, {

    root_id: '',
    anim: null,

    constructor: function(root_id) {
        this.root_id = root_id;
        this.resetAnim();
        this.wireUpButtons();
    },
```

The preceding code starts the declaration of a class named withEvents that will encapsulate all the connections and handlers needed for running the interface.

Notice that the constructor of this class accepts a root_id parameter. The value of this will be given anim_events from the markup in the preceding example. This class is not quite a proper widget, but since the root_id is parameterized you might like to try making multiple copies of the markup with different IDs and instantiate one of these objects for each. You can run many events in parallel and play with them each independently.

The other two duties of the constructor are to reset the animation with .resetAnim() and wire up all the buttons with .wireUpButtons(). The first of these, .resetAnim(), begins with this code:

```
resetAnim: function(ev) {
    console.log("Resetting animation");

    // If there's an existing animation, stop it.
    if (this.anim) this.anim.stop();

    // Build the new animation object.
    var root_id = this.root_id;
    this.anim = dojo.animateProperty({
        node: dojo.query('.toAnim', root_id)[0],
        duration: 10000,
        properties: {
            left: { start: '0', end: '300', unit: 'px' },
        },
        beforeBegin: function() {
```

```
                           console.log(root_id + ': beforeBegin fired!');
                   },
                   onBegin: function() {
                       console.log(root_id + ': onBegin fired!');
                   },
                   onAnimate: function() {
                       // No console.log here - too noisy!
                   },
                   onPause: function() {
                       console.log(root_id + ': onPause fired!');
                   },
                   onStop: function() {
                       console.log(root_id + ': onStop fired!');
                   },
                   onEnd: function() {
                       console.log(root_id + ': onEnd fired!');
                   }
               });
```

In `.resetAnim()`, the first thing done is to check if there's a preexisting animation in `this.anim`. If found, that animation is stopped. Then, work begins on building a new animation.

Here, the animation is a simple left-to-right slide over the course of 10 seconds created using the `dojo.animateProperty()` utility. The new feature illustrated here is that the properties accepted by this utility include named handlers for each of the events offered by the resulting animation object. Since you've never seen them used this far in the chapter, they are of course all optional. Just to cover the bases, though, a handler is provided for each that generates log messages.

The one exception to this is the `onAnimate` handler: This handler fires quite a lot — many times a second, in fact. This rate might be a bit too high and yield a log transcript that's a bit too noisy, so this handler in the preceding code does nothing. It's present just to illustrate that it's available to use.

However, in the second half of the `.resetAnim()` method, you can see another way to connect to the events offered by the animation object:

```
           // Wire up connections for each event fired by the animation.
           var anim_events = [
               'beforeBegin', 'onBegin', 'onPause',
               'onStop', 'onAnimate', 'onEnd'
           ];
           dojo.forEach(anim_events, function(ev_name) {
               var handler = dojo.hitch(this, function(val) {
                   this.setStatus(ev_name, val);
               });
               dojo.connect(this.anim, ev_name, handler);
           }, this);
       },

       setStatus: function(ev_name, val) {
           var str = ev_name + ' ' + this.anim.status();
           if (val) str += ' ' + dojo.toJson(val);
           dojo.query('.status', this.root_id)[0].value = str;
       },
```

The code here is a bit dense, but in short: The final half of `.resetAnim()` uses `dojo.connect()` to hook up a handler to each of the methods offered by the animation object, each of which calls the new `.setStatus()` method to update the text field in the user interface with a message reporting on the last event to fire, the current result of the animation's `.status()` method, as well as a representation of the parameter (if any) passed to the handler.

An interesting bit here is the use of `dojo.toJson()` utility. This is covered in more depth in the next chapter, but basically this function takes a JavaScript data structure and converts it into a JSON string representation that's convenient here for watching what happens with the parameter given to each event handler.

So, along with providing handlers at the time of creating the animation, you can later use `dojo.connect()` to attach handlers to the set of synthetic events fired by the animation.

Next up is the definition of the `.wireUpButtons()` method promised earlier:

```
wireUpButtons: function() {

    dojo.forEach(['reset', 'play', 'pause', 'stop'], function(name) {
        dojo.query('.'+name, this.root_id)
            .onclick(this, 'handle' + name);
    }, this);

    dojo.forEach(['0', '25', '50', '75'], function(perc) {
        dojo.query('.go'+perc, this.root_id).onclick(
            dojo.hitch(this, function(ev) {
                return this.handlego(ev, perc);
            })
        );
    }, this);

},
```

The `.wireUpButtons()` method works in two parts:

The first part wires up the click events of the `reset`, `play`, `pause`, and `stop` buttons to handler methods named with the prefix "`handle`" and a suffix of the button name.

The second part builds and connects intermediate handlers that each call the `.handlego()` method with a precooked percentage parameter and the incoming event. This helps cut down on unique handlers in need of implementation, since only the percentage varies. The same could have been done with all of the other handlers, but it seems useful to spell those out a bit more for illustration.

Speaking of handlers, the following code provides them and wraps up the `withEvents` class:

```
handlereset: function(ev) {
    dojo.stopEvent(ev);
    this.resetAnim();
},

handleplay: function(ev) {
    dojo.stopEvent(ev);
    this.anim.play();
},
```

```
handlepause: function(ev) {
    dojo.stopEvent(ev);
    this.anim.pause();
},

handlestop: function(ev) {
    dojo.stopEvent(ev);
    this.anim.stop();
},

handlego: function(ev, perc) {
    dojo.stopEvent(ev);
    this.anim.gotoPercent( perc / 100.0, true);
}

});

var obj = new decafbad.ch4.animation.withEvents('anim_events');
```

In the preceding code, the handlers needed for buttons are defined. The first, `.handlereset()`, wraps a call to `.resetAnim()` to start the animation over from scratch. The rest each wrap a call to a method on the animation object — including `.play()`, `.pause()`, `.stop()`, and `gotoPercent()`, respectively.

The `.handlego()` handler is a little bit of a special case, since it accepts a percentage from 0-100 from the intermediate handlers wired up previously. It also hardcodes the `andPlay` parameter to `true`, enabling each of the "Jump to" buttons in the interface to jump the animation around in its course without the need to click the play button.

And, finally, after the declaration of the class is complete, an instance of the class is created using the ID `anim_events` as the parameter to tie the instance to the markup provided at the start of this section. You may have noticed that all attempts to acquire nodes for events and such like throughout the code used CSS class names with `dojo.query()` calls rooted on this ID. This is what enables the code to be portable and reusable between multiple instances of the markup, as promised earlier.

This exploratory interface should give you some hands-on sense of how to interact with animation events and methods. Watch the status field and log messages for cues and try various combinations of method calls with the buttons.

Summary

In this chapter, you were introduced to the tools Dojo offers for composing animations and visual transitions. Demonstrations were offered for the various animation primitives in Dojo, along with ways to chain and combine animations and apply easings to the flow of animations. The extended `NodeList` methods were then introduced, showing how `dojo.query()` can be used to construct animations with specific sets of nodes. Finally, an in-depth look at the workings of animation objects was given along with a simple interface to play with them.

Coming up in the next chapter, it's time to add external data sources to the mix. You'll be introduced to the utilities provided by Dojo for accessing server-side data through the use of AJAX and IFrames, as well as invoking remote-procedure calls on a variety of web-based services.

27

Working with AJAX and Dynamic Data

The first crop of web applications employing Dynamic HTML and DOM scripting were certainly more interesting than scrolling status bar tickers, but in the browser they were essentially closed systems. That is, everything needed for the user interface had to be present at the time of page load, and form submissions were the only way to get data back to the server. Thus, the only way to combine client-side user interaction with server-side processing was to regularly blow away the entire carefully constructed interface with a page reload.

To improve this situation, several approaches have arisen to enable smaller, in-place interactions between web client and server. Though varied and diverse, these have generally fallen under the umbrella initialism "AJAX."

The original expansion of the term, coined from "Asynchronous JavaScript and XML", is a bit of a misnomer in use lately — almost every part of the concept, save perhaps JavaScript itself, has been swapped at one point or another for other technologies and data formats. In any case, the basic concept remains: Rather than reloading the whole page, perform just what small and focused web client-server dialog is needed for a given user interface interaction.

In Dojo, you have at your disposal several ways to request and handle dynamic data, both using the same domain from which your pages are served and across domains from third-party data providers. As you'll see in this chapter, the Dojo toolkit offers abstractions for using XMLHttpRequest objects, IFrames, and JSON data feeds, as well as a number of ways to automatically parse and handle the data provided by these means.

In this chapter, you'll learn about:

❑   Making simple web requests

❑   Handling web responses

❑   Augmenting forms

Making Simple Web Requests

One of the simplest of AJAX transactions is fetching a resource via HTTP GET. Thanks to the XMLHttpRequest object available in most modern browsers, most kinds of HTTP requests can be made back to the server domain from which a page was loaded. This restriction is notable as an effort to limit the security scope and traffic implications for a given web page — though, later in the chapter, you'll see ways to fetch data that get around the cross-domain limitations.

At any rate, leading into exploring Dojo's simplest XMLHttpRequest facility, consider the following markup:

```
<style type="text/css">
    .success {
        background-color: #dfd;
        border: 2px solid #000;
    }
    .error {
        background-color: #fdd;
        border: 2px dotted #000;
    }
</style>

<div id="xhrget1">
    <h2>Simple xhrGet</h2>
    <p class="content_found">Loading...</p>
    <p class="content_not_found">Loading...</p>
</div>
```

As you've seen in previous chapters, Dojo offers plenty of tools for doing anything you like with this markup, including animation and modifying the content. In this chapter, it's where you get the content that counts.

Speaking of content, consider the following as residing on the server in a file named "`data.txt`" relative to the page bearing the markup in the preceding example:

```
Hello world, this is some text available for load.
```

Examples throughout the rest of the chapter will refer back to this simple text file.

Making Simple Requests and Handling Responses

The use of XMLHttpRequest is asynchronous in nature, thus explaining the first "A" in AJAX. What this means is that making a request and accepting a response are separated in time and execution context — requests are launched by method calls that return immediately, and responses are handled by callback functions not entirely unlike those used with DOM events.

This allows you to launch multiple simultaneous requests in parallel and continue to maintain a responsive user interface while the web requests are still running their respective courses — a *synchronous* web request would freeze everything on the page while the browser waits for completion.

While this is possible to do, it's not usually desirable, so juggling asynchronous flows is the way of life for modern web UIs.

Getting down to it, take a look at this code:

```
dojo.xhrGet({
    url: 'data.txt',
    timeout: 5000,
    load: function(resp, io_args) {
        dojo.query('.content_found', 'xhrget1')
            .addClass('success')
            [0].innerHTML = resp;
    },
    error: function(error, io_args) {
        dojo.query('.content_found', 'xhrget1')
            .addClass('error')
            [0].innerHTML = error.message;
    }
});
```

This attempts to fetch the `data.txt` resource using a call to `dojo.xhrGet()`, which returns immediately, firing up the web request in the background. The following parameters are used:

❑ `url` — The URL to which a request will be made

❑ `timeout` — For how long in milliseconds the browser should wait for a response

❑ `load` — A callback function to be called upon receipt of a successful response

❑ `error` — A callback function called in case of a failure or error response

If the request eventually yields a successful response, the function defined as the `load` parameter will be called. With respect to the previous markup, this function will switch the first <div>'s CSS class to "success" and replace its contents with the fetched data. The first parameter to the callback, `resp`, contains the response data returned by the web request.

The second callback parameter, `io_args`, is interesting in that it provides additional context on the request. It is an instance of an internal Dojo class, whose properties include:

❑ `args` — A copy of the original parameters passed to `dojo.xhrGet()`—which also includes custom parameters not understood by `dojo.xhrGet()`. You can use this to pass data through to your response handlers.

❑ `xhr` — The XMLHttpRequest object used in the request, useful for digging up headers and other details of the response.

❑ `url` — The final URL used for the request, subject to redirects and other changes and often different than the original parameter.

❑ `query` — An object representing query parameters sent in the request.

The second callback named `error` will be called in case of a problem with the request. In this case, the <div>'s CSS class will be switched to "error", and the resulting error message will replace the <div>'s contents.

For the `error` handler, the first parameter will be an object of type `Error`, a native JavaScript object with properties including these:

❑ `message` — A human-readable description of the error

❑ `fileName` — The name of the file where the error occurred

❑ `lineNumber` — The number of the line in the file where the error occurred

In this context, only the message property is really helpful. Now, given this explanation of the `dojo.xhrGet()` call, take a look at Figure 27-1 to see what effect a successful request has on the page.

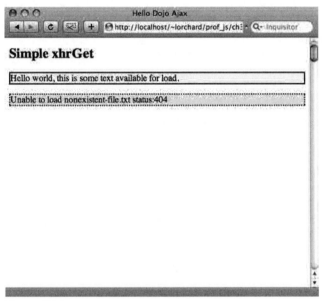

Figure 27-1

Using a Single Handler for Both Error and Success

In some cases, it's overkill to define two separate handler callbacks for both error and success conditions. For this reason, `dojo.xhrGet()` also allows you to supply a single function for both conditions like so:

```
dojo.xhrGet({
    url: 'nonexistent-file.txt',
    timeout: 5000,
    handle: function(result, io_args) {
        if (result instanceof Error){
            dojo.query('.content_not_found', 'xhrget1')
                .addClass('error')
                [0].innerHTML = result.message;
        } else {
```

```
                dojo.query('.content_not_found', 'xhrget1')
                    .addClass('success')
                    [0].innerHTML = result;
            }
        }
    });
```

This code is basically identical to the previous example, with the exception that `load` and `error` handlers have been replaced with a single callback named `handle`. This function checks the type of its first parameter, which will be an instance of `Error` if the request has failed. Thus, the single handler can take care of both the error and success conditions in one shot.

Notice that Figure 27-1 also depicts the result of this second call, intentionally attempting to fetch what should be a nonexistent resource that results in an error.

Handling Web Responses with Deferreds

Although `dojo.xhrGet()` makes it simple, there is a bit more going on with handling responses in Dojo. As it turns out, the `dojo.xhrGet()` call returns an object of a class called `Deferred`. This object represents the eventual success or error outcome of a background task, accepting a number of callbacks registered against either branch.

To see what this means, exactly, start by considering this HTML that will be updated in the code examples to come:

```
<div id="xhrget2">
    <h2>Deferred xhrGet</h2>
    <p class="content_found1">Loading...</p>
    <p class="content_found2">Loading...</p>
    <p class="content_not_found1">Loading...</p>
    <p class="content_not_found2">Loading...</p>
</div>
```

Registering Handlers for Success and Error Responses

When you supply callbacks in `load` and `error` parameters to `dojo.xhrGet()`, something equivalent to the following is automatically done for you:

```
var defer1 = dojo.xhrGet({
    url: 'data.txt', timeout: 5000
});

defer1.addCallback(function(resp) {
    var io_args = defer1.ioArgs;
    dojo.query('.content_found1', 'xhrget2')
        .addClass('success')
        [0].innerHTML = resp;
```

```
        return resp;
    });

    defer1.addErrback(function(error) {
        var io_args = defer1.ioArgs;
        dojo.query('.content_found1', 'xhrget2')
            .addClass('error')
            [0].innerHTML = error.message;
        return error;
    });
```

Internally in Dojo, the `Deferred` object is created and the `.addCallback()` and `.addErrback()` methods are called to register the parameter-supplied `load` and `error` handlers. In the preceding code, this is made explicit by using the `Deferred` returned by `dojo.xhrGet()` directly.

Notice that each of the success and error callbacks receive a single parameter for the response content or `Error` object, respectively — what was passed as `io_args` in the second parameter for handlers passed in the `dojo.xhrGet()` call can now be accessed via the `ioArgs` property of the `Deferred` object itself.

Also note that each of these handlers returned the values passed in as parameters. This is significant, because you can register additional handlers in series like so:

```
    defer1.addCallback(function(resp) {
        dojo.query('.content_found2', 'xhrget2')
            .addClass('success')
            [0].innerHTML = resp;
        return resp;
    });

    defer1.addErrback(function(error) {
        dojo.query('.content_found2', 'xhrget2')
            .addClass('error')
            [0].innerHTML = error.message;
        return error;
    });
```

The handlers registered in this example will fire after the previously registered handlers. Additionally, the parameters they receive will be those returned by the previous handlers. In this way, you can build up chains of callbacks that have the option of filtering results on the way down to subsequent handlers.

This is also worth paying extra attention to because leaving out the return statements at the end of the `Deferred`-based callbacks is an easy error, and will leave chained callbacks with no access to response data.

Registering Error and Success Handlers in One Call

If you find yourself using the `Deferred` interface, and often register both success and error handlers, the following convenience method may be of use:

```
var defer2 = dojo.xhrGet({
    url: 'nonexistent-file.txt', timeout: 5000
});

defer2.addCallbacks(
    function(resp) {
        dojo.query('.content_not_found1', 'xhrget2')
            .addClass('success')
            [0].innerHTML = resp;
        return resp;
    },
    function(error) {
        dojo.query('.content_not_found1', 'xhrget2')
            .addClass('error')
            [0].innerHTML = error.message;
        return error;
    }
);
```

In the preceding code, the single `Deferred` method `.addCallbacks()` takes the place of both the `.addCallback()` and `.addErrback()` methods. In the first parameter to `.addCallbacks()`, the success callback handler is expected. The error handler is expected in the second parameter.

Registering a Single Handler for both Error and Success

If you find yourself wanting to register a single callback to take care of both error and success conditions, the following is basically equivalent to using the `handle` parameter with `dojo.xhrGet()`:

```
defer2.addBoth(function(result) {
    if (result instanceof Error){
        dojo.query('.content_not_found2', 'xhrget2').addClass('error')
            [0].innerHTML = result.message;
    } else {
        dojo.query('.content_not_found2', 'xhrget2').addClass('success')
            [0].innerHTML = result;
    }
    return result;
});
```

The single parameter to `.addBoth()` is expected to be the handler function called in either error or success cases. As with the handle parameter to `dojo.xhrGet()`, this function branches on the type of its single parameter to determine error or success cases.

Figure 27-2 shows the results of all this `Deferred` action in the example HTML page.

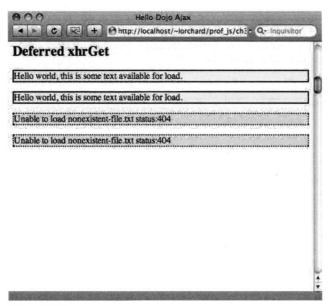

Figure 27-2

Working with Response Formats

So far, in making simple HTTP GET requests, the success handlers in this chapter have been treating the response content as plain text. And, by default, this is how Dojo handles responses. However, Dojo also knows about a number of other data formats useful for web responses, and can automatically translate from raw response data to more useful objects.

Consider the following markup as a framework to display results from upcoming examples:

```
<div id="xhr_handle_as">
    <h2>xhrGet with handleAs</h2>
    <p class="content_text">Loading...</p>
    <p class="content_xml">Loading...</p>
    <p class="content_json">Loading...</p>
    <p class="content_js">Loading...</p>
    <p class="content_json_comment">Loading...</p>
</div>
```

Additionally, keep in mind the following helper function for updating the contents of this markup:

```
function updateContent(result, handle_as, sel) {
    if (result instanceof Error){
        dojo.query(sel, 'xhr_handle_as').addClass('error')
            [0].innerHTML = result.message;
    } else {
        dojo.query(sel, 'xhr_handle_as').addClass('success')
            [0].innerHTML = handle_as + ' [' + (typeof result) + '] ' + result;
    }
}
```

This code will handle the success or error cases of a web request, updating the given element identified by CSS class with either the error message or a report on the data handling and contents returned for a request.

Working with Text Responses

Handling response data as text is the default case for dojo.xhrGet(), as you've already seen. To make things explicit, the following introduces the handleAs parameter with its default value of "text":

```
dojo.xhrGet({
    url:      'data.txt',
    handleAs: 'text',
    timeout:  5000,
    handle: function(result, io_args) {
        return updateContent(result, 'text', '.content_text');
    }
});
```

Assuming a successful fetch of the same contents for data.txt used so far in the chapter, this code will use the updateContent() helper to replace the contents of <p class="content_text"> with something like the following:

```
text [string] Hello world, this is some text available for load.
```

No real surprises here: The content is handled as type text, the JavaScript type of the response data parameter is string, and the content itself appears as expected.

Working with XML Responses

Where things get interesting is in changing the value for handleAs, and fetching a different kind of data. In this case, consider XML, which puts the "X" in AJAX:

```
<?xml version="1.0"?>
<foo>
    <bar>hello</bar>
    <baz>world</baz>
</foo>
```

Assuming that this simple XML document resides in a file named data.xml, consider this code example meant to fetch it:

```
dojo.xhrGet({
    url:      'data.xml',
    handleAs: 'xml',
    timeout:  5000,
    handle: function(result, io_args) {
        console.log("Fetched XML data, root tag is:");
        console.log('<' + result.firstChild.tagName + '>');
        return updateContent(result, 'xml', '.content_xml');
    }
});
```

Given a successful request, the following will be the result placed into the "content_xml" paragraph:

```
xml [object] [object XMLDocument]
```

You'll also see the following messages logged when the callback runs:

```
Fetched XML data, root tag is:
<foo>
```

Notice what's different here in contrast to handleAs: 'text' — when the response received, rather than simply passing the data into the callback, Dojo takes handleAs: 'xml' as a cue to first attempt to parse the data as an XML document and return *that* object as the response to the callback.

Something interesting to note about XML response in particular is that there's a little bit of cross-browser trickery that needs to go on behind the scenes to normalize this behavior. Although native XMLHttpRequest objects come with a responseXML property, some browsers refuse to provide an XML document here unless the Content-Type header is correct in indicating XML content.

In contrast, Dojo's handleAs behavior ensures that an XML document is available no matter what the Content-Type header says, as long as the content can be parsed as such.

Working with JSON Responses

Responses with XML documents aren't the only game in town, though. JSON — or JavaScript Object Notation (http://json.org) — is another alternative to packaging up structured data.

Take a look at this example, residing in a file named data.json:

```
{"url":"http:\/\/decafbad.com","title":"0xDECAFBAD"}
```

In a nutshell, this is a way of expressing data structures using a subset of JavaScript syntax. Although practice may vary, the format is executable JavaScript code by definition.

To fetch this data, the handleAs parameter is used with "json" like so:

```
dojo.xhrGet({
    url:      'data.json',
    handleAs: 'json',
    timeout:  5000,
    handle: function(result, io_args) {
        console.log("Fetched JSON data:");
        console.dir(result);
        return updateContent(result, 'json', '.content_json');
    }
});
```

With a successful response, the following will appear in the <p class="content_json"> element:

```
json [object] [object Object]
```

Additionally, you'll see the following output in your log transcript, providing a bit more detail on what was fetched in terms of the data structure:

```
Fetched JSON data:

title
        "0xDECAFBAD"
url
        "http://decafbad.com"
```

Although there is a rich toolset available for working with XML data, JSON data is often much quicker and simpler to work with. After all, this data format is expressed using JavaScript itself, so the parser comes free with a call to `eval()`.

Working with Comment-Filtered JSON Responses

To backpedal for a moment, use of `eval()` to parse JSON can be asking for trouble, unless you have complete control over both the server and the client in your web application — it is executable code, after all, and `eval()` makes no distinction between simple JSON data and more complex JavaScript containing potential exploits against your application.

Additionally, allowing the web host to serve up data easily used with `eval()` can expose the data to being used by unanticipated agents outside the loop between your application's client and server halves. A technique dubbed *JavaScript Hijacking* can be used to include a script tag loading your JSON data into a page on another domain and, through overriding some native object constructors, access the data outside your application.

The danger posed by this technique may be overblown — but if your application depends solely on cookies as authentication to private data available via simple JSON fetches, for instance, you may have a problem lurking. Read more about JavaScript Hijacking here:

```
www.fortify.com/security-resources/javascripthijacking.jsp
```

Whatever the threat to your application (or lack thereof) Dojo supports a variant on JSON called `"comment-filtered"` JSON. It looks like this:

```
/*{"url":"http:\/\/decafbad.com","title":"0xDECAFBAD"}*/
```

The only real change is that the JSON data is wrapped in JavaScript comments, rendering it impossible to access with a `<script>` tag across domains or direct use with `eval()` without first stripping the comment markers. Dojo offers a `handleAs` type named "`json-comment-filtered`" that does this exact thing.

Assuming this data is made available as `data.json-comment-filtered`, the following code fetches it:

```
dojo.xhrGet({
    url:     'data.json-comment-filtered',
    handleAs: 'json-comment-filtered',
    timeout: 5000,
    handle: function(result, io_args) {
        console.log("Fetched JSON data:");
```

```
            console.dir(result);
            return updateContent(result, 'json-comment-filtered',
                '.content_json_comment');
        }
    });
```

Just as before with JSON, a successful response inserts the following content into the `"content_json_comment"` paragraph:

```
json [object] [object Object]
```

And in the log transcript, the same messages as with raw JSON appear:

```
Fetched JSON data:

title
        "0xDECAFBAD"
url
        "http://decafbad.com"
```

Working with JavaScript Responses

In direct contrast to what the comment-filtered JSON convention seeks to *prevent*, Dojo also offers the ability to dynamically load and execute arbitrary JavaScript. As long as you've got control over what the server sends back from your domain, this is less alarming than it sounds — and can be quite useful for injecting on-demand code into the page based on server-side decisions.

Consider the following, assumed to reside in the file `data.js`:

```
(function() {
    console.log("Executable JavaScript ahoy!");
    dojo.query('.content_js', 'xhr_handle_as')
        .addContent('<p>Look, a side-effect!</p>', 'after');
    return "Hello! Today is " + ( new Date() );
})();
```

Notice that along with a return value built on the client side, it sends a message to the log console, and inserts some content into the page as a side effect.

This content is fetched — and executed — the same as every other response format, with an appropriate value for `handleAs`:

```
dojo.xhrGet({
    url:      'data.js',
    handleAs: 'javascript',
    timeout:  5000,
    handle: function(result, io_args) {
        return updateContent(result, 'javascript', '.content_js');
    }
});
```

A successful response for this fetch will result in content like the following appearing in the content_js paragraph:

```
javascript [string] Hello! Today is Tue Mar 11 2008 21:33:23 GMT-0700 (PDT)
```

Also, directly after this paragraph, a new paragraph will appear with the following content:

```
Look, a side-effect!
```

And, finally, this message will appear in the log:

```
Executable JavaScript ahoy!
```

All of this just serves to reinforce the flexibility of this particular response handling type. A JavaScript response from the server can do just about anything to the page and the user interface on the client, from altering content to updating classes and code resident in memory.

Figure 27-3 shows what all of these response format handlers have done in the markup.

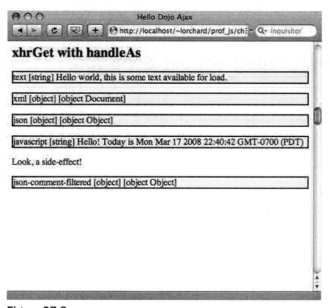

Figure 27-3

Specifying Request Methods

Up to this point in the chapter, only HTTP GET requests have been demonstrated, using the `dojo.xhrGet()` utility. However, there's more to HTTP than just GET — using forms in a browser will at least introduce you to the POST method, while exploring REST-style web services will require the use of further methods like PUT, DELETE, HEAD, and OPTIONS.

For these additional methods, Dojo offers these utility functions:

- ❑   `dojo.xhrPost(params)`

- ❑   `dojo.xhrPut(params)`

- ❑   `dojo.xhrDelete(params)`

These basically work in the same way as `dojo.xhrGet()`: The data structure passed with parameters for the request is expected to contain the same information, such as `url`, `timeout`, `handleAs`, `load`, `error`, `handle`. These functions also each return an instance of `Deferred`, just like `dojo.xhrGet()`.

In fact, all of these method-specific utilities are wrappers for the following function:

```
dojo.xhr(method, params, has_body)
```

The first parameter, `method`, expects the HTTP method (such as GET, POST, PUT). The second parameter expects the same data structure describing the request, as has been used so far in `dojo.xhrGet()` examples.

The third and final parameter, `has_body`, is a Boolean flag, indicating whether the request should expect to be sent with a request body. The methods POST and PUT should be made with this flag set as `true`, though actually sending request bodies will be covered in the next section.

Building a Server-Side Request Echo Tool

Now, before you get into any experiments with these calls, it might help to take a diversion into a small amount of server-side code. The examples up to this point have all worked fine with static data files, but now it's time to see a little more out of the HTTP request/response dialog.

Thanks to its ubiquity and popularity, you most likely have access to a web server running PHP. So, consider the following start to an exploration tool named `echo.php`:

```php
<?php
// Assemble a report of what was received in the request.
$out = array(
    'method' => $_SERVER['REQUEST_METHOD'],
    'post_params' => $_POST,
    'query_params' => $_GET,
    'accept' => $output_type,
    'x_requested_with' => $_SERVER['HTTP_X_REQUESTED_WITH'],
);

// If a request body was present include it in the response.
if ($_SERVER['CONTENT_LENGTH']) {
    $out['content_type']   = $_SERVER['CONTENT_TYPE'];
    $out['content_length'] = $_SERVER['CONTENT_LENGTH'];
    $out['request_body']   = file_get_contents('php://input');
}
```

This code assembles some key data points describing the request being made to the script, in preparation for echoing them back out in some form in the response. They include:

❏   HTTP method used in the request

❏   Any POST parameters sent in the request body

❏   Any query parameters passed in the URL

❏   The `Accept:` header sent along with the request

❏   The value of a header named `X-Requested-With`, which Dojo sets to "`XMLHttpRequest`", and may be useful for distinguishing AJAX requests from other page requests in your server-side code

And finally, if content is sent along in the request body, its length, type, and the content itself is included in the data collected for the response.

Next, in order to further exercise some of the asynchronous features of Dojo's AJAX helpers, the script includes an option to fake long-running processes:

```
// If a ?wait parameter passed, wait that number of seconds
// This lets us pretend there's work going on to allow animated
// spinners to spin for a little while.
if ($_GET['wait']) {
    sleep(intval($_GET['wait']));
}
```

With the preceding code, supplying a `?wait=10` parameter to the script will cause it to wait for 10 seconds. In the meantime, code on the client-side can display loading messages, show animated GIFs with spinning indicators, or do whatever else it wants while the work gets done. At any rate, throwing in a delay will allow you to slow things down a little to see what is happening.

Finally, it's time for the script to assemble a response:

```
// Accept either a ?type query parameter or an Accept: header
if ($_GET['type']) {
    $output_type = $_GET['type'];
} else {
    $output_type = $_SERVER['HTTP_ACCEPT'];
}

// Now, decide what output format to use.
switch($output_type) {

    case 'text':
    case 'text/plain':
        header('Content-Type: text/plain');
        echo var_export($out, true);
        break;

    case 'json-comment-filtered':
    case 'text/json-comment-filtered':
        header('Content-Type: text/json-comment-filtered');
```

```
        echo '/*'.json_encode($out).'*/';
        break;

    case 'iframe-text':
        header('Content-Type: text/html');
        ?><html><body><textarea><?php
            echo htmlentities(var_export($out, true));
        ?></textarea></body></html><?php

    case 'iframe-json':
        header('Content-Type: text/html');
        ?><html><body><textarea><?php
            echo htmlentities(json_encode($out));
        ?></textarea></body></html><?php

    default:
        header('Content-Type: application/json');
        echo json_encode($out); break;

}
```

The preceding code expects either an `Accept:` header sent in the request, or a parameter named `type` to be included in the URL query string. This corresponds roughly to the options made available by the `handleAs` parameter accepted by `dojo.xhr()`:

❏ `text` or `text/plain` — Sends the response in text format

❏ `json-comment-filtered` or `text/json-comment-filtered` — Uses the `"comment-filtered"` JSON format

❏ `iframe-text` — Sends a text response wrapped in an HTML `<textarea>`, which will make more sense toward the end of the chapter

❏ `iframe-json` — Sends a JSON response wrapped in an HTML `<textarea>`, which will also make more sense toward the end of the chapter

Anything not covered by one of the preceding options will result in a JSON format response. In all cases, the response is a quick-and-dirty dump of the data points collected on the request, either with a PHP `json_encode()` or a `var_export()`. You can work on a prettier report if you like, but this should serve for most experimental purposes.

This small utility allows you to try out various combinations of parameters and HTTP methods, with the response offering details you can expect to see in actual working server-side application code. If you can't run this directly in PHP, hopefully you can get the idea from the code if you need or want to implement something similar in your server-side environment of choice.

Trying Out Request Methods

Rather than just list examples of code making requests with various methods, it might be more interesting to build a small lab for trying each out interactively and see what the server responses look like.

To begin, consider the following markup:

```
<div id="xhr_methods">
    <h2>xhr methods</h2>

    <form>
        <button class="GET">GET</button>
        <button class="POST">POST</button>
        <button class="PUT">PUT</button>
        <button class="DELETE">DELETE</button>
        <button class="HEAD">HEAD</button>
        <button class="OPTIONS">OPTIONS</button>

        <br />

        <textarea class="results" cols="70" rows="25"></textarea>
    </form>

</div>
```

This code provides a user interface consisting of a number of buttons devoted to HTTP methods, followed by a <textarea> that will serve as a display for responses received from requests.

Next, take a look at this JavaScript code beginning the definition of a class that will drive the user interface:

```
dojo.declare('decafbad.ajax.ajax.MethodPlay', null, {

    root_id: '',

    url: 'echo.php?type=text&wait=1',

    constructor: function(root_id) {
        this.root_id = root_id;
        this.wireUpButtons();
    },

    wireUpButtons: function() {
        dojo.forEach(this.methods, function(method) {
            dojo.query('.'+method, this.root_id)
                .onclick(this, 'handleButtonClick');
        }, this);
    },
```

This code declares a new MethodPlay class. Its constructor expects a root ID for the preceding markup, which it uses to wire up all the HTTP method buttons to a handler method .handleButtonClick(). Additionally, there's a property pointing at the location of the echo.php script.

Continuing on, the following code defines the `.handleButtonClick()` method:

```
handleButtonClick: function(ev) {
    var method = ev.currentTarget.className;

    dojo.stopEvent(ev);

    dojo.query('.results', this.root_id)
        .style('backgroundColor', '#ffd')
        [0].value = 'loading...';

    dojo.xhr(method, {
        url:     this.url,
        handleAs: 'text',
        load:     dojo.hitch(this, 'handleResponse'),
        error:    dojo.hitch(this, 'handleError')
    });
},
```

This button click handler method first uses the target button's CSS class name to figure out which HTTP method it should be using. Then, it updates the display `<textarea>` with a loading message and a light yellow background color — note that the URL for `echo.php` specified earlier has a `wait=1` parameter, which will cause this loading message to hopefully stick around long enough for you to see it.

The method finishes off with a call to `dojo.xhr()` with the appropriate method and URL. Something interesting to note here is the use of `dojo.hitch()` to wire up object methods as callback handlers for the response — unlike other event handling code in Dojo, an object reference and method name cannot be used directly here, so the `dojo.hitch()` utility is needed to come up with a wrapper function to adapt to the requirements of `dojo.xhr()` and the `Deferred` objects it uses.

The following defines the `.handleResponse()` method used to handle successful responses:

```
handleResponse: function(resp, io_args) {
    var out =
        "Response Headers:\n\n" +
        io_args.xhr.getAllResponseHeaders() + "\n" +
        "Response body:\n\n" +
        resp;
    dojo.query('.results', this.root_id)
        .style('backgroundColor', '#dfd')
        [0].value = out;
},
```

Upon receiving a successful response, the `.handleResponse()` method assembles a quick-and-dirty report on the response headers and body content. It then switches the `<textarea>` color to light green and replaces its contents with this report.

Finally, the class declaration is wrapped up with the definition of `.handleError()` in the following:

```
handleError: function(error, io_args) {
    dojo.query('.results', this.root_id)
        .style('backgroundColor', '#fdd')
```

```
                    [0].value = error.message;
        }

    });

    var method_play = new decafbad.ajax.ajax.MethodPlay('xhr_methods');
```

This final method turns the `<textarea>` light red and displays the error message upon receiving a response failure. And then, after the end of the class declaration, a new instance of the class is created using the root ID of the markup introduced at the beginning of this section.

Figure 27-4 shows the resulting page.

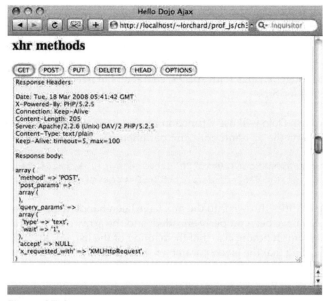

Figure 27-4

Using Request Parameters and Content

Now that you've seen how to make requests, handle response content in varied ways, and change the method used in the request, it's time to check out how to send query parameters and request body content. As with the other aspects of making HTTP requests and dealing with responses, Dojo offers a few convenient features to make passing data in requests easier as well.

Making GET Request with Query Parameters

One of the simplest ways to get parameters into a request is by way of the query string portion of the URL. You're probably already familiar with this, and you saw it earlier with the `wait` and `type` parameters passed to the `echo.php` script. But, of course, these were hand-coded into the request URL and luckily required no escaping of any kind.

Consider the following example, which includes parameters of significantly greater complexity:

```
dojo.xhrGet({
    url: 'echo.php?type=text',
    content: {
        alpha:      'one two three',
        beta:       '!@#$%^&*()',
        'splat[]':  ['uno', 'dos', 'tres'],
        glob:       { what:1, who:2, where:23 }

    },
    handle: function(resp, io_args) {
        console.log("Response from xhrGet with request parameters:");
        console.log(resp);
    }
});
```

In the preceding code, one query string parameter is already included in the URL itself. Beyond that, a further set of request parameters are provided under the content parameter passed to dojo.xhrGet(). Note that these include longer strings with spaces, characters in need of URL encoding, and even an array of values thrown in for fun.

In constructing the request, Dojo will use a function named dojo.objectToQuery() to come up with the following URL based on the url and content parameters:

```
echo.php?type=text&alpha=one%20two%20three&beta=!%40%23%24%25%5E%26*()
&splat%5B%5D=uno&splat%5B%5D=dos&splat%5B%5D=tres&glob=%5Bobject%20Object%5D
```

Notice that all the little oddities thrown into the mix have been handled: Spaces and other characters relatively exotic for URLs have been properly encoded, and the array of values has been transformed into multiple parameters. It's worth noting also that the naming of the list, splat[], is not a convention of Dojo but rather of PHP, indicating that the given parameter should be expected to have multiple values.

There are some limitations to the magic provided by dojo.objectToQuery(), however, as the final parameter glob was rendered as %5Bobject%20Object%5D — which is probably somewhat less than desirable. But, that's not so much a failing of Dojo itself as it is a limitation of expressing parameters in a URL query string.

Finally, here's what you should see in the log after a successful response from running the previous code:

```
Response from xhrGet with request parameters:
array (
  'method' => 'GET',
  'post_params' =>
  array (
  ),
  'query_params' =>
  array (
    'type' => 'text',
    'alpha' => 'one two three',
    'beta' => '!@#$%^&*()',
    'splat' =>
```

```
        array (
          0 => 'uno',
          1 => 'dos',
          2 => 'tres',
        ),
        'glob' => '[object Object]',
      ),
      'accept' => NULL,
      'x_requested_with' => 'XMLHttpRequest',
    )
```

This should give you an idea of how these parameters will be received and handled by a server-side language like PHP.

Making POST Requests with Response Body Parameters

Another way of getting parameters into a request is via body content in a POST request. This is done just like the previous example, but swapping `dojo.xhrPost()` for `dojo.xhrGet()` like so:

```
dojo.xhrPost({
    url: 'echo.php?type=text',
    content: {
        alpha:      'one two three',
        beta:       '!@#$%^&*()',
        'splat[]':  ['uno', 'dos', 'tres'],
        glob:       { what:1, who:2, where:23 }
    },
    handle: function(resp, io_args) {
        console.log("Response from xhrPost with request parameters:");
        console.log(resp);
    }
});
```

To see how this call to `dojo.xhrPost()` compares and contrasts with the previous call to `dojo.xhrGet()`, take a look at what shows up in the Firebug log after a successful request:

```
Response from xhrPost with request parameters:
array (
  'method' => 'POST',
  'post_params' =>
  array (
    'alpha' => 'one two three',
    'beta' => '!@#$%^&*()',
    'splat' =>
    array (
      0 => 'uno',
      1 => 'dos',
      2 => 'tres',
    ),
    'glob' => '[object Object]',
  ),
  'query_params' =>
```

```
       array (
         'type' => 'text',
       ),
       'accept' => NULL,
       'x_requested_with' => 'XMLHttpRequest',
       'content_type' => 'application/x-www-form-urlencoded',
       'content_length' => '127',
       'request_body' => 'alpha=one%20two%20three&beta=!%40%23%24%25%5E%26*()
           &splat%5B%5D=uno&splat%5B%5D=dos&splat%5B%5D=tres
           &glob=%5Bobject%20Object%5D',
   )
```

The first thing to notice is that, although there is still a single query parameter `type`, the rest of the parameters have been separated out into `post_params`. This is because PHP interprets parameters given in the URL and those passed in the request body into separate collections.

The other thing to notice is that this request has body content now — which is reflected in the appearance of a content type, length, and body data. The body data itself looks like the query string in the URL, which is basically how the `application/x-www-form-urlencoded` content MIME type is defined.

Unfortunately, this means that the parameter encoding magic is limited to the same rules as a GET request. However, since the length of a URL is limited to various lengths in various browsers, and the body content of a POST request can be as large as you like, using a POST request gives you more flexibility in that respect at least.

Making POST Requests with Raw Body Content

With all this mention of the limitations of the usual ways to pass parameters, it's about time to take a look at a less-than-usual way to improve upon the situation. You can do this by sending raw data in the request body using the encoding of your choice. This can include text, XML documents, binary data, or maybe even JSON — using `dojo.rawXhrPost()` like so:

```
dojo.rawXhrPost({
    url: 'echo.php?type=text',
    headers: {
        'Content-Type': 'application/json'
    },
    postData: dojo.toJson({
        alpha: 'one two three',
        beta:  '!@#$%^&*()',
        splat: ['uno', 'dos', 'tres'],
        glob:  { what:1, who:2, where:23 }
    }),
    handle: function(resp, io_args) {
        console.log("Response from rawXhrPost with request parameters:");
        console.log(resp);
    }
});
```

This time around, the code uses `dojo.toJson()` to encode the data structure as a JSON string, passed to `dojo.rawXhrPost()` in the `postData` parameter. This data doesn't *have* to be JSON, but this example provides an easy contrast to the previous two.

In the Firebug log, the following should appear upon the success of this request:

```
Response from rawXhrPost with request parameters:
array (
  'method' => 'POST',
  'post_params' =>
  array (
  ),
  'query_params' =>
  array (
    'type' => 'text',
  ),
  'accept' => NULL,
  'x_requested_with' => 'XMLHttpRequest',
  'content_type' => 'application/json',
  'content_length' => '113',
  'request_body' => '{"alpha":"one two three","beta":"!@#$%^&*()",
    "splat":["uno","dos","tres"], "glob":{"what":1,"who":2,"where":23}}',
)
```

Although the `echo.php` script doesn't use it, PHP 5 offers a `json_decode()` function. You can use this to decode the `request_body` content in your scripts. Most modern web application environments offer something similar, so JSON can be a good choice to provide a pretty seamless transfer of data structures from client-side JavaScript to server-side code with none of the limitations of plain old URL-encoded query strings.

Finally, it's worth noting that along with `dojo.rawXhrPost()`, there's also a `dojo.rawXhrPut()` function that does the same thing as the previous code for a request using HTTP PUT instead of POST. All of the parameters and the pattern of use are identical. There are no "rawXhr" equivalents for other HTTP methods such as GET, DELETE, or HEAD — but those methods don't support request bodies either.

Augmenting Forms with In-Place Requests

All of the previous means for getting parameters and data sent in a request to the server are great for working with server-side resources built for the express purpose of being used in a client-side user interface, or built as REST-style web services. But, one of the ideals of modern web development is to introduce some degree of unobtrusive augmentation of the page, with graceful fallback to non-AJAX functionality.

Apropos of this, one of the techniques used by some sites is the construction of a form that, where possible, submits its data to the server and displays the result in place without disturbing the entire page. Where the enhancement is not possible, the form falls back to a full-page reload.

To give you a preview of how Dojo helps accomplish this, consider the following code:

```
dojo.xhrPost({
    form:    dojo.query('form')[0],
    handle: function(resp, io_args){ ... }
});
```

The main attraction here is that `dojo.xhrPost()` — and, in fact, all of the helper functions wrapped around `dojo.xhr()` — accept a parameter named `form`, which is expected to either be an ID or a reference to a `<form>` node from the DOM.

Given this, Dojo uses a function named `dojo.formToObject()` to dig through the form and convert all of its contained data into a JavaScript object. This process skips buttons and disabled form fields, finds currently selected checkboxes and drop-down options, and scoops up the contents of text fields. This, then, is run through `dojo.objectToQuery()` in order to come up with the body content for the POST request. Additionally, the URL for the request is taken from the form's `action` attribute.

Moving things along, consider the following start to a demonstration of this feature:

```
<style>
    form li {
        list-style-type: none;
        line-height: 3.5ex;
    }
    form li.submit {
        margin-left: 6ex;
    }
    form label {
        display: block;
        text-align: right;
        width: 5ex;
        padding-right: 1ex;
        float: left;
    }
    .shown {
        display: block;
    }
    .hidden {
        display: none;
    }
</style>
```

This markup provides some simple CSS styling for a form, as well as a hidden panel that will provide in-place feedback for a form submission. The markup styled by the preceding code appears in the following example:

```
<div id="xhr_request_form">
    <h2>xhr request form</h2>

    <div id="magic_form1">

        <form class="form_post" method="post"
                action="echo.php?wait=1&amp;type=text">
```

```html
        <h3>magic ajax form #1</h3>
        <ul>
            <li>
                <label for="foo">foo:</label>
                <input type="text" name="foo" value="Hello" size="20" />
            </li>
            <li>
                <label for="disabled_thing">disabled:</label>
                <input type="text" name="disabled_thing"
                    value="Ignore me" disabled="true" size="20" />
            </li>
            <li>
                <label for="bar[]">bar:</label>
                <input type="checkbox" name="bar[]" value="world" /> world
                <input type="checkbox" name="bar[]" value="planet" /> planet
            </li>
            <li>
                <label for="baz">baz:</label>
                <select name="baz">
                    <option value="one">Number one</option>
                    <option value="two">Number two</option>
                    <option value="three">Number three</option>
                </select>
            </li>
            <li class="submit">
                <input type="submit" value="submit" />
            </li>
        </ul>
    </form>
```

The form constructed here is not too elaborate, but it does include a few representative elements: a text field, a disabled element, a pair of checkboxes, and a drop-down selector. Note, again, that the name `bar[]` reflects a PHP convention to denote an expectation of multiple values for the field. Figure 27-5 shows what this form looks like.

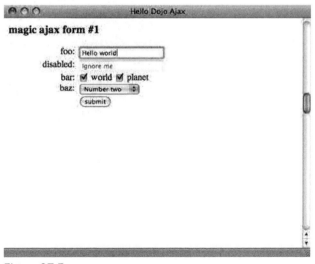

Figure 27-5

The next part will be hidden at first, but contains elements necessary to report on the form submission:

```
<form class="form_results hidden">
    <h3>magic ajax form #1 results</h3>
    <a class="reset_form" href="#">click here to try the form again</a>
    <br />
    <textarea class="results" cols="70" rows="25"></textarea>
</form>

</div>

</div>
```

This also finishes off the markup for this example. At the end, there's an initially hidden form consisting of a link that will reset the form when clicked, as well as a `<textarea>` into which the results of the response will be inserted.

Now, it's time to start the JavaScript code that will impart functionality to the preceding markup:

```
dojo.require('dojo.NodeList-fx');

dojo.declare('decafbad.ajax.ajax.MagicForm', null, {

    root_id: '',

    constructor: function(root_id) {
        this.root_id = root_id;
        this.wireUpForm();
    },

    wireUpForm: function() {
        dojo.query('.form_post', this.root_id)
            .connect('submit', this, 'handleSubmit');
        dojo.query('a.reset_form', this.root_id)
            .onclick(this, 'resetForm');
    },
```

This code first requires the `dojo.NodeList-fx` module, which will integrate animations into the `dojo.query()` and `dojo.NodeList` system. Next, the declaration of a class named `MagicForm` is begun. The constructor of this class expects a root ID (for example, `magic_form1`) identifying the container within which it will wire up handlers to take care of the form submission and clicks on the form reset link.

The next part defines the `.handleSubmit()` method, meant to take care of form submission:

```
handleSubmit: function(ev) {
    dojo.stopEvent(ev);

    // Disable the submit button while this is working.
    dojo.query('input[type="submit"]', this.root_id)
        .attr('value', 'loading...')
```

```
                    [0].disabled = true;

            // Find the form, submit using XHR
            dojo.query('form.form_post', this.root_id)
                .forEach(function(form) {
                    dojo.xhrPost({
                        form:    form,
                        handle: dojo.hitch(this, 'displayResults')
                    });
                }, this);
        },
```

The `.handleSubmit()` method first uses `dojo.stopEvent()` to intercept and take care of the form submission. Note that this `submit` event includes clicks on the form submit button, as well as the user hitting the return key from within any text field in the form.

Next, the method finds the form submit button, changes its label to read `"loading..."`, and sets it as disabled. This grays out the button in most browsers and prevents it from being clicked again.

After this, the method locates the form and fires off a `dojo.xhrPost()` call given the form, with the `.displayResults()` method registered to handle any responses.

The following defines the `.displayResults()` method:

```
displayResults: function(result, io_args) {
    // Hide the submitted form.
    dojo.query('.form_post', this.root_id)
        .addClass('hidden').removeClass('shown');

    var msg, clr;
    if (result instanceof Error){
        // Display error message and flash red color.
        clr = '#f88'; msg = result.message;
    } else {
        // Display response and flash green color.
        clr = '#8f8'; msg = result;
    }

    // Reveal the results pane container.
    dojo.query('.form_results', this.root_id)
        .removeClass('hidden').addClass('shown');

    // Inject the results into the results pane.
    // .attr() doesn't seem to work with textareas
    var pane = dojo.query('.results', this.root_id);
    pane[0].value = msg;

    // Make the textarea flash to attract attention.
```

```
            pane.animateProperty({
                duration: 750,
                properties: {
                    backgroundColor: { start: clr, end: '#fff' }
                }
            }).play();
    },
```

The `.displayResults()` method shows off just a little more Dojo flair. First, upon receipt of a response, the method hides the form. Then, it determines whether the response was an error or a success and picks a red or green color and the appropriate message.

After this, the form results pane is made visible. Once visible, the `<textarea>` within that pane has its contents replaced with either an error message or the body of the successful response. As a bonus feature, the background color of the `<textarea>` is briefly flashed red or green as appropriate to indicate error or success.

Finally, the following defines the method `.resetForm()`, which is connected to the form reset link:

```
    resetForm: function(ev) {
        // Show the form again.
        dojo.query('.form_post', this.root_id)
            .removeClass('hidden').addClass('shown');

        // Hide the results pane.
        dojo.query('.form_results', this.root_id)
            .addClass('hidden').removeClass('shown');

        // Re-enable the submit button.
        dojo.query('input[type="submit"]', this.root_id)
            .attr('value', 'submit')
            [0].disabled = false;

        dojo.stopEvent(ev);
    },

    EOF:null

});

    var mf1 = new decafbad.ajax.ajax.MagicForm('magic_form1');
```

Figure 27-6 shows how things look after a successful form submission. Along with reporting on the response, this also makes the form reset link visible. Clicking this link is handled by the `.resetForm()` method defined in the preceding code, which reveals the form again and hides the results pane. It also re-enables the submit button and changes its label back to read "submit", thus resetting the form for another try.

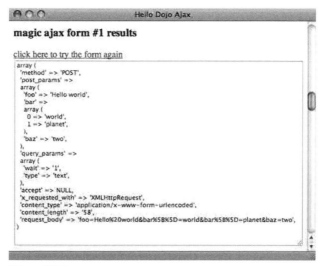

Figure 27-6

Finally, after the end of the class definition for `MagicForm`, there's a statement creating a new instance of the class using `magic_form1` as the root ID, thus completing the circle and wiring up the markup.

Although it may be legible in Figure 27-6, the following offers a closer look at the results from `echo.php` from this sample request:

```
array (
  'method' => 'POST',
  'post_params' =>
  array (
    'foo' => 'Hello world',
    'bar' =>
    array (
      0 => 'world',
      1 => 'planet',
    ),
    'baz' => 'two',
  ),
  'query_params' =>
  array (
    'wait' => '1',
    'type' => 'text',
  ),
  'accept' => NULL,
  'x_requested_with' => 'XMLHttpRequest',
  'content_type' => 'application/x-www-form-urlencoded',
  'content_length' => '58',
  'request_body' => 'foo=Hello%20world&bar%5B%5D=world&bar%5B%5D=planet&baz=two',
)
```

Now, if you're curious to see what happens when the form enhancement fails, try commenting out the final line of the code in the preceding example to prevent the form from getting wired up. Submitting the form without the benefit of the in-place Dojo form submission magic will send you to a completely new page consisting entirely of output like the following:

```
array (
  'method' => 'POST',
  'post_params' =>
  array (
    'foo' => 'Hello world',
    'bar' =>
    array (
      0 => 'world',
      1 => 'planet',
    ),
    'baz' => 'two',
  ),
  'query_params' =>
  array (
    'wait' => '1',
    'type' => 'text',
  ),
  'accept' => NULL,
  'x_requested_with' => NULL,
  'content_type' => 'application/x-www-form-urlencoded',
  'content_length' => '56',
  'request_body' => 'foo=Hello+world&bar%5B%5D=world&bar%5B%5D=planet&baz=two',
)
```

The thing to notice is that the unadorned form submission is identical to the previous one facilitated by dojo.xhrPost(), with just a few highlighted exceptions:

❑   The X-Requested-With header was not provided.

❑   The Content-Length was a bit shorter.

❑   As predicted by the previous point, the body content itself was shorter because the browser chose to use "Hello+world" as opposed to "Hello%20World" as chosen by Dojo. These two are basically equivalent, as the rest of the report on the request indicates.

This is where the X-Requested-With header can be useful: For instance, your web application framework can make some automated decisions whether or not to use a full-page template in the absence of the header or produce a simpler markup fragment if "XMLHttpRequest" is detected as the value for the X-Requested-With header.

On the whole, techniques such as the one presented in this section can provide tools to build pleasing user interfaces that still function in degraded form in less capable browsing environments.

Using Cross-Domain JSON Feeds

This chapter has provided an introduction to the various ways Dojo makes AJAX easier through abstractions and utilities wrapped around XMLHttpRequest objects. One glaring limitation of the XMLHttpRequest facility in browsers, however, is that it's limited to making requests back to the same domain, protocol, and port from which the page was loaded. That is, assuming the address of your page is `http://example.com/foo/bar.html`, all of the code presented in this chapter so far would be limited to URLs based at `http://example.com` and restricted from any other parts of the Web.

This restriction, in short, is an attempt to limit the risk of allowing client-side code to access the Web. By allowing requests only back to its server of origin, JavaScript in a browser-based application is made less capable of launching attacks against other sites on the Web — or even accessing information otherwise available to the client, behind firewalls and home routers.

It's a frustrating restriction, however, limiting the scope of mashups and cross-service integrations. It's also a restriction that can be overcome with proxies. Imagine a PHP script on the origin web server that accepts a URL as a parameter, fetches that URL, and returns the contents — though this satisfies the same-domain restriction, it's not always the safest or most convenient method.

This is an area where JSON can provide a boost. JSON is, in essence, executable JavaScript code and `<script>` tags have no cross-domain restrictions. So, you can use `<script>` tags to load JSON data structures from any domain on the Web — the only tricky part is making something happen once the inert arrays and object literals of JSON have loaded in.

There are basically two ways Dojo provides for handling this: polling a variable on script load or firing a callback script on load.

Loading JSON by Polling Variables

To get an idea of what sort of JSON feed can be handled by polling for the existence of a variable, check out the following help page at `delicious.com`, which describes a JSON feed of bookmarks:

> `http://delicious.com/help/json/posts`

As an example of what to expect from the feed, take a look at the following list of bookmarks for a user:

> `http://feeds.delicious.com/feeds/json/deusx?raw`

Fetching this URL should produce a JSON data structure like the following:

```
[{"u":"http://blog.simonshea.com/2005/09/holly-shelf-unit-batman.html","n":"&quot;I
have always wanted to build a concealed room or have secret trapdoors or similar in
a house, well this is my first (very amateur) attempt.&quot;","d":"Per Vivere [To
Live]: Holly Shelf Unit, Batman!","t":["funny","home","projects","furniture"]},...]
```

This feed is an array of object literals, each of which represents a bookmark. Each of these object literals offers properties including the following:

- ❏ u — The bookmark URL
- ❏ d — A title for the bookmark
- ❏ n — Extended notes for the bookmark
- ❏ t — An array of tags attached to the bookmark

This would be great if you could use a `dojo.xhrGet()` call with a `handleAs` parameter of `json` to load up this data and parse it, but it's highly unlikely that your code will be hosted on the `delicious.com` domain.

So, try removing the `?raw` parameter from the URL, and the content you should see from the feed will change to include a wrapper like the following:

```
if(typeof(Delicious) == 'undefined') Delicious = {}; Delicious.posts = [...]
```

The important part here is the `Delicious.posts = [...]` variable assignment. When this JSON feed is included with a `<script>` tag, the variable `Delicious.posts` will get initialized with the data included in the feed.

In other words, as long as you haven't defined `Delicious.posts` beforehand, the variable will be *undefined* before the script loads and will *become defined* afterward — thus, providing a way to detect that the data has loaded. This is what Dojo depends on for this first JSON loading technique.

To demonstrate, consider the following markup:

```
<h3>delicious posts (checkString)</h3>
<ul class="checkstring_posts"></ul>
```

Now, consider the following code, which loads up the feed and watches for the `Delicious.posts` variable:

```
dojo.require('dojo.io.script');

// Update this with your delicious.com username
var del_user = 'deusx';

// Establish the Delicious namespace, so checkString works with Delicious.posts
Delicious = {};

dojo.io.script.get({
    url: 'http://feeds.delicious.com/feeds/json/' + del_user,
    checkString: 'Delicious.posts',
    handle: function(io_args) {

  var list = dojo.query('.checkstring_posts', 'xhr_request_script');
        dojo.forEach(Delicious.posts, function(post) {
            list.addContent(
                '<li>'+
```

```
                        '<a href="' + post.u + '">' + post.d + '</a>'+
                        ( (post.n) ? '<br /><span>' + post.n + '</span>' : '' ) +
                        '</li>'
                );
            });

            delete Delicious.posts;
        }
    });
```

First, in the preceding code is a `dojo.require()` call loading up the `dojo.io.script` module. This module provides for loading and handling JSON feeds via `<script>` tags.

From this module, the use of the `dojo.io.script.get()` method resembles the use of the `dojo.xhrGet()` utility in that it accepts these parameters:

❑   url — A URL to load as a JSON feed script

❑   handle — A function called when the requested script has loaded

However, the parameter that drives this script loading technique is the following:

❑   checkString — The value of this parameter names a variable in the global namespace, which will be initialized when the URL is loaded in a `<script>` tag.

After the call to `dojo.io.script.get()`, Dojo starts periodically checking this variable, named `Delicious.posts` in the preceding code. The test used in these checks is implemented like so:

```
eval("typeof(" + checkString + ") != 'undefined'")
```

This means that as soon as the specified variable becomes defined with a type, the test is `true` and the `handle` function is called.

This specific implementation detail is important: The JSON data can even consist entirely of the value `false`, and the `handle` callback will still be called. What's also important to remember is that you must clean up the variable with the `delete` statement if you want to load another of the same kind of feed.

The implementation of the handler callback in the previous code accepts the single parameter, io_args, which resembles the same io_args parameter used with `dojo.xhr()`. Also note that this call to `dojo.io.script.get()` returns a `Deferred` object, which can be used just as described with `dojo.xhrGet()`.

Inside the callback, the variable `Delicious.posts` is used directly with a `dojo.forEach()` loop. This loop populates a list with HTML renderings of the bookmarks found in the feed. Note that, as advised in the previous paragraph, a `delete` statement is applied to the variable `Delicious.posts` after the data is processed, so that this code may be reused with more such feeds.

Figure 27-7 shows an example run of this code.

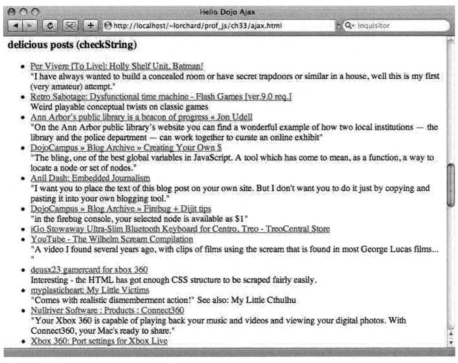

Figure 27-7

Loading JSON with Callbacks

Watching for a variable to appear before firing a callback function is one way to handle a `<script>` tag loading. What would be better, though, is to cause the loading script to fire a callback directly. Among other things, this technique has been dubbed JSONP (or "JSON with padding") about which you can read more here:

```
http://bob.pythonmac.org/archives/2005/12/05/remote-json-jsonp/
```

The basic idea is that you can pass a parameter to a JSON feed naming a local callback function. The JSON structure will be wrapped with a call to this function, thus firing your callback on load.

For an example, take a look at the help page for another JSON feed from `delicious.com`:

```
http://delicious.com/help/json/tags
```

The following URL is an example instance of the feed described on this page:

```
http://feeds.delicious.com/feeds/json/tags/deusx?raw
```

The data from this URL will resemble the following JSON structure, representing a user's tags associated with usage counts:

```
{"webdev":1051,"funny":971,"gaming":947,"politics":777,"nifty":472,"osx":435,
"music":389,"metablogging":339,"odd":331}
```

Apropos of the JSONP pattern, one of the parameters available for use with this feed is named ?callback. Replacing ?raw with ?callback=display_tags in the preceding JSON URL results in the following:

```
display_tags({"webdev":1051,"funny":971,"gaming":947,"politics":777,"nifty":472,
"osx":435,"music":389,"metablogging":339,"odd":331})
```

Notice that the JSON data structure has been prepended with display_tags and a single parenthesis. The data is bracketed on the other end with a closing parenthesis, which completes the function call wrapper. This means that when the URL is loaded with a <script> tag, the global function display_tags() will be called with the JSON data structure as a parameter.

Dojo offers another variant of dojo.io.script.get() that facilitates the previous scenario. The following markup sets the stage for a quick demonstration:

```
<h3>delicious tags (callback)</h3>
<ul class="callback_tags"></ul>
```

Next, the following code offers another call to dojo.io.script.get():

```
dojo.require('dojo.io.script');

// Update this with your delicious.com username
var del_user = 'deusx';

dojo.io.script.get({
    url: 'http://feeds.delicious.com/feeds/json/tags/' + del_user,
    callbackParamName: 'callback',
    content: {
        count: 10,
        sort: 'count'
    },
    handle: function(resp, io_args) {
        var list = dojo.query('.callback_tags', 'xhr_request_script');
        for(tag in resp) {
            list.addContent(
                '<li><a href="http://del.icio.us/deusx/'+tag+'">' +
                tag + ' (' + resp[tag] + ')' +
                '</a></li>'
            );
        }
    }
});
```

Again, like calls to `dojo.xhr()`, the parameters accepted here include `url`, `handle`, and `content`. In the preceding code, content is used to pass a few additional query parameters to the JSON feed, which cause the list of tags to consist of the top 10 in order of most used.

The distinguishing parameter that enables callbacks is the following:

❑   `callbackParamName` — Name of the parameter accepted by the URL used to wrap a JSON structure with a function call

This parameter allows `dojo.io.script.get()` to work almost like calls to `dojo.xhr()`. Dojo will automatically create and manage a callback function and pass it in the request with the query string parameter named by `callbackParamName`. This managed callback calls the `handle` function defined inline — but since `dojo.io.script.get()` also returns a `Deferred` object just like calls to `dojo.xhr()`, the managed callback actually does this by firing the appropriate success and error callbacks registered on the `Deferred` object.

In the previous example, the callback handler processes the returned list of tags by rendering each as a list item. Unlike the previous variable polling demo, this one requires no `delete` statement because there is no intermediate global variable involved.

Figure 27-8 shows an example run of this code.

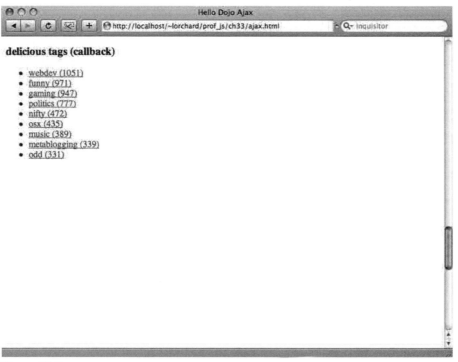

Figure 27-8

Making Requests with IFrames

Before the XMLHttpRequest object became widely available in most modern browsers, there were alternative approaches to making small requests back to the server after page load. One of these is the use of an `<iframe>`, hidden from view with CSS. This invisible `<iframe>` can facilitate HTTP GET requests through manipulation of its `src` attribute, and can even help perform HTTP POST request by being the target of a form submission.

In most ways, the use of hidden `<iframe>` elements is superseded by the use of XMLHttpRequest objects where available. An `<iframe>` can't offer a way to get around the cross-domain restriction, since the contents of an `<iframe>` loaded from another domain cannot be accessed in JavaScript. Additionally, an `<iframe>` can't really help in performing any requests with an HTTP method other than GET and POST.

However, besides offering a mostly functional backup technique for XMLHttpRequest objects, there is at least one situation where using an `<iframe>` offers a unique trick: Since an `<iframe>` can be the target of a form submission, it can help augment forms that include file upload fields with in-place feedback to avoid page reloads. This is something that can't be done at all with XMLHttpRequest objects, because JavaScript can't access the contents of a file upload field directly. This is useful for things such as uploading a personal avatar image for a bulletin board or forum.

So, with all of this in mind, this section introduces Dojo's support for making requests with hidden `<iframe>` elements, which aims to work as much like `dojo.xhr()` as possible.

Using a Proxy Script to Package IFrame Data

There is at least one major catch to using Dojo's IFrame support: Raw data of various formats cannot be reliably handled in an `<iframe>`, so Dojo requires that the data be wrapped in an HTML page containing a single `<textarea>`.

Leaning on PHP again, consider the following script, named `iframe_proxy.php`, as explanation of this packaging scheme:

```php
<?php
$path = $_GET['path'];
if (realpath($path) != realpath('./'.$path)) {
    header('Status: 403 Forbidden'); exit;
}
?>
<html><body><textarea><?php
    echo htmlentities(file_get_contents($path));
?></textarea></body></html>
```

This code accepts a query string parameter named `?path` that names a file under the same directory as the script — a requirement enforced by the `realpath()` conditional at the start of the script.

The file named in `?path` is read in with `file_get_contents()`, run through `htmlentities()` to make the data appropriate for inclusion in HTML, and then wrapped with a `<textarea>` element in a simple HTML page.

So, for example, trying to fetch `iframe_proxy.php?path=data.json` would result in the following:

```
<html><body><textarea>{&quot;url&quot;:&quot;http:\/\/decafbad
.com&quot;,&quot;title
&quot;:&quot;0xDECAFBAD&quot;}</textarea></body></html>
```

By using this packaging scheme for data, Dojo can scoop out the `<textarea>` contents in a consistent and predictable way and handle the chosen data format appropriately.

There is one exception to all the above, however, and that's using a `handleAs` parameter with a value of `html` — in this case, the HTML DOM for the `<iframe>` is itself passed along as the response, so you can perform any custom handling you like through `dojo.query()` and DOM traversal.

Handling Response Formats with IFrames

Dojo attempts to make working with `<iframe>` elements as similar to working with `dojo.xhr()` as possible. As part of this, it offers a number of options for the `handleAs` parameter. Consider the following code exercising Dojo's `<iframe>` abstraction module:

```
dojo.require('dojo.io.iframe');

var resources = [
    [ 'data.txt',   'text' ],
    [ 'data.json', 'json' ],
    [ 'data.js', 'javascript' ],
    [ 'data.xml', 'html' ]
];

dojo.forEach(resources, function(resource) {
    var url       = resource[0];
    var handle_as = resource[1];

    var dfd = dojo.io.iframe.send({
        url: 'iframe_proxy.php',
        content: {
            path: url
        },
        handleAs: handle_as,
        handle: function(resp, io_args) {
            console.log("Response via an iframe, handled as " + handle_as + ":");
            console.log(resp);
        }
    });

});
```

The first line in the preceding code loads in the `dojo.io.iframe` module. This module provides the `dojo.io.iframe.send()` utility function, which will be used shortly.

The next part of the code builds a list of lists, each sublist containing a URL and a value for `handleAs`. This is a subset of what's available with `dojo.xhr()`, including the following:

❑   `text` — Handle as plain text content.

❑   `json` — Parse as JSON data into a JavaScript object.

❑   `javascript` — Execute as JavaScript code.

❑   `html` — Return the DOM of the loaded `<iframe>` element. Note that this is not the same as XML parsing, and loading an XML document directly into the `<iframe>` may offer mixed results.

After defining this list, a `dojo.forEach()` loop is used to process each. A call is made to the `dojo.io.iframe.send()` function, which returns a `Deferred` object such as `dojo.xhr()` and accepts similar parameters including `url`, `content`, `handleAs`, and `handle`.

When called, `dojo.io.iframe.send()` first ensures that a hidden `<iframe>` is available in the page, either by dynamically inserting one into the document or finding one that it had inserted earlier. It then queues up the request — although Dojo uses a single `<iframe>` for this abstraction, it does maintain an internal queue of requests waiting to use it.

When a request gets a turn with the `<iframe>`, Dojo changes the element's `src` attribute for a GET request. If the request involves using a form, the form's target is changed to point at the `<iframe>` and it gets programmatically submitted to fire off a POST request. In either case, Dojo watches for the `<iframe>` to finish loading in order to get the response for the request and fire the appropriate `Deferred` success or error callback branch. Note again that if you use the `handle`, `load`, or `error` parameters, callbacks defined inline are automatically registered as handlers on the `Deferred` object.

When running the preceding code, you should see something like the following appear in your Firebug log transcript:

```
Response via an iframe, handled as text:
Hello world, this is some text available for load.
Response via an iframe, handled as json:
Object url=http://decafbad.com title=0xDECAFBAD
Executable JavaScript ahoy!
Response via an iframe, handled as JavaScript:
Hello! Today is Sun Mar 16 2008 21:53:31 GMT-0700 (PDT)
Response via an iframe, handled as HTML:
Document iframe_proxy.php
```

This should give you a quick idea how to start using hidden `<iframe>` elements and how to handle the results from such requests. The next section introduces one of the main advantages an `<iframe>` has over the use of XMLHttpRequest objects.

Uploading Files with Forms and IFrames

As shown earlier in this chapter, it's possible to simulate a form submission with a call to the `dojo.xhrPost()` utility function, supplying a reference to or the ID of the `<form>` element in the function's `form` parameter.

For most purposes, this technique works just fine. However, there's at least one kind of form field that can't be usefully read or manipulated from JavaScript: file selection input fields. Sure, you might be able to get the name of a selected file out of the field, but there's no way to then read the file contents from the local filesystem — and what's the point of using the file selection field if you can't get the file data uploaded to the server?

This is where the use of `<iframe>` elements for AJAX-style requests really shines: Although you can't access the contents of the selected file from JavaScript, you can point the form's target attribute at a hidden `<iframe>` and programmatically submit the form. Thus, the need to reload the whole page is avoided, and the selected file's contents can be uploaded to the server via the browser's normal form submission machinery. And, once the form submission has completed in the hidden <iframe>, you can handle the response that arrives there.

In preparation for a demonstration of this technique, check out the following markup:

```
<div id="magic_upload_form">

    <form class="form_post" method="post"
            enctype="multipart/form-data" action="upload_avatar.php">
        <h3>magic upload form</h3>
        <ul>
            <li>
                <label for="nickname">nickname:</label>
                <input type="text" name="nickname" value="biff" size="20" />
            </li>
            <li>
                <label for="avatar">avatar:</label>
                <input type="file" name="avatar" size="20" />
            </li>
            <li class="submit">
                <input type="submit" value="submit" />
            </li>
        </ul>
    </form>

    <form class="form_results hidden">
        <h3>magic upload form results</h3>
        <a class="reset_form" href="#">click here to try the form again</a>
        <br />
        <div class="results"></div>
    </form>

</div>
```

The preceding markup should look somewhat familiar: It's basically the same as what was provided for the previous in-place form submission example. The form fields have replaced with a text field and a file selection field, and the `<textarea class="results">` element used to display textual results has now become a `<div class="results">` element.

Also, note the `enctype="multipart/form-data"` attribute on the `<form>` element — this attribute is required to enable file uploads with a form in general, and it's a very common error to leave this out. Figure 27-9 shows what this markup looks like.

Figure 27-9

Now, before getting into the JavaScript code to handle the markup in the previous example, it might be useful to take a deeper look at what the form's action, `upload_avatar.php`, might look like. The following code offers the first part of such a script, which might be useful in accepting the upload of an avatar image for a discussion forum or a personal profile:

```php
<?php
// Find the location of this script and the uploads
// directory relative to it.
$BASE_DIR    = dirname(__FILE__);
$uploads_dir = $BASE_DIR . '/uploads';

// Determine if upload is of acceptable type and decide on
// extension, or decide if the type is not acceptable.
switch($_FILES['avatar']['type']) {
    case 'image/gif':
        $avatar_ext = 'gif'; break;
    case 'image/jpeg':
        $avatar_ext = 'jpeg'; break;
    case 'image/png':
        $avatar_ext = 'png'; break;
```

```
        default:
            $avatar_ext = FALSE; break;
    }

    if (!$avatar_ext) {

        // Since no acceptable type was found for the upload,
        // report that it was unacceptable.
        $out = array(
            'error' => true,
            'message' => "Avatar upload ".
                $_FILES['avatar']['name'].
                " is not an acceptable image type"
        );
```

This script assumes that a directory named `uploads/` will exist in the same path as the script itself, and that the script will have permission to write to files in this directory. You may want to move this directory, but watch throughout the rest of the script for references to this directory.

Next, a check is made of the MIME type reported by the browser for the file upload submitted from the field named `avatar`. The script requires that this type match one of three known image types:

❑   `image/gif`

❑   `image/jpeg`

❑   `image/png`

From the known image types, the script picks a file extension. If the uploaded file type matched none of those image types, no extension is chosen and instead an error message is constructed reporting on the rejection of the upload.

If and when the upload passes the gauntlet in the preceding code, it's time to actually do something with the file data:

```
    } else {

        // Get the chosen nickname and come up with a safe
        // filename for the image based on the nickname.
        $nickname  = $_REQUEST['nickname'];
        $avatar_fn = 'avatar-'.md5($nickname).".".$avatar_ext;

        // Move the uploaded file into an appropriately named file
        // under the uploads directory.
        $rv = move_uploaded_file(
            $_FILES['avatar']['tmp_name'],
            $uploads_dir . '/' . $avatar_fn
        );

        if (!$rv) {
            // Report an error if the upload move failed.
            $out = array(
```

```
                'error' => 'Could not process avatar upload.'
            );
        } else {
            // Report details of success if the move worked.
            $out = array(
                'nickname' => $nickname,
                'avatar_fn' => $avatar_fn
            );
        }

    }
```

To pick a relatively safe filename for the uploaded image, the MD5 hash of the chosen nickname is used. This will always be a 32-character long string made up of letters and numbers, derivable from the value of the user-supplied `nickname` field but never containing dangerous characters such as "." and "/" that might affect the file path itself. This also has the added benefit of obscuring database identifiers, should you choose to use something other than the nickname. In addition to this nickname-based filename, the extension chosen from the MIME type is appended to the final name.

Next, the PHP function `move_uploaded_file()` is used to move the uploaded image file from a temporary location into the proper directory under the chosen filename. If this was successful, a report is prepared that includes the nickname and the filename constructed for the upload. If the file move failed, then an error message is prepared that says as much.

Finally, it's time to actually produce some output:

```
switch($_REQUEST['type']) {

    case 'iframe-json':
        ?><html><body><textarea><?php
            echo htmlentities(json_encode($out))
        ?></textarea></body></html><?php
        break;

    default:
        ?><html>
            <body>
                <?php if ($out['error']): ?>
                    <h1>Error accepting avatar upload:</h1>
                    <p><?php echo htmlentities($out['error']) ?></p>
                <?php else: ?>
                    <h1>Avatar upload accepted</h1>
                    <dl>
                        <dt>Nickname</dt>
                        <dd>
                            <?php echo htmlentities($out['nickname']) ?>
                        </dd>
                        <dt>Avatar</dt>
                        <dd>
                            <img src="uploads/<?php echo $out['avatar_fn'] ?>" />
                        </dd>
                    </dl>
```

```
            <?php endif ?>
        </body>
    </html><?php
    break;

}
```

The preceding code splits into two main output templates, based on the value of an optional type form field. If the value is "iframe-json", then a simple JSON encoding of the output variables is wrapped in Dojo's required <iframe> data packaging. Otherwise, a full HTML page is constructed based on the output variables.

At this point, given the markup and the upload_avatar.php script, you might want to try things out to see what happens. Without any JavaScript or AJAX yet in play, all of the above should work as a system that accepts image uploads for given nicknames. Figure 27-10 shows what the preceding script produces when given a valid image.

Figure 27-10

Notice that between Figure 27-9 and Figure 27-10 that the URL in the address bar changed — this is because, as expected in a normal form submission, a completely new page loaded.

But, as you should already suspect, there's a way to augment this user interface to reflect the results of the form submission and the file upload all in place without leaving the page. The following code is the beginning of that effort:

```
dojo.require('dojo.io.iframe');

dojo.declare('decafbad.ajax.ajax.MagicUploadForm', decafbad.ajax.ajax.MagicForm, {

    handleSubmit: function(ev) {
        dojo.stopEvent(ev);

        // Disable the submit button while this is working.
        dojo.query('input[type="submit"]', this.root_id)
            .attr('value', 'loading...').attr('disabled', true)

        // Find the form, dig up its method and URL, submit using XHR
        dojo.query('form.form_post', this.root_id)
            .forEach(function(form) {
                dojo.io.iframe.send({
                    form: form,
                    content: {
                        type: 'iframe-json'
                    },
                    handleAs: 'json',
                    handle: dojo.hitch(this, 'displayResults')
                });
            }, this);
    },
```

The preceding code declares a class named `MagicUploadForm`, which is a subclass of `MagicForm` declared earlier in the chapter.

In this subclass, the first thing to do is to replace the `.handleSubmit()` method: Here you have a call to `dojo.io.iframe.send()` given a reference to the avatar upload form, as well as an additional `content` parameter setting a type field to "`iframe-json`". If you recall the other output branch of `upload_avatar.php`, this value results in a JSON response packaged up for Dojo, which will be properly parsed into a JavaScript data structure thanks to the `handleAs` parameter of "`json`".

The important thing to note here is that, although a reference to a form is given to `dojo.io.frame .send()`, you can still specify additional fields to include in the request. To maintain the consistency of the form submission, the utility function will create and insert hidden form fields for each additional field before the submission, keep track of those inserted fields, and remove them when the form submission has gotten a response.

In order to get that response, the call to `dojo.io.frame.send()` changes the form's `target` attribute to point to a managed hidden `<iframe>` element and then programmatically submits the form. From there, things proceed generally as you've seen from the `dojo.io.frame.send()` examples presented thus far. The big win, though, is that since the entire form was submitted, the `avatar` file selection field is allowed to upload its data as usual.

When that response is received, the following replacement for `.displayResults()` will handle it:

```
displayResults: function(result, io_args) {

    // Hide the submitted form.
    dojo.query('.form_post', this.root_id)
        .addClass('hidden').removeClass('shown');

    var msg, clr;
    if (result instanceof Error || result.error){
        // Display error message and flash red color.
        clr = '#f88';
        msg = '<p>' + result.message + '</p>';
    } else {
        // Display response and flash green color.
        var avatar_url = result.avatar_fn + '?' +
            (new Date()).valueOf();
        clr = '#8f8';
        msg = '<img src="uploads/' + avatar_url + '" />';
    }

    // Update the results content.
    dojo.query('.results', this.root_id)
        .empty().addContent(msg);

    // Reveal the results pane container.
    dojo.query('.form_results', this.root_id)
        .removeClass('hidden').addClass('shown')
        .animateProperty({
            duration: 750,
            properties: {
                backgroundColor: { start: clr, end: '#fff' }
            }
        }).play();
},

EOF:null

});

var mf2 = new decafbad.ajax.ajax.MagicUploadForm('magic_upload_form');
```

The big difference between this implementation and the one used previously with `MagicForm` is that this one doesn't just update a `<textarea>` — instead, given a successful avatar image upload result, this method inserts an `<img>` element reflecting the uploaded file. By the way, if you moved the `uploads/` directory in `upload_avatar.php`, this is a part you'll need to tweak to reflect that new location.

Additionally, this code recognizes the presence of an `error` property in the response as an error condition. This enables cooperation with the server-side script in indicating faults in validating the uploaded file.

Finally, with the end of the new subclass, an instance is created using the root ID from the markup presented earlier. Now that all the pieces are together, you should be able to submit the form to upload a new image, and see something like what's depicted in Figure 27-11.

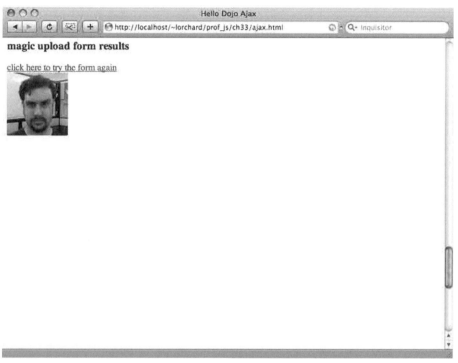

Figure 27-11

In contrast to Figure 27-10, note that the URL in the location bar has not changed in Figure 27-11. The results of this image upload have been displayed in place, and the form reset link is ready for a click to start it all over again without leaving the page.

Summary

In this chapter, you were given a tour of Dojo's facilities for fetching data from server-side resources without the need for full page loads that tear down your carefully constructed client-side user interfaces. Among these AJAX-enabling features, you saw how Dojo eases the use of XMLHttpRequest objects to perform a variety of HTTP requests, how to abstract away the loading of JSON feeds across domains, as well as how to use hidden `<iframe>` elements to load data and submit forms with file upload fields.

The next facet of Dojo introduced in the next chapter puts almost everything together that's been explained so far: You'll see how the Dojo widget system, Dijit, combines Dojo's packaging, inheritance, markup parsing, events, and data facilities to enable a declarative style of application assembly that can require very little code — and sometimes can make do with nothing but markup.

28

Building User Interfaces with Widgets

The previous chapters gave you an introduction to the core offerings of the Dojo toolkit. These modules and helpers provide all the parts you need to piece together a modern web application with a responsive user interface and access to server-side resources. However, these features are not essentially distinctive with respect to other JavaScript frameworks presented in the book.

There is at least one part of Dojo that's relatively unique: As you saw briefly back in Chapter 23, Dojo offers a module named `dojo.parser`, which facilitates the declaration of JavaScript objects in HTML markup. This aspect of the toolkit takes center stage in the Dijit subproject of Dojo, which collects together a broad palette of user interface components — or widgets — that each either wrap UI elements native to the browser or encapsulate completely new UI elements built with HTML, CSS, and JavaScript.

Dijit widgets can be instantiated programmatically in conventional code, or declared as augmentations of existing nodes in markup. This duality allows Dijit to support the "unobtrusive" paradigm of keeping JavaScript and HTML as separate as possible, while introducing a more integrated approach where behavior and data handling can be defined and declared in-context alongside user interface elements.

In this chapter, you'll learn about:

❑   Building and validating forms

❑   Managing application layout

❑   Creating application controls and dialogs

Building and Validating Forms

One of the first and most practical uses for Dijit is in the construction of forms with built-in input validation and formatting. So as a reminder to highlight how HTML pages are constructed using Dojo and Dijit, the following starts a complete document to prepare for some form building:

```html
<html>
    <head>
        <title>Hello Dojo Forms</title>

        <style type="text/css">
            @import "../dojodev/dojo/resources/dojo.css";
            @import "../dojodev/dijit/themes/tundra/tundra.css";
            @import "forms.css";
        </style>

        <script type="text/javascript">
            djConfig = {
                isDebug:      true,
                parseOnLoad:  true,
                modulePaths:  { "decafbad": "../../ex-dojo-widgets/decafbad", },
            };
        </script>

        <script type="text/javascript" src="../dojodev/dojo/dojo.js"></script>

        <script type="text/javascript">
            dojo.require("dojo.parser");
            dojo.require("decafbad.widgets.forms");
        </script>

    </head>
```

The preceding markup can be broken up into the following main chunks:

The base style sheet for Dojo is loaded, followed by the style sheet defining the "tundra" widget theme. You've seen this before, but themes will be explored in greater depth at the end of the chapter.

The djConfig variable is constructed, establishing configuration settings for the Dojo toolkit. Remember that the module paths are defined relative to the path from which the toolkit is loaded.

❏ The Dojo toolkit is loaded with a <script> element.

❏ Once Dojo itself is loaded, the modules dojo.parser and decafbad.widgets.forms are declared as requirements.

The file providing the second module, decafbad/widgets/forms.js, starts out like this:

```
dojo.provide("decafbad.widgets.forms");

dojo.require('dojo.behavior');

dojo.require("dijit.form.Form");
dojo.require("dijit.form.ValidationTextBox");
dojo.require("dijit.form.NumberTextBox");
dojo.require("dijit.form.NumberSpinner");
dojo.require("dijit.form.CurrencyTextBox");
dojo.require("dijit.form.DateTextBox");
dojo.require("dijit.form.TimeTextBox");
dojo.require("dijit.form.CheckBox");
dojo.require("dijit.form.Textarea");
dojo.require("dojo.data.ItemFileReadStore");
dojo.require("dijit.form.ComboBox");
dojo.require("dijit.form.FilteringSelect");
dojo.require("dijit.form.Slider");
dojo.require("dijit.Editor");
dojo.require("dijit._editor.plugins.TextColor");
dojo.require("dijit._editor.plugins.LinkDialog");

decafbad.widgets.forms = function() {

    return {

        init: function() {
            dojo.addOnLoad(this, 'onLoad');
            return this;
        },

        onLoad: function() {
            console.log("* Welcome to Chapter 28 and forms!");

            /**
             * Startup code goes here.
             */
        },

        EOF: null // I hate trailing commas.

    };

}().init();
```

The laundry list of `dojo.require()` statements here load in all the Dijit modules that will be used throughout the rest of the chapter. You could put them in the `<head>` of the page itself, but putting them here helps reduce clutter a bit. Additionally, in the module `.onLoad()` method, you can add whatever startup code you find necessary along the way.

The following provides CSS declarations for `forms.css` imported toward the top of the page:

```
form
    { float: left; clear: both; width: 400px; }
form fieldset.main
    { border: 1px solid #ccc; margin: 1em; padding: 0.5em 1em; }
form ul li
    { list-style-type: none; padding-top: 1em; clear: both; }
form ul li.first
    { padding-top: 0em; }
form ul li label
    { width: 10ex; margin-right: 1ex; text-align: right; float: left; }
form ul li label.inline
    { width: auto; margin-right: 0; text-align: left; float: none; }
form ul li div.RichTextEditable
    { margin-left: 11ex; width: 225px; height: 25em; border: 1px solid #ccc; }
form ul li.buttons
    { text-align: right; }
hr
    { clear: both }
```

This provides some styling for simple HTML form markup, presenting a two-column layout of labels and fields. Along with the theme style sheet, this CSS helps demonstrate that Dijit widgets are amenable to conventional styling.

Returning to the HTML page, it's time to start composing the form itself:

```
<body class="tundra">
    <h1>Hello Dojo Forms</h1>

    <form id="form1" method="post" action="echo.php?type=text"
            dojoType="dijit.form.Form">

        <fieldset class="main">
            <legend>Book inventory management</legend>
            <ul>
```

So far, so good — this looks like the preamble to a pretty standard HTML form. There are two touches of Dojo here, though:

❑   The `class="tundra"` attribute on the `<body>` tag establishes that the "tundra" widget theme should be used throughout the page. The CSS for this theme was loaded earlier.

❑   The `dojoType="dijit.form.Form"` attribute on the `<form>` tag will cause this element to be wrapped in a Dijit widget. The implications of this will be explained more fully later in the chapter.

Instantiating Widgets with JavaScript

Moving along, it's time to take a closer look at getting widgets into this form, first trying things out with JavaScript code. Consider the following additions to the form markup:

```
<li class="first">
    <label for="title">Title</label>
    <input type="text" name="title" id="title" />
</li>
<li>
    <label for="author">Author</label>
    <input type="text" name="author" id="author" />
</li>
```

To wire these elements up as widgets, take a look at the following code, intended for inclusion in the .onLoad() method of the module decafbad.widgets.forms:

```
dojo.behavior.add({
    '#title': function(el) {
        new dijit.form.ValidationTextBox({
            name:          el.name,
            required:      true,
            properCase:    true,
            promptMessage: "Enter the book title"
        }, el);
    },
    '#author': function(el) {
        new dijit.form.ValidationTextBox({
            name:          el.name,
            required:      true,
            properCase:    true,
            promptMessage: "Enter the author's full name"
        }, el);
    }
});
```

The preceding code uses dojo.behavior to build two widgets corresponding to form fields on the page. Each is a new instance of the Dijit widget dijit.form.ValidationTextBox. The first parameter to the constructor is an object bearing parameters for the widget, while the second parameter passes a reference to the DOM node meant to be managed by the widget.

If you recall the end of Chapter 23, this should look familiar. This constructor method signature is used by dojo.parser() when objects are declared in markup. There's no magical requirement that the constructor be used in that way — so instantiating a widget programmatically in JavaScript works fine.

In fact, you may prefer the use of dojo.behavior in the previous code to the declarative markup style presented throughout the rest of the chapter. Keep in mind that any example done with markup can also be done with code like in the previous example.

Figure 28-1 shows the results of the code in the previous example. You should see that, beyond the form styles defined inline in the page <head>, the form fields have gained some subtle gradients from the "tundra" widget theme.

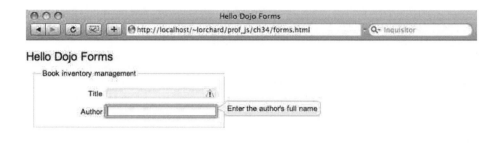

Figure 28-1

When either field is selected, the `promptMessage` property is used to create a tooltip floating to the right of the field. Thanks to the `required` property, leaving one of the fields empty after having been selected will produce a warning highlight. And finally, the `properCase` property will cause each word of text input into the field to be capitalized when focus leaves the field, which is useful for book titles and author names.

Declaring Widgets in HTML Markup

To try out the `dojo.parser` approach to widget creation, replace the second of the form fields from the previous example with the following markup:

```
<li>
    <label for="author">Author</label>
    <input type="text" name="author"
        dojoType="dijit.form.ValidationTextBox"
        required="true"
        properCase="true"
        promptMessage="Enter the author's full name" />
</li>
```

There's no JavaScript necessary here, so you can get rid of the `dojo.behavior` code invoked for this field as well.

As described at the end of Chapter 23, the `dojo.parser` module scans the page on load and finds all elements bearing a `dojoType` attribute, like the one in the previous example. For each of these, the parser instantiates a new object of the type specified on the `dojoType` attribute, passing a collection of the element's attributes, and a reference to the element itself, to the object's constructor call.

Also, in case it's not clear, all of the modules referenced by `dojoType` attributes must be loaded via `dojo.require()` statements before `dojo.parser` performs its scan on page load. You should see each widget module used in this chapter appear in the `<head>` markup provided earlier.

Although this integrated approach definitely seems like the direct opposite of the "unobtrusive" approach advocated by many web developers, it does have advantages in keeping all the context in one spot. This markup entirely describes the desired widget and its intended behavior, without a need to track intention between files. It's also pretty compact code and degrades gracefully in absence of `dojo.parser`, since browsers will ignore the nonstandard HTML attributes.

Validating Input with a Regular Expression

Another more useful feature of this `ValidationTextBox` widget in particular is offered in the following markup example:

```
<li>
    <label for="sku">SKU</label>
    <input type="text" name="sku"
        dojoType="dijit.form.ValidationTextBox"
        required="true"
        regExp="^[0-9\-]+$"
        invalidMessage="Invalid stock ID (eg. 00-00000-000-0)"
        promptMessage="Enter the stock ID (eg. 00-00000-000-0)" />
</li>
```

With the `regExp` attribute, you can specify a regular expression describing what is acceptable valid input for this field. In the preceding markup, numbers and dashes are required. With each key press, the field content is subjected to this test, and if the content fails the validation test, the field is given a highlight and a tooltip indicating the error.

Notice that in this widget, there's both a `promptMessage` and an `invalidMessage` attribute. The `invalidMessage` is presented in the tooltip whenever the field content fails the test defined by the regular expression. This is demonstrated in Figure 28-2. This attribute is optional: If you omit it, Dojo will use a generic message.

> ### Regular Expressions in JavaScript
>
> A decent guide to regular expressions in JavaScript is far beyond the scope of this chapter, and in fact serves as the topic for a number of full-length books. However, you can get a good primer on the subject at the following web site:
>
> ```
> http://developer.mozilla.org/en/docs/Core_JavaScript_1.5_Guide:
> Regular_Expressions
> ```

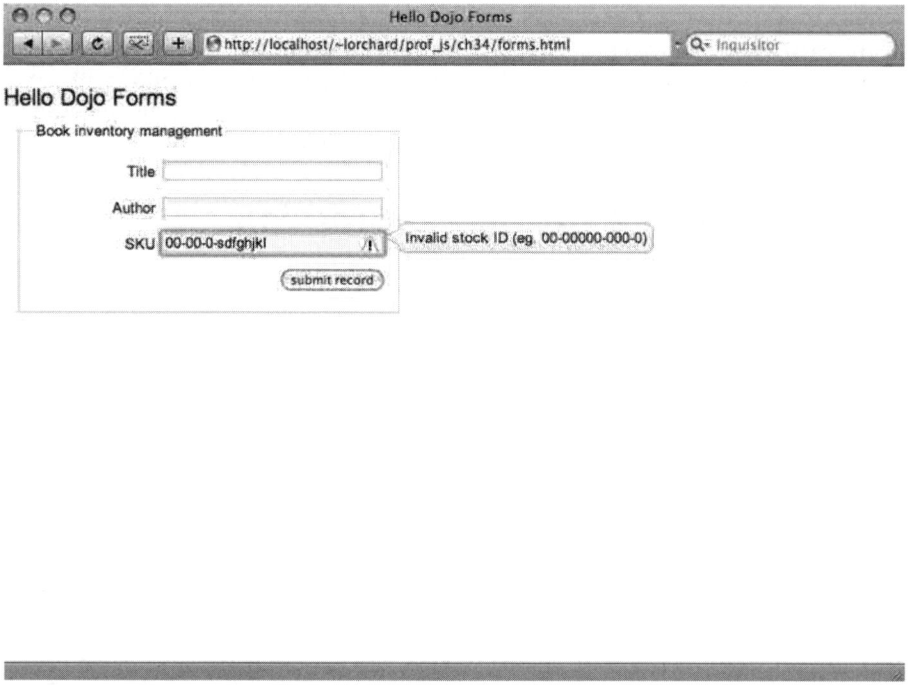

Figure 28-2

Enforcing Form Validation on Submit

Although there are more fields to come for this form, it seems like a good time to take a look at enforcing valid form data on submission before going further. Consider the following markup, which finishes off the form and the page itself:

```
                            <li class="buttons">
                                <input type="submit" value="submit record" />
                            </li>

                    </ul>
                </fieldset>

                <script type="dojo/method" event="onSubmit" args="ev">
                    if (!this.validate()) {
                        dojo.stopEvent(ev);
                        alert("Form not yet valid! (defined in markup)");
                    }
                </script>

            </form>

        </body>
    </html>
```

The form is finished off with a plain vanilla submit button, not wrapped in any kind of widget. You could use a button widget here, but this should serve as a reminder that widgets coexist with native elements.

The Dojo magic appears here in the form of a `<script>` element with a custom `dojo/method` type. This is a convention handled by `dojo.parser` — since it's an unrecognized type of script, the browser itself ignores it, but `dojo.parser` picks it up during its page scan.

The `<script>` element appears as a direct descendant of the `<form>` element, and that position in the DOM tree is important. The `<form>` was declared earlier as a `dijit.form.Form` widget, and `dojo.parser` treats the body of this `<script>` child node as a function parameter for the widget constructor.

The `event="onSubmit"` attribute of the `<script>` element indicates that the `.onSubmit()` method of the widget instance should be replaced by this code. The `args="ev"` attribute specifies that the method itself should accept one parameter, named `ev`. Since the widget's `.onSubmit()` method handles the `submit` event handler on the `<form>` node it manages, this is an ideal place to enforce the validity of form input.

And finally, what the handler itself does is trigger the Form widget's `.validate()` method. This method iterates through the field widgets within the form, asking each if it contains valid data. If any one of the fields reports invalid data, this method returns a value of `false` — and thus, the `submit` event is stopped, and an error message is thrown up in an alert dialog. As a side effect, all fields with invalid data are highlighted, and cursor focus is given to the first invalid field. Figure 28-3 shows the result of an invalid form submission.

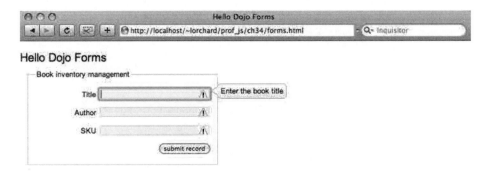

Figure 28-3

Again, if this custom markup isn't your cup of tea, here's another way to do it:

```
dojo.behavior.add({

    '#form1': function(el) {
        new dijit.form.Form({
            onSubmit: function(ev) {
                if (!this.validate()) {
                    dojo.stopEvent(ev);
                    alert("Form not yet valid! (connected in JS)");
                }
            }
        }, el);
    }

});
```

In case it's not clear, remember that use of `dojo.behavior` in the preceding code replaces the `dojoType` attribute used earlier with the `<form>` tag.

Handling Numbers and Currency Values

So, at this point, you have a complete form with several required fields, a field with a regex-based validity test, and a form submission handler that enforces data validity.

Now, it's time to take a look at some more specialized fields. The first of these deals with numbers:

```
<li>
    <label for="pages">Pages</label>
    <input type="text" name="pages"
        dojoType="dijit.form.NumberTextBox"
        required="true"
        promptMessage="Enter the number of pages in the book"
        constraints="{min:1,max:999}"
        rangeMessage="Too many pages - we only carry books under 1000 pages" />
</li>
```

This widget is named `dijit.form.NumberTextBox`, and it manages an input field intended for numbers. Using the `constraints` attribute, you can establish the minimum and maximum values allowed for the field. While it's conceivable that you could do this with a regular expression, this approach is somewhat more natural. Paired with the constraints is the `rangeMessage` attribute, allowing you to specify a tooltip message to be displayed when the value lies outside the defined constraints.

Closely related to `NumberTextBox` is this next widget, specializing in currency amounts:

```
<li>
    <label for="price">Price</label>
    <input type="text" name="price"
        dojoType="dijit.form.CurrencyTextBox"
        required="true"
        currency="USD"
        constraints="{min:1.00, max:199.00}"
        rangeMessage="Books must be priced between $1 and $199"
        promptMessage="Enter the book's price (in USD)" />
</li>
```

Notice that the attributes of this `CurrencyTextBox` widget closely matches the `NumberTextBox` in the last example — and they serve all the same purposes. The `constraints` and `rangeMessage` attributes manage validity in terms of `min` and `max` values.

The new attribute here is `currency`, which accepts ISO 4217 currency codes — such as USD, CAD, GBP, and EUR. You can find a list of these on Wikipedia, here:

```
http://en.wikipedia.org/wiki/ISO_4217
```

The main purpose for this attribute is not for enforcing valid data, however. You can enter any numeric value here that lies within the constraints. Instead, the widget will reformat the numeric value to match the conventions of the specified currency type. Try various currency types here to see what happens.

Easing into more advanced controls, take a look at this next widget:

```
<li>
    <label for="stock">Stock</label>
    <input type="text" name="stock"
        dojoType="dijit.form.NumberSpinner"
        required="true"
        value="0"
        smallDelta="5"
        constraints="{min:0,max:200}"
        rangeMessage="Shelves will only hold up to 200 books"
        promptMessage="How many of this book are in stock?" />
</li>
```

Like the `NumberTextBox` before it, this `NumberSpinner` widget manages a numeric value with constraints. The new feature here, though, includes a pair of up and down buttons at the end of the field. When clicked, the numeric value shows up in increments and decrements by the amount specified in `smallDelta`. When the field is has focus, you can also use the up and down arrow keys to perform the same action.

Figure 28-4 shows a preview of the three new numeric field widgets presented in this section of the chapter, complete with an out-of-range value to demonstrate the tooltip message.

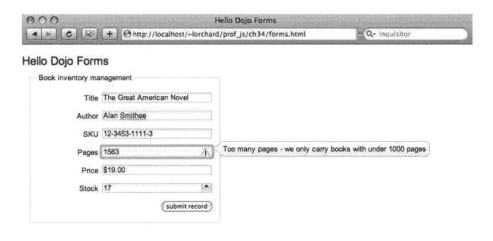

Figure 28-4

Working with Date and Time Fields

A little more complex than numbers, dates and times are often necessary parts of constructing forms. Dijit does not disappoint in this area; it offers two more widgets with custom interfaces.

The first of these offers a calendar interface for selecting dates:

```
<li>
    <label for="pubdate">Date</label>
    <input type="text" name="pubdate"
        dojoType="dijit.form.DateTextBox"
        required="true"
        constraints="{min:'2008-03-19', max:'2008-06-20'}"
        rangeMessage="Store is only open between March 19 and June 20"
        promptMessage="Select the book's publication date" />
</li>
```

This widget named `dijit.form.DateTextBox` offers a custom calendar-based UI element built from HTML, CSS, and JS for selecting a date that appears in the input field it manages. You can see a quick preview of this widget in Figure 28-5.

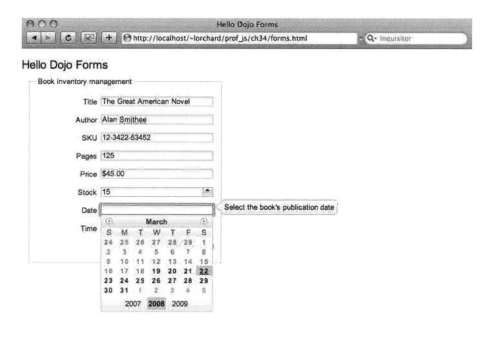

Figure 28-5

Like the numeric widgets before it, it honors a definition of constraints on acceptable values for the field. These constraints are expressed in terms of the ISO8601 format, which basically amounts to the following pattern:

```
yyyy-MM-ddTHH:mm:ssZ
```

So, for example, the current date and time might be represented as:

```
2008-03-24T06:29:15-08:00
```

You can read more about Dojo's specific implementation of this format in documentation for the `dojo` `.date.stamp.fromISOString` function, found here:

```
http://redesign.dojotoolkit.org/jsdoc/dojo/HEAD/dojo.date.stamp.fromISOString
```

In playing with the calendar widget, you should also notice that it minds the constraints, graying out and disallowing selection of dates that fall outside its valid range.

The next field allows the selection of a time of day:

```
<li>
    <label for="reltime">Time</label>
    <input type="text" name="reltime"
        dojoType="dijit.form.TimeTextBox"
        required="true"
        constraints="{min:'T09:00', max:'T17:00'}"
        rangeMessage="Books are shelved only between 9AM and 5PM"
        promptMessage="Select the shelving time of the book" />
</li>
```

The widget in the preceding example is named `dijit.form.TimeTextBox`, and it offers a sort of fisheye lens selector strip of hours throughout the day. The value selected ends up in the text input field managed by the widget. You can see what it looks like in Figure 28-6. Like the calendar widget, it also accepts time value constraints expressed in the ISO8601 format. However, unlike the calendar widget, it does not prevent invalid selections at the time of this writing.

Both of these time-based widgets are illustrations of what kinds of advanced widgets are possible with Dijit, since they're instantiated from bundles of templated HTML, CSS, and JS. This will be explained in greater detail toward the end of the chapter. These widgets are also very useful because the data selected with them ends up as the value of a native browser text input field, thus getting sent along with the form submission like every other field.

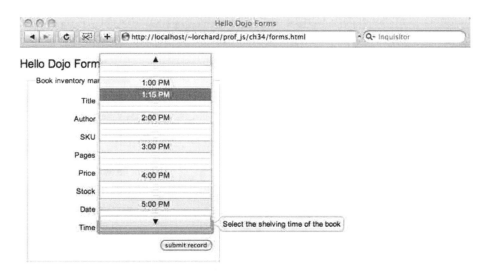

Figure 28-6

Enhancing Radio Buttons and Checkboxes

The widgets offered by Dijit for radio buttons and checkboxes are by no means as dramatic as the calendar and time selectors, but they do offer at least one subtle advantage. Consider the following markup defining a pair of radio buttons:

```
<li>
    <label for="cover">Cover</label>

    <input type="radio" name="cover" id="cover-paperback"
        value="paperback"
        dojoType="dijit.form.RadioButton" />
    <label for="cover-paperback" class="inline">Paperback</label>

    <input type="radio" name="cover" id="cover-hardback"
        value="hardback" checked="checked"
        dojoType="dijit.form.RadioButton" />
    <label for="cover-hardback" class="inline">Hardback</label>
</li>
```

There's not much here that departs from normal radio buttons, beyond the `dojoType` attribute value of `dijit.form.RadioButton`. The same is true of Dijit's checkbox widgets:

```
<li>
    <label for="features[]">Features</label>

    <input type="checkbox" name="features[]" id="features-slipcover"
        value="slipcover"
        dojoType="dijit.form.CheckBox" />
    <label for="features-slipcover" class="inline">Slipcover</label>

    <input type="checkbox" name="features[]" id="features-cdrom"
        value="cdrom"
        dojoType="dijit.form.CheckBox" />
    <label for="features-cdrom" class="inline">Computer media</label>
</li>
```

These are also fairly nondescript, with the exception of the `dijit.form.CheckBox` value for `dojoType`. Again, the `features[]` name for the fields is a PHP-based naming convention providing a cue to the server that this should be treated as offering potentially multiple values.

The primary reason for using these widgets, however, is that it renders these normally hard-to-style form elements able to participate in Dijit's widget themes. You should be able to see this in Figure 28-7, which shows that the radio button and checkbox pairs both have been given a look and feel that's much different from the native platform UI.

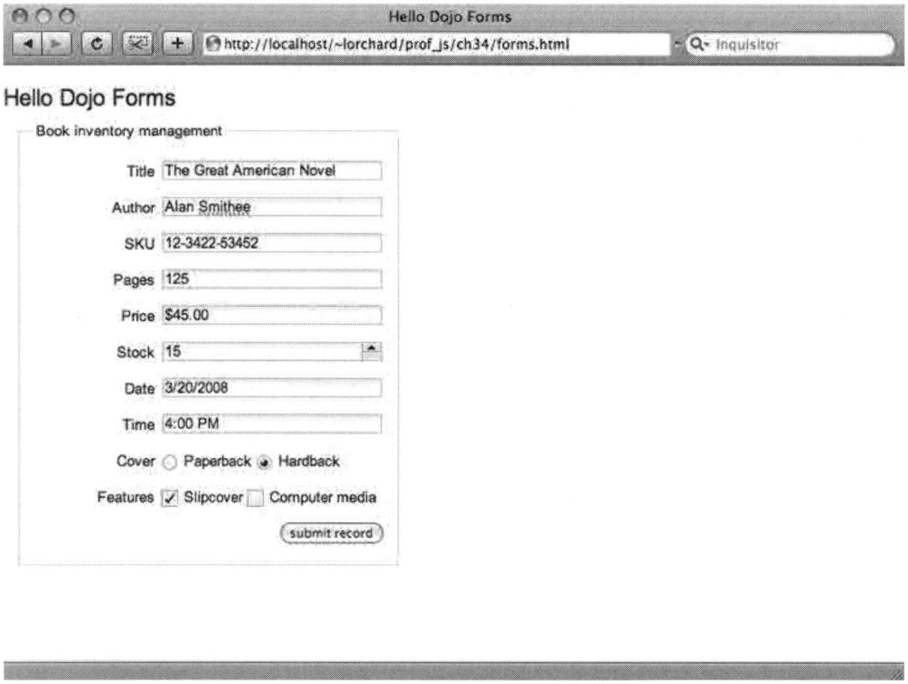

Figure 28-7

Working with Selection Fields and Data Sources

The next form element to get the Dojo treatment is the drop-down selection box. These elements are often some of the most data-intensive fields on the page, so Dijit offers some interesting tricks to use in constructing them. Check out the following markup:

```
<li>
    <div dojoType="dojo.data.ItemFileReadStore" jsId="genre_store"
        url="genres.json"></div>

    <label for="genre">Genre</label>
    <input name="genre" value="Misc"
        dojoType="dijit.form.ComboBox"
        store="genre_store"
        searchAttr="name"
        autoComplete="true"
        required="true" />
</li>
```

The first thing to notice in this example is an empty `<div>` used to declare an instance of the class `dojo.data.ItemFileReadStore` — while not technically a widget itself, the markup will still be interpreted by `dojo.parser` to create an object.

A full description could take up a chapter on its own, but in short the `dojo.data` package provides a way to access server-side data resources locally in a way not entirely like using a simple database. The usage here only scratches the surface, and you may want to check out the Dojo documentation on the `dojo.data` API, in the following pages:

❑ `http://redesign.dojotoolkit.org/jsdoc/dojo/HEAD/dojo.data`

❑ `www.dojotoolkit.org/book/dojo-book-0-9/part-3-programmatic-dijit-and-dojo/data-retrieval-dojo-data-0`

Although the data sources used in the examples here are based on static JSON structures, it is possible to implement subclasses that repeatedly query remote server-side resources for partial data — such as searching for a subset of choices from a large set, which start with the letters typed so far in a field.

To keep things simple in the example, though, the markup creates a data source object that fetches content from a JSON resource named `genres.json`. Thanks to the `jsId` attribute, a reference to that object instance is put into the global JS variable `genre_store`.

The result of fetching the `genres.json` resource should look something like this:

```
{
    "identifier": "name",
    "items": [
        { "name": "Misc",    },
        { "name": "Scifi" },
        { "name": "Mystery" },
        { "name": "Romance" },
        { "name": "Tech" },
        { "name": "Self-Help" }
    ]
}
```

If you think of this data as a table in a relational database, the `identifier` property is basically the primary key of the set, and the array of objects under `items` are the rows. Each item in the set is an object whose properties make up the columns. In this case, it's a very simple table — just a list of book genre names, in fact.

Now, consider the declaration of the `dijit.form.comboBox` widget. It has a `store` property with the value "genre_store", which corresponds to the `jsId` of the data store described previously. It also has a `searchAttr` property with the value "name", which corresponds to the column in the data set containing genre names.

When you put it all together, and you get what's shown in Figure 28-8: a text field with a button that, when clicked, pops up a list of choices based on the items made available in this data source. You can also type anything into this field, and it will offer suggestions from the list as you type if any are available.

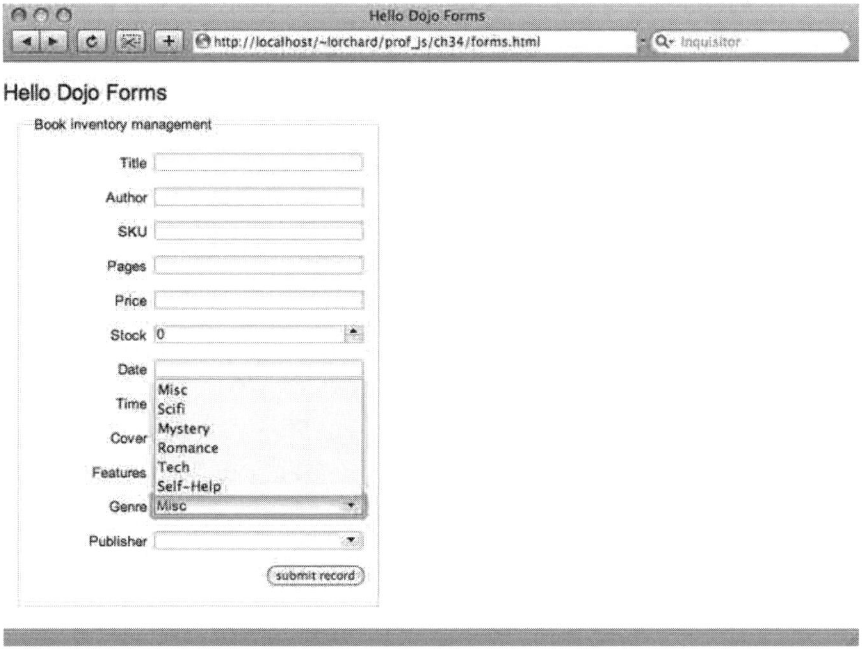

Figure 28-8

Slightly different, yet related, is the widget declared in this next bit of markup:

```
<li>
    <div dojoType="dojo.data.ItemFileReadStore" jsId="publisher_store"
        url="publishers.json"></div>

    <label for="publisher">Publisher</label>
    <select name="publisher" value="Wiley"
        dojoType="dijit.form.FilteringSelect"
        store="publisher_store"
        searchAttr="name"
        labelAttr="label"
        labelType="html"
        required="true">
        <option value="001">Wiley</option>
    </select>
</li>
```

Like the previous example, this field relies on a data source, provided this time by a resource named publishers.json. This time, though, the JSON is a little more complex:

```
{
    "identifier": "code",
    "items": [

        { "code": "001", "name": "Wiley",
            "label": "<b>Wiley<\/b>"},

        { "code": "a08", "name": "Sybex",
            "label": "<i>Sybex<\/i>"},

        { "code": "fdd", "name": "Wrox",
            "label": "<u>Wrox<\/u>"},

        { "code": "010", "name": "Pfeiffer",
            "label": "<small>Pfeiffer<\/small>"},

        { "code": "00f", "name": "Frommer\'s",
            "label": "<big>Frommer\'s<\/big>"},

        { "code": "00a", "name": "CliffsNotes",
            "label": "<center>CliffsNotes<\/center>"},

        { "code": "101", "name": "Audel",
            "label": "<sup>Audel<\/sup>"}

    ]
}
```

613

The `dijit.form.FilteringSelect` widget looks just like the `ComboBox` widget, but it acts more like a standard `<select>` element. In further contrast to the `ComboBox` widget, the `FilteringSelect` widget allows separate definitions for each of the following:

❑ How items are presented in the pop-up menu and suggestions while typing

❑ The text that appears in the visible form field when an item is selected or typed

❑ The value submitted with the form, based on the item selected

You can see each of these three things defined in the JSON data source as the respective properties `label`, `name`, and `code`. You can name these whatever you like in the data source — the following conditions establish how things are used:

❑ The `labelAttr` attribute on the widget names the property in the data source to be used in constructing the pop-up menu, and `labelType` may be either `text` or `html` to determine how to handle presenting the value from the data source.

❑ The `searchAttr` attribute on the widget determines what appears in the text field, just as it did with the `ComboBox` widget.

❑ The `identifier` header property of the data source determines which property of the selected item will be sent to the server on successful form submission.

As you can see in Figure 28-9, the `FilteringSelect` widget allows for styling and markup in each menu item shown in the pop-up menu. Additionally, since the widget's `searchAttr` can differ from the data source `identifier`, you can display the choice with more readable text than the value that is eventually submitted — in this example, it's a user-hostile database code that needs some dressing up.

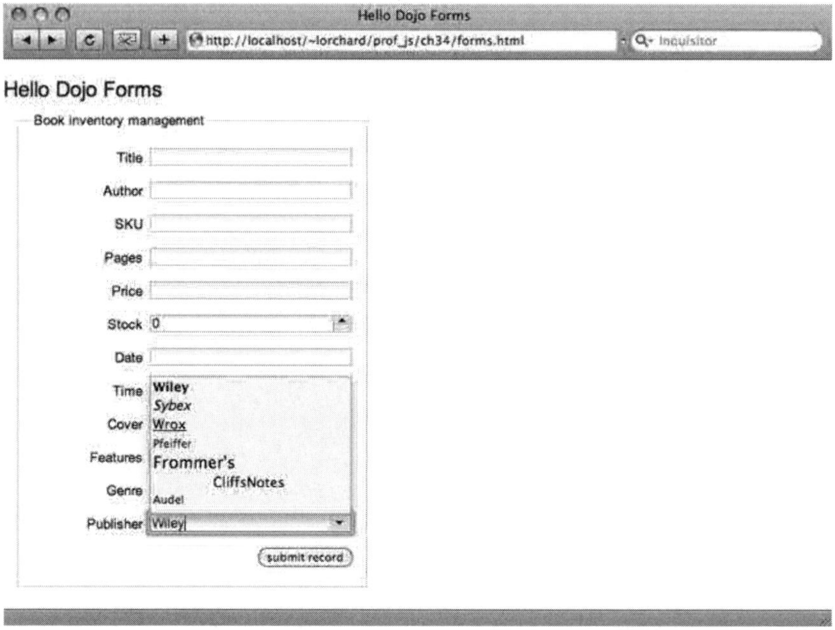

Figure 28-9

Given the relationship between display and submitted value, consider that this widget also imposes validation requirements based on the list that it's given. Figure 28-10 depicts what happens when a value is typed that does not appear in the data source items.

So, the `ComboBox` widget simply allows data entry with suggestions from a list supplied by data source. Building upon this, the `FilteringSelect` widget allows data entry based on menu items marked up in HTML or in plain text, with the choice mapped to a non-visible value and validation enforced within the constraints of the items in the data source.

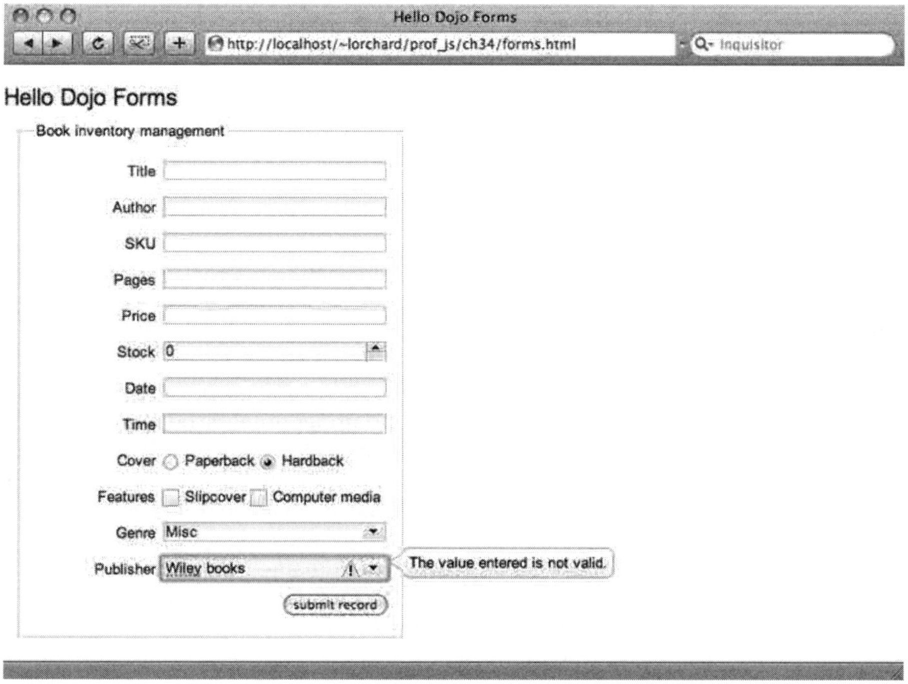

Figure 28-10

Using Sliders to Allow Discrete Value Selection

When you've got a set or spectrum of discrete choices, sometimes neither a number spinner nor a selection box is quite the right UI element to use. This is where the slider widget comes in, defined with the following markup:

```
<li>
    <label for="rating">Rating</label>
    <input type="hidden" name="rating" id="rating" value="0" />

    <div id="rating_slider" dojoType="dijit.form.HorizontalSlider"
        value="3" style="width: 225px;"
        minimum="0"
        maximum="5"
```

```
            discreteValues="11"
            showButtons="true">

        <script type="dojo/connect" event="onChange">
            dojo.byId('rating').value = this.getValue();
        </script>

        <ol dojoType="dijit.form.HorizontalRuleLabels"
            style="height:1em; font-size:75%; color:#333;">
            <li>awful</li>
            <li>bad</li>
            <li>so-so</li>
            <li>okay</li>
            <li>good</li>
            <li>great</li>
        </ol>

    </div>
</li>
```

The slider is a user interface element that allows a handle to be dragged back and forth across either a horizontal (`dijit.form.HorizontalSlider`) or vertical (`dijit.form.VerticalSlider`) track, snapping to one of a set of discrete positions.

In the previous markup, these positions are defined by the `minimum`, `maximum`, and `discreteValues` attributes. The `minimum` and `maximum` define the lower and upper numeric bounds for the slider. The `discreteValues` attribute specifies into how many equal parts the numeric range between the two should be divided. Given the previous markup, numeric values from 0 to 5 are possible, with 0.5 half-steps along the way — thus, values like 0, 0.5, 1, 1.5, and so on are to be expected.

Notice that in the previous markup, there's a hidden form field named `rating`. This field exists because the `dijit.form.HorizontalSlider` widget is not itself a form element. Instead, it's a separate UI element altogether, and so a little glue scripting is required to tie changes in its state to the hidden form field for eventual inclusion in the form submission.

Here's where a custom `<script>` element again makes an appearance: This time it's got a `type` of "`dojo/connect`" with an event attribute of "`onChange`". Rather than completely replacing the `.onChange()` method of the widget, this kind of script is attached to the method by `dojo.parser` with a call to `dojo.connect()`. In Chapter 27, you saw how connecting handlers to method calls worked — and that's exactly what this is, expressed in declarative markup and carried out by the `dojo.parser` page scan.

As for the handler code itself, it simply grabs the slider's current value with a call to the widget's `.getValue()` method and updates the hidden form field every time the slider signals a change.

The final part of the markup is the declaration of a `dijit.form.HorizontalRuleLabels` widget inside the `HorizontalSlider` widget. This associates with the slider a number of positional markers, declared as an ordered list. These list items will be laid out evenly along the track, and the slider will have positions where it rests on these labels. Notice that only six labels are included here; — with respect to the 11 discrete positions defined, this counts only the odd positions on the track. So, the slider handle will offer positions that lie in between the labels.

Figure 28-11 depicts how this declared widget appears in a browser.

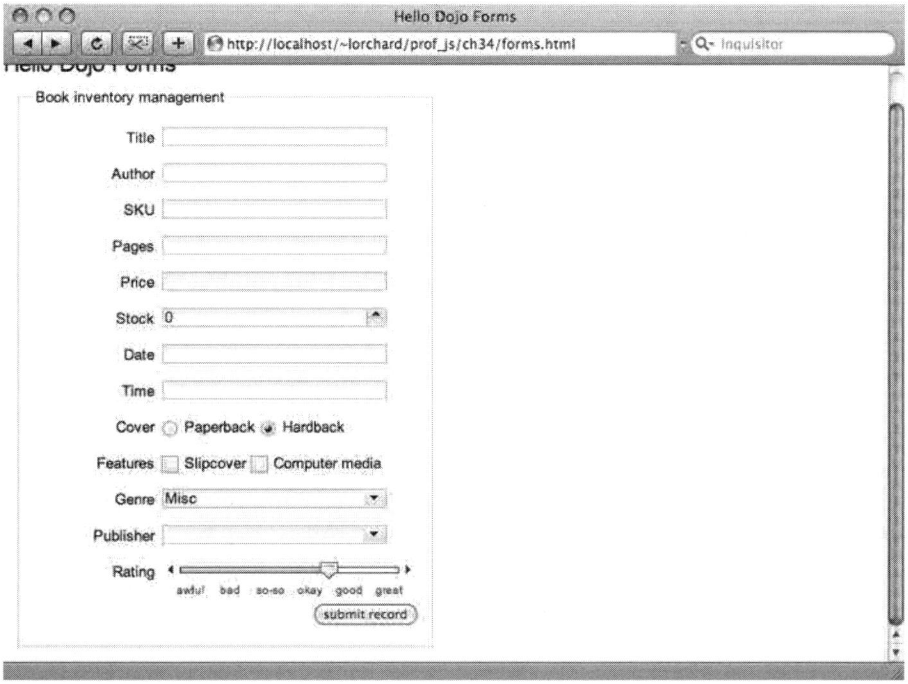

Figure 28-11

Using Dynamic Textareas and Rich Text Editors

Another slight upgrade to a native browser element is the `textarea` widget, declared in markup like so:

```
<li>
    <label for="abstract">Abstract</label>
    <textarea name="abstract" style="width:50ex; height: auto"
        dojoType="dijit.form.Textarea"></textarea>
</li>
```

This widget, `dijit.form.Textarea`, does not honor the `cols` and `rows` attributes of the standard `<textarea>` element, instead requiring that you use CSS style `width` and `height`. What the widget offers in exchange is the ability to grow automatically to fit the content entered into it.

In the preceding markup, the width is constrained to `50ex`, but the height has been set to `auto`. This means that as you type in this text area, the height will increase line by line to accommodate your text entry. This allows you to include fields that start out compact, but can expand as needed.

While useful, this `textarea` widget is not all that exciting as a text editor. What's much more interesting is the widget declared in the following:

```
<li>
    <label for="review">Review</label>
    <input type="hidden" name="review" id="review" value="" />

    <div id="review_editor"
        dojoType="dijit.Editor"
        plugins="[
            'undo','redo','|',
            'bold','italic','underline','|',
            'indent', 'outdent', '|',
            'foreColor', 'hiliteColor', '|',
            'createLink', 'insertImage'
        ]"
        onChange="dojo.byId('review').value = dojo.trim(this.getValue());">

        Compose your book review here.

    </div>
</li>
```

Like data sources, an entire chapter could be devoted to this one widget. The `dijit.Editor` widget provides a rich text editor like a miniature word processor that allows you to work with fonts, formatting, links, and images with the results produced as HTML.

At the time of this writing, this widget is under active development, and some features may be a bit unstable — but it's still a very useful widget to have on hand. You may wish to read more about it on the following Dojo documentation pages:

❑   http://redesign.dojotoolkit.org/jsdoc/dijit/HEAD/dijit.Editor

❑   www.dojotoolkit.org/book/dojo-book-0-9/part-2-dijit/advanced-editing-and-display/editor-rich-text

In the previous markup, the editor widget is treated not unlike a slider widget, in that a little glue code attached to the `onChange` event relays changes in the editor into a hidden form field.

Additionally there's a `plugins` attribute listing the following items to be included in the widget's toolbar:

❑   `undo, redo` — Provides buttons to undo and redo changes

❑   `bold, italic, underline` — Applies formatting changes to the text

❑   `indent, outdent` — Manipulates the indentation level of the text

❑   `foreColor, hiliteColor` — Sets text and background colors provided by the module `dijit._editor.plugins.TextColor` declared earlier as a requirement

❑   `createLink, insertImage` — Turns text into hyperlinks, and embeds images provided by the module `dijit._editor.plugins.LinkDialog` declared earlier as a requirement

As you can see, there are some plug-ins that come out of the box with the editor, and more can be loaded separately from modules external to the editor core package. If you omit the `plugins` attribute, the complete set of built-in buttons will be included — you may want to try that to see what is available.

There's a lot going on behind the scenes with both of these text editing widgets, but they're both pretty easy to declare on the page. Figure 28-12 shows a preview of what these look like on the page.

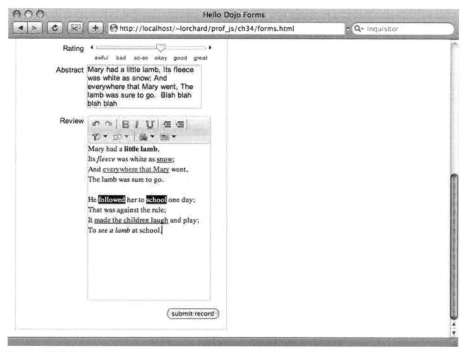

Figure 28-12

Managing Application Layout

One way to look at creating a web page is as a document, using CSS styles to build up columns and sections, counting on the browser's main scroll bar to navigate through your many pages of content. Another way is to treat the browser as an application window, fully managing the available space for your own user interface elements and contained content displays.

While you can use the techniques for content-based pages to build full-window applications, the two are different enough that it's worth approaching in different ways. This is where Dijit's layout widgets come in. Instead of worrying about the construction of your user interface in granular terms of CSS styles and ground-up element positioning, Dijit offers a set of widgets that each define a different kind of top-down window space management. Some divide the space up into flexible regions, while others manage the visibility of whole subpanels in the application.

Also, thanks to the declarative style of widget construction offered by `dojo.parser`, you can create quite complex arrangements of user interface elements without a single extra line of CSS or JavaScript code.

Setting Up an Application Layout Page

Establishing the scaffolding for a full-window application using Dijit is not much different than any other page — in fact, it's a bit simpler than most. The following markup starts off such a page:

```
<html>
    <head>
        <title>Hello Dojo Layouts</title>

        <style type="text/css">
            @import "../dojodev/dojo/resources/dojo.css";
            @import "../dojodev/dijit/themes/tundra/tundra.css";
        </style>

        <style type="text/css">
            html, body, #main {
                /* make the body expand to fill the visible window */
                width: 100%; height: 100%;
                padding: 0; margin: 0;
                /* erase window level scrollbars */
                overflow: hidden;
            }

            h1, h2, h3 { margin: 0.5em 0 1em 0 }
            p   { margin: 0 0 1em 0 }

            .box     { border: 1px #bbb solid; }
            .content { padding: 0.5em; overflow: auto }

            #header  { height: 40px; }
            #sidebar { width: 150px; }
            #content { padding: 1em; }
            #footer  { height: 25px; padding: 0.25em; text-align: right; }

            #sidebar ul { margin-left: -1em; }

            #mainstack { width: 75%; height: 75%; border: 1px #888 solid }
        </style>
```

This first half of the page header is concerned mostly with CSS. The base Dojo style sheet is imported, along with the widget theme "tundra".

Then, it's time for the page-specific styles, of which there are very few: First, styles are applied to the page at large, specifying that the page and the main <div> containing the user interface should fill the browser window from edge to edge. Then, there are a few styles tweaking margins and establishing the sizes of a few major page regions. And, that's it — Dijit widgets declared entirely in markup will manage the rest of the layout concerns of the page, with no need for further CSS.

In this next chunk of markup, the overall setup of the page is completed:

```
<script type="text/javascript">
    djConfig = {
        isDebug:      true,
        parseOnLoad:  true
    };
</script>

<script type="text/javascript"
    src="../dojodev/dojo/dojo.js"></script>

<script type="text/javascript">
    dojo.require("dojo.parser");

    dojo.require("dijit.layout.ContentPane");
    dojo.require("dijit.layout.BorderContainer");
    dojo.require("dijit.layout.StackContainer");
    dojo.require("dijit.layout.AccordionContainer");
    dojo.require("dijit.layout.SplitContainer");
    dojo.require("dijit.layout.TabContainer");
    dojo.require("dijit.layout.LinkPane");
</script>

</head>

<body class="tundra">
    <!-- content goes here -->
</body>

</html>
```

The preceding code presents the usual pattern for pulling in the Dojo toolkit, as well as declaring a handful of Dijit modules as requirements. As with the CSS, there's not much need for more code here beyond getting dojo.parser into the page and loading up the widgets that will be used.

Using ContentPanes as Layout Building Blocks

The first of the widgets loaded, named dijit.layout.ContentPane, is the basic building block for displaying content in Dijit layouts. At a minimum, it can act as a simple container, existing on its own or offering hooks to a parent widget managing its position and size.

However, the `ContentPane` widget does offer at least one built-in trick worth noting:

```
<div class="content"
    dojoType="dijit.layout.ContentPane"
    loadingMessage="Loading content..."
    errorMessage="Content load failed!"
    href="content.html"
    preventCache="true"
    refreshOnShow="true">

    <!-- content will be loaded dynamically -->

</div>
```

Using the `href` attribute, the `ContentPane` widget can be populated with content fetched from an external resource via `dojo.xhrGet()`. As opposed to using an `<iframe>`, this content is usually expected as a document fragment and is injected right into the page DOM inside the `ContentPane` widget body.

This content loading mechanism displays the `loadingMessage` attribute while waiting for the fetch request to complete, injecting the content on success or the contents of `errorMessage` on failure. Both of these are optional attributes, and there are defaults that will be used for either if absent.

The next attribute shown, named `preventCache`, will append a time-based parameter onto the fetched URL in order to make the request unique and circumvent caching to help ensure that the fetched content is fresh. This attribute defaults to `false`, thus allowing browser caches to operate normally otherwise.

The final attribute `refreshOnShow` is useful when the `ContentPane` is managed as part of another widget that controls the visibility of its contained elements. When `true`, this `ContentPane` will attempt to fetch its contents over again fresh whenever it has been hidden from view and then subsequently revealed again.

Managing Layout Regions with BorderContainer

The next layout widget listed in the page head is named `dijit.layout.BorderContainer`. This widget offers the ability to easily construct a layout with a header, footer, left/right sidebars, and a central content area. The following markup begins the declaration of one of these widgets:

```
<div id="main" dojoType="dijit.layout.BorderContainer"
    design="headline"
    persist="true"
    liveSplitters="false">
```

The first optional attribute, design, expects one of the following two values:

❑   headline (the default) — The top header and bottom footer stretch across the entire layout. Think of this shape as the letter "I".

❑   sidebar — Left and right sidebars extend to the very top and bottom of the layout, bookending the header and footer regions. Think of this shape as the letter "H".

The next attribute, persist, is concerned with splitters. Each boundary between regions can be given draggable splitters, allowing the user to customize the proportions of the layout. The persist attribute causes this widget to remember dragged splitter positions in cookies, so that the user-customized state of the layout can be restored when the application is visited again.

And speaking of splitters, the liveSplitters attribute switches between two styles of splitters. When set to true (the default value), a splitter will cause the layout to update itself in real time while being resized. Proportionally sized elements will grow and shrink, and text will reflow itself within containers. When dealing with simple content, this can offer very responsive feedback to the user.

However, if the regions contain complex subordinate layouts that are somewhat computationally expensive to resize, you should set liveSplitters to false. This mode waits to adjust layout until the user has stopped dragging the splitter, instead offering just a ghosted avatar of the splitter as it's moving.

Now, it's time to define a few content regions for this widget:

```
<div id="header" class="box"
    dojoType="dijit.layout.ContentPane"
    region="top">
    <h1>Hello Dojo Layouts</h1>
</div>

<div id="footer" class="box"
    dojoType="dijit.layout.ContentPane"
    region="bottom">
    <p>This is a footer!</p>
</div>

<div id="maincontent" class="box"
    dojoType="dijit.layout.ContentPane"
    region="center">
    <h3>This is center content</h3>
    <p>
        Cras ut mauris vitae nisl mattis vulputate. Duis urna
        pede, iaculis vitae, tristique a, tempor eget, leo.
    </p>
</div>
```

Each of the content regions for the BorderContainer in the preceding markup are simple instances of dijit.layout.ContentPane — but as you'll see further on in the chapter, these can be nearly any other layout widgets.

For each of these ContentPane widgets, the most significant feature with respect to the BorderContainer is the region attribute. It expects one of the following values:

❑ center — At least one region of this type is required, and will be placed in the center of the layout, to be surrounded by all other region types.

❑ top — This region will form the header at the top of the layout.

❑ bottom — This region forms the bottom footer of the layout.

❑ left — This region appears as a sidebar on the left-hand side of the layout.

❑ right — This region appears as a sidebar on the right-hand side of the layout.

❑ leading — Based on the direction in which text flows in the layout — that is, left-to-right in English and right-to-left in Hebrew — this region appears in the position where text begins.

❑ trailing — Based on the direction in which text flows in the layout — that is, left-to-right in English and right-to-left in Hebrew — this region appears in the position where text ends.

Beyond the region attribute, a BorderContainer watches for a few more attributes on its contained widgets:

```
<div id="sidebar" class="box"
    dojoType="dijit.layout.ContentPane"
    region="left"
    splitter="true"
    minSize="160"
    maxSize="300">

    <p>This is the sidebar!</p>

    </div>
</div>
```

As mentioned earlier, the BorderContainer widget can provide draggable dividers between regions. For any region but center, setting the splitter attribute to true is how you do it. Accompanying the splitter attribute are the minSize and maxSize attributes. These define constraints on the splitter for the minimum and maximum sizes allowed for the region.

Figure 28-13 shows how the BorderContainer declared in the previous example turns out once it's dropped into the body of the page.

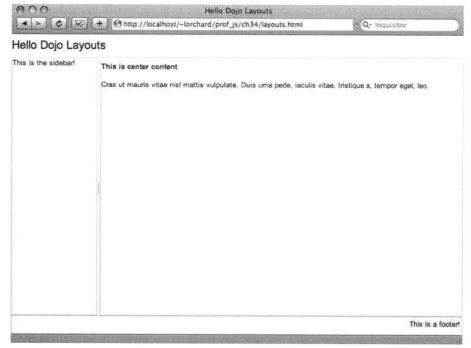

Figure 28-13

Managing Content Visibility with StackContainer

The `BorderLayout` widget is great for organizing layouts with headers and sidebars. But, beyond simply slicing space into regions, it's often useful to manage space by swapping in and out different sets of elements altogether.

The basic building block for this in Dijit is `dijit.layout.StackContainer`, which serves as the parent class for number of widgets offering related functionality. The `StackContainer` can be used by itself, however, as presented in the following markup:

```
<div id="maincontent" class="box"
    dojoType="dijit.layout.ContentPane"
    region="center">

    <h2>StackContainer ahoy!</h2>

    <div id="mainstack"
        dojoType="dijit.layout.StackContainer">

        <div class="content"
            dojoType="dijit.layout.ContentPane"
            title="Page 1">
            <h3>Page 1</h3>
```

```
            <p>Proin suscipit gravida quam. Quisque nec enim.</p>
        </div>

        <div class="content"
            dojoType="dijit.layout.ContentPane"
            selected="true"
            title="Page 2">
            <h3>Page 2</h3>
            <p>Phasellus suscipit mollis turpis.</p>
        </div>

        <div class="content"
            dojoType="dijit.layout.ContentPane"
            title="Page 3">
            <h3>Page 3</h3>
            <p>Pellentesque consectetuer, ligula eget adipiscing pharetra</p>
        </div>

        <div class="content"
            dojoType="dijit.layout.ContentPane"
            title="Page 4">
            <h3>Page 4</h3>
            <p>Magna magna suscipit nibh, et fermentum massa ante a tortor.</p>
        </div>

    </div>
```

Like `BorderContainer`, a `StackContainer` manages a number of `ContentPane` children. Only one of these is visible at a time, like a stack of cards with only the top card showing.

Out of the box, the `StackContainer` comes with no navigation controls. However, there exists a companion widget named `dijit.layout.StackController` that can be wired up to offer buttons managing the currently visible card in the stack:

```
<div dojoType="dijit.layout.StackController"
    containerId="mainstack">
</div>
```

The `StackController` a pretty bare-bones widget, mainly meant as a parent class for more advanced and elaborate widgets. It expects an attribute named `containerId`, referencing the ID of the `StackContainer` meant to be controlled. On its own, though, the `StackController` only provides a simple set of buttons, one for each page in the stack. When the appropriate button is clicked, the corresponding page is shown and all others are hidden. When new children are added to the stack, the `StackController` automatically adds new buttons.

Building a Pagination Control for a StackContainer

To exercise a few more features of the `StackController` widget, it would be useful to augment this controller with a few more bits of prototyped user interface. Consider the following markup as a start:

```
<div id="stackpaging" class="content"
    containerId="mainstack"
    dojoType="dijit.layout.ContentPane">

    <a href="#" class="prev">&lt; prev</a> <span>--</span>

    <span class="currpage"></span> <span>--</span>

    <a href="#" class="next">next &gt;</a> <span>--</span>

    <a href="#" class="add">add child</a> <span>--</span>

    <a href="#" class="remove">remove child</a>
```

This markup declares a new ContentPane widget containing the following simple elements:

❑   A link to navigate to the previous card

❑   An element to indicate the title of the currently visible card

❑   A link to navigate to the next card

❑   A link to add a new card

❑   A link to remove the current card

With the user interface parts established, it's time to start wiring things up:

```
<script type="dojo/method">

    var root_id      = this.srcNodeRef.id;
    var container_id = this.srcNodeRef.getAttribute('containerId');

    var stack = dijit.byId(container_id);

    dojo.query('.prev', root_id)
        .onclick(function(ev) {
            dojo.stopEvent(ev);
            stack.back();
        });

    dojo.query('.next', root_id)
        .onclick(function(ev) {
            dojo.stopEvent(ev);
            stack.forward();
        });
```

The preceding code starts off with one more kind of custom <script> tag understood by dojo.parser. This time it's a type of "dojo/method" with no event attribute — dojo.parser executes code within this kind of <script> tag immediately after the creation of the widget containing the script.

While this collection of user interface elements is not itself a new class of widget, the code here attempts to follow some widget conventions by grabbing both the ID of the container widget itself and the ID of the StackContainer from attributes in markup.

Also, note the use of `dijit.byId()` to get a reference to the widget instance, as opposed to `dojo.byId()`, which returns a DOM node reference.

Inside the script block, the scope variable `this` is available as a reference to the widget just created. Given this, one of the base properties of Dijit widgets is `srcNodeRef`, offering a reference to the original DOM node. The user interface elements themselves are identified by class name, conveniently found via `dojo.query()` using the widget's root ID.

This whole arrangement forms a sort of protowidget, allowing the whole rig to be easily portable to multiple instances of itself and other `StackController` instances in the future. Fully massaging this into a proper Dijit widget is a topic beyond the scope of this chapter, but consider it an advanced exercise for later exploration.

Finishing off the previous code, both the previous and next pagination links are wired up, with clicks handled by calling the `.back()` and `.forward()` methods of the `StackContainer` respectively. These two methods cycle through the cards in the stack, hiding the current and revealing the previous or next in the list.

Next, the following code introduces event topics published by the `StackContainer` widget:

```
dojo.subscribe(
    container_id + '-startup',
    function(params) {
        if (params.selected) {
            var title = params.selected.title;
            dojo.query('.currpage', root_id)
                [0].innerHTML = title;
            console.log("Starting up, selected child '" + title + "'");
        }
    }
);

dojo.subscribe(
    container_id + '-selectChild',
    function(page) {
        dojo.query('.currpage', root_id)
            [0].innerHTML = page.title;
        console.log("Selected child '" + page.title + "'");
    }
);
```

Whereas the code block shown earlier wired up user interface elements to *cause* the `StackContainer` to page through its contents, the code in this example wires up event topic subscribers to *react* to the `StackContainer` initially waking up and subsequently paging through its contents. Both of the event subscribers in this code log messages in reaction to visibility changes in the `StackContainer`, as well as update the current page indicator in the user interface.

Along with providing callable methods to control it, the StackContainer widget publishes a number of topics to announce what it's doing. Since all of these happenings are published as global event topics, it's pretty easy to wire up multiple loosely coupled handlers to react to changes in this widget. The event topics include the following:

❑   {id}-startup — When the widget wakes up, it publishes this event that contains an object detailing the widget's children and may be currently selected.

❑   {id}-selectChild — When a child card is made visible, this event topic is published with a reference to the child selected.

❑   {id}-addChild — This event is published when a new child card is added, including a reference to the new child and the numeric insertion index as parameters.

❑   {id}-removeChild — This event is published when a child card is removed, including a reference to the removed card.

Note that the string {id} in the preceding list should be replaced with the ID of the StackContainer widget.

Continuing on, the following code deals with adding to and removing from the stack:

```
dojo.query('.add', root_id)
    .onclick(function(ev) {
        dojo.stopEvent(ev);
        var widget = new dijit.layout.ContentPane({
            title: "child " + parseInt(Math.random() * 1000),
            href: 'random.php'
        });
        stack.addChild(widget, 0);
        stack.selectChild(widget);
    });

dojo.query('.remove', root_id)
    .onclick(function(ev) {
        dojo.stopEvent(ev);
        var widget = stack.selectedChildWidget;
        stack.removeChild(widget);
    });
```

The first part of this code block wires up the add link to programmatically create a new ContentPane widget, loading content dynamically from a resource named random.php. Additionally, a random and unique title is provided for the pane. The .addChild() method of the StackContainer is used to insert this new pane at the head of the list, and the .selectChild() method is called to make the new addition visible.

The second part of this block wires up the remove link, which grabs the currently visible card with the
StackContainer's selectedChildWidget property and then calls the .removeChild() method to
remove it from the stack.

Completing the circle, the following code offers subscribers to react to the previous actions:

```
dojo.subscribe(
    container_id + '-addChild',
    function(page, index) {
        console.log("Added child '" + page.title + "' at " + index);
    }
);

dojo.subscribe(
    container_id + '-removeChild',
    function(page) {
        console.log("Removed child '" + page.title + "'");
    }
);

</script>

</div>
```

As described earlier, the {id}-addChild and {id}-removeChild event topics are published whenever
the StackContainer is caused to add or remove a card from its stack. The preceding code simply
creates subscribers that report such activity in the log.

To help demonstrate these features with changing content, the following is an implementation for the
random.php resource that's referenced by the href property, which was used in creating a new
ContentPane child widget earlier:

```
<?php
// Wait for a number of seconds to fake work.
if ($_GET['wait']) {
    sleep($_GET['wait']);
}

// Take a list of words and shuffle them all up.
$words = explode(" ",
    "Lorem ipsum dolor sit amet, consectetuer adipiscing elit. ".
    "Maecenas porta, sapien bibendum adipiscing rutrum, ".
    "est nunc congue nibh, nec faucibus magna turpis sed arcu."
);
shuffle($words);
?>
```

```
<ul>
    <?php if ($_GET['dojo_preventCache']): ?>
        <li>preventCache: <?php echo $_GET['dojo_preventCache'] ?></li>
    <?php endif ?>
    <?php foreach ($words as $word): ?>
        <?php if (rand(0, 10) > 5 ): ?>
            <li><?php echo $word ?></li>
        <?php endif ?>
    <?php endforeach ?>
</ul>
```

This PHP script accepts a parameter `?wait` that causes a delay for a number of seconds, in order to fake processing time and draw out loading messages in the demonstration. The rest of the script builds a bulleted list out of random words from a sample paragraph. Keep this script around — it will be useful in demonstrating dynamic content throughout the rest of the chapter.

Figure 28-14 shows a preview of how all the above should turn out in a browser. After playing around a bit with the interface, the event subscribers will produce a log transcript with messages like these:

```
Added child 'child 290' at 0
Selected child 'child 290'
GET http://localhost/~lorchard/prof_js/ch34/random.php
Added child 'child 904' at 0
Selected child 'child 904'
Selected child 'Page 2'
Removed child 'Page 2'
Selected child 'child 904'
GET http://localhost/~lorchard/prof_js/ch34/random.php
Added child 'child 596' at 0
Selected child 'child 596'
Selected child 'child 904'
Removed child 'child 904'
Selected child 'child 596'
```

You should be able to get a good idea of the sequence of events that fire during the course of navigating and managing the contents of the `StackContainer`.

Also, as you read about more layout widgets through the rest of this chapter, keep in mind that `StackContainer` is the parent class for a few of these — meaning that all the above applies to them as well, including methods for manipulation and event topics available for subscription.

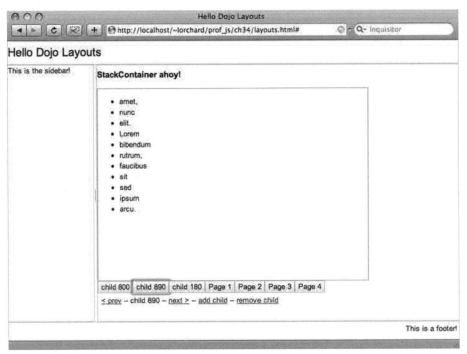

Figure 28-14

Swapping Content Panes with AccordionContainer

Another widget available for managing visibility is named `dijit.layout.AccordionContainer`. This is a `StackContainer` subclass that provides a vertical stack of content panes, of which only one is visible at a time. Other panes collapse into title bars that, when clicked, cause the visible pane to collapse and the clicked pane to expand in a combined animation.

Consider the following markup, intended to replace the `<p>` content of the `BorderLayout` widget's left-hand sidebar in the previous example:

```
<div id="sideaccord"
    dojoType="dijit.layout.AccordionContainer">

    <div id="side1" dojoType="dijit.layout.AccordionPane"
        title="Pane #1">
        <ul>
            <li>foo</li>
            <li>baz</li>
        </ul>
    </div>

    <div id="side2" dojoType="dijit.layout.AccordionPane"
```

```
            loadingMessage="Loading content..."
            href="random.php?wait=1"
            preload="true"
            preventCache="false"
            refreshOnShow="false"
            title="Pane #2 (dynamic content)">
    </div>

    <div id="side3" dojoType="dijit.layout.AccordionPane"
            title="Pane #3">
        <ul>
            <li>bar</li>
            <li>baz</li>
        </ul>
    </div>

    <div id="side4" dojoType="dijit.layout.AccordionPane"
            title="Pane #4"
        <ul>
            <li>foo</li>
            <li>bar</li>
            <li>baz</li>
        </ul>
    </div>

</div>
```

The `title` attribute in each of the panes shown in this example is what gets used in the clickable accordion title bars. Beyond that, it's useful to note that the `dijit.layout.AccordionPane` widget is a subclass of `ContentPane`, tweaked slightly to work in the accordion-style navigation element. You can include other non-layout widgets here — a restriction of the `AccordionContainer` itself — and use all other base attributes accepted by a `ContentPane`.

Another thing worth recalling is the use of the `href` attribute for loading dynamic content. Since the `AccordionContainer` widget fully hides and reveals content, the `refreshOnShow` attribute of a `ContentPane` comes into play. Because the second pane of the accordion loads dynamic content with `refreshOnShow` set to `true`, you should be able to navigate between the various panes and watch the second one reload itself each time you come back to it.

Figure 28-15 shows how an `AccordionContainer` is rendered, this time also with the `design` attribute of the parent `BorderContainer` switched to "sidebar" in order to give the accordion element more vertical space. Notice that the header and footer have been displaced to allow the sidebar to stretch to both the top and bottom borders of the window.

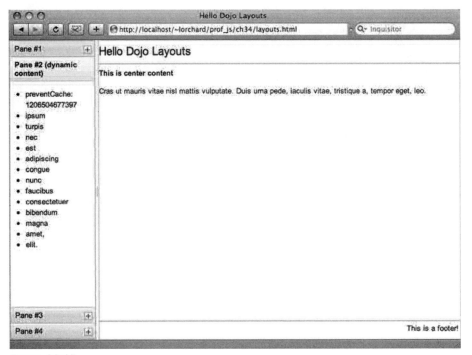

Figure 28-15

Building Tabbed Content Panes with TabContainer

Whereas the `AccordionContainer` best manages hiding and showing panes in vertical spaces like sidebars, the `StackContainer` widget subclass `dijit.layout.TabContainer` is better suited for managing wider spaces with clickable tabs laid out in a horizontal or vertical bar.

Consider the following markup, which declares a `TabContainer` widget, intended to replace the center region `ContentPane` in the `BorderContainer` from earlier in the chapter:

```
<div id="maincontent"
    dojoType="dijit.layout.TabContainer"
    tabPosition="bottom"
    region="center">

    <div class="content"
        dojoType="dijit.layout.ContentPane"
        title="Tab #1">
        <h3>Praesent aliquet</h3>
        <p>
            Cras ut mauris vitae nisl mattis vulputate. Duis urna
            pede, iaculis vitae, tristique a, tempor eget, leo.
        </p>
    </div>
```

```
<div class="content"
    dojoType="dijit.layout.ContentPane"
    closable="true"
    selected="true"
    title="Tab #2 (closable)">
    <h3>Duis urna pede</h3>
    <p>
        Nam imperdiet, lectus sit amet feugiat adipiscing,
        turpis mi ornare enim,
    </p>
</div>

<div class="content"
    dojoType="dijit.layout.ContentPane"
    loadingMessage="Loading content..."
    href="random.php?wait=1"
    preventCache="true"
    refreshOnShow="true"
    title="Tab #3 (dynamic content)">
</div>

</div>
```

Note that the `TabContainer` can directly replace a `ContentPane` in a `BorderContainer`, bearing the `region="center"` attribute. Additionally, the `TabContainer` widget accepts an attribute named `tabPosition`, whose value may be one of the following:

❑   `top` — Tabs are laid out horizontally across the top of the widget.

❑   `bottom` — Tabs are laid out horizontally across the bottom of the widget.

❑   `left-h` — A vertical strip of tabs appears on the left-hand side.

❑   `right-h` — A vertical strip of tabs appears on the right-hand side.

The tab children of the `TabContainer` are `ContentPane` widgets. The `title` attribute supplied with each of these becomes the title displayed in the clickable tabs. The first tab is pretty simple, supplying only a `title` and some content.

The second tab, however, supplies a pair of new attributes:

❑   `closable` — When `true`, this tab can be closed and removed from display altogether.

❑   `selected` — When the page loads, the first tab with this attribute set to `true` will be made visible. Otherwise, the first tab in the list will be made visible.

Finally, the third tab in the set loads dynamic content just like one of the sections of the accordion in the previous section. You should notice similar behavior: Switching away from the dynamic content pane and later returning to it will cause its contents to be reloaded.

Figure 28-16 shows what the previous markup produces as a widget.

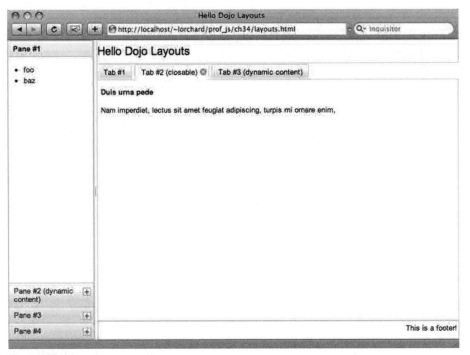

Figure 28-16

Dividing Up Layout Regions with SplitContainer

If you appreciated using the draggable region borders provided by BorderContainer, then you may like this next widget named dijit.layout.SplitContainer — its sole purpose is to provide draggable split borders. Consider the following markup, intended as a new tab for the previous section's TabContainer widget:

```
<div id="splittab"
    dojoType="dijit.layout.SplitContainer"
    orientation="vertical"
    activeSizing="true"
    persist="false"
    title="Tab #4 (SplitContainer)">

    <div class="content"
        dojoType="dijit.layout.ContentPane"
        sizeShare="15"
        sizeMin="65">
        <h3>Another section</h3>
        <p>Lorem ipsum dolor sit amet, consectetuer adipiscing elit.</p>
    </div>
```

```
<div class="content"
    dojoType="dijit.layout.ContentPane"
    sizeShare="55"
    loadingMessage="Loading content..."
    href="content.html"
    preventCache="true">
</div>

<div class="content"
    dojoType="dijit.layout.ContentPane"
    sizeShare="30">
    <h3>Duis urna pede</h3>
    <p>
        Nam imperdiet, lectus sit amet feugiat adipiscing,
        turpis mi ornare enim,
    </p>
</div>

</div>
```

The `SplitContainer` widget demonstrated in the preceding markup accepts the following attributes controlling the behavior and layout of its draggable borders:

❑   `orientation` — This value can be either `horizontal` (default) or `vertical`, specifying in which direction the split regions should be laid out. Unlike a `BorderContainer`, a `SplitContainer` allows split regions in only one direction.

❑   `activeSizing` — Similar to `liveSplitters` used with `BorderContainer`, this flag decides between live resizing of region contents or a ghosted avatar until the drag has completed.

❑   `persist` — When true, the user-selected dimensions of regions will be retained with cookies.

❑   Looking at the child widgets defining the split regions, there are a few attributes useful for managing the relative sizes of the splits:

❑   `sizeMin` — This is the minimum size allowed for the region when resized.

❑   `sizeShare` — This attribute is a proportional value that, when added up with the `sizeShare` values of all other split regions, represents how much space the particular region should take up.

The `sizeShare` attribute may be a bit hard to understand at first. The values in the previous markup all add up to 100, so they look like percentages. This is a convenient way to manage things — but technically, it's just about the total and the proportions. Beyond the initial page load, this attribute also allows a `SplitContainer` to grow and shrink as a fluidly when the browser window is resized.

Figure 28-17 shows how the widget declared in the previous markup fits into the layout as a `TabContainer` pane.

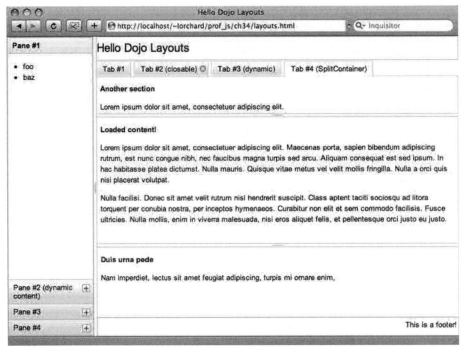

Figure 28-17

Creating Application Controls and Dialogs

Using Dijit widgets, you've seen how to build forms with built-in validation handling and hooks for CSS styling, and you've seen how to manage window space with top-down layout widgets. Now, it's time to cover the remaining widgets concerned with application control and feedback.

Since the layout built up in the last section has gotten fairly complex, the following markup offers a new start to continue playing with more widgets:

```
<html>
    <head>
        <title>Hello Dojo Widgets</title>

        <style type="text/css">
            @import "../dojodev/dojo/resources/dojo.css";
            @import "../dojodev/dijit/themes/tundra/tundra.css";
        </style>

        <script type="text/javascript" src="../dojodev/dojo/dojo.js"
            djConfig="parseOnLoad: true"></script>

        <script type="text/javascript">
            dojo.require("dojo.parser");
```

```
        dojo.require("dijit.Menu");
        dojo.require("dijit.Toolbar");
        dojo.require("dijit.form.Button");

        dojo.require("dijit.Dialog");
        dojo.require("dijit.ProgressBar");
        dojo.require("dijit.TitlePane");
    </script>

    <style type="text/css">
        h1, h2, h3 { margin: 0.5em 0 1em 0 }
        p  { margin: 0 0 1em 0 }
        hr { clear: both }
        #loader {
            padding: 0; margin: 0;
            top: 0; left: 0;
            position: absolute;
            width: 100%; height: 100%;
            background: #fff;
            z-index: 999;
        }
        .menu_target {
            padding: 1em; margin: 1em;
            width: 75px; float: left;
            border: 1px solid #333;
            background-color: #ddd;
        }
    </style>

</head>

<body class="tundra">

            <div id="loader"><h1>Loading widgets demo...</h1></div>
                <script type="text/javascript">
        dojo.addOnLoad(function() {
            var loader = dojo.byId('loader');
            loader.style.display = "none";
        });
    </script>

    <h1>Hello Dojo Widgets</h1>

    <!-- body content goes here -->

</body>

</html>
```

This markup looks pretty straightforward with respect to other pages using Dojo and Dijit. The one new feature worth explaining is the loader element appearing first thing in the <body> of the page.

Depending on how fast things have loaded up for you this far in this chapter, you may start to notice a "flash of unstyled content" as the widgets pile in. That is, you will see content on the page in between various stages of getting CSS applied and the `dojo.parser` module completing its sweep through the page to instantiate widgets.

This simple loading `<div>` presents an opaque curtain over the stage until Dojo has signaled that everything has been loaded, at which point the loader `<div>` is made invisible. You could make this mechanism more sophisticated by applying a fade-out at the end of page load and maybe even including some indication of progress along the way or at least an animated spinner — but for the sake of this demonstration, the loader stays simple.

Building and Scripting Clickable Buttons

Beyond data entry forms, one of the fundamental building blocks of any user interface is a clickable button. Recall that during the exploration of Dijit's form widgets, only plain old submit buttons were used in order to keep things simple and to show how to hook up an `onSubmit` handler to invoke form validation.

As it turns out, Dijit does offer a flexible set of buttons that are useful both in forms and in an application in general. The first of these centers around the `dijit.form.Button` widget, declared like so:

```
<button id="button1" dojoType="dijit.form.Button">
    Click me #1!
    <script type="dojo/method" event="onClick">
        console.log('Clicked '+this.id);
    </script>
</button>
```

This markup declares a new `<button>` element with a `dojoType` of `dijit.form.Button`. It's best to use a `<button>` element over, say, an `<input type="button">` because the former is so much more amenable to styling with CSS than the latter — and that's just what happens when a widget theme is applied.

In the body of the `<button>` element, there's some text, which forms the label for the button. After this, there's a `<script>` of type "dojo/method", implementing a handler for the button's onClick method. This implementation simply sends a message to the log, but it should suffice as a demonstration.

This button is pretty simple, but the Button widget does accept a few more attributes:

```
<button id="button2" dojoType="dijit.form.Button"
    showLabel="false"
    iconClass="dijitEditorIcon dijitEditorIconCopy"
    onClick="console.log('Clicked '+this.id);">
    Click me #2!
</button>
```

In the preceding markup, the `iconClass` attribute is given the CSS class names of an icon from the widget theme for the rich text editor toolbar. This causes the icon for the "copy" operation to appear. And, while there is a label provided in the body of the widget declaration, the `showLabel` attribute set to false will prevent it from being displayed.

The end result is a button consisting only of an icon, with no text label. Also notice that this time, instead of a `<script>` element within the button, there's an `onClick` attribute specifying the code to be executed when the button is clicked.

To give a taste of widget theme construction, the following is what the "tundra" CSS code looks like with respect to the icon usedpreviously:

```
.tundra .dijitEditorIcon {
      background-image: url('images/editor.gif'); /* editor icons sprite image */
      background-repeat: no-repeat;
      width: 18px;
      height: 18px;
      text-align: center;
}
.tundra .dijitEditorIconCopy { background-position: -72px; }
```

Widget themes will be discussed a bit more in this chapter, but this gives some hints on what you can do to use your own icons when building buttons.

Moving along, the following shows how you can programmatically create a new button:

```
<button id="button3">Click me #3!</button>

<script type="text/javascript">
    dojo.addOnLoad(function() {
        var button3 = new dijit.form.Button({
            onClick: function(ev) {
                console.log('Clicked '+this.id);
            }
        }, dojo.byId('button3'));
    });
</script>
```

There's nothing much new here: You can create a new instance of `dijit.form.Button` in JavaScript code like any other object, passing in a set of properties and a reference to a DOM node just as `dojo.parser` does during its sweep through the page.

Figure 28-18 shows what all three of these buttons look like in a browser.

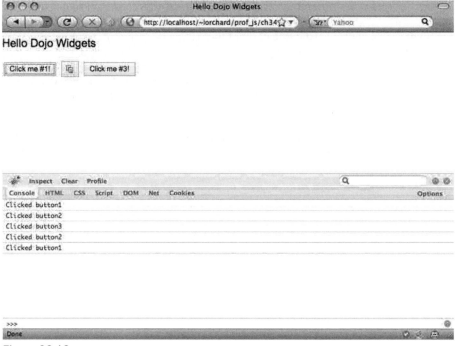

Figure 28-18

Composing Pop-up Context Menus

Buttons are already offered in various native forms by browsers, with or without augmentation in widgets or CSS styles. However, so far no kind of native pop-up menu structure is offered by browsers. So, Dijit offers a widget to fill your hierarchical command menu needs.

The following markup offers a look at declaring such a widget:

```
<div id="menu_target1" class="menu_target">Target #1</div>
<div id="menu_target2" class="menu_target">Target #2</div>
<div id="menu_target3" class="menu_target">Target #3</div>

<div dojoType="dijit.Menu"
    targetNodeIds="menu_target1, menu_target2, menu_target3"
    contextMenuForWindow="false"
    style="display: none">

    <div id="foo_item" dojoType="dijit.MenuItem">
        <span>Foo</span>
        <script type="dojo/method" event="onClick">
            console.log('Menu clicked: '+this.id);
        </script>
    </div>
</div>
```

The first thing to notice in this markup is that there are three `<div>` elements, each with a CSS class of `menu_target`. Following them is a widget declaration with a `dojoType` of `dijit.Menu`, whose first attribute named `targetNodeIds` lists the IDs of those first three `<div>` nodes.

As demonstrated earlier, the `targetNodeIds` attribute accepts a list of node IDs to which the menu will be attached. When a user right-clicks one of these elements, the declared menu is activated.

Following this attribute is `contextMenuForWindow` set to "`false`". As opposed to the behavior of the `targetNodeIds` attribute, if `contextMenuForWindow` is set to "`true`" a right-click anywhere in summons this menu, overriding the browser's native context menu for the window.

Last but not least in the list of attributes, you'll notice that the element's style is set to make it invisible. If this is not done, the context menu will appear initially visible in the page layout, which is usually not the desirable behavior.

Once the `Menu` widget is established, it's time to declare an instance of `dijit.MenuItem`. Notice that this works almost like a `dijit.Button` widget — it accepts a label in markup or as an attribute, and can be given an `onClick` handler with a custom `<script>` block or an attribute.

A `Menu` widget can contain any number of `MenuItem` instances. However, deeper menu structure comes from `MenuItem` subclasses, like this one:

```
<div dojoType="dijit.PopupMenuItem">
    <span>Edit</span>

    <div dojoType="dijit.Menu" id="context_edit">

        <div dojoType="dijit.MenuItem" label="Copy"
            onClick="console.log('Menu clicked: '+this.id);"
            iconClass="dijitEditorIcon dijitEditorIconCopy"></div>

        <div dojoType="dijit.MenuItem" label="Paste"
            onClick="console.log('Menu clicked: '+this.id);"
            iconClass="dijitEditorIcon dijitEditorIconPaste"></div>

    </div>
</div>
```

This instance of `dijit.PopupMenuItem` introduces a new item, which cannot be clicked, but instead reacts to mouse rollover by revealing the otherwise hidden `dijit.Menu` widget it contains. Also akin to the `Button` widget, the `MenuItem` widgets contained in this submenu offer items bearing image icons supplied by the CSS widget theme and handlers defined via `onClick` attributes.

Something worth noting here is that neither the "Copy" nor "Paste" menu items here have been given IDs, yet their `onClick` handlers refer to IDs. When created, these `MenuItem` widgets will come up with their own unique IDs, so you should see these appear in the log when you click on these items.

Moving on to something a little bit more complex, check out this self-modifying menu:

```
<div dojoType="dijit.PopupMenuItem">
    <span>Windows</span>

    <div dojoType="dijit.Menu" id="context_windows">

        <div dojoType="dijit.MenuItem" id="new_window"
            label="New Window..."
            iconClass="dijitEditorIcon dijitEditorIconInsertImage">

            <script type="dojo/method" event="onClick">
                var rand = parseInt(Math.random() * 1000);
                console.log("Adding a new window item, window_"+rand);
                this.getParent().addChild(
                    new dijit.MenuItem({
                        id: 'window_'+rand,
                        label: 'Window '+rand,
                        onClick: function() {
                            console.log('Removing clicked: '+this.id);
                            this.getParent().removeChild(this);
                        }
                    })
                );
            </script>

        </div>
    </div>
</div>
```

As with any other widget, it's possible to programmatically create new MenuItem widgets. Additionally, Menu widgets offer both .addChild() and .removeChild() methods for modifying the contents of a menu.

The markup in the preceding example allows a user to add new items by clicking the "New Window ..." item, and the items created will remove themselves when clicked. Although it's not exercised here, you can also call a .setDisabled() method on MenuItem widgets to set whether or not the item should be clickable or grayed out.

Figure 28-19 shows the finished menu in action in Firefox, along with an open Firebug log transcript showing some of the messages produced in the course of interacting with the menu.

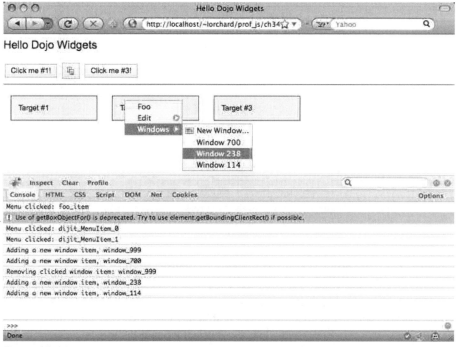

Figure 28-19

Combining Buttons and Menus

If buttons and menus are useful, then how about buttons that spawn menus? Dijit offers two kinds of buttons for this purpose, the first of which is offered in the following markup:

```
<div dojoType="dijit.form.DropDownButton" id="edit_dropdown">
    <span>Edit</span>

    <div dojoType="dijit.Menu">

        <div dojoType="dijit.MenuItem" label="Copy"
            onClick="console.log('Menu clicked: '+this.id);"
            iconClass="dijitEditorIcon dijitEditorIconCopy"></div>

        <div dojoType="dijit.MenuItem" label="Paste"
            onClick="console.log('Menu clicked: '+this.id);"
            iconClass="dijitEditorIcon dijitEditorIconPaste"></div>

    </div>
</div>
```

The `dijit.form.DropDownButton` widget reveals a menu when clicked, though does not itself handle clicks. The following widget does handle clicks, as well as a menu:

```
<div dojoType="dijit.form.ComboButton" id="edit_combo"
    onClick="console.log('Menu clicked: '+this.id);">
    <span>Edit</span>

    <div dojoType="dijit.Menu">

        <div dojoType="dijit.MenuItem" label="Copy"
            onClick="console.log('Menu clicked: '+this.id);"
            iconClass="dijitEditorIcon dijitEditorIconCopy"></div>

        <div dojoType="dijit.MenuItem" label="Paste"
            onClick="console.log('Menu clicked: '+this.id);"
            iconClass="dijitEditorIcon dijitEditorIconPaste"></div>

    </div>

</div>
```

As evidenced by the `onClick` attribute in the declaration of the `dijit.form.ComboButton` widget in the preceding markup, this widget handles clicks within its main body like a normal button. However, it also offers a region to one side that, when clicked, reveals the menu it contains.

Building Toolbars from Buttons and Menus

There is no widget built especially to provide horizontal style application menus. However, there is a toolbar widget that can contain any of the buttons presented so far:

```
<div dojoType="dijit.Toolbar">

    <button dojoType="dijit.form.Button"
        showLabel="true">File</button>

    <button dojoType="dijit.form.DropDownButton">
        <span>Edit</span>
        <div dojoType="dijit.Menu">

            <div dojoType="dijit.MenuItem" label="Copy"
                iconClass="dijitEditorIcon dijitEditorIconCopy"></div>

            <div dojoType="dijit.MenuItem" label="Cut"
                iconClass="dijitEditorIcon dijitEditorIconCut"></div>

            <div dojoType="dijit.MenuItem" label="Paste"
                iconClass="dijitEditorIcon dijitEditorIconPaste"></div>

        </div>
    </button>

    <div dojoType="dijit.ToolbarSeparator"></div>
```

```
<button dojoType="dijit.form.Button"
    iconClass="dijitEditorIcon dijitEditorIconBold"
    showLabel="true">Bold</button>

<div dojoType="dijit.ToolbarSeparator"></div>

<button dojoType="dijit.form.Button"
    iconClass="dijitEditorIcon dijitEditorIconCopy"
    showLabel="false">Copy</button>

</div>
```

More flexible than a simple horizontal menu bar widget, this `dijit.Toolbar` widget can play host to multiple Button widgets. If you wanted just a horizontal application menu, you could compose one by solely using `dijit.DropDownButton` widgets. You can also include buttons with icon images, and group similar buttons together with `dijit.ToolbarSeparator` widgets.

Figure 28-20 depicts an assemblage of buttons in a toolbar, including the `ComboButton` and `DropDown` button widgets from the previous section.

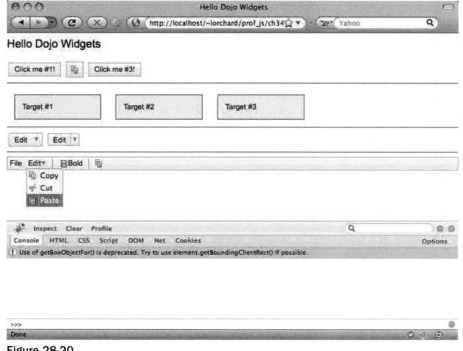

Figure 28-20

Giving Feedback on Completion with Progress Bars

When initiating an action that will take some time to complete, or loading some data from a remote source, it's often useful to provide some animated indicator that there's work going on. You can do this with a simple animated GIF image, but it's also nice to try to provide some accurate measure of progress toward finishing. To this end, Dijit offers the following widget:

```
<div id="progress1" dojoType="dijit.ProgressBar"
    style="width: 250px;">
</div>

<button dojoType="dijit.form.Button">
    <span>Start thinking</span>
    <script type="dojo/method" event="onClick">
        dijit.byId('progress1').update({
            indeterminate: true
        });
    </script>
</button>
```

This markup declares an instance of dijit.ProgressBar, a user interface element, which should be familiar from other applications. When the button in the preceding example is clicked, the ProgressBar widget is thrown into an "indeterminate" state, which means that it shows an animation to indicate something's happening but it doesn't indicate any measure of completion. This is the "barber pole" style seen in many applications.

The next example of the widget is somewhat more complex, this time attempting to simulate some measure of progress over time:

```
<div id="progress2" dojoType="dijit.ProgressBar"
    style="width: 250px;">
</div>

<button dojoType="dijit.form.Button">
    <span>Start loading</span>
    <script type="dojo/method" event="onClick">

        var prog_done  = 0;
        var total_prog = 1000;

        this.setLabel("Loading...");
        this.setDisabled(true);

        var prog_int = setInterval(dojo.hitch(this, function() {
            prog_done += Math.random() * 100;

            dijit.byId('progress2').update({
                indeterminate: false,
                progress: prog_done,
                maximum:  total_prog,
                places:   2
            });
```

```
            if (prog_done >= total_prog) {
                clearInterval(prog_int);
                this.setLabel("Start loading");
                this.setDisabled(false);
            }
        }), 100);

    </script>
</button>
```

When the button in this example is clicked, it starts a timer that progresses in increments, counting in random amounts over a course of time until it reaches a total value of 1000. Each time this routine fires, it calls the `.update()` method of the `ProgressBar` widget with a set of properties to report on the following:

❑ `indeterminate` — The value is false here because the progress is a known range.

❑ `progress` — This value represents the work done so far.

❑ `maximum` — This value represents the work expected to be done by the end.

❑ `places` — Since the bar displays a numerical percentage from 0 to 100, this value specifies to how many decimal places the percentage should be displayed. Thus, given a value of 2, you'll see percentages like 12.34 percent.

Figure 28-21 shows both forms of the `ProgressBar` widget in action.

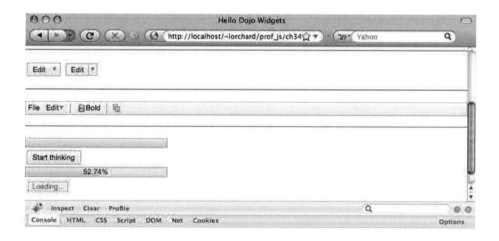

Figure 28-21

Applying Themes to Widgets

Dojo and Dijit offer a growing selection of CSS-based themes available to apply various looks and feels across the entire selection of widgets available. This is possible because each widget is designed to offer a rich set of CSS class names and patterns of markup that facilitate complete control of appearance in CSS.

Examining Widget DOM Structure

For example, recall the following declaration of a button in HTML:

```
<button id="button2" dojoType="dijit.form.Button"
    showLabel="false"
    iconClass="dijitEditorIcon dijitEditorIconCopy"
    onClick="console.log('Clicked '+this.id);">
    Click me #2!
</button>
```

Once `dojo.parser` has scanned through the page and instantiated a widget to manage this button, the DOM structure will have been reworked to look something like this:

```
<div widgetid="button2"
    class="dijit dijitLeft dijitInline dijitButton dijitButton"
    dojoattachevent="onclick:_onButtonClick,onmouseenter:_onMouse,
        onmouseleave:_onMouse,onmousedown:_onMouse">
    <div class="dijitRight">
        <button aria-disabled="false" aria-valuenow="" title="Click me #2!"
            tabindex="0" id="button2" aria-labelledby="button2_label"
            role="button"
            class="dijitStretch dijitButtonNode dijitButtonContents"
            dojoattachpoint="focusNode,titleNode" type="button"
            wairole="button" waistate="labelledby-button2_label">
            <span class="dijitInline dijitEditorIcon dijitEditorIconCopy"
                dojoattachpoint="iconNode">
                <span class="dijitToggleButtonIconChar">✓</span>
            </span>
            <span class="dijitButtonText dijitDisplayNone"
                id="button2_label" dojoattachpoint="containerNode">
                Click me #2!
            </span>
        </button>
    </div>
</div>
```

You'll find that this is standard operating procedure for Dijit widgets, transforming simple markup declarations into rich DOM structures that serve multiple goals including the facilitation of visual themes.

This is a spot where another Firebug feature in Firefox comes in very handy. As shown in Figure 28-22, you can inspect this button element and see not only what the widget has done to it in terms of the DOM, but also get a report on what CSS declarations from which style sheets apply to various parts of this widget in the DOM.

Figure 28-22

Loading and Applying a Theme to Widgets

So far, you've mostly seen the "tundra" theme used throughout the book, but there's a growing collection of alternatives available in Dojo. Consider the following markup loading two different themes:

```
<html>
    <head>
        <style type="text/css">
            @import "../dojodev/dojo/resources/dojo.css";
            @import "../dojodev/dijit/themes/tundra/tundra.css";
            @import "../dojodev/dijit/themes/soria/soria.css";
        </style>
    </head>

    <body>
        <div class="tundra">
            <!-- tundra-themed widgets here -->
            <button id="button2" dojoType="dijit.form.Button"
                showLabel="false"
                iconClass="dijitEditorIcon dijitEditorIconCopy"
                onClick="console.log('Clicked '+this.id);">
                Click me #2!
            </button>
        </div>
```

```
        <div class="soria">
            <!-- soria-themed widgets here -->
            <button id="button3" dojoType="dijit.form.Button"
                showLabel="false"
                iconClass="dijitEditorIcon dijitEditorIconCopy"
                onClick="console.log('Clicked '+this.id);">
                Click me #3!
            </button>
        </div>
    </body>

</html>
```

As shown earlier, this is a snippet of CSS that applies an image icon to the previous example, which is found under the Dojo resource `dijit/themes/tundra/Editor.css`:

```
.tundra .dijitEditorIcon {
        background-image: url('images/editor.gif'); /* editor icons sprite image */
        background-repeat: no-repeat;
        width: 18px;
        height: 18px;
        text-align: center;
}
.tundra .dijitEditorIconCopy { background-position: -72px; }
```

Notice the `.tundra` prefix to each declaration in the CSS. This should appear as a class name somewhere in the parent nodes containing the button — either on the `<body>` tag itself, or somewhere further down the tree if you'd like to mix themes as shown in the preceding HTML.

Another theme available is called "soria", which offers the following alternative to the preceding example in the file named `dijit/themes/soria/Editor.css`:

```
.soria .dijitEditorIcon {
        background-image: url('images/editor.gif'); /* editor icons sprite image */
        background-repeat: no-repeat;
        width: 18px;
        height: 18px;
        text-align: center;
}
.soria .dijitEditorIconCopy { background-position: -72px; }
```

While not substantially different than the "tundra" variant in this case, you can see that the `.soria` class name selector is used here. Loading this theme and switching to a container node class to "soria" will switch everything over to this subtly different look and feel.

Customizing and Examining Available Themes

Creating a new theme from scratch is a large topic beyond the scope of this chapter. The CSS declarations matching up with widgets are exhaustive, and you'll need to work with a combination of existing examples and the DOM inspector functionality of Firebug to get a sense of what gets applied where.

Your best bet is to stick to overriding parts of an otherwise acceptable theme with a few CSS declarations of your own — or, if you must build your own comprehensive look and feel, try exploring the `dijit/themes/` directory of your Dojo installation to see what other themes are available as a base. Either way, the good news is that the CSS hooks in widgets are numerous and well structured, and creating or tweaking a theme involves nothing more complex than building cascading style sheets.

If you want to explore available themes, take a look at the demo page named `dijit/themes/themeTester.html` that comes with Dojo. As you can see in Figure 28-23, the demo page offers a look at most available widgets and a selection of available themes to switch between. You can use a combination of this tool and your own pages to experiment with themes and see what works best for you.

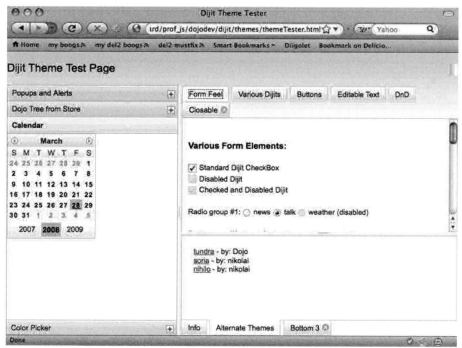

Figure 28-23

Summary

In this chapter, you were given a tour of the Dijit subproject of Dojo. Dijit offers a broad palette of widgets offering advanced form fields, layout managers, and other user interface controls. Each can be created with programmatic JavaScript code or, more in the spirit of Dojo, as declarative HTML markup handled by the `dojo.parser` module. Once instantiated, the Dijit family of widgets offers plenty of options for integration with your JavaScript code, as well as rich CSS hooks for the application of extensive CSS themes.

In the next chapter, you'll read about making custom builds of the Dojo framework based on your projects and see what advanced and experimental functionality is lurking in the DojoX subproject.

29

Building and Deploying Dojo

The custom build tools offered by the Dojo toolkit provide options to minimize and shrink the toolkit — and your own packaged code — down to just the bits you need for your deployed web application. As you've seen so far, you can get by perfectly well with a single script tag and a laundry list of `dojo.require()` declarations to load what you need.

Under the hood, Dojo manages loading JavaScript modules and other miscellaneous assets such as HTML widget templates. But, of course, all that on-demand loading activity takes time and bandwidth. To ease the burden, custom builds of the Dojo toolkit attempt to include all the most important parts demanded by your application in one compact and self-contained bundle.

In this chapter, you'll learn about:

- ❏ Creating a custom build profile
- ❏ Producing a custom build
- ❏ Examining and using a custom build

Explaining Dojo Builds

There's a lot to the Dojo toolkit. By the time you've built up a decent size web application, you'll have easily created dependencies on a dozen or more separate Dojo modules.

If you're using a "source" distribution of Dojo, or working from a Subversion checkout of the latest and greatest, loading modules translates into web requests — and usually more than one request per module, because modules often declare further requirements and even load in resources such as HTML templates for widgets. All of these HTTP requests add up fast, loading your application down with latency and bandwidth demands.

For these reasons, Dojo's custom build tools offer a better alternative: Thanks to the namespace and module structure in Dojo, along with dependency declaration, modules in Dojo are very amenable to having their source files all combined into one big include. Once joined together, this JavaScript code can be further optimized and compressed in a way that, while no longer suitable for human eyes, is much more efficient to load up.

The really nice thing about this build system is that, like the module and class system provided by Dojo, it's not limited only to Dojo internal code. You can bundle in your own project's modules and resources along with everything you use from Dojo. Additionally, the build system understands the concept of "layers", wherein you can selectively bundle parts used in different arrangements throughout your project. Even while creating efficiently loaded toolkit compilations, you can choose to only load the code that will be used in any given section of your site.

Finding the Build System

To get started with the build system, you'll need a full "source" distribution of Dojo or a checkout from the Subversion repository. A review of the beginning of Chapter 23 will tell you how to get your hands on one of these, if you're not already using one or the other.

Under the root directory of the Dojo distribution, you'll find a directory structure something like the following:

- ❑ `dijit/` — The Dijit subproject
- ❑ `dojo/` — The Dojo core
- ❑ `dojox/` — The DojoX subproject
- ❑ `util/` — Build, testing, and documentation tools
    - ❑ `buildscripts/` — Build tools

Under `util/buildscripts/` is where all the building fun begins — specifically with the scripts `build.bat` for Windows and `build.sh` for systems like Linux or Mac OS X.

The build system works as a command-line tool, so you won't find a point-and-click interface here. But, if you're already comfortable using a terminal window or shell, the process is not very complicated. Additionally, the build system requires that you have Java 1.4.2 or later installed. Beyond that, everything you need to run it should be included with Dojo.

Creating a Custom Build Profile

The Dojo build process performs a dependency analysis, checking for `dojo.require()` statements found in modules to gather an inventory of all modules necessary to construct a comprehensive set. But, it needs to know where to start — and this is where a build profile comes in. A build profile lays out module namespaces and their locations, as well as providing the definitions of "layers" to be produced by the process.

Layers, by the way, are nothing more complicated than additional .js resources intended for inclusion on a page via <script> tag alongside dojo.js. These additional includes layer code atop dojo.js and preload modules and assets that would otherwise be loaded dynamically when dojo.require() statements appear.

The build process allows you to produce multiple layers, each containing a different aggregate set of dependencies, so that you can load up individual layers with functionality you know will be used by specific sections of your site. This can help you minimize code loaded on every page. For instance, if you know that one part of the site will use dojox.dtl while another will use dijit.form, you can create two different layers in this case, and thus refrain from loading unused modules.

For your perusal, you can find a number of sample profiles under the directory util/buildscripts/ profiles, including the following:

❑   layers.profile.js — Example profile showing how the structure works

❑   base.profile.js — Empty profile that results simply in a layer containing Dojo core

❑   offline.profile.js — Profile including everything needed to use dojox.offline

❑   standard.profile.js — Profile including all of Dijit along with some other often-used modules

Check out these profiles to get some more up-to-date ideas about what can be included. Consider the following example profile:

```
dependencies ={
    prefixes: [
        [ "dijit", "../dijit" ],
        [ "dojox", "../dojox" ],
        [ "decafbad", "../../ex-dojo-expand-deploy/decafbad" ]
    ],
    layers:  [
        {
            name: "decafbad-expand.js",
            dependencies: [
                "decafbad.expand.encodings",
                "decafbad.expand.templates",
                "decafbad.expand.jsonpath"
            ]
        },
        {
            name: "decafbad-io-common.js",
            dependencies: [
                "dojo.io.script",
                "dojo.io.iframe"
            ]
        },
        {
            name: "decafbad-fx-common.js",
            dependencies: [
                "dojo.fx",
```

```
                    "dojox.fx.easing",
                    "dojo.NodeList-fx",
                    "dojo.behavior"
                ]
        },
        {
            name: "decafbad-form-common.js",
            dependencies: [
                "dijit.form.Form",
                "dijit.form.ValidationTextBox",
                "dijit.form.NumberTextBox",
                "dijit.form.NumberSpinner"
            ]
        }
    ]
};
```

Conveniently, profiles are defined as JavaScript objects. The first property of the dependencies object is `prefixes`, listing all the module namespaces to be used in the profile beyond Dojo core itself. Each item in the list provides the name of a module namespace, as well as a directory path relative to the Dojo core. As you can see, the Dijit and DojoX subprojects are included, as well as a module outside of the Dojo directory tree altogether containing sample code for this chapter.

Once the module namespaces are described, it's time to define the layers — this is done as a list named, appropriately enough, `layers`. Each item of the list is a structure naming the layer and offering a further list detailing the base modules to be included in the layer. Remember that you don't need to include everything in the world here, though: The modules listed should include just the essentials. In building the layer, the Dojo build process will begin dependency analysis with these modules, including not only those listed but chasing down anything for which there's a `dojo.require()` call inside the module.

So, for example, the code for `decafbad.expand.encodings` contains `dojo.require()` calls for the following additional modules:

❑   `dojo.io.script`

❑   `dojox.encoding.base64`

❑   `dojox.encoding.crypto.Blowfish`

❑   `dojox.encoding.digests.MD5`

Thus, simply listing `decafbad.expand.encodings` as part of the layer will result in these four additional modules — as well as any further requirements *they* list — being pulled into the layer.

Producing a Custom Build

The build process is launched via command-line script. This script fires up the Java-based Rhino JavaScript interpreter (www.mozilla.org/rhino/), which executes the JavaScript code that runs the show. In case you're curious, this is implemented in a file named build.js in the same directory as build.sh.

The following is a sample invocation of the build script, with line breaks added for clarity:

```
./build.sh \
    profileFile=../../../ex-dojo-expand-deploy/decafbad.profile.js \
    action=clean,release \
    releaseDir=../../../ex-dojo-expand-deploy/build/ \
    releaseName=prof_js
```

As you can see, this script accepts a number of parameters to control its behavior and its output. This invocation doesn't include all the options available, but here are a few of the more useful ones:

❑ profile — This is the optional name of a profile from the util/buildscripts/profiles directory, minus the .profile.js suffix. This, profile=base would read from base. profile.js.

❑ profileFile — This replaces profile, and allows you to specify the full path and filename to a build profile, possibly outside of the Dojo tree altogether.

❑ action — This determines whether the build removes and replaces an existing one (clean,replace), simply deletes existing files (clean), or simply overwrites files (replace).

❑ releaseDir — Optionally specifies the path where the build process should create the release directory. The default is a directory named release at the root of the Dojo tree, or "../../ release/" relative to the buildscripts/ directory.

❑ releaseName — Optionally specifies the name of the release directory. The default is "dojo".

❑ optimize — This accepts one of the following options for streamlining and compressing code:

　❑ comments — Comments are removed from the code.

　❑ packer — Dean Edwards' Packer (http://dean.edwards.name/packer/) is used to compress the code. This system applies a few simple techniques to raw JS source to minimize size at the expense of code obfuscation.

　❑ shrinksafe (default) — The Dojo ShrinkSafe system (http://dojotoolkit .org/docs/shrinksafe) is used to compress the code. ShrinkSafe is a system that parses JS code into bytecode with the Rhino JS interpreter, and then attempts to streamline things in the bytecode. This bytecode is then reconstituted again as JS source, which should be smaller and more efficient to load.

Given this explanation of options, then, reviewing the sample invocation shown earlier should reveal that it produces a new build using the decafbad.profile.js profile from this chapter's sample code directory and generates a fresh release under the directory ../../../ex-dojo-expand-deploy/ build/prof_js.

Upon running this command, you should see output something like the following abridged sample:

```
$ ./build.sh profileFile=../../../ex-dojo-expand-deploy/decafbad.profile.js \
    action=clean,release releaseName=prof_js \
    releaseDir=../../../ex-dojo-expand-deploy/build/

clean:   Deleting: ../../../ex-dojo-expand-deploy/build/prof_js
release: Using profile: ../../../ex-dojo-expand-deploy/decafbad.profile.js
release: Using version number: 0.0.0.dev for the release.
release: Deleting: ../../../ex-dojo-expand-deploy/build/prof_js
release: Copying: ../../dojo/../dijit to:
    ../../../ex-dojo-expand-deploy/build/prof_js/dijit
release: Copying: ../../dojo/../dojox to:
    ../../../ex-dojo-expand-deploy/build/prof_js/dojox
release: Copying: ../../dojo/../../ex-dojo-expand-deploy/decafbad to:
    ../../../ch35/build/prof_js/decafbad
release: Copying: ../../dojo to: ../../../ex-dojo-expand-deploy/build/prof_js/dojo
release: Building dojo.js and layer files
...
release: Files baked into this build:
dojo.js:
...

decafbad-expand.js:
...

decafbad-io-common.js:
...

decafbad-fx-common.js:
...

decafbad-form-common.js:
...
release: Build is in directory: ../../../ex-dojo-expand-deploy/build/prof_js
Build time: 67.238 seconds
```

This output will provide you with a long-running commentary about everything that's done during the build process.

Examining and Using a Custom Build

So, now you've seen how to specify a profile for a custom build, as well as how to produce the build from the profile. But, what is it that you get at the end of the process?

Well, the first thing to notice is that in the build process transcript, there are several messages announcing that it's "Copying" various collections of files. This signifies that a custom build includes all the individual modules normally included with Dojo — meaning that calls to dojo.require() for modules not part of any layer will still be available and can still be loaded dynamically.

But, the next thing to notice are the newly built "layer" files that are written into the `dojo/` subdirectory at the root of the build. In the transcript shown earlier, these included the following files corresponding to layers defined in the profile:

- ❑ `dojo/dojo.js`
- ❑ `dojo/decafbad-expand.js`
- ❑ `dojo/decafbad-io-common.js`
- ❑ `dojo/decafbad-fx-common.js`
- ❑ `dojo/decafbad-form-common.js`

The preceding files have all been compressed, but you should also find corresponding files with a suffix of `.uncompressed.js`, which are the concatenated yet uncompressed JS files that may be useful for visual debugging because they're still somewhat readable while still containing all the code made available in the fully compressed versions.

For further consideration of what's happened during the build, take a look at `dojo/dojo.js` in particular. You should notice that this file has expanded from a tiny 5k bootstrap in its source form to around 76k of aggregated and compressed code.

If you search for `dojo.provide()` calls in the `.uncompressed.js` version, you'll find over 20 instances — versus none in the original bootstrap source. All of the code from these modules is now part of the `dojo/dojo.js` bootstrap. When loaded with a `<script>` tag in the head of your page, `dojo.require()` calls for these modules will not cause further dynamic fetches.

So, in order to use all of these new layers produced by the build, you just need something like the following in the `<head>` of your pages:

```
<script type="text/javascript"
    src="build/prof_js/dojo/dojo.js"></script>
<script type="text/javascript"
    src="build/prof_js/dojo/decafbad-expand.js"></script>
<script type="text/javascript"
    src="build/prof_js/dojo/decafbad-io-common.js"></script>
<script type="text/javascript"
    src="build/prof_js/dojo/decafbad-fx-common.js"></script>
<script type="text/javascript"
    src="build/prof_js/dojo/decafbad-form-common.js"></script>
```

These includes will layer in all the modules processed by the build — and once they've been loaded by the browser, there will be no need for additional dynamic fetches to satisfy `dojo.require()` declarations. On the other hand, note that the beauty of this arrangement is that if you leave out any of these includes — with the exception of `dojo/dojo.js` — the requirements system will still find and fetch any desired modules.

In this way, the build system is a clean post hoc way to enhance load times and efficiency, without requiring any pre-planned action or discipline during development beyond using `dojo.require()` and `dojo.provide()` calls. But, if you've bought into the Dojo way of doing things, you'll have already gotten benefits from using the module system while developing your application — and thus have naturally paved the way for the build process.

To get more in-depth information on the build system, check out the official documentation at:
`http://dojotoolkit.org/book/dojo-book-0-9/part-4-meta-dojo/package-system-and-custom-builds`

Summary

And so, with this chapter, the part of the book devoted to the Dojo toolkit comes to a close. You were given a quick trip through the DojoX subproject and many of the varied and experimental code packages made available there. Then, you saw how the Dojo custom build process works to help make loading both Dojo's and your own code more efficient in your deployed projects.

30

Expanding Dojo

The DojoX subproject encompasses the expanding frontier of Dojo, including new modules and experimental code. While this project is too large and too fast a moving target to fully cover in a single chapter, an attempt will be made here to offer a tour of some of the more interesting modules and to give a taste of where the Dojo toolkit as a whole is headed. The optional code found in the DojoX subproject is not yet a part of Dojo core, and you can certainly create compelling web applications without it. However, the modules found here can certainly enhance your development, and in some cases open up entirely new kinds of applications.

In this chapter, you'll learn about:

- ❑   The DojoX subproject
- ❑   Trying out advanced widgets
- ❑   Producing content from templates

Exploring the DojoX Subproject

The core of the Dojo toolkit offers nearly everything essential to developing responsive modern web applications. Adding Dijit into the mix offers a richly expanded set of user interface and layout management components. Beyond this solid foundation, the DojoX subproject introduces a variety of interesting and innovative modules that push the boundaries of your browser and application design. Included among these modules are such features as:

- ❑   Advanced user interface and layout widgets
- ❑   Template handling and rendering
- ❑   Vector drawing and data-driven charts
- ❑   Alternatives to AJAX

❑   Expanded form data validation helpers

❑   Local in-browser storage and offline application support

❑   Encoding and hashing functions

❑   Advanced data structures

This list is far from complete, and even this list won't be entirely covered here, but you may find something in the DojoX subproject that fills an unusual or challenging need in your application.

Trying Out Advanced Widgets

In DojoX, you'll find a number of experimental UI widgets that aren't yet a part of Dijit. They're in various stages of development and documentation, but one or more of them may be worth checking out for your projects.

As with most of the offerings in the DojoX subproject, it's worth digging into the Dojo distribution itself to see what's there — especially if you're working with a distribution checked out of the Subversion repository. The DojoX widgets live under the path `dojox/widget/` and it's especially worthwhile to peek into the `dojox/widget/tests/` directory, where you'll find demonstrations of most if not all of the DojoX widgets available.

Building Fisheye Menus

To start getting a taste for these widgets, take a look at this first bit of markup:

```
<div dojoType="dojox.widget.FisheyeList"
    itemWidth="50" itemHeight="50"
    itemMaxWidth="150" itemMaxHeight="150"
    orientation="horizontal"
    effectUnits="2"
    itemPadding="10"
    attachEdge="top"
    labelEdge="top"
    id="fisheye1">

    <div id="item1" dojoType="dojox.widget.FisheyeListItem"
        onclick="console.log('clicked '+this.id)"
        label="Item 1"
        iconSrc="../dojodev/dojox/widget/tests/images/icon_browser.png">
    </div>

    <div id="item2" dojoType="dojox.widget.FisheyeListItem"
        label="Item 2"
```

```
    onclick="console.log('clicked '+this.id)"
    iconSrc="../dojodev/dojox/widget/tests/images/icon_calendar.png">
</div>

<div id="item4" dojoType="dojox.widget.FisheyeListItem"
    label="Item 3"
    onclick="console.log('clicked '+this.id)"
    iconSrc="../dojodev/dojox/widget/tests/images/icon_email.png">
</div>

</div>
```

The preceding markup declares an instance of `dojox.widget.FisheyeList` with contained instances of `dojox.widget.FisheyeListItem`. This creates a horizontal or vertical set of icons not unlike the Mac OS X dock: When the mouse approaches a point in the list, it enlarges and bulges out. The icon closest to the mouse grows larger, and icons to either side expand to lesser degrees, thus creating a "fisheye" effect. The icons are clickable and can be given text labels.

This next widget is sort of a lightweight cousin compared to the previous example:

```
<ul id="fisheye_list">
    <li>Foo bar</li>
    <li>Baz foo</li>
    <li>Quux xyzzy</li>
    <li>Plugh thud</li>
    <li>Hello world</li>
</ul>

<script type="text/javascript">
    dojo.addOnLoad(function() {
        dojo.query('li', 'fisheye_list').forEach(function(el) {
            new dojox.widget.FisheyeLite({
                durationIn:  350,
                easeIn:      dojox.fx.easing.bounceOut,
                durationOut: 600,
                easeOut:     dojox.fx.easing.elasticOut
            }, el);
        });
    });
</script>
```

Rather than declare a parent list with child widgets, the `dojox.widget.FisheyeList` widget declares independent elements that each expand on mouseover. In the preceding code, `dojo.query()` is used to create instances of the widget programmatically for each item in an HTML list.

Creating Animated Notifications with the Toaster Widget

Here's one more widget for your consideration:

```
<div id="toast1" dojoType="dojox.widget.Toaster"
    positionDirection="br-up"
    messageTopic="decafbad/toasterMessage"></div>

<div id="toast2" dojoType="dojox.widget.Toaster"
    positionDirection="tl-right"
    messageTopic="decafbad/toasterMessage"></div>

<button dojoType="dijit.form.Button">
    <span>Message</span>
    <script type="dojo/method" event="onClick">
        dojo.publish("decafbad/toasterMessage", ["Hello toaster!"]);
    </script>
</button>

<button dojoType="dijit.form.Button">
    <span>Warning</span>
    <script type="dojo/method" event="onClick">
    dojo.publish("decafbad/toasterMessage", [{
        message: "I'm warning you toaster!",
        type: "warning",
        duration: 1500
    }]);
    </script>
</button>
```

This declares a pair of `dojox.widget.Toaster` widgets and companion `dijit.form.Button` widgets. The Toaster widget works like many unread e-mail notification systems, sliding in an element from one of the corners of the window. The widget in the preceding example can be configured to listen to a global event topic and provide an animated notification for styled messages of various types including plain informative messages, warnings, and errors.

Figure 30-1 depicts all of the widgets shown in this chapter so far. Also remember that these are far from all of the widgets available in DojoX, so be sure to take a look around inside your Dojo directories to find more modules and demonstrations.

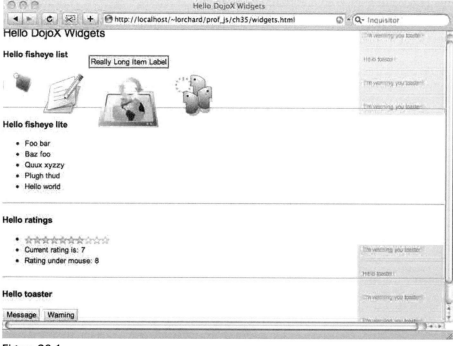

Figure 30-1

Employing Advanced Form Validation Helpers

As you saw in the previous chapter, the Dijit subproject offers a wide range of form widgets that have built-in form validation options. You can specify a few kinds of data, as well as define constraints based on regular expression and value ranges.

The DojoX subproject expands upon these capabilities, offering a collection of additional validation tests as well as an alternative to markup-based validation rules altogether. To demonstrate, consider that the following modules should be declared as requirements:

```
<script type="text/javascript">
    dojo.require("dojo.parser");

    dojo.require("dijit.form.Form");
    dojo.require("dijit.form.ValidationTextBox");

    dojo.require('dojox.validate');
    dojo.require('dojox.validate.web');
    dojo.require('dojox.validate.us');
    dojo.require('dojox.validate.check');
</script>
```

Next, partially revisiting the kind of form built in Chapter 28, take a look at this markup:

```
<form id="form1" method="post" action="echo.php?type=text"
    dojoType="dijit.form.Form">

    <fieldset class="main">
        <legend>Registration form</legend>
        <ul>

            <li>
                <label for="homepage">Homepage</label>
                <input type="text" name="homepage"
                    dojoType="dijit.form.ValidationTextBox"
                    required="true"
                    validator="dojox.validate.isUrl"
                    promptMessage="Enter a URL" />
            </li>

            <li>
                <label for="email">Email</label>
                <input type="text" name="email"
                    dojoType="dijit.form.ValidationTextBox"
                    required="true"
                    validator="dojox.validate.isEmailAddress"
                    constraints="{ allowCC: false }"
                    promptMessage="Enter an email address" />
            </li>
```

This markup declares a form as a widget of type `dijit.form.Form`. Within it are two field widgets of type `dijit.form.ValidationTextBox`, each with a new attribute named `validator`.

This attribute, `validator`, accepts the name of a function that can serve as the validity check for this field. A function used in this way should accept two parameters: the value of the field and the value of the field's `constraints` attribute.

So, for example, the first field requires a valid URL as a value. It defines no constraints, so any valid URL is accepted. However, thanks to the constraint attribute value of "`{ allowCC: false }`", the second field will reject any e-mail address whose domain name ends with a country code. This is implemented in the code behind the `dojox.validate.isEmailAddress` function. The documentation on this feature may be a bit confusing to navigate, so your best bet is to dive right into your Dojo distribution and see what's available.

This next bit of markup eschews widgets altogether and falls back on plain old input fields:

```
            <li>
                <label for="homepage2">Homepage2</label>
                <input type="text" name="homepage2" />
            </li>
            <li>
                <label for="email2">Email2</label>
                <input type="text" name="email2" />
            </li>
            <li>
```

```
            <label for="password">Password</label>
            <input type="password" name="password" />
        </li>
        <li>
            <label for="passsword_check">Password (again)</label>
            <input type="password" name="password_check" />
        </li>
```

The fields in the preceding example are less exciting now that they're no longer widgets, but the validation concerns have now moved entirely into the form submit handler:

```
        <li class="buttons">
            <input type="submit" value="submit record" />
        </li>

    </ul>
</fieldset>

<script type="dojo/method" event="onSubmit" args="ev">
    var profile = {
        required: [
            'homepage2',
            'email2'
        ],
        constraints: {
            homepage2: dojox.validate.isUrl,
            email2:    dojox.validate.isEmailAddress
        },
        confirm: {
            password_check: 'password'
        }
    };

    var validate_result = window.foo =
        dojox.validate.check(dojo.byId('form1'), profile);
    if (!this.validate() || !validate_result.isSuccessful()) {
        dojo.stopEvent(ev);
        alert("Form not yet valid! (connected in markup)");

        console.log(validate_result.getMissing());
        console.log(validate_result.isMissing('email2'));

        console.log(validate_result.getInvalid());
        console.log(validate_result.isInvalid('password_check'));
    }

</script>

</form>
```

Just like the form built in Chapter 28, this form implements a form validation check in a handler for the form's submit event. And, like that previous form, it requires that all the field widgets on the page report validity. However, the new thing is the validation profile and the call to the helper function dojox.validate.check() that uses it.

This validation profile replaces most, if not all, of the form widget attributes concerned with post-processing and validation of field values. The profile shown here does not fully exercise the functionality — but as you can see it defines required fields, validation handler functions, and which fields should have matching values (for example, password and password_check).

The call to dojox.validate.check() returns an object bearing several methods useful in determining the validation state of the form. The first method called is .isSuccessful(), which reports on the overall validity of the form in terms of passing the profile gauntlet. After that, there are the methods determining which fields were missing or containing invalid data.

Unlike widget-based forms, this means of validation refrains from doing anything to indicate or highlight which fields were invalid or missing required data. For better or worse, this method leaves all of that up to you, to handle in whatever way you see fit. So, if widgets and declaring the requirements of your form in custom markup are not your cup of tea, dojox.validate.check() places it all completely under your direct control.

Producing Content from Templates

Most modern web application frameworks on the server side have some concept of a Model-View-Controller architecture. The basic idea is that your design should keep separate the data, business logic, and display rendering involved so that you can flexibly alter or swap out components in any of those three areas.

One such web application framework implementing such a model on the server-side is Django, written in Python. And, as it turns out, there's a cloned implementation of the Django Template Language in the DojoX subproject. You can read more about the original system here:

www.djangoproject.com/documentation/templates/

The dojox.dtl module provides a complete transliteration of Django's built-in template system, with a few additions to make it work even better in a browser. To prepare for a demonstration, consider this example of a Django template:

```
<li>
    Total results:
    <i>{{ ResultSet.totalResultsAvailable }}</i>
</li>

{% for result in ResultSet.Result %}
    <li>
        <h4><a href="{{ result.Url }}">{{ result.Title }}</a></h4>
```

```
        <div>
            <p>{{ result.Summary }}</p>
            <div class="meta">

                <b>{{ result.DisplayUrl }}</b> -

                {% ifnotequal result.MimeType 'text/html' %}
                    <i>{{ result.MimeType }}</i> -
                {% endifnotequal %}

                {{ result.ModificationDate|timesince }} -

                {% if result.Cache.Size %}
                    {{ result.Cache.Size|filesizeformat }} -
                    <a href="{{ result.Cache.Url }}">Cached</a>
                {% endif %}

            </div>
        </div>
    </li>
{% endfor %}
```

It might help to consult the Django template language documentation to understand exactly what's going on here, but this template produces markup for what looks like the results of a web search. It expects to be given a data structure named `ResultSet`, which will contain various metadata about the search results, as well as a list of the search results themselves.

The template accepts the search results data and renders them out as an HTML list, including all sorts of detail about each result — such as the title as a link to the page, the content type of the page, how long ago the page was indexed, and a link to the page in the search engine's cache with an indication of the page size in cache. The template language also offers output filters to convert times and file sizes into more human-friendly presentations, and all variable data gets HTML-escaped so as to help prevent unfortunate XSS security exploits.

In the end, this template produces something that looks an awful lot like a Yahoo! search engine results page. Accordingly, this demonstration uses the JSONP version of the Yahoo! Web Search API to populate the template.

Now, consider the following markup, which builds a simple interface for performing web searches:

```
<div id="ex_search">

    <form class="search_form">
        Search:
        <input type="text" size="30" class="search" />
        <input type="submit" value="search" />
    </form>

    <ul class="results">
    </ul>

</div>
```

Next, the following JavaScript code grants functionality to the search form in the preceding example:

```
dojo.require('dojo.io.script');
dojo.require('dojox.dtl');
dojo.require('dojox.dtl.Template');
dojo.require('dojox.dtl.Context');

// Fetch the external template source and instantiate a new DTL object.
var tmpl = null;
dojo.xhrGet({
    url: 'templates.dtl',
    handleAs: 'text',
    load: function(resp, io_args) {
        tmpl = new dojox.dtl.Template(resp);
    }
});
```

The first thing to do here is declare some requirements. Since this code will eventually need to use the JSONP version of the Yahoo! Web Search API, it's useful to pull in `dojo.io.script`. Following this are declarations to load up various parts of the `dojox.dtl` namespace.

After the requirements, a call to `dojo.xhrGet()` is made to load up the template shown a little earlier. Assuming that it will be available at the URL `templates.dtl`, it should be saved under that name or you should update this code to point to wherever you saved it. Once it is loaded, its text is used to instantiate a `dojox.dtl.Template` object. This object will be used to render the template once data is available.

Now, it's time to wire up that search form:

```
dojo.query('.search_form', 'ex_search')
    .connect('onsubmit', function(ev) {
        dojo.stopEvent(ev);

        // Don't work until the template has arrived.
        if (!tmpl) return;

        // Build up the JSON URL for search results.
        var search_url = 'http://search.yahooapis.com/'+
            'WebSearchService/V1/webSearch?'+
            dojo.objectToQuery({
                appid: 'appid_goes_here',
                output: 'json',
                results: 5,
                query:  dojo.query('.search', 'ex_search')[0].value
            });
```

The preceding code looks up the search form in the page and provides it with a handler function which fires upon submission. Preempting the usual handling, this code takes the `search` field value and prepares a URL for use shortly in calling the Yahoo! Web Search API.

For more information on how this API works, and what parameters are accepted, take a look at the documentation available here:

```
http://developer.yahoo.com/search/web/V1/webSearch.html
```

Finally, it's time to fetch the data and put that template to work:

```
// Insert a loading message.
dojo.query('.results', 'ex_search')
    .empty().addContent('<li>Loading...</li>');

// Fetch the JSON feed for search results...
dojo.io.script.get({
    url: search_url,
    callbackParamName: 'callback',
    handle: function(resp, io_args) {
        // HACK: Search result times are in seconds, but JS
        // times are in milliseconds.  Patch the data.
        dojo.forEach(resp.ResultSet.Result, function(r) {
            r.ModificationDate *= 1000;
        });
        console.log(resp);
        var ctx = new dojox.dtl.Context(resp);
        var out = tmpl.render(ctx);
        dojo.query('.results', 'ex_search')
            .empty().addContent(out);
    }
});

});
```

In this last piece of the code, the contents of the search results list is emptied and replaced with a loading message. Then, a call to `dojo.io.script.get()` is made using the Yahoo! Web Search API URL composed in the previous listing. Once the data has arrived, it invokes the callback function defined under the `handle` parameter.

The final part is where the template comes into play: First, the data structure returned by the search API is used to create a `dojox.dtl.Context` object. This object is a holder for data to be passed into the template for rendering. Then, the `.render()` method of the template object instantiated earlier is called, which returns the final rendered content. This content is then inserted into the page to replace the loading message.

As shown in Figure 30-2, the end result of all of this is a dynamically rendered display of search results, all done on the client side.

Although this is the sort of thing you probably want to do on the server most of the time, this template system has a lot of flexibility and allows you to produce or update content on the client side. It also comes in handy if you start creating your own Dijit widgets.

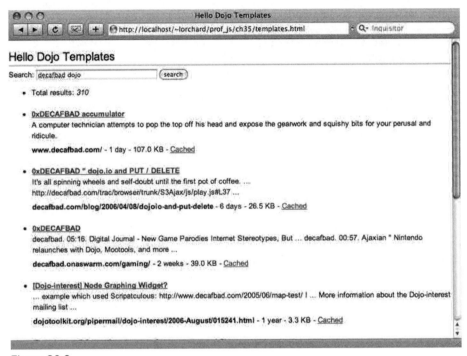

Figure 30-2

Drawing Shapes and Rendering Charts

Drawing arbitrary shapes and lines is a task where plain old HTML, CSS, and JavaScript have generally been pushed aside in favor of plug-in-based technologies such as Java applets and Flash movies. However, modern browsers have been gaining more and more native capabilities in this area. These capabilities have yet to completely converge across browsers, but the functionality is similar enough that it's possible to abstract away differences in a common interface that's of practical use.

With that in mind, the `dojox.gfx` package offers an encapsulation of drawing facilities across browsers as swappable rendering engines — employing SVG, VML, Silverlight, or the `<canvas>` tag as appropriate. On top of these engines, the `dojox.gfx` module provides a wide variety of declarative drawing primitives for describing lines, curves, closed and filled shapes, images, and text. There's support for various transformations and rotations, as well as the connection of event handlers to throw interactivity into the mix.

Going further, the facilities of `dojox.gfx` and a few other modules are employed to build `dojox.charting`. This package offers the ability to plot and present data from various sources as line, bar, and pie charts. It includes options for tweaking the appearance of representations of data and labeled axes, as well as updating displays dynamically. Also, thanks to other technologies made available under Dojo, data can be fetched from server-side sources on demand, or baked right into the page as declarative markup.

Drawing Shapes and Lines

To get a small sample of what the `dojox.gfx` package can do, start with the following markup:

```
<div id="mycanvas" style="width: 400px; height: 400px"></div>
```

This provides a blank canvas for `dojox.gfx` to manage in the following code:

```
dojo.require("dojox.gfx");

var g = dojox.gfx.createSurface(dojo.byId("mycanvas"), 400, 400);

g.createCircle({ cx: 200, cy: 200, r: 195 })
    .setFill([255, 255, 128, 1])
    .setStroke({ color: [0, 0, 0, 1], width: 2 });

g.createCircle({ cx: 125, cy: 120, r: 25 })
    .setFill('white')
    .setStroke({ color: 'black', width: 2 });

g.createCircle({ cx: 275, cy: 120, r: 25 })
    .setFill('#fff')
    .setStroke({ color: "#000", width: 2 });

g.createPath()
    .setStroke({color: "#000", width: 2})
    .setFill('white')
    .moveTo(100, 225)
    .curveTo(100, 225, 200, 400, 300, 225)
    .curveTo(300, 225, 205, 500, 100, 225);
```

This code doesn't do much more than draw a happy face, as shown in Figure 30-3. But, it's likely to be more than you're used to having at your disposal with the usual arrangement of HTML, CSS, and JavaScript.

Figure 30-3

The sample provided here just barely scratches the surface — a chapter or two could be devoted entirely to dojo.gfx alone. To really get a sense of what dojox.gfx offers, you should explore the package in your Dojo distribution. In particular, there are some interesting demos and detailed tests available for perusal under the following paths:

- ❏ dojox/gfx/demos/
- ❏ dojox/gfx/tests/

Made available under demos/ are hands-on and interactive examples combining parts of dojox.gfx. Alternatively, under the tests/ directory, you'll find exhaustive and focused tests exercising each aspect of the package, useful for viewing source and seeing what's available and how various things are used.

As with most things made available under DojoX, the documentation for this package is still undergoing polish — so digging into these demos and tests is really the best way to wrap your head around this experimental yet still useful code.

Rendering Charts and Graphs

Moving on from raw graphics to structured charts, consider the following markup:

```
<div dojoType="dojox.data.HtmlStore"
    dataId="tableExample" jsId="tableStore"></div>

<table id="tableExample" style="display: none;">
```

```
    <thead>
        <tr><th>value</th></tr>
    </thead>
    <tbody>
        <tr><td>6.3</td></tr>
        <tr><td>1.8</td></tr>
        <tr><td>3.0</td></tr>
        <tr><td>0.5</td></tr>
        <tr><td>4.4</td></tr>
        <tr><td>2.7</td></tr>
        <tr><td>2.0</td></tr>
    </tbody>
</table>
```

This is another glimpse at the data capabilities in Dojo and DojoX. As you saw in Chapter 28, you can create data sources either with markup or by programmatic means, fetching data from external JSON data sources. In this case, everything's self-contained in the markup. The data widget `dojox.data. HtmlStore` is given the ID of a hidden table, and the data source populates itself from the rows and columns of that table's structure in the DOM.

However, rather than populating a drop-down selection widget, this data is used for more visually interesting purposes:

```
<table><tr>
    <td>

        <div dojoType="dojox.charting.widget.Chart2D"
                style="width: 300px; height: 300px;">
            <div class="series" name="Series A" store="tableStore"
                    valueFn="Number(x)"></div>
        </div>

    </td><td>

        <div dojoType="dojox.charting.widget.Chart2D"
            theme="dojox.charting.themes.PlotKit.glue"
            fill="'#999'" style="width: 300px; height: 300px;">
            <div class="axis" name="x" font="italic normal bold 10pt Tahoma"></div>
            <div class="axis" name="y" vertical="true" fixUpper="major"
                includeZero="true" font="italic normal bold 10pt Tahoma"></div>
            <div class="plot" name="default" type="Areas"></div>
            <div class="plot" name="grid" type="Grid"></div>
            <div class="series" name="Series A" store="tableStore"
                valueFn="Number(x)*100" stroke="'#666666'" fill="'#b3b3b3'"></div>
        </div>

    </td>
</tr></table>
```

In the preceding markup, two widgets are declared. The first is much simpler than the second, simply declaring an instance of the widget `dojox.charting.widget.Chart2D` with a connection to the data source defined earlier. This will be shown as a simple line graph, unadorned by axes or labels of any kind.

The second widget, by contrast, has a few more bells and whistles. It defines both a horizontal and vertical axis, including fonts and a smattering of other options. The chart is also given a grid background, and the line itself is given an area fill beneath it. Besides the colors defined for the line and area, there's also a new function through which the data is passed before being plotted on the graph.

Figure 30-4 renders of both of these widgets.

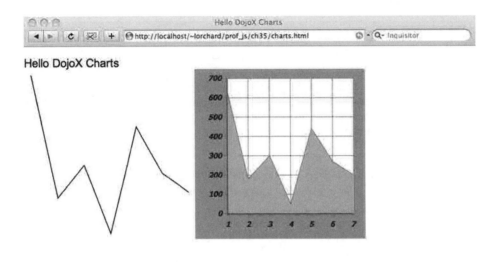

Figure 30-4

As with the demonstration of dojox.gfx, this quick example of the charting widget just shows one tiny piece of what dojox.charting offers and is beyond the scope of this book. Be sure to poke around in your Dojo distribution for examples and tests, particularly in the following directory:

```
dojox/charting/tests/
```

You find a set of samples and tests here showing the various aspects of dojox.charting, including more programmatic construction of charts and the use of three-dimensional graphics for richer charts and representations of data.

Using Encoding and Crypto Routines

A variety of modules useful in encoding, encrypting, and compressing data are available in the DojoX subproject. These modules might seem of limited use in browser-based applications, but you might be surprised where they come in handy.

Generating MD5 Hashes

The `dojox.encoding.digests.MD5` module implements the MD5 cryptographic hash algorithm, which is useful in providing some assurance of the integrity of a set of data as well as offering a pretty convenient way to produce a safe and unique identifier for a given string.

To illustrate this, consider this markup and the code that follows:

```
<div id="ex_md5">
    <h2>Hello MD5</h2>
    <form class="url_form">
        URL:
        <input type="text" size="50" class="url"
            value="http://decafbad.com/blog/" />
        <input type="submit" />
    </form>
    <dl class="urlinfo"></dl>
</div>
```

This markup builds a small form that accepts the entry of a URL, which is used by the following code to fetch a JSON feed from the social bookmarking site Delicious:

```
dojo.require("dojox.encoding.digests.MD5");
dojo.require('dojo.io.script');

dojo.query('.url_form', 'ex_md5')
    .connect('onsubmit', function(ev) {
        dojo.stopEvent(ev);

        var url = dojo.query('.url', 'ex_md5')[0].value;

        var url_md5 = dojox.encoding.digests.MD5(
            url, dojox.encoding.digests.outputTypes.Hex
        );

        var json_url =
            'http://feeds.delicious.com/feeds/json/url/data?hash='+url_md5;

        dojo.query('.urlinfo', 'ex_md5')
            .empty()
            .addContent('<dt>Loading...</dt><dd>'+url_md5+'</dd>');

        dojo.io.script.get({
            url: json_url,
            callbackParamName: 'callback',
```

```
            handle: function(resp, io_args) {
                dojo.forEach(resp, function(urlinfo) {
                    dojo.query('.urlinfo', 'ex_md5').empty();
                    for (key in urlinfo) {
                        var val = urlinfo[key];
                        if (key == 'top_tags') {
                            var tags = [];
                            for (tag in val)
                                tags.push(tag + ' (' + val[tag] + ')');
                            val = tags.join(", ");
                        }
                        dojo.query('.urlinfo', 'ex_md5')
                            .addContent("<dt>"+key+"</dt><dd>"+val+"</dd>");
                    }
                });
            }
        });

    });
```

The key to the preceding code is the use of `dojox.encoding.digests.MD5`: Delicious offers a set of JSON feeds that report summary details on the number of bookmarks being saved for a given URL and what top tags are used in those bookmarks. The catch is that you need to hash the URL in question with MD5 in order to form the JSON feed URL.

So, using `dojo.io.script.get()` and `dojo.query()`, the JSON feed is fetched and the resulting data is used to update the page dynamically with details on the URL for which the MD5 was calculated.

Encoding Data with Base64

The Base64 encoding scheme provides a way to express full 8-bit data using a set of only 64 characters. The character set used in Base64 consists of A-Z, a-z, 0-9, +, and / — all characters that tend to avoid escape characters and sequences that belong to the structures and statements of container and transfer formats.

Basically, anywhere it's safe to transfer plain-vanilla 7-bit ASCII content, Base64 can be used to transfer full 8-bit data such as images and non-English text. This includes e-mail, XML, and even the clipboard on just about every modern operating system. You can read more about Base64 here:

```
http://en.wikipedia.org/wiki/Base64
```

The following markup sketches out a test bed to try out the Base64 implementation in DojoX:

```
<div id="ex_base64">
    <h2>Hello Base64</h2>
    <form>
        Raw: <br />
```

```
            <textarea cols="70" rows="3" class="raw"></textarea>
            <br />
            Base64: <br />
            <textarea cols="70" rows="3" class="base64"></textarea>
            <br />
            <button class="encode">encode with base64</button>
            <button class="decode">decode from base64</button>
        </form>
    </div>
```

The preceding markup is given functionality with the following code:

```
    dojo.require("dojox.encoding.base64");

    dojo.query('.encode', 'ex_base64')
        .onclick(function (ev) {
            dojo.stopEvent(ev);

            var raw = dojo.query('.raw', 'ex_base64')[0].value;

            var byte_array = [];
            for(var i=0; i<raw.length; i++) {
                byte_array.push(raw.charCodeAt(i));
            }

            dojo.query('.base64', 'ex_base64')
                [0].value = dojox.encoding.base64.encode(byte_array);
        });

    dojo.query('.decode', 'ex_base64')
        .onclick(function (ev) {
            dojo.stopEvent(ev);

            var byte_array = dojox.encoding.base64.decode(
                dojo.query('.base64', 'ex_base64')[0].value
            );

            var raw_array = [];
            for(var i=0; i<byte_array.length; i++) {
                raw_array.push(String.fromCharCode(byte_array[i]));
            }

            dojo.query('.raw', 'ex_base64')
                [0].value = raw_array.join("");
        });
```

DojoX offers its Base64 implementation in the `dojox.encoding.base64` module, and the preceding code wires up the buttons in the markup to respectively encode and decode content in the given text areas.

Note that the Base64 encoder deals with arrays of numbers representing 8-bit bytes, and so both the encoding and the decoding functions above must respectively convert from string to array and from array to string in order to interface with the text areas.

There's a flaw in this simple-minded code, however: It assumes that the data in the "raw" text area will be plain old ASCII and that each character in the string corresponds directly to a single 8-bit byte. But, if you paste or enter non-ASCII Unicode characters — Japanese-language text, for example — the demonstration will break down because Unicode characters require more than a single byte to express, and thus the return value from `raw.charCodeAt()` will exceed 8 bits in this case.

But, rather than get into the details of Unicode encodings such as UTF-8, this will be left as an exercise to the reader. In case you're curious, you can find an implementation of a UTF-8 encoding routine in JavaScript from this public domain cryptography package:

```
www.fourmilab.ch/javascrypt/index.html
```

Look for the `utf-8.js` file, which contains Unicode/UTF-8 encoding and decoding routines you can use to make the previous code more robust.

Encrypting Data with Blowfish

Whereas the previous two sections dealt with one-way hashing and two-way encoding of data, this next module deals with symmetrical encryption using a secret key. The stage is set with the following example markup:

```
<div id="ex_blowfish">
    <h2>Hello Blowfish</h2>
    <form>
        Key:<br />
        <input type="text" value="asecretkey" width=20" class="key" />
        <br />
        Clear: <br />
        <textarea cols="70" rows="3" class="clear"></textarea>
        <br />
        Crypt: <br />
        <textarea cols="70" rows="3" class="crypt"></textarea>
        <br />
        <button class="encrypt">encrypt with blowfish</button>
        <button class="decrypt">decrypt with blowfish</button>
    </form>
</div>
```

This markup consists of three text fields expecting the following information: The secret key, the clear text, and the encrypted data encoded as Base64. The preceding markup can then be given functionality with the following code:

```
dojo.require("dojox.encoding.crypto.Blowfish");

dojo.query('.encrypt', 'ex_blowfish')
    .onclick(function(ev) {
        dojo.stopEvent(ev);

        var key   = dojo.query('.key', 'ex_blowfish')[0].value;
        var clear = dojo.query('.clear', 'ex_blowfish')[0].value;

        dojo.query('.crypt', 'ex_blowfish')[0].value =
            dojox.encoding.crypto.Blowfish.encrypt(clear, key);
    });

dojo.query('.decrypt', 'ex_blowfish')
    .onclick(function(ev) {
        dojo.stopEvent(ev);

        var key   = dojo.query('.key', 'ex_blowfish')[0].value;
        var crypt = dojo.query('.crypt', 'ex_blowfish')[0].value;

        dojo.query('.clear', 'ex_blowfish')[0].value =
            dojox.encoding.crypto.Blowfish.decrypt(crypt, key);
    });
```

This code wires up the encrypt and decrypt buttons with handlers that exercise the implementation of the Blowfish algorithm provided by the dojox.encoding.crypto.Blowfish module in DojoX. You should be able to drop text into the first textarea and view the encrypted result in the second, and vice versa, as long as the key stays the same. Enter a new key, and previously encrypted data will not come back as expected.

Note that this demonstration will also fall over if you try to use non-ASCII text as cleartext or the key. This is because the DojoX implementation of Blowfish expects strings to consist of 8-bit bytes, just like the previous demo did. You can solve this by encoding strings as UTF-8 on the way into the encrypt() function and decoding from UTF-8 to Unicode on the way out of the decrypt() function.

These are just a few of the routines available under the dojox.encoding namespace. Be sure to take a look around, where you'll find compression algorithms and a few other potentially useful data manipulation tools.

Navigating JSON Data Structures

Where CSS and dojo.query() have selectors to assist in identifying elements in the DOM, dojox.jsonPath offers a declarative expression language for identifying data in JavaScript and JSON data structures. This package is a contributed port from a previously independent project, and as such you can find some documentation and articles on this XPath-like expression language at the following URLs:

❑ http://code.google.com/p/jsonpath/

❑ http://goessner.net/articles/JsonPath/

To help offer some understanding of this package, this next bit of markup provides a variation on the search form used to demonstrate Django template support:

```
<div id="ex_search">

    <form class="search_form">
        Search:
        <input type="text" size="30" class="search"
            value="decafbad" />
        <br />

        Path:
        <input type="text" size="30" class="path"
            value="$.ResultSet.Result..Title" />
        <br />

        <input type="submit" value="search" class="search_button" />
        <br />

        <textarea cols="70" rows="15" class="results"></textarea>
    </form>

</div>
```

The primary change to this form is the addition of another form field, which expects a JSONPath expression. The results of this expression will appear in the results `textarea` at the bottom of the form.

Now, the following code offers a variation on using the Yahoo! web search feed in order to give this form functionality:

```
dojo.require('dojo.io.script');
dojo.require("dojox.jsonPath");

dojo.query('.search_button', 'ex_search')
    .onclick(function(ev) {
        dojo.stopEvent(ev);

        // Build up the JSON URL for search results.
        var search_url = 'http://search.yahooapis.com/'+
            'WebSearchService/V1/webSearch?'+
            dojo.objectToQuery({
                appid: 'appid_goes_here',
                output: 'json',
                results: 5,
                query:  dojo.query('.search', 'ex_search')[0].value
            });
```

```
                    // Insert a loading message.
                    dojo.query('.results', 'ex_search')
                        [0].value = 'Loading...';

                    // Fetch the JSON feed for search results...
                    dojo.io.script.get({
                        url: search_url,
                        callbackParamName: 'callback',
                        handle: function(resp, io_args) {
                            var matches = dojox.jsonPath.query(
                                resp, dojo.query('.path', 'ex_search')[0].value
                            );
                                        dojo.query('.results', 'ex_search')
                                [0].value = dojo.toJson(matches, true);

                        }
                    });
                });
```

Once you've gotten it all running, try out a few different JSONPath expressions like the following:

❑   Refer to the root of the data structure:

    ```
    $
    ```

❑   Find the value of this specific property:

    ```
    $.ResultSet.totalResultsAvailable
    ```

❑   Dig up all properties named Title throughout the data structure:

    ```
    $..Title
    ```

❑   Find Result object with the given value for Title:

    ```
    $.ResultSet.Result[?(@.Title=="0xDECAFBAD")]
    ```

Check out the files made available with the package itself for further examples and documentation. In particular, take a look at some of the samples available here:

```
dojox/jsonPath/README
```

This package gives you a powerful tool for sifting through data on the client side, rather than making multiple requests back to the server for custom views and slices of content. You can have the server deliver a complete set of the data, then query and expand using JSONPath expressions.

Exploring Further DojoX Offerings

This chapter has offered just a sample of what's lurking in the DojoX subproject. It can't be said enough — dig into the directories and see what's waiting to be used in there. Though there's likely to be more evolution by the time you look, the following offers a partial inventory of additional packages percolating in the experimental wing, at the time of this writing:

❑ dojox.analytics — Live browser-to-server measurement of user behaviors and interactions.

❑ dojox.av — Abstractions and wrappers for dealing with audio and video resources.

❑ dojox.collections — Advanced data types and iterators for JavaScript.

❑ dojox.color — Utilities for converting and dealing with various expressions of colors.

❑ dojox.cometd — Code for working with Cometd, a persistent-connection alternative to AJAX.

❑ dojox.data — Utilities for handling data from XML feeds, web services, the DOM, and more.

❑ dojox.date — Date manipulation utilities.

❑ dojox.flash — Facilities for two-way communication between JavaScript and Flash objects.

❑ dojox.gfx3d — Modules for working with 3D graphics.

❑ dojox.grid — A powerful grid and table-based widget for navigating sets of data.

❑ dojox.highlight — A syntax highlighting engine.

❑ dojox.image — Widgets and utilities for working with images and collections of images.

❑ dojox.lang — Conceptual extensions for JavaScript, including functional programming helpers.

❑ dojox.layout — Additional experimental layout managers.

❑ dojox.math — Advanced math functions.

❑ dojox.off — Dojo offline, a package made to help create web applications that work with and without network connectivity.

❑ dojox.presentation — Dojo Presentation, a package offering the start of a slideshow and presentation engine.

❑ dojox.sketch — A cross-browser drawing editor.

❑ dojox.storage — A module for dealing with various kinds of local client-side storage offered across browsers. This goes far beyond cookies.

❑ dojox.string — String manipulation, including sprintf and tokenize.

❑ dojox.timing — Advanced timing constructs and sequencing.

❑ dojox.uuid — Generation of universally unique identifier strings as per RFC 4122.

❑ dojox.wire — A generic data binding and service invocation library.

❑ dojox.xml — XML manipulation utilities, including an XML parser implemented in JavaScript.

As an incubator for functionality and experimental features, DojoX is bursting at the seams. Some of these packages offer one or two simple new functions (that is, `dojox.string`) — while others offer entire applications (that is, `dojox.sketch`) or radical new ways of building web applications (that it, `dojox.off`). If you keep up to date with a Subversion checkout, you're sure to see many more such packages appear in your `dojox` subdirectory.

Summary

With this chapter, the part of the book comes to a close. You were given a quick trip through the DojoX subproject and many of the varied and experimental code packages made available there.

Keep in mind that this particular chapter will age fast — if you're interested in the leading edge of Dojo work, be sure to check out news on these developments at the Dojo Project web site itself at `http://dojotoolkit.org/` and you'll also find some ongoing Dojo toolkit work by SitePen Labs at `http://sitepen.com/labs/dojo.php`.

Part V

MooTools

Part V: MooTools

As its homepage claims, MooTools is a compact, modular, object-oriented JavaScript framework. And more than perhaps any other framework presented in this book, MooTools is a *native* JavaScript toolkit. Unlike jQuery, which implements a domain-specific language of its own, MooTools stays firmly rooted in standard JavaScript and augments it. As opposed to the near Java-esque system of isolated modules and on-demand dependencies offered by YUI and imposed by Dojo, MooTools is loaded with HTML script tags and relies on JavaScript's built-in facilities for namespaces and modularity through object literals and closures.

MooTools is often compared to Prototype, because of the way it injects functionality into the prototypes of native objects in the JavaScript environment. But, far from a simple Prototype clone, MooTools provides a clean and powerful API that's built with a strong standard of consistency throughout. On top of that, MooTools offers animation and UI facilities similar to those provided to Prototype by Scriptaculous — and still manages to offer a more lightweight alternative.

The modular and extendable design of MooTools allows you to include just the parts of the framework you need — as well provides the ability to introduce your own custom functionality by creating a subclass or by injecting your own functions into an existing MooTools prototype at run-time. Here, MooTools makes good use of JavaScript as a dynamic prototype-based language without trying to mold it into the patterns of other languages. In the coming chapters, you'll see this particularly demonstrated in the extendibility offered by the framework's CSS selector code, DOM property manipulation, and custom events.

Finally, the incrementally constructed nature of MooTools means that all the little conveniences and building blocks used to implement the higher-level DOM and AJAX tools are themselves made available as standalone utilities for use in your own code. MooTools is, all in all, an expansion pack for JavaScript — from the environment basics all the way up to the flashy features of a modern framework.

Oh, and the "Moo" in MooTools, in case you were wondering, stands for "My Object Oriented" JavaScript Tools.

31

Enhancing Development with MooTools

More than just a page manipulation toolkit or AJAX utility library, MooTools offers basic enhancements to development in JavaScript. This includes new data structures like hashes and augmentations to existing types like arrays, strings, and numbers. Additionally, MooTools provides a set of tools for working with object-oriented programming concepts such as classes, inheritance, and mixins.

In this chapter, you learn about:

❑   Getting MooTools

❑   The MooTools Core

Getting MooTools

If MooTools sounds like the thing for you, there are a few ways to get your hands on either a stable or in-development version of the code.

Downloading the Latest MooTools Release

The latest release of MooTools, as shown in Figure 31-1, is available for download at:
`http://mootools.net/download`

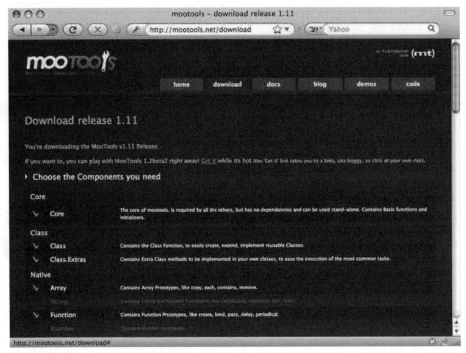

Figure 31-1

Here, you'll find the MooTools Core library provided with a variety of compressions and code reduction schemes applied for faster download when used in your pages. However, if you like, you can build a personalized copy of MooTools at the following URL:

```
http://mootools.net/core
```

From here, you can see the modular structure of the framework advertised in Figure 31-2. This download page offers a customizable checklist of all core modules made available in this release. You can pick and choose just the parts you need, and dependencies will be automatically selected as well. This on-the-fly download builder also offers a choice of compression to apply to the library you receive.

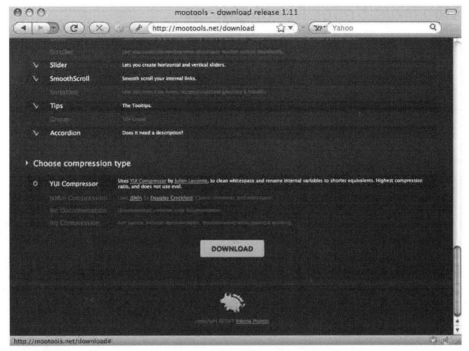

Figure 31-2

You can get an additional set of plug-ins and modules from the MooTools More collection, available in another build tool here:

```
http://mootools.net/more
```

This will give you a second JavaScript library suitable for inclusion after MooTools Core, which can include any or all of the extended components made available by the MooTools team. Most of these will also be covered in the coming chapters, so you might want to grab all of them — you can always go back to the builder if you need a reduced library for your own projects.

So, unlike some frameworks, you get the build version of MooTools custom assembled and optimized straight from the factory. Depending on how hands-on you like to get with the build process, this may be more or less desirable. In any case, you may wish to download a few versions of MooTools — for instance, one with all the modules included and no compression applied, for development, and another with just a few hand-picked and compressed modules for your production site.

You can start using the downloaded files with the following in the <head> of your page:

```
<script type="text/javascript" src="../mootools-1.2.1-core-yc.js"></script>
<script type="text/javascript" src="../mootools-1.2-more.js"></script>
```

Trying MooTools Under Development

If you want to skip past the handy custom release build tool and dig right into the bleeding edge, MooTools offers public access to the developers' code in progress.

Fetching a Git Checkout

Using a command-line Git client, invocations such as the following will fetch everything for you:

```
git clone git://github.com/mootools/mootools-core.git
git clone git://github.com/mootools/mootools-more.git
```

This will deliver all the documentation, tests, and raw source code that make up the MooTools framework. However, unlike the custom build process offered by the web site, this Git repository will not offer a single-include version of the framework — you'll need to build that yourself using the included `build.rb` script written in Ruby. The operation of that script will be left as an exercise to the reader.

Downloading an Edge Build

If you don't want to bother with building MooTools from source, there's an hourly build of MooTools Core made available at the following address:

```
http://mootools.net/download/get/mootools-core-edge.js
```

The library you receive as a download from this method can be used as an include, like the following:

```
<script type="text/javascript" src="../mootools-core-edge.js"></script>
```

Note that this hourly build doesn't include the plug-ins or modules provided by MooTools More.

Examining MooTools Core

The MooTools Core is small, but it packs in a lot of useful functionality — useful not only in setting the stage for the rest of the framework, but also for use in enhancing your own JavaScript development in general.

In preparation for taking a look at what's offered in MooTools Core and beyond, here are a couple of MooTools-style global shortcuts that produce log messages:

```
function $log(msg) {
    return console.log(msg);
}

function $log_json(obj) {
    return $log( JSON.encode(obj) );
}
```

These shortcuts will be used extensively to offer some visibility on the data structures and return values involved in demonstrating features in this chapter. The first, `$log()`, is a just a shorter form of Firebug's `console.log()` call. The second, `$log_json()`, exercises MooTools' `JSON.encode()` tool to turn objects and their properties into representative strings.

Checking the MooTools Version

Relatively new to the MooTools framework is the ability to check what version has been loaded:

```
$log("** Checking MooTools version");

if (MooTools) {
    switch(MooTools.build) {
        case '%build%':
            $log("*** SVN checkout, current version " + MooTools.version);
            break;
        default:
            $log("*** Version " + MooTools.version + ", build " + MooTools.build);
            break;
    }
} else {
    $log("*** Unknown version/build of MooTools");
}
```

You can follow the logic that's used in the preceding code or something similar to fork code between different versions of MooTools, or just to verify what version is available before attempting to run at all. Usually, you should be able to pair the version of MooTools desired with your own code, but this version detection may nonetheless come in handy at some point.

Determining Types

JavaScript offers the native `typeof` operator for determining the types of various values and objects — but in a lot of cases, it just falls back to reporting "`object`" for quite different things. This is among the reasons why MooTools offers the useful `$type()` function:

```
$log( $type( null ) );                     // false
$log( $type( arguments ) );                // "arguments"
$log( $type( { foo: 'bar' } ) );           // "object"
$log( $type( [ 1, 2, 3 ] ) );              // "array"
$log( $type( "hello" ) );                  // "string"
$log( $type( 123 ) );                      // "number"
$log( $type( true ) );                     // "boolean"
$log( $type( function() { } ) );           // "function"
$log( $type( /^hello(.*)World$/ ) );       // "regexp"
$log( $type( $('para1') ) );               // "element"
$log( $type( $('para1').firstChild ) );    // "textnode"
$log( $type( $('para1').childNodes ) );    // "collection"
```

As you can see, the global function `$type()` can report on whether a value is undefined (`false`) or whether the "`object`" is actually an array, string, number, function, or something else. Some combination of the types detected with this utility will come in handy eventually.

For example, you could detect between an array type and others to decide whether a function is receiving a single parameter or a list, and wrap the single value in an array if necessary.

Checking for Defined Values

You can detect whether a given variable contains a defined value either with the native JavaScript construct `typeof obj == 'undefined'` or with MooTools' `$type(obj)==false`, but there's another convenience function provided by MooTools for this purpose:

```
var foo = null;
$log( $defined(foo) ); // false

foo = "Hi there";
$log( $defined(foo) ); // true
```

Picking a Defined Value

Once you're able to detect defined values, one of the first uses to which the ability is applied is in selecting a defined value from a range of parameters and defaults. For this task, MooTools offers the global function `$pick()`:

```
$log( $pick(    1,    2, 3) ); // 1
$log( $pick( null,    2, 3) ); // 2
$log( $pick( null, null, 3) ); // 3
$log( $pick(false,    2, 3) ); // false
$log( $pick(    0,    2, 3) ); // 0
$log( $pick( "",    2, 3) ); // ""
```

In the preceding code, you can see that the `$pick()` function accepts multiple parameters. Each of these parameters is evaluated with `$defined()`, and the first one to come up as defined is returned. As mentioned before the code, this can be useful in choosing between a set of user-supplied parameters, configuration values, and defaults in order to come up with the first defined value in the set.

Choosing Random Numbers

It's a small thing, but this expression to pick a whole number between 10 and 100 is a bit verbose:

```
parseInt( Math.random() * (100 - 10) ) + 10
```

Depending on what you're building, you may need to do this sort of thing frequently — in games, for instance, or in creating randomized animations. For this, MooTools defines the `$random()` function:

```
$log( $random(0, 10) );     // Integer between 0 and 10
$log( $random(10, 100) );   // Integer between 10 and 100
$log( $random(100, 1000) ); // Integer between 100 and 1000
```

Getting the Current Time

Along the same lines as picking random numbers, the following is a rather verbose way to get the current clock time in milliseconds:

```
Date.now(); // Not always available
(new Date()).getTime();
```

So, MooTools offers the $time() function for quick access to the current time:

```
$log( $time() );
```

This can be pretty handy in setting up timers and measuring performance. Additionally, including a time stamp in log messages can help in reviewing the sequence of events fired in an application.

Clearing Timers and Intervals

Since JavaScript isn't technically a threaded environment, multitasking needs to be cooperatively managed in small steps set to execute on timers or repeating intervals. For this, the native window. setTimeout() and window.setInterval() methods are made available.

Each of these methods returns a different kind of opaque handle used for aborting the next execution. One-shot timers are canceled with window.clearTimeout() and repeating intervals are canceled with window.clearInterval().

It can occasionally get confusing as to whether a given handle belongs to a one-shot timer or a repeating interval, so for this reason MooTools offers a unified $clear() function that can be applied to either:

```
var timer = setTimeout(function() {
    alert('Alert never happens');
}, 1000);
timer = $clear(timer);

var interval = setInterval(function() {
    alert('Alert never happens');
}, 1000);
interval = $clear(interval);
```

Merging and Extending Objects

MooTools offers support for object-oriented programming, and inheritance is a big part of that paradigm. But sometimes, rather than diving fully into that practice, it's useful to at least get the inheritance part in merging or extending data structures. Say, for instance, you'd like to establish a set of default configuration values and then layer a user-supplied set on top.

This is what the global functions $merge() and $extend() are useful in accomplishing. In preparation for a demonstration, consider the following data structures:

```
var alpha = {
    foo: 'bar',
    baz: 'quux',
    test: { one: 1, two: 2 }
};
var beta = {
    thud:  'splat',
    xyzzy: 'magic',
    test:  { three: 3, four: 4 }
};
```

Notice that each of the preceding code snippets has two different properties and each shares one containing an object, itself bearing different properties in each structure. Now, take a look at what the $merge() function does with these structures:

```
// Returns recursively merged copy of alpha and beta, no side-effects.
var gamma = $merge(alpha, beta);

$log_json(alpha);
// {"foo":"bar","baz":"quux","test":{"one":1,"two":2}}

$log_json(gamma);
// {"foo":"bar","baz":"quux","test":{"one":1,"two":2,"three":3,"four":4},
// "thud":"splat","xyzzy":"magic"}
```

Neither the alpha nor beta structures were modified in the preceding code, but the return value in gamma has received the results of recursively merging both alpha and beta — right down to the object contained under the test property.

The $extend() function does things a little differently, modifying one of the original structures:

```
// Returns modified copy of alpha, with properties overwritten by beta.
var delta = $extend(alpha, beta);

$log_json(alpha);
// {"foo":"bar","baz":"quux","test":{"three":3,"four":4},"thud":"splat",
// "xyzzy":"magic"}

$log_json(delta);
// {"foo":"bar","baz":"quux","test":{"three":3,"four":4},"thud":"splat",
// "xyzzy":"magic"}
```

As you can see in the preceding code, the alpha structure has been modified by having its properties overwritten by beta. The variable gamma at this point simply contains a copy of the alpha structure.

In a way, this $extend() function works like class inheritance in object-oriented programming, but maybe a bit in reverse: alpha is injected with the features of beta, rather than beta establishing a subclass.

Using Array Extensions

Up to this point, everything seen from the core of MooTools has been a collection of global convenience functions. From here on, though, you'll start to see how MooTools extends native browser objects by adding new methods that either bring consistency to functionality across browsers or introduce new features altogether.

The first native feature to get this treatment is the `Array` object. In modern versions of JavaScript, this object has quite a few convenient methods for manipulating and processing its contents. You can, for example, read all about what's available in Mozilla browsers here:

```
http://developer.mozilla.org/en/docs/Core_JavaScript_1.5_Reference:Objects:Array
```

In fact, many of the extensions added by MooTools are redundant implementations of native `Array` methods described in the preceding document. These are provided so that the few browsers without native implementations can be patched to offer consistent functionality. You may wish to also refer to this documentation for another perspective on some of these methods.

In addition, be sure to check out the MooTools documentation, since not every `Array` extension method is covered in this section.

Processing Array Items with .each() and .forEach()

One of the most useful things to do with a list of items is to do something useful with each of the items in the list. For this purpose, the `Array` methods `.forEach()` and its alias `.each()` are made available:

```javascript
var list = [
 'foo', 'bar', 'baz', 'quux',
 'xyzzy', 'plugh', 'thud', 'splat'
];

var someObj = {

    someThing: 'value of some thing',

    doIt: function() {

        list.forEach(function(item, idx) {
            $log(idx + ': ' + item + ' (' + this.someThing + ')' )
        }, this);

        list.each(function(item, idx) {
            $log(idx + ': ' + item + ' (' + this.someThing + ')' )
        }, this);

    }

};
someObj.doIt();
```

The log transcript output from the preceding code should be the following repeated twice:

```
0: foo (value of some thing)
1: bar (value of some thing)
2: baz (value of some thing)
3: quux (value of some thing)
4: xyzzy (value of some thing)
5: plugh (value of some thing)
6: thud (value of some thing)
7: splat (value of some thing)
```

The first parameter to .forEach() and .each() is a function to which the item and the current index in the list will be passed. In this function, you can do whatever you like with the item, and the return value will be ignored.

The second parameter to .forEach() and .each() is an optional object scope. If given, it will become the local value for the variable inside the function passed in the first parameter. As demonstrated in the preceding code, this allows the anonymous function access to the scope of the object in which the .forEach() and .each() loops are called.

Using the $each() Shortcut

It's also worth noting that there's a global shortcut $each() that can be applied to nearly anything that looks list-like:

```
$each(
    ['foo', 'bar', 'baz'],
    function(item, idx) {
        $log( idx + ': ' + item );
    }/*,
    optional_scope */
);
// 0: foo
// 1: bar
// 2: baz

$each(
    {oof:'foo', rab:'bar', zab:'baz'},
    function(value, key) {
        $log( key + ': ' + value );
    }/*,
    optional_scope */
);
// oof: foo
// rab: bar
// zab: baz

$each(
    document.getElementsByTagName('p'),
    function(el) {
        $log( el.firstChild.nodeValue );
    }/*,
    optional_scope */
```

```
);
// Open your Firebug console for log messages!
// Here's another paragraph for reference.
```

This `$each()` shortcut works with arrays, objects, and even node collections resulting from DOM lookup methods.

Using the $A() Shortcut to Create Arrays

Speaking of shortcuts, there's also the `$A()` shortcut function, which is useful in turning almost anything list-like into a native array:

```
function foo() {
    $A(arguments).each(function(item, idx) {
        $log(idx + ': ' + item);
    });
}
foo('bar', 'baz', 'quux', 'xyzzy');
// 0: bar
// 1: baz
// 2: quux
// 3: xyzzy
```

Just like `$each()`, the `$A()` function can be applied to DOM node lists and other collections.

Filtering and Mapping Array Items

In the `.forEach()` and `.each()` methods, the return value from the function processing items was ignored. However, in the next two methods, `.filter()` and `.map()`, the return value becomes very important.

Using the .filter() Array Method

You can use the `.filter()` method to produce a subset of a list whose items match criteria implemented in a function:

```
$log(
    list.filter(
        function(item, idx) {
            return item.length <= 3
        } /*, optional_scope */
    )
    .join(', ')
);
// foo, bar, baz
```

In the preceding code, only items whose length is 3 or below are admitted into the subset. The `true` or `false` value decides, respectively, whether or not a particular item in the list is included in the subset. Just like `.forEach()`, this function is given the item and current array index. Although it's not used here, an object scope for the function can be given as the second parameter.

Using the .map() Array Method

In this next method, whereas `.filter()` decides on the presence of items, `.map()` determines the value of items that make it into a resulting list:

```
$log(
    list.map(
        function(item, idx) {
            return item.length
        } /*, optional_scope */
    )
    .join(', ')
);
// 3, 3, 3, 4, 5, 5, 4, 5
```

In the preceding code, each item from the original list is transformed by the supplied function into its respective string length in the resulting array. In addition, the optional object scope parameter is accepted here as well.

Checking the Content of Array Items

In the previous two methods, the return value from the function processing each array item was used in influencing a resulting output array. However, in these next functions, the output is a single Boolean `true`/`false` value or an integer.

Using the .some() Array Method

Consider the following demonstration of the `.some()` method:

```
$log(
    list.some(
        function(item, idx) {
            return item.length < 4
        }/*, optional_scope*/
    )
);
// true

$log(
    list.some(
        function(item, idx) {
            return item.length > 5
        }/*, optional_scope */
    )
);
// false
```

The purpose of the `.some()` method is to determine whether *some* of the items in the list meet the criteria of a given function. If this function returns `true` for *any* of the items in the list, the ultimate return value of `.some()` is also `true`.

Using the .every() Array Method

The inverse of `.some()` is the `.every()` method, demonstrated in the following code:

```
$log(
    list.every(
        function(item, idx) {
            return item.length > 2
        }/*, optional_scope */
    )
);
// true

$log(
    list.every(
        function(item, idx) {
            return item.length < 4
        }/*, optional_scope */
    )
);
// false
```

With the `.every()` method, for the return value to be true, *all* items in the array must cause the function to evaluate to true. If *any* value results in false, the entire `.every()` method returns a false value.

Using the .indexOf(), .contains(), and .erase() Array Methods

These next methods are useful for checking for the existence of specific items in the list:

```
$log( list.indexOf('xyzzy') );  // 4
$log( list.contains('xyzzy') ); // true

list.erase('xyzzy');

$log( list.indexOf('xyzzy') );  // -1
$log( list.contains('xyzzy') ); // false
```

The `.contains()` method returns whether or not an item is found in the list, while the `.indexOf()` method returns the position where the given value was found, or –1 if it wasn't found at all.

The other method introduced here, `.erase()`, is used to remove all instances of a given value.

Converting Array Items into Object Properties

This next method, `.associate()`, converts an array into an object by *associating* the values of a given list as keys for the items of the list on which the method is called. Consider the following code:

```
var obj = list.associate([
  'oof', 'rab', 'zab', 'xuuq'
]);
$log_json(obj);
// {"oof":"foo", "rab":"bar", "zab":"baz", "xuuq":"quux"}
```

As you can see, the first parameter of the method is an array. Each of these values is paired up as a key with each value of the array on which `.associate()` was called, resulting in an object returned.

Extending and Combining Arrays

Having processed array items and interrogated their contents, now it's time to look into mingling the contents of arrays together.

Using the .extend() Array Method

The array extension method `.extend()` is useful for appending values to an array:

```
var list = [
  'foo', 'bar', 'baz', 'quux', 'xyzzy', 'plugh', 'thud', 'splat'
];
list.extend([ 'foo', 'alpha', 'beta', 'gamma' ]);
$log( list );
// ["foo", "bar", "baz", "quux", "xyzzy", "plugh", "thud",
//      "splat", "foo", "alpha", "beta", "gamma"]
```

An array is accepted as a parameter to the `.extend()` method, which appends each value of that array to the array on which the method was called. Note that the list is changed in place, and the return value from `.extend()` is the original list itself.

Using the .include() Array Method

What's worth noting is that `.extend()` does nothing to prevent duplicate values. This next method, `.include()`, refrains from appending values already found in the array:

```
var list = [
  'foo', 'bar', 'baz', 'quux', 'xyzzy', 'plugh', 'thud', 'splat'
];
list.include('alpha').include('foo');   // Notice the chaining?
$log( list );
// ["foo", "bar", "baz", "quux", "xyzzy", "plugh", "thud",
//      "splat", "alpha"]
```

Note that although there were two calls to `.include()`, one with the parameter 'alpha' and another with 'foo', only the first of the two was added to the list. This is because the second, 'foo', was already present in the list.

Using the .combine() Array Method

The list-based equivalent of this functionality is offered in the .combine() method:

```
var list = [
    'foo', 'bar', 'baz', 'quux', 'xyzzy', 'plugh', 'thud', 'splat'
];
list.combine(['alpha', 'foo', 'bar', 'baz', 'beta']);
$log( list );
// ["foo", "bar", "baz", "quux", "xyzzy", "plugh", "thud",
//     "splat", "alpha", "beta"]
```

Like the .extend() method, the .combine() method accepts a list. However, like the .include() method, this one does not allow duplicate values into the list.

Flattening Nested Arrays

Occasionally, it's useful to take a list of lists and flatten it into one array of values. This is where the .flatten() method comes in:

```
var list = [ ];

list.push(['foo', 'bar', 'baz']);
list.push(['alpha', 'beta', 'gamma']);

$log( list );
// [["foo", "bar", "baz"], ["alpha", "beta", "gamma"]]

$log( list.flatten() );
// ["foo", "bar", "baz", "alpha", "beta", "gamma"]
```

As you can see, the preceding code constructs an array containing two nested arrays. A call to the .flatten() method produces a single list containing all the values from the nested lists. The following is an even more complex example:

```
$log(
    list.map(function(i) {
        return i.map(function(j) {
            return [ j, j.length ]
        })
    })
    .flatten()
);
// ["foo", 3, "bar", 3, "baz", 3, "alpha", 5, "beta", 4, "gamma", 5]
```

In this code, a nested pair of .map() calls builds a nested list of items and their lengths. The call to the .flatten() method at the end produces a simple list of values alternating with lengths.

Applying Selection Rules with .link()

The .link() array extension method allows for some fairly complex selection rules in building an object's properties:

```
var list = [
 'foo', 'bar', 'baz', 'quux',
 'xyzzy', 'plugh', 'thud', 'splat'
];
var obj = {
    'three1': function(key) { return key.length == 3 },
    'three2': function(key) { return key.length == 3 },
    'foo' : function(key) { return key == 'foo' },
    'x1'    : function(key) { return key.indexOf('x') != -1 },
    'x2'    : function(key) { return key.indexOf('x') != -1 }
};

var obj2 = list.link(obj);

$log_json(obj);
// {}

$log_json(obj2);
// {"three1":"foo", "three2":"bar", "x1":"quux", "x2":"xyzzy"}
```

The .link() method allows for a set of selection rules to be applied against a list. The object returned at the end is the result of all the rules' applications.

In the preceding code, a list is defined, as well as an object literal consisting of named functions. When the .link() method on the list is called with the object as a parameter, each item in the array is passed into each of the named functions in turn.

The first function to return true causes the list item to be the value of the corresponding property name in the return value object. Once matched, a rule is removed from the set. Thus, since there are duplicate rules here, such as three1 and three2 — each matches a different three-letter value, because each rule is removed after a successful match.

This method can be useful if, for example, you'd like to accept parameters to a function in any order but match values with parameter names based on types — such as object, string, and so on.

Using Hash Data Structures

Although you can use a plain object as a hash or associative array structure in JavaScript, objects are missing a few of the useful methods found in other languages' implementations of these structures. For example, it's not altogether natural to get a list of just the keys or the values present in an object, to determine whether a given value is present, or what the key is for a given value.

Defining Hashes and the Hash Shortcut

Rather than extending the base object prototype itself, MooTools offers a `Hash` class as a wrapper around JS objects. The following code offers several ways to create `Hash` objects:

```
var h1 = new Hash({
    foo: 'bar',
    baz: 'quux',
    xyzzy: 'thud',
    plugh: 'fred',
    x123: 'y456'
});

var h2 = $H({
    foo: 'bar',
    baz: 'quux',
    xyzzy: 'thud',
    plugh: 'fred',
    x123: 'y456'
});

var h3 = $H(h1);
```

The first means of creating a `Hash` object is simply with the new keyword, while the second uses a global shortcut function named `$H()` — both of these are equivalent in functionality.

The third example produces a copy of an existing hash or object, but the interesting thing is that the copy is *independent*, meaning that changes to values of any native type — array, string, object, and so on — will not change the nested data type in the original. This is done using a global function named `$unlink()`, which produces a nested copy of a given data structure.

Getting and Setting Keys and Values

While you can access a `Hash` object just like a plain JavaScript object, the `Hash` object offers a few convenience methods that make your intentions a bit clearer in code:

```
$log( h2.hasValue('fred') );  // true
$log( h2.hasValue('alpha') ); // false

$log( h2['foo'] );            // "bar"
$log( h2.get('foo') );        // "bar"
h2.erase('foo');
$log( h2['foo'] );            // typeof h2['foo'] == "undefined"
$log( h2.get('foo') );        // null

h2.set('foo', 'bar');
$log( h2.keyOf('bar') );      // "foo"

$log( h2.getKeys() );         // ["foo", "baz", "xyzzy", "plugh"]
$log( h2.getValues() );       // ["bar", "quux", "thud", "fred"]
```

In the preceding code, the `.hasValue()` method is used to determine whether a given value exists under any key name in the structure. Next, the `.get()` method is used to get a value for a key, all but identical to using `h2['foo']` or `h2.foo` as direct access expressions. Then, the `.set()` method is used to set a value for a key, and the `.keyOf()` method reports the key of a given value. And, finally, the `.getKeys()` and `.getValues()` methods each report on the keys and values used in the hash, respectively.

It's worth noting here that the main way in which `Hash` methods differ from using a plain JavaScript object is that each `Hash` method makes use of the base JS object method `.hasOwnProperty()`. This means that if anything *does* extend the base JS object — unlike the `Hash` wrapper — those extensions would show up in a naïve `"for key in obj"` loop. But, the methods of `Hash` watch for this, reporting only on the specific keys and values introduced in that particular data structure.

You can read more about this distinction and its implications at this blog entry:

```
http://yuiblog.com/blog/2006/09/26/for-in-intrigue/
```

Mapping and Filtering Hashes

Like the `Array` extensions, `Hash` instances offer a few similar methods that use values and keys rather than values and numeric indexes. The first of these are the `.map()` and `.filter()` methods:

```
$log_json(
    h1.map(
        function(value, key) {
            return value + " (" + key + ")";
        }/*, optional_scope */
    )
);
// {"foo":"bar (foo)","baz":"quux (baz)","xyzzy":"thud (xyzzy)",
//     "plugh":"fred (plugh)"}

$log_json(
    h1.filter(
        function(value, key) {
            return key.length <=3
        }/*, optional_scope */
    )
);
// {"foo":"bar","baz":"quux"}
```

In the preceding code, you can see that `.map()` works like its `Array` equivalent, operating on the values of the hash through the function's return value. Notice that it works *only* on the values, though — the keys of the hash are not easily modified with this method.

Also like its `Array` equivalent, the `.filter()` method determines which keys and values make it into a return value hash. Neither `.map()` nor `.filter()` modify the original hash.

Checking Hashes with .every() and .some()

Also like their `Array` cousins, the `.every()` and `.some()` methods offered by the `Hash` class serve to interrogate all values and keys for criteria defined in a function:

```
$log(
    h1.every(
        function(value, key) {
            return /(\d+)/.test(key)
        }/*, optional_scope */
    )
); // false

$log(
    h1.some(
        function(value, key) {
            return /(\d+)/.test(key)
        }/*, optional_scope */
    )
); // true
```

As you can see in this example, again, the functions used with `.every()` and `.some()` expect value and key as parameters instead of value and index used in the `Array` equivalents. And, again, the `.every()` and `.some()` methods respectively expect *all* or *any* value/key pair to match the criteria implemented in the given function.

Extending and Combining Hashes

Like the Array extensions, hashes offer the methods `.extend()`, `.include()`, and `.combine()`. The following code demonstrates how these work:

```
h2.extend({
    foo: 'alpha', bar: 'beta', thingy: 'gamma'
});
$log_json( h2 );
// {"baz":"quux","xyzzy":"thud","plugh":"fred","x123":"y456",
// "foo":"alpha","bar":"beta","thingy":"gamma"}

h2.include('foo', 'ignored_value');
h2.include('stuff', 'delta');
$log_json( h2 );
// {"baz":"quux","xyzzy":"thud","plugh":"fred","x123":"y456",
// "foo":"alpha","bar":"beta","thingy":"gamma","stuff":"delta"}

h2.combine({
    foo: 'ignored',
    stuff: 'ignored',
    more: 'added value'
});
$log_json( h2 );
// {"baz":"quux","xyzzy":"thud","plugh":"fred","x123":"y456",
// "foo":"alpha","bar":"beta","thingy":"gamma","stuff":"delta",
// "more":"added value"}
```

The .extend() method accepts a hash or a JS object and modifies the original hash, overwriting keys found there from the data structure accepted as parameter. The .include() method accepts individual key / value pairs, but refuses to replace any existing data in the hash. And, finally, the .combine() method works like a cross between .extend() and .include(), accepting a hash to mingle into the original hash yet refusing to clobber any existing data.

Converting Hashes into URL Query Strings

Since query strings figure so importantly into making web requests and constructing URLs, .toQueryString() is a particularly useful method of the Hash class:

```
$log(
    $H({
        foo: "The quick",
        bar: "brown fox",
        baz: "@#$%^&*",
        thud: [ 'alpha', 'beta', 'gamma' ]
    })
    .toQueryString()
);
// foo=The%20quick&bar=brown%20fox&baz=%40%23%24%25%5E%26*&thud[0]=alpha
// &thud[1]=beta&thud[2]=gamma
```

In the preceding code, a Hash is quickly constructed using the $H() shortcut, and then the Hash's .toQueryString() method is called. The return value is a string containing all of the keys and values of the hash, with each properly URL-escaped. Also notice that the nested array has been flattened into enumerated parameters, somewhat like the PHP style of specifying multiple values for a given named parameter.

Using String Extensions

MooTools also offers a handful of useful extensions to the native String type. These are useful for performing a few tests, conversions, and even some simple template-based formatting.

Checking String Contents

This first method, .contains(), is useful for determining whether a given substring is present in a string:

```
var str2 = "brown, bluegreen, black, red";
$log( str2.contains("blue") );          // true
$log( str2.contains("blue", ", ") );       // false
$log( str2.contains("bluegreen", ", ") ); // true
```

The first parameter to .contains() is a substring for which to search. The optional second parameter, however, can be used to specify a delimiter to use in searching for the substring.

In the preceding code, the string being searched contains a comma-separated list. So, the first example looks for the simple substring "blue", while the second two look for specific delimited items "blue" and "bluegreen". This can be useful when investigating what classes are present in CSS class names, or just simple list searches.

Getting a bit more general, the .test() method offers the ability to look for a substring or apply a regular expression against a string:

```
var str = "The quick brown fox jumps over the lazy dog";
$log( str.test("brown") );            // true
$log( str.test("bar") );              // false
$log( str.test(/^([a-zA-Z\s]+)$/) ); // true
$log( str.test(/^(\d+)$/) );          // false
```

The first two calls to the .test() method simply search for substrings. The second two apply regular expressions, with the first checking for letters and whitespace and the second checking for all numbers. Note that regular expression objects offer a .test() method, too, so this method on the string prototype is basically an alternate expression of that.

Converting Strings to Numbers and Colors

JavaScript offers the parseInt() and parseFloat() functions for converting string values to numbers, but as a convenience MooTools wraps these up as string extensions .toInt() and .toFloat() like so:

```
$log( "100".toInt() );     // 100
$log( "99.96".toInt() );   // 99
$log( "100".toFloat() );   // 100
$log( "99.96".toFloat() ); // 99.96
```

Writing the code this way may read a bit more cleanly than using the native JavaScript functions.

The next pair of methods, .hexToRgb() and .rgbToHex(), are useful when manipulating colors on elements and styles:

```
$log('*** String.hexToRgb and String.rgbToHex');
$log( "#aabbcc".hexToRgb() );          // "rgb(170,187,204)"
$log( "#abc".hexToRgb() );             // "rgb(170,187,204)"
$log( "rgb(170,187,204)".rgbToHex() ); // "#aabbcc"
$log( "rgb(186,218,85)".rgbToHex() );  // "#bada55"
```

It's usually easier to do math with the numeric RGB equivalents of hexadecimal colors, yet it's often easier to remember the hexadecimal equivalents when writing markup and CSS. So, these two methods are helpful in converting back and forth as the situation demands.

Using Simple Substitution Templates

It's often awkward to build a string with a long series of string and variable concatenations, and yet it's usually overkill to call in a full-featured template language for doing so. MooTools offers a happy medium in the `.substitute()` method:

```
var str = "Hello, my name is {name}, and I am a {sign}.";
$log(
    str.substitute({
        name: "l.m.orchard", sign: "Scorpio"
    })
);
// Hello, my name is l.m.orchard, and I am a Scorpio.

var str = "Hello, my name is %%name%%, and I am a %%sign%%.";
$log(
    str.substitute(
        { name: "l.m.orchard", sign: "Scorpio" },
        /\\?%%([^%]+)%%/g
    )
);
// Hello, my name is l.m.orchard, and I am a Scorpio.
```

The `.substitute()` method accepts an object or `Hash` as its first parameter, the values of which will be used to replace named placeholders in the string. The optional second parameter accepts a regular expression to be used to redefine the placeholder pattern. The preceding code demonstrates both the use of default placeholders, as well as specifying a new pattern.

This method can be useful in separating format templates from where they're used, allowing for internationalization or just plain cleaner code.

Performing Miscellaneous Transformations

Although this section doesn't promise to cover every extension available, the following miscellaneous transformations are worth pointing out:

```
$log( "    lots   of   space ".trim() );  // "lots   of   space"
$log( "    lots   of   space ".clean() ); // "lots of space"

$log( "this-is-a-test".camelCase() ); // thisIsATest
$log( "thisIsATest".hyphenate() );    // this-is-a-test

$log( "this is a test".capitalize() ); // This Is A Test
```

The `.trim()` method lops off extra whitespace at the ends of a string, while `.clean()` does the same and collapses multiple spaces into single spaces as well.

The methods `.camelCase()` and `.hyphenate()` are a complementary pair, converting strings between camel case and hyphenated-expressions. This comes in most handy when referring to CSS properties as used in JavaScript and CSS itself, since the general rule there is that the properties are named with camel case in JavaScript and hyphenated-naming in CSS.

Finally, the `.capitalize()` method is available for ensuring the right case for titles and proper nouns.

Using Function Extensions

Since functions are themselves objects with a prototype in JavaScript, it's possible to attach some extended methods to them. With that in mind, MooTools has a few improvements to offer in this area as well.

Binding Functions to Object Contexts

A useful, but tricky aspect of functions in JavaScript is the scope variable `this`. In general, the accessible value of the variable `this` during the execution of a function reflects the relevant context in which it was called. When called as a method of an object, `this` usually refers to that object. But, when a function is used as the handler for an event, `this` can refer to an element or the browser window itself.

However, often when using an object method as a handler, you'd like `this` to remain pointing at the object to which the method belongs. Apropos of this, consider the following code:

```javascript
var SelfDestructTimer = {
    count:    5,
    interval: null,

    tick: function(msg) {
        $log(msg + " Tick... " + this.count);
        if (this.count-- <= 0) {
            $log("Boom!");
            $clear(this.interval);
        }
    },

    lightFuse: function(msg) {
        /* This doesn't work - 'this' for tick() will be the window itself:
        this.interval = setInterval(
            this.tick, 1000
        );
        */
        this.interval = setInterval(
            this.tick.bind(this, [ msg ]), 1000
        );
        $log("The fuse is lit!");
    }
};

SelfDestructTimer.lightFuse('Oh noes!');

// The fuse is lit!
// Oh noes! Tick... 5
// Oh noes! Tick... 4
// Oh noes! Tick... 3
// Oh noes! Tick... 2
// Oh noes! Tick... 1
// Oh noes! Tick... 0
// Boom!
```

The object that's defined in the preceding code implements a countdown timer, built around the `.bind()` method and the `setInterval()` function. Normally, a function passed into `setInterval()` as a handler will see a reference to the browser window as its value for the variable `this`.

However, this new `.bind()` method on the functions builds a wrapper function as a closure that retains the original object reference as this when called. Thus, when *that* function is supplied as a handler to `setInterval()`, the object method is called by the wrapper with the proper context to access the counter and the interval time for eventual cancellation. Notice also that an array of parameters can be passed as an optional second argument to `.bind()` — these get passed to the bound method when the wrapper is called.

Note that all of this is essentially the same thing done for the second optional argument accepted by `.forEach()` methods on `Arrays` and `Hashes`, just broken out for use in other situations.

Delaying and Setting Function Calls on Intervals

Since the previous example made use of a timer, it's apropos that the next pair of extension methods deal with timers and intervals. Named `.delay()` and `.periodical()`, these methods ease the use of `setTimeout()` and `setInterval()` with respect to functions and the use of `.bind()` shown in the preceding code.

As a demonstration, take a look at this revised timer object:

```
var SelfDestructTimer_v2 = {
    count:   10,
    interval: null,

    tick: function(msg) {
        $log(msg + " Tick... " + this.count);
        if (this.count-- <= 0) {
            $log("Boom!");
            $clear(this.interval);
        }
    },

    cancel: function(msg) {
        $log(msg + " Self-destruct cancelled!");
        $clear(this.interval);
    },

    lightFuse: function(msg) {
        this.interval =

            this.tick.periodical(1000, this, [ msg ]);
        $log("The fuse is lit!");

        this.cancel.delay(5000, this, [ msg ]);
        $log("Considering cancellation!");
    }
};

SelfDestructTimer_v2.lightFuse('Banzai!');
```

Rather than using `setInterval()` to start the timer, the function method `.periodical()` is called. The first parameter is the time in milliseconds between repeating calls to the `.tick()` method. The second parameter is used to bind the object context, and the final parameter accepts a list of parameters to pass when the `.tick()` method is called.

Similarly, there's a new delayed call to the `.cancel()` method using the function method `.delay()`, which takes the place of a `setTimeout()` call. All of the same parameters are accepted by the `.delay()` method as by `.periodical()`. Also, note that both of these return the appropriate handle for use with `$clear()` to eventually cancel such a timed action.

Attempting Function Calls with Potential Exceptions

Occasionally, it's useful to attempt a potentially exception-prone operation, yet absorb and silence the exception itself when it happens:

```
function bad_function() {
    window.thisDoesntExist();
}
$log( bad_function.attempt() );
```

Using the `.attempt()` method in the preceding code, the usual error condition caused by attempting to call a nonexistent window method is silently trapped with a `try/catch` block inside MooTools.

This becomes most useful in the related global function `$try()`, when used to find a usable object across browsers like so:

```
function(){
    return $try(
        function(){ return new XMLHttpRequest() },
        function(){ return new ActiveXObject('MSXML2.XMLHTTP') }
    );
};
```

The `$try()` function attempts each function passed to it in turn until one of them successfully returns a defined value. The preceding case is an attempt to find the current browser's implementation of the XMLHttpRequest object, which varies between vendors and versions.

Using Object-Oriented Programming

Although JavaScript does support object-oriented programming, it's based on prototypes rather than classical inheritance. So, for programmers more used to the latter, the former can be a bit confusing. However, class-based inheritance itself can be implemented under a prototype-based system.

So, MooTools augments the base prototype system of JavaScript with a few bits of class-based inheritance programming, as well as some ways to implement post hoc augmentation of existing classes.

Building Classes and Subclasses

First, consider the following code that constructs a simple base class:

```
var Furniture = new Class({

    name: 'Furniture',

    isSelfAssembled: false,

    initialize: function() {
        $log("Furniture init!");
    },

    describe: function() {
        return '[' + this.name + '] ' +
            ( (this.isSelfAssembled) ? '(self assembled)' : '(pre-built)' );
    }

});
```

In MooTools, all classes are themselves instances of a class named `Class`. When an instance of this `Furniture` class is created using the new keyword, the `.initialize()` method is called. However, beyond that, there's nothing very special in the preceding code.

Now, consider how a subclass of `Furniture` is declared:

```
var CheapBookshelf = new Class({

    Extends: Furniture,

    name: 'CheapBookshelf',

    isSelfAssembled: true,

    initialize: function() {
        this.parent();
        $log("CheapBookshelf init!");
    }

});

$log('*** Creating a CheapBookshelf');
var a_bookshelf = new CheapBookshelf();
$log( a_bookshelf.describe() );

// *** Creating a CheapBookshelf
// Furniture init!
// CheapBookshelf init!
// [CheapBookshelf] (self assembled)
```

By virtue of the Extends property supplied in the definition of this class, the CheapBookshelf class begins by inheriting everything from the Furniture class and then selectively overriding things. This is not entirely unlike the global function $extend() introduced earlier.

Thus, the CheapBookshelf class is given a .describe() method without needing to declare one. But, notice that this class overrides its parent's implementation of .initialize() — within the body of that method implementation, the statement this.parent() causes the execution of the parent function that's been overridden, thus allowing extension of the parent class' behavior rather than simply replacing it.

To further demonstrate the point, consider the following demonstration of another Furniture subclass named Chair, which also provides a new implementation for the .describe() method:

```
var Chair = new Class({

    Extends: Furniture,

    name: 'Chair',

    initialize: function() {
        this.parent();
        $log("Chair init!");
    },

    describe: function() {
        var desc = this.parent();
        return desc + " (I'm a chair!)";
    }

});

$log('*** Creating a Chair');
var a_chair = new Chair();
$log( a_chair.describe() );

// *** Creating a Chair
// Furniture init!
// Chair init!
// [Chair] (pre-built) (I'm a chair!)
```

As you can see, the statement this.parent() applies in any method, not just .initialize() — it calls the appropriate method in the parent class, wherever it's used. As shown in this new implementation of .describe(), the return value can be captured and manipulated on the way to being returned.

With the behavior demonstrated in the preceding code, the Class object in MooTools forms the simple foundation of classical inheritance and the ability to override parent behavior.

Injecting Methods and Properties into Existing Classes

Beyond plain vanilla classical inheritance, however, MooTools also offers a way to inject new behavior into existing classes with the .implement() method of the Class object:

```
Chair.implement({
    owner: null,
    assignSeating: function(name) {
        this.owner = name;
    },
    describe: function() {
        var desc = this.parent();
        return desc + " (owner: "+ this.owner +")";
    }
});

$log('*** Creating another Chair, with assigned seating');
var b_chair = new Chair();
b_chair.assignSeating("Alan Smithee");
$log( b_chair.describe() );

// *** Creating another Chair, with assigned seating
// Furniture init!
// Chair init!
// [Chair] (pre-built) (owner: Alan Smithee)
```

As shown in the preceding code, calling .implement() on the Chair class allows the supplied properties and methods to be mixed into the existing class — causing subsequently instantiated objects to be granted the new data and functionality. Something to notice, though: In the newly implemented .describe() method, this.parent() refers to the parent class Furniture and not the Chair class.

The really interesting thing about this feature is that this is post hoc augmentation of an existing class. The class could be part of the MooTools framework or from some other third-party library — but no modifications to the original source are needed, and there's no need for coordination with the original authors. This new stuff just plugs right into existing classes and patches preexisting functionality.

Extending Native Browser Objects

Another thing that's interesting to note is that the .implement() method also works as an extension method on many native types as well, like so:

```
String.implement({
    join: function(list) {
        return list.join(this);
    }
});

$log( " -- ".join([1, 2, 3, 4, 5]) );
// 1 -- 2 -- 3 -- 4 -- 5
```

This is basically how all of the previously described native extensions on the Array, String, and Function prototypes get installed by MooTools — but you can use this functionality, too. The one thing that MooTools attempts to avoid is installing anything custom in the prototype of the base `Object` type, opting instead for the `Hash` wrapper class in that case.

Implementing Mixin Classes

So, in defining subclasses, supplying the `Extends` property is the way to declare a parent class. But, notice that the expected value of the `Extends` property is a single `Class` instance, which means that a class can only inherit from one parent class — in object-oriented programming terms, this is called *single inheritance*.

However, often it's useful to accumulate functionality from multiple parent classes as "mixed-in" functionality using *multiple inheritance*. In MooTools, this can be done with the `Implements` property in a class definition like so:

```
var Reclinable = new Class({
    recline: function() { $log('Reclining chair...'); }
});

var Massaging = new Class({
    massage: function() { $log('Initiating massage...'); }
});

var Heated = new Class({
    activateHeat: function() { $log('Warming up chair...'); }
});

var ComfyChair = new Class({
    Extends: Chair,
    Implements: [
        Reclinable, Massaging, Heated
    ]
});

$log('*** Creating a ComfyChair');
var c_chair = new ComfyChair();
$log( c_chair.describe() );
c_chair.recline();
c_chair.massage();
c_chair.activateHeat();

// *** Creating a ComfyChair
// Furniture init!
// Chair init!
// [Chair] (pre-built) (owner: null)
// Reclining chair...
// Initiating massage...
// Warming up chair...
```

Unlike the concept of an "implements" keyword in Java, the mixin classes here are not abstract interface classes. The `Implements` property in a MooTools class definition is acted upon in the Class constructor by using the `.implement()` method described earlier, injecting copies of the properties and methods of the specified classes into the newly defined class.

Keep in mind how the `.implement()` method works, though: The copied properties and methods overwrite what was defined in the class itself, rather than overriding them. Any calls to `this.parent()` will refer to the parent class, and not the new subclass. The same applies to anything mixed in with the `Implements` property in the class definition.

Using the Events Mixin Class

One particularly useful mixin class provided by MooTools is the `Events` class, which allows for the implementation of events on an object as attachment points for handler functions that get called when the event is fired. Consider this implementation of a class using the `Events` mixin:

```
var Firework = window.Firework = new Class({

  Implements: [ Events ],

    fuse_lit: false,
    delay:    null,
    color:    null,

    lightFuse: function(color) {
        this.fuse_lit = true;
        this.delay    = $random(500, 5000);
        this.color    = color;

        this.fireEvent('burst', this.color, this.delay);

        $log("Fuse lit @ {time}, {delay}ms delay, color {color}".substitute({
            time: $time(), delay: this.delay, color: this.color
        }));

    }
});
```

Notice the use of the `.fireEvent()` method in the preceding code — this comes courtesy of the `Events` mixin class. The `.fireEvent()` method accepts as parameters the name of an event, an optional parameter to send along to event handlers, and an optional delay in milliseconds to wait before actually firing the event.

Now, take a look at how event handlers are attached with the `.addEvent()` method:

```
var rocket1 = new Firework();
var rocket2 = new Firework();
var rocket3 = new Firework();

function watchFirework(color) {
    $log("Saw firework @ "+$time()+" burst "+color);
}

rocket1.addEvent('burst', watchFirework);
rocket2.addEvent('burst', watchFirework);
rocket3.addEvent('burst', watchFirework);

rocket1.addEvent('burst', function(color) {
    $log("Also saw firework @ {time} burst {color} after {delay}ms".substitute({
```

```
        time: $time(), color: this.color, delay: this.delay
    }));
});

rocket1.lightFuse('red');
rocket2.lightFuse('white');
rocket1.lightFuse('blue');

// Fuse lit @ 1207749778446, 3040ms delay, color red
// Fuse lit @ 1207749778447, 1195ms delay, color white
// Fuse lit @ 1207749778447, 3731ms delay, color blue
// Saw firework @ 1207749779638 burst white
// Saw firework @ 1207749781482 burst red
// Also saw firework @ 1207749781485 burst red after 3040ms
// Saw firework @ 1207749782174 burst blue
```

The first three calls to `.addEvent()` connect a pre-defined handler function to respond when the "burst" event fires. The fourth call to `.addEvent()` connects an inline function, within which you can see that the value of `this` points to the object on which the event was fired. This facility will later come in handy in dealing with DOM events, but as demonstrated here it's a generic facility you can use to build event-driven code not limited directly to user interface happenings.

Providing Options and Defaults in Classes

Another useful mixin is the `Options` class. The `Options` mixin class offers the ability to establish a default set of options for an object, with an easy way to layer in user-specified values on initialization of a new object:

```
var NiftyThing = new Class({
    Implements: [ Options ],

    options: {
        rating:   50,
        color:    'red',
        duration: 1000
    },

    initialize: function(options) {
        this.setOptions(options);
    },

    describe: function() {
        return "[NiftyThing] " + JSON.encode(this.options);
    }

});
```

The `Options` mixin class provides a `.setOptions()` method that accepts a set of properties in an object or `Hash`. These are merged into the options property of the object. When called as part of the `.initialize()` method as shown in the preceding code, this makes for a quick and easy initialization process.

Now, take a look at this functionality in action:

```
var nifty1 = new NiftyThing();
$log( nifty1.describe() );
// [NiftyThing] {"rating":50,"color":"red","duration":1000}

var nifty2 = new NiftyThing({ rating: 100 });
$log( nifty2.describe() );
// [NiftyThing] {"rating":100,"color":"red","duration":1000}

var nifty3 = new NiftyThing({ rating: 25, quacks: false });
$log( nifty3.describe() );
// [NiftyThing] {"rating":100,"color":"red","duration":1000,"quacks":false}
```

If no options are given, the defaults are all used. In the second object instance, just the rating property is given, and so that value is used with defaults for the rest. In the third object instance, a default is replaced and a new property named quacks is merged in. Given these sample cases, you can see how the .setOptions() method handles each of these cases, merging defaults and user-supplied properties.

Building Method Call Chains

One more mixin worth attention is the Chain class, which becomes particularly useful later on for composing animations from sequences of method calls. Consider the following class definition using the Chain class:

```
var Poet = new Class({

    Implements: [ Chain ],

    reader_name: null,

    initialize: function(reader_name) {
        this.reader_name = reader_name;

        // Compose the method call chain
        this.chain(this.line1);
        this.chain(this.line2);
        this.chain(this.line3);
        this.chain(this.line4);
    },

    read: function() {
        // Call the next method in the chain
        return this.callChain();
    },

    line1: function() {

        // The scope of 'this' is the Poet object, no need for .bind()
        $log(this.reader_name + ': Mary had a little lamb,');

        // The return value here is passed along by this.callChain()
        return true;
```

```
        },

    line2: function() {
        $log(this.reader_name + ': Its fleece was white as snow;'); return true;
    },
    line3: function() {
        $log(this.reader_name + ': And everywhere that Mary went,'); return true;
    },
    line4: function() {
        $log(this.reader_name + ': The lamb was sure to go.'); return true;
    }
});
```

The `Chain` mixin provides two new methods. The first, `.chain()`, allows you to add methods to an internal list and the second, `.callChain()`, calls the first method in the list and removes it afterward. Two things to notice in particular: Methods in the chain are called with `this` pointing at the object instance to which the methods belong, and the return value from the method itself is passed along by the `.callChain()` method.

The following code demonstrates how the `Poet` class in the preceding code may be used:

```
var poet1 = new Poet('Alan Smithee');
while (poet1.read()) {
    $log('next line...');
}
$log('done!');

poet1.read();  // Nothing happens; the chain is empty.

// Alan Smithee: Mary had a little lamb,
// next line...
// Alan Smithee: Its fleece was white as snow;
// next line...
// Alan Smithee: And everywhere that Mary went,
// next line...
// Alan Smithee: The lamb was sure to go.
// next line...
// done!
```

Since each method in the chain defined by the `Poet` class returns the value `true`, the end of the chain is signified by the first instance where the `.callChain()` method call in `.read()` fails to return `true`. So, a `while` loop is sufficient here to process through the call chain. You could also set this up with an interval timer that cancels itself after the chain runs out.

Summary

This chapter offered an in-depth look into the MooTools Core, as well as how to get a copy of the framework in either release or developmental form and how to use it in your pages. The classes and extensions detailed here provide the foundation for the features to be detailed in the coming chapters.

In the next chapter, you'll start to see how MooTools employs all the basics from its core to ease manipulating the DOM and building user interfaces that respond to events.

32

Manipulating the DOM and Handling Events

By extending browser objects and DOM elements, MooTools augments the built-in capabilities of browser-based JavaScript with a host of convenient methods for finding and manipulating elements and handling native and custom events. This close integration with DOM scripting allows you to perform some very powerful page modifications and user interface construction with concise and minimal code.

Within the enhancements provided by MooTools, you'll find some convenient hooks for tying in your own augmentations within the framework.

In this chapter, you'll learn about:

❑   Finding elements

❑   Manipulating styles and properties

Finding Elements in the DOM

As you'll see in this chapter, MooTools offers a comprehensive and convenient toolkit for finding elements and negotiating the DOM structure of a page. To prepare for demonstrations to follow, consider the following markup:

```
<div id="div2">
    <h2>Some list</h2>
    <ul id="list1" class="first-list">
        <li class="foo">Foo</li>
        <li class="bar">Bar</li>
        <li class="sublist">
            <span class="baz">Baz</span>
```

```
            <ol>
                <li>Alpha</li>
                <li>Beta</li>
                <li>Gamma</li>
            </ol>
            <span class="zab">Zab</span>
        </li>
        <li class="xyzzy">Xyzzy</li>
        <li class="quux">Quux</li>
    </ul>
</div>
```

This markup provides enough complexity to show off a few of the tricks facilitated by MooTools.

Finding Elements with $() and IDs

The first and simplest DOM navigation tool offered by MooTools is the $() function, common to many other JavaScript frameworks, and used like so:

```
$log( $('div2') );
// <div id="div2">
```

In case you didn't see it in the previous chapter, recall that the $log() function is not provided by MooTools. Instead, it is defined as a shortcut to wrap console.log() statements.

Getting back to the code example, when called with a string parameter, the function $() is useful for looking up DOM elements by ID. However, the $() function can also be given an existing DOM element reference, acting as a pass-through operation returning the element basically unmodified:

```
$log( $( document.getElementsByTagName('div')[0] ) );
// <div id="div2">
```

Well, it's not entirely true that the element is left unmodified — there's an important distinction between using native browser and MooTools methods for fetching elements.

MooTools augments elements by providing a whole host of methods for dealing with DOM nodes and structure, sets up a handler to dispose of element references on page unload to prevent memory leaks, as well as creates a unique ID for element metadata storage.

This is where the second form of $() really comes in handy, offering a way to bring DOM elements acquired outside MooTools' methods into the toolkit's fold. If you're already mostly using MooTools' methods for DOM traversal, however, you usually don't need to think about this.

Finding Elements with $$() and CSS Selectors

The next useful function for finding elements is named $$(), and can be used like this:

```
$log( $$('li') ); // Only accepts tag names without Selectors
// [li.foo, li.bar, li.sublist, li, li, li, li.xyzzy, li.quux]
```

In its most basic form, the $$() function allows you to look up lists of elements by tag name. However, if you include the Element.Selectors module in your MooTools build, you can make further use of the $$() function to locate elements with CSS3 selectors, like so:

```
$log( $$('ol>li') );
// [li, li, li]
```

The implementation of Element.Selectors and $$() in MooTools do not support the full CSS3 specification, but they do support a large and useful subset. The following table provides a description of some selectors known to work with MooTools:

Selector	Purpose
*	Matches all elements
.class	Matches elements whose CSS classes contain 'class'
#foo	Matches elements with id="foo"
E	Matches <E> elements
E F	Matches elements <F> that are descendants of elements <E>
E>F	Matches elements <F> that are direct descendants of elements <E>
E+F	All elements <F> immediately preceded by an element <E>
E~F	All following element <F> siblings of elements <E>
E[foo]	Matches elements <E> bearing attribute foo
E[foo="bar"]	Matches elements <E foo="bar">
E[foo!="bar"]	Matches elements <E> with no attribute foo="bar"
E[foo~="bar"]	Matches elements <E> whose attribute foo is a space-separated list containing the value bar — useful for attributes constructed like CSS class names
E[foo^="bar"]	Matches elements <E> whose attribute foo begins with bar
E[foo$="bar"]	Matches elements <E> whose attribute foo ends with bar
E[foo*="bar"]	Matches elements <E> whose attribute foo contains bar
E:nth-child(n)	Matches elements <E> that are the nth child of the parent element
E:nth-child(odd)	Matches elements <E> that are the odd-numbered children of the parent element
E:nth-child(even)	Matches elements <E> that are the even-numbered children of the parent element
E:nth-child(3n+1)	Matches every third element <E>, starting with the first child.
E:first-child	Matches elements <E> that are their parent element's first child
E:last-child	Matches elements <E> that are their parent element's last child
E:only-child	Matches elements <E> that are their parent element's only child
E:empty	All elements <E> with empty text content
E:contains(TXT)	All elements <E> with direct descendant textnodes containing TXT
E:not(...)	Negates any of the above selectors

Using and Creating Custom CSS Pseudoselectors

The preceding table offers a subset of CSS3 selectors usable with MooTools, but the toolkit also offers a few additional pseudoselectors not defined by the specifications. These extended pseudoselectors are included in the following table:

Selector	Purpose
`E:index(n)`	Matches elements `<E>` appearing as the nth child of a parent element
`E:even`	Matches elements `<E>` appearing as even-indexed children
`E:odd`	Matches elements `<E>` appearing as odd-indexed children

Since these psuedoselectors are just implemented as JavaScript functions in a hash named `Selectors.Pseudo`, provided by the `Element.Selectors` module, it's not too hard create new pseudoselectors of your own. As a working explanation, consider the following:

```
Selectors.Pseudo.multicontains = function(text) {

    return text.split('|').some(function(part) {

        return (this.innerText || this.textContent || '').contains(part)

    }, this);

};
```

This code adds a new function named "`multicontains`" to the MooTools hash collection `Selectors.Pseudo`, which is part of the `Element.Selectors` module.

There's a lot packed into this handful of lines: The function expects to be called in the context of an element and accepts a pipe-delimited string. It returns `true` when the context element's text content contains at least one of the values in the pipe-delimited list. As a custom selector, you can use it like so:

```
$log( $$('li:multicontains(Foo|Bar|Quux)') );
// [li.foo, li.bar, li.quux]
```

The CSS selector parser in MooTools looks up the custom pseudoselector in the `Selectors.Pseudo` hash, extracts the parameter string, and calls the custom function to get a decision on whether or not to include any particular `<li>` element in the results.

Navigating the DOM Structure

Native DOM elements provide basic means to navigate the parent, child, and sibling relationships of the document tree. However, what's offered is just that: basic. Along with locating elements by ID and CSS selectors, MooTools provides enhanced methods attached to elements to allow easy traversal from one element to other single elements or groups of elements in the DOM structure of a page.

Consider that all DOM nodes offer a property named `parentNode` that points at the node containing the node in question. You can build loops that chase this pointer from node to node to traverse child-to-parent relationships all the way up to the root of the document.

With that in mind, take a look at the following code using the `.getParent()` and `.getParents()` methods offered by MooTools:

```
var ol = document.getElement('ol');

$log( ol.getParent() );
// <li class="sublist">

$log( ol.getParent('ul') );
// <ul id="list1" class="first-list">

$log( ol.getParents() );
// [li.sublist, ul#list1.first-list, div#div2, body, html]

$log( ol.getParents('div') );
// [div#div2]
```

As you can see, the `.getParent()` method returns a single parent element and accepts an optional parameter specifying a tag name as a filtering criteria. This method will continue traversing upward through the parent element hierarchy until it finds a parent matching the criteria — or return nothing once it's reached the root element of the document.

Accordingly, the `.getParents()` method returns multiple parent elements, traversing the document upward through parent elements and returning all that meet the specified tag name criteria (if any) along the way.

MooTools offers a full set of navigation tools such as the two mentioned earlier, which enhance the use of DOM navigation pointers already present on elements; each accepts an optional filter criteria and each traverses a different dimension or direction in the DOM structure, as described in the following table:

Method	Purpose
`el.getElement(selector)`	Finds the first descendant element matching the given CSS selector
`el.getElements(selector)`	Finds all descendant elements matching the given CSS selector
`el.getFirst(tag_name)`	Gets the first child element matching the optional tag name
`el.getLast(tag_name)`	Gets the last child element matching the optional tag name.
`el.getChildren(tag_name)`	Gets all child elements matching the optional tag name
`el.hasChild(child_el)`	Returns whether the given child is a direct child of the context element
`el.getParent(tag_name)`	Gets the first parent element matching the optional tag name
`el.getParents(tag_name)`	Gets all parent elements matching the optional tag name

Method	Purpose
`el.getPrevious(tag_name)`	Gets the first previous sibling matching the optional tag name
`el.getAllPrevious(tag_name)`	Gets all previous siblings matching the optional tag name
`el.getNext(tag_name)`	Gets the first next sibling matching the optional tag name
`el.getAllNext(tag_name)`	Gets all next siblings matching the optional tag name

Filtering Lists of Elements by Tag Name

Although it may be obvious, it's worth noting that all lists of elements returned by the methods and helpers described so far are basically JavaScript arrays. This means that all the usual array methods can be applied to lists of DOM elements — including methods such as `.each()`, `.filter()`, `.map()`, `.some()`, and `.every()`.

A more accurate statement, however, would be to say that lists of elements in MooTools are instances of a *subclass* of the built-in JavaScript array, named `Elements`. One enhancement offered by this subclass is that the `.filter()` method can either be used with a function implementing selection criteria like usual, — or it can be given a tag name like the DOM navigation methods described earlier, used like so:

```
$log( $$('*').filter('li') );
// [li.foo, li.bar, li.sublist, li, li, li, li.xyzzy, li.quux]

var eles = $$('*')
    .filter('li')
    .filter(function(el) {
        return el.getParent().get('tag') == 'ol';
    })
    .map(function(el) {
        return el.get('text');
    });
$log( eles );
// ["Alpha", "Beta", "Gamma"]
```

Throughout the rest of this chapter, you'll continue to see further array methods introduced by the `Elements` subclass, wherever some method appears capable of acting on both individual elements and lists of elements.

Manipulating Styles and Properties

Once you've got a handle on one or more DOM elements, it's time to actually do something with them. One of the first useful things you can do is manipulate the presentation styles, CSS classes, and other attributes and properties belonging to the elements. As you may have guessed, MooTools offers a broad suite of tools for doing all of those things and more.

Manipulating Element CSS Classes

Since CSS class names are specified in the class attribute of an element, you could simply use the native `className` property or maybe `.getAttribute()` and `.setAttribute()` methods to access and manipulate classes. However, since CSS classes are sets expressed as space-separated strings, there's potential complexity lurking even just to detect the presence of a single class:

```
$log( /\s?first-list\s?/.test( $('list1').className ) );
// true
```

For this exact reason, MooTools provides extension methods that take care of checking, adding, removing, and toggling members of a set of CSS classes. Consider the following MooTools' solution for the previous code example:

```
$log( $('list1').hasClass('first-list') );
// true
```

The `.hasClass()` method on elements accepts a string and returns whether or not that CSS class appears in the element's set.

Now, keeping in mind the markup presented at the start of the chapter, toss in the following CSS to offer a bit of style to play with in considering the rest of the CSS methods MooTools provides:

```
<style type="text/css">
    .bordered { border: 2px dotted #000 }
    .grayed   { background-color: #ccc; margin: 0.25em 0 }
</style>
```

The following code demonstrates how the `.addClass()` method can be used:

```
var first_item = document.getElement('ol>li');

first_item.addClass('bordered');

first_item.getAllNext().addClass('grayed');
```

The variable `first_item` is used to hold the first child of the first ordered list in the markup. On this element, the `.addClass()` method is called to add the CSS class "`bordered`" into its set. This, as defined in the CSS provided earlier, places a simple dotted border around the element.

The second application of `.addClass()` in this example is a bit more interesting: It's a call chained on the return value of `.getAllNext()` — which means that `.addClass()` can be called both on single elements and lists of elements. This is, by the way, another array extension offered by the `Elements` array subclass.

As you can see in Figure 32-1, the effect is that all following siblings of the first element are given the "grayed" class, which gives each a gray background color.

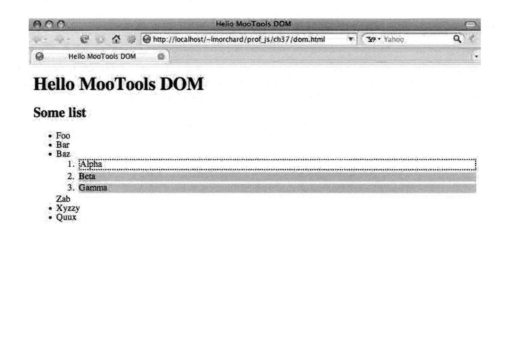

Figure 32-1

The inverse to .addClass() is the .removeClass() method, which is used like so:

```
$$('li.foo').addClass('bordered');
$$('li.foo').removeClass('bordered');
```

The net effect of the preceding two lines is nothing — the first line adds the class "bordered" to an element, while the second removes it. Note that .removeClass() is also usable in a list context just like .addClass().

Finally, as a complement to both .addClass() and .removeClass(), MooTools offers the . toggleClass() method for alternately adding and removing a CSS class:

```
var ele = document.getElement('li.quux');

ele.toggleClass('bordered');

var timer = ele.toggleClass.periodical(500, ele, [ 'bordered' ]);

$clear.delay(5000, ele, [ timer ]);
```

The preceding code first makes a straightforward call to the element method .toggleClass(). This is followed by the setup of a repeating timer toggling the "bordered" class off and on every half-second, until it gets canceled 5 seconds later with a second one-shot timer. If you try it out, this should easily show off the toggling feature visually.

Although Figure 32-2 is not animated, you can see that the final element in the list will receive the toggling treatment.

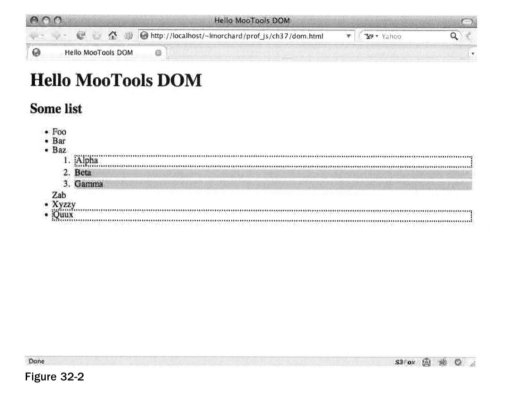

Figure 32-2

Manipulating Element Visual Styles

Although defining styles in a separate cascading style sheet and manipulating element classes is the cleanest and most loosely-coupled way to deal with visual styles from JavaScript, there are times when it's more convenient or necessary to manipulate the visual styling of elements directly. And, in this department, MooTools happily obliges with a set of handy extension methods.

The first of these is the .setStyle() method, which is used like so:

```
$$('li.bar').setStyle('font-weight: bold');
```

Like the .addClass() and .removeClass() methods shown in the previous section, .setStyle() can be called in either a single element or element list context. The effect of the preceding statement is to render bold text in list elements with a "bar" CSS class.

While setting one style on one or more elements is useful, it's often even more useful to apply a set of styles all at once. For this purpose, the .setStyle() method is accompanied by the .setStyles() method. This accepts a hash of styles like so:

```
$$('li.bar').setStyles({

    fontWeight: 'bold',

    fontStyle: 'italic'

});
```

The preceding code applies a combination of both bold and italic rendering to the text contained in all list nodes with a CSS class of "bar". This call can be very powerful, applying large collections of styles to a wide variety of elements, all in one efficient call. Also note that the keys of the style hash are expressed in camelCase rather than the hyphen-separated names of CSS — this is a fairly consistent conversion rule to allow the easy expression of style property named in JavaScript.

Now that you've set styles, it's also useful to be able to check what styles have been set for an element. For this, the methods .getStyle() and .getStyles() are provided:

```
$log( $$('li.bar').getStyle('font-weight') );
// ["bold"]

$log_json( $$('li.bar').getStyles(

    'font-weight',

    'font-style'

));
// [{"font-weight":"bold","font-style":"italic"}]
```

Using these two methods is pretty straightforward, considering the methods presented so far:

The first method, .getStyle(), fetches the value of a single style. If called for a single element, the value is a single string. If called for a list of elements, the return value is a list of strings listing style values.

The second method, .getStyles(), accepts a list of style names. If called for a single element, it returns a hash of named styles and their values. If called for a list of elements, the result is a list of hashes of named styles and values.

Manipulating Element Opacity

Although the transparency or opacity of an element is essentially just another visual style, it's one whose implementation varies enough between browsers to be a pain for how often it's called into use in fading transitions and animations. So, to help address this, MooTools offers a pair of methods to normalize access to element opacity:

```
$$('ol>li').setOpacity(0.75);

$log( $$('li').getOpacity() );
// [1, 1, 1, 0.75, 0.75, 0.75, 1, 1]
```

Like the `.setStyle()` and `.getStyle()` methods, `.getOpacity()` and `.setOpacity()` can be called on either single elements or in a list context. The value expected is a decimal number between 0 and 1, representing the degree to which the element should appear transparent (0) or opaque (1).

Manipulating Element Properties and Attributes

After CSS classes and style properties, the attributes in general are the next aspect of elements worth attention and enhancement. MooTools provides some interesting extension methods and cross-browser normalization to assist in this area, as you'll see in just a bit.

To start things off, consider this new sample of attribute-rich markup:

```
<div id="div3">
    <h2>Some form</h2>
    <form id="form1">
        <ul>
            <li>
                <label for="alpha">Alpha</label>
                <input type="text" id="alpha" name="alpha" value="Some value" />
            </li>
            <li>
                <label for="beta">Beta</label>
                <input type="checkbox" id="beta" name="beta" />
            </li>
            <li>
                <label for="gamma">Gamma</label>
                <input type="text" id="gamma" name="gamma" readonly="readonly" />
            </li>
            <li>
                <label for="delta">Delta</label>
                <input type="checkbox" id="delta" name="delta" checked="checked" />
            </li>
        </ul>
    </form>
</div>
```

Getting Element Property and Attribute Values

With the preceding markup in mind, take a look at this demonstration of the `.getProperty()` method introduced into elements by MooTools:

```
$log( $('alpha').getProperty('type') );
// text

$log( $('alpha').getProperty('value') );
// Some value

$log( $('gamma').getProperty('readonly') );
// true

$log( $('alpha').getPrevious().getProperty('text') );
// Alpha

$log( $('alpha').getPrevious().getProperty('for') );
// alpha
```

The `.getProperty()` method is very similar to the native `.getAttribute()` DOM method or accessing element object properties. In fact, what the `.getProperty()` method offers is a merged namespace, each property name mapped automatically to a DOM object property access or a call to the DOM object `.getAttribute()` method.

Property names handled as direct access to DOM object properties are defined as keys of the internal MooTools object `Element.Attributes.Props` — so you can produce a list for yourself like so:

```
$log( $H(Element.Attributes.Props).getKeys() );

["html", "class", "for", "text", "compact", "nowrap", "ismap", "declare",
"noshade",
"checked", "disabled", "readonly", "multiple", "selected", "noresize", "defer",
"value",
"accesskey", "cellpadding", "cellspacing", "colspan", "frameborder", "maxlength",
"rowspan", "tabindex", "usemap"]
```

Each of the property names listed by the preceding code is mapped to a DOM object property when `.getProperty()` is called. Additionally, a few of these MooTools properties get special internal handling beyond simple name mapping (see the following table).

Property	Mapping
`el.getProperty("html")`	`el.innerHTML`
`el.getProperty("text")`	`el.innerText` or `el.textContent`, depending on the browser
`el.getProperty("class")`	`el.className`
`el.getProperty("for")`	`el.htmlFor`, useful mostly for `<label>` elements.

There's also a subset of these properties that are handled as Boolean values based on whether a value exists. These are defined under the `Element.Attributes.Bools` object, so a list can be produced like this:

```
$log( $H(Element.Attributes.Bools).getKeys() );
["compact", "nowrap", "ismap", "declare", "noshade", "checked", "disabled",
"readonly",
 "multiple", "selected", "noresize", "defer"]
```

This is why, in the code example presented earlier, getting the `readonly` property resulted in a value of true rather than the literal value "`readonly`" attribute value offered by the markup.

Finally, if the property name given to `.getProperty()` fails to match any of the mappings described previously, the fallback is to call the element's `.getAttribute()` method. In the code example demonstrating the `.getProperty()` method, this is the case where the "`type`" property is fetched.

Getting Multiple Properties at Once

As a companion to the `.getProperty()` method offered by MooTools, there also exists a method named `.getProperties()`, which is useful for fetching multiple properties in one call:

```
$log_json( $$('label').getProperties('for', 'text') );
// [{"for":"alpha","text":"Alpha"},{"for":"beta","text":"Beta"},
// {"for":"gamma","text":"Gamma"},{"for":"delta","text":"Delta"}]
```

In this example, the `.getProperties()` method is called on a list of elements, thus fetching multiple properties for a set of elements all at once. The return value is a list of hashes, each hash offering the requested property names and respective values for each element in the list.

Setting Property Values

The complement to `.getProperty()` is the `.setProperty()` method attached to elements by MooTools, used to set property values like so:

```
$('gamma').setProperty('value', 'Another value');

$('gamma').setProperty('disabled', true);
```

Note that all of the property and attribute mappings used by `.getProperty()` apply here as well: The `html` and `text` MooTools properties are mapped accordingly, and Boolean properties like `disabled` are converted to Boolean values before assigning to element properties.

Removing Property Values

You can effectively remove a property by setting its value to null, false, or an empty string. However, a simpler way is to use the `.removeProperty()` method like so:

```
// Equivalent to .setProperty('checked', false)
$('delta').removeProperty('checked');
```

Again, like both `.getProperty()` and `.setProperty()`, all the property and attribute mappings are honored by `.removeProperty()`.

Building a Query String from a Form

Since the markup in the preceding example is a form, the `.toQueryString()` method offers one more trick to demonstrate:

```
$('beta').setProperty('checked', true);

$log( $('form1').toQueryString() );
// alpha=Some%20value&beta=on
```

After first ensuring that there's a checkbox checked to exercise it, the form's `.toQueryString()` method is called, which results in a query string based on the form's contents. One scenario where this method can come in very handy is in attempting to unobtrusively convert a form submit into a lighter-weight AJAX request, on which you'll see more details in Chapter 33.

Manipulating Extended Element Properties

The `.getProperty()`, `.setProperty()`, and `.removeProperty()` methods provided by MooTools offer a merged namespace of properties mapped to either DOM object properties or DOM node attributes.

However, layered atop these methods and others is a powerful and an even further abstracted property access system provided by the deceptively simple `.get()`, `.set()`, and `.erase()` methods.

Getting Extended Property Values

The `.getProperty()` method falls back to using the native `.getAttribute()` method when no mapping to a DOM object property has been defined. In a similar spirit, the `.get()` method falls back to using the `.getProperty()` method when no extended property is defined for a given name.

Thus, for most purposes, the `.get()` method can be used as a replacement for the `.getProperty()` method. The crucial difference, though, is that the `.get()` method is backed by a pluggable extension scheme that allows for the creation of new property handlers. These handlers are used instead of calling `.getProperty()`, so you may occasionally still need to call `.getProperty()` to get at the original property. If this is at all confusing, it will hopefully make more sense as you see the system in action.

Using the `.get()` method itself is pretty straightforward, as shown in this code example:

```
$log( $$('li').get('class') );
// ["foo", "bar", "sublist", "", "", "", "xyzzy",
// "quux", "", "", "", ""]

$log( $$('ol>li').get('text') );
// ["Alpha", "Beta", "Gamma"]

$log( $$('li>*').get('tag') );
// ["span", "ol", "span", "label", "input", "label",
// "input", "label", "input", "label", "input"]
```

The first two calls to `.get()` in the preceding code each result in `.getProperty()` calls, fetching the `class` and `text` properties respectively for lists of elements. The third `.get()` call, however, makes use of an extended property handler named `tag` to get the tag names for the elements in the list.

Although you'll see how to define your own extended property handlers very shortly, it's worth getting a sense for what extended properties are provided by MooTools modules. The following table provides a list of properties that are associated with the modules that provide them — by including the module in your build, the extended property is made available.

Property	Provided by	Purpose
style	Element	Gets and sets CSS styles
tag	Element	Gets the tag name of elements
href	Element	Gets relative URLs from an element
html	Element	Accepts a list of strings to concatenate as the element's HTML
styles	Element.Style	Maps to `.setStyles()` and `.getStyles()` calls
opacity	Element.Style	Maps to `.setOpacity()` and `.getOpacity()` calls
events	Element.Event	Maps to `.addEvents()` calls
send	Request	See Chapter 33 for more details on AJAX handling.
load	Request.HTML	See Chapter 33 for more details on AJAX handling.
tween	Fx.Tween	See Chapter 34 for details on animation.
morph	Fx.Morph	See Chapter 34 for details on animation.
slide	Fx.Slide	See Chapter 34 for details on animation.

To reinforce the difference between `.getProperty()` and `.get()`, consider the following markup:

```
<div id="div5">
    <a href="http://decafbad.com/">decafbad</a>
    <a href="/~lmorchard/prof_js/ch30/dom.html">this page</a>
</div>
```

Notice that there's an extended `href` property handler listed in the preceding table. This handler is used instead of `.getProperty()`, so the following demonstrates that each of these methods produces slightly different results:

```
$log( $$('a').getProperty('href') );
// ["http://decafbad.com/", "http://localhost/~lmorchard/prof_js/ch30/dom.html"]

$log( $$('a').get('href') );
// ["http://decafbad.com/", "/~lmorchard/prof_js/ch30/dom.html"]
```

The second link in the markup was declared with a relative URL, but the `.getProperty()` method returns an absolute URL — this is because of browser behavior in handing the `href` property. However, when `.get()` is used, the extended handler automatically strips the URL for the current page from the `href` value, thus converting it back to a relative value.

Setting Extended Property Values

The `.set()` method is the direct complement to the `.get()` method, honoring all the same property mapping characteristics describedearlier. You can use it to set a single property like so:

```
$$('#div2 .bar').set('class', 'grayed');
```

Setting Multiple Extended Properties at Once

Where the `.set()` method really shines, though, is in setting multiple properties all at once — especially when used with a list of elements like so:

```
$$('ol>li').set({

    // This falls back to .setProperty()
    text: $time() + '-' + $random(0,1000),
    class: 'bordered',

    // Uses Element.Properties.html.set()
    html: '<b>Hello there</b>',

    // Uses setOpacity from Element.Style
    opacity: 0.75,

    // Uses setStyles from Element.Style
    styles: {
        lineHeight: '1.5em',
        textAlign: 'center'
    }

});
```

In a sense, this use of `.set()` is the payoff for this extended property handler system. By supplying a simple hash of named properties and values, you can fire off a complex arrangement of handlers with a minimum of declarative code.

The simple `.set()` call in the preceding code causes several method calls to `.setProperty()`, `Element.Properties.html.set()`, `.setOpacity()`, and `.setStyles()` — all via a single unified and consistent interface that abstracts away those complexities and individual calls.

You'll also see that calls to the `.set()` method are embedded in other places, such as in the `Element` constructor and the `document.newElement()` method, thus further exploiting the elegance offered by the `.set()` method in manipulating elements.

Erasing Extended Property Values

Last but not least in this trio is the `.erase()` method. This operates very similarly to the `.removeProperty()` method, removing a property or attribute like so:

```
document.getElement('ol>li:first-child').erase('style');
```

But, again, the main distinction between `.erase()` and `.removeProperty()` is contained in the extension system powering `.get()`, `.set()`, and `.erase()`.

Creating a Custom Property Handler

Now that you've seen how the `.get()`, `.set()`, and `.erase()` methods use extended property handlers, it's time to take a look at how to define one of your own.

MooTools defines a hash collection named `Element.Properties`, whose keys name extended properties. The value for each of these keys is a further hash, which can bear keys named `get`, `set`, and `erase` — each of which is optional. Each of these keys, in turn, points at functions used by the `.get()`, `.set()`, and `.erase()` methods, respectively, to ultimately get their jobs done.

Better to show than tell, though, so consider the following example of a custom property handler:

```
Element.Properties.color = {

    get: function() {
        $log("get color called");
        return this.style.color;
    },

    set: function(clr) {
        $log("set color called");
        this.style.color = clr;
    },

    erase: function() {
        $log("erase color called");
        this.style.color = '';
    }

};
```

The preceding code defines a new custom extended property named "color", which supports all three of the extended property methods. Each of these methods expects to be called in the context of the element intended for manipulation. Also remember that each of these is optional: Any left undefined will fall back to the respective `.getProperty()`, `.setProperty()`, and `.removeProperty()` methods.

To see this new property handler in action, take a look at the following example code:

```
var item = document.getElement('li');

item.set('color', 'green');
// set color called

$log( item.get('color') );
// get color called
// green

item.erase.delay(2000, item, ['color']);
// erase color called
```

Since logging statements were included in the custom handler, you can see when the methods are called in your log transcript.

This ability to define your own property handlers in MooTools offers a powerful mechanism for extending one of the toolkit's core conveniences. Although MooTools provides means to manipulate just about any property you'd normally need, this system allows you to implement support for anything unusual you find necessary to handle.

Using Element Storage to Safely Manage Metadata

Speaking of handling unusual things, MooTools also provides a system called "element storage" for associating arbitrary metadata and objects with elements. This might seem superfluous since DOM elements offer the ability to set values on arbitrary *expando* properties, allowing you to stash away whatever you like along with elements.

The problem with using DOM expando properties, however, is that they're prone to causing memory leaks and other issues. For example, if you store a reference to an element in an object, then stash a reference to that object on the element, you've then created a circular reference that's not always handled gracefully by garbage collection when the user navigates away from the page — in other words, a memory leak. And then, there's the small matter of namespace collision with the existing properties belonging to DOM objects.

MooTools seeks to address these issues by constraining itself to a single expando property, named uid. This property is assigned a unique identifier whenever an element is first encountered by MooTools' methods, and is used as the key to a global hash. This global hash, in turn, can contain any arbitrary data at all. When the page is unloaded, MooTools then cleans up its own global storage hash, thus breaking circular references and preventing memory leaks.

So, having established the backstory, demonstrating the use of this element storage facility is very simple:

```
$('list1').store('database_id', '12345');

$log( $('list1').retrieve('database_id') );
// 12345
```

Each element is given `.store()` and `.retrieve()` methods, used for storing and retrieving entries in the global storage hash, respectively. The preceding code uses the key `database_id`, but you can use whatever string you like as a key.

Although you'll never need to do this normally, you can see a bit more into the machinery by checking out the unique ID assigned to the element like so:

```
var ele_uid = $('list1').uid;

$log( ele_uid );
// 3

$log_json( Element.Storage.get(ele_uid) );
// {"database_id":"12345"}
```

Each element is also given an `.eliminate()` method to clear the data for a key, used like this:

```
$('list1').eliminate('database_id');

$log( $('list1').retrieve('database_id') );
// null

$log_json( Element.Storage.get(ele_uid) );
// {}
```

MooTools uses this system extensively in its internal implementation, so you may benefit from its use as well.

In fact, rather than using the `.store()` and `.retrieve()` methods directly, you may wish to create new extended property handlers to integrate your special-purpose metadata needs into the core property handling system. Either way, this element storage system makes it easier to tie information and DOM objects to elements, all while avoiding common browser issues and memory leaks.

Modifying DOM Structure

So far, this chapter has shown you how to find elements with MooTools and then how to manipulate their properties once you've found them. Now it's time to examine how MooTools facilitates creating elements themselves and modifying the structure of the DOM.

Setting the stage for demonstrations, consider this short example of markup:

```
<div id="div4">
    <h2>Another list</h2>
    <ul>
        <li><span>First list item</span></li>
    </ul>
</div>
```

Creating New Elements

The preceding list is mostly empty, since one of the first things to investigate is how to create new elements with MooTools. One way to create a new element under MooTools is with the `document.newElement()` method, like so:

```
var item1 = document.newElement('li', {
    class: 'bordered',
    text: 'Second list item'
});
```

The first parameter to the `document.newElement()` method is the name of the element to create, followed by an optional hash. When supplied, this hash is used to call the new element's `.set()` method after creation, thus reinforcing the importance and power of the `.set()` method described earlier.

The internal use of `.set()` means that immediately upon creating an element, you can do a variety of things from setting the element's text and HTML contents to attaching events and setting CSS classes and styles. Of course, you can just omit the second parameter and manipulate the new element by other means, but this provides an elegant all-in-one creation and refinement step.

Along with the `document.newElement()` method, you can also create new elements by creating an instance of the MooTools `Element` class:

```
var item2 = new Element('li', {
    style: 'font-weight: italic',
    html: '<a href="http://decafbad.com">A link</a>'
});
```

The parameters for the `Element` constructor are basically the same as `document.newElement()`, including the optional hash parameter that will be supplied to `.set()` internally.

There's no real advantage to using one approach over the other, except that the `Element` constructor can also accept a native DOM element as its first parameter along with a tag name. So, a new `Element` instance can wrap an existing native DOM element, whereas `document.newElement()` cannot be used in that way.

Cloning Elements

Once you've created an element, cloning it is almost always the fastest way to get more of the same — especially if you need a lot of them. MooTools makes this simple:

```
var item3 = item2.clone();
```

Thus, if you need to build up a list or some other structure with a lot of similar elements, a good practice is to create an initial model element with `document.createElement()` or a new `Element` instance, and then create an army of clones from that initial model.

The `.clone()` method accepts two optional Boolean parameters:

❑   The first, when `false`, will prevent the recursive cloning of child elements. Otherwise, by default, the new clone will contain all of its original's contents, also all newly cloned.

❑   The second, when `true`, will cause the clone to retain the `id` attribute of the original. This attribute will otherwise be discarded by default in the clone, thus helping keeping the original's `id` unique.

The final caveat to note about `.clone()` is that data associated with the original in element storage is not copied along with the new element. All of native attributes are copied, with the exception of the unique element storage ID. Thus, the newly cloned element will receive a new element storage ID, but it won't get a copy of the element storage data from its original.

This has some interesting implications, since MooTools uses element storage to attach events and a few other housekeeping bits. So, you should only expect basic DOM features such as attributes and child elements to be carried over into cloned elements.

This really is a blessing in disguise as a limitation, since the construction of events and other objects associated with elements often have complexities and references to other elements that make construction from scratch much easier to deal with than an attempt at cloning.

Grabbing Elements

The next thing is to get this new element into the DOM structure of the page. One way to do this is with the `.grab()` method of an element that's already residing in the DOM:

```
var list = $$('#div4>ul')[0];
list.grab(item1, 'inside'); // see also: .grab{Inside,Before,After,Bottom,Top}
```

MooTools provides elements with a method named `.grab()` that, as its name suggests, grabs a given element and places it in one of several relative positions according to the optional second parameter:

❑   `before` — Previous sibling

❑   `after` — Next sibling

❑   `top` — First child

❑   `bottom` — Last child

❑   `inside` — Last child, the default and an alias for `bottom`

There are also named functions for each of these positions, which can be used instead of supplying a named position to the more general `.grab()` method:

❑   `.grabBefore(el)`

❑   `.grabAfter(el)`

❑   `.grabTop(el)`

❑   `.grabBottom(el)`

❑   `.grabInside(el)`

Using these partially-applied functions can be easier when creating delayed function calls or other less-than-usual cases where passing parameters may be challenging.

Injecting Elements

The inverse of `.grab()` is the `.inject()` method, by which you can inject an element into position relative to another element residing in the DOM:

```
item2.inject(list, 'inside'); // see also: .inject{Before,After,Bottom,Top}
```

Just like the `.grab()` method, `.inject()` accepts a target element as its first parameter and an optional string declaring the desired relative position. The following partially-applied versions of `.inject()` are available as well:

- `.injectBefore(el)`
- `.injectAfter(el)`
- `.injectTop(el)`
- `.injectBottom(el)`
- `.injectInside(el)`

Both `.grab()` and `.inject()` and their respective families of associated methods work together as an interesting set of alternatives to the `.appendChild()` and `.insertBefore()` methods offered by the native DOM. The same sorts of placements would involve multiple lines of element location and native calls.

Creating and Appending Text Nodes

Although you can manipulate the text contents of an element by using the `.set()` method, you can also handle text as DOM nodes with the method `document.newTextNode()`, like so:

```
var txt1 = document.newTextNode(' - some random text');
item2.grab(txt1);
```

These two steps can be combined into one with the `.appendText()` method:

```
item3.appendText('Prepended text - ', 'top');
```

Note that, like the `.grab()` method, `.appendText()` accepts an optional second parameter declaring the relative position at which the newly created text node should be placed — in this case, as the first child of the parent element.

Replacing and Wrapping Elements

Along with `.grab()` and `.inject()`, there are a few more interesting structural tools MooTools offers. With the tools shown so far, you can insert new content into the page, but the `.replaces()` method offers a way to swap one element out for another:

```
var new_title = new Element('span', {
    text: 'New sublist'
});

new_title.replaces(span1);
```

The .replaces() method accepts one parameter, an element that will be removed and replaced with the context element. The return value from this method is the context element, thus allowing call chaining.

Building on the .replaces() method, the .wraps() method can be used to place an element into a new parent and insert the new parent in place of the element — thus creating a new in-place wrapper for an element:

```
var span1 = $$('#div4>ul>li>span')[0];

var strong = new Element('strong');

strong.wraps(span1, 'top');
```

The .wraps() method first parameter is expected to be an element. The context element for which .wraps() is called becomes at once the replacement and new parent for this element. As you can see in this code example, you can use this method for things such as wrapping a text node or other element in a new formatting element or other container.

Adopting Elements

The .grab() method is great for getting new elements placed into a parent node one-by-one, but the .adopt() method offers an even easier way to add multiple children all at once:

```
var new_list = new Element('ul', {
    html: '<li>First item</li>'
});

$$('#div4>ul>li')[0].grabBottom(new_list);

var new_items = [ 1, 2, 3, 4 ].map(function(num) {
    return new Element('li', { text: 'Item ' + num });
});

var extra_item = new Element('li', {
    text: 'And one more item!'
});

new_list.adopt(new_items, extra_item);
```

In the preceding code, a new list is created and inserted as a new sublist. Then, a handful of new list items are created in a list using .map() on a list of numbers. A single element is also created in a separate variable. Both of these are passed as parameters to the .adopt() method of the new parent list.

The interesting thing here is that `.adopt()` accepts multiple parameters, which all can be either single elements or lists of elements. These are all flattened into a single list and then added as children to the context element. This offers a lot of flexibility in how you build list or single instances of elements, making it a single-step process to get all the elements into the page.

Destroying and Emptying Elements

The final two DOM manipulation methods left to describe are the `.destroy()` and `.empty()` methods, used to remove an element and remove its children, respectively.

The `.destroy()` method is used like so:

```
new_items[1].destroy();
```

This method removes the context element from the DOM and cleans up any associated resources MooTools knows about — including child elements and attached events and functions. Because of this extra cleanup, the `.destroy()` method is better to use than the native DOM function `.removeChild()` called on the parent node.

On the other hand, if all you want to do is clean out the contents of an element, you can make a call to the `.empty()` method:

```
new_list.empty();
```

This method basically applies the `.destroy()` method to each child node contained by an element. Note that `.destroy()`, in turn, employs the `.empty()` method internally to effect recursive cleanup on child nodes.

Attaching Listeners and Handling Events

All this work tweaking elements and manipulating the DOM structure is interesting, but it's not entirely useful until you can put it all into service building a responsive user interface. This is where MooTools' convenience methods for DOM event handling come into play, smoothing over cross-browser differences and simplifying the whole process of wiring up event listeners to elements.

Reacting to Page Load and Unload

Most browser-based applications start with the loading of the page. Since browsers support attaching handlers to page load and unload events, these are the most convenient points at which to begin initialization and to later clean things up, respectively.

Here's how to register handlers on page load and unload in MooTools:

```
window.addEvent('load', function() {
    $log("** window load event fired");
    $log(this == window); // true
});

window.addEvent('unload', function() {
    alert("** window unload event fired");
    alert(this == window); // true
});
```

There's not much to it — the `.addEvent()` method accepts the name of an event as its first parameter and a function to be called as a handler as the second parameter. The names "load" and "unload" identify the events of page load and unload, respectively. For each of these, the handler function is called without parameters in the context of the window object itself.

You can call `.addEvent()` as many times as you like to add as many handlers as you like. MooTools maintains internal lists in element storage, and calls them all with its own single real event listener.

Reacting to DOM Readiness

A bit more advanced than simple page load and unload is the point of DOM readiness. The page load event itself only fires after all images and embedded objects have loaded — but before the images have finished loading, the user will see the page appear and have a chance to start interacting with it.

The problem with this is that your JavaScript will not have had a chance to wire up user interface elements and perform other initializations and page tweaks before that point. And, depending on the number of images and other assets embedded on the page, there can be quite a delay until that happens. Thus, users will potentially experience an interface that is "broken" because it's not yet completed initialization.

However, as it happens, there's a point in the process of loading a page where page DOM has completed loading and is ready to be manipulated by JavaScript, even though there are images and other objects still loading. Detecting and acting upon this milestone in the loading of the page varies between browsers, but there is a way in most modern browsers to detect it.

MooTools offers a cross-browser implementation of this as a custom event that, at worst, works just like a window load event — but, at best, it catches the DOM at just the right point.

Explaining the concept is more difficult than using it, since MooTools makes it just as simple as a registering a window load handler:

```
// Requires Domready module
window.addEvent('domready', function() {
    $log("** window domready event fired");
});
```

The one caveat is that you must include the Domready module as part of your MooTools build. If you'd like to read more about the DOM readiness concept in general, check out this blog post by Dean Edwards, entitled "The window.onload Problem - Solved!":

```
http://dean.edwards.name/weblog/2005/09/busted/
```

Adding and Removing Event Handlers

Working with window load, unload, and DOM readiness events gives you a taste of MooTools' simplified event handing, but there's a lot more to explore. In preparation for demonstrations of MooTools' event tools, consider the following markup:

```
<style type="text/css">
    #ex1 .clickme {
        padding: 0.5em; margin: 0.5em;
        display: block; background-color: #ddf;
        border: 2px dashed #fff;
        color: #000;
    }
    #ex1 .clickcolor {
        background-color: #dfd;
        border: 2px dashed #000;
    }
</style>

<div id="ex1">
    <h2>Add / Remove events</h2>

    <a id="link1" class="clickme color0" href="#">Click me!</a>
    <a id="link2" class="clickme color0" href="#">Click me!</a>
    <a id="link3" class="clickme color0" href="#">Click me!</a>
    <a id="link4" class="clickme color0" href="#">Click me!</a>
    <a id="link5" class="clickme color0" href="#">Click me!</a>
</div>
```

The examples ahead will attach various handlers to the links defined in the preceding code, and offer some feedback by toggling CSS classes and styles.

Adding Event Handlers

MooTools' event handling tools are simple, which is great because they cover over a lot of cross-browser inconsistencies and oddities. The following offers a demonstration of how to hook up a quick mouse-click handler to a link element:

```
var first_handler = function(ev) {

    ev.stopPropagation();
    ev.preventDefault();

    var el = ev.target;
    el.toggleClass('clickcolor');

    $log('Click handler #1');
    $log( this == ev.target ); // true

};

$('link1').addEvent('click', first_handler);
```

Many of the major features of MooTools DOM event handling are demonstrated in the preceding code:

❑ The first parameter to the event handler function is an `Event` object, a custom MooTools wrapper that normalizes cross-browser event object differences.

❑ The `Event` object offers both `.stopPropagation()` and `.preventDefault()` methods, which cancel event bubbling and the default behavior of an event, respectively.

❑ Among the properties made available by the `Event` object, the `target` property gives access to the element directly involved in the event.

❑ The context of the event handler function is normalized across browsers to reflect the element on which the event was registered.

❑ Event handlers can be registered using the `.addEvent()` method given to elements, with the first parameter naming the desired event and the second parameter providing the handler function.

For an even more concise yet sweeping example, consider this code:

```
$$('.clickme').addEvent('click', function(ev) {

    ev.stop().target.toggleClass('clickcolor');

    $log('Click handler #2');
    $log( this == ev.target ); // true

});
```

Where the previous `.addEvent()` call was made in the context of a single element, this one is made against a list of elements — thus attaching the event handler to every element in the list.

In addition, both the `.stopPropagation()` and `.preventDefault()` method calls have been combined by using the shortcut `.stop()` method. Since this method returns the event object itself, the call can be chained to access the target element, which in turn allows a call to the `.toggleClass()` method. This is showing off a little, but it demonstrates some of the conciseness and power offered by MooTools.

Adding Multiple Event Handlers at Once

Even more powerful than adding one handler to a list of elements is adding a list of handlers to a list of elements, like so:

```
$$('.clickme').addEvents({
    mouseover: function(ev) {
        $log("Mouseover " + ev.target.id);
    },
    mouseout: function(ev) {
        $log("Mouseout " + ev.target.id);
    }
});
```

Where the `.addEvent()` method accepts a single event name and handler, the `.addEvents()` method accepts a hash of named handlers and can be called in the context of either a single element or a list of elements. This allows you to register a complex map of handlers to a wide variety of elements all in one go.

Furthermore, if you recall that one of the extended property handlers supported by the `.set()` method on elements was "`events`", consider that the following is possible as well:

```
$$('.clickme').set({

    html: '<strong>No, really click me!</strong>',

    styles: {
        color: 'green',
        border: '1px solid #ddd'
    },

    events: {
        mouseover: function(ev) {
            $log("Mouseover " + ev.target.id);
        },
        mouseout: function(ev) {
            $log("Mouseout " + ev.target.id);
        }
    }

});
```

Using the `.set()` method, you can register a set of event handlers in the same call that you perform tweaks on the properties, attributes, styles, and contents of one or more elements on the page.

Also, remember that the `.set()` method can be used in the construction of a new element, and so you can even register events at the time of element creation. It's hard to overstate that the `.set()` method is one of the most powerful aspects of the MooTools toolkit.

Adding Object Methods as Event Handlers

Up to this point, all of the functions attached as event listeners have been anonymous functions. But, often, it's useful to register the methods of objects as event listeners. The problem with this, though, is that MooTools automatically corrects the contexts of handler functions to reflect the element on which the events are registered.

For this reason, the `.bindWithEvent()` method on functions is offered to help retain the correct object context, ensure that the MooTools event wrapper is passed, and even allow optional parameters to be passed just like the `.bind()` method on functions. Consider the following code to see the method `.bindWithEvent()` in use:

```
var obj = {
    handler: function(ev, optional) {
        ev.stop();

        $log('Object method handler');
```

```
        $log( this == obj ); // true

        if (optional)
            $log("Optional parameter: " + optional);
    }
};

$('link3').addEvent('click',
    obj.handler.bindWithEvent(obj, "hello there"));
```

After running the preceding code, any clicks to the third link in the markup example will include the following messages in the log transcript:

```
Object method handler
true
Optional parameter: hello there
```

The value of `this` has been bound to the object to which the method belongs, and the optional parameter has been passed along with the Event object.

Cloning Event Handlers

Once you've assigned a set of events to an element, it's often faster and more convenient to just clone the arrangement onto other elements. MooTools facilitates this with the `.cloneEvents()` method like so:

```
$('link2').cloneEvents($('link1'), 'click');
```

After this code runs, all handlers attached to the first link will be copied and attached to the second link.

It's worth noting, also, that since the `.clone()` method for cloning elements doesn't carry over events, a subsequent call to `.cloneEvents()` can help remedy this shortcoming.

Removing Event Handlers

Finally, it's occasionally useful to remove event listeners after a certain point. There are two ways to do this — the first is to remove a specific handler for a specific event type with the `.removeEvent()` method, and the second is to remove all handlers for a certain event type using `.removeEvents()`. You can use these methods like so:

```
// Note that a reference to the function is needed
$('link1').removeEvent('click', first_handler);

// All click events removed, no references needed.
$$('.clickme').removeEvents('click');
```

So, if you have retained a reference to a specific handler, such as the `first_handler` variable, you can selectively remove one handler with `.removeEvent()` — note that there's no such thing as a `.getEvents()` method provided by MooTools to fetch attached event handlers, so retaining the handler reference is key.

After `.removeEvent()`, the call to `.removeEvents()` removes all `click` handlers for the list of elements. As with the other event handling methods, `.removeEvent()` and `.removeEvents()` can be called for individual elements as well as whole lists of elements.

Creating Custom Event Types

Before getting deeper into the realm of the Event object, there's one more trick offered by MooTools event handling, and that's the ability to define custom events based conditionally on existing native DOM events. This is perhaps best explained in code, so first consider the following markup:

```
<style type="text/css">
    #shift_listener {
        padding: 0.5em; margin: 0.5em;
        display: block; background-color: #ddf;
        border: 2px dashed #fff;
        color: #000;
    }
    #ex3 .clickcolor {
        background-color: #dfd;
        border: 2px dashed #000;
    }
</style>

<div id="ex3">
    <h2>Custom events</h2>
    <div id="shift_listener">Shift-click on me!</div>
</div>
```

Now, check out this code wiring up an event listener:

```
Element.Events.shiftclick = {

    base: 'click',

    condition: function(ev) {
        return ev.shift;
    }

};

$('shift_listener').addEvent('shiftclick', function(ev) {

    ev.stop().target.toggleClass('clickcolor');

    $log(ev.target.id + " was shift clicked!");

});
```

The first thing to notice is that there's a hash maintained by MooTools named `Element.Events`, which allows the definition of new named event types. These event types are themselves defined as hashes, containing values for the keys `base` and `condition` — the first, `base`, declares a real DOM event on which this event is based and the second, `condition`, defines a function which is intended to examine event conditions besides type to decide whether the custom event has fired.

Registering a handler for a custom event type actually results in a handler being registered for the declared base type, but it fires only when the condition function returns true. Thus, in the preceding code, a shiftclick custom event type is created, whose registered handlers will only be called in the case of a mouse click where the shift key is held down.

This mechanism is used internally in MooTools to offer a mousewheel event normalized across browsers, as well as custom mouseleave and mouseenter events that don't consider passing over or out of child element as leaving a parent element.

Investigating the Event Wrapper Object

The last part of the MooTools event handling system that's gone mostly without in-depth discussion so far in the chapter is the Event object wrapper passed to all event handlers. But, if ever there was an aspect of MooTools worth showing over telling, this is it.

So, this last part of the chapter is devoted to building the demonstration application previewed in Figure 32-3. The construction of this application will hopefully help explain what the Event object offers, as well as show what it offers once you see the code in action.

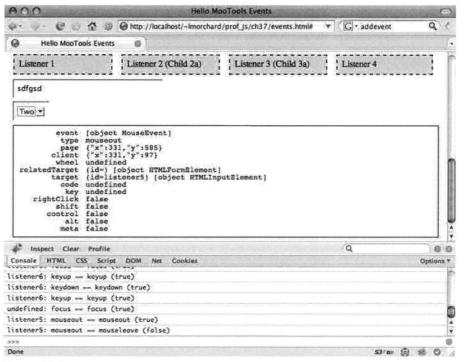

Figure 32-3

Constructing the Application Page

The first piece of the puzzle is the following chunk of markup, which provides sample elements and a framework from which to hang the demonstration:

```
<div id="ex2">
    <h2>Event wrapper</h2>

    <div id="listener1" class="listener">Listener 1</div>
    <div id="listener2" class="listener">
        Listener 2
        <span id="listener2a">(Child 2a)</span>
    </div>
    <div id="listener3" class="listener">
        Listener 3
        <span id="listener3a">(Child 3a)</span>
    </div>
    <div id="listener4" class="listener">Listener 4</div>

    <form>
        <input type="text" id="listener5" class="listener" size="30" />
        <select id="listener6" class="listener">
            <option>One</option>
            <option>Two</option>
            <option>Three</option>
        </select>
    </form>

    <dl id="listener_status"></dl>

</div>
```

The first few `<div>` elements and the `<form>` element on the page will provide anchors to which event listeners will be attached — notice that all of these elements bear a CSS class name of "listener", which will be used later in selecting elements for event handler attachment.

Appearing after these elements, the final `<dl>` element will serve as the information readout describing the state of events firing, in conjunction with the Firebug browser log.

Next, consider a few CSS styles to make the application a bit more attractive and compact:

```
<style type="text/css">
    #ex2 .listener {
        padding: 0.5em; margin: 0.5em; display: block;
    }
    #ex2 div.listener {
        background-color: #ddf; border: 2px dashed #333;
        color: #000; width: 20%; float: left;
    }
```

```
            #ex2 input.listener {
                clear: both;
            }
            #listener_status {
                padding: 0.5em; margin: 0.5em; border: 2px solid #666;
                font-family: monospace;
            }
            #listener_status dt {
                float: left; text-align: right;
                width: 18ex;
            }
            #listener_status dd {
                margin-left: 20ex;
            }
    </style>
```

These styles impose the layout, borders, and shading shown in Figure 32-3. The CSS is, of course, optional with respect to the functionality of this demonstration, but it should help fit everything on one page.

Preparing an Event Object Inspector

The next step in the demonstration application is to build some way of inspecting event objects when handlers fire. The following array lists significant properties offered by the MooTools Event object:

```
// Properties made available by Mootools Event wrappers
var event_props = [
    'event',                    // Native browser event object
    'type',                     // Type of event, normalized by MooTools
    'page', 'client',           // Mouse position in page and viewport coordinates
    'wheel',                    // Normalized to [-3 ... 3] movement speed
    'relatedTarget', 'target',  // Elements involved in the event
    'code',                     // Original which or keyCode from key event
    'key',                      // Events.Keys used for translation of key event
    'rightClick',               // Derived by MooTools from mouse state
    'shift', 'control',         // Keyboard modifiers
    'alt', 'meta'
];
```

The comments in the code should help describe what each of these properties is for, though their purposes will be even clearer once you're able to see events in action and check out the resulting values for these various properties.

The following code converts this list of `Event` object properties into a set of elements added to the `<dl>` element appearing toward the end of the application's markup:

```
// Inject status display fields for each Event property
var event_prop_fields = $H(event_props.map(
    function(name) {

        var label =
            document.newElement('dt', { text: name });

        var field =
            document.newElement('dd', { text: '...' });
        $('listener_status').grab(label).grab(field);

        // Note that MooTools purges all element wrapper
        // references on page unload, so this should be safe.
        return field;

    }
).associate(event_props));
```

As a definition list, this arrangement of dynamically constructed markup displays `Event` property names as terms and will soon be used to display values as definitions. The CSS styles provided earlier will present this as a two-column table.

This chained arrangement of `.map()` and `.associate()` method call adds the appropriate markup to the page — and results in a hash where property names are associated with the `<dd>` elements inserted into the page. This may be a little hard to follow at first, but it's a concise demonstration of the array and hash methods introduced in the previous chapter.

Note also that these element references in a hash are relatively safe from memory leak conditions thanks to MooTools' handling of `Element` objects and cleanup on page unload.

Building a Generic Handler to Inspect Event Objects

Now that you've got a nice and neat hash structure tying `Event` properties to DOM elements ready to display their contents, it's time to build an event handler that will do the job of populating these fields when events happen. Consider the following code for that task:

```
// Create a generic event handler to report on Event
var base_handler = function(event, expected_type) {

    // Update each status display field with Event properties.
    event_prop_fields.each(function(el, name) {

        var value = event[name];
        switch ($type(value)) {
```

```
            case 'element':
                // Display the ID of elements.
                value = '(id=' + value.id + ') ' + value; break;

            case 'object':
                // Show JSON for more complex objects.
                value = JSON.encode(value); break;

            default:
                // Coerce undefined and others to string.
                value = ''+value; break;

        }

        el.set('text', value);
    });

    // Report the event with a log message.
    $log(
        event.target.id + ': ' +
        event.type + ' == ' + expected_type +
        ' (' + (event.type == expected_type) + ')'
    );

};
```

The event handler defined in the preceding example uses the `event_prop_fields` hash constructed in the previous block of code to inspect an incoming `Event` object's properties one by one.

The type of each property value is checked to decide how to display it:

❑   Elements are represented by a string including the element's ID.

❑   Objects are converted to a JSON representation for readability.

❑   Every other type of value is simply coerced to a string.

Finally, once a suitable string representation of the value has been constructed, the text content of the associated inspector field is updated with the value. After this, a log message is constructed to report on the ID of the target element, the type of event, and the event type expected by the handler.

Overall, this handler has the effect of constantly updating the definition list with the contents of whatever `Event` objects are handled by it, as well as producing a running commentary on the event stream in the browser log transcript.

Creating Handlers for Specific Event Types

Now that there's a generic event handler created, it's time to produce handlers bound specifically to each kind of expected event type. This will help show the distinction between custom and native event types. It's also a handy excuse to list some event types known to be handled by MooTools.

Consider the following code, which employs .bindWithEvent() to bundle expected event type names with specific handlers:

```
// A subset of event types available for listeners/
var event_types = [

    'mouseup', 'mousedown',

    'click', 'dblclick', 'contextmenu',

    'mouseover', 'mouseout', 'mousemove',

    'mouseenter', 'mouseleave', 'mousewheel', // Custom event types

    'selectstart', 'selectend',

    'keydown', 'keypress', 'keyup',

    'focus', 'blur', 'change'

];

// Build a set of event handlers associated with types.
var event_handlers = event_types.map(
    function(type) {
        return base_handler.bindWithEvent(
            event_handlers, type
        );
    }
).associate(event_types);
```

As in the construction of the Event property inspector fields, this code uses the combination of the methods .map() and .associate() to convert a simple list into a hash of event handler functions based on the list of event names.

Attaching the Application Event Handlers

Finally, it's time to wire the whole thing up with events, like so:

```
// Finally, wire up the event handler set to listener elements.
$$('#ex2 .listener').addEvents(event_handlers);

// Stop the form from submitting.
$$('#ex2 form').addEvent('submit', function(ev) {
    ev.stop();
});
```

Using the convenient power of the .addEvents() method with a list of events and a handy hash of named event handlers, all of the elements with a class name of "listener" should now be wired up with every type of event contained in the event_types list.

Using the Event Object Inspector Application

The effect after all the above should be that interacting with the various elements provided in the markup will cause the Event object property inspector to be continually updated, while the browser log scrolls away with a record of the event stream.

This may be too much information at first, so you might want to selectively comment out some of the event types named in the event_types list to focus on a few at a time. But, as you interact with this page, you should be able to get a sense for what things the MooTools Event object can tell you about your interactions with the page.

You can watch coordinates change with mouse moves, see keyboard modifiers reported, and check out what elements are involved in various combinations of events. Also notice that when custom events fire, their expected types do not match the actual event types reported by the Event object.

This should help give you some idea of what you can do in your own applications with the Event object wrapper provided by MooTools.

Summary

In this chapter, you were introduced to the many tools and abstractions MooTools brings to easing the manipulation of elements and nodes in the DOM structure of a page, as well as wiring up event handlers to those elements and nodes to build responsive user interfaces.

Some of the major themes recurrent in these tools include concise and powerful expressions that can operate on large numbers of elements all at once, affecting complex arrangements of changes and event handler connections. All of the array, hash, and function methods presented in the previous chapter are built upon by the tools presented in this chapter to offer a lot of expressive power in a few short lines of code.

In the next chapter, you'll see how MooTools deals with the matter of facilitating AJAX and JSON requests and other forms of dynamic data requests.

33

Simplifying AJAX and Handling Dynamic Data

Each of the frameworks presented in this book offer slightly different approaches to dealing with AJAX — that is, firing off small web requests for new data after a page has loaded, using dynamic data to selectively update page content and interface elements without reloading the entire page from scratch.

The YUI and Dojo frameworks, for instance, offer a full-featured and verbose set of tools for dealing with various approaches to making requests and dealing with various data formats. On the other hand, Prototype provides a much simpler and straightforward interface that focuses on simple requests, rather than attempting to cover every possibility.

The MooTools framework offers something in between: The full range of same-domain web requests can be performed, along with just a bit of special handling for HTML content and JSON data. Page assets such as CSS, images, and additional JavaScript includes are easy to pull into the page, and extended element methods make it easy to update page content on the fly.

In this chapter, you'll learn about:

❑   Manipulating browser cookies
❑   Dynamically loading page assets

Manipulating Browser Cookies

While not always considered alongside AJAX and JSON data exchanges, cookies nonetheless provide an interesting mechanism for both sending data to the server on requests as well as retaining some data between requests to maintain state between pages on the client.

A relatively venerable mechanism in terms of browser support, cookies allow you to set name/value pairs with JavaScript that reside in the specially formatted `document.cookie` string. The name/value pairs set on the client are sent along with the next request to the server with a `Cookie:` header. Conversely, the server can include new cookie data for the client a `Set-Cookie:` header, and thus both client and server can communicate and maintain persistent state between them.

Although you may already be familiar with how cookies work, you can read more about them at the following URLs:

```
http://en.wikipedia.org/wiki/HTTP_cookie
http://wp.netscape.com/newsref/std/cookie_spec.html
```

Using Cookie Functions

One thing that makes dealing with cookies a bit of a pain is the specially formatted string found in `document.cookie`: Although it's basically a collection of name/value pairs, the data is encoded similarly to URL query strings. On top of that, there are a few bits of metadata available for each cookie to specify from where on the Web the cookie can be used and when it should expire.

MooTools offers a simple interface that takes care of these small complexities for you.

Writing Cookies

The following is the simplest way to write a cookie using MooTools:

```
Cookie.write('demo_cookie', $time());
```

This code sets a cookie named "`demo_cookie`" with the current time as its value. The default metadata options are used — which means that the cookie will expire when the browser is closed, and the cookie will be made available for the current page.

However, if necessary, you can supply your own values for the cookie options, using an object or hash as the third parameter like so:

```
Cookie.write('demo_cookie_2', 'value #2', {
    domain: 'localhost', // domain from which cookie accessible
    path: '/',           // path under which cookie accessible
    duration: 7,         // 7 days
    secure:    false,    // whether or not HTTPS is required
    document: document   // document for which to set cookie
});
```

The preceding code makes a few different choices with respect to defaults. The domain from which the cookie is made available is `localhost`, and any page from the root of the site on up will have access thanks to the value of path. Also, thanks to secure, there's no requirement that HTTPS and SSL be used, but you can set this to true to require an `https://` URL be used for access to this cookie.

Additionally, the cookie will last seven days with the given value of `duration`. Although there are many ways to express expiration time and date for cookies, they're often confusing and hard to remember. So, MooTools normalizes this situation by expecting a number of days from the current time — which is often what you want to do anyway. The downside is that the `Cookie.write()` function doesn't accept any other way to express expiration times, so you may face rare cases where this convenience becomes a hindrance.

Disposing of Cookies

Erasing a cookie is simple in MooTools as well:

```
Cookie.dispose('demo_cookie');
```

Note also that, just like `Cookie.write()`, the `Cookie.dispose()` function accepts options as its second parameter like so:

```
Cookie.dispose('demo_cookie_2', {
    domain: 'localhost', // domain from which cookie accessible
    path: '/',           // path under which cookie accessible
    secure:   false,       // whether or not HTTPS is required
    document: document     // document for which to set cookie
});
```

Notice that the `duration` option is omitted with respect to the `Cookie.write()` example. Disposing of a cookie is done by setting its expiration into the past, thus causing it to be automatically dropped by the browser.

Reading Cookies

Reading a cookie is even simpler than writing or disposing of them:

```
var the_value = Cookie.read('demo_cookie');
```

There are no options involved in reading a cookie — all of the details set along with writing a cookie determine whether or not a given cookie can be read depending on the page environment and expiration time, so all that needs to be done at the time of reading the data is to supply the name.

Using Cookie Objects and Methods

The `write`, `dispose`, and `read` functions provided by the `Cookie` module are actually just a convenient facade for the `Cookie` object defined by MooTools. You can use this object directly if you prefer:

```
var ck = new Cookie('cookie_obj_demo', {
    domain: 'localhost', // domain from which cookie accessible
    path: '/',           // path under which cookie accessible
    duration: 7,         // 7 days
    secure:   false,       // whether or not HTTPS is required
    document: document     // document for which to set cookie
});

var val_read = ck.read();
$log("*** Obj cookie value: " + val_read );
```

```
var obj_val = $time();
ck.write( obj_val );

$log("*** New obj cookie value: " + obj_val );

$log("*** Disposing of object cookie");
ck.dispose();
```

The main advantage of using the object-oriented interface over the functional equivalents is that you only need to set up the cookie name and options once, in the parameters to the object constructor. This can come in handy if you'll end up doing any complex logic to decide whether or how to write a value for a cookie, and want to prevent repeating the same options setup at every turn.

Using Cookie-Backed Hashes

Along with setting simple name/value pairs for cookies, MooTools also offers an interesting Hash subclass whose contents can be saved to a cookie either automatically or with a manual call. The utility of this class is limited to the amount of data accepted in a cookie — which seems to be around 4KB per cookie across browsers. But, still, this is plenty of room to do some interesting things:

```
var ch1 = new Hash.Cookie('hash_cookie_1');

ch1.set('alpha', 'foo');                    // cookie changed
ch1.set('beta', [ 'bar', 'baz', 'quux' ]); // cookie changed
```

The preceding code creates a new instance of the Hash.Cookie class, accepting all the same parameters as the Cookie object constructor. This new hash is initialized with any data available to be read from the cookie. After construction, the .set() method can be used to store data as with a normal MooTools hash — but the new special trick is that the cookie backing the hash is written to with every data change by default.

Notice that one of the values stored in the hash is an array. The chief advantage to using a cookie-backed hash versus setting individual cookies is that MooTools encodes all the data in the hash as JSON before updating the associated cookie. Thus, you can store structured data in a cookie without needing to do any kind of parsing or interpretation when you fetch it again.

Just to underscore what happens to the actual cookie value, try using Cookie.read() to take a look at what's stored, like so:

```
$log( Cookie.read('hash_cookie_1') );
// {"alpha":"foo","beta":["bar","baz","quux"]}
```

To illustrate a few more options of the Hash.Cookie class, consider the following code:

```
var ch2 = new Hash.Cookie('hash_cookie_2', {
    autoSave: false, // must call .save() before changing.
    duration: 2      // 2 days
});
```

```
ch2.set('alpha', 'foo');
ch2.set('beta',  [ 'bar', 'baz', 'quux' ]);

ch2.save();  // cookie changed
```

As mentioned before, the constructor for the `Hash.Cookie` accepts the same parameters as the constructor for the Cookie class, with the addition of an `autoSave` flag. When `false`, the cookie is no longer written to with each `.set()` call. Instead, a call to the `.save()` method is required for changes to the hash to be reflected in the cookie.

Turning off the `autoSave` flag can come in handy when you plan to perform a number of manipulations on the hash, before finally deciding on whether to update the cookie. It can also help save a small performance hit of a cookie update with every change.

Dynamically Loading Page Assets

Although you can include references to various JavaScript libraries, cascading style sheets, and images directly in your markup, it's often very handy to pull in new page resources after load in response to user interactions. MooTools provides a set of functions useful for this purpose, allowing you to load JavaScript and JSON feeds on demand, link new cascading style sheets into the page, as well as preload any single image or set of images.

Loading JavaScript and JSON Feeds

Like the Dojo toolkit, MooTools offers a way to load JavaScript modules and JSON data feeds on demand. Unlike the Dojo toolkit, MooTools does not make it a central feature of the framework, nor does it offer a dependency tracking system. MooTools simply offers a convenience function named `Asset.javascript()` that creates a new `<script/>` element in the head of the page.

Loading JSON Feeds with Callbacks

When loading a new JavaScript module or JSON data feed, it's very useful to perform some action upon completion of the resource load. One increasingly common way to do this depends on the server facilitating a callback parameter that causes a call to a client-side JavaScript function with the loaded data as a parameter, as shown in the following code:

```
var cb_name = 'feed_cb_' + $random(1, 1000);

window[cb_name] = function(data) {
    $log('*** Loaded ' + data.length + ' bookmarks');
};

$log('*** Loading delicious bookmarks JSON feed...');
Asset.javascript(
    'http://del.icio.us/feeds/json/deusx?callback=' + cb_name
);
```

In the preceding code, a unique name is created for a callback function defined to process the data from a JSON feed of bookmarks from `delicious.com`. The MooTools function `Asset.javascript()` is then used in conjunction with the callback function name to fetch the feed. When the feed is loaded, it will be wrapped in a call to the callback, which produces a log message with the count of bookmarks present in the feed.

The log transcript will offer messages like the following:

```
*** Loading delicious bookmarks JSON feed...
*** Loaded 15 bookmarks
```

As mentioned earlier, the mechanism behind this JavaScript asset loading is basically the addition of a new `<script/>` element to the `<head/>` of the page. You can use this to load up JSON feeds or additional on-demand JavaScript modules that weren't included in the markup originally.

Loading JSON Feeds with Load Checks

There's a little more to the story behind `Asset.javascript()`, though. Where callback functionality is not made available on the server — either because the data itself is a static file or the server's web API just doesn't support callbacks — MooTools offers the ability to detect the successful load of JavaScript code or JSON data. Consider the following code:

```
Asset.javascript(
    'http://del.icio.us/feeds/json/tags/deusx',
    {
        check: function() {
            return $defined(window.Delicious) &&
                $defined( Delicious.tags );
        },
        onload: function() {
            var tags = $H(Delicious.tags);
            $log('*** Loaded ' + tags.getKeys().length + ' tags');
            delete Delicious.tags;
        }
    }
);
```

When run, you should expect to see log transcript messages something like this:

```
*** Loading delicious tags JSON feed...
*** Loaded 4989 tags
```

As a second parameter, `Asset.javascript()` accepts an object or hash defining the properties `check` and `onload`. The first, `check`, is expected to be defined as a function that returns true once the desired JavaScript code has successfully loaded. The second, `onload`, is expected to be the definition of a function to be run when a successful load has been detected.

Note that some browsers define the `onLoad` event on `<script />` tags natively — for these browsers, a listener for that native event will be used to fire the `onload` function. However, for other browsers, a periodic call to `check` will be made until a successful load is detected.

Including Additional CSS Style Sheets

Consider a simple style sheet like the following:

```
body { font: 12px arial; }
```

If it were named `ajax.css`, you could load it with MooTools like so:

```
Asset.css('ajax.css');
```

This MooTools utility function, named `Asset.css()`, simply adds a new `<link />` tag to the `<head />` of the page to pull in the specified cascading style sheet on demand.

Controlling Style Sheet Include Attributes

Along with simply constructing and inserting the `<link/>` tag, `Asset.css()` also accepts some options for element attributes as a second parameter. Consider the following example:

```
Asset.css('ajax.css', {
    rel:   'stylesheet',
    media: 'screen',
    type:  'type/css'
});
```

Used in the preceding code are options basically matching the defaults. However, you could attach a new style sheet for a different media type (that is, `print`) or tweak the relation or content type attributes — though changing the `rel` or `type` values would depart from the function's named purpose in loading CSS assets and work instead as a general `<link/>` element injector.

Fetching Images and Image Sets

A common task in complex modern web applications is preloading images upon page load for use in user interface elements like rollovers and animations. While you can embed the images you need in markup, it's often more useful to decide on the fly what images you need and wait until they've all loaded before building the user interface, preferably displaying a loading message to keep the user appraised of how long before the application is ready for use.

Fetching a Single Image

For a quick demonstration of how MooTools enables you to fetch individual images on demand, consider markup including the following `<div/>`:

```
<div id="images"></div>
```

You can load an image for inclusion in this `<div/>` with MooTools like so:

```
var img1 = Asset.image(
    'http://decafbad.com/images/decafbad-title.gif',
    {
        onload: function(el) {
            $log('*** Image loaded ' + el.src );
            $('images').grab(el);
        }
    }
);

$log( img1 );
// <img src="http://decafbad.com/images/decafbad-title.gif">
```

The `Asset.image()` function accepts the URL to an image as its first parameter. The second parameter expected is an object or hash defining event handlers, with `onload` being the only one defined in the preceding code.

In this example, once the image has been loaded, an instance of an `<img/>` element referring to the image is passed to a call to the `onload` handler, which then uses the `.grab()` method to insert the image into the page content.

You can also define a few other event handlers, as shown in the following example:

```
var img2 = Asset.image(
    'http://example.com/nonexistent.jpg',
    {
        onload: function(el) {
            $log('*** Image loaded ' + el.src );
        },
        onabort: function(el) {
            $log('*** Image aborted ' + el.src );
        },
        onerror: function(el) {
            $log('*** Image error ' + el.src );
        }
    }
);
// *** Image error http://example.com/nonexistent.jpg
```

In the preceding code, the image URL should result in a failure, causing a call to the `onerror` handler with a reference to the `<img/>` element whose image was not found. The `onabort` handler also exists to handle cases where the user has clicked the browser stop button or otherwise aborted the load of this image manually.

Fetching Sets of Images

Loading an image on demand is useful. But, if a user interface needs to use one image, there's usually a whole pile of them that needs to be loaded. Setting up a fetch for each one would be tedious, so MooTools also offers a mechanism for preloading and tracking an entire list of image URLs with the `Asset.images()` function.

Consider the following code demonstrating the use of `Asset.images()`:

```
var imgs = Asset.images(
    [1, 2, 3, 4, 5, 6, 7, 8, 9].map(function(n) {
        return 'http://decafbad.com/images/coffee-stains-'+n+'.gif'
    }),
    {
        onProgress: function(counter, idx) {
            // The function context is the image element.
            $('images').grab(this);

            $log(
                "*** Loaded #" + idx + ", " + (counter + 1) + " so far, "
                + this.src
            );
        },

        onComplete: function() {
            $log("*** Completed all images!");
        }
    }
);
```

In the preceding code, the `.map()` array method is used to construct a quick list of numbered image URLs, supplied as the first parameter to the `Asset.images()` function. The second parameter is an object or hash defining event handlers called during the process of loading the images. The first of these handlers, named `onProgress`, is called each time one of the images in the set has successfully loaded. The second, `onComplete`, is called once the full set has finished loading.

As defined in the previous example, log transcript messages something like these should appear:

```
*** Loaded #4, 1 so far, http://decafbad.com/images/coffee-stains-5.gif
*** Loaded #2, 2 so far, http://decafbad.com/images/coffee-stains-3.gif
*** Loaded #5, 3 so far, http://decafbad.com/images/coffee-stains-6.gif
*** Loaded #0, 4 so far, http://decafbad.com/images/coffee-stains-1.gif
*** Loaded #7, 5 so far, http://decafbad.com/images/coffee-stains-8.gif
*** Loaded #1, 6 so far, http://decafbad.com/images/coffee-stains-2.gif
*** Loaded #3, 7 so far, http://decafbad.com/images/coffee-stains-4.gif
*** Loaded #6, 8 so far, http://decafbad.com/images/coffee-stains-7.gif
*** Loaded #8, 9 so far, http://decafbad.com/images/coffee-stains-9.gif
*** Completed all images!
```

The interesting things about the call to the `onProgress` event handler include the following:

❑ The context variable, `this`, is set to point at the `<img/>` element representing the image that's finished loading. In the previous example, this is used to add the image to the page content.

❑ The first parameter, `counter`, indicates progress in how many images have loaded so far, starting at zero.

❑ The second parameter, `idx`, indicates which image in the list supplied to `Asset.images()` was just loaded.

Using Firebug, you can see the resulting network requests for these additional images, as shown in Figure 33-1.

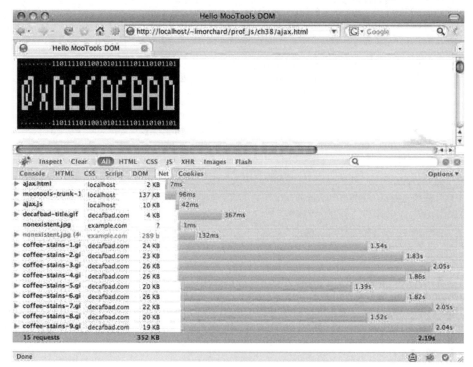

Figure 33-1

On initial load, the images can arrive in any random order, as shown in the log transcript. After that first load, the images should be cached locally, and so they usually arrive in the same order as they were loaded. Either way, this is where the `counter` parameter comes in handy, because you can't count on the order of the images as originally supplied to determine how close to completion things are.

Making Web Requests

Manipulating cookies and fetching page resources on demand is quite useful, but a modern web application can't claim to be fully buzzword-compliant without the use of the highly versatile XmlHTTPRequest object to make same-domain AJAX web requests in offering a responsive and data-driven user interface.

MooTools offers a very lightweight but sufficient cross-browser interface for making on-demand web requests, including a few special MooTools-flavored shortcuts to incorporating dynamic content fetched via AJAX in your pages.

Performing Basic Web Requests

MooTools offers the `Request` class for use in making basic web requests. When creating a new instance of `Request`, a single hash or object parameter is expected as definition of options to use in constructing the object. Consider the following example of a simple HTTP GET request:

```
var req1 = new Request({
    method: 'GET',
    url:     'data1.txt',

    onRequest: function() {
        $log("*** Firing request for " + this.options.url);
    },
    onSuccess: function(result_text, result_xml) {
        $log("*** Loaded " + this.options.url);
        $log("*** Data: " + result_text);
    },
    onFailure: function() {
        $log("*** Request failed: " + this.status);
    },
    onException: function() {
        $log("*** Exception occurred!");
        $log(arguments);
    }
});

req1.send();
```

With this example, the log transcript will offer messages such as the following for a successful request:

```
*** Firing request for data1.txt
*** Loaded data1.txt
*** Data: Hello there, have some sample data!
```

The first two options to the `Request` constructor supply the URL ("`data1.txt`") and HTTP method ("`GET`") for the request, and the rest of the options define event handlers for the request:

❑   `onRequest` — Fired when the request is sent, which doesn't happen until the `.send()` method is called.

❑   `onSuccess` — Called when the request completes successfully. The text and/or XML data sent back in the response are given as parameters to the handler.

❑   `onFailure` — Called if the request completes unsuccessfully. This occurs if the request resulted in a 404 Not Found or other HTTP error status code.

❑   `onException` — Called if any JavaScript exception occurred as part of processing the request or response.

Note that for each of these event handlers, the context variable `this` points at the `Request` object, as if the event handlers were methods of the object itself. As you can see in the event handlers, this gives access to things beyond the handler parameters, like the HTTP status code and initial options given to the object constructor.

Using Event Listeners with Web Requests

Whereas the previous code example constructs an HTTP request and its handlers all in one shot, you can piece things together more incrementally using event listeners and HTTP object methods like so:

```
var req2 = new Request()
    .addEvent('success', function(txt, xml) {
        $log("*** Data loaded: " + txt);
    })
    .addEvent('failure', function() {
        $log("*** Request failed: " + this.status);
    });

req2.addEvent('success', function(txt, xml) {
    $log("*** Me too! Data loaded: " + txt);
});

req2.GET('data1.txt', { /* options */ })

/* req.{get,post,GET,POST,PUT,DELETE}() */
```

In the log transcript, you can expect to see messages such as the following upon running this code:

```
*** Data loaded: Hello there, have some sample data!
*** Me too! Data loaded: Hello there, have some sample data!
```

Notice that the `Request` object is created in the preceding example without any options supplied to the constructor. This results in a generic instance to which you can attach event handlers for any of the `request`, `success`, `failure`, and `exception` events just as if they were native DOM events on an element.

Note also that you can attach multiple handlers to the same event, as demonstrated by the second handler attached to the `success` event.

Finally, the `Request` can be sent with a call to the `.GET()` method. There are `Request` object methods corresponding to each of the HTTP methods `GET`, `POST`, `PUT`, and `DELETE`. The expected parameters to these methods are the URL for the request, followed by an optional hash or object containing the options that would have otherwise been supplied to the object constructor.

Since only the URL, HTTP method, and event handlers have been shown as options so far, the options hash is empty in the previous example — but you'll see what additional options are available in the next sections.

Sending Headers and Request Data

Up to this point, the examples using `Request` have only dealt with simple URLs, HTTP methods, and event handlers. But, there's more to an HTTP request than that: You can supply both headers and additional data in the body of the request. Beyond that, MooTools offers a few more special features in handling both the HTTP request and response.

Consider this example showcasing additional features for the `Request` object:

```
var req3 = new Request({
    url: 'echo.php',
    method: 'PUT',
    emulation: false, // default true
    urlEncoded: false, // default true
    encoding: 'utf-8',
    data: 'This is some sample data!',
    headers: {
        'Content-Type': 'text/plain',

        'X-Alpha': 'foo',
        'X-Beta': 'bar',
        'X-Gamma': 'baz'
    },
    onSuccess: function(txt, xml) {
        $log("*** Text: " + txt);
        $log(xml);
    }
});
req3.send();
```

The first option, url, is set to "echo.php" — this is intended to be used with a request echo script such as the one offered back in Chapter 27 under the section "Building a Server-Side Request Echo Tool." You can build one of your own, but the basic idea is that the script produces a response whose content reports on the request it received. This can help you investigate what happens in HTTP requests made by MooTools, as well as any other framework.

The second and third options, method and emulation, are somewhat related: The HTTP method in this example is set to "PUT", which is a valid HTTP method in the specifications — yet not all browsers support the HTTP PUT method. Thus, when the emulation flag is set to true — as it is by default — the HTTP method actually used in the request is switched to "POST". Then, the method originally desired is included by adding a parameter such as the following to the start of request data:

```
_method=PUT&
```

Of course, to properly use this emulation hack, the application on the server side must support the convention by honoring the _method parameter in HTTP POST requests as the true intended method. Additionally, the request data must be in URL-encoded format as if it were submitted from a form — something that precludes the use of raw data in the request.

The urlEncoded option, true by default, will set the Content-Type header in the request to application/x-www-form-urlencoded, as well as include the value of encoding in the header. These defaults generally work for AJAX-style form submission — a very common scenario — but they need to be tweaked as in the preceding example code if you want to send raw data.

This example supplies the urlEncoded option with a value of false, along with raw text supplied using the option named data. This, of course, conflicts with the use of the emulation flag.

Submitting a Form via AJAX

Since many of the default options in the Request object seem geared toward facilitating AJAX-style form submissions, it might be useful to offer a demonstration of how such a thing might work with MooTools.

First, consider the following markup establishing a form for AJAX submission:

```
<div id="ex_form" class="form_widget">

    <form method="put" action="echo.php?type=text">

        <label for="foo">Foo</label>
        <input type="text" name="foo" id="foo" />
        <br />

        <label for="bar">Bar</label>
        <input type="text" name="bar" id="bar" />
        <br />

        <input type="submit" value="submit this form!" />

    </form>

    <div class="results">
        <pre></pre>
        <a href="#">Reset form</a>
    </div>

</div>
```

This markup establishes a sort of quasi-widget consisting of a simple form and a results section to confirm the form submission by displaying what the server returns from a successful request.

Next, consider the following CSS styles for use with this markup:

```
<style type="text/css">
    .form_widget  .results { display: none }
    .show_results form     { display: none }
    .show_results .results { display: block }
</style>
```

When initially displayed, the widget will show only the form itself. After successful form submission, adding the CSS class "show_results" will hide the form and reveal the results confirmation and the form reset link.

Now, it's time to wire up all of the above with code to give it the desired functionality:

```
function ajaxifyFormWidget(widget_id) {

    // Wire up the form submission with AJAX instead of native submit.
    $$("#"+widget_id+" form")
        .addEvent('submit', function(ev) {

            // Intercept the usual form submission process.
            ev.stop();
```

This first chunk of code begins the definition of a function named `ajaxifyFormWidget()`, which accepts an element ID as the basis for building its event handlers. The first thing it does is it builds a handler to intercept the `submit` event of the form in the widget.

Continuing on with the implementation of this function, the following introduces the desired AJAX form submission code:

```
// Set Request options for the form AJAX request
this.set('send', {

    onSuccess: function(txt) {

        // Swap classes to hide the form and show results.
        $$('#'+widget_id).addClass('show_results');

        // Populate the results with server response content.
        $$('#'+widget_id+' .results pre').set('text', txt);

    }

}).send();

});
```

This is new and interesting: Thanks to an extended property handler provided by the `Request` module, the "send" property supported on form elements creates an implicit `Request` object with the given options. For what it's worth, this implicit `Request` object resides in element storage, a feature introduced in the previous chapter.

If not otherwise supplied in explicit options, the `url` and `method` options for the implicit `Request` object are automatically derived from the form's `action` and `method` attributes in markup, respectively. The `data` option for the Request object is supplied as a reference to the form element itself.

Since the form element itself is passed as the `data` option, the `.send()` method of `Request` will automatically use the form's `.toQueryString()` method. This gets the content of the form's fields encoded as a query string ready for submission to the server. It's also worth noting that if an arbitrary object is supplied for the `data` option, MooTools uses the `.toQueryString()` method of the `Hash` class.

The `onSuccess` handler supplied to the `Request` object adds the "show_results" class to the widget, thereby hiding the form and revealing the results section. After this, the results section is populated with the text response from the server, thus providing feedback on what happened in the request.

Along with the "send" property, elements also support a `.send()` method. When called, the element method in turn calls the `.send()` method of the `Request` object created implicitly by the extended property handler.

So, directly after constructing the options for the implicit `Request` object in the preceding code, the element's `.send()` object is called to fire off the AJAX request.

Wrapping things up, the following finishes off ajaxifyFormWidget() and puts it to use:

```
// On click of the reset form link, swap back to form display.
$$("#"+widget_id+" .results a")
    .addEvent('click', function(ev) {
        $$('#'+widget_id).removeClass('show_results');
    });

}

ajaxifyFormWidget('ex_form');
```

The final thing done in the ajaxifyFormWidget() function is to wire up the "reset form" link. This link is part of the results section revealed with a successful form submission. When clicked, the event handler attached in the preceding code removes the "show_results" class on the widget, thus hiding the results and again revealing the form for another try.

Then, with the completion of ajaxifyFormWidget(), the function is called with the ID "ex_form" used in the markup provided earlier. This gets the form widget all set up and ready to use.

If you're using the echo.php script from Chapter 27, entering some data into the form and submitting it should yield results something like the following:

```
array (
  'method' => 'POST',
  'post_params' =>
  array (
    '_method' => 'put',
    'foo' => 'sadf asdf as',
    'bar' => 'as dfasd f',
  ),
  'query_params' =>
  array (
    'type' => 'text',
  ),
  'x_requested_with' => 'XMLHttpRequest',
  'content_type' => 'application/x-www-form-urlencoded; charset=utf-8',
  'content_length' => '51',
  'request_body' => '_method=put&foo=sadf%20asdf%20as&bar=as%20dfasd%20f',
)
```

Some interesting things to notice from the details reported on the request include:

❑ The X-Requested-With header was set to XMLHttpRequest by MooTools, allowing you to detect AJAX-based requests on the server side and thus automatically alter the kind of content sent back in response.

❑ The Content-Type header was set to application/x-www-form-urlencoded, thanks to the urlEncoded option default value of true.

❑ The request body data came through as URL-encoded thanks to the form's .toQueryString() method.

❑ Thanks to the default value of `true` for the option `emulation`, the request was sent with the HTTP method POST instead of the PUT method as specified in markup. Also, the request body data was prepended with "`_method=put&`" to indicate the original HTTP method.

Submitting a form via AJAX in MooTools is very simple, and thanks to extended properties and methods is actually integrated right into the form element itself. In fact, notice that the bulk of the code here was involved in setting up the user interface for the form, rather than in building the AJAX request based on a form.

Loading and Executing JavaScript

There are two more interesting options made available by `Request`, both of which safely default to a value of `false`, and both of which deal with the automatic execution of JavaScript in response content:

❑ `evalResponse` — When `true`, executes the entire contents of the response body as JavaScript.

❑ `evalScripts` — When `true`, extracts any `<script/>` tags found in the response body and executes their contents as JavaScript code.

So, for example, consider a file named "`data1.js`" with the following contents:

```
alert("hello world!");
```

Then, consider the following code used to fetch the preceding content:

```
var req_js = new Request({
    method: 'get',
    url:            'data1.js',
    evalResponse: true,
});
req_js.send();
```

This would result in an alert message of "hello world!" upon a successful fetch.

Next, consider the following file named "`data2.html`":

```
<script>alert("hello world!");</script>

This is some sample content.
```

The following code used to fetch this file would also result in a "hello world!" alert message:

```
var req_js2 = new Request({
    method: 'get',
    url:            'data2.html',
    evalScripts:  true,
    onSuccess:    function(txt) {
        $log("content fetched was " + txt);
    }
});
req_js2.send();
```

However, the `evalScripts` flag also causes the executed scripts to be stripped from the resulting content. Thus, the following message would appear in the log when `onSuccess` is executed:

```
content fetched was This is some sample content.
```

Notice that the `<script/>` tag content is missing from the text data supplied to the `onSuccess` event handler.

Fetching and Updating HTML Content

One of the things done in the AJAX form submission example was to update the contents of an element on the page with text contents. Somewhat related to this, MooTools offers a `Request` subclass named `Request.HTML` that makes it easy to update the content of any element on the page with content fetched on demand via AJAX.

Using Element Methods to Update Content

Consider the following markup on a page:

```
<div id="content"></div>
```

Next, consider the following markup made available under the URL "`data.html`":

```
<script>alert("Script executed!");</script>
<div>
    <h2>Some headline</h2>
    <p>Here is some sample text!</p>
</div>
```

The easiest way to get the contents of "`data.html`" inserted into the previous `<div/>` on demand is with the `.load()` element method like so:

```
$('content').load('data.html');
```

This call to `.load()` creates an instance of `Request.HTML`, fires off a request for the URL supplied, and injects the content from a successful request into the context element.

However, if you try this, you'll notice a call to `.load()` does more than just insert content into the page: The code in the `<script/>` tag is executed as well, producing an alert message. As mentioned earlier, the execution of scripts found in responses is thanks to the `evalScripts` option understood by the `Request` class. What's new here is that the `Request.HTML` subclass flips the `evalScripts` flag to `true` by default.

So, behind the scenes, an instance of `Request.HTML` is used in the element `.load()` method. As a subclass of `Request`, this object accepts all the options of `Request` and a few more. The following expanded example shows how you can set some of these options before firing off the request to load content:

```
$('content').set({
    load: {
        url:        'data.html',
```

```
            method: 'post',
            filter: 'p',
            evalScripts: false
    }
});

$('content').load();
```

An element property named "load" can be manipulated with the .set() method, establishing the options to be used in the Request.HTML object that's created in the subsequent call to the .load() method. The options usable here include all of those understood by the superclass Request, with some additions and changes to defaults:

❑ filter — When HTML in the response is parsed into DOM elements, apply this CSS selector filter to the results.

❑ evalScripts — Defaulting to true in Request.HTML, this option causes the execution of <script/> tags present in the response.

Thus, in the previous example, the alert message will no longer occur, and only the paragraph element from the HTML loaded will be injected into the page.

Fetching HTML and JavaScript Content

After seeing the Request.HTML object put to use behind the scenes, it's time to take a look at the object in a more center-stage role. Consider the following code example:

```
var req1 = new Request.HTML({

    url:        'data.html',
    evalScripts: false,

    onSuccess: function(tree, elements, txt, js) {
        $log('Document: ' + tree);
        $log('Elements: ' + elements.length);
        $log('Text: ' + text);
        $log('JS: ' + js);
    }

});
req1.send();
```

And, once executed, this code will produce a log transcript like the following:

```
Document: [object NodeList]
Elements: 3
Text:
<div>
    <h2>Some headline</h2>
    <p>Here is some sample text!</p>
</div>
JS: alert("Script executed!");
```

781

The parameters supplied to the onSuccess handler are changed with respect to what the superclass Request does. These new parameters are as follows:

- ❏ tree — A document fragment representing the parsed HTML structure of the content fetched
- ❏ elements — A flat list of all the elements found in the HTML content, suitable for filtering
- ❏ text — Raw text content from the response, including HTML tags, but not script tags
- ❏ js — JavaScript code stripped from <script/> tags, which would be executed if evalScripts is true

As you can see, these revised parameters are a bit more useful for HTML content, which is automatically parsed into DOM nodes behind the scenes when it's loaded.

Updating Content with a Request Object

Whereas the combination of .set() and .load() for an element uses a Request.HTML object implicitly behind the scenes, the following code makes that usage explicit:

```
var req2 = new Request.HTML({
    url:            'data.html',
    update:         $('content'),
    filter: 'p',
    evalScripts: false
});
req2.GET();
```

This code does basically the same thing as the .set() and .get() example shown earlier: Content is loaded from the URL 'data.html', the content is parsed as HTML, the HTML is filtered for <p> elements, and the filtered elements are used to replace the contents of the element with an ID of 'content'.

You've seen the new filter option before, which applies a filter to the list of elements found in the parsed HTML. What's new is the update option, which basically does the same thing as calling .load() on the supplied element: The element's contents are replaced by the document fragment loaded and parsed from the server response body.

Requesting and Using JavaScript and JSON Data

While it's true that you can fetch JavaScript and JSON resources from third-party domains using script tags injected into the header via the Asset.javascript() function, that approach is limited to HTTP GET and whatever parameters you can supply using the query string. And on top of that, detecting whether a resource has completed loading successfully requires either a server-supported callback hack or a periodic existence check function.

If you don't need the flexibility of cross-domain resources, you can use the Request.JSON class to take more explicit control of your web requests to a local API. As a subclass of Request, this gives you all the same options and event handlers, with the added benefit of automatic JSON data handling.

Encoding and Decoding JSON Data

But, before diving into the `Request.JSON` class, it's worth spending a little time with the `JSON` module. This module facilitates the encoding and decoding of JavaScript objects to and from the JSON text format.

For example, consider the use of the `.toJSON()` method added by the JSON module to native `String` and `Number` data types:

```
$log( 'string with "quotes" and \\backslashes\\ and /slashes/'.toJSON() );
// "string with \"quotes\" and \\backslashes\\ and \/slashes\/"

$log( (105.3).toJSON() );
// 105.3
```

This isn't very exciting, since the JSON encodings aren't much different than the original JavaScript. However, the `.toJSON()` method is also available for `Array` and `Hash` instances:

```
var some_array = [
    'foo', 'bar', 'baz'
];
$log( some_array.toJSON() );
// ["foo","bar","baz"]

var some_hash = $H({
    alpha: 'foo',
    beta: 'bar',
    gamma: 'baz'
});
$log( some_hash.toJSON() );
// {"alpha":"foo","beta":"bar","gamma":"baz"}
```

However, the `.toJSON()` method is not made available when using native generic objects:

```
var some_obj = { some_key: 'some_value' };

try {
    some_obj.toJSON();
} catch(e) {
    $log( "Exception: " + e );
    // Exception: TypeError: some_obj.toJSON is not a function
}
```

Instead, if you want to encode a native JavaScript object as JSON, you can use the `JSON.encode()` function directly:

```
$log( JSON.encode(some_obj) );
// {"some_key":"some_value"}
```

The widely available .toJSON() method is actually just a facade for this JSON.encode() function, which you can use with just about any other data type:

```
$log( JSON.encode(some_array) );
// ["foo","bar","baz"]

$log( JSON.encode(some_hash) );
// {"alpha":"foo","beta":"bar","gamma":"baz"}
```

Conversely, to get JavaScript objects and data types from a given string of JSON data, use the JSON.decode() function like so:

```
var str     = some_hash.toJSON();
var new_obj = JSON.decode(str);

$log( some_hash.every( function(v,k) {
    return new_obj[k] == v
}) );
// true
```

The preceding code demonstrates the inverse relationship between .toJSON() and JSON.decode() by first encoding a hash and then decoding it. A comparison of data between the original and the new decoded object should reveal that everything in the original is in the new object that's undergone encoding and subsequent decoding.

But, just to be thorough, the following checks to see that everything in the new object can be found in the original:

```
// new_obj is not yet a hash...
var new_hash = $H( new_obj );

$log( new_hash.every( function(v,k) {
    return some_hash[k] == v
}) );
// true
```

The one trick in the preceding code is that the object returned by JSON.decode() is not, in fact, a Hash object like the original: Instead, it's a generic JavaScript object, requiring a pass through the $H() convenience function to be transformed into a Hash object bearing the custom MooTools .every() method. So, there's one caveat to watch out for — JSON has no concept of MooTools custom classes, and so will not produce them when decoded.

Sanity Checking JSON Data

The way MooTools parses JSON is simple — it uses the JavaScript function eval(), which unless given predigested input or otherwise chaperoned will blithely execute any code given to it:

```
var result1 = JSON.decode(
    "window.alert('sideeffect #1')"
);
// throws up an alert
```

When executed, the preceding code does not result in JSON data, but instead produces an alert message.

If you can trust data produced by your own code and returned by your own services, using `eval()` is not a bad choice. It exploits the JavaScript parser supplied by the browser, so it should be quite fast and handle any JSON construct.

However, if you plan to consume JSON whose source is less trusted than you like, you can supply a second parameter of true, which forces the JSON string passed into `JSON.decode()` to first pass a whitelist of characters allowed in JSON:

```
var result2 = JSON.decode(
    "window.alert('sideeffect #2')", true
);
// no alert, null returned, tests 'JSON' with a regex
```

As it happens, this function call fails the test, and so the call to `eval()` is aborted. This should make your JSON processing a bit more resistant to attempts to subvert the machinery.

Making Requests for JSON Data

Now that you've seen how to deal with JSON data in MooTools, it's time to take a quick look at the `Request.JSON` object. Consider a file named "data.json" with the following contents:

```
{
    "first":"hewey",
    "second":"dewey",
    "third":"louie",
    "fourth":[
        1, 2, 3, 4, 5
    ]
}
```

You can use a `Request.JSON` object to fetch this data like so:

```
var req_json = new Request.JSON({

    url:    'data.json',
    secure: true, // true by default anyway

    onSuccess: function(json, txt) {
        $log("*** Loaded JSON data");

        $log_json( json );
        // {"first":"hewey","second":"dewey","third":"louie","fourth":[1,2,3,4,5]}

        $log( json == this.response.json );
        // true
    }

});
req_json.GET();
```

As a subclass of `Request`, everything else said about that class so far in this chapter applies to `Request`. `JSON`, with just a few additions:

❑ A header of `X-Request:` `JSON` is added to the request.

❑ A header of `Accept:` `application/json` is also added to the request.

❑ A call to `JSON.decode()` is made implicitly, the results of which are placed in the `response.` `json` property of the `Request.JSON` instance, as well as passed as the first parameter to the `onSuccess` handler when called.

❑ The option `secure` is a Boolean flag passed along as the second parameter the `JSON.decode()` call used to parse the response body content. As described earlier, this forces the incoming JSON to first pass a whitelist test to determine whether the JSON data is sane. Note that this option is `true` by default if omitted.

But, beyond these tweaks, every other aspect of the `Request` object is usable here — including all the methods supported by HTTP, additional headers and response body handling, and the method emulation feature. Additionally, the secure flag adds just a little more sanity checking to your consumption of JSON data, which is nice.

None of these things are supported by the `Asset.javascript()` call, so using `Request.JSON` is clearly the best choice when dealing with web APIs that speak JSON and share the same domain with your pages. And, even in those cases where cross-domain access is unavoidable and absolutely necessary, you can often build a local-domain proxy that relays some of those calls from your pages on a limited basis.

Summary

In this chapter, you were introduced to some of the AJAX and dynamic data facilities offered by MooTools. These included the `Request`, `Request.HTML`, and `Request.JavaScript` family of classes wrapping web requests and responses made using XmlHTTPRequest objects. You were also given demonstrations of the cookie manipulation and hash persistence mechanisms MooTools offers, as well as functions for dynamically loading page assets on the fly.

In the next, and final chapter, you'll be given a tour of the visual effects facilities offered by Moo Tools — considered by many to be one of the deciding features that make this framework worth using.

34

Building User Interfaces and Using Animation

Last but certainly not least in this book's MooTools story are the modules that enable visual effects and provide compact yet quite useful user interface widgets. This part of MooTools actually predates the toolkit itself, having been originally released as Moo.Fx, a lightweight and full-featured companion for the Prototype JS framework. So, these effects and UI modules have had even longer to mature and receive attention to performance and developer usability.

The animation and user interface modules provided by MooTools build on all of the other toolkit conveniences to which you've been introduced up to this point. In this chapter, you'll see how the extended properties and methods of elements can be used to easily integrate smooth visual transitions and other small touches into your web applications.

In this chapter, you'll learn about:

❑ *Composing animations*
❑ *Using user interface widgets*

Composing Animations

In preparation for demonstrating the ways in which MooTools enables you to build animations, it might be useful to provide a few shortcuts to build elements to animate without a lot of redundant markup.

First, consider the following CSS:

```
<style type="text/css">
    .mover {
        position: relative;
        margin: 0.25em;
        padding: 1em;
        width: 150px;
        float: left;
        border: 2px dotted #000;
        background-color: #ddf;
        text-align: center;
    }
</style>
```

This establishes a simple style useful for putting MooTools effects through all of its paces. Next, to create such elements on the page, consider the following JS function:

```
function createMoverDivs(parent_el, num, id_pre) {
    parent_el = $(parent_el);
    for (var i=1; i<=num; i++) {
        parent_el.adopt(
            document.newElement('div', {
                'class': 'mover',
                'id':    id_pre + i,
                'text': 'Click me'
            }),
            document.newElement('br', {
                'style': 'clear: both'
            })
        )
    }
}
```

The function defined in the preceding code will be used throughout the chapter in lieu of markup in many spots. Its purpose is simple: Given a parent element, a count of elements to create, and an ID prefix, create and insert a number of elements with unique IDs and a CSS class of "mover". This will come in handy in illustrating many variations of MooTools techniques.

Figure 34-1 provides an example of a page on which this function was used.

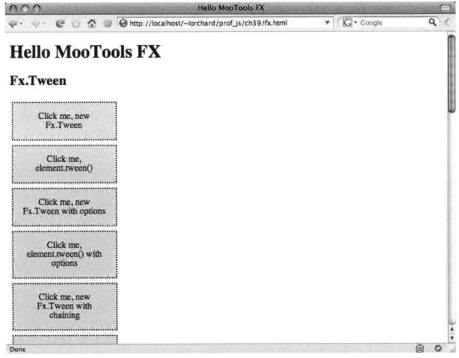

Figure 34-1

Examining Element Size and Position

Another brief stop before diving into animations: Since many animations depend heavily on manipulating the position, size, and scrolling of elements, it's worth spending a little time examining the Element.Dimensions module provided by MooTools for dealing with all the above.

Consider the following markup as a demonstration platform:

```
<style type="text/css">
    #ex_element_dimensions .scrolling {
        width: 100px;
        height: 100px;
        overflow: auto;
    }
</style>
<div id="ex_element_dimensions">
    <h2>Element.Dimensions</h2>

    <div class="mover scrolling">
        I can has dimensions!
        Lorem ipsum dolor sit amet, consectetuer adipiscing elit. Cras
        imperdiet velit at arcu. Nullam viverra lectus ac felis. Cum sociis
        natoque penatibus et magnis dis parturient montes, nascetur ridiculus
```

```
        mus. Nullam eu sapien dictum purus consequat cursus. Etiam non sapien
        sed elit dignissim tristique.
    </div>

    <br style="clear: both" />
</div>
```

The markup defined in the preceding example constructs an element with enough content to force overflow and scroll bars as declared in the CSS. This should provide enough structure to try out all the utilities provided by `Element.Dimensions`. Take a look at these utility method calls first:

```
var el = $$('#ex_element_dimensions .mover')[0];

$log('*** el.getScrollSize()');
$log( el.getScrollSize() );
// Object x=117 y=512

$log('*** el.scrollTo()');
el.scrollTo( 0, el.getScrollSize().y / 3 );
//

$log('*** el.getScrolls()');
$log( el.getScrolls() );
// Object x=0 y=170
```

As you can see, this module provides element methods to interrogate the scrolling limits offered by an element (`.getScrollSize`); to programmatically scroll an element to a given position (`.scrollTo`); and to get the current scrolling position (`.getScrolls`). You can use these functions with an element as shown above, or even with the `document` or `window` objects to control the browser overall.

Next, check out this code dealing with element position and size:

```
$log('*** el.getCoordinates()');
$log( el.getCoordinates() );
// Object left=12 top=65 width=136 height=136 right=148

$log('*** el.getSize()');
$log( el.getSize() );
// Object x=136 y=136

$log('*** el.getPosition()');
$log( el.getPosition() );
// Object x=12 y=65

$log('*** el.position()');
el.position({ x: 150, y: 10 });
```

The first element method `.getCoordinates()` returns a single object listing all the details about the element's size and position within the page. Since the element in question isn't positioned absolutely, these numbers are relative to its parent element, as well as its scrolling position. The methods `.getSize()` and `.getPosition()` return size and position as separate objects, respectively.

To really get a sense for these methods, you should try them out with different combinations of relative and absolute positioning, as well as combinations of margins and padding on parent elements. You can see a sample run of all the previous code in Figure 34-2.

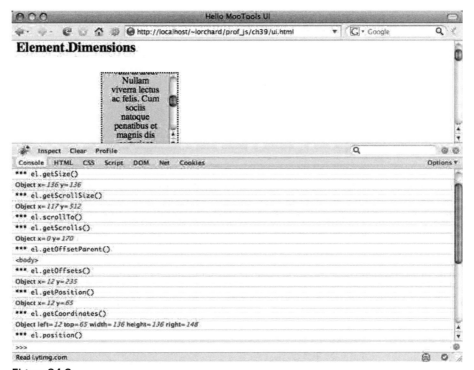

Figure 34-2

Using MooTools Fx to Compose Animations

Now, on to the meat of MooTools animations: The `Fx.Tween` module, along with the `Fx` and `Fx.CSS` modules on which it's based, provides the basic means for producing animation by way of varying the value of a CSS property over time. Since this includes positions, size, and colors, this is a very powerful basis for producing motion and other transitions.

To get started, consider the following markup:

```
<div id="ex_tween">
    <h2>Fx.Tween</h2>
</div>
```

Then, recalling the `createMoverDivs()` function, check out this call:

```
// Create a set of divs for this demo
createMoverDivs('ex_tween', 11, 'tween_mover');
```

The preceding code adds 11 numbered `<div>` elements to the parent declared in markup, all of which will be used in the examples to follow. Refer back to Figure 34-1 to get an idea of what this will look like.

Using Fx.Tween Instances

Take a look at this first example using the `Fx.Tween` module:

```
$('tween_mover1').set({
    text: 'Click me, new Fx.Tween',
    events: {
        click: function(ev) {
            var tweener = new Fx.Tween(ev.target);
            tweener.start('left', '0px', '300px');
        }
    }
});
```

Most of the code in the preceding example consists of setup to attach an event listener responding to clicks on the first of the `<div>` elements created earlier, as well as changing its text contents to something a little more descriptive. Consider this another demonstration of the `.set()` method introduced in Chapter 32 — there will be more of it in this chapter.

But, inside the click handler, an instance of `Fx.Tween` is created. The constructor for this class takes an element as its first parameter, which in this case the target of the click event is passed.

Once constructed, the object's `.start()` method is called. This method takes three parameters:

❑ The name of a CSS property

❑ A starting value for the property

❑ An end value for the property

Once called, MooTools begins transitioning the named CSS property from the starting value until it equals the end value. In this particular case, the `left` position property of the element travels from 0 to 300 pixels across the page over the default duration of 500ms, or 1/2 a second. Thus, by varying the position property, animated motion is achieved.

Although it's pretty simple to use, this explanation glosses over a few details deep within MooTools. Most importantly, it has a set of handlers implemented in the `Fx.CSS.Parsers` namespace that understand how to interpret numeric values with units like "300px" and even colors like "#338833" — and, once parsed, these handlers understand how to transition a property value between two end points over the duration of an animation.

This means that not only can you produce animations with motion, but you can also transition between colors, sizes, scroll positions, and any other numeric properties.

For the most part, you'll never need to worry about the CSS parsers themselves, since most properties worth animation are covered by the set that comes with MooTools. Of course, there are a few properties for which no form of animated transition really makes sense — for example, font-face and list-style-type — but MooTools still tries to oblige by at least ensuring that the element begins the tween with the starting value and ends with the ending value when the animation duration has finished.

Using the Tween Element Method

As you've seen so far in this part of the book about MooTools, wherever there's a class available for use with elements, there's usually another way to do the same thing integrated right into the element itself. In the Fx.Tween module, there's no exception to this pattern:

```
$('tween_mover2').set({
    text: 'Click me, element.tween()',
    events: {
        click: function(ev) {
            ev.target.tween('left', '0px', '300px');
        }
    }
});
```

As before, most of the code here is bound up in setting up a proper description for the <div> involved in the demonstration, as well as setting up a click event handler. Within that handler function, there's a simple call to the element's .tween() method, to which are passed the same three parameters as were supplied to the .start() method of an Fx.Tween object.

This is no coincidence because, in fact, the .tween() method creates an instance of Fx.Tween behind the scenes and calls its .start() method with the CSS property name and its start and finish values. And, just like the previous example, the code here causes the second <div> on the page to travel from 0 to 300 pixels across the screen when clicked.

Specifying Tween Options

Along with specifying the CSS property to animate with start and finish values, a number of other options are available for use with Fx.Tween using the optional second parameter of its constructor, which has not yet made an appearance until this example:

```
$('tween_mover3').set({
    text: 'Click me, new Fx.Tween with options',
    events: {
        click: function(ev) {
            var tweener = new Fx.Tween(ev.target, {
                duration:   1000,
                transition: Fx.Transitions.Elastic.easeOut
            });
            tweener.start('left', '0px', '300px');
        }
    }
});
```

As in the first example usage, you can see that the first parameter to the `Fx.Tween` constructor in this click handler is a reference to the `<div>` being clicked. However, the second parameter is an object containing further options to be applied once the animation is initiated.

Returning to the element method approach of initiating `Fx.Tween` animations, you can use the extended element property `"tween"` to set options to be used when the `.tween()` method is called, like so:

```
$('tween_mover4').set({
    text: 'Click me, element.tween() with options',
    tween: {
        duration:    1000,
        transition: 'elastic:out'
    },
    events: {
        click: function(ev) {
            ev.target.tween('left', '0px', '300px')
        }
    }
});
```

Using the `.set()` method and the `tween` property creates an instance of `Fx.Tween` using the context element and the given options, then stashes it in element storage for use when the `.tween()` method is called. This lets you create a tweening animation all in the same context as manipulating other element properties and handlers.

The following is a quick summary of common options useful in most animations derived from the `Fx` class, which includes `Fx.Tween`:

❑   `fps` — Frames per second, defaults to 50.

❑   `unit` — Which unit to use in property animation, that is, "px", "em", or "%". Defaults to `false`, using whatever is supplied the values passed to `.start()`.

❑   `link` — Accepts one of three string values:

  ❑   `cancel` — Multiple calls to `.start()` interrupt running animations (the default).

  ❑   `chain` — Multiple calls to `.start()` are added to the call chain.

  ❑   `ignore` — Multiple calls to `.start()` are ignored.

❑   `duration` — Duration in milliseconds for how long the animation should last.

❑   `transition` — Reference to a function that customizes the linear progress of an animation, default is a smooth and gradual acceleration and stop.

The options `duration`, `link`, and `transition` are probably the ones you'll use the most. The `duration` option is easiest to understand, but `link` and `transition` will be explained in better detail later in the chapter.

Chaining Tween Animations

Once you've gotten a basic animation up and running, one of the next useful things to do is chain it with subsequent animations in a series to build up more complex motions and transitions. This is facilitated within the `Fx` base class using the `Chain` mixin class, introduced in Chapter 31. You can use this functionality with `Fx.Tween` like so:

```
$('tween_mover5').set({
    text: 'Click me, new Fx.Tween with chaining',
    events: {
        click: function(ev) {
            var tweener = new Fx.Tween(ev.target, {
                duration:   1000,
                transition: 'elastic:in:out'
            });

            tweener
                .start('left', '0px', '300px')
                .chain(function(){
                    tweener.start('left', '300px', '0px')
                });
        }
    }
});
```

The preceding code constructs a chained pair of animations such that, when the element in question is clicked, it slides out 300 pixels from the left and then immediately returns back to the left edge of the page.

Since `Fx` implements the `Chain` mixin class, and `Fx.Tween` inherits from the `Fx` class, you can use the `.chain()` method on `Fx.Tween` instances, as shown in the preceding code.

A call to the `.chain()` method expects a reference to a function, which will be called with a subsequent call to the `.callChain()` method. Conveniently, since an instance of the `Fx` class makes a call to its own `.callChain()` method whenever an animation has completed, you can use this feature to chain one animation after another — as well as trigger other code at the end of an animation.

Using this chaining feature in the context of extended element properties and methods is possible, and made even easier with setting the `link` option to "chain", with code like the following:

```
$('tween_mover6').set({
    text: 'Click me, element.tween() with chaining',
    tween: {
        link: 'chain',
        duration:   1000,
        transition: Fx.Transitions.Bounce.easeOut
    },
    events: {
        click: function(ev) {
            ev.target
                .tween('left', '0px', '300px')
                .tween('left', '300px', '0px');
        }
    }
});
```

The return value of an element's .tween() method is the element itself, not a reference to the Fx.Tween object created in the background. However, this object is available from element storage, so a call to .get('tween') will return the desired Fx.Tween instance — and thus, you can call the .chain() method on that instance to attach subsequent animations just like the previous example.

This is slightly less than elegant, so you may want to stick with directly creating Fx.Tween instances when you want to compose complex animation chains, and use element methods and properties when you want to fire off quick and simple transitions.

Exploring Pre-Built Animations and Effects

While you have the freedom to compose whatever sort of single-property animation you like using Fx.Tween, there are a few particular kinds of animation that come in handy for web applications. So, MooTools offers a few pre-built animations that are very easy to fire off without all the required preamble of constructing a more custom animation.

Using Fade Animations

The following code causes the given element to fade out and back in by varying its opacity:

```
$('tween_mover7').set({
    text: 'Click me, element.fade()',
    events: {
        click: function(ev) {
            ev.target.fade();
            ev.target.fade.delay(1000, ev.target);
        }
    }
});
```

The click handler calls the .fade() method on the element, which constructs and starts an animation using an instance of Fx.Tween behind the scenes. The method accepts one of the following options for its only expected parameter:

❑   in — Animate opacity from 0.0 to 1.0, fading the element into visibility.

❑   out — Animate opacity from 1.0 to 0.0, fading the element out of visibility.

❑   toggle — Alternately animate opacity in and out of visibility on subsequent calls.

❑   show — Set the element's opacity to 1.0, with no animation.

❑   hide — Set the element's opacity to 0.0, with no animation.

❑   0.0 - 1.0 — Animate the element's opacity from its current value to the given value.

The .fade() method uses the extended property "tween" to deal with Fx.Tween — so as shown earlier in the chapter, you can use this to set some options to override defaults, like duration.

Also note the second call to .fade(), by way of the .delay() function method. Although not as clean or exact as chaining animations, this is another quick-and-dirty way to schedule one animation after the completion of another.

Using Highlight Animations

Along with fades, another kind of animation made popular with modern web applications is a quick flash of color highlighting that something's happened on the page. This can be done with MooTools like so:

```
$('tween_mover8').set({
    text: 'Click me, element.highlight()',
    events: {
        click: function(ev) {
            ev.target.highlight();
            // ev.target.highlight('#8f8');
        }
    }
});
```

Using the preceding code, when the element in question is clicked, it will briefly flash a pale yellow color before fading back to its original color. This is done with a call to the element's `.highlight()` method, which also accepts a color as its single optional parameter to use instead of the default yellow color.

Again, like `.fade()`, the `.highlight()` method makes use of the implied `Fx.Tween` object involved in using the "tween" extended property.

Using Fx.Slide Animations

Whereas fades and highlights cause changes to the opacity or color of an element that stays motionless, sliding animations hide or reveal an element by expanding it into or shrinking it out of the page layout.

Unlike the other pre-built animations, `Fx.Slide` is implemented as an independent subclass of the `Fx` base class, rather than just a variation of `Fx.Tween`. You can use an instance of the class like so:

```
$('tween_mover9').set({
    text: 'Click me, new Fx.Slide()',
    events: {
        click: function(ev) {
            var slider = new Fx.Slide(ev.target, {
                duration:   1000,
                transition: Fx.Transitions.Bounce.easeOut,
                mode:       'vertical'
            });
            slider
                .slideOut()
                .chain(function() {
                    slider.slideIn();
                });
        }
    }
});
```

As you can see, this class supports all of the features inherited from the Fx parent class, including options and animation chaining. However, notice that there's a new option "mode", which can be either "vertical" (the default if omitted) or "horizontal" — this specifies whether the element should grow or shrink along the vertical or horizontal axis, respectively.

Beyond a new option, though, the main thing that Fx.Slide offers is the following set of method calls each providing a slightly different effect:

- ❑   .slideIn() — Slide the element into the page layout by growing it.
- ❑   .slideOut() — Slide the element out of the page layout by shrinking it.
- ❑   .toggle() — Alternately slide the element in and out of the page layout with subsequent calls.
- ❑   .hide() — Hide the element from the page layout with no animated transition.
- ❑   .show() — Insert the element into the page layout with no animated transition.

Note that, for each of these methods, the element must already be part of the DOM — this class provides hiding and revealing transitions, but it does not actually adopt, grab, or insert the element. The Fx.Slide class simply affects the element's visibility and size within the visible page layout.

Of course, along with using Fx.Slide objects directly, you can make use of extended element properties and methods provided by the module like so:

```
$('tween_mover10').set({
    text: 'Click me, element.slide()',
    slide: {
        link:       'chain',
        duration:   1000,
        transition: Fx.Transitions.Elastic.easeOut,
        mode:       'horizontal'
    },
    events: {
        click: function(ev) {
            ev.target
                .slide('out')
                .slide('in');
        }
    }
});
```

Like an Fx.Tween animation, you can supply options using the "slide" extended property, and initiate the animation with a call to the .slide() method. The .slide() method accepts an optional string parameter naming one of the animation methods supported by the Fx.Slide class — namely in, out, toggle (the default), hide, or show.

Also, just like an Fx.Tween animation, the link option set to "chain" facilitates animation chaining with subsequent calls to .slide(), and the implicit instance of Fx.Slide can be fetched by using the "slide" property.

Using Fx.Scroll Animations

Another useful kind of animation offered by MooTools involves scrolling content within elements, as well as programmatically scrolling the browser window itself. This is implemented in another Fx subclass named Fx.Scroll, used like so:

```
$(' tween_mover10').set({
    text: 'Click me to scroll!',
    events: {
        click: function(ev) {

            var scroller = new Fx.Scroll(window, {
                duration: 1500,
                transition: Fx.Transitions.Bounce.easeOut
            });

            scroller
                .toTop()
                .chain(function(){
                    scroller.start(0, 200);
                })
                .chain(function(){
                    scroller.toBottom();
                })
                .chain(function(){
                    scroller.toTop();
                })
                .chain(function(){
                    scroller.toElement(ev.target);
                });

        }
    }
});
```

When the element involved in the preceding code is clicked, nothing actually happens to the element itself. Instead, the browser window starts scrolling all on its own. First, it scrolls to the top of the page, then somewhere about 200 pixels down, then all of the way to the bottom, and then finally back up to a spot where the element clicked rests at the top of the browser window.

This helps illustrate the methods made available by Fx.Scroll:

❑ .start(x, y) — Initiate an animation scrolling to the desired horizontal and vertical location.

❑ .toElement(el) — Fire off an animation scrolling to make the given element visible.

❑ .toTop() — Scroll up to the top of the vertical space.

❑ .toBottom() — Scroll down to the bottom of the vertical space.

❑ .toLeft() — Scroll over to the left edge of horizontal space.

❑ .toRight() — Scroll over to the right edge of horizontal space.

Unlike the other animation tools presented so far, however, there are no associated element properties or methods provided by the `Fx.Scroll` module. Instead, you'll need to use the class directly.

Exploring MooTools Fx.Transitions

So far, this chapter has used the "`transition`" option accepted by all `Fx` subclasses but has not explained much about it. You may already understand the purpose of this option, since many other JavaScript frameworks offer something similar — Dojo and YUI call these functions "easings", for instance.

In a nutshell, linear motion in animations is boring. Simply watching an object crawl from point A to point B is tedious and less than eye catching. It's much more interesting to watch an on-screen object move in some way that approximates something physical with inertia or momentum — or even in an unnatural way that at least introduces variety into the thing's progress.

Thus, in MooTools, the general Fx "`transition`" option expects to be given a reference to a function which, when called with a value from 0.0 to 1.0, will introduce some transformation varying the result in an interesting way.

But, rather than trying to express what *interesting* means in prose, it might be more useful to offer a small tool that can interactively demonstrate the effect of all the transition functions offered out of the box by MooTools under the `Fx.Transitions` namespace.

Consider the following markup as the start of such a tool:

```
<div id="ex_transitions">
    <h2>Fx.Transitions</h2>

    <form>
        <select class="transitions"></select>
        <button class="animate">Animate</button>
    </form>

    <div class="mover">
        <div>Watch me!</div>
    </div>

    <br style="clear: both" />

</div>
```

The preceding markup establishes a simple test bed, offering a selection widget to pick a transition function and a button to fire off an animation using that function. The animation is applied to the single "mover" <div> element in the markup.

Now, the following code digs up all of the transitions available under `Fx.Transitions` and constructs a hash of names and functions for use in further constructing and powering this testing interface:

```
// Collect candidates for MooTools transition functions.
var base_name   = 'Fx.Transitions.';
var transitions = $H();
Fx.Transitions.getKeys().each(function(name) {
    ['', 'easeIn', 'easeOut', 'easeInOut'].each(function(func) {
        var t_name = base_name + name;
        if (func == '') {
            var t_func = Fx.Transitions[name];
        } else {
            var t_func = Fx.Transitions[name][func];
            t_name += '.' + func;
        }
        if ($type(t_func) == 'function')
            transitions[t_name] = t_func;
    });
});
```

The `Fx.Transitions` namespace is actually a MooTools hash object, so the `.getKeys()` method works to dig up all the names of transitions defined. At the time of this writing, these include the following

- ❑   `Fx.Transitions.linear`
- ❑   `Fx.Transitions.Pow`
- ❑   `Fx.Transitions.Expo`
- ❑   `Fx.Transitions.Circ`
- ❑   `Fx.Transitions.Sine`
- ❑   `Fx.Transitions.Back`
- ❑   `Fx.Transitions.Bounce`
- ❑   `Fx.Transitions.Elastic`
- ❑   `Fx.Transitions.Quad`
- ❑   `Fx.Transitions.Cubic`
- ❑   `Fx.Transitions.Quart`
- ❑   `Fx.Transitions.Quint`

Under each of these keys is a function, but usually defined as properties attached to each function are further functions named "easeIn", "easeOut", and "easeInOut". Each of these serves as a modifier to the base transition function — applying it unmodified, reversing it, or applying it in mirrored directions.

The end result of this preceding code is to produce a hash of names for use in the drop-down selector, tied to the actual functions useable in animations. The following code uses those keys to build the selector contents:

```
// Build selector options from the collected transitions.
$$('#ex_transitions .transitions').adopt(
    transitions.getKeys().map(function(name) {
        return document.newElement('option', {
            'text': name, 'value': name
        });
    })
);
```

For each key scooped up from the list of transitions, a new <option> element is created and injected into the drop-down selector. This is made simple thanks to a combination of the element .adopt() method and the array .map() method.

Finally, the following code wires up the "animate" button with a handler that fires off the animation with the currently selected transition function:

```
// Wire up the button to animate using the selected transition.
$$('#ex_transitions .animate').addEvent('click', function(ev) {
    ev.stop();

    var t_name = $$('#ex_transitions .transitions').get('value')[0];
    var trans  = transitions.get(t_name);

    $$('#ex_transitions .mover').set('tween', {
        transition: trans,
        duration: 500
    }).tween('left', '0px', '500px');
});
```

There's not much in the preceding code that differs from the Fx.Tween examples you've seen so far in this chapter, beyond the bit that grabs the current value of the selection box and maps it to an available transition function. But, once these pieces are put together, you should be able to try out a number of different transition and easing types to see what each does to the kind of motion displayed by the animation.

Figure 34-3 shows the finished product of all of the above, listing many of the transition functions available.

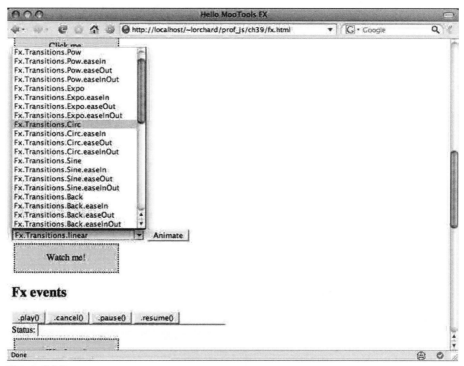

Figure 34-3

Expressing Transition Choices as Strings

There's one additional small trick to the "transition" option that seems interesting and may come in handy, and has been used at least once in this chapter so far:

```
var tweener = new Fx.Tween(ev.target, {
    duration:   1000,
    transition: 'elastic:inOut'
});
```

Notice that, rather than using the reference to an actual function, a string is used to identify a transition. The format of this string can be described something like this:

```
{transition name}[:in][:out]
```

So, rather than using a reference to an Fx.Transitions key directly, you can just use the name and optionally follow it with a colon and one of in, out, or inOut to use one of the easing modifiers.

803

Exploring Animation Events

While you can register code for execution at the end of an animation by way of the `.chain()` method, animations based on the Fx class also offer a number of events for use with the `.addEvent()` method thanks to the Events mixin class introduced in Chapter 31. Additionally, Fx animations offer a number of methods that can be called to control an animation in progress.

Setting the stage for an interactive example, consider the following markup:

```
<div id="ex_events">
    <h2>Fx events</h2>

    <form>
        <button class="start">.start()</button>
        <button class="cancel">.cancel()</button>
        <button class="pause">.pause()</button>
        <button class="resume">.resume()</button>

        <br style="clear: both" />

        <label for="status">Status:</label>
        <input class="status" type="text" size="40" />
    </form>

    <div class="mover">
        <div>Watch me!</div>
    </div>

    <br style="clear: both" />

</div>
```

You can see this markup rendered in Figure 34-4. As you may expect from the names of the buttons, Fx animations offer the following methods:

❏   `.start()` — Starts an animation

❏   `.stop()` — Stops an animation

❏   `.pause()` — Pauses an animation

❏   `.resume()` — Resumes a paused animation

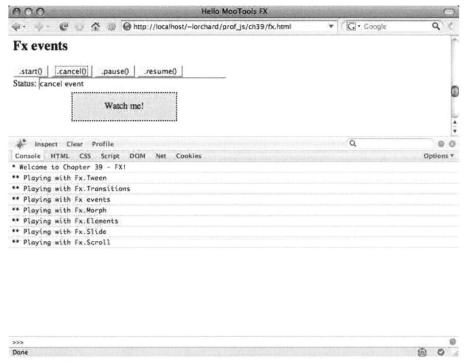

Figure 34-4

Next, the following code sets up the animation to be used as an experimental subject:

```
var anim = $$('#ex_events .mover')[0]
    .set('tween', {
        duration:    2000,
        transition: Fx.Transitions.linear
    })
    .get('tween');
```

In the preceding code, the animation is given a longer duration than usual so that there's time to play with things, and the transition is set to the boring straight "linear" transformation to make it simply crawl across the screen.

Now that the animation object is available, it's time to wire up those buttons in the markup to issue commands to the animation:

```
$$('#ex_events .start)
    .addEvent('click', function(ev) {
        ev.stop();
        anim.start('left', '0px', '500px');
    });

$$('#ex_events .cancel')
    .addEvent('click', function(ev) {
```

```
                  ev.stop();
                  anim.cancel();
            });

      $$('#ex_events .pause')
            .addEvent('click', function(ev) {
                  ev.stop();
                  anim.pause();
            });

      $$('#ex_events .resume')
            .addEvent('click', function(ev) {
                  ev.stop();
                  anim.resume();
            });
```

The preceding code is pretty straightforward: Each button is given a click handler that calls a different method offered by the animation object, beginning with the .start() method that kicks off the animation as a left-to-right movement.

Now, it's time to wire up some event handlers to monitor the animation:

```
var status = $$('#ex_events .status')[0];
anim.addEvents({
      start: function() {
            status.set('value', 'start event');
      },
      complete: function() {
            status.set('value', 'complete event');
      },
      chainComplete: function() {
            status.set('value', 'chainComplete event');
      }
      cancel: function() {
            status.set('value', 'cancel event');
      }
});
```

As shown in the preceding code, Fx-based animations in MooTools fire one or more of the following events during the course of their execution:

❑   start — Fired at the start of the animation

❑   complete — Fired when the animation has finished completely

❑   chainComplete — Fired when a chain of animations has finished completely

❑   cancel — Fired when the animation is stopped early

The handlers for each of these events in the preceding code update the contents of the text input field with the CSS class "status" with a message indicating the last event to fire. You should see this change appropriately as you click the buttons to start and stop the animation, as well as when it runs its course. You can use handlers attached to these events to coordinate the execution of other parts of your application, including further animations or other functionality such as firing off AJAX requests.

Animating Multiple Properties with Fx.Morph

Where Fx.Tween offers the ability to animate a single CSS property on an element, the Fx.Morph module expands this to allow the animation of multiple properties. As another Fx.CSS subclass, Fx.Morph is very similar to Fx.Tween in use.

To get into a couple of examples, consider this markup:

```
<div id="ex_morph">
    <h2>Fx.Morph</h2>
</div>
```

Then, consider this function call creating <div> elements for animation:

```
createMoverDivs('ex_morph', 2, 'morph_mover');
```

Now, it's time to try out the Fx.Morph class like so:

```
$('morph_mover1').set({
    text: 'Click me, new Fx.Morph()',
    events: {
        click: function(ev) {
            var morph = new Fx.Morph(ev.target, {
                duration: 1000
            });

            morph
                .start({
                    left:  [ '0px', '300px' ],
                    width: [ '150px', '300px' ],
                    backgroundColor: [ '#ddf', '#dfd' ]
                })
                .chain(function() {
                    morph.start({
                        left:  [ '300px', '0px' ],
                        width: [ '300px', '150px' ],
                        backgroundColor: [ '#dfd', '#ddf' ]
                    })
                });

        }
    }
});
```

When using the Fx.Tween class, the .start() method expects three parameters: the name of a CSS property, followed by a start and end value for the property. This is expanded in Fx.Morph through the use of a hash or an object as the only parameter. The keys of this hash name CSS properties, and the values are expected to be two element arrays listing the desired start and end property values.

In the preceding code example, the registered click handler causes the element in question to simultaneously move left, grow wider, and shift to a green color. Then, in a chained animation, it returns back to its original position, size, and color.

And also like Fx.Tween, the Fx.Morph class can be used with extended element properties and methods like so:

```
$('morph_mover2').set({
    text: 'Click me, element.morph()',
    morph: {
        duration: 1000,
        link:      'chain'
    },
    events: {
        click: function(ev) {
            ev.target
                .morph({
                    left:  [ '0px', '300px' ],
                    width: [ '150px', '300px' ],
                    backgroundColor: [ '#ddf', '#dfd' ]
                })
                .morph({
                    left:  [ '300px', '0px' ],
                    width: [ '300px', '150px' ],
                    backgroundColor: [ '#dfd', '#ddf' ]
                });
        }
    }
});
```

Options can be set using the "morph" element property, which implicitly creates an instance of Fx. Morph managed in element storage. Then, the element method .morph() can be called with a hash or object specifying the properties and values to initiate the animation. And, in the same way as was done with Fx.Tween, you can chain subsequent animations using the object fetched via the "morph" property.

By tracking changes in multiple properties at once, the Fx.Morph class offers a useful upgrade to Fx. Tween to compose more detailed animations. Figure 34-5 shows one of the animations explained earlier caught in mid-transition.

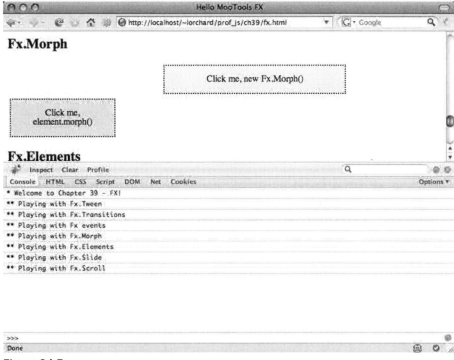

Figure 34-5

Animating Multiple Elements with Fx.Elements

Going even further than `Fx.Morph` is the `Fx.Elements` class, which enables you to compose animations that affect multiple CSS properties on multiple elements all at once.

The following markup helps set the stage for the code coming up:

```
<div id="ex_elements">
    <h2>Fx.Elements</h2>
</div>
```

And the following function call creates a number of `<div>` elements for use in the animation:

```
createMoverDivs('ex_elements', 4, 'elements_mover');
```

Now, with all of the above in place, you can try out the `Fx.Elements` class:

```
$$('#ex_elements .mover').addEvent('click', function(ev) {

    var fx_ele = new Fx.Elements('#ex_elements .mover', {
        duration:    750,
```

```
        transition: Fx.Transitions.Bounce.easeOut
    });

    fx_ele.start({
        '0': {
            left:   [ '0px', '300px' ],
        },
        '1': {
            width: [ '150px', '300px' ],
        },
        '2': {
            backgroundColor: [ '#ddf', '#dfd' ]
        },
        '3': {
            left:   [ '0px', '300px' ],
            width: [ '150px', '300px' ],
            backgroundColor: [ '#ddf', '#dfd' ]
        }
    });

});
```

The preceding code sets up a click event handler on all four <div> elements created such that, when any one of them is clicked, all four of them animate simultaneously in different ways. The first moves left, the second grows wider, the third changes color, and the fourth does all the above.

The effect can be pretty dramatic, but creating it is relatively simple. An instance of Fx.Elements can be created by using either a list of elements — such as what the $$() function returns — or by supplying a CSS selector string that would produce a list of elements. And, as yet another Fx.CSS subclass, the second parameter of the constructor expects the same options as the other Fx classes presented so far.

Describing the desired animation is straightforward as well: The .start() method of an Fx.Elements instance expects a hash or object, with keys derived from the numeric indices of elements in the list supplied at the time of construction. Each of these keys, in turn, points at a hash or object describing one or more CSS properties to animate, just like the Fx.Morph class.

You can also chain animations using Fx.Elements, subscribe to animation lifecycle events, and call the methods introduced earlier to pause or stop the animation. Thanks to the inheritance system offered by MooTools, it's easy to build up on one simple convention after another to arrive at something as powerful and complex as the animations offered by the Fx.Elements class.

Figure 34-6 shows what the animation in the previous example looks like as it nears completion.

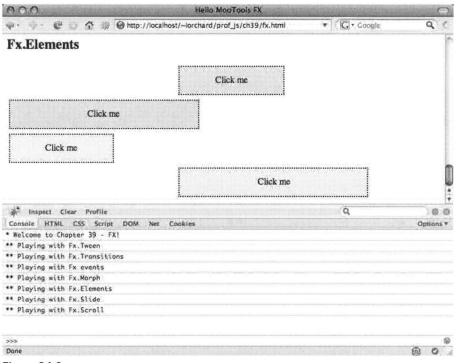

Figure 34-6

Using User Interface Widgets

Some frameworks, such as Ext JS and Dojo, provide a rich and extremely flexible library of user interface components or widgets. Some of these widgets can reach the level of replacing native browser controls and facilitating the construction of something very close to full desktop applications.

Although MooTools doesn't go as far as those frameworks, it does offer a minimal yet very handy set of user interface widgets that encapsulate a convenient interaction with patterns and controls. If building a desktop application is not *quite* what you're after, then what MooTools provides might be just enough for what you need.

Building Accordion Layouts

The accordion layout widget offered by MooTools provides a way to display a lot of information in a limited amount of vertical space, allowing the user to navigate through the content by clicking on headers to expand the relevant section and collapse all others. This leaves only one block of content visible at a time, with the rest reduced just to headers, thus minimizing the room needed to present the widget.

Laying the groundwork for a demonstration, consider the following CSS and HTML markup constructing a few blocks of viewable content:

```
<style type="text/css">
    #accordion { width: 33%; }

    p { margin: 0; padding: 0; }

    dl.has_items dt {
        font-weight: bold;
        background: #ccc; margin: 0.25em; padding: 0.5em;
    }

    dl.has_items dd {
        background: #eee; margin: 0.25em; padding: 0.5em;
    }
</style>

<div id="ex_accordion">

    <h2>Accordion</h2>

    <dl id="accordion" class="has_items">

        <dt id="acc_item1">First Item</dt>

        <dd id="acc_content1"><p>
            Lorem ipsum dolor sit amet, consectetuer adipiscing
            elit. Cras imperdiet velit at arcu. Nullam viverra lectus ac
            felis.
        </p></dd>

        <dt id="acc_item2">Second Item</dt>

        <dd id="acc_content2"><p>
            Cum sociis natoque penatibus et magnis dis parturient
            montes, nascetur ridiculus mus.
        </p></dd>

        <dt id="acc_item3">Third Item</dt>

        <dd id="acc_content3"><p>
            Nullam eu sapien dictum purus consequat cursus. Etiam non
            sapien sed elit dignissim tristique.
        </p></dd>

    </dl>

</div>
```

The preceding markup builds a tall, narrow block of content with three sections, each bearing a header title. As you can see in Figure 34-7, the content takes up most of the height of the browser window. If there were much more content here, you'd need to scroll down the page to see it all.

While this is not the end of the world, it might be more interesting to get all of the title headers onto the same page to at least give the user an idea of what content is available for perusal. This is where the accordion layout comes in handy.

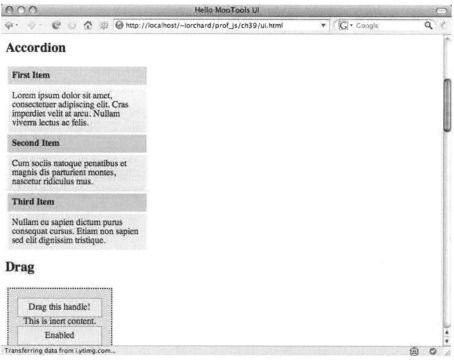

Figure 34-7

Having established the preceding preamble, it seems a bit anticlimactic to actually put the Accordion class to work:

```
var accordion = new Accordion(
    $$('#ex_accordion dt'), $$('#ex_accordion dd'), {
        duration: 500,
        transition: Fx.Transitions.Bounce.easeOut,
        display: 1
    }
);
```

The constructor for the Accordion class accepts three parameters:

❑   A list of elements to be used as headers

❑   A list of elements to be used as content associated with headers

❑   Animation options understood by the Fx.Elements class, as well as a few more

The additional options supported by `Accordion` include the following:

❏ `display` — The index (default 0) of the element to show first, with a visual transition.

❏ `show` — The index (default 0) of the element to show first, with no visual transition.

❏ `height` — If set to true, the height of shown/hidden sections will be animated. Defaults to true.

❏ `width` — If set to true, the width of shown/hidden sections will be animated. Defaults to false.

❏ `opacity` — If true, opacity will be involved in hiding and revealing sections. Defaults to true.

❏ `fixedHeight` — The widget overall will maintain a fixed height. Defaults to false.

❏ `fixedWidth` — The widget overall will maintain a fixed width. Defaults to false.

❏ `alwaysHide` — If true, the single visible section may also be closed. Defaults to false.

With various combinations of these options and some CSS styling of your own, you can customize the initial state of the widget, in what directions it animates, and tweak the effects used during the animation. Like other animations, the `Accordion` widget supports a number of events to which you can attach your own listeners for reacting to user interaction:

```
accordion.addEvents({
    start: function() {
        $log('starting animation');
        $log(arguments);
    },
    complete: function() {
        $log('completed animation');
        $log(arguments);
    },
    cancel: function() {
        $log('canceled animation');
        $log(arguments);
    },
    active: function(header, content) {
        $log("showing " + header.get('text'));
    },
    background: function(header, content) {
        $log("hiding " + header.get('text'));
    }
});
```

Along with the set of events provided by Fx.Elements, the following pair is specific to the Accordion class:

❏ `active` — Fired for the header element clicked and content element made visible.

❏ `background` — Fired for each header element not clicked and content element hidden.

These events are called before the animated transition starts, so you could do something interesting like dynamically update the content of the section that's about to appear just before it's revealed.

Figure 34-8 shows what `Accordion` does to the size of the content, as well as shows a sample run in Firebug with a log transcript of messages resulting from a few clicks on the widget.

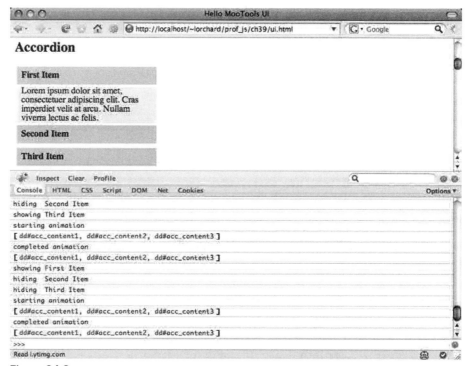

Figure 34-8

Adding Smooth Scrolling to Page Navigation

This next widget isn't as much of a layout utility as a transitional flourish. Consider the following markup, which defines content with internal anchor links:

```
<div id="ex_smoothscroll">
    <h2>SmoothScroll</h2>
    <ul>
        <li><a href="#scroll1">Scroll to #1</a></li>
        <li><a href="#scroll2">Scroll to #2</a></li>
        <li><a href="#scroll3">Scroll to #3</a></li>
    </ul>
</div>

<div id="scroll1">
    <h3>Scroll link destination #1</h3>
    <p>
        Cum sociis natoque penatibus et magnis dis parturient
        montes, nascetur ridiculus mus.
    </p>
</div>

<div id="scroll2">
    <h3>Scroll link destination #2</h3>
```

```
    <p>
        Lorem ipsum dolor sit amet, consectetuer adipiscing
        elit. Cras imperdiet velit at arcu. Nullam viverra lectus ac
        felis.
    </p>
</div>

<div id="scroll3">
    <h3>Scroll link destination #3</h3>
    <p>
        Nullam eu sapien dictum purus consequat cursus. Etiam non
        sapien sed elit dignissim tristique.
    </p>
</div>
```

In fact, what's most interesting with the preceding content is if you intersperse the linked `<div>` elements among other content, you give some room for vertical scrolling. Doing this will make the use of the following widget even more dramatic, as instantiated in the following code:

```
var smooth = new SmoothScroll({
    links:      $$('#ex_smoothscroll a'),
    duration:   1000,
    transition: Fx.Transitions.Bounce.easeOut
});

['start', 'cancel', 'complete'].each(function(ev_name) {
    smooth.addEvent(ev_name, function(ev) {
        $log('SmoothScroll fired event ' + ev_name);
    })
});
```

The `SmoothScroll` widget accepts `Fx` options in its constructor, with an additional option named `links`. This additional option is expected to be a list of clickable links, which are each given a special click handler.

When one of these links is clicked, rather than simply snapping to the linked content, an animation is fired up that scrolls the window until the desired element is made visible. Since transition functions are supported, the preceding code makes this scrolling a little more interesting by making the window bounce on each section of content to which the user navigates.

This widget adds a small bit of visual flair to large pages of content, while at the same time providing some awareness of where in the page the internal links send the user.

Enabling Draggable Elements

One of the expected essentials in modern JavaScript framework user interface is some way to enable draggable elements. Consider the following markup, which defines just such an element:

```
<style text="type/css">
    .mover .handle {
        background: #eee;
        padding: 0.5em;
```

```
        border: 1px dotted #333;
    }                  .
</style>
<div id="ex_drag">

    <h2>Drag</h2>

    <div class="mover dragger">
        <div class="handle drag">Drag this handle!</div>
        <p>This is inert content.</p>
        <div class="handle toggle">Enabled</div>
    </div>

    <br style="clear: both" />

</div>
```

This markup, which can be seen rendered in Figure 34-9, constructs a draggable box with a handle, some inert content, and a box to enable and disable dragging. Getting the dragging to work is pretty easy:

```
var dragger = new Drag( $$('#ex_drag .dragger')[0], {
    handle: $$('#ex_drag .mover .drag')[0],
    snap: 25,
    grid: 25
});
```

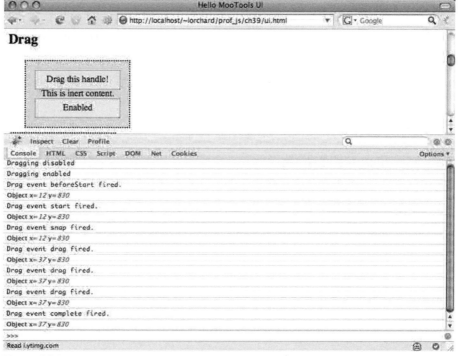

Figure 34-9

The first parameter expected by the Drag object constructor is a reference to the element to be moved by dragging, and the second parameter is an object or hash of options including the following:

- ❏ handle — Reference to an element that will accept drag gestures. Defaults to the first element passed into the constructor.

- ❏ Grid — Distance in pixels forming a regular grid of positions to which the element can be dragged. Defaults to false.

- ❏ Snap — Distance in pixels the element must be dragged before it will start responding to the gesture. Defaults to 6.

- ❏ Limit — An object or hash defining x and y limits constraining the drag.

- ❏ Modifiers — An object specifying CSS properties modified by the x and y coordinates of the drag. This defaults to { x: 'left', y: 'top' }, which directly controls the element's position.

- ❏ Style — If true (the default), the style properties of the element with the specified modifiers. If false, element attributes are updated instead.

- ❏ Invert — If true, invert the x and y values reported on drag. Defaults to false.

- ❏ Unit — The CSS unit to append to reported values. Defaults to px.

If you simply go with the defaults for the Drag object, a given element can be made freely draggable across the page. However, you can alter this behavior in interesting ways by tweaking the options.

As shown in the previous example, you can make the element draggable only with a handle element, such as a title bar or other child element. Dragging can be constrained to a defined area, and locked to a specified grid of positions. With the modifiers and style options, you can change what happens on drag altogether.

The Drag object also offers a pair of methods, .detach() and .attach(), which disable and enable the object's mouse event listeners, respectively:

```
$$('#ex_drag .mover .toggle').addEvent('click', function(ev) {
    if (/Enabled/.test(ev.target.get('text'))) {
        dragger.detach();
        $log('Dragging disabled');
        ev.target.set('text', 'Disabled');
    } else {
        dragger.attach();
        $log('Dragging enabled');
        ev.target.set('text', 'Enabled');
    }
});
```

The preceding code wires up a `<div>` element provided in the markup earlier with an event handler that alternately disables and enables dragging. You can use these two methods to conditionally allow or disallow dragging under whatever conditions you require, without needing to create or destroy the `Drag` object overall.

Finally, after you've got a `Drag` widget set up to your satisfaction, you can attach event listeners to react to various stages of user interaction with the widget:

```
[ 'beforeStart', 'start', 'snap', 'drag', 'complete' ]
    .each(function(ev_name) {
        dragger.addEvent(ev_name, function(drag_el) {
            $log("Drag event " + ev_name + " fired. ");
            $log( drag_el.getPosition() );
        })
    });
```

As shown in the preceding code, the following events are supported by the Drag widget:

❑   beforeStart — Fired when the user depresses the mouse button over the element, but before the dragging gesture has started

❑   start — Fired once the user has started the drag gesture

❑   snap — Fired if and when the user has dragged far enough to satisfy the snap option distance

❑   drag — Fired for each mouse event dragging the element

❑   complete — Fired once the user releases the mouse button after a drag gesture

The handler for each of these events is given the element passed as the first parameter into the `Drag` object constructor. By reacting to a combination of these events, you can either listen in on the default element dragging behavior, or implement your own dragging behavior entirely.

Making Elements Resizable

To customize drag behavior, MooTools provides an element method that uses a `Drag` object. By calling the `.makeResizable()` method, you can cause an element to grow and shrink on drag, rather than moving around on the page.

To demonstrate, consider the following markup declaring an element to be resized on drag:

```
<div class="mover resizer">
    <div class="handle drag">Drag to resize me</div>
</div>
<br style="clear: both" />
```

Now, take a look at how this element can be made resizable:

```
$$('#ex_drag .resizer').makeResizable({
    handle: $$('#ex_drag .resizer .handle')[0],
    snap: 25,
    grid: 25,

    onComplete: function(el) {
        $log("Element resized!");
        $log( el.getSize() );
    }
});
```

The .makeResizable() element method accepts as its only parameter a hash or object of options, matching those accepted by the Drag object — including handle, snap, grid, and onComplete. The onComplete event handler defined previously reports on the completion of any resizing drag gesture, displaying the resulting element size in the log transcript.

You can see a snapshot of this in action in Figure 34-10.

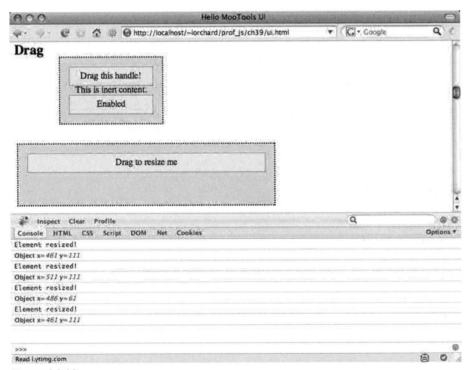

Figure 34-10

Automatically Scrolling the Window and Elements

One thing you may have noticed in the previous example is that if you drag the element toward the edges of the window, you need to drop the element and scroll if you want to move it beyond the bounds of the currently visible portion of the page. Many applications avoid this by automatically scrolling the view for you when your mouse gesture reaches a certain close proximity to the edges of the window.

In MooTools, this can be achieved by using the `Scroller` class in conjunction with the `Drag` class. Consider the following construction of a draggable element:

```
<div id="ex_scroller">

    <h2>Scroller</h2>

    <div class="mover dragger">
        <div class="handle drag">Drag this handle!</div>
        <p>This is inert content.</p>
    </div>

    <br style="clear: both" />

</div>
```

Now, before creating a `Drag` instance to make this element movable, take a look at this code:

```
var my_scroller = new Scroller(window, {
    area:     Math.round(window.getWidth() / 10),
    velocity: 1,
    /*
    onChange: function(x, y){
        this.element.scrollTo(x, y);
    }
    */
});
```

The first parameter to the `Scroller` constructor is expected to be a DOM element, in this case a reference to the window itself. You could use a reference to some other scrolling element here, say a <div> with its `overflow` style property set to "auto" containing a large amount of content.

The second parameter to the `Scroller` constructor is expected as a hash or object of options, including the following:

❑   area — The distance from the edges of the element within which automatic scrolling begins. In the previous example, this is set to one-tenth the width the current window size.

❑   velocity — A multiplier to the speed at which the scroll position is moved.

❑   onChange — A function that will be used to affect scrolling on the managed element. The default, as shown in the code commented out in the example is to call the element's `.scrollTo()` method — but you can replace this behavior by defining this option.

The `Scroll` class also provides two methods, `.start()` and `.stop()`, to control whether or not the automatic scrolling is active, respectively. The following code wires up a `Drag` object with event handlers defined to call these methods:

```
var dragger = new Drag(
    $$('#ex_scroller .dragger')[0],
    {
        handle: $$('#ex_scroller .mover .drag')[0],
        onBeforeStart: function(drag_el) {
            my_scroller.start();
        },
        onComplete: function(drag_el) {
            my_scroller.stop();
        }
    }
);
```

In the preceding code, automatic window scrolling is activated with the `.start()` method when a drag gesture is started, and then deactivated again with `.stop()` when the user releases the mouse button. This ensures that the window scrolling happens only during a drag gesture and not otherwise.

Enabling Drag-and-Drop Targets

In discussions of graphical user interfaces, the word most often following *drag* is *drop* — which describes what is generally the point of making an object in a user interface draggable in the first place, offering the ability to drag something from point A and drop it at point B or point C, and then do something interesting with that user choice.

In MooTools, this can be achieved with the `Drag.Move` class. Take a look at the following markup providing the pieces for a small drag-and-drop interface:

```
<style type="text/css">
    #ex_drag_move .container {
        width: 400px;
        padding: 1em;
        margin: 1em;
        border: 2px dotted #333;
    }
</style>
<div id="ex_drag_move">

    <h2>Drag.Move</h2>

    <div class="container">

        <div class="mover drop" id="dest1">Bucket #1</div>
        <div class="mover drop" id="dest2">Bucket #2</div>
        <div class="mover drop" id="dest3">Bucket #3</div>
        <div class="mover drop" id="dest4">Bucket #4</div>
        <br style="clear: both" />

        <div class="mover dragger">Drag me!</div>
```

```
                <br style="clear: both" />

            </div>

        </div>
```

In the preceding markup, four boxes are defined that will be wired up as drop targets for a fifth draggable box. This promised functionality is provided by the following code instantiating a `Drag`.`Move` object:

```
var dragger = new Drag.Move(

    $$('#ex_drag_move .dragger')[0], {

        droppables: $$('#ex_drag_move .drop')

    }

);
```

The `Drag`.`Move` constructor expects an element to make draggable as its first parameter, and an object or hash of options as the second. As a subclass of `Drag`, the `Drag`.`Move` class accepts all of the options of a `Drag` constructor — including `snap`, `grid`, `limit`, and `handle`. Other options may not make as much sense, as the functionality of `Drag`.`Move` depends on its own defaults.

The new option introduced by `Drag`.`Move` is named `droppables`, and expects a list of elements to be monitored for drag and drop of the managed element. This monitoring is made useful through the addition of a few new events, used like so:

```
[ 'enter', 'leave', 'drop' ]
    .each(function(ev_name) {
        dragger.addEvent(ev_name, function(drag_el, drop_el) {
            $log(
                "Drag fired " + ev_name + " event" +
                ( (drop_el) ? ", element " + drop_el.id : '' )
            );
        });
    });
```

While the `Drag`.`Move` class supports all the events of `Drag`, the most interesting ones here are the following:

❑   `enter` — Fired when the dragged element is passed over one of the `droppables` elements.

❑   `leave` — Fired when the dragged element is moved away from a `droppables` element.

❑   `drop` — Fired when the dragged element is released within a `droppables` element.

Between these three events, the `Drag`.`Move` class gives you everything you need to build some very complex and effective drag-and-drop interfaces. Figure 34-11 gives you a preview of what this code looks like running in the browser window and the log transcript.

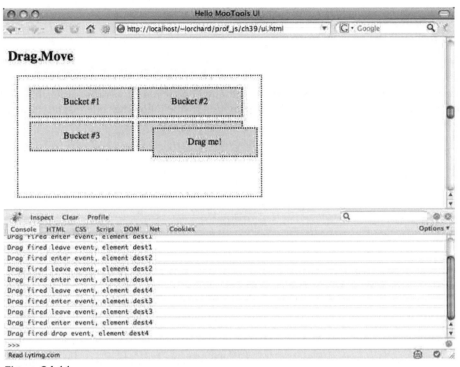

Figure 34-11

Building Sortable Lists

Sortable lists are another useful implementation of drag and drop, allowing users to interactively arrange items of a list. To help build these lists, MooTools offers the `Sortable` class.

Getting down to business, consider the following markup, which constructs a set of content blocks:

```
<div id="ex_sortables">

    <h2>Sortables</h2>

    <div id="sortables">

        <dl class="has_items" id="sortable_item1">
            <dt>First Item</dt>
            <dd><p>
                Lorem ipsum dolor sit amet, consectetuer adipiscing
                elit. Cras imperdiet velit at arcu. Nullam viverra lectus ac
                felis.
            </p></dd>
        </dl>

        <dl class="has_items" id="sortable_item2">
            <dt>Second Item</dt>
```

```
        <dd><p>
            Cum sociis natoque penatibus et magnis dis parturient
            montes, nascetur ridiculus mus.
        </p></dd>
    </dl>

    <dl class="has_items" id="sortable_item3">
        <dt>Third Item</dt>
        <dd><p>
            Nullam eu sapien dictum purus consequat cursus. Etiam non
            sapien sed elit dignissim tristique.
        </p></dd>
    </dl>

    </div>

</div>
```

In the preceding markup, dictionary lists are used to define content blocks. The <dt> elements are used as the title bars, and the <dd> elements hold content for the blocks. The Sortables class is not constrained to using this particular pattern of markup, but a pattern similar to this makes it easy to identify parts with CSS selectors.

Now, take a look at the following code example, which creates an instance of the Sortables class:

```
var sortable = new Sortables( $('sortables'), {

    handle:     'dt',
    clone:      true,
    revert:     true,
    opacity:    0.25,
    constrain:  true

});
```

The constructor of the Sortables class expects as its first parameter either one or more elements, or a CSS selector string identifying elements to be wired up as sortable lists. This means that you can actually wire up more than one list at once with the same Sortables instance. In the preceding code, only one element is supplied as a sortable list, that being the container <div> from markup with an ID of "sortables".

The second parameter of the constructor is expected to be a hash or an object containing options. These options include the following:

❑   handle — This option can be used with a CSS selector to specify a child element inside each list item to be used as a dragging handle.

❑   snap — Like the Drag class, this is the distance an item must be dragged before sorting starts.

❑   `opacity` — This is the level of opacity to use on the preview of where an element will land if dropped.

❑   `clone` — If `true`, the dragged element will be cloned and follow the mouse until dropped. If `false`, dragging to rearrange elements will swap with no transition.

❑   `revert` — If the `clone` option is `true`, this option determines whether to fire off a short animation of the cloned element moving in for a landing when the mouse button is released.

❑   `constrain` — If `true`, the dragging motion of list items will be constrained to their parent lists, and dragging items between lists will not be allowed.

Once you've got a sortable list working, it's useful to get an update from the list when the user has finished moving something around. For this purpose, the Sortables class offers a set of events ready for listeners, as well as a convenient method for getting a list of element IDs to reflect the new sort order.

Consider the following code, which wires up the significant events and reports on them at each stage:

```
[ 'start', 'sort', 'complete' ]
    .each(function(ev_name) {
        sortable.addEvent(ev_name, function(el_dragged) {
            $log('Sortable fired event ' + ev_name);
            $log( el_dragged );
            $log( sortable.serialize() );
        });
    });
```

The events wired up in the preceding code include the following:

❑   `start` — Fired when the user first starts dragging an element

❑   `sort` — Fired when the dragged element is in position to swap places with another

❑   `complete` — Fired when the user releases the dragged element

Notice that in the event handler the `Sortables` object method `.serialize()` is called — this returns a list of IDs of the elements in their current arranged order. When called during the `start` or `sort` event handler, one of the IDs may be `null`, reflecting the optional cloned element in the gap.

However, once the `complete` event fires, the `.serialize()` method should return the complete clean list — this is the best place to update other data structures, fire off AJAX requests to save the changed order, or whatever you'd like to do with it.

Figure 34-12 shows a snapshot of a manual sort in progress, along with a sample log transcript showing a few messages from events fired.

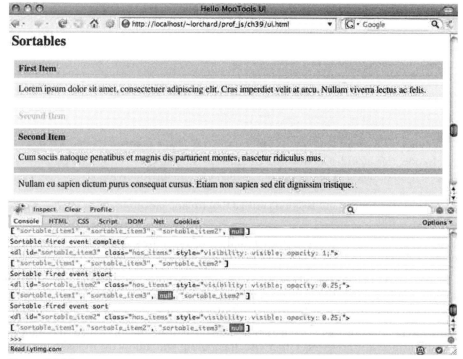

Figure 34-12

Using Tool Tips

When you're confused about some aspect of a user interface, a natural thing to do is to hover around the elements that present the source of confusion. In this scenario, tool tips offer an unobtrusive way to include help text in a temporary panel floating near the mouse. MooTools offers the Tips class to help you build tool tips without much code.

Consider the following markup presenting a set of links:

```
<div id="ex_tips">

    <h2>Tips</h2>

    <a class="mover" title="Tip #1" href="#" rel="some text">Hover on me!</a>
    <a class="mover" title="Tip #2" href="#" rel="some text">Hover on me!</a>
    <a class="mover" title="Tip #3" href="#" rel="some text">Hover on me!</a>
    <a class="mover" title="Tip #4" href="http://decafbad.com">Hover on me!</a>

    <br style="clear: both" />

</div>
```

Now, take a look at the following code that creates an instance of the `Tips` class:

```
var tips = new Tips( $$('#ex_tips .mover'), {
    className:  'mytool',
    showDelay:  250,
    hideDelay:  250,
    offsets:    { x: 20, y: 20 },
    fixed:      false
});
```

The first parameter to the `Tips` constructor should be a list of elements for which tool tips are needed. In the preceding code, this includes all the links declared in the markup. The second parameter to the constructor is a hash or object defining options, which include the following:

❑ `showDelay` — Time in milliseconds until a tool tip appears after a user hovers over an element. Defaults to 100.

❑ `hideDelay` — Time in milliseconds a tool tip lingers on the screen after the mouse leaves the element. Defaults to 100.

❑ `offsets` — An object specifying horizontal and vertical distance away from the mouse where a tooltip should appear. The `Tips` class manages in what direction the tip panel appears, based on the mouse position in the window. Defaults to `{ x: 20, y: 20 }`.

❑ `fixed` — If `true`, the tool tip will appear at an offset from the top-left corner of the element over which the mouse is hovering. Otherwise, the tool tip will follow the mouse.

❑ `className` — To implement the tool tip panel, MooTools creates a new DOM element. The value for this option is used as a CSS class on the container for the tool tip, which allows you to style the tip and its contents.

With respect to that last option, `className`, the following CSS offers an example of how the automatically injected tool tip panel can be styled:

```
<style type="text/css">
    #ex_tips a {
        cursor: help;
    }
    .mytool .tip {
        opacity: 0.75;
        background: #333;
        color: #fff;
        z-index: 1000;
        padding: 0.25em;
    }
    .mytool .tip-title {
        font-weight: bold;
        font-size: 13px;
    }
    .mytool .tip-text {
        font-size: 13px;
    }
</style>
```

The CSS in the preceding example provides styling for the links themselves, the tool tip panel overall, a title in the tool tip, and some additional text in the tool tip.

By default, the `Tips` class derives the title for the tip from the elements' `title` attributes, and derives the text for the tip from elements' `rel` or `href` attributes. However, you can specify your own titles and text for tips programmatically using element storage like so:

```
$$('#ex_tips .mover')[1]
    .store('tip:title', 'Custom title');

$$('#ex_tips .mover')[2]
    .store('tip:text', 'Custom text here');
```

The preceding code sets the title of the tip for the second link and sets the text for the third link's tool tip. This gives you a choice between defining tool tip content in markup or setting it up in your code.

Finally, the `Tips` class offers a few events ready for handlers, as the following code shows:

```
tips.addEvents({
    show: function(el_tip) {
        var tip_title =
            el_tip.getElement(".tip-title").get("text");
        $log("Tip shown: " + tip_title);
    },
    hide: function(el_tip) {
        var tip_title =
            el_tip.getElement(".tip-title").get("text");
        $log("Tip hidden: " + tip_title);
    }
});
```

Although the preceding code attaches event listeners after the `Tips` object is created, you can actually override the default behavior entirely like so:

```
var tips = new Tips( $$('#ex_tips .mover'), {
    className:  'mytool',
    showDelay:  250,
    hideDelay:  250,
    offsets:    { x: 20, y: 20 },
    fixed:      false,

    onShow: function(tip){
        tip.setStyle('visibility', 'visible');
    },

    onHide: function(tip){
        tip.setStyle('visibility', 'hidden');
    }

});
```

If you specify `show` and `hide` event handlers in the constructor's options, those handlers will replace the default behavior, which is actually shown in the preceding code. So, you can either override default behavior altogether or later attach new listeners to react to tool tip actions.

Figure 34-13 shows a tool tip in action, along with a log transcript produced by the event handlers defined previously.

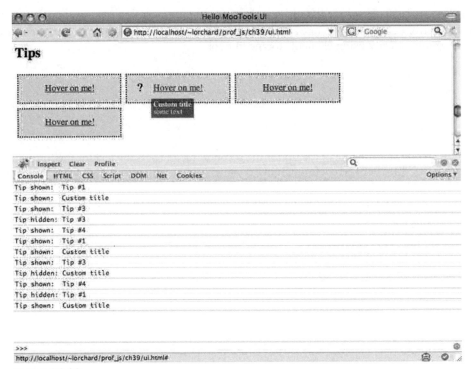

Figure 34-13

Building Slider Controls

Although MooTools doesn't provide a large set of user interface or form controls, it does offer a few useful and lightweight widgets. Another one of these is the Slider class, which implements a simple one-dimensional value slider consisting of a draggable knob element constrained within a track.

Take a look at the following markup laying out a slider:

```
<style type="text/css">
    .slider {
        width: 300px;
        height: 25px;
        background: #ccc;
    }
    .knob {
        width: 25px;
        height: 25px;
        text-align: center;
        background: #333;
        color: #fff;
    }
```

```
    .status {
        margin: 1em 0 0 0;
    }
    .status code {
        font-weight: bold
    }
</style>

<div id="ex_slider">
    <h2>Slider</h2>

    <div class="slider">
        <div class="knob">*</div>
    </div>

    <div class="status">
        Value = <code>--</code>
    </div>

</div>
```

The markup in the preceding example defines a horizontal slider track <div> element, within which there's a knob element. The CSS provides some simple presentation for this, but you can apply whatever styles you like to match your own design — the Slider class doesn't impose any themes or styles of its own on this control.

With the markup in place, it's time to create an instance of the Slider class:

```
var slide = new Slider(
    $$('#ex_slider .slider')[0],
    $$('#ex_slider .knob')[0],
    {
        snap:   true,
        range:  [10, 200],
        wheel:  true,
        steps:  10,
        mode: 'horizontal',

        onChange: function(pos) {
            $log("Slider set to " + pos);
            $$('#ex_slider .status code').set('text', pos);
        }

    }
).set(50);
```

The first parameter of the Slider constructor is a reference to the slider container element, and the second parameter should point to the knob contained within the slider. The third and final parameter expects an object or hash of options, which include the following:

❑ range — Expects a value of false, or an array of the minimum and maximum values to use for the slider. Defaults to false.

❑ steps — Along with range, this value can be used to supply the number of chunks into which the range can be cut up. Defaults to 100.

- ❏ snap — If true, the slider will snap to the discrete steps in the slider range when dragged. Defaults to false.

- ❏ offset — By default, this uses the offsetHeight or offsetWidth of the knob for deciding its position during a drag. However, you can supply your own offset position with this option.

- ❏ wheel — If true, the mouse wheel can be used to move the slider. Defaults to false.

- ❏ mode — Can be either horizontal or vertical. Defaults to horizontal.

The Slider class also supports events including the following:

- ❏ change — Fired for each change in the slider
- ❏ complete — Fired at the end of a drag of the slider

The slider's current numeric value is passed as a parameter to handlers for both of these events.

Shown in Figure 34-14 is a preview slider built by the code in this section, along with a sample log transcript displaying values produced by dragging the slider knob.

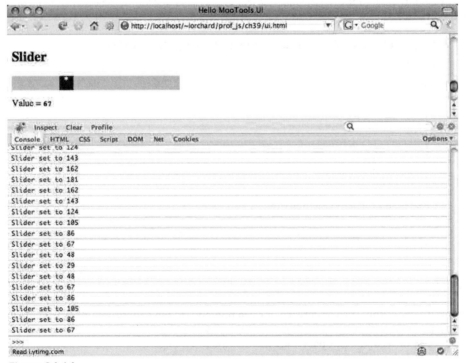

Figure 34-14

Summary

In this chapter, you were taken on a tour through the animation tools and user interface widgets offered by MooTools. For many developers and fans of this framework, the features presented in this chapter are the payoff for everything built up from the previous chapters in this part of the book.

Using the Fx family of classes, you can compose some very complex and rich visual transitions based on manipulating CSS properties over time. But, if just a few flourishes are all you need for a page, MooTools offers a set of quick shortcuts to commonly used transitions without the need to construct a complete animation from scratch. Beyond animations, this chapter also introduced the set of user interface layouts and controls offered by MooTools for managing content and interactive user input.

Index

841

M